THE AGE OF ENLIGHTENMENT

1715–1789

HENRY B. GARLAND

RONALD GRIMSLEY
(EDITOR)

JOHN PRESTON

D. MAXWELL WHITE

PENGUIN BOOKS

Penguin Books Ltd, Harmondsworth, Middlesex, England
Penguin Books, 625 Madison Avenue, New York, New York 10022, U.S.A.
Penguin Books Australia Ltd, Ringwood, Victoria, Australia
Penguin Books Canada Ltd, 2801 John Street, Markham, Ontario, Canada L3R 1B4
Penguin Books (N.Z.) Ltd, 182–190 Wairau Road, Auckland 10, New Zealand

—

First published 1979

—

—

Made and printed in Great Britain by
Hazell Watson & Viney Ltd,
Aylesbury, Bucks
Set in Monotype Bembo

Contents

Contents

PART FOUR: THE NOVEL

PART FIVE: AESTHETIC IDEAS

Note

THIS volume concentrates almost exclusively on the literature of England, France, Germany and Italy. While the editor has determined the general plan, each contributor has been given responsibility for his own sections.

Introduction

SUSTAINED by a steadfast faith in absolute values and the universality of objective principles, the classical age had been one of comparative cultural stability. Even when a thinker like Descartes questioned the validity of traditional philosophy, he still retained confidence in the power of reason (as 'naturally equal in all men') and in the possibility of reaching complete intellectual certainty. In the same way few writers and artists doubted the existence of good taste and the technical means of attaining it. The subject-matter of art did not depend on immediate social and political reality, but on apparently indestructible values. If artists sought inspiration in the remote past, it was because the great genres of antiquity – the tragedy and the epic poem – were deemed to be the perfect expression of an imperishable ideal. Whenever concessions were made to everyday life – when, for example, an ode was prompted by an important event or the writer of comedies portrayed some aspect of contemporary society – it was always with a view to transcending it: the ode would launch out into reflections on life and death and the comedy would emphasize the moral aspects of human nature. Moreover, what gave art its ultimate value was not simply its 'eternal' content but the formal perfection in which it was embodied – a formal perfection controlled by 'reason' and 'nature', and obtainable only through the observation of clearly defined principles. These cultural values were also protected by powerful social and political influences. Not only was the age of Louis XIV one of absolutism, so that an all-powerful monarch and Church prevented any serious examination of political and religious beliefs, but art itself was dominated by the aristocratic taste of *l'honnête homme*. A stable, well-ordered society thus seemed to lend powerful support to a view of art that required the exclusion of subjective deviations from universally accepted principles.

The Enlightenment, on the other hand, was a time of cultural ferment, for the religious, philosophical and social ideas of the previous century were subjected to a close and, for the most part, hostile scrutiny. This critical spirit had already begun to emerge in the last decades of the previous century, but it was henceforth to become one of the most characteristic features of the new age. Thinkers were no longer prepared to accept ideas on the mere authority of the past, but insisted on testing them in the light of their intellectual validity. Whereas religious authority presupposed the acceptance of revelation as mediated through the Church, the *esprit philosophique* relied solely on human reasoning. 'We are men before we are Christians', said the author of the article 'Reason' in the *Encyclopédie*. Although reason had certainly been admired in the classical period, for the whole of Cartesian philosophy was based on its universal power, the new 'philosophical spirit' would not admit any necessary link between philosophy and traditional metaphysics. The old rationalism was rejected because of its alleged failure to relate the activity of reason to the field of everyday experience; rationalism henceforth seemed to stand for an empty abstraction divorced from the concrete facts of real life. If the Enlightenment was proud to call itself 'the age of philosophy', it no longer understood 'philosophy' in the traditional metaphysical sense; apart from exercising his reason to criticize unproved assumptions about ultimate reality, the philosopher had the more positive task of exploring the 'system of the world' and the many different aspects of human existence. Science, art and society were deemed to function in accordance with the laws of cause and effect and did not need to look beyond the finite world for their explanatory principles. Yet because the philosopher was concerned with life on earth rather than with the revealed truths of eternity, he had to take into account the link between reason and the observation of accessible facts. As the article 'Philosopher' in the *Encyclopédie* puts it, 'the philosopher forms his principles on an infinite number of observations and to do this he has to take a maxim at its source and examine its origins'; he does not deal with empty abstractions but with the 'science of facts'. 'The *esprit philosophique*', insists the same article, 'is the spirit of observation and accuracy which relates everything to its true principles.'

The Enlightenment considered itself fortunate to have inherited two geniuses who could provide them with new insights into human existence and the nature of the physical world. The names of John

Locke (1632–1704) and Isaac Newton (1643–1727) dominate the early decades of the century. Reacting against the metaphysical pretensions of Descartes, Locke had demonstrated the advantage of studying ideas in relation to their origins and of seeing how they emerge from the mind's response to the data of sense-experience; intellectual truth no longer depended on the universal principles of abstract reason, but on mental reactions to the external world. This genetic method was to be extended to other intellectual disciplines such as natural history and psychology. Newton had also revealed the amazing fertility of a scientific method which abandoned the elaboration of vague and unsupported hypotheses for a close and systematic examination of the physical world by means of mathematics, observation and experiment. Henceforth, the universe could be explored in the light of its own inherent properties. Although both Locke and Newton themselves were sincere Christians and stressed the importance of God's existence (Newton believed that God could intervene directly to modify the working of physical laws), other thinkers, impressed by the order and rationality of the physical universe, were prepared to disregard the question of its divine origin, and to concentrate their attention upon nature rather than upon the supernatural.

'Nature' was one of the most widely used terms of the period, although it was invested with different and occasionally contradictory meanings. Very often it was linked with the critical function of reason already mentioned: nature warned men not to go beyond the realm of observation and experiment in order to probe the ultimate mystery of things. On the other hand, it opened up a vast territory for intellectual endeavour, since nature included all finite reality – 'the system of the world and the collection of all created things', as d'Alembert put it in the *Encyclopédie*. As such, nature seemed to offer an important unifying principle which included a vast range of phenomena – both physical and human – and yet served as a guide and inspiration for their further exploration. Moreover, thanks to Newton, nature was believed to contain a harmony and order which lent support to man's efforts to penetrate its secrets. Admittedly, this notion was intended to provide a warning as well as encouragement, for the examination of nature had to be confined to the observable aspects of the physical world and man's existence; but the territory accessible to investigation was very extensive and when approached in the right way – in the modest confidence that the powers of the human mind were great enough to understand at least limited aspects of the natural order – it could provide the basis of a fruitful scientific method. Indeed, science was henceforth to replace metaphysics as a means of extending man's understanding of his own existence and his relationship with the universe.

The considerable scientific advances of the previous age seemed to justify this confidence in nature and provided the eighteenth century with strong reasons for believing in the possibility of yet greater progress. Sustained by the spectacular achievements of Newton, the physico-mathematical sciences continued to move forward: mathematicians such as Euler, d'Alembert, the Bernouillis and especially Joseph Lagrange, with his *Mécanique analytique* (1799–1805) were outstanding, while Laplace's *Système du monde* was an ambitious attempt to give Newtonian principles a cosmic dimension. In spite of the work of Priestley and Cavendish, chemistry had to wait for Lavoisier (1743–94) before it could enter a really creative period, E. G. Stahl's notorious theory of 'phlogiston' as the explanation of fire having been a serious obstacle to fruitful experiment. On the other hand, such names as Linnaeus, Buffon and Von Haller testify to important work in botany, zoology and physiology, while biology and the sciences of life came to the fore in the second half of the century as the traditional theory of 'preformation' gradually gave way to the idea of epigenesis. Perhaps more important for the literature of ideas than the developments of specific sciences was the extension of the scientific outlook and method to particular aspects of human life. Montesquieu has been hailed with some justification as a forerunner of sociology, while the empiricism of Locke encouraged interest in psychology, as is evident from the work of philosophers like Condillac and Hume; history and language also became the objects of more systematic study as they freed themselves from theological presuppositions; and there was a growing confidence in the possibility of applying the scientific principle of causal explanation to many areas of human experience.

Although scientific progress involved, for the most part, an intellectual prudence which acknowledged the need to respect the lessons of observation and experiment, it did not check all rash speculation, even among scientists; nor did it prevent thinkers from accepting the need to establish universal principles. Newton, for example, made metaphysical assumptions concerning the absolute nature of time and space. The very fact that nature was a unifying concept helped to strengthen belief in its objectivity and permanence. Moreover, the old school of Natural Law philosophers continued to exercise a strong influence upon eighteenth-century thought, even upon thinkers who, like Rousseau, criticized their basic tenets; the very idea of 'the state of nature' presupposed that man was provided with a fixed essence which made his true being capable of resisting historical change and social influence. The 'noble savage' himself was endowed with qualities which were said to be more natural and universal than the artificial characteristics of his European counterpart. The rejection of the old metaphysical and religious absolutes did not necessarily mean the complete rejection of the rationalist spirit on which they were based.

The faith of the Enlightenment in the power of natural order is often demonstrated in unexpected ways. The political economy of the Physiocrats, for example, rested on the assumption that a benevolent God had created a natural order involving an ultimate harmony of interests, so that self-seeking and social good were not incompatible; the Physiocrats also believed that agriculture should be given precedence over industry and commerce because it lay closer to the principle of natural order. In England Adam Smith showed the same confidence in nature; in *The Wealth of Nations* (1766), he maintained that the unrestricted exercise of economic self-interest would lead, by a natural process, to the prosperity and happiness of the whole community. A pessimist such as Mandeville did not hesitate to affirm that 'private vices' could become 'public benefits' and that nature could help society to function harmoniously in spite of the presence of conflicting elements. Thinkers as far removed from the Physiocrats as were utopian socialists such as Morelly, with his *Code de la Nature* (1755) and *La Basiliade* (1751), or Mably who wanted to replace private property by some form of agrarian communism, still based their ideas on the principle of 'nature'.

Although this confidence in nature provides one of the main themes of the Enlightenment, the concept itself underwent considerable modification in the course of the century. The rigidly mechanistic outlook associated with Descartes and Newton gradually yielded to a conception that interpreted the universe in more dynamic terms. Philosophically, the ground had been prepared for this change by Leibniz and Spinoza who had already stressed the idea of energy and striving rather than the Cartesian notion of 'extension'; a revival of interest in the works of ancient thinkers such as Epicurus and Lucretius also served to encourage this transformation of intellectual attitudes. Later eighteenth-century thinkers began to replace the image of the clock by that of the animal or organism. The notion of evolution made a hesitant appearance in the work of Buffon, Maupertuis and Diderot, although it tended to be remote from the minds of most thinkers of the time. When biology began to replace physics as the developing science, the universe was seen as a centre of energy rather than of order: it was the constant creation and destruction of its various elements – and not the orderly working of its complex mechanism – which began to command attention. Imagination – as well as reason – now began to play a large part in the interpretation of the world. In this respect it is interesting to compare the old-fashioned mechanistic materialism of d'Holbach's *Système de la Nature* (1770) with the animistic view of the world contained in Robinet's *De la Nature* (1761). The gap between man and animal rigidly maintained by the Cartesians and reaffirmed by Montesquieu and Voltaire, who still accepted a hierarchical view of the world (in spite of important concessions to the influence of man's physical being upon his philosophy of life) was gradually being closed by thinkers such as Robinet and Diderot. The soul of the world, it was believed, spread throughout the whole of creation and included all forms of existence, both animate and inanimate. In Germany Goethe came to see nature no longer in mechanistic terms, but as an infinitely rich and spontaneous source of creative energy; the origins of conflict did not lie in man himself (as Kant had believed in his separation of morality and nature) but in a world that frustrated the feelings and aspirations of the heart; given the right conditions, man could find a harmonious fulfilment of his being. Herder also set the life of the individual within the wider context of the history of mankind as a whole; he affirmed that as soon as men saw their lives in this way, they could achieve harmony and peace. Confidence in nature thus continued to dominate the age, but it no longer provided the basis of a rigidly hierarchical universe.

This persistent tendency to dwell on the unity of nature, whether conceived in mechanistic or dynamic terms, had to reckon with the rapidly expanding knowledge of man's situation in the world. Whereas writers of the classical age had tended to ignore contemporary achievements (since artistic perfection had already been realized in antiquity), the eighteenth century saw a spectacular growth of interest in other cultures and civilizations. Men's outlook was broadened and modified by the thought that the world contained a remarkable variety of hitherto unknown customs and ways of life. The tremendous popularity of books written by travellers from the Far and Near East made people increasingly aware of the relativism of their own moral ideas. Jesuit missionaries in China disseminated information about Oriental religion; travellers like Cook and Bougainville gave accounts of their voyages around the world; Chardin and Tavernier fascinated readers with their descriptions of Persian life; the Baron de la Hontan, with his *Dialogues curieux* and other works, described the outlook of the American savages. As writers became more familiar with other cultures, they were able to take a detached and often critical look at their own; a favourite satirical pastime was to expose the naïve and one-sided viewpoint of those who thought that the customs of their country had timeless validity. Typical of these satirical attacks upon contemporary complacency were Swift's *Gulliver's Travels*, Defoe's *Robinson Crusoe* and Montesquieu's *Lettres persanes*.

Apart from drawing upon these exotic sources of new knowledge, Europe itself was recognizing its own differences of outlook. The prestige of French classicism was being rapidly undermined by the growing enthusiasm for English culture. Major writers like Voltaire and Montesquieu visited England and helped to spread knowledge of its philosophical, religious and political life: with the publication of his *Lettres philosophiques* in 1734, Voltaire was one of the first writers to give the French public a panoramic view of English culture, while Montesquieu, in *De l'esprit des lois* of 1748, wrote at length about the English political constitution. Apart from the tremendous prestige of Locke and Newton in philosophy and science, other aspects of English life aroused great sympathy and interest. Voltaire was struck by the liberalism of the English religious outlook and contrasted it with the intransigence of Roman Catholicism in France; constitutional English monarchy also appeared to have advantages over French political absolutism; a more reasonable attitude towards trade and commerce and the constant stress upon the principle of social utility made England a liberal country which could offer many salutary lessons to less enlightened régimes. English literature also began to enjoy a hitherto unprecedented vogue. In *Le Pour et contre* (1733–40) the journalist and novelist the abbé Prévost undertook to give French readers up-to-date information about English authors; and later on he translated several of Richardson's novels. Translations of other novelists such as Fielding, Goldsmith and Sterne, soon followed. Before the end of the century the name of Shakespeare was also to become familiar to French readers, even though translations were usually adapted to their taste; at the same time the domestic tragedy of Otway, Lillo and Moore became known in France and the 'pre-Romantic' poetry of Thomson, Young and Ossian began to exert an important influence upon French sensibility. In the second half of the century, German influence, though much more limited than the English, began to make itself felt with the translation of Haller's *Die Alpen* in 1750, of the German-Swiss Gessner's *Idylls* in 1762 and with fifteen translations of Goethe's *Werther* between 1776 and 1797.

With the weakening of national barriers, the eighteenth century tended to appear as an age of cultural cosmopolitanism. There was an active interchange of writers and thinkers between France and England and most educated people were European rather than nationalist in their intellectual outlook; in spite of important social and political differences, they were conscious of sharing the same ideas and, thanks to common mental attitudes, men could cross physical frontiers without difficulty.

This broadening of cultural horizons is revealed not simply by the way in which writers looked beyond their national boundaries, but also by their growing consciousness of links with the past. Judged by modern standards, the historical studies of the time may often appear to be inadequate, but they certainly constitute a considerable advance on the theological conception of the previous century. Whereas Bossuet's *Universal History* related human events to the direct working of divine Providence, a more scientific and philosophical attitude towards history emerges with the publication of such works as Gibbon's *Decline and Fall of the Roman Empire* (1776–88), Voltaire's *Siècle de Louis XIV* (1751), Vico's *Scienze nuova* (1725) and Herder's *Ideen zur Philosophie der Geschischte der Menschheit* (1784–91). Apart from his extended essay on the rise and fall of the Roman Republic and Empire, Montesquieu revolutionized the study of law with his *De l'esprit des lois* (1748) which set the interpretation of the laws within the context of their physical and historical origins. In a still more important way this rapid change of temporal perspective not only related contemporary culture to that of the past, but also accustomed men to vast time-scales which would have been inconceivable to their predecessors. When Buffon, in his *Époques de la nature* (1779), put the age of the earth at the absurdly modest figure of 75,000 years, he still shocked his contemporaries, although his fear of ecclesiastical censorship made him conceal his real opinion that a million years would have been more accurate. Likewise, Voltaire's *Essai sur les moeurs* treated European history as only one phase in the history of mankind.

Whether it was a question of seeing human existence as a part of nature in the widest sense or in the light of its specific aspects, this new outlook, with its constant emphasis upon man's involvement with the problems of this world rather than the next, gave priority to the problem of happiness. In spite of occasional violent reactions against the austerity and discipline of the previous period – in France, for example, the Regency which followed the death of Louis XIV was a time of frenzied pleasure-seeking and wild financial speculation, as a novel like *Manon Lescaut* makes clear – the Enlightenment was not to be an age of mere self-indulgence, for the preoccupation with happiness led writers and thinkers to ponder the deeper human implications of this new outlook. It was soon realized that nature involved more than man's rational being and that his feelings and passions had as much right to expression as his intellect. Voltaire's polemic against Pascal is a striking example of the confrontation of the old and new philosophies: Voltaire attacked his illustrious predecessor as a 'sublime misanthropist' who had failed to accept the reality of man's full participation in nature; to attempt to suppress human passions, he declared, was to pursue the foolish chimera of creating an angel! Man, insisted Voltaire, is a part of nature, and, in spite of his potential nobility, is in many ways closer to the animal world than to his divine creator; his problem, therefore, is not to abolish or ignore the passions but to control them. Other thinkers came to see the heart as the source of noble behaviour. The young philosopher, Vauvenargues (1715–47), extolled heroic actions as a means of attaining happiness; will and instinct spur men on to greater achievements than the deceptive and hesitant counsels of reflection; decisively rejecting any idea of original sin, he had complete confidence in man's ability to attain his own salvation. In a less precise way other thinkers and writers began to consider morality in terms of feeling rather than of reason.

As soon as happiness was related to man's emotions and feelings, thinkers were faced with the problem of reconciling the demands of the individual with his obligations to society. If a materialist such as La Mettrie openly affirmed the supremacy of hedonism, the majority accepted the need to subordinate selfish impulse to some kind of social ideal. Some thinkers at first tried to bring worldly happiness into harmony with religious principles by developing a view that was both epicurean and Christian, but with the decline of Christianity, serious attempts were made to find a more truly 'philosophical' solution to the problem: there was a persistent effort to defend the possibility of establishing a harmonious relationship between man and the universe, the individual and society. Considerable importance was henceforth attached to the notion of sociability; nature, it was believed, places man in society and it is only in society that he can find true fulfilment. 'In whatever state the philosopher may find himself,' says the *Encyclopédie* on that subject, 'his needs and well-being engage him to live in society.' If the philosopher is *un honnête homme*, he must also make himself useful, and be 'filled with ideas about the good of civil society'. Even though Rousseau questioned the notion of innate sociability, he agreed that man did not become a rational and intelligent being until he entered society. Although many moralists would have hesitated to accept Shaftesbury's idea of a social instinct, they were quite prepared to advocate some form of *la bienfaisance* as the basis of universal morality; in fact, 'beneficence' became one of the most characteristic concepts of the time, for it seemed to be in accord with the idea of a harmonious natural order. This social element also led some thinkers to espouse utilitarianism. Bentham's famous principle of 'the greatest happiness of the greatest number' aptly epitomizes this aspect of Enlightenment thought.

Yet this emphasis upon the social aspect of morality could not conceal the emergence of a serious dilemma as soon as happiness was equated with the pleasure–pain principle rather than with virtue. The doctor-philosopher La Mettrie boldly affirmed that morality had no connection with notions of virtue or spiritual need, but was based directly on the search for happiness and pleasure; since physical sensations ought always to be given precedence over intellectual and moral notions, the only sensible philosophy seemed to be some form of hedonism. Still more disturbing was the appearance of a writer such as the Marquis de Sade who transformed the idea of nature into an impersonal power which justified the most perverse acts of violence and cruelty as long as they were carried out in the name of personal happiness.

Admittedly Sade was an extreme case and most thinkers were prevented from espousing such a radical reversal of traditional concepts by their continued confidence in the power of universal principles and the essential stability of human nature as well as by their view of man as a social being. Nevertheless, whatever the particular answer given to the question of ultimate moral values, both theoretical principles and their specific practical applications were bound up with one of the major preoccupations of the period – the question of freedom. It was widely believed that the demands of social life had to be compatible with the requirements of human dignity. The struggle for basic freedoms – the individual's right to choose his own religious beliefs and the thinker's right to pursue the truth in his own way – lay behind the assaults upon the Roman Catholic Church; there was fierce hostility to the idea that revelation, being tied to the notion of eternal truth, presupposed the Church's right to defend it by the active suppression of heresy. Likewise, most enlightened thinkers were anxious to protect freedom by making all individuals equal before the law; they insisted that membership of a particular social class ought not to exempt anyone from being subjected to the laws governing the lives of others.

In a more general way, the Enlightenment fought for man's right to throw off all those metaphysical and religious constraints which prevented him from exercising his essential humanity. The love of freedom thus tended to express itself in a distinctly humanitarian sense. This affected not simply the domain of ideas but various efforts to achieve practical reforms; thinkers who were unwilling to advocate radical political changes still denounced particular abuses. In France there were protests – some of them inspired by the Italian publicist Beccaria's *Treatise on Crimes and Punishment* (1764) – against the inhuman severity of the criminal code; these included Voltaire's indefatigable campaigns on behalf of Calas, the Chevalier de la Barre and other unfortunate victims of judicial barbarity. Equally vigorous were attacks upon the educational monopoly of the Church and demands for the abolition of slavery. In the *Encyclopédie*, slavery was denounced as an offence to human dignity and freedom. 'Every man possessing a soul has the right to be free', says one author. 'Men and their freedom are not objects of commerce: they cannot be sold, bought or paid for at any price.' Because man was becoming aware of himself as a finite being concerned with achieving happiness on this earth, philosophers were opposed to the intolerance and injustice which prevented him from expressing his true nature.

In spite of its prominence in the literature and thought of the century, the notion of liberty should not be given undue political significance, for, on the whole, the eighteenth century was one of comparative political stability. The only thinkers to make lasting contributions to the development of political theory were Montesquieu and Rousseau, and the latter's political writings created little interest before the Revolution. There was certainly a broad current of liberalism flowing from Locke and affecting many areas of European thought, but most thinkers were able to consider political ideas in fairly general terms and reconcile them with the acceptance of the existing order. Montesquieu's genuine admiration for republicanism did not prevent his acceptance of the French monarchy; Voltaire's eulogy of English liberalism was accompanied by his advocacy of some form of enlightened despotism. Indeed, few thinkers had any serious faith in the power of the people to help themselves, and Voltaire was not alone in treating them as *la canaille*. Rousseau's democratic ideas were exceptional and even he agreed that monarchy was probably the best form of government for a large country. Most writers believed that the most effective way of achieving reforms was through the activity of a powerful ruler who was wise enough to heed the counsels of men like the *philosophes*. Perhaps that is why Voltaire and d'Alembert paid court to the philosopher-king, Frederick, and Diderot visited the Empress Catherine of Russia.

If one is to judge by the space accorded to the subject in the *Encyclopédie*, liberty was still a philosophical and moral rather than a political issue. There is an article of enormous length on philosophical freedom (most attention being focused on the question of freedom and determinism), while the articles on civil and political freedom are quite brief, consisting for the most part of extracts or summaries of Montesquieu and the jurist of the school of Natural Law, Burlamaqui. Diderot's most radical article 'Autorité politique' confined itself to the discussion of general principles. Certainly a few utopian socialists and communists were to be found among the *philosophes* – for example, Morelly with his *Code de la Nature* (1755) and Mably with *De la législation, ou principes des lois* (1776), but these were idealist dreamers whose work had little bearing on the political reality of the time. It was probably in the field of economics that the notion of freedom had greater influence. Adam Smith's *Wealth of Nations* made a much greater impact on the thought of the time than any specifically political work, while in France economists like Turgot strove to remove irksome restrictions from trade and commerce rather than to develop any general political theory.

Perhaps the most important single social factor contributing to the development of this new outlook was the rise of the bourgeoisie which, though still denied political power in a country like France, constituted a new and important reading public whose needs and desires could no longer be ignored. As a class, the bourgeoisie was difficult to define; its social attitude was sometimes ambiguous and, in any case, tended to vary from one country to another. In France, for example, it included wealthy financiers who were often close to the aristocracy and occasionally married into it, merchants and a large group of lawyers, doctors, writers and craftsmen; the French bourgeoisie was becoming more influential and was increasingly resentful at its exclusion from political power and privilege. In England, on the other hand, the middle classes enjoyed much greater prestige and were already influencing the cultural, social and political life of the nation. The geographical and political divisions of Germany made it much more difficult for a comparatively uneducated and often impoverished social class to present an effectively unified attitude towards contemporary problems. In general, the rise of the bourgeoisie led to a considerable enlargement of the reading public and a rapid expansion of intellectual curiosity by encouraging the production of new books and journals intended for the serious-minded reader. Steele's *Tatler* and Addison's *Spectator* are two of the best-known periodicals of the time and they had several imitators. Moreover, specialized publications like the *Journal des savants* were constantly attracting new readers and an ambitious commercial enterprise like the publication of the *Encyclopédie* would have been impossible without the support of the bourgeoisie. The same class provided members for the Academies which were being established in various European countries: apart from the new French provincial *Académies*, there was the Berlin Academy founded by Frederick the Great and the new Academy of Science at Stockholm, as well as a Society for the Advancement of Science in Denmark; well-established societies like the famous Royal Society of London and the Parisian Académie des Sciences were either strengthened or reorganized. Even such a traditional and aristocratic institution as the *salons* could not resist this new influence, as is clear from the bourgeois *salons* of Mme Geoffrin and Mlle de Lespinasse. At a lower social level the multiplication of the Parisian cafés and the English coffee-houses provided yet further evidence of new and broader cultural activity, for they were often centres of literary and intellectual discussion.

In the purely literary sphere the bourgeoisie also exercised an important influence by demanding a literature that was closer to its own interests than the aristocratically orientated culture of the previous period: authors were henceforth to describe such familiar aspects of everyday life as a man's involvement with his family, profession and society. Furthermore, the bourgeois's predilection for a certain type of moralizing sentimentality led to the creation of new genres like *la comédie larmoyante* and *le drame bourgeois*, whilst the history of the novel in both France and England bears eloquent testimony to the influence of this new social class. The novels of Richardson, for example, deal with the lives of ordinary people, usually set against their family background; there is no exceptional heroism and the author expends his main effort on the analysis of his characters' feelings, taking care at the same time to stress the moral implications of his work. Other works such as Goldoni's *Pamela* and Lessing's *Miss Sara Simpson* show the same concern with the description of the familiar social world. In a still more general way, these social themes were often accompanied by a greater concern with physical reality: money, clothes, professional problems, family habits, all were given new prominence. Although the universal aspects of man's existence continued to exercise many writers' talents, they were henceforth to be located in a precise physical or psychological setting.

Pictorial art too began to draw its subject-matter from the world of ordinary human beings and to detach itself from the portrayal of gods and heroes. Hogarth's pictures and engravings, with their vivid and often satirical portrayal of contemporary life, are those of an artist who, in his own words, was anxious to treat 'modern moral subjects', while Greuze was hailed by Diderot as the supreme painter of domestic life.

The importance of these new social factors in literature and art ought not to make us lose sight of the continued presence of some of the old traditions. Many novels continued to portray the aristocracy; one of the finest novels of the period, Laclos's *Les Liaisons dangereuses*, is an example. In painting there was no sudden change to new bourgeois subjects. Characteristic of the early Enlightenment was the rococo style, which still retained the elegance and elaborate decorative elements of the classical period. One of the greatest painters of the period, Watteau, still moves in the aristocratic world, even though he introduces a new psychological dimension into the portrayal of character.

The Enlightenment was not only a period of changing intellectual and social values, but also a time when men were beginning to experience a new mode of feeling, a new sensibility which helped to prepare the way for Romanticism. It is now customary to speak of the 'pre-Romantic' aspects of the eighteenth century, but these did not represent any organized or systematic attempt to replace intellectual values by subjective feelings; the new sensibility emerged slowly and sporadically and, existing alongside the old outlook, it led at no point to a decisive break with the traditional order. Partly encouraged by the influence of bourgeois sentimentality, it was also rooted in a deep reaction against classicism and even against the excessive intellectualism of the Enlightenment itself. As men began to explore their reality as finite human beings, they became conscious of more than merely mental needs. Already the philosopher Locke with his stress upon sensation had opened up the possibility of a less stable conception of the self. The novels of Prévost, the comedies of Marivaux, the growing interest in Shakespeare and the novels of Richardson, the popularity of the bogus Celtic poetry of Ossian, the vogue of Gessner's

Idylls and the sympathetic reception of Goethe's *Werther* were all signs of this sensibility, which found its most eloquent expression in the personal writings of Jean-Jacques Rousseau.

The influence of English poetry – Young's *Night Thoughts*, Thomson's *Seasons*, Gray's *Elegy* – strengthened this resistance to intellectualism by encouraging indulgence in melancholy yearning. A new feeling for nature was also emerging. Significant of this trend was the love of the artful disorder of English gardens which seemed more 'natural' than the geometrical lines of the French gardens of Le Nôtre. Painters such as Vernet began to portray wild, picturesque scenes – shipwrecks, storms and rugged landscapes. In a more general way other painters – Chardin and Fragonard, for example – attempted to capture on their canvases the play of light and shade and to use vivid colour to render the sensuous beauty of physical objects. English and Swiss travellers like Coye and Saussure revealed the attractions of mountain scenery. With his poem *The Alps*, Haller stimulated interest in a hitherto neglected part of Europe. The curiosity directed upon primitive peoples, including the 'noble savage', was often accompanied by a new-found enthusiasm for their exotic surroundings. Bernardin de Saint-Pierre's description of Mauritius in *Paul et Virginie* contributed as much to the success of the book as his portrayal of simple characters. Rousseau made his readers feel the close bond which existed between the beauty of physical nature and their inner feelings: a landscape became *un état d'âme*. The cult of nature spread to the love of night, a predilection for ruins and tombs and aspects of the external world which were capable of arousing deep emotions. Eventually this sensibility led to a new attitude, a deepening dissatisfaction with life as it was and the experience of a melancholy inspired by unfulfilled longings.

This new mood was also partially responsible for the renewal of the religious spirit, usually in response to the promptings of the heart rather than of the mind. In England Methodism sought to revitalize the established Church; in Germany pietism exerted an increasingly strong influence on men's inner life, whilst in France there was a growing interest in occultism and illuminism, often inspired by the writings of Swedenborg. Rousseau's *Profession de foi* and *La Nouvelle Héloïse*, with its strong religious emphasis, helped to reawaken dormant feelings from which even orthodox Christianity itself was to derive great benefit with the eventual publication of Chateaubriand's *Le Génie du Christianisme* in 1802. All these movements were prompted by a widespread desire for an emotional satisfaction which could not be found in the intellectualism of the Enlightenment.

It was inevitable that with these changes in outlook, the conception of art itself should be greatly modified. Undoubtedly, the enormous prestige of classicism still weighed heavily even upon those writers who, in the domain of ideas, were striving to emancipate themselves from traditional principles, and the eighteenth century never freed itself completely from the tutelage of the old aesthetic conservatism. It is enough to recall that Voltaire, in spite of many radical views, still considered himself a defender of classical taste (however liberal his interpretation of it) and that he was esteemed by his contemporaries mainly as a writer of tragedies and serious poetry. The classical notion of 'imitation' still remained a cardinal principle of literary theory, and this was buttressed by the continuing belief in the universality of human nature. At the same time it was recognized by many writers that the permanent features of human existence had to be adapted to various aspects of contemporary life: art itself could no longer remain aloof from historical, geographical and social influences.

There was a growing recognition that the appreciation of art depended on a number of factors which, though perhaps universal, involved more than the rational criteria of classicism. Feeling was as important as reason in judging the worth of a work of art, which had to satisfy both aspects of man's being. Moreover, due account had to be taken of the physical circumstances which help to give art its diversity. The very notion of beauty itself was considerably modified as the balance and harmony traditionally associated with the formal principles of classicism were replaced by a conception that allowed greater room for the expression of sensibility and emotions stimulated by the experience of the grandiose and the terrible. Reflection upon the nature of beauty itself was being developed more systematically as the creation of the term 'aesthetics' by Baumgarten in 1735 clearly shows. Although the classical genres continued to enjoy considerable prestige, there was an increasing desire to create new genres having a closer connection with the needs of the age. Classical tragedy, though diligently pursued by Voltaire, tended to give way to the *drame bourgeois* which, as its name implies, was deemed to be closer to the interests of the rising social class. The novel, too, a minor and somewhat despised genre during the classical period, gave evidence of remarkable vitality and renewal. As it dealt with subjects closest to real life – love, money and social advancement – it was one of the most popular genres of the period. Novelists made use of new forms – the memoir, the first-person narrative and letters. Writers like Diderot and Sterne did not hesitate to make still bolder experiments, while Voltaire and Montesquieu used the novel as a vehicle for the presentation of philosophical ideas or the satirical portrayal of contemporary viewpoints. Respect for the classical tradition was still very strong, but writers were beginning to realize that a full understanding of nature and its relation with the modern world required a changed aesthetic outlook as well as a new philosophy of life.

This new approach to literature was accompanied by an important change of attitude towards the function of the writer himself. The emphasis upon feeling, though not destroying the traditional respect for the principle of 'imitation', meant that artists hitherto looked more and more to the resources of their inner life for the inspiration of their work. The growing interest in the psychological origins of art and the recognition of the variety of cultural phenomena inevitably made artists sceptical about the value of the old absolutes. The notion of genius henceforth emerged as a significant new concept in artistic theory, although it was only in the Romantic Movement that it achieved its real apotheosis. True art was impossible without 'enthusiasm' and enthusiasm itself depended on the innate power of 'genius'. Genius alone, declared Diderot, was able to penetrate the true mystery of 'nature'. Likewise, Edward Young, in his *Conjectures on Original Composition*, praised the writer for being more than an ordinary human being.

One important consequence of this new development was to give writers much greater independence; they could henceforth write with the knowledge that there was a market for their books. Admittedly, poverty remained an ever-present threat: Samuel Johnson's early struggles, the bohemianism of the young Diderot and the desperate plight of the poet Thomson, compelled to sell his poem *The Seasons* for a pair of shoes, are but a few examples of the precarious nature of the literary profession. However, the old system of patronage was on the decline. In England it was virtually at an end by 1750, although the first part of the period saw writers still dependent on pensions and sinecures. In general there was a growing recognition that a book was a commodity of commercial value and the establishment of a new relationship between writers and publishers helped to increase the independence of the former. If the eighteenth century lacked the exalted view of the artist which was to be characteristic of Romanticism, it was none the less gradually according him a far higher status than that of the 'skittle-player' to whom he had been compared in the classical age. Writers were now being treated as the purveyors of truth and enlightenment and as men who were working – or could work – for the happiness and well-being of their fellow-men.

PART ONE

LITERATURE OF IDEAS

ONE

Literature of Ideas

As has already been indicated in the Introduction, there is no difficulty in naming the two thinkers who were to dominate the early decades of the Enlightenment, for Locke and Newton were held by many to be (in the expression of the Encyclopedists) 'demi-gods'. These intellectual giants were to oust from his growing position of eminence the philosopher whom many had already hailed as the founder of modern philosophy – Descartes. After being received with considerable distrust by his seventeenth-century contemporaries, Descartes had gradually been accepted as an ally of Christianity. More especially, the French Jesuits had given their approval to Cartesianism, which consequently began to find favour among the supporters of 'revelation'; the idea of reconciling philosophy and theology (for Descartes himself had insisted that the notion of God's existence was the ultimate basis of all valid philosophizing) attracted those who were impressed by the Cartesian stress on the autonomy of mind and spirit. Various attempts – including that of Malebranche, with his notion of the vision of all things 'in God' – were made to give Cartesian principles a more specifically religious character. Nevertheless, the universality of rational principles raised difficulties for the defenders of 'revelation'; and the influence of Descartes inclined many thinkers to accept broader religious principles than those of traditional Christianity. Consequently, Cartesianism often took the form of deism, so that if 'revelation' was not explicitly rejected, it was allowed to fall quietly into the background, prominence being given to those universal principles which seemed to be part of the fundamental beliefs of all reasonable men.

As Newtonianism began to replace Cartesianism, more and more thinkers tended to see in Descartes a pioneer rather than a constructive philosopher. The abstract *a priori* character of his metaphysical system was deemed to be incompatible with the scientific and empirical outlook of Newton and Locke, so that Cartesian philosophy was rejected by Voltaire as a mere 'romance', and the product of an uncontrolled imagination, whilst the real value of Cartesianism was alleged to lie in its method – the bold method of doubt, which, by substituting reason for authority, seemed to prepare the way for future intellectual advances. For many thinkers progress would be achieved only when attention was turned from abstract metaphysics towards a philosophical and scientific method based on experience and observation.

In spite of the rejection of Descartes's metaphysics, he continued to exercise an important influence upon the interpretation of the physical world. Because many philosophers were prepared to accept his mechanistic view of matter while ignoring his insistence on the autonomy of mind, he became the unwitting supporter of a materialist outlook which reduced all reality to matter in movement. The Cartesian principle of matter as extension was given universal validity and made to exclude any theological stress upon the role of Providence or 'final causes'. 'Natural laws' were deemed to offer an adequate explanation of everything that existed and, with the abandonment of mind as a unique substance, the way was prepared for the development of materialism. Many thinkers, it is true, believed that this complex piece of universal mechanism still needed a creator, but others were content to accept it as self-regulating: how or when it had been created was of no interest to those who were concerned solely with its present mode of working.

The influence of other rationalist thinkers who were opposed to Descartes in their fundamental ideas sometimes reinforced the development of another kind of materialism. Such was the case with Spinoza – who was considered by most eighteenth-century thinkers as an atheist. His work was known only imperfectly, being restricted mostly to the *Tractatus philosophico-theologicus* and a part of the *Ethics* and usually read in adaptations and interpretations which distorted its real meaning. Nevertheless, Spinoza's monism seemed to lend support to the notion of universal necessity and his works, severely proscribed by the authorities, were at first available only in clandestine manuscripts.

In the early decades of the century, however, materialism made only limited progress, for philosophical optimism was still a powerful intellectual force. Unlike Spinoza, Leibniz, while retaining the broad concept of determinism, had tried to preserve the notion of God's omnipotence and reconcile it with the autonomy of human freedom; he thus emerged as the protagonist of a fundamentally religious view of the universe. As in Spinoza's case, knowledge of his work was limited, in spite of the wide diffusion of the *Theodicy* and the considerable interest aroused by the controversy with Bayle; in France he was known largely through the adaptations of Christian Wolff and his followers. Moreover, like other philosophical movements of the time, Leibniz's influence merged with that of optimistic viewpoints to which it was not directly related: as the defender of religious and philosophical optimism, Leibniz was associated with Pope and other writers who stressed the idea of the universe as a vast system working for the good of the whole.[1]

As well as these complex philosophical developments, there were also many attempts to combine the religious and scientific views of the universe in a more popular manner. The 'final causes' which had apparently been banished from philosophy by Cartesianism re-entered through another intellectual door. In particular, there was a widespread demand for books which combined science and theology. Typical of these were the *Physico-theology* and the *Astro-theology* of Derham; the Dutch scientist Bernard Nieuwentyt produced a very popular work which sought to prove God's existence from the marvels of nature, while one of the most widely read books of this kind was the abbé Pluche's *Spectacle de la Nature* (1732–42) which went through many editions.

Deism, therefore, rather than atheism and materialism, was the characteristic attitude of the early part of the Enlightenment and it found valuable support in the work of Newton whose influence overshadowed all other scientific developments of the time. Not only did Newton reject the *a priori* character of Cartesianism, but the apparently objective principle of gravitation seemed to demolish a metaphysical system that relied on 'innate ideas' and the analysis of human consciousness. Henceforth philosophical and scientific progress was judged to depend on the discovery of the 'how' rather than of the 'why' of natural phenomena; it was believed that fresh knowledge of the universe could be obtained only from the results of observation and experiment. At the same time, it seemed possible to combine this

1. On Leibniz see pp. 93–8.

scientific attitude with the religious interpretation of nature, for Newton had affirmed not only that God could – and did – intervene directly in the workings of the universe, but that nature itself had been created by an omnipotent and all-wise God.

Yet at a time when metaphysics was on the retreat and religious belief itself was being increasingly exposed to attack, the ultimate influence of Newtonianism could be expressed in different ways. The universal validity of the principle of gravitation inspired many thinkers with the hope of finding a single principle which would explain all the mysteries of the universe. It is interesting to observe how, in the *Discours préliminaire* he wrote for the *Encyclopédie*, the usually cautious d'Alembert pointed out that anyone who could achieve the superhuman feat of taking in the whole universe at a glance might be able to explain it in terms of a single truth. Henceforth nature was to be conceived as a vast unity, even though many aspects might still remain hidden from our limited minds. Other thinkers, however, were not content to restrict this unity to the physical world, but were prepared to extend it to the explanation of human nature. When Condillac gave pride of place to 'sensation' as the key-concept of his psychological system, he saw himself as a follower of Newton's scientific method.

It was not only the impressive range of Newtonian science and the remarkable variety of its achievements which led thinkers to consider the universe – and more particularly matter – as being composed of something more fundamental than 'extension'; new intellectual paths were to be opened up by the development of other sciences, especially in the latter half of the century. Particularly important were the rapidly expanding 'sciences of life', which helped to undermine still further the mechanistic concepts of Cartesianism. Already in his book *De generatione* (1651) Harvey had questioned the validity of traditional (and especially Aristotelian) ideas about generation and the following century was to witness vigorous and often passionate debates on the subject. Especially prominent was the attempt to break down the barrier between human and vegetable life. Abraham Trembley's researches on the freshwater hydra or 'polyp', by revealing its remarkable regenerative power, seemed to open up the possibility of abolishing the absolute distinction between plants and animals and so of establishing a mode of reproduction that owed nothing to sexual activity. Moreover, Trembley's work was eagerly accepted by the opponents of the old theory of 'preformation' or *emboîtement*, according to which all the 'seeds' of future generations had already been present in the very first human beings. Still more remarkable was the impact of experiments carried out by the abbé Needham, who claimed to have discovered 'spontaneous generation'. Once again a scientist was believed, albeit mistakenly, to have shown that living organisms could be produced from vegetable substances. Critics of Cartesianism such as Maupertuis – probably an unjustly neglected thinker of the time – also helped to encourage the idea that matter had hitherto unsuspected properties of growth and vitality.

The effect of all this was to strengthen the idea that matter could be analysed in terms of its own inherent characteristics, for it no longer depended on some quality (such as movement) imposed upon it from the outside. It is, therefore, not surprising to find developments in biology being used to further the cause of materialism, but of a materialism based on a vitalistic, dynamic principle and not upon the physico-mathematical and mechanistic conception of Cartesianism. The attribution of a new vitality to matter was also encouraged by certain philosophical influences. Leibniz, whose support of philosophical optimism has already been noted, had been firmly opposed to the mechanistic views of Descartes: he had treated the 'monads' as 'immaterial atoms' which were centres of force and energy. Although this system of monads was made the basis of a view of the universe which involved the notion of a universal harmony ultimately controlled by God, it could be detached from its theological context and used in the analysis of the physical world. In this Leibniz was made an unwitting supporter of materialism. Likewise, Spinoza, with his conception of reality as a form of *nisus* or striving, encouraged the same dynamic view of matter. To these modern rationalists ought also to be added ancient thinkers such as Lucretius and Epicurus who had defended a non-mechanistic conception of the physical world. Philosophic ideas thus began to impinge on scientific theories with which they had seemingly only a very remote connection.

Such developments inevitably helped to weaken the traditional idea of the world as a complex piece of mechanism, the work of a divine clockmaker. Instead of being a clock, it was now treated as a living 'soul' or 'animal', whose parts were often in active relationship with one another. Nevertheless, the controversies aroused by old-fashioned materialists such as Helvétius and d'Holbach show that the Enlightenment was a period when many different views of the world were striving for recognition.

The introduction of non-rational concepts into philosophy and science was not restricted to general views of nature, for it began to exert a profound influence on man's ideas about his own existence. John Locke helped to demolish the rationalist view of man by attacking the Cartesian notion of innate ideas and by starting his philosophical inquiry at the level of sensation rather than of abstract mental activity. Instead of assuming that it was possible to obtain direct insight into the meaning of mental or physical substances or of deciding whether man is first and foremost a thinking substance, Locke proposed to set about the more modest task of explaining the origin and development of his ideas. He did not ignore the activity of the mind or deny that it had a unique function, but he related it closely to the realm of sense-experience; this advocate of the 'plain historical method', who claimed to be no more than 'an under-labourer' engaged in 'clearing ground a little and removing some of the rubbish that lies in the way to knowledge', was enthusiastically praised by Voltaire as the 'historian of the human mind' and as the thinker who had boldly rejected the abstractions of traditional metaphysics. As d'Alembert was later to say, he had reduced metaphysics to its true role of 'the experimental physics of the soul'. Although Locke himself had been a sincere Christian, many of his successors did not hesitate to make the priority accorded to sensations an argument for materialism. Even an opponent of materialism like Condillac believed that Locke had not been radical enough in his approach and he set himself the task of explaining all mental and psychological functions as developing forms of 'sensation'. In a more general way, however, Locke's influence certainly encouraged thinkers and writers to look more closely at the working of the human mind and to relate it to immediate experience rather than to rational thought.

The repercussions of this attitude upon moral philosophy were often very profound. If the method of genetic explanation was applied to moral notions, priority was likely to be given to pleasure and pain and not to virtue and vice. The materialist doctor-philosopher La Mettrie (1709–51) affirmed that morality had no connection with traditional notions of virtue or spiritual contemplation, but was directly connected with the search for happiness and pleasure; since physical sensations ought always to be given precedence over intellectual and moral notions, he believed that some form of hedonism was the only sensible philosophy.

Although La Mettrie's extreme position would have shocked most of his contemporaries, his insistence on the importance of earthly happiness was a commonplace notion. As soon as men began to see their problems in the light of possibilities open to them in this world rather than in the next, it was natural for them to focus their attention on the problem of happiness. Moreover, since happiness involved the fulfilment of the whole man and not just his rational or moral aspect, particular emphasis was placed on his affective nature. The eighteenth century was an age when thinkers accepted passion and feeling as essential constituents of man's being. Moreover, Hobbes and Spinoza had already insisted upon the non-moral attributes of 'natural' man; for them morality was the product of social development, not an innate impulse; if men were left to themselves, they would simply destroy one another. Certainly this pessimistic view was not shared by all thinkers and it is enough to recall Rousseau's vigorous opposition to Hobbes, but even Rousseau was forced to admit that primitive man lacked morality and was little more than a creature of instinct.

In spite of this growing desire to rehabilitate the passions and the affective side of human nature, few writers were prepared to deny the need to adapt them to the requirements of social life. Many thinkers who were not greatly interested in political theory were very much concerned with the problem of social morality and its effect upon humanity as a whole. An active social conscience was often accompanied by political conservatism. Most of the *philosophes* tended to be supporters of the monarchy, and some were prepared to defend the notion of 'enlightened despotism'. The visits of d'Alembert and Voltaire to Frederick the Great and of Diderot to the Empress Catherine of Russia remind us that the *philosophes* did not have any confidence in the ability of the lower classes to help themselves. Nevertheless there was a growing desire to bring greater rationality and justice into the existing social system, for an acceptable political order required just laws. Many thinkers judged the existing criminal code to be barbarous and inhuman; and the use of torture was explicitly condemned in the *Encyclopédie*. Denunciation of religious intolerance was also frequent among the *philosophes*. There was widespread opposition to all institutions which degraded man by depriving him of a freedom which was his inalienable right.

If literature tended to lack specific political content, it granted a large place to social morality. Humanitarianism became of great concern to the eighteenth century. Although it was agreed that happiness was the worthy object of human endeavour, it was also maintained that the individual ought not to seek it at the expense of other people. As the idea of moral autonomy was weakened under the influence of the pleasure–pain principle, the emphasis upon social relations became correspondingly greater. Materialist philosophers, in particular, stressed the importance of judging men's actions by their effect on society. Those who still believed in some kind of providential order or universal harmony were also inclined to see society as part of this wider unity. Happiness became a worthy moral goal as soon as it involved the idea of seeking the happiness of all. Self-love, when properly organized and controlled, was perfectly consistent with the love of others. Some writers were prepared to follow Shaftesbury in his view that men possessed a social instinct or innate feeling which spontaneously impelled them towards benevolence. Even those who, like Mandeville, took a more pessimistic view of human nature, still believed that 'private vices' could be made to contribute to the 'public good'.

Seen as a whole, this extensive literature of ideas shows a greater concern for specifically human problems than for abstract philosophical notions. Since the broad concept of 'nature' is usually considered to be inseparable from that of 'human nature', thinkers inevitably tended to concentrate on themes related to the history of man, his position in the world and his efforts to achieve earthly happiness. Although the major thinkers sometimes linked up their particular interests with wider philosophical issues, others were content to explore some limited but, as they believed, fundamental aspect of the human condition. This is why the 'sciences of man' were gradually taking the place of traditional metaphysics.

TWO

France

As Paul Hazard has convincingly shown in his classical study of the European consciousness, the first signs of these intellectual changes were already evident in the last decades of the seventeenth century. Even in France, the bastion of absolutism, traditional values were gradually being called into question; in particular, doubts were being voiced about the truth of certain Christian dogmas. Admittedly, the *libertins*, who were among the first to protest against the Christian way of life, did not constitute an influential group of thinkers; many of them were for the most part pleasure-loving aristocrats more concerned with practical and personal activities than with the theoretical and general implications of their epicurean outlook, and if they were severely condemned by the orthodox, it was as much for their example as for their precept. Nevertheless, the *libertins* could count some men of letters among them – Saint-Évremond, the essayist, and the poet Théophile de Viau. Apart from advocating epicurean ideas, Saint-Évremond, in his *Réflexions sur les divers génies du peuple romain*, attempted a philosophical analysis of Roman history and dared to criticize many traditions and legends hitherto accepted by most writers as historical fact. Often writers of unimpeachable orthodoxy unwittingly helped to undermine the uncritical acceptance of the old absolutes: such was the case with the work of the Roman Catholic priest Richard Simon (1638–1712) in the field of biblical criticism: to subject the books of the Bible to objective scrutiny – however honest and impartial – was likely to disturb the prevailing mood of obedience to authority and helped to furnish enemies of the Church with some valuable ammunition for their later attacks. When Fénelon, in his turn, conceived the idea of writing a novel (*Télémaque*, 1699) for the instruction of the young Duc de Bourgogne, he did not hesitate to look critically at the political system of Louis XIV; by advocating the limitation of royal power, he was challenging the widely accepted principle of the divine right of kings. In a more general way, influences such as these were to merge with the widening of intellectual horizons effected by the increased knowledge of foreign cultures; the many travel books which were to become such a popular feature of the eighteenth century began to make the French realize that culture was much more varied and relative than the advocates of absolute truth had previously supposed; although thinkers continued to search for the universal principles of human nature, they became increasingly reluctant to look for them in the fixed domain of supernatural religious beliefs; the mystery of human existence, it was argued, could only be resolved – if at all – by a full and impartial examination of its many varied and contradictory forms.

In France censorship could still be very strict and after the Revocation of the Edict of Nantes it would have been impossible for any thinker to defend openly the cause of religious toleration. Yet by forcing Protestants to flee from France in order to escape persecution and death, the authorities had involuntarily prepared the way for widespread attacks upon the exclusive authority of the Roman Church; exiles who had taken refuge in England and Holland not only began to translate critical works into French but also to write for journals which were being secretly introduced into France. To such activities should be added the more aggressive and radical clandestine literature which was being circulated in manuscript and which was eagerly read by those who could afford to buy it. When such factors are related to the more specific philosophical developments already mentioned in the Introduction, it becomes clear that even before the death of Louis XIV, France was destined for great intellectual changes.

One of the first major writers to express this new spirit was probably Pierre Bayle (1647–1706), whose work was to be constantly used by the *philosophes.* After criticizing superstition in his *Pensées sur la comète* (1682), he went on to produce his major work, the *Dictionnaire critique et historique* (1695–97); ostensibly containing inoffensive articles on history and geography, it subjected to close scrutiny (especially in its copious footnotes) many sacrosanct religious ideas; more especially, it cast doubt on many traditional Roman Catholic beliefs – by showing, for example, that certain widely revered saints had never existed! Bayle was also fond of pointing out how Roman Catholicism had maintained itself only through tyranny and bloodshed. In a more general way, he criticized the whole idea of a philosophical and theological optimism based on the activity of divine Providence and, in particular, he challenged Leibniz's ideas, suggesting that Manicheism might offer a more credible explanation of human history than providentialism. Bayle's work was significant not simply for its critical emphasis but also for the way in which this criticism relied on the careful examination of historical evidence. Furthermore, Bayle concluded from his painstaking research that, since it was impossible for any single man or group of men to prove the absolute validity of their viewpoint, the wisest and most moral attitude was to tolerate the expression of all beliefs; he even suggested extending such toleration to sincere atheists on the grounds that they could constitute a virtuous society.

Bayle is often associated with Fontenelle (1657–1757) as a forerunner of the Enlightenment. With his *Histoire des oracles* (1687), Fontenelle already cast doubt on pagan superstition and, by implication, upon Christian miracles, and a great deal of his subsequent work was to be imbued with the same sceptical spirit. Involved in the famous Quarrel of the Ancients and the Moderns, he was a resolute supporter of the latter, declaring that, because of the advance of reason and science, the modern world was in many ways superior to the old; even in those spheres in which the ancients had achieved perfection – in the arts and literature – Fontenelle believed that their feats could still be equalled. Impressed by the remarkable achievements of science, he became an influential popularizer of scientific ideas; the principles of astronomy, for example, were presented in his *Entretiens sur la pluralité des mondes* (1686). He praised the virtues of 'experimental philosophy' based on the study of 'things' at the expense of vague metaphysical concepts. Fontenelle, like Bayle, still belonged in some respect to the seventeenth century in so far as he remained attached to Cartesianism and never showed any sympathy for Newtonianism, preferring the theory of the 'vortices' to that of 'attraction', and basing his interpretation of nature largely on mechanistic principles; but he discreetly left aside Descartes's religious views and limited himself to a philosophical interpretation of the world which replaced supernaturalism by rational laws. In a still wider sense, Fontenelle's attachment to the universality of natural laws did not prevent him from adopting a critical attitude towards religious beliefs; he believed that religion would be constantly weakened by man's expanding knowledge of the physical world and his understanding of the errors and ignorance of the past.

In spite of their importance, thinkers such as Bayle and Fontenelle remain precursors of the new spirit rather than its principal exponents. Their influence eventually merged with that of the major thinkers of the Enlightenment as well as with the new intellectual and cultural forces which were beginning to make themselves felt in the early decades of the eighteenth century. One of the most important of these new thinkers and writers was undoubtedly Montesquieu.

MONTESQUIEU (1689–1755)

Unlike most of the *philosophes*, Montesquieu – or, to give him his full name, Charles-Louis de Secondat, Baron de la Brède et de Montesquieu (1689–1755) – was of aristocratic origins, being born into the *noblesse de robe*, that is, the nobility associated with the law and the *parlements*. Never knowing financial hardship, he always remained a property-owner who devoted considerable time and energy to the preservation and development of his lands and vineyards; all his life too he was closely identified with his native region of Guyenne and, while still a young man, he read papers on scientific subjects at the Bordeaux Academy of Sciences; on the death of his uncle in 1716 he inherited the position of *président à mortier* in the Bordeaux *parlement*. Although he spent some time in Paris, from 1721 to 1725, and subsequently travelled throughout Europe (a stay in England from 1729 to 1731 stimulated his interest in the English constitution), he eventually settled at La Brède where he composed his major works. On the whole, Montesquieu had a well-balanced contented character which showed little sign of deep anxiety and stress; he considered himself to be a happy man who, with his trust in reason and nature, had no difficulty in accepting the limitations of human existence. At the same time, he was sustained by a steadfast intellectual purpose and spent many years in the studious preparation of his masterpiece, *De l'esprit des lois*. He effectively summarized his outlook when he wrote in his notebooks: 'Study has been for me a sovereign remedy against discouragement and I have never had any trouble which an hour's reading has not taken away.'

Montesquieu made a brilliant literary debut with his *Lettres persanes* (1721), first published anonymously but then – after its astonishing success – with its author's name; it was a novel which appealed immediately to the newly awakened interest in the East (it had as its fictional framework a harem-intrigue) and to the rapidly developing critical awareness and the moral licence of the Regency period.[1] Although this epistolary novel contained in embryonic form some of Montesquieu's most important ideas, it was only with the publication of his *Considérations sur les causes de la grandeur des Romains et de leur décadence* (1734) that he gave some indication of his ultimate intellectual objectives. Written in an incisive style reminiscent of its Latin sources, it is one of the first serious historical works of the period and breaks sharply with the theological view of history exemplified by Bossuet's *Discours sur l'histoire universelle* – according to which human history, being guided by Providence, unfolds in obedience to a divine plan. The *Considérations* exclude any appeal to supernatural principles as they seek to explain the rise and fall of Roman power in purely natural terms; history is dominated neither by chance nor by Providence, but by 'general causes, either physical or moral'. Any specific cause – for example, some momentous battle – which seems to determine the fate of a particular state is simply part of a 'general cause'; 'particular accidents' of history, therefore, have to be interpreted in the light of its 'general movement'. Admittedly, the value of Montesquieu's explanatory principle is sometimes impaired by the obscurity of his conception of general causes, but his attempt to base his historical analysis on the use of original documents makes him a forerunner of 'scientific' history. No doubt his attitude to original sources was often uncritical when judged by modern standards (for example, he accepted Livy's speeches as authentic and treated Romulus and Remus as historical characters), but the *Considérations* tried to approach history objectively and to understand it in rational terms.

This historical work – like the extensive period of study and travel which followed its completion – was only a preliminary to Montesquieu's final and most ambitious production, *De l'esprit des lois*, which, though apparently finished about 1743, was not published until 1748. In spite of its somewhat sprawling and loosely organized form, this work is one of the intellectual landmarks of the age and represents a

1. See p. 17.

decisive change of mental attitude towards problems of law and government. As in the case of his earlier historical work, Montesquieu excludes, on the one hand, all recourse to supernatural theories of explanation and, on the other, any attempt to abandon the subject to the domain of mere chance and accident; he is convinced that the problem of law is inseparable from a systematic examination of the psychological and physical consequences of man's involvement in the finite world. Yet as the title of his work makes clear, Montesquieu is concerned with those deeper and broader principles which make the laws what they are in all their unity and diversity. This does not mean that he rejects all metaphysical notions, for he believes that there is a universal human nature which, in its turn, is related to still more fundamental aspects of the world; at the very outset he defines laws as 'the necessary relations which derive from the nature of things'. Yet this definition, though broadly metaphysical, rejects theological postulates, for it restricts itself to the finite world; even more important, it presupposes the idea of a causal connection between the various forms of observable phenomena. Montesquieu believes that law and politics are governed by principles capable of rational analysis and elucidation. Although this concern for an absolute explanation seems to hark back to Descartes and the old metaphysical tradition, his obvious anxiety to avoid the rash use of *a priori* assumptions brings Montesquieu close to Newton; like Newton, he wants to understand laws scientifically and to discover, by a close scrutiny of particular facts, the underlying principles which will enable him to understand their manifold forms. Ultimately, therefore, it is a question of grasping the 'spirit' of the laws rather than of merely describing their many different aspects.

In his initial effort to relate the problem of legislation and particular laws to the general 'laws of nature' governing 'the constitution of our being' and the structure of the universe in which we live, Montesquieu still belongs to the rationalist tradition; however precise and scientific any particular explanations may be, they have to take into account man's involvement in this wider metaphysical context. In spite of his keen interest in particular aspects of human experience, Montesquieu never abandoned his reliance on 'nature' and 'reason'. In this respect, he remained indebted not only to the rationalist tradition but also to the school of Natural Law thinkers who had attained prominence and influence in the seventeenth century. Like Grotius and Puffendorff, for example, he tried to describe the nature of man before his entry into society and, like them, he made use of the well-known concept of 'the state of nature'.

Yet Montesquieu was not content to consider such problems in merely abstract terms. This is interestingly brought out in the early chapters of *De l'esprit des lois* when he takes issue with Hobbes concerning man's character in the state of nature: he dismisses the Hobbesian view of man's innate aggressiveness as a theory which ignores the complexity of human experience. The 'idea of mastery and domination' is far from being a simple primordial urge, for it is made up of various psychological components and appears only at a late stage of human development; a careful examination of man's nature, argues Montesquieu, reveals that his essential need is to be close to his fellows; men are brought together by weakness, the pressure of primordial needs, sexual attraction and a conscious desire to live in society. Positive laws thus emerge from the adaption of these 'natural laws' to particular circumstances and social relations. No doubt man continues to retain his essential human characteristics in social life, but they are modified by particular conditions. In his conscientious search for the causal explanation of social phenomena – whether at the physical or psychological level – Montesquieu may be justifiably described as a 'precursor of modern sociology'.

Montesquieu's stress upon the role of causal explanation led him to attach considerable importance to physical factors in the formation of government and law. In particular, he emphasized the decisive influence of climate. The idea was not new and had already been developed by the sixteenth-century political thinker, Jean Bodin; the abbé Du Bos – the author of *Réflexions critiques sur la poésie et la peinture* (1719)[2] – had also stressed the role of climate in the development of aesthetic taste; Montesquieu was influenced, too, by the work of an English friend, the doctor, John Arbuthnot (1667–1735), author of an *Essay on the Effects of Air* (1733). Hot climates, maintains Montesquieu, have a weakening effect upon the population; people living in hot climates therefore accept despotism more easily than northern peoples

2. See pp. 393–6.

who are spurred on to hard work and political independence by their cold climate and inhospitable terrain; free peoples are thus found more frequently in the north than in the south.

Some ambiguity and confusion in Montesquieu's work is due to his desire to remain a moralist, in spite of his historical and scientific outlook. A good example of this appears in his classification of governments and the principles sustaining them. It had been customary to classify various forms of government since the time of Aristotle, who had already distinguished between monarchy, aristocracy and republic with their corresponding corrupt forms of tyranny, oligarchy and ochlocracy; Montesquieu divides governments into republics (which include democracy and aristocracy), monarchy and despotism. The sustaining principle of a republic must be virtue, the civic strength which allows the individual to subordinate selfish interests to the common good; monarchy has to rely on the principle of honour which encourages worthy ambition and a striving for 'preferences and distinctions', so that 'each one contributes to the common good, while believing that he is contributing to his own interests' (III, 7); despotism rests on the simple psychological motive of fear, for it has no need of virtue or honour. The underlying principle of government will help to explain the different types of education and laws; each state must develop the system of education most appropriate to its own needs, whilst laws will also vary from one country to another. Particular laws – for example, criminal and sumptuary laws – will reveal the same diversity. Furthermore, each type of government will deteriorate as soon as its guiding principle is weakened or lost; a democracy which ceases to respect virtue will disintegrate; a monarchy which neglects honour will soon become despotism, whilst a despot who can no longer inspire fear in his subjects will be rapidly overthrown. Thus any government wishing to survive has to maintain the principle on which it is founded. Yet this elaborate explanation of the different forms of government cannot conceal Montesquieu's hatred of despotism and his ultimate preference for those states which respect man's essential dignity as a human being.

Another theme which shows the uneasy alliance of the scientist and moralist in Montesquieu is that of freedom – a central preoccupation of *De l'esprit des lois*. In his treatment of this subject he not only appears as an objective thinker who is trying to account for its different forms

– 'liberty', he declares, 'is not meant for every nation' – but he also seeks to be the earnest advocate of a human value which transcends political considerations. As he admits, his heart is sometimes in conflict with his mind. While allowing that there may be rational grounds for accepting the existence of unfree societies, he clearly believes in the superiority of those which are free. Freedom, then, is not a purely abstract problem for Montesquieu. Not only does he show little interest in the philosophical problem of 'free will', but he also refuses to treat it as a matter for the individual alone; being free does not mean 'doing what one pleases'. In a state – that is, in a society where there are laws – freedom can consist only 'of being able to do what one ought to want to do, and not of being compelled to do what one ought not to want to do'. In other words, freedom and independence are not the same thing. Although every individual has the right to security, this cannot be achieved outside the law. Political freedom is, in Montesquieu's opinion, inseparable from law. 'Freedom is the right to do what the laws permit; and if a citizen had the right to do what they forbid, he would no longer have freedom because others would also have the same power' (XI, 3). This explains why the 'formalities of justice' are necessary to freedom. On the other hand, freedom and the laws must not run counter to the 'nature of things'; all societies must respect fundamental human rights.

The effective expression of political freedom always involves, in Montesquieu's opinion, the acceptance of balance and moderation. This is one of the essential principles determining his whole outlook. True freedom, whether political or moral, 'is found between two limits'. That is why he lays such great stress upon the idea of political checks and balances. Every political society is threatened by the abuse of power, for 'any man who has power is inclined to misuse it'.

Montesquieu believed that the English constitution had been particularly successful in solving this problem. Already, upon his return from England in 1731, he had thought of writing a separate treatise about political freedom in that country and of appending it to the *Considérations*. Whether his knowledge of the English constitution was historically accurate has been disputed, but he obviously saw it – or wanted to see it – as an example of the advantageous separation of powers – executive, legislative and judiciary – and in this interpretation of English political life he seems to have followed the ideas of Bolingbroke and *The Craftsman*. In any case, he was convinced that any stable political constitution required a proper balance among its various elements and that the separation of powers seemed the most satisfactory way of achieving this end.

In spite of his admiration for England, Montesquieu realized that freedom in that country depended on conditions peculiar to it and that other states – for example, in Asia and the Orient – would not enjoy the same advantages. Even in Europe, circumstances varied greatly and in spite of his predilection for the English constitution, Montesquieu was aware that the French monarchy could not be the same as the English. He thought that, in France, effective government could be maintained only if the king relied on the support of the aristocracy and the clergy. In this respect, no political constitution could ignore its historical origins, for these helped to determine its present form. This no doubt explains Montesquieu's late decision to add the historical chapters to the end of the *De l'esprit des lois*. Although the modern reader is apt to find them tedious since they seem to be only marginally related to the main theme of the work, they provide an interesting indication of Montesquieu's conception of the origins of the French state – a subject that was passionately discussed by historians of the time; some saw the French monarch as the heir of the Roman constitution and so the holder of absolute authority by hereditary right (Du Bos was a supporter of this view); others – like the historian Boulainvilliers – traced the authority of the monarch to Germanic sources (which were hostile to Rome) so that, in their view, ancient monarchs had always relied on the support of the aristocracy. Montesquieu favoured this interpretation, for it seemed to lend weight to his conception of a properly balanced state in which the aristocrats would play an influential role. At the same time he believed – and this is already apparent in the *Lettres persanes* – that the French monarch could easily become a despot if he ignored the historical traditions which had brought him to power. The way for despotism had already been prepared (according to Montesquieu) by the political activities of Richelieu and Louvois who had made possible the incipient tyranny of Louis XIV.

In spite of its lofty intellectual purpose, *De l'esprit des lois* is not a dry abstract treatise. However historical and objective he tries to be,

Montesquieu leaves his personal imprint on every page of his work. His historical sense does not exclude deep humanitarian feelings, and it is this humanitarian impulse which often gives his style warmth, vigour and irony. It is characteristic of Montesquieu that, at the end of his long account of slavery as an institution explicable in terms of particular historical and physical causes, he should admit that he still finds it reprehensible. In his famous chapter on 'The slavery of the Negroes' (XV, 5), he makes a biting attack upon the European society which is prepared to support such exploitation of human beings for the sake of material gain.

Apparently a deist as far as his own personal religious beliefs were concerned, Montesquieu was prepared to judge particular religions by their social effects. Since he feared the disruptive effects of religious strife, he tended to support the dominant religion in each country. He believed that all existing religions should be tolerated, but that no new one should be introduced. In spite of his strictures upon the Roman Catholic Church in France, he continued to give it his support. At the same time, he remained a firm opponent of religious intolerance and his 'very humble remonstrance to the Inquisitors of Spain and Portugal' (XXV, 13) is a good example of his scathing criticism of fanaticism and bigotry. Yet his often severe criticism of traditional attitudes never carried him beyond the bounds of prudence. In no sense a revolutionary, he was opposed to violent change; the reforms he desired were to be achieved gradually in a spirit of enlightened rationality.

His growing interest in particular aspects of historical and physical causation never made Montesquieu a mere relativist. His search for the 'spirit' of the laws revealed his steadfast desire to establish broad principles. Like so many thinkers of the Enlightenment, he never abandoned his faith in the existence of a universe based on reason and nature; he also clung tenaciously to the notion of man as a being with a permanent essence. Even his insistence on the importance of causal explanation presupposed a stable and coherent universe. His awareness of the multiplicity and complexity of particular causes did not weaken his acceptance of some kind of absolute: he maintained that men's tendency to become lost in the many relativities of their daily lives ought not to make them doubt the permanence of the universal order of which they formed part. In this combination of relative and absolute elements, Montesquieu is a typical thinker of the early French Enlightenment.

VOLTAIRE (1694–1778)

If posterity has confirmed the judgement of Voltaire's contemporaries that he was a great writer, it is for reasons very different from theirs: whereas in his day he was hailed as a poet capable of matching the achievements of the classical age in tragedy and epic, most modern readers see him as one of the most brilliant representatives of the Enlightenment, the disseminator of a critical and irreverent spirit, the author of remarkable *contes* such as *Candide* and *Zadig* and the supreme master of literary irony; today his tragedies and serious poetry have little more than historical interest, but the prose-writer is very much alive, not only in his formal works but in his vast and fascinating correspondence. Whatever we may now think of his 'classical' writings, there is no denying the prodigious range and abundance of his output. As well as considering himself to be the heir and defender of the classical literary tradition, Voltaire was very much aware of what was happening in the world around him and if a great deal of his work has an improvisatory quality, it is because of his restless curiosity, his ceaseless desire to be involved in the events of his time and his determination to change men's outlook.

One of Voltaire's aims was to enlighten his fellow-countrymen about some of the most remarkable cultural achievements of the time; he wanted to make them aware of the most recent developments in philosophy, science and literature, and to broaden their intellectual horizon by opening their eyes to the wonders of European – and especially English – culture. Since he believed that knowledge of other cultures would make Frenchmen turn a critical gaze upon their own, his purpose was not simply didactic, for he wanted his contemporaries to revise their attitude towards fundamental philosophical, religious and social values. Consequently, he expended a great deal of energy in making fierce onslaughts upon complacency and ignorance; his remarkable literary gifts and extraordinary mental agility made him a formidable opponent of outworn institutions and modes of thought.

The great breadth of Voltaire's interests and his passionate desire to change existing attitudes inevitably limits his achievement as a 'philosopher' in the technical sense but explains his importance as a *philosophe*. In spite of strong convictions, Voltaire was not a profound or systematic thinker inasmuch as he did not undertake a detailed analysis of a limited number of philosophical problems, and it may be doubted whether he ever attained – or sought to attain – a rigidly consistent philosophical outlook. As a thinker, he was always concerned with the human and practical implications of ideas rather than with their intrinsic brilliance or value. Capable of wide intellectual curiosity, he let his mind range freely from one topic to another: his persistent effort to relate other thinkers' ideas to the immediate human situation prevented him from limiting his use of them to mere exposition or discussion. This is clearly brought out in his first major work, the *Lettres philosophiques* (1734), in which he sought to give the French public a synoptic view of English culture and institutions. Deeply impressed during his stay in England from 1728 to 1731 by the extent of that country's liberalism, he presented his readers with a brief but clear account of the work of Locke and Newton as well as of the religious and political institutions of England. Several vivid letters on the Quakers and shorter ones on the Church of England and the nonconformists stressed the tolerance of English religious attitudes; a brief account of the British constitution brought out the benefits of a limited monarchy, while a description of various social attitudes emphasized Englishmen's enlightened approach to such matters as trade, social habits, literature and the theatre. He also added a number of letters on English authors, which included an acknowledgement of Shakespeare's originality, 'barbarous' though Voltaire deemed it to be.

Yet this account of English life and thought was intended not only to inform the French public about a foreign culture, but also to make them aware of the shortcomings of their own way of life. The eulogy of English liberalism was but a means of criticizing French absolutism and intolerance. The work of Locke and Newton was praised at the expense of Descartes's 'romance' about metaphysics and astronomy; the variety of religious beliefs in England was contrasted with the exclusive authority of the Roman Catholic Church in France; an account of constitutional monarchy in England served to remind Frenchmen of the absolute power of their own king, who claimed to reign by divine right; the enlightened attitude of the English towards trade and social problems was also opposed to the absurd prejudices of the French aristocracy. The *Lettres philosophiques*, therefore, contain a remarkable blend of factual exposition and biting satire; both are expressed in a clear, varied and often brilliantly ironic style.

Other philosophical works devoted to the direct analysis of traditional problems usually have the same critical purpose. More especially, they seek to show the futility of metaphysics. Although the *Traité de métaphysique* (probably written in the 1730s, but not published during Voltaire's lifetime) contains a substantial section on the notion of God's existence as a necessary intellectual concept, it pours scorn on traditional metaphysics; believing (like Locke) that the resolution of such problems as the definition of God's essence or the nature of freedom (as opposed to the rational attempt to prove their actual existence) is beyond the capacity of the human mind, Voltaire's constructive thought is devoted to a consideration of practical moral issues; he is interested in human rather than in divine justice. The same emphasis appears in *Le Philosophe ignorant* (1766) which, as its title shows, is intended to be a lesson in intellectual modesty; the major part of this work seeks to show the absurdity of trying to find answers to insoluble philosophical problems; Voltaire points out that, whereas thinkers have always been hopelessly divided on metaphysical questions, they have shown a far greater measure of agreement in their discussions of universal moral principles; he contrasts the absurd and irrational opinions of metaphysicians and theologians with the fact that the 'whole universe' agrees that 'it is necessary to be just'. Likewise, the full title of his work on toleration, the *Traité de la tolérance à l'occasion de la mort de Jean Calas* (1763), shows that Voltaire does not wish to discuss the problem of religious tolerance in merely general terms, but to call attention to the shocking aspects of a particular case. The strength – as well as the weakness – of Voltaire's philosophical and religious writings lies in their concern with the practical human implications of the subjects discussed.

Of Voltaire's 'philosophical' works perhaps the *Dictionnaire philosophique* (1764) (on which he worked for many years and produced a number of versions) is the most effective, since it is perfectly adapted to his need for the incisive and witty exposition and discussion of philosophical and religious problems. It seems likely that the form of the work – a series of comments on a wide range of topics arranged in alphabetical order – owes something to his desire to compete with the *Encyclopédie*; although he had contributed some purely literary articles to that work, he had begun to doubt the effectiveness of its huge folio volumes as an instrument of 'philosophical' propaganda. The *Dictionnaire*, together with his *Questions sur l'Encyclopédie*, was intended to be a more concise and effective statement of ideas which Voltaire deemed essential to the betterment of mankind.

Voltaire did not possess strong religious feeling except in an inverted way; he showed a passionate, often obsessive hatred of traditional Christianity, especially in its Roman Catholic form. (His biographers relate that he had to retire to bed, physically and emotionally ravaged, on every anniversary of the St Bartholomew's Day massacre of the Protestants.) He never seems to have understood the nature of Pascal's spiritual anguish, as is clear from the comments appended to the *Lettres philosophiques*: Pascal, for Voltaire, is a gloomy, misanthropic thinker anxious to involve men in the sterile contemplation of their religious situation rather than in an active effort to eradicate the actual evils of intolerance and bigotry. Man, declares Voltaire, is born for action just as naturally as fire tends upwards; he does not need the support of supernatural powers, for reason is capable of telling him all he needs to know about religion (the existence of God and morality, the need for justice and the difference between good and evil). Men (at least enlightened men) have to be entrusted with the task of working out their own salvation, for there is no other way. Religious people who accept the authority of 'revelation' will (in Voltaire's opinion) not only be led to a supine acquiescence in existing injustice but, by remaining the victims of ecclesiastical tyranny and wickedness, will simply help to perpetuate fanaticism and intolerance. The same fear of a passive acceptance of present evils prompts Voltaire to make a sustained, ironical attack upon the metaphysical optimism of Leibniz in his philosophical tale *Candide*.

Voltaire's hostility to metaphysics and theology did not prevent him from being a deist. While believing that the human mind could not penetrate the secret of God's essence, he did not doubt its ability to establish the fact of his existence. The *Traité de métaphysique* interprets the presence of order in the universe as incontrovertible proof that it has been created by an intelligence greater than itself. In this respect, Voltaire's religious views link up with his acceptance of Newtonian science, for both presuppose the idea of an orderly universe governed by fixed laws. (Voltaire also stressed the importance of God's existence for a less praiseworthy reason: without the restraint of this belief, men might ignore all moral principles, so that even wise philosophers would no longer be able to sleep peacefully in their beds!)

Sometimes Voltaire's writings were simply intended to support his active personal efforts to obtain justice for the innocent. His views on toleration, for example, were prompted by his interest in the case of Jean Calas, the French Protestant who was brutally and unjustly executed for the alleged murder of his son; he also campaigned vigorously and successfully to rehabilitate the memory of such men as Sirven and the Chevalier de la Barre who had been put to death for offences against religion. Equally indignant about the barbarity of the French criminal code, he wrote an enthusiastic *Commentaire sur le livre des délits et des peines* (1766) which gave support to the Italian jurist Beccaria's plea for a more enlightened attitude towards penal reform.[3]

Even Voltaire's 'classical' works cannot be ignored by any student of his thought, for the traditional form often serves as a vehicle for the expression of his ideas. Such was the case with the *Discours en vers sur l'homme* (1738), a didactic poem partly inspired by Pope's *Essay on Man*. It is worth recalling that the author of the article 'Liberté' (probably the abbé Yvon) in the *Encyclopédie* did not hesitate to include extracts from this *Discours* in his detailed intellectual defence of free-will. Likewise, the tragedies – especially the later ones – often refer to favourite ideas such as the condemnation of intolerance and the evils of war. Voltaire's poems on *Le Désastre de Lisbonne* and *La Loi naturelle* (1755) provide valuable information about his intellectual development at a time when he was moving towards pessimism. (Their rejection of divine governance prompted Rousseau to reply to his illustrious contemporary with a *Lettre sur la Providence* in 1756.) Events such as the Lisbon earthquake of 1755, the horrors of the Seven Years War and Voltaire's own personal disappointments (especially with the King of Prussia) made him reject the idea that a world full

3. On Beccaria, see pp. 150–54.

of so much misery and pain could be ruled by Divine Providence. Nevertheless, his growing inclination to favour some kind of determinism did not make Voltaire accept it in any absolute sense. However great and numerous the evils of life might be, he believed that it was man's duty to oppose them and to work for happiness on this earth. The famous conclusion of *Candide* that 'we must cultivate our garden' expresses his practical solution to the problem; being always concerned with the improvement of the human lot, he could never be content to accept the world as it was. The reality of freedom might be difficult to prove at a strictly philosophical level, but it presented no problem for the man who was prepared to strive for its practical extension. There was no need, thought Voltaire, to waste time and energy demonstrating how and why men had this precious attribute; far more urgent was the task of teaching them how best to use it.

In the whole of Voltaire's work we detect the same overriding concern with man and, in this respect, he is at one with most of the thinkers of the Enlightenment. Attention has already been called to the humanitarianism of Montesquieu. In Voltaire's case, his restless energy, persistent curiosity and strong feelings did not allow him to remain content with the mere dissemination of general ideas or with an ironical attack upon traditional absolutes. Like Montesquieu, he was very much preoccupied with the spectacle of man's history and with his ceaseless efforts, sometimes successful, often unsuccessful, to rise above cruelty, ignorance and bigotry. Voltaire, however, was not content to record man's successes and failures, for he also tried to be a genuine historian and to develop a 'philosophy of history'. His early work, *Histoire de Charles XII* (1731), being for the most part a biography of the Swedish king, gave no indication of the breadth of his later approach to history, but it already revealed his love of accurate detail in its effort to present an authentic picture of the character and career of this strange monarch. *Le Siècle de Louis XIV* (1751) shows a significant shift from the narration of political and military events to the analysis of the essential characteristics of a particular historical period; included in this work is an account of the artistic and cultural achievements of the age as well as of its specifically historical aspects; *Le Siècle de Louis XIV* is thus one of the first serious attempts to describe the main features of a particular European civilization. Yet Voltaire tried to take a still wider view of historical phenomena, for he was greatly interested in the history of the human mind. With the *Essai sur les moeurs* (first published in 1756 and then republished in an expanded form in 1769) he undertook a still more ambitious task – the history of humanity. Whereas in his previous work he had made a serious effort to consult original documents and surviving witnesses of the age, he was henceforth forced to rely on secondary sources; but he sought to set European civilization within the context of world history as a whole. Needless to say, one of his main objects was to belittle the achievements of Christianity. In order to do this he denied any privileged place to Jewish history, which he considered to be less important than the ancient civilization of Egypt. Like many of the writers of the period, he also cast scorn on the Middle Ages. At the same time, he tried to show that the history of mankind contains much more than the feats of kings and generals, for it involves the complex reality of 'civilization'. However, since Voltaire, like so many of his contemporaries, was constantly preoccupied by the idea of 'universal' man, he tended to see civilization as a fixed concept manifesting itself in various ways at different stages of history. In this respect he still remained under the influence of the rationalist tradition and, in a yet more general sense, his approach to history was in harmony with his general view of the universe as an ordered whole.

The limitations of Voltaire's achievements as a historian have often been noted. His hostility to religion made it difficult for him to give an adequate account of human psychology; he saw priests as wicked exploiters of the credulous and believers as their foolish dupes. Likewise, his rejection of Bossuet's notion of Providence as a guiding force in history made him rely too much on the role of chance in determining the course of human affairs; unlike Montesquieu, therefore, he had no clear grasp of historical causation even though he realized that the interpretation of events needed some kind of guiding principle. On the whole he was wont to exaggerate the influence of 'great men' upon the course of history. It was probably Louis XIV's protection of such men which made Voltaire praise him so warmly. In Voltaire's opinion, civilization did not come about as a matter of course or as a result of widespread human activity, but through the efforts of the enlightened few. Later generations owed so much to Louis XIV and Peter the Great because these rulers had been able to discipline man's crude, animal-like nature. If, therefore, Voltaire's philosophy of history remains rather superficial, it still represents a considerable advance on the older theological approach. Moreover, Voltaire can be justifiably treated as the forerunner of modern 'scientific' history in so far as he made a steadfast effort to ascertain the truth of historical events; he not only criticized the acceptance of the miraculous and improbable as historical evidence, but he also refused to be overawed by traditional authority.

In any case, Voltaire never had a purely detached view of history, for he was aware that if the study of the past showed mankind struggling towards the light, its achievements remained precarious. Always likely to slip back into barbarism, man would maintain progress only if he remained watchful of himself and his situation. Civilization, insisted Voltaire, had to be supported and extended by ceaseless effort. By relating the history of the past, therefore, Voltaire wished to call attention to the shortcomings of the present and to the enormous tasks of the future. He hoped that even the eighteenth century – the 'age of philosophy' – would find useful lessons in *Le Siècle de Louis XIV*.

In view of Voltaire's constant desire to improve men's lot, it may be asked to what extent he intended his action to be political. In his early years he had spent considerable time in kings' courts and ministers' anterooms, but he had never been given serious political responsibility. The tragi-comedy of his relationship with Frederick the Great remained one of the more sobering experiences of his long life. His eventual decision to withdraw from the political scene still left him with a keen and active interest in contemporary affairs and with a strong desire to play his part in the resolution of practical issues. He does not seem to have given careful and systematic consideration to general problems of political theory and he never produced anything to match Rousseau's *Contrat social*; nor did his concern for humanity make him a 'democrat' in the same way as Rousseau may be said to have been a democrat in his doctrine of sovereignty of the people and the 'general will'. Voltaire always distrusted the masses – *la canaille*, as he was wont to call them; since their ignorance and brutishness made it impossible for them to help themselves, the only hope of improving their lot lay in the action of an enlightened monarch, perhaps a despot, who was ready to heed the advice of intelligent *philosophes*. The 'spirit of a nation' always resided, in Voltaire's view, in a minority of enlightened people who could bring benefits to the rest and the only person able to make a direct and effective impact upon the nation was a monarch invested with the requisite power. Voltaire conceded that democracy might be possible in very small states, but he believed that a large country like France required a strong monarchy.

In many respects Voltaire remained a typical bourgeois who, fearing internal disruption and anarchy, was anxious to maintain a stable political order. If he wanted the king to make the necessary improvements to the state, he was firmly opposed to the nefarious influence of privileged bodies, especially the clergy. The aristocracy was to be tolerated only if it made itself socially and economically useful, as it had done in England. While he remained friendly with many French aristocrats, Voltaire's unhappy experience with others made him critical of their role.

In general Voltaire was much more eager to eradicate contemporary abuses than to modify the essential structure of society. He considered that the *philosophes*' primary task was to work for the spread of enlightened attitudes and to help to change people's way of thinking about the human condition. In the name of 'reason' and 'humanity' he was prepared to attack any outlook which ran counter to the principle of enlightened 'nature': he fought for the rehabilitation of unjustly executed and persecuted Protestants; he attacked the iniquities of the criminal code; he was relentlessly opposed to religious intolerance and urged his fellow-*philosophes* 'to crush the infamous thing'; he strove for a society which would grant writers and thinkers genuine freedom of thought.

If he was able to do more to attain his objectives than other contemporary writers, it was because of his remarkable literary gifts; his clear, precise and rapid style rarely faltered, even when dealing with obscure subjects. Most striking of all was his extraordinary mastery of irony. No French writer has more effectively undertaken the oblique criticism of established ideas and institutions; he could demolish a point of view in a single verbal thrust; he could destroy an idea at the very moment when he seemed to be espousing it; his irony was indefatigable in hunting down pretentiousness and cant. Yet while Voltaire sought to arouse his reader's indignation, his irony also brought into play his intelligence, so that the abuses he attacked were made to seem irrational as well as inhuman. Writing, therefore, was for him not the creation of mere literary effect, but an instrument for changing man's attitude towards his position in the world.

ROUSSEAU (1712–78)

In retrospect many of Jean-Jacques Rousseau's ideas (for example, on philosophy and religion) often seem unexceptional when placed in the context of contemporary thought, whilst others (such as his political theories), though much more original, were couched in an abstract form which prevented them from achieving wide diffusion during his lifetime. Yet, whatever the subject on which he wrote, he managed to imbue it with an urgency and intensity which could not leave his readers indifferent. At the same time, the strong link between his personality, ideas and style often hindered – and still hinder – a proper understanding of his achievement as a thinker. In his last years Rousseau himself, with the composition of his autobiographical writings, perhaps unwittingly encouraged misunderstanding of his didactic work by presenting himself as a lonely, unique figure destined to be misunderstood and vilified by a hostile world.

Although the difference between certain of Rousseau's ideas and those of the Enlightenment must not be exaggerated, there is no doubt that, on some issues, especially those appertaining to the nature of society, he was at odds with the *philosophes*. Moreover, his origins and character made him hostile to the cultural values of eighteenth-century France. Born in the Protestant republic of Geneva, he never completely escaped its influence, even though he left it at the age of sixteen: on the title-page of several of his major works he proudly described himself as 'Citizen of Geneva'. Since his mother died a few days after his birth and his erratic father had to leave Geneva in 1722 as the result of a quarrel, young Jean-Jacques received very little formal education. This may help to explain his later distrust of the French intellectuals, and his rejection of the title of 'philosopher' in favour of that of a simple 'friend of the truth'. He was also endowed with a highly developed sensitivity which often wrought havoc with his personal relationships and, when taken in conjunction with his painful bladder complaint, made it difficult for him to adapt himself to the conventional social life of his time. When, therefore, he eventually went to Paris in 1742 for a prolonged stay, he could look upon the life and outlook of the capital with the critical detachment of an 'outsider'. Admittedly, he did not escape the influence of the *philosophes* but towards the end of his life he insisted that they had merely 'shaken' him, never 'convinced' him, with their irreligion.

From the very outset Rousseau provoked controversy by challenging one of the cherished assumptions of the Enlightenment: far from being a sign of progress, modern culture was, in his view, an unmistakable symptom of moral disease. The essay which won Rousseau the Academy of Dijon prize in 1749, the *Discours sur les sciences et les arts*, established the fundamental principle of his 'system' – the antithesis between cultural achievement and natural human need. More especially, by abandoning the development of his true nature for an anonymous existence in an artificial, unequal and unjust society, man had transformed himself into a mere cipher, a simple numerical unit devoid of individuality and genuine humanity; living henceforth 'outside himself', he was the slave of 'opinion' instead of being the free man of 'nature'.

Having indicated the errors of modern culture, Rousseau was still faced with the problem of explaining their origin. Accordingly, the *Discours sur l'origine de l'inégalité* (1755) attempted a hypothetical and imaginary reconstruction of man's history, beginning with the traditional concept of the 'state of nature' and ending with contemporary society. In this approach to his subject, Rousseau was following the genetic method already adopted by Locke, Condillac and Buffon in their examination of other aspects of human nature. Rousseau pointed out that primitive man was an innocent animal-like being, knowing neither good nor evil, not only because he was governed by his instincts, but also because he was independent of other human beings: since he was largely self-sufficient and content with his immediate existence, he never had to face the problems of modern man who, being constantly divided against himself, is a permanent prey to anxiety. However, primitive man was not a 'man' in the full sense of the term and it was only when he abandoned his primitive state for participation in a simple communal life centred on the family that he found genuine fulfilment: this was probably the happiest period of human existence, for it was 'half-way between the stupidity of the brutes and the fatal enlightenment of civil man'. Yet this first social revolution was in no sense political, for political society did not appear until the advent of property and the legal separation of rich and poor; this new situation arose with the invention of agriculture and metallurgy and the consequent division of labour. In Rousseau's opinion, the great inequality resulting from this new society meant that the eventual foundation of a stable political order was little more than a gigantic confidence-trick perpetrated by the rich against the poor, who were persuaded to give up freedom for the sake of security. In this way inequality was given legal sanction and the majority of men were doomed to slavery and misery by the very act through which they had hoped to free themselves from uncertainty and conflict.

Yet Rousseau was not content to denounce modern civilization in merely general terms. The publication of d'Alembert's article 'Geneva' in the seventh volume of the *Encyclopédie* in 1757, with its suggestion that a theatre should be established there, immediately prompted Rousseau to spring to the defence of his native republic with his *Lettre à d'Alembert sur les spectacles* (1758). He affirmed that a theatre in Geneva would inevitably bring corruption to a small Protestant republic that was already exposed to the insidious influence of French culture. The *Lettre* thus contained an indictment of French society as well as a defence of Genevan values. In Rousseau's eyes, the theatre, a typical symbol of modern decadence, illustrated the 'reversal of natural relations' characteristic of contemporary society. By making love its chief subject, it thrust women into a position of unnatural prominence, and drew them from that retired domestic life which, according to him, suited their natural character. Yet the dominant role of women in the theatre was simply one aspect of their overwhelming influence in modern society as a whole. Rousseau paints a satirical picture of effeminate men cringing in the *salons* before some 'female idol' whom they accept as the arbiter of their lives. The popularity of the theatre thus indicates the existence of a much greater social evil. Even the shape of the theatre and the physical posture of its frequenters – its prison-like form and the immobility of a silent audience fascinated by the performers on the stage – is a sign of human servitude. Rousseau contrasts this artificial form of entertainment, the product of a society based on luxury and inequality, with the true entertainment which is 'derived from man's nature, needs and daily life'. The ancients had already known this authentic form of enjoyment: unlike the artificial and pernicious plays of the servile modern theatre, their tragedies were enacted 'in the open air', beneath the sky and in the presence of the whole people and were inspired by subjects drawn from the nation's historical heritage; men of old thus felt themselves to be part of nature and active members of their own communities. Rousseau urged the Genevans to draw their entertainment from their own national resources, especially from the public festivals which were remarkable for their joyful spontaneity and for their power to engage all the citizens in the same act of simple happiness and freedom.

If in his early works Rousseau was concerned mainly with an analysis of the maladies of modern civilization, he realized that it was still necessary to propose some constructive alternative and that, even if no genuine remedy were possible, he had to suggest some means of arresting further decline. This was the purpose of *Émile* and *Du contrat social* – works which set out the ideal principles necessary for the satisfactory development of a genuine human being and a just political community. As Rousseau himself carefully pointed out, *Émile* was not intended to be a mere educational manual: it was a 'philosophical treatise' on human nature. More especially it was based on the assumption that man's original being was good and that it had been perverted by social institutions. Consequently, if the individual could be brought up in an environment free from these evil influences – that is, if he could be brought up in the country and not in the town – he would eventually become a true man. Evil came to man from outside, not from within his own sinful self. Rousseau described the child's early education as 'negative' because it was concerned with keeping away harmful influences and allowing him to develop in accordance with his own physical and instinctive needs. This did not mean that there would be no discipline, but that he would be disciplined by 'things' – by that physical 'necessity' which imposed limits on every human existence – rather than by an arbitrary human will that produced inequality and injustice. In thus affirming his confidence in 'nature', Rousseau clearly reflected the view of many thinkers of the Enlightenment, but he differed from most of them in his stress upon the antithesis between 'man' and present society; he also imbued his vision of regenerated man with a fervent idealism which made it seem far more than a merely abstract or utopian concept.

Unlike most of his contemporaries, Rousseau did not consider 'nature' in static terms, for he stressed the progressive features of education, pointing out that each phase of human existence had its own distinctive characteristics. The child, for example, is not just a man in miniature, but a being in his own right, with his own kind of 'perfection' and his own forms of behaviour; as such, he is much more responsive to the promptings of feeling and sensation than to the demands of abstract reason. At the same time, the educator has to consider the child's ultimate destiny in relation to the greater reality – the universal order – of which he is to form part. This principle of natural order is a fundamental aspect of Rousseau's philosophy as a whole and serves to refute an excessively individualistic interpretation of his ideas. In man himself order is ultimately linked up with the primordial impulse of 'self-regard' or *amour de soi* – the only 'passion natural to man'; it is 'always good and always in conformity with order', revealing itself at the lowest level as mere self-preservation and ultimately assuming the form of 'gentle and loving passions'. *Amour de soi*, as a natural impulse, stands in striking contrast to the false 'pride' (*amour-propre*) generated by society. The educator's task is to keep at bay the 'hateful, irascible passions' produced by pride and to encourage the development of the natural needs and feelings inspired by genuine self-regard. Whereas society is dominated by *amour-propre*, which involves the artificial and harmful attitude through which men vie with one another in accordance with a destructive competitive principle, the true individual will follow the primordial human impulse of *amour de soi*, and allow it to develop in accordance with the growing complexity of his personal needs.

It was Rousseau's religious views, as expressed through the 'Profession de foi du vicaire savoyard' inserted in the fourth book of *Émile*, which aroused the greatest hostility on the part of his contemporaries. He first of all shocked the orthodox by refusing to allow the child to receive any religious instruction until he was mentally and spiritually capable of profiting by it; most children, said Rousseau, are merely idolatrous because they are taught religious doctrines which they do not properly understand, he, therefore, proposed to delay the child's religious education until the age of fourteen. Even more offensive to the orthodox was the nature of Rousseau's religious beliefs. Although his defence of 'natural religion' was in no way exceptional as far as the *philosophes* were concerned, for even Voltaire and Montesquieu readily accepted some form of deism, Rousseau's insistence that the tenets of natural religion were independent of the idea of original sin and dispensed with the need for any supernatural revelation inevitably offended the traditionalists. On the other hand, he genuinely hoped to reconcile Christians and unbelievers, for he was convinced that his defence of God's existence and the immortality of the soul would be enough to satisfy Christians and that his espousal of universal religious principles would save the *philosophes* from being seduced by the materialism which was making such rapid inroads into their midst. Needless to say, he pleased neither party: the devout were offended by his cavalier treatment of revelation, whilst the *philosophes* who still accepted some form of natural religion as an intellectual framework for their humanistic ideas, rejected his bold assertion that religious fanaticism was in some ways preferable to the spiritual sterility of philosophical scepticism.

Rousseau's sense of deep inner commitment, even to ideas which in themselves were not exceptional, made him a disturbing figure and few people could remain indifferent to his works, whether they became his followers or his opponents: he constantly challenged his readers to re-examine the essential nature of their experience. This is very evident in one of the main principles of his religious and moral thought: the idea of conscience as a 'divine instinct' which could guide men through all moral difficulties was not a notion likely to commend itself to thinkers who were looking for a utilitarian or social basis for morality, but it had a strong attraction for those contemporaries who were anxious to escape from the stultifying and depressing limitations of abstract philosophizing and social convention. To an age of rational or utilitarian ethics Rousseau thus proposed a deeper and more intense form of morality – a morality based ultimately on the notion of conscience as a kind of innate spiritual feeling.

More radical than his religious principles were Rousseau's political views, which were given much less attention during his lifetime. The highly abstract nature of the *Contrat social* may partly account for this neglect, although the general lack of enthusiasm for any radical political changes (the *philosophes* wanted reform, not revolution) meant that the climate of opinion was not yet favourable to the discussion of ideas which did not come into their own until the advent of the

French Revolution. However, Rousseau always insisted upon the great importance of politics in determining the nature of human existence and, more especially, he established a close link between politics and morality; it was only in political society, he insisted, that man could attain genuine moral fulfilment and replace instinct by justice, appetite by right; only thus could he be transformed, in the words of the *Contrat social*, from a 'stupid limited animal' into 'an intelligent being and a man'.

The society envisaged by Rousseau differed fundamentally from the institutions he saw around him; whereas these had originated in inequality and injustice, so that political and material advantage always remained with the richest and most powerful members of the community, Rousseau insisted on the need for a just society in which the citizens would enjoy equal rights and equal security. The basis of this new society must be freedom – not the 'natural freedom' of primitive man living in the forests, but the 'civil' and 'moral' freedom of mature individuals who, in order to obtain fulfilment, willingly accept restraints provided that they are shared by all the members of the community. For Rousseau, therefore, political freedom is inseparable from equality: in a just society all citizens have the same rights and the same obligations. This does not mean that there will be complete economic equality; the determining principle, insists Rousseau, will be that no citizen should be rich enough to buy another or so poor that he has to sell himself.

The citizens, therefore, alienate their power and rights as independent individuals in order to invest them in the community as a whole; in Rousseau's opinion, they need not fear to do this because the society of which they will form part is largely their own creation and one to which they have initially given their free consent. Moreover, they will find an important safeguard in the knowledge that sovereignty, or supreme power, resides in the people as a whole, and, as such, is absolute, indivisible and inalienable. The community is protected from the arbitrary and unjust pressure of sectional interests because it is sustained by the moral power of the 'general will', which always aims at the good of society as a whole. The general will, in its turn, is given objective expression through the laws.

As soon as these essential principles are accepted, Rousseau admits the possibility of different forms of 'government', for these will be determined by particular needs and situations. Government is, in any case, simply the instrument of the people's will and has no absolute authority in its own right. It is only the principle of sovereignty itself which can never be changed.

While not doubting the validity of his political ideas, Rousseau always acknowledged the difficulty of putting them into practice. Aware of the dangers of selfishness, he realized that the problem of persuading men to put the law above their own petty interests was almost as insoluble as the mathematical one of squaring the circle. This probably explains why, at the very last moment, he decided to add the chapter on civil religion to his political treatise: men would need a religious sanction to keep them obedient to the principles acknowledged by their reason and conscience.

If Rousseau's personal writings seem to stand in such sharp contrast to the didactic works, this is simply because they were written with a very different intention. Their subsequent repercussions on the psychological and literary outlook of Romantic and post-Romantic generations was something that cannot have been foreseen by a writer who was striving to understand and express his own unique personality. No doubt Rousseau thought that he was throwing light upon the nature of man and that his own exceptional position was due mainly to the incomprehension and hostility of a world which had forgotten the true meaning of natural goodness. In his very last years Rousseau came to see himself as a 'man of nature' who had been preserved from the corruption of his time by his own innocence and goodness. Yet his use of the terms 'men' and 'nature' shows his steadfast belief in the universality of the 'order' that lay at the heart of God's creation. Works such as the *Confessions*, *Dialogues*, and the *Rêveries du promeneur solitaire* give nature and man a new, or at least hitherto neglected, dimension by expressing the complexity of a sensibility and consciousness which go beyond a merely rational and intellectual comprehension of man's being and of the universe in which he lives. In all his writings, therefore, Rousseau challenged his readers to re-examine the ultimate quality of their own experience and to distinguish between its artificial aspects and those original elements which made it a part of their own true nature. Moreover, he held out the hope that, if only they would firmly grasp the full implications of natural goodness, they could reasonably hope to draw close to the reality of which they glimpsed the real meaning on the depths of their own being.

DIDEROT (1713–84)

In an age of polymaths Denis Diderot was certainly one of the most remarkable, and all the more remarkable because the true extent of his genius and achievement was not known to his contemporaries. To them he was chiefly the editor of the *Encyclopédie* and the author of 'philosophical' works of an irreligious character; few would have compared him to Voltaire and the majority would have placed him after d'Alembert. Yet to modern readers he is a writer of astonishing originality, energy and versatility. Not only did he make important contributions to philosophical problems as he sought to incorporate the new findings of science into his view of the world and to tackle the grave moral difficulties raised by materialism, but he also interested himself in the theory as well as in the practice of literature: he tried to revitalize the theatre by creating a new drama and, in spite of his many years' labour with the editorship of the *Encyclopédie*, he wrote a number of important novels; he also found time to engage in art criticism and he composed a series of 'Salons' for the *Correspondance littéraire* edited by his friend Grimm.

Although his particular achievements in the domain of the theatre, the novel and the *Encyclopédie* are discussed elsewhere, it may be helpful to give a brief indication of his philosophical ideas. His early work, the *Pensées philosophiques* (1746), already betrays his dissatisfaction with religious orthodoxy; he declares that superstition is more offensive to God than atheism; like other contemporary thinkers, he rejects the sterility of traditional metaphysics which should be replaced, he affirms, by the rational and critical use of scientific method. Whereas the *Lettre sur les aveugles* (1749) examines in detail – and with an ultimately materialistic emphasis – the role of sensations in the formation of intellectual and moral ideas, the *Pensées sur l'interprétation de la nature* (1754) develop still further his conception of philosophical and scientific method; they also give prominence to an idea which plays a major role in his subsequent philosophy, the unity of nature. His reflections on this subject were prompted by the work of the scientist Maupertuis who was visiting France at this time. 'The absolute independence of a single fact', declares Diderot, 'is incompatible with the idea of the whole: without the idea of the whole, there is no more philosophy.' Of Diderot's philosophical works the *Rêve de d'Alembert* (which includes the *Entretien entre d'Alembert et Diderot* and the *Suite de l'Entretien*), written in 1769 but not published during his lifetime, is certainly the most original in both form and content. A striking use of the dialogue-form which portrays real characters in a contemporary setting shows that Diderot had found a vehicle particularly suited to his genius, whilst the philosophical content expresses a view of the universe which foreshadows the later theory of evolution. Other shorter dialogues such as the *Entretien d'un père avec ses enfants* (1773) and the *Entretien d'un philosophe avec la Maréchale de* * (1776) undertake a bold examination of moral problems.

Diderot took a much greater interest in science than any other *philosophe* except d'Alembert and Buffon. Although Voltaire was a popularizer of Newtonian ideas and did some fitful experimenting of his own at Cirey, his deistic philosophy did not rest on a scientific basis, whilst Rousseau's view of the universe depended on religious postulates; Montesquieu's early addiction to scientific experiments led to no original discovery and the scientific aspects of the *Esprit des lois* are closer to sociology than to physical science. Although one of Diderot's early interests was mathematics (in 1748 he published his *Mémoires sur différents sujets de mathématiques*), he had already prophesied in the *Pensées sur l'interprétation de la nature* 'a great revolution in the sciences' that would replace mathematics by 'ethics, *belles-lettres*, the history of nature and experimental physics' (IV). 'Abstract sciences have occupied the best minds for too long and with too little profit' (XVII). The lasting achievements of science are to be found in 'experimental' rather than in 'rational philosophy', for it is facts which have always provided the basis of true scientific discovery. Later on Diderot came to believe that it was chemistry, biology and anatomy which would replace the deposed science of mathematics. If, like many of his contemporaries, he rejected vague systems, whether metaphysical or theological, he laid greater stress on the role of scientific method in the discovery and interpretation of facts.

For Diderot the domain of facts was vast and varied and he made serious efforts to follow the latest scientific discoveries in a number of different fields – physics, chemistry (he attended the famous chemist Rouelle's lecture-courses for three years), anatomy, physiology and biology; he was also interested in what is now known as psychopathology. With the rapid development of so many sciences Diderot believed that great changes were about to take place not only in the formulation of a scientific view of the world, but also in philosophy and ethics. In one of his last works, the *Réfutation suivie de l'ouvrage d'Helvétius intitulé 'De l'homme'* (written in 1773–4, but not published until 1875), he affirmed: 'It is very difficult to do any good metaphysics or good ethics without being an anatomist, naturalist, physiologist and doctor.' Any worthwhile explanation of the world and human existence had to take into account the latest findings in many scientific fields and to assess them in the light of observation and experiment.

While condemning mere abstraction, Diderot emphasized that facts could not be considered in isolation, but had to be related to and developed by the use of hypotheses. This interaction between fact and hypothesis is, in Diderot's view, one of the most fruitful sources of scientific progress. Hypotheses, when valid, help the scientist to extend the range of his researches and investigations and to link together new discoveries. In spite of his interest in particular branches of science, Diderot never abandoned this wider philosophical perspective. In this respect, he was clearly influenced by the unity of vision which was so influential in the outlook of the Enlightenment; whatever their devotion to particular disciplines, the thinkers of the time were always seeking for a principle which would enable them to unify their view of the universe. In Diderot's case, the search for a unifying principle became of paramount importance and it is the particular nature of his cosmic vision which constitutes his real originality. From the very outset he had been fascinated by the ideal of a unified body of knowledge based on the exploration of the universal 'chain of beings'. Departing from the traditional conception which had treated the 'chain of beings' as a fixed qualitative hierarchy stretching from inanimate matter to the highest forms of spiritual life, Diderot was increasingly attracted by the possibility of finding a single principle which would account for the whole of reality. After his early abandonment of deism and subsequent conversion to atheism, he became a supporter of philosophical materialism.

Materialist philosophies were certainly not lacking in the eighteenth century, as the work of La Mettrie, Helvétius, d'Holbach and many others shows. Indeed Cartesianism itself had unwittingly fostered their emergence. Although Descartes had based his dualistic philosophy, with its rigid separation of mind and matter as absolutely distinct substances, on the notion of God's existence, he had given prominence to a mechanistic conception of matter as a substance characterized solely by its spatial qualities; he had explained the physical world by movement and matter alone. The influence of physico-mathematical science had reinforced this mechanistic view which many thinkers were prepared to accept as an adequate explanation of all reality: rejecting the existence of mind as a separate substance, they maintained that mental and physical phenomena were explicable in terms of a single mechanistic and materialistic principle which obviated any need for the Cartesian notion of two substances. On the other hand, the deists, while accepting a mechanistic interpretation of matter, rejected materialism on the ground that matter, being essentially passive and inert, could not generate its own movement; being external to matter, movement had to be initiated by some spiritual power. Moreover, many believed that the organization of matter itself provided evidence for the existence of a supreme intelligence as its originator. For a long time, therefore, deism seemed to offer a satisfactory alternative to materialism, but in the second part of the century materialism steadily gained ground.

Diderot's originality is to have supported materialism while modifying its mechanistic form. It has been suggested that he was influenced in this by the dynamic concepts of such philosophers as Leibniz, Spinoza and Lucretius for whom every substance was a source of energy; in the opinion of Leibniz, for example, the monad was not the passive occupant of space, but a centre of autonomous activity. Diderot took over this notion of the energy of matter and separated it from the religious context in which Leibniz had set it: for Diderot movement became an intrinsic property of matter and generated its own momentum. At the same time he was struck by the idea that movement did not exist in isolation and that the more highly developed forms of matter – living organisms, for example – were also endowed with a special kind of sensitivity. Diderot saw this principle of 'sensitivity' extending throughout the whole physical realm; there was thus no definite break in nature, which was made up of sensitive matter at different stages of development and still evolving into other forms. This was the idea developed with such lyrical enthusiasm in the *Rêve de d'Alembert*. Later on, especially in his *Eléments de physiologie*, Diderot was to place greater emphasis on the principle of organization as a means of explaining the detailed structure of matter, although he did not see this as conflicting with his earlier ideas.

Diderot's theory of matter shows that he was a bold – at times rash – speculative thinker, as well as an advocate of the experimental method. He admitted that the idea of the sensitivity of matter was a hypothesis, but he believed that it would prove a fruitful means of explaining the unity and structure of the universe as a whole and that it would eventually be confirmed by observation and experiment. Mental and physical phenomena differed only in degree, not in quality; the mind was simply a highly refined and elaborately organized form of sensitive matter. From an early period Diderot had been interested in psycho-physical phenomena and had stressed the action of the brain upon the mind; consciousness could be demonstrably related to the physical activity of the brain, as he tried to point out through the person of Dr Bordeu in the *Rêve de d'Alembert*. The *Lettre sur les aveugles* had also shown how a blind man's view of the universe and the moral consequences he deduced from it were determined by his own limited sensations; the mind was constantly affected, in Diderot's opinion, by the action of the senses and the body. 'The soul is nothing without the body', he declared in the *Éléments de physiologie* which strove to demonstrate the physical origins of all psychological phenomena.

In spite of his respect for empiricism and his firm belief in the importance of scientific experiment, Diderot thus remained in many ways sympathetic to the metaphysical outlook; he could not help being fascinated by the idea of the cosmic process and, more especially, by what he believed to be its essential unity; he longed for a unifying principle of explanation which could be verified by scientific evidence.

The comprehensive hypothesis of sensitivity, with its rejection of any absolute qualitative distinction between the various forms of matter, whether animate or inanimate, is elaborated with imagination, enthusiasm and literary skill in the remarkable *Rêve de d'Alembert*. This scientific conversation-piece takes place between real people

(Diderot and his friends d'Alembert, Dr Bordeu and Mlle de Lespinasse) in a contemporary *salon*. The cautious scientist d'Alembert, though interested in Diderot's notion of the sensitivity of all matter, treats it with some scepticism. Yet the idea continues to preoccupy him, for when he goes to bed, he begins to talk excitedly in his sleep as he works out the implications of this revolutionary scientific concept. Mlle de Lespinasse, puzzled and alarmed by the sleeping man's ramblings, jots down his words and eventually discusses them with Dr Bordeu, who, as a scientist, takes them up and develops their consequences. Early in the conversation it is recognized that the main problem is to explain the existence of forms of matter which, at first sight, seem irreducible to one another; it is necessary not only to account for the difference between living and inanimate matter, but also to distinguish psychological and mental from merely physiological phenomena. Diderot attempts to overcome the difficulty by treating matter as an active force developing over vast periods of time.

While admitting that everything is interconnected in space, he suggests that it assumes various forms because of an enormous temporal evolution which has gradually enabled different kinds and levels of physical organization to come into being. We are prevented from understanding this process not only by our reluctance to use such a time-scale, but also by the restrictive influence of our conventional notions of individuality and normality; for example, evolution will not heed the traditional distinction between the normal and the abnormal, for the monstrous, though less frequent, is as much a part of nature as the normal; Diderot boldly affirms that there is no absolute difference between the sexes, for 'man is woman's monster just as woman is man's'. Likewise, he considers that life and death are relative concepts which must be seen in the context of a universe in which 'everything passes and changes'. The usual distinction between the animal, vegetable and mineral kingdoms must be eliminated in favour of a more fluid conception of matter. 'To be born, to live and to pass away is to change form.' Diderot firmly rejects the widely accepted eighteenth-century theory of biological genesis as 'preformation' or *emboîtement* – a mechanistic theory which supposed that all later generations were also contained in the *germes* of the first;[4] he stresses, on the other hand, the chemical origin of life and the role of adapta-

4. See p. 12.

tion in determining its various forms ('organs produce needs and needs produce organs'); by a process of natural selection, organisms unfitted for survival disappear and give way to more adaptable ones. Clearly this evolutionary concept of nature, which has only a general resemblance to the Darwinian theory, owed a great deal to Diderot's interest in chemistry and, more particularly, biology. Admittedly, his enthusiasm sometimes led him to the injudicious espousal of scientific 'discoveries' which later proved to be without foundation; such was the case with the theory of 'spontaneous generation' put forward by the scientist Joseph Needham.

Diderot's dynamic materialism, although it did not exclude all mechanistic concepts, was far less dependent than earlier materialist views upon a physico-mathematical conception of the world based on the Cartesian notion of matter as 'extension'. Certainly Diderot's view of the universe contained a visionary and poetic element, for it went far beyond the range of observable phenomena. While considering physical reality in terms of a vast whole, he was fascinated by its constantly changing elements; if the ultimate unity of the universe was undeniable, it was also involved in a perpetual process of growth and decay, creation and destruction. Ultimately, everything is interrelated, but this notion of universal interdependence does not exclude the inexhaustible energy and variety of nature whose ever-changing forms seem to defy man's efforts to fix and understand them.

Diderot's materialism had serious repercussions upon his moral philosophy, for it committed him to some form of determinism and so to the rejection of the traditional notions of 'good' and 'bad'. Instead of judging people as good or bad, he proposed to consider them as being 'fortunately' or 'unfortunately born'. He admitted that this created problems for a philosopher who, like himself, wanted to defend the cause of virtue, and nowhere are the consequences of this difficulty more clearly expressed than in *Le Neveu de Rameau*, where the 'philosopher' is confronted with a man who, unashamedly basing his personal existence upon the supremacy of selfish appetite, claims to find support for his views in the general conduct of a society that simply hides its egoism behind a hypocritical respect for moral principles. Diderot recognized that his philosophical ideas, by leading him to determinism, made it extremely difficult for him to defend the notion of freedom. He put the point very forcibly in a famous letter to his friend Landois: 'The word "freedom" is a word devoid of meaning; there are not and cannot be free beings; we are what is in accordance with the general order, organization, education and the chain of events.' When he let his mind and imagination dwell upon this problem, he considered – for example, in *Le Neveu de Rameau* and in some of the stories included in his novel, *Jacques le fataliste* – that it was possible for us to obtain some rational insight into our given nature and, thereby, to let us control it more efficiently, but, at the same time, more selfishly and ruthlessly. Unfortunately people who managed to achieve this kind of egoistic fulfilment would be criticized by traditionalists as 'wicked' or 'evil', since they would be seeking a personal satisfaction that owed nothing to the dictates of traditional morality. Even Diderot himself, in spite of his materialism, remained a passionate defender of 'virtue' and often appealed to the very freedom which his philosophy seemed to repudiate. In one of his last works – the *Réfutation d'Helvétius* – we find him protesting against an over-simplified materialism which would abolish some of man's most distinctive characteristics: man does not need to be the slave of crude physical appetites, for he can achieve a certain measure of selfless devotion to causes greater than his own petty interests.

All this does not alter the fact that, in Diderot's view, man is nothing but a biological system, with feelings and emotions explicable in terms of his 'diaphragm'; his mental reactions are merely the molecular activity of his brain; nothing else is required for a completely adequate explanation of his character. Thought is simply an expression of the physical power of the brain, that is, of a mere biological function. The unity of the self can be explained by the activity of memory. Since morality itself has a physical or psychological origin, Diderot insists that it must be related first of all to those basic impulses which make men pursue happiness. When this notion of happiness is extended to other people and society at large, it assumes the form of beneficence which can thus replace goodness as a moral goal. Nevertheless, Diderot never gave up his attempt to reconcile happiness and virtue, even though virtue was regarded in some sense as its own reward and a feeling that generated its own satisfaction.

Since Diderot had increasing difficulty in safeguarding morality as an autonomous activity, he was often tempted to link it up with aesthetic principles. He believed that it might be possible to carry over to human behaviour some of the principles which governed existence in general. More especially, the human being achieved true selfhood in so far as he gave unified and consistent expression to the innate energy of his character; a man is not respected for any goodness he may have, but for his ability to establish the unity and energy of his character. No doubt this explains Diderot's admiration for genius as a primordial force. As his imaginative writings make clear, however, he acknowledged that 'genius' expressed itself in ways which placed it outside the range of normal moral judgements and that, at the highest level of experience, art and morality were in certain essential respects the same.[5]

Of all the *philosophes*, Diderot was certainly one of the most forward-looking in his views. His conception of the world lay much closer in many ways to the later Romantic outlook with its emphasis upon the dynamic unity of all forms of being than to the mechanistic conception of most eighteenth-century thinkers, and unlike the latter, he envisaged the universe nor as a complex machine, but as a huge organism. Although his vision of the world was in many ways poetic rather than scientific, his remarkable intuitions enabled him to anticipate, if only in a general way, one of the most distinctive achievements of nineteenth-century science – the theory of evolution. His restless curiosity and boundless energy impelled him to explore intellectual and aesthetic regions of which most of his contemporaries had little or no comprehension.

BUFFON (1707–1788) AND MINOR PHILOSOPHES

Of the major figures of the French Enlightenment the one with the closest affinity to Diderot was perhaps Buffon – not of course at the social level (Georges-Louis Leclerc Comte de Buffon, like Montesquieu, was connected with the magistrature or *noblesse de robe*, and eventually assumed the title of 'Comte'), but in the domain of scientific thought. Unlike Diderot, however, Buffon was a pure scientist, which may explain why he no longer commands the enormous prestige accorded to him in his lifetime when his discoveries still seemed strikingly original. Moreover, being a cautious man (he was always anxious to avoid offending authority and constantly sought to advance his per-

5. See p. 404.

sonal position; he was for many years curator of the Jardin du Roi and he never forgot that he was the prosperous *seigneur* of the château of Montbard), he tended to remain aloof from the Encyclopedists, even though was not unfriendly towards them; the much-heralded article on 'Nature' which he undertook to write for the *Encyclopédie* was never published. When the Sorbonne threatened to condemn his work, he did not hesitate to disavow his ideas as a 'pure philosophical speculation'; at the same time he went on publishing as though nothing untoward had happened! Yet the thirty-six volumes of his *Histoire naturelle* (1749–89), which include his *Époques de la nature*, constitute an impressive intellectual achievement: Buffon not only wrote the history of the earth, which allowed for its evolution over several geological periods, but his detailed descriptions of the animal kingdom made him a forerunner of modern zoology. During his long career, his views underwent some changes and he gradually moved away from the conservatism of his earlier attitude towards a hesitant and limited acceptance of the notion of evolution.

In spite of his intellectual ambitions, Buffon always recognized (at least in theory) the need for a rigorous scientific method, and he saw himself as Newton's successor, that is, as a scientist who was applying Newtonian principles to the history of the earth and the origins of the solar system. He did not believe, however, that there was a single method valid for all branches of science; each had to have its own characteristic features and techniques. The truths of mathematics differed from 'physical truths'; whereas the former, as 'truths of definition', are largely abstract productions of our own minds, the latter do not depend upon us but 'rest only on fact'; the scientist's main task is to separate 'what is real in a subject from what we put into it arbitrarily'. Buffon also criticized the loose and vague use of nomenclature: he maintained that the botanist Linnaeus's classification was too broad to do justice to the rich diversity of nature; in Buffon's opinion, classification of this kind substituted definition for description. In biology he did not hesitate to reject the widely accepted theory of 'preformation', or *emboîtement*, as being too mechanistic to account for the complexity of generation. In his view, scientific theories had to be flexible and adaptable enough to assimilate the discovery of new facts; they ought not to remain rigidly imprisoned in some narrow concept.

However important 'exact description' and 'particular facts' may be, Buffon believed that the scientist must look beyond them, for facts have to be linked together and extended to new areas of investigation; this can be done only if he is willing to determine relationships and make fruitful comparisons and analogies. The scientist's ultimate aim must be to understand 'the great operations of nature' and, to achieve this, he requires superior powers – a powerful imagination, a highly developed reason, a tenacious memory and great determination; he must be able to form 'general views' and to establish distant relationships as well as to observe and interpret detailed facts. Buffon himself combined devotion to observation and experiment with a predilection for broad theories: 'the great views of an ardent genius who takes in everything at a glance' will be inspired by his comprehension of the 'great laws of the universe'.

Nowhere is Buffon's indifference to religious orthodoxy more apparent than in his treatment of the history of the earth. His theory of the 'seven ages' presupposed a time-scale vastly greater than the one to which the devout were accustomed and, in spite of his professed acceptance of the Mosaic chronology, he made no effort to reconcile his own views with the biblical account. Nevertheless, it would probably be wrong to see him as an opponent of religion. He was filled with awe at the wonders of nature and he believed that the universe had been created in accordance with a divine plan. Of particular importance was the unity which God had given his creation. As a thinker, therefore, Buffon was able to reconcile deism with the single-mindedness of the scientist who examined nature from within; the unity of nature could be discovered in the light of its own internal principles, even though these had ultimately to be referred to God as the original creator. There was no direct connection between theology and science, which was a purely secular human activity requiring its own methods and techniques. Buffon had no hesitation in rejecting the traditional notion of 'final causes'; the scientist, he believed, should examine the world without the help of religious postulates; nature – and not the supernatural – must be his constant guide.

In spite of the modernity of his approach to science, it would probably be wrong to see Buffon as a forerunner of Darwin, for he was prevented from reaching a definite theory of biological evolution by his firm belief in certain unchanging aspects of nature. Maintaining that life was a physical property of matter endowed with the spontaneous power to organize itself into different forms, he thought that it consisted of 'organic molecules' which, in the case of individual organisms, were shaped by an 'inner moulding force' (*le moule intérieur*); he admitted that the exact nature of this force was obscure, but it did not seem to him more incomprehensible than the widely accepted principle of gravitation; he found confirmation of his theories in the experiments carried out by the priest Joseph Needham, the 'discoverer' of 'spontaneous generation' to which Buffon – like Diderot – gave his support.

Ideas such as these provided Buffon with a stable conceptual framework for his scientific thought, but, within the limits of these ideas, he gradually introduced the notion of variation; he began to ask whether certain species of animals might not have common ancestors and whether, in particular, the observable differences between the same species existing on different continents might not be due to precise physical factors; he attributed, for example, the 'deterioration' of certain species to the influence of temperature, food and domestication. These ideas, however, never led to any explicit repudiation of the notion of the fixity of species; the possibility of variations was contained within definite limits. In any case, his theory of organic molecules and the fixed property of matter blocked the way to any genuine theory of evolution.

An important factor influencing Buffon's outlook was undoubtedly his view of man as the 'master of the earth'. Many of his theories – even those which seemed only remotely connected with human existence – revealed this preoccupation with the need to give man a place of honour in the universal creation. At the end of the *Époques de la nature*, he stressed man's capacity for modifying and controlling his environment. He did not hesitate, for example, to attribute the climatic differences between Roman and modern times to the clearing of forests and the building of cities: these activities were enough to account for the colder conditions of ancient times. Man, he believed, is 'the only living being whose nature is strong, extensive and flexible enough to adapt itself to the influences of all the climates of the earth'.

Yet this strongly anthropocentric cast of thought did not prevent Buffon from being increasingly impressed by the movement and power of nature; he tended to change from a static to a dynamic conception of the world; like Diderot, he attached more importance to biology than to physical science and he rejected a purely mechanistic interpretation of nature in favour of a view which made it a source of force and energy and a vast cosmic power engaged in a continuous process of destruction and renewal; he liked to contemplate nature in its imposing grandeur and this visionary attitude may help to explain his love of vast theories embracing the whole of creation. Matter took the form of an infinite number of relationships extending to all parts of the universe; to understand its working, the scientist had not only to look outwards to the distant parts of space, but also to consider the existence of the earth over vast periods of time. Nevertheless, Buffon held fast to the notion that nature was orderly, and not chaotic, in form; and that it was governed by regular laws. Consequently, although he never abandoned his deism, Buffon elaborated scientific views which were perfectly consistent with a materialistic conception of nature.

The celebrity of the principal figures of the French Enlightenment ought not to obscure the importance of many minor thinkers whose contemporary influence was often considerable, even though their lack of literary talent confines them to the history – and not the literature – of ideas. The *philosophes* constituted a widely diffused and varied group of thinkers united by a common determination to challenge traditional ideas and prejudices rather than by any agreed philosophical programme. While some considered themselves 'philosophers' in the narrow sense of the term, the majority were preoccupied with social, economic and other practical issues. A particularly influential thinker was Condillac (1714–80), whose *Essai sur l'origine des connaissances humaines* (1746) and *Traité des sensations* (1754) attempted, under the influence of Locke, to do for psychology what Newton had done for natural science: to reduce all mental phenomena to a single explanatory principle – sensation. An original feature of the first work is to have called attention to the importance of language in the formation of ideas, language itself being rooted in man's affective rather than in his rational nature; in the *Traité* he made use of a psychological model that was to become famous: a 'statue inwardly organized like ourselves was allowed to bring its sense-organs into use one at a time', so that the specific function of each could be clearly defined and illustrated in relation to man's psychological and mental development. Unfortunately Condillac's obsession with systematization often impugned the value of his sometimes penetrating psychological analyses.

Baron d'Holbach (1723–89), a fanatical enemy of Christianity who achieved notoriety with *Le Système de la Nature* (1770) and *La Morale universelle ou les devoirs de l'homme formé sur la Nature* (1776) tried to construct a materialistic philosophy on the basis of a strict empiricism and to draw from it a hedonistic morality which would combine individual happiness with social utility. Helvétius (1715–71), a wealthy tax-farmer turned philosopher, whose major work *De l'esprit* (1758) was condemned by the ecclesiastical authorities and the Parlement, wrote *Le Bonheur*, a poem recapitulating his ideas, and a treatise *De l'homme*, both of which were published posthumously in 1772; he was also a materialist who maintained that all ideas originated in sensations and that men, being governed by the search for happiness, could base their entire moral outlook on the principle of enlightened self-interest. Like d'Holbach, his materialism was of an old-fashioned kind and the main interest of their work lies in their efforts to apply their ideas to the field of education and social philosophy. The doctor-philosopher La Mettrie (1709–51), to whom reference has already been made,[6] advocated his own brand of materialism with *Histoire naturelle de l'âme* (1745) and *l'Homme-machine* (1747), works which swept aside all traditional moral ideas in favour of a thorough-going hedonism. *L'Homme-machine* expounds an evolutionary materialism based on diversity of 'organization' rather than on the Cartesian mechanism suggested by its title. Because of the scandal aroused by his irreligious ideas, La Mettrie fled to the court of Frederick the Great.

Another thinker deserving mention is Turgot (1727–81) who, in addition to his fame as economist and politician, outlined some interesting ideas on the theme of historical progress in his *Discours sur les progrès de l'esprit humain* (1750): this is one of the first systematic treatments of a subject implicit in much Enlightenment thought. The same subject is developed by the Marquis de Condorcet (1743–94), whose early achievements as a mathematician gave way to an increasing interest in social questions; and after being made (largely through d'Alembert's influence) secretary of the French Academy, he became actively involved with the events of the French Revolution and seems

6. See pp. 36–7.

to have escaped execution only through suicide. The last of the *philosophes* – in fact the only one to have seen the Revolution – he is known chiefly for his *Tableau historique des progrès de l'esprit humain*, which he wrote in 1793–4 while he was being hunted as a Girondin. In it the history of humanity is traced through ten periods beginning with primitive times and ending with a prophetic account of 'the future progress of mankind'; this buoyantly optimistic work, written in such desperate circumstances, offered its readers an entrancing view of human perfectibility.

Other thinkers had less ambitious aims, being content to deal with more limited subjects such as political and economic theory. Such was the case of Mably (1709–85) who criticized the evils of land-ownership and put forward radical communistic views in *De la législation, ou principes des lois* (1776); and of Morelly (dates unknown) who also developed a theory of communism in *Le Code de la Nature* (1755). The Physiocrats, of whom Francois Quesnay (1694–1774) was the originator and the Marquis de Mirabeau (1715–89) with *L'Ami des hommes* (1756) and *La Philosophie rurale* (1763), one of the chief supporters, stressed the importance of agriculture as the source of national wealth and free trade as a means of fostering economic prosperity.

Some of the boldest ideas of the period were disseminated through a kind of intellectual underground in the form of a clandestine literature that sought to circumvent the censorship by being circulated in manuscript and sold surreptitiously. One of the most famous of these works was the *Testament* of the priest Jean Meslier (1664–1729) who denounced Christianity and espoused the cause of philosophical materialism. Many of these aggressively atheistic manuscripts were obviously anonymous, although some were – or purported to be – translations and adaptions of foreign works; they often owed a great deal to the influence of Spinoza, whose imperfectly known ideas were interpreted in a materialistic sense. Other clandestine works, more favourable towards religion, though critical of Christianity, were of deistic inspiration. Such was the case with the *Militaire philosophe* (available in manuscript about 1710 and eventually published in London in 1767), a work which caught Voltaire's eye and earned his approbation.

THE ENCYCLOPÉDIE

Nowhere is the spirit of the French Enlightenment more apparent than in the *Encyclopédie*. In clear and unmistakable terms this vast enterprise expressed some of the most persistent and characteristic aspirations of the age: it bore witness not only to the extension and diffusion of the new critical spirit but also to a firm determination that all knowledge should contribute to the betterment of humanity. To achieve this aim the Encyclopedists considered it necessary to remove the serious obstacles, especially outmoded ideas, that stood in the way of intellectual progress. Although the *Encyclopédie* would never have been completed without the tireless energy, enthusiasm and devotion of its editor-in-chief, Diderot, its ultimate significance does not depend on the activity of any single man, or of the great writers whose names were associated with it – Montesquieu, Voltaire, Rousseau and Buffon. Upon close examination we find that Montesquieu did not contribute a great deal: although he was invited to write articles on 'Despotism' and 'Democracy', he promised nothing more than an article on 'Taste', which was unfinished at his death. This did not prevent the editors – and especially d'Alembert, in an 'Éloge de Montesquieu' which headed the third volume – from skilfully making this tenuous link a reason for hailing Montesquieu as an active supporter of the enterprise. Moreover, *De l'esprit des lois* is used and quoted extensively throughout the whole work. If Voltaire's articles were more numerous, they were confined to purely literary topics, and practically ceased in 1758; apart from an article on 'Political Economy', Rousseau wrote only on music, whilst Buffon's much-heralded article on 'Nature' never appeared. For the most part, the success of the *Encyclopédie* depended on the collaboration of a host of now forgotten contributors, many of whom, in any case, wanted to remain anonymous from the very beginning. It was this wider co-operative appeal of the *Encyclopédie* which made it particularly significant; as the title-page proudly stated, it was the work of 'a society of men of letters'.

Many contemporaries were already convinced that the moment had come for the publication of such a work. The rapid growth of knowledge, especially in science, the rise of a new social class, the bourgeoisie, eager to learn about the latest intellectual advances, and a marked increase in the size of the reading public, made the undertaking of a large-scale encyclopedia seem an intellectually feasible as well as a commercially profitable enterprise. Although it now seems unlikely that the freemasons were responsible for the inception of the *Encyclopédie*, they had certainly envisaged its possibility, for one of their members, Ramsay, spoke in 1737 of the desirability of producing a 'vast work for which no academy or university would suffice', since it would be incapable of 'embracing such a vast object'; a genuine encyclopedia ought to aim at 'the enlightenment of all the nations' and to be a 'general storehouse and universal library of all that is fine, great and luminous, solid and useful in every natural science and in every art'.[7] At first, the *Encyclopédie* was planned as a mere translation (perhaps revised and extended) of an English work, the two-volume *Cyclopaedia* of Ephraim Chambers, published in 1728. As soon as Diderot became associated with the project, however, its character changed, for he persuaded the publishers to undertake a completely new work. Diderot himself, although known only as a translator and the author of a short book, *Pensées philosophiques* (1746), was eventually made editor-in-chief, the other editor being Jean d'Alembert who had already achieved European fame as a mathematician and scientist; officially the latter was willing to accept responsibility only for the scientific and mathematical sections, but he contributed articles on other subjects until he withdrew from the editorship in 1757.

A prospectus (written by Diderot) appeared in 1750, and in 1751 the first volume was published, with a preface by d'Alembert, an extensive *Discours préliminaire* which was a remarkable attempt at a synthesis of modern thought. The next volumes were produced at approximately yearly intervals, so that by November 1757 seven volumes had been published. From the outset, however, the whole work aroused fierce hostility on the part of the Roman Catholic Church and the Parlements who were constantly pressing the government to suspend it. Particularly persistent were the attacks of the Jesuits, who perhaps saw the *Encyclopédie* as a rival to their own *Dictionnaire de Trévoux*, whilst the Jansenists also provided some fierce opposition with their journal, *Les Nouvelles ecclésiastiques*. In 1752 the *Encyclopédie* was suspended for a time by the government, but it soon

7. Quoted in J. Lough, *The Encyclopédie*, London, 1971, pp. 5–6.

started up again. At last, in 1757, after years of relentless and unceasing opposition, an official ban was placed on its continuation. Owing to the protection of a well-disposed minister, Malesherbes, Diderot was able to carry on in secret, even though d'Alembert, made weary by all the obstacles and difficulties, had abandoned the work in 1757. Diderot's doggedness and enthusiasm eventually led to the publication of the last volumes of text in 1765; but the final volume of plates did not appear until 1772. The whole work consisted of seventeen volumes of folio text and eleven volumes of plates.

The faults of the *Encyclopédie* have often been stressed and some were already acknowledged by the editors. Diderot called attention to the lack of balance in the articles, great space often being given to trivial subjects, whilst important ones were apt to be dismissed in a few lines. The uneven quality of the work was admitted by d'Alembert when he called it a 'Harlequin's cloak' – a patchwork of good and bad material. Many of the articles are disorganized and occasionally incoherent. Several of these shortcomings were no doubt due to the difficulties of publication, especially in the case of the last volumes; fear of the censor's disapproval often made it impossible for the contributors to express their true opinions. Certain articles, which purport to be new contributions to their subject, are merely plagiarized from other works. Sometimes articles on major subjects are difficult to find, because of the absence of a biographical method, especially in the first volumes: thus Shakespeare appears under 'Stratford' and Newton under 'Wolstrope'. Many geographical articles are astonishingly brief – for example, 'England' and 'America' are given little more than half a column each! Essential cross-references are sometimes lacking or given to articles which do not exist.

More significant for the modern reader than these obvious defects are the techniques adopted for eluding the censor's eye. The *Encyclopédie* was not intended solely as a source of information but as the expression of a new critical attitude towards man's position in the world; it was intended, in Diderot's expression, to 'change the common way of thinking'. Since, under an absolute monarchy, it was impossible to make direct criticisms of the existing order, the contributors sought to outwit the censors by making the main articles on well-known religious or philosophical subjects completely orthodox; and by inserting at the same time real criticisms in less obvious places, to which the reader's attention was sometimes called by means of discreet cross-references. In this way, it was hoped, in Diderot's words, to 'attack, shake and overthrow secretly some ridiculous opinions which could not be openly insulted'. Another device was to set unorthodox views alongside of the orthodox ostensibly with the intention of refuting them but really in order to give them wider diffusion. The ironical use of elaborate detail could also be quite effective; the article on 'Noah's Ark' contains such a wealth of arithmetical data that it makes the whole subject ridiculous. Very often, therefore, the perspicacious reader was required to read between the lines in order to grasp the writer's real meaning.

For the understanding of the Enlightenment, the story of the publication of the *Encyclopédie* is perhaps less important than the spirit animating it. Even a rapid glance at some of the major articles shows that the supporters of traditionalist ideas were justifiably apprehensive about the subversive effect of this new work. Although they were wrong to suppose that the Encyclopedists were trying to undermine the religious and moral basis of national life, they were rightly convinced that most of the contributors were challenging traditional ideas. One of the simplest and (as it seems to us today) one of the most reasonable of the Encyclopedists' demands, namely, their right to seek truth in their own way, offended the zealous supporters of religious and political absolutism; to the latter it seemed shocking that writers should demand freedom of thought and expression for ideas which were inconsistent with the traditional teaching of Church and State; in the same way the request for religious toleration angered the defenders of Roman Catholicism who still considered that it was the state's duty to protect – if necessary, by force – the exclusive authority of the Church.

As has already been pointed out, traditional metaphysics was rapidly retreating before the advance of the new empiricism founded by Locke, whilst the metaphysically inspired Cartesian view of the universe was being destroyed by the scientific outlook of Newtonianism; it was no longer possible to accept absolute but obscure concepts as a valid way of explaining the ultimate meaning of reality; philosophy had henceforth to concern itself with the 'how' rather than with the 'why' of phenomena, both in the analysis of human experience and in the examination of the physical world. As Diderot was responsible for many of the articles on the history of philosophy, his influence is obviously very marked in the formulation of the new outlook; but his admiration for such thinkers as Bacon, Locke and Newton, and his contempt for the old scholasticism and metaphysics merely echoed a point of view that had been common in France since the publication of Voltaire's *Lettres philosophiques* in 1734. The development of philosophical ideas was becoming increasingly dependent on the findings of modern science. It was, however, the general spirit, as well as the particular aspects of the new philosophy which were being disseminated by the *Encyclopédie*: ideas could no longer be accepted on the basis of authority alone, but had to be justified by an appeal to reason. Admittedly, the critical spirit of the *Encyclopédie* did not exclude the publication of many inoffensive traditional articles. The early volumes, for example, contained many orthodox theological contributions by the abbé Mallet. Yet the very habit of subjecting ideas to rational scrutiny suggested the possibility of extending this attitude to matters which had hitherto been considered sacrosanct.

The concept underlying the Encyclopedists' claim to undertake the independent examination of philosophical and scientific principles was the pervasive, if sometimes obscure, notion of 'nature'. Curiously enough, the article on 'Nature' was for the most part taken from Chambers' *Cyclopaedia*, but it is a term which constantly recurs in every volume of the work. In the first place, 'nature' was opposed to the supernatural; instead of relying on sources of knowledge which had been hitherto judged to lie outside the range of ordinary experience because they were transmitted through an institution with direct and unique access to divine truth, the Encyclopedists insisted upon a strictly human approach to philosophical problems; 'nature' meant what was immediately related to the observable world and to the powers with which man was endowed for investigating it. Diderot effectively summed up the role of nature when he asked: 'What is the authority which the philosopher must have for himself? That of reason, nature, observation and experience.'[8] 'The philosopher', he wrote elsewhere, 'neither denies nor admits anything without examination; he has just confidence in his reason; he knows by experience that the search for truth is hard; but he does not believe it to be

8. Article on 'Syncrétistes' (xv, 750a), quoted in J. Lough, *The Encyclopédie*, London, 1971, p. 155.

impossible.' The thinker's function is thus different from the theologian's. 'Nature is the philosopher's only book; the sacred Scriptures are the theologian's only book.'[9] Unlike the directness of revelation, the truth of nature can be known only through the activity of reason, observation and experience; there is no other means of attaining sound knowledge.

Since experience is as indispensable as reason, it is nature's observable effects – not its occult properties – which must be the subject of the philosopher's immediate inquiry. 'Philosophy', wrote d'Alembert, 'must not lose itself in general properties of being and substance, in futile questions concerning abstract notions, etc. It is either the science of facts or a chimera.' The philosopher cannot penetrate the ultimate mystery of things and, in this respect, the Encyclopedists criticized the scholastics and metaphysicians for having deluded themselves with merely verbal accounts of the absolute. Yet, even though any sudden metaphysical leap into the transcendent and supernatural is forbidden, the philosopher-scientist is sustained by a firm belief in the ultimate unity of all things. He confidently assumes that there is a hidden unity which, though perhaps never completely comprehensible, lies behind the disconcerting complexity and variety of all phenomena. That is why d'Alembert, in his *Discours préliminaire*, presents the search for this unity as a worthy intellectual ideal. 'The universe, for the man who can envisage it from a single point of view, would be . . . only one great truth.' 'It is undeniable', he wrote in the article 'Qualité cosmiques', 'that all the bodies of which this universe is made up form a single system, whose parts are interdependent and whose interrelations derive from the harmony of the whole.' Nevertheless, the exploration of this 'nature' in which 'everything is interconnected' is a long and arduous process, for the universe is 'a vast ocean' on the surface of which we can discern only 'a few more or less large islands' while the vast 'continent lying beneath remains hidden from us'. In 'the great riddle of the universe' we can make out no more than a 'few syllables'.

This notion of the ultimate unity of the universe suggests the method to be followed in any attempt to seek knowledge about it. In the first place, the *Encyclopédie* itself proposes to demonstrate the interconnec-

9. Article on 'Mosäique et chrétienne (Philosophie)'; quoted in J. Lough, op. cit., p. 155–6.

tion and interrelationship of the various branches of knowledge. *Enchaînement* is a word frequently used by the editors when they describe their task. 'As an encyclopedia, it must expound, as far as possible, the order and interconnection of human knowledge.' That is why the *Discours préliminaire* tries to analyse the 'genealogy and filiation of our ideas'. As in the case of Locke, the Encyclopedists seek to use the genetic method; tracing ideas back to their origins seems to them the most fruitful way of acquiring a sound basis for the advancement of philosophical and scientific knowledge.

Interest in the interconnection and ultimate unity of all knowledge does not exclude a serious effort to present a systematic account of the 'elements and details of each branch'; as a 'rational dictionary', the *Encyclopédie* 'has to contain on each science and art, whether liberal or mechanical, the general principles which are its basis and the essential details which form its body and substance'. A good example of an attempt to determine such principles is d'Alembert's article 'Éléments des sciences'. At the same time there is an effort (inspired by Bacon) to relate the organization of knowledge to the three human faculties: memory (history), reason (philosophy) and imagination (fine arts).

A spirit of intellectual optimism is clearly reflected in the concluding section of d'Alembert's *Discours préliminaire* which outlines the history of modern culture from the time of the Renaissance and gives prominence to such famous figures as Bacon, Descartes, Newton, Locke and Leibniz; among the contemporary writers praised are Fontenelle, Montesquieu, Voltaire and Buffon. For d'Alembert this period marked a definite step towards a more adequate understanding of man and the world, and the eighteenth century could proudly call itself 'the age of philosophy'. In using this term he intended to equate it with 'enlightenment'. The Encyclopedists were inspired by what they called *l'esprit philosophique* – a critical, rational approach to problems which are related to this world rather than to the next. More particularly, they held up science and its methods as examples to be followed by all thinkers.

It was the eulogy of this *esprit philosophique* which aroused the wrath of the Encyclopedists' enemies, for they saw in it a grave threat to religious orthodoxy. The rejection of the supernatural as irrelevant to the search for secular knowledge was certainly a distinctive feature of the *Encyclopédie*, which professed to be concerned with 'the history of the human mind'. Even contributors who were still sympathetic to religion often favoured a liberal and rational interpretation of Christianity and emphasized its moral, rather than its dogmatic, content. This stress upon morality enabled atheists like Diderot and d'Holbach, who could give only indirect expression to their irreligious views, to call attention to the inhuman consequences of traditional attitudes; revealed religion was treated as a source of intolerance and bigotry as well as of intellectual obscurantism – in short, as an offence to both humanity and reason. Not only were many particular abuses of the Church – its intolerance, wealth, exclusive control of education and support of unacceptable doctrines such as that of eternal punishment – the target of constant criticism, but considerable prominence was also given to the ideas of non-Christian religions, which were often shown to encourage attitudes more in conformity with the true Christian spirit than the practices of the Church itself! Likewise, persistent efforts were made to prove that the Bible, far from being a unique book, contained many examples of human weakness and ignorance.

This general hostility to revealed religion, and especially to Roman Catholicism, was inspired by the Encyclopedists' determination to concentrate on the problem of man. Apart from tracing 'the history of the human mind', they sought to deal with all aspects of man's existence. 'It is man's presence which makes the existence of beings interesting', declares Diderot in his long article 'Encyclopédie'. 'Why shall we not introduce man into our work as he is placed in the universe?' In the same article he states that the *Encyclopédie* seeks 'to treat everything appertaining to man's curiosity, duties, needs and pleasures'.

The Encyclopedists' preoccupation with human values explains the strong current of humanitarian feeling flowing through their work. A respect for human dignity means a rejection of all forms of tyranny and oppression and a corresponding need to affirm the right to freedom. As Diderot points out, 'freedom is a present from heaven and every individual of the same species has the right to enjoy it as soon as he enjoys reason' (article on 'Autorité politique'). Another contributor, the Chevalier de Jaucourt, who wrote numerous articles for the later volumes, condemns the exploitation of human beings for material gain. 'Men and their freedom are not an object of trade; they cannot be sold, bought or paid for at any price' (article on 'Traité des Nègres'). 'Everything conspires to leave man the freedom which is natural to him.' It is its denial of this unique human attribute which makes slavery so reprehensible; a slave cannot lose his freedom because no man, however exalted his position, has the right to take it from him; nothing is more blameworthy than the pernicious argument which seeks to justify the enslavement of the negroes by maintaining that 'the salvation of their souls' outweighs every other consideration. The Encyclopedists believe that the principles of natural right which are 'engraved in the human heart' provide permanent support to those who fight to uphold man's desire to be a true human being. As Diderot observes, nothing is more striking than the contrast between a 'society of men united by reason, inspired by virtue and governed by justice', and a 'herd of animals brought together by habit, driven on by the whip and subservient to the whim of an absolute master'. It is the same concern for the 'sacred rights of humanity' which leads the Encyclopedists to condemn the barbarous rigour of the penal code and the use of torture. Why could not France follow the example of a nation 'as enlightened as respectful towards humanity' (England) which has abolished torture 'without inconvenience'. The evils of war are also severely condemned by Jaucourt in his article on that subject, because 'war stifles the voice of nature, justice, religion and humanity'. The article on 'Humanity' (probably by Diderot) sums up the whole matter when it points out that 'this noble and sublime enthusiasm is concerned about the pains of others and the need to relieve them; it would like to go out into the whole universe to abolish slavery, superstition, vice and misfortune'.

It is probably this interest in humanity which explains one of the most original technical features of the *Encyclopédie* – the large place given to the detailed description of the mechanical arts and trades. Although some controversy has arisen over the question of possible plagiarism, there seems no doubt that the editors believed that in calling attention to this technological aspect of modern man's achievements they were giving their due to those who worked with their hands as well as to those who achieved recognition through the power of their minds.

The Encyclopedists' humanitarianism did not make them political revolutionaries. It is unlikely that any of them wanted to overthrow the monarchy. Even the important concept of freedom is not given a detailed and sophisticated political definition, but tends to remain a broadly human concept. It is noteworthy that the twenty-page article devoted to that subject concentrates exclusively on its philosophical aspects, while the more specialized articles on political and civil freedom are extremely brief and do little more than reproduce extracts from Montesquieu and the Genevan jurist, Burlamaqui, the popularizer of the ideas of the School of Natural Law. There are, of course, more extended articles on subjects such as 'Political Authority' and 'Natural Right', and Rousseau's important contribution on 'Political Economy', but these had only a general bearing upon the problems of contemporary France. Professor John Lough has pointed out that political issues tend to become more prominent in the later volumes of the *Encyclopédie*. Broadly speaking, the Encyclopedists seem to have been anxious to protest against the abuse of absolute power and to place some restraint upon the king's authority. Perhaps this is why many of them gave limited support to the Parlements in their struggle against the Crown, while also condemning them for their religious intolerance.

The general influence of the School of Natural Right is very obvious in the constant approval given by the Encyclopedists to the principle of government by consent. Man, as a rational free being, has the right to choose the kind of government under which he wishes to live, for it is the duty of every government to provide for the security and well-being of all its citizens. This is clearly brought out in Diderot's article 'Autorité politique' when he affirms: 'The power which comes from the consent of the nation necessarily supposes conditions which make its use legitimate, useful to society, advantageous to the commonwealth and which fix and restrict it within proper limits'. There is no such thing as absolute arbitrary power, for all power is limited by 'the laws of nature and the state'; every ruler ought to be bound by the terms of the 'social contract' which gives him authority. Other writers do not hesitate to follow Montesquieu in his praise of the English constitution or to approve of such typical English institutions as the jury system and representative government. All contributors would thus seem to be opposed, in their support of a rational human exercise of power, to the traditional theory of the divine right of kings. Authority must be both 'legitimate and reasonable'. It follows also that some importance is attached to the notion of equality – that is, equality before the law. Jaucourt argues that it is the 'violation of this principle of natural equality which is responsible for political and civil slavery'.

Support for moral and legal equality in no way involved the acceptance of economic equality, which was dismissed as an absurd chimera. In general the Encyclopedists wanted moderate but specific reforms rather than any radical change; they pressed for freedom of trade, the development of agriculture, a more equitable system of taxation and the secular control of education. Although they did not want to abolish the aristocracy, they sought to remind the nobles of their obligations to society; a man is superior to others only through the usefulness of his activity, not through some inherent right. At the same time the Encyclopedists, like most of the *philosophes*, had little confidence in the masses. Any improvement in man's lot must be brought about by those in authority and the enlightened members of the nation. Few Encyclopedists were willing to place any confidence in the masses themselves.

Although, as a source of information, the *Encyclopédie* has suffered the fate of all such compilations, it still remains a valuable testimony to the essential spirit of the French Enlightenment and to the essentially human and intellectual ideals by which it was constantly inspired. More particularly, it was an act of confidence in man himself, for it presupposed that, with the spread of enlightenment and knowledge, he would be able to find happiness in his life on earth.

THREE

Germany

THE prestige of German philosophy, so high in the nineteenth century, dates from the 1780s, the years of the publication of Kant's great *Critiques*. Before Kant there is no German philosopher of originality after Leibniz, who essentially belongs to the seventeenth century. And even after the advent of Kant it is scarcely correct to write of a literature of ideas, since exposition of 'ideas' is taken so far that it becomes virtually unintelligible. The French had a very notable literature of ideas, which flourished in social conditions suited to the discussion and interchange of ideas; but these conditions were absent from Germany, where there was no single intellectual centre comparable, even remotely, with Paris. Instead there were numerous small courts, university towns and trading cities. Conversation at the courts was often gross, and where it was not, it was in French and nourished itself from French books. The universities, too numerous and too small, were homes of pedantry. The rising middle class in the towns, having no metropolitan standard to look up to, remained provincial. In these conditions a diverse and dynamic creative literature could and did arise through the unconstricted efforts of individuals, but a literature of ideas could not take root in a soil so unpropitious. The record is rather that of thinkers than of a continuous strand of developing thought.

LEIBNIZ (1646–1716)

Gottfried Wilhelm Leibniz possessed a universal mind endowed with a marked predisposition for harmony and concord. At university he studied mathematics and law, but his mind ranged over the whole field of available knowledge. In 1666 he took a doctorate at Altdorf and in the following year entered the service of the Electoral Archbishop of Mainz, who favoured him because he was acquainted with the beliefs and practices of alchemy. The archbishop employed him on a political mission to Paris in 1672. To the ministers of Louis XIV he put forward the proposal that the princes of Europe should cease to war among themselves and unite to expel the infidel Turk, then harrying the eastern marches of central Europe. Much as he admired Descartes, he could not accept the sharp dualism of Cartesian thought and devoted himself to a philosophy of harmonization. In 1676 Leibniz transferred his services to the Duke of Brunswick-Lüneburg, for whom he made an exhaustive study of genealogy, examining sources as far afield as Modena and Rome. From 1690 he was librarian of the Ducal Library, a post in which Lessing was to follow him some eighty years later. Not long before becoming librarian he devised his *System theologicum* (1686),[1] an interesting, though abortive, attempt to reconcile the Roman, Lutheran and Reformed Churches. It testifies both to his desire to harmonize and to his tolerance in an age still much inclined to bigotry and persecution. Leibniz also demonstrated his versatility by devising a system of international law arising out of historical legal studies which he had first formulated in *Nova methodus discendae docendaeque jurisprudentiae* (1667).

Leibniz had a complete command of French and Latin, which he used in his multifarious manuscripts and publications to the complete exclusion of his native German. He also maintained an abundant correspondence with scholars and men of eminence at home and (more often) abroad, all of which was written in French. His mind teemed with projects and was constantly seeking to explore new fields, and, as a consequence, a number of his schemes are not taken to their conclusion, and inconsistencies and even contradictions occur. He was a mathematical genius of the first order and the inventor (independently of and simultaneously with Newton) of the calculus.

The two principal systems of the eighteenth century were the dualistic philosophy of Descartes and the monistic pantheism of Spinoza. Leibniz devoted himself to devising a new conception to accommodate and harmonize both, and in doing so shows the acuteness of his mathematical mind and the brilliance of his speculative imagination. The general lines of Leibniz's thought are not too difficult to summarize, but it must be realized that his fecund mind teemed with other schemes besides philosophy. He expressed his ideas in a diversity of

1. Circulated in manuscript, but not published until 1819.

essays, published and unpublished, which represent aspects and facets of his thought without ever organizing it into a coherent system. The only philosophical work which he published is *Essais de Théodicée sur la bonté de Dieu, la liberté de l'homme, et l'origine du mal* (1710). Among unpublished papers are 'Considérations sur la doctrine d'un esprit universel' (1702) and 'Nouveaux essais sur l'entendement humain' (1696).

The eighteenth century was influenced mainly by Leibniz's published essay, the *Théodicée*, and to a lesser extent by the *Monadologie*, published in a German translation (1720) after his death. The *Théodicée* is nowadays best known through Voltaire's mockery in *Candide*. It is concerned with the problem of evil and the justification of God. When we contemplate the evil in the world, is it possible to believe that it is the creation of a beneficent deity? Thanks to Voltaire's irony Leibniz's phrase 'le meilleur des mondes possibles' is generally regarded as a foolish cliché. Nevertheless, if abstract argumentation is accepted, as it was in Leibniz's day, his case is a reasonable one. God only is perfect. If God creates something other than himself it must be less than perfect. God could create an infinity of worlds, all of which would, in varying degree, be imperfect. But God's perfection implies that he can only be satisfied with that which, though imperfect, comes nearest to perfection. Therefore the world, as it exists, with all its shortcomings must be the best possible. But however neat the logic, the conclusion is expressed in words of a complacency which would not now be acceptable. As well as being ridiculed by Voltaire, the validity of such proofs in the sphere of metaphysics was rejected definitively by Kant, but at the time at which Leibniz wrote such reasoning was widely accepted as a means of establishing ultimate truth. And it was the *Théodicée* which the early pioneers of the German Enlightenment disseminated in their own interpretation.

Leibniz's essay *La Monadologie* was written in 1714 in response to an inquiry from Marlborough's military colleague Prince Eugene of Savoy. Speculative and imaginative, it seemed to most readers (who encountered it in its published German form after Leibniz's death) to be in part crazy or at least incomprehensible. Leibniz's aim was to solve the problem of causation, to which Cartesianism gave no satisfactory answer. Descartes conceded free-will to man, but conceived matter to be subject to a mechanistic law of cause and effect. Man, however, was also in part material, and the dualism of matter and spirit was accepted. This problem was bound to haunt a congenital monist, as Leibniz was, and in the *Monadologie* he attempts a solution. Leibniz used the well-known image of two clocks which keep perfect time, one of which corresponds to the material and the other to the spiritual substance of the world. Their conformity may be explained in one of three ways. The one may be mechanically connected with the other, or there may be concealed in one clock a cunning artificer who ensures that it keeps time with the other, or the clock-maker made them with such skill that from the beginning of time they agree without further adjustment. Leibniz opts for the last solution, to which he gives the name 'prästabilierte Harmonie', and the clock-maker is, of course, God the Creator. Leibniz's contemporaries had no difficulty in accepting the idea of 'pre-established harmony'; their troubles began with the theory of monads which he invented to support it. In a curious way foreshadowing Kant's *Erkenntnistheorie* and, still more remarkably, seeming to anticipate conclusions of modern physics, Leibniz suggests that perceived matter is illusory, being the sensory appearance of a much more complex and intangible reality. To every perceived object there corresponds a monad, and to all the particles of that object correspond further monads, and these contain still others which extend downwards to the infinitely small. He compares each monad to 'a garden full of plants' and 'a pond full of fish'. The monads themselves do not change but their relationship to each other changes, and such shifts in monadic structure account for the changes in objects observed by the senses. And the whole conspectus of monads extends from the infinitely small to the infinitely great, all aspiring upward to the greatest monad, God, and so teleologically, and not mechanically, caused.

Leibniz made explicit the political analogy with the pyramidal grouping of his monadological metaphysics, indicating that it corresponded to benevolent monarchy in which each has his proper and useful place, so that this brilliant and rather fanciful essay draws attention at the very beginning of the Age of Enlightenment to the ideal of the enlightened and benevolent despot, who was to be embodied in greater or less degree in such figures as the Emperor Joseph II, Frederick II of Prussia and Count William of Schaumburg-Lippe.

WOLFF (1679–1754)

Christian Wolff was the principal disseminator of Leibniz's stimulating, but scattered and unsystematic, ideas, but his capacity to grasp them was limited and he himself conceded that he could make nothing of the theory of monads. Like Leibniz, Wolff was also a mathematician, and it was Leibniz who recommended him in 1707, for appointment to the chair of mathematics and natural sciences at Halle University. The publication of the *Théodicée* in 1710 made a great impression upon Wolff and in the following years he devoted more and more of his time to the study of philosophy, making Leibniz's justification of the ways of God to man the central feature of his system. Wolff lacked his master's brilliance, imagination and instant response to new ideas, possessing instead patience, thoroughness and the capacity to organize his material. In 1712 he published his treatise on logic under the title *Vernünftige Gedanken von den Kräften des menschlichen Verstandes*. This was followed by metaphysics (*Vernünftige Gedanken von Gott, der Welt und der Seele des Menschen*, 1720), ethics (*Vernünftige Gedanken von des Menschen Tun und Lassen*, also 1720), politics (*Vernünftige Gedanken von dem gesellschaftlichen Leben der Menschen*, 1721), physics (*Vernünftige Gedanken von der Wirkungen der Natur*, 1723) and teleology (*Vernünftige Gedanken von den Absichten der natürlichen Dinge*, also 1723). The parallelism in this list of titles indicates clearly enough the methodical nature of Wolff's acute and yet extremely limited mind. He accepted, and indeed believed firmly in, a theocentric universe, and yet his arguments imply a mechanistic conception. Unable to appreciate the importance of the monads (since God and men are related as monads in Leibniz's theory), Wolff retains the pre-established harmony (though changing the term to 'predetermined' – 'vorherbestimmt') which in his hands becomes a simple determinism. The human soul is for Wolff the rational intellect, and in propagating this view he gave strong support to the primacy of reason, which played so strong a part in the earlier phases of the Enlightenment. Though the homocentric utilitarianism with which Wolff regarded the 'lower orders of creation' is not only repugnant in itself but inadequately argued, Wolff's rationalism leads him in the ethical field to a praiseworthy advocacy of tolerance and understanding, and he is a firm opponent of bigotry. Through the intrigues of intolerant enemies Wolff became a figure of some historical importance in the development of the Enlightenment. Suspected of atheism, he was dismissed in 1723 by King Frederick William I of Prussia at the instigation of a faction in the university. He found refuge at Marburg University and was recalled in triumph to Halle on the accession of Frederick II in 1740.

Although Wolff was mainly responsible for initiating the diffusion of Leibniz's optimistic rationalism (in a simplified form) to a wider circle of readers, the sheer bulk of his volumes and the weight of their style still made heavy demands upon the reader. The role of popularizer was filled by Gottsched.

GOTTSCHED (1700–1766)

Born in Königsberg in East Prussia, Johann Christoph Gottsched grew up under a Prussian King, Frederick William I, who had an obsession for things military and a mania for acquiring tall grenadiers. By the time Gottsched graduated at Königsberg he was a very tall man, and in 1724 he thought it wise to slip over the frontier and make his way to Saxony, a land with a more favourable intellectual climate. Determined to make an academic career for himself, he settled in Leipzig, and by 1730 was a supernumerary professor of poetry at Leipzig University, and by 1734 the professor of logic and metaphysics. Though he is best known for his treatise on aesthetics, published in 1732,[2] Gottsched made his mark with a philosophical work, *Erste Gründe der gesamten Weltweisheit*, which appeared in two volumes in 1730. Gottsched made no pretence to originality, offering in effect a condensed version of Wolff's rationalistic system in readable and convenient form. It would hardly be true to say that this was philosophy for the common man, but the task of reading the six volumes of Wolff's *Rational Thoughts* was a daunting one, which was not made easier by the author's desiccated style. To Gottsched belongs the credit, not only of having given considerable assistance in spreading the gospel of rationalism, but of reaching a public which would otherwise scarcely have been aware of the nature and scope of philosophy.

2. See p. 408f.

LESSING (1729–81)

Gotthold Ephraim Lessing is the first German writer of the Age of Enlightenment who may be said to represent a literature of ideas. He made no claim to be a philosopher, though his attitude of rationalism tempered by common sense and his awareness of the limits of reason put him in the van of intellectual developments at the mid-century. He claimed to be a devotee of truth, and campaigned through many years to expose cant, hypocrisy and pretentiousness, and to rehabilitate reputations of poets, publicists or theologians who had been the victims of calumny. Most of his writings were critical or concerned themselves with aesthetics and these will be examined later.[3] Apart from aesthetics, it is primarily in the field of theology that Lessing appears as a writer on ideas.

Early in his career Lessing embarked on a didactic poem entitled *Die Religion*. The decision to write it is not surprising. Lessing's father, who enjoyed his son's life-long respect, was a Lutheran pastor, and Lessing himself began his university career at Leipzig as a student of theology. In later years he was at loggerheads with certain representatives of the Lutheran Church, but none of his works contains at any point an attack upon religion as such. He failed to complete his poem *Die Religion*, publishing in 1751 only a fragment of 347 lines from the first canto of what was originally intended to be a long poem. The reason for his failure to complete it lies partly in his inadequate poetic equipment and gifts, partly in his preference at all times for specific aspects to comprehensive surveys, and partly in his own uncertainty; for the fragment reveals a conflict between his orthodox upbringing and the impact upon him of Wolffian deism.

A few years later Lessing published in *Schriften* (1754) three essays concerned with long defunct theologians. They were Hieronymus Cardanus (1501–76), Johann Cochläus (1479–1552) and the anonymous author of a tract published in 1656 with the title *Ineptus religiosus*. They were in no way connected with one another, but Lessing believed all three to have incurred unjustified censure by their contemporaries for their religious views, and his essays were intended as *Rettungen*, or rehabilitations, rectifying injustice. The preoccupation

3. See pp. 411–16.

with these obscure figures may show Lessing's unwillingness, for reasons of genuine respect, to make any direct attack upon religion; it certainly indicates a life-long disposition to denounce intolerance. It is perhaps significant of his wish to be fair that in his early comedy *Der Freigeist* (1755, written in 1748) an orthodox pastor displays tolerance and an atheist lacks it, whereas in the play *Die Juden* (1754, written in 1749) a Christian's anti-semitic intolerance is corrected.

For a great part of his life Lessing was occupied with criticism, aesthetics and the writing of plays, and it was only when his appointment as Ducal Librarian at Wolfenbüttel (Brunswick) in 1770 gave him a fixed stipend that he had leisure to gratify hitherto neglected interests. Among these was the championship of tolerance, particularly in a theological context. His first opportunity came from the inspection of uncatalogued manuscripts, and one of his earliest publications of these years was a rehabilitation, on an altogether larger scale than the earlier essays, of the reputation of Berengar of Tours (died 1088), who was twice convicted of heresy (*Berengarius turonensis*, 1770). There followed a number of minor theological publications based on papers found in the library and, in 1774, a document which purported to have its origin in the archives, but had in fact no connection with the library (*Von Duldung der Deisten*). Lessing had come into possession of the manuscript of a treatise written by a well-known Hamburg schoolmaster, H. S. Reimarus (1694–1768); entitled *Apologie oder Schutzschrift für die vernünftigen Verehrer Gottes*,[4] it was a defence of deism conducted with much hostile comment on the Christian faith. Reimarus was a rationalist of early-eighteenth-century cast and his views were by no means identical with Lessing's. They suited, however, Lessing's purpose, which was to provoke a fruitful discussion on two important questions, the historical approach in theology and the nature of belief. He adopted the fiction that the manuscript was discovered in Wolfenbüttel in order to protect Reimarus's family from probable persecution.

Lessing's intention was to provoke controversy which would clarify in an arresting manner the distinction between experimentally derived knowledge and faith, and particularly to attack the literal interpretation of the Bible on which the orthodox Lutherans insisted. In this he at first failed. *Von Duldung der Deisten* passed unnoticed. In 1777 he

4. First published 1972.

tried again, and was this time all too successful. The second set of extracts from Reimarus's manuscript appeared under the title *Ein Mehreres aus den Papieren eines Ungenannten, die Offenbarung betreffend* and was concerned with divergences of fact between the Gospels. To his first critic (J. D. Schumann, 1714–87) Lessing replied with courtesy, to his second (J. H. Reiss, 1723–1803) with irony; the third, Pastor J. M. Goeze (1717–86) of Hamburg was not a man to be brushed aside. To Goeze's forthright condemnation Lessing published a rejoinder; Goeze retorted, Lessing countered, and so developed an acrimonious campaign in which the original issue was replaced by that of religious toleration, intolerantly debated by both parties. Lessing styled his pamphlets *Anti-Goeze*, giving each issue a number; when they had reached eleven the Duke of Brunswick, embarrassed by the controversial role of his librarian and under pressure from the orthodox Lutheran wing, ordered a cessation. The *Anti-Goeze* papers remain as a monument of polemical literature and of skilled invective, but they do not contribute to the detached debate which Lessing had originally sought. His most positive contributions were made in the supplement, headed *Gegensätze*, which he appended to the extracts from Reimarus, notably the sentence: 'The Christian religion is not true because the Evangelists and Apostles taught it, but they taught it because it is true.' Lessing excelled at such lapidary formulation, but one should hesitate to accept such a statement in such a context as a personal confession of faith. For all his forthrightness he had a streak of reticence in what concerned him personally and an instinct to screen himself spiritually from the public gaze. From the whole controversy there emerges the conviction of the limitations of historical truth. Beneath it lies a clear distinction between faith and experimental proof, and hence a denunciation of rationalistic metaphysics.

Lessing eventually circumvented the duke's ban on writing on religious matters by writing a play. *Nathan der Weise* (1779), written in blank verse, is a noble plea for humanity and tolerance which completely transcends the controversy in which Lessing had become entangled.

Lessing's last religious work is a pamphlet consisting of a hundred numbered paragraphs, occupying in all some twenty pages. It appeared in 1780 without indication of the author's name, a fact which, in view of Lessing's ingrained reluctance to write publicly of his own deep convictions, is consonant with the generally held opinion that it represents his final testament in the matters which he had so ardently and energetically discussed in the years 1777–9. *Die Erziehung des Menschengeschlechts* sustains a thesis of the development of religion, allotting a place to the Christian faith in its scheme, whilst denying that it is the ultimate revelation. Lessing sees the history of mankind as a process of education, beginning in the religious sphere with the first intimations of divinity, expressed in idolatry and polytheism. The monotheism of Judaism was the next stage of revelation (Lessing uses the word *Offenbarung*), to be succeeded in its turn by Christianity. This in turn will yield to a new gospel ('die Zeit eines *neuen ewigen* Evangeliums') corresponding to the perfection of mankind, realized in an altruistic ethic, when men will do right because they recognize it as right, needing neither promise of reward nor threat of punishment. It is an attitude characteristic of the Enlightenment, and anticipates the ethical views to be expressed by Kant in closely argued form a few years later.

HAMANN (1730–88), HERDER (1744–1803) AND PESTALOZZI (1746–1827)

Lessing was at the centre of attention for more than two decades and represented (though with important but concealed reservations of a religious, almost mystic character) the trend of a perfectionist, progressive rationalism. Johann Georg Hamann, an eccentric and unstable character only eighteen months younger than Lessing, was a peripheral figure, whose writings were nevertheless to prove seminal for movements yet to come. While in England in 1758–9, Hamann suffered an emotional and spiritual crisis, and all his writings are subsequent to this period of disturbance. He is the first German writer of the eighteenth century outside clerical and pietistic circles to reject reason for intuition. His curiously entitled *Sokratische Denkwürdigkeiten für die lange Weile des Publikums zusammengetragen von einem Liebhaber der langen Weile* (1759) is in part a criticism of the rationalism of the age; it is also one of the first works to separate and virtually to place learning and genius in opposition to each other. 'What in Homer', writes Hamann, 'makes up for his ignorance of the rules of art, which Aristotle later invented, and what in Shakespeare makes up for his ignorance of these rules or his infringement of them? Genius is the only answer.' Hamann, who already in his life-time was referred to as 'The Magus in the North', applied his conception of genius to the philosopher Socrates. He influenced the *Sturm und Drang* chiefly through Herder, whose primary considerations were aesthetic. Because of his predominating preoccupation with literature and the arts, Johann Gottfried Herder (1744–1803) is discussed in Part Five,[5] though it should be mentioned here that his thought, in spite of its aesthetic bias, had considerable influence in the nineteenth century upon attitudes to the history of civilization. Herder, who, under the impact of Rousseau's writings, had abandoned his clerical appointment in Riga in 1769, returned to theology in 1774–6 with *Die älteste Urkunde des Menschengeschlechts* and made from time to time further contributions to the subject, notably in *Christliche Schriften* (five volumes, 1794–8). Towards the end of his life an attempt to refute Kant's *Kritik der reinen Vernunft* failed dismally (*Eine Metakritik zur Kritik der reinen Vernunft*).

An early sociologist, possessing literary gifts, was the Swiss Johann Heinrich Pestalozzi (1746–1827), whose views are contained in *Meine Nachforschungen über den Gang der Natur in der Entwicklung des Menschengeschlechts* (1797). Though chiefly remembered for his contribution to modern education, Pestalozzi was also a humane reformer in other fields, and made a deep impression upon his contemporaries with his pamphlet on infanticide, *Über Gesetzgebung und Kindermord* (1782). He propagated his views, not only in essays and treatises, but also in the novels *Lienhard und Gertrud* (1781–7) and *Wie Gertrud ihre Kinder lehrt* (1801).

KANT (1724–1804)

Immanuel Kant, a man of humble origin and insignificant presence, became the first real philosopher of Germany – far greater (as a philosopher) than Leibniz, not for the span of his intellect, but for his power to organize and systematize the profound conclusions achieved by a first-class intelligence with a full command of logic and completely at home in the realm of abstract thought. In temperament and

5. See below, pp. 411–18.

activity he exhibited a complete contrast to Leibniz's restless inquiring mind, which achieved brilliant results in many fields of study but denied its possessor the leisure and repose necessary to produce a philosophy.

Kant's biography is virtually without interest. From 1747 to 1754 he was a private tutor; in 1755 he qualified to lecture and was given an appointment at Königsberg University; in 1770 he became professor of logic and metaphysics and in 1796 he retired. All his life he lived in his native city of Königsberg, the capital of Prussia's easternmost province. He never visited Berlin and never set foot in any foreign country. He never married, and his daily bachelor routine continued unchanged through the years. His regularity almost reached the point of eccentricity, and anecdotes about him are common. The best known are the story that the citizens checked their watches by Kant's morning walk, which always took the same route at the same pace and at the same time, and the connected episode that the only occasions when he failed to appear at the recognized time were the result of absorption in Rousseau's *Émile*. These anecdotes may well be apocryphal, but they are nevertheless characteristic.

It must be supposed that Kant's restricted environment and set routine were congenial to his nature and gifts. He was able, provincialism notwithstanding, to give German philosophy the prominent place in European abstract thought which it retained for a century through a series of thinkers, all of whom were profoundly influenced by him. Nor was he narrow in his interests or illiberal in his views: he wrote on meteorology, cosmology, mysticism, copyright and politics. His tract *Zum ewigen Frieden* (1795) presents a draft for a universal treaty, barring aggression and annexation, abolishing standing armies, advocating a universal federation of states, and guaranteeing the rights of man. Kant could not have believed that his proposals would be adopted at the time of the wars of the French Revolution, but he was undoubtedly an opponent of war and wished to arouse discussion in the hope of an eventual solution.

Kant's reputation and achievement, however, rests on his three great 'Critiques', *Die Kritik der reinen Vernunft* (1781, the basic work of the whole system), *Die Kritik der praktischen Vernunft* (1788), dealing with ethics, and *Die Kritik der Urteilskraft* (1790, a treatise in great part concerned with aesthetics). The similarity in the titles indicates his basic method: a critical examination of the current ideas of rationalism and empiricism, preparing the ground for the construction of his own transcendental philosophy, which itself is developed in a process of self-scrutiny.

This is not the place to expound Kant's arguments, which are of a character to interest only professional philosophers. It is necessary, however, to summarize some of his conclusions, especially those which bear upon literature. Kant was originally trained in the rationalist philosophy of Wolff, which had its antecedents in the thought of Leibniz and, indirectly, Descartes. The scepticism of Hume made a deep impression upon him, and his own philosophy, worked out over many years but written down in haste (hence, according to some, the obscurity of his style), provides an answer to the problems of previous philosophers. Kant's transcendental philosophy accepts, with restrictions, the mechanical causation of the empiricists and, at the same time, finds room for a reality not apprehended by the senses: a moral world, which is also the true world, in which the highest being is God. In denying that metaphysics could be an exact science, Kant, in his own words, set out to 'abolish knowledge to make room for faith'.

The most important aspects of Kant's philosophy, in so far as it concerns literature, are his theory of knowledge (*Erkenntnistheorie*) and the categorical imperative. Knowledge, which the empiricists held to be derived from experience, is according to Kant not absolute or objective, but conditioned by the apparatus of perception of the human being. The early-nineteenth-century dramatist Heinrich von Kleist put it succinctly in a famous passage in a letter written to his fiancée in March 1801: 'If all men had green glasses instead of eyes, they would have to esteem that the objects they behold *are* green – and they would never be able to decide whether their eyes show them things as they are, or whether they do not confer on things something which pertains, not to the things, but to the eye – so it is with the mind.' Kant denied, in fact, that we could perceive things as they really are, since our cognitive structure gives its own shape to the perception. What we see is, he claimed, a phenomenon or '*Erscheinung*'. This was not a denial of the existence of things: indeed, he maintained that it is possible to apprehend the true nature which lies, so to speak, behind the phenomenon and to which he gave the term noumenon or 'Ding an sich' (an untranslatable expression, usually rendered as 'thing-in-itself'). The means by which the noumenon is known is not, however, through the senses, but by the intuitive moral sense. Though the subtleties and difficulties of Kant's thought were and remain considerable, the message of idealism spread rapidly, through the writings and lectures of his disciples, and exercised a powerful influence, not only on the next generation of Romantic writers and philosophers, but on Goethe and Schiller, men whose roots were in the Age of Enlightenment. This is the more remarkable in respect of Goethe, who was temperamentally opposed to Kant's methods, and acquired his idealistic attitude through the intellectual climate of the time.

The 'categorical imperative' was the ethical maxim of idealism. Every action we undertake, ought, according to Kant, to be such as we are able to will to be a general law. This morality, a refinement on 'Do unto others as you would be done by', is the ethical apogee of the Enlightenment. Kant's high altruism eliminated pleasure from virtue, asserting that, in so far as an act is done for motives of pleasure, it is to that degree not virtuous. He is not, however, so stern as to deny that pleasurable feelings may *afterwards* be aroused by a virtuous action in the person who performs it. It was over the point of pleasure and morality, that Schiller, in *Über Anmuth und Würde* (1793), took issue with the *Kritik der Urteilskraft*. Using the terms duty (*Pflicht*) and inclination (*Neigung*), which implies pleasure, Schiller maintained that virtue, as the quality of a person (rather than an appurtenance to an act), is 'an inclination to duty' ('eine Neigung zur Pflicht').[6]

6. See p. 419.

FOUR

Italy

In 1700 Italy, unlike France and England, was not a united and power ful nation, but a region divided into a loose agglomeration of states- isolated by customs barriers and an infinite number of local allegian-, ces; and each, for the most part, subject to foreign domination, the claims of dynastic legitimism through divine right and of political absolutism. During the seventeenth century, in the years of Spanish domination, Italy's markets in Europe and the Levant and the international trade, had largely been lost to France, England and Holland: great nation states, operating in a spirit of enterprise and speculation, whose development had been assured through the encouragement of navigation and the pursuance of a mercantile system which sought to increase national wealth by regulation of the balance of trade. Italy, with a trade in luxury goods, art industries, wool and silk, all produced on traditional lines, had been driven out of her markets; and by 1700 the peninsula was in economic decline.

In the first half of the eighteenth century, the peninsula became politically involved, like the rest of Europe, in the three great wars of succession: the Spanish (1701–13/14), the Polish (1733–4) and the Austrian (1740–48). With the Treaty of Utrecht (1713), Milan and Naples, long ruled by Spain, passed to Austria; though in 1734 Spain restored Bourbon rule to Naples, with Don Carlos, and Austria was ousted. Sicily was awarded to Savoy, which, after a period of eclipse, re-emerged in the eighteenth century as a strong military state. The duke took the royal title; and in 1720, when Sicily was exchanged with Austria for Sardinia, Victor Amadeus II also became king of that island. With the Treaty of Aix-la-Chapelle (1748), which brought an end to the War of Austrian Succession and ushered in a period of peace, at least until Napoleon began his Italian campaign in 1796, even more far-reaching changes took place. In Tuscany, with the extinction of the House of Medici in 1737, the Grand Duchy passed to Francis, Duke of Lorraine (1708–65), as compensation for his hereditary dominions, which had been seized by France. After 1740, through the marriage of Maria Theresa, the duchy became an apanage of the Austrian family. Francis was succeeded in 1765 by his son Peter Leopold (1747–92), who became emperor after the death of his brother Joseph II in 1790. At Parma, after 1748, when the duchy was lost to the Farnese and became another Bourbon possession, Don Philip of Bourbon (1748–65), son of Philip V of Spain and Elizabetta Farnese, rendered the state prosperous, with the help of the Frenchman Du Tillot, and turned Parma into the so-called 'Athens of Italy'.

In the cultural and intellectual sphere the Italian eighteenth century was in part the heir of the Italian seventeenth century, laying great stress on classical erudition, historical scholarship and archaeological research, and in part a period of transition, achieved largely through a growing involvement in the great ferment and confrontation of new ideas. In the last decade of the seventeenth century and the early part of the eighteenth century, in Italy, as elsewhere in Europe, the period of the Counter-Reformation and the Baroque fell into disrepute and 'Reason' and 'Nature' came into fashion. War began to be waged on traditional values; institutions, both religious and secular, were subjected to critical scrutiny.

The century as a whole may be divided into three phases. The first of these, covering the years 1690 to 1740, has often been typified as the 'Age of Arcadia', deriving its name from a celebrated academy, of phenomenal social and cultural influence, founded in Rome on 5 October 1690, with the aim of purifying by example Italian letters, especially poetry, eradicating the excesses of the seventeenth-century style. The philosophical, scientific, economic, literary and aesthetic movements of seventeenth-century Europe and their attendant publicists – such as Bayle, Fontenelle, Malebranche and Bouhours – had their champions and critics in Italy. And it is doubtless significant, as Carlo Dionisotti has noted, that 'all the major figures in Italian literature born in the second half of the seventeenth century – G. V. Gravina, G. B. Vico, L. A. Muratori, F. S. Maffei and P. Giannone – should have been men who were also, and in many cases principally, concerned with subjects other than literature'. At this time, and for the greater part of the eighteenth century, press censorship, first introduced in the sixteenth century, remained in force throughout the states of Italy. Every manuscript was perused by two or more revisors appointed by the civil and ecclesiastical authorities before a licence to print was authorized. This practice did not entirely preclude, however, the publication of new and interesting works, though many were brought out, with or without the connivance of the licensing authorities, under a false imprint. In the seventeenth century distinguished scholars had flourished in all the main centres of the peninsula and the Age of Arcadia inherited a remarkable tradition of erudition in antiquarian and other matters. Three such scholar-historians, who belonged to both the seventeenth and eighteenth centuries, were Antonio Magliabecchi (1633–1714), librarian to the Duke of Tuscany; the Benedictine Domenico Bacchini (1651–1721), friend and adviser to Muratori and historiographer to the Duke of Modena; and Monsignor Francesco Bianchini (1662–1721), the author of some sixty works of historical erudition, including the *Istoria universale provata con monumenti e figurata con simboli degli antichi* (1697). Bianchini travelled throughout Europe, met Sir Isaac Newton, and became one of the few Italian members of the French Academy of Sciences. In the early eighteenth century press censorship did not impede, but rather stimulated, erudition and the compilation of such monumental works of scholarship. Characteristic areas of study were ecclesiastical and medieval history, archaeological research and investigation of ancient cultures and artefacts, regional historical studies and jurisprudence. In the Age of Arcadia historical and antiquarian research also began to be conducted in a more scientific and systematic manner than hitherto. Medieval and Etruscan studies developed; Ludovico Antonio Muratori (1672–1750) laid the foundations of modern Italian historiography; and with Giambattista Vico (1668–1744), who made a genuine attempt to discover the past of mankind, a philosophy of history was formulated. At this time too a main instrument of cultural popularization and divulgation, both literary and scientific, was the periodical – which was to become an increasingly effective channel and promoter of new ideas. In the Age of Arcadia the most important periodical, with contributions on scholarly topics from men of science and letters all over the peninsula was the *Giornale dei Letterati d'Italia* (Venice, 40 vols., 1710–40), founded by the Venetian scholar Apostolo Zeno (1668–1750), in collaboration with the Paduan naturalist Antonio Vallisnieri (1661–1730) and with the Veronese 'cavaliere erudito', Francesco Scipione Maffei (1675–1755). Each volume of the *Giornale dei Letterati* was erudite and academic in tone, solid and authoritative, with an index and between fifteen and twenty articles, some of which dealt with new publications. Book news, eulogies of famous men and literary news were also plentiful. The journal was edited by Apostolo Zeno, with his brother Caterino, until 1719; after which, with the departure of Apostolo for Vienna as Poet Laureate, Caterino Zeno carried on alone. Its aim was to compete effectively with foreign periodicals, which at that time showed scant interest in Italian writers; or, as in the case of the *Mémoires de Trévoux*, were offensively antagonistic to Italian matters. Another compilation of outstanding merit, started some years later, was the *Raccolta di opuscoli scientifici e filologici* (Venice, 50 vols., 1728–54; vol. 51, Index, 1757), which was continued, embracing in all a span of almost sixty years, under the title *Nuova raccolta di opuscoli scientifici e filologici* (Venice, 1755–87). The *Raccolta* was edited, up to Volume 15 of the *Nuova raccolta*, by Angelo Calogerà (1699–1768), a Benedictine monk of the Camaldolesian order living in the convent of San Michele in Isola, who for decades was a leading promoter of journalistic and allied activities in Venice. The *Raccolta* was a vast miscellany which provided a forum for articles and pamphlets on medicine, philosophy, history, natural science and antiquarian matters. The second cultural phase of the eighteenth century, which may be said to terminate in 1764 with the foundation of *Il Caffè* (74 numbers, May 1764–June 1766), the polemical organ of the Società dei Pugni ('The Punch-hards'), a group of young Milanese aristocrats imbued with the spirit of French encyclopedism, was largely one of transition from the Age of Arcadia to the so-called Age of Reforms. In the years 1740 to 1760 men of the older generation, such as Vico, Muratori, and Maffei, brought out the works of their maturity and passed away; and new figures emerged. Such were the Neapolitan political economist Antonio Genovesi (1713–69), born at Castiglione near Salerno, Ferdinando Galiani (1728–97), the Istrian Gian Rinaldo Carli (1720–95) and the Florentine Pompeo Neri (1706–76). Journalism also progressed with Gasparo Gozzi (1713–86), editor of the *Gazzetta Veneta* (1760–61) and the *Osservatore Veneto* (1761–2). At the same time the popularization of the 'New Science' was furthered by the cosmopolitan and cultured publicist Francesco Algarotti (1712–64), one of the most representative polymaths of the century, who is especially remembered for his three influential essays on architecture (1756), painting (1762) and music (1762), and for his youthful *Newtonianismo per le dame* (1737), an entertaining and instructive dialogue in the vein of lightly written scientific divulgation first cultivated by Fontenelle.

Between 1760 and 1800, with the gradual diffusion of the thought of the English and French *philosophes,* and with the conflicting claims on the one hand of neo-classic and on the other of pre-Romantic modes of thought, notable advances were made in all spheres. Confronted with the contrast between the Italian inherited order and the new culture and flourishing economic state of Europe, the Italian intelligentsia and the foreign monarchs by whom they were supported were faced with the task of meeting new requirements. In this task the 'literature of ideas' was subsidiary. Interest developed in agricultural, economic and juridical reform. Translations were made from the English and French classics of political economy – that branch of the art of government which dealt with public revenue and the enrichment of the community. Works of scientific divulgation were published. In the more vital centres movements developed to suppress the old trade guilds, with their entrenched medieval economic structures; and governments began to issue patents and privileges to favour new types of industrial production. The spirit of reform naturally varied from state to state. It was especially strong at the mid-century in Naples, with Genovesi and his followers; and later, with such men as Pietro Verri (1728–97) and Cesare Beccaria (1738–94), at Milan and in Tuscany, subject to Austria and the enlightened princes of Lorraine; but elsewhere also extensive and on the whole beneficial reforms were introduced. By the turn of the century there were in Italy signs of a marked recovery. In the words of the historian Luigi Salvatorelli: 'In the eighteenth century the spiritual life of Italy woke to new activity and returned to the spiritual life of Europe'. This life had in the meantime evolved independently of Italy and the Italians could not now escape its influence; the principal phenomenon of this spiritual reawakening was the wide penetration of foreign culture. From this was generated a new national life, more closely linked to the life of Europe.

SCHOLARS AND HISTORIANS

Ludovico Antonio Muratori (1672–1750)

Muratori, an industrious scholar-priest of prodigious output and a central figure in the intellectual ferment of pre-Illuminist Italy, was born at Vignola, a village in the duchy of Modena, into a family of modest station. An archivist and librarian by profession, he soon began to show his preference for literary and historical pursuits. At the age of thirteen, he was sent to school in Modena, where he studied with the Jesuits and the Franciscans. In 1688–9 he took minor and major orders. Three years later he met the Benedictine archaeologist Benedetto Bacchini, who was to play an important part in his life, directing his studies towards historical inquiry, especially to the history of religion. In 1692 Muratori entered Modena University as a law student. He also took a course in Greek and began to publish his first works: three short treatises in Latin which gave evidence of his encyclopedic interests and desire for cultural and educational renewal. In the first and most interesting of these, entitled *De graecae linguae usu et praestantia*, dated 15 July 1693, he deplored the decline of Greek while advocating its study as an indispensable tool for all serious learning and historical investigation. In 1694 Muratori graduated with a doctorate in civil and canon law. In the same year, at the age of twenty-two, having been admitted to the Order of Deacons, he was invited to Milan by Count Carlo Borromeo, where he spent five years as one of the librarians in the Ambrosiana. Availing himself of the resources at his disposal, he prepared the first two volumes of a much-praised collection of unpublished Latin and Greek fragments, known as the *Anecdota latina* (5 vols., 1697–1713) and the *Anecdota graeca* (1709). He also wrote a *Vita* (1700) of the celebrated Milanese dialect poet and playwright Carlo Maria Maggi (1630–99). This was the first of a number of biographies composed by Muratori which were designed to introduce a reprint of the works of the writer concerned. Among these may be noted the biographies of Petrarch, Tasso, Ludovico Castelvetro, Alessandro Tassoni, and the sixteenth-century Modenese medievalist Carlo Sigonio, who is often regarded as a precursor of Muratori.

Muratori's most important scholarly labours began in 1700 when he left the Ambrosiana for the rich but disordered Estense Library in Modena, where he spent the rest of his life. The move was occasioned by the visit to Modena of the German philosopher Leibniz, sent by the Elector of Hanover, whose librarian he was, to clarify obscure points in the genealogy of the Brunswick–Este families. Duke Rinaldo I d'Este, an erudite and austere man, was anxious to aid the Elector and his distinguished representative. He remembered Muratori; and at the instigation of the ageing Bacchini, he invited him to return to the cultivated court of Modena as archivist and librarian. Years later, in 1716, Muratori accepted, in addition, his first and only ecclesiastical benefice. He became priest of the impoverished parish of the dilapidated church of Santa Maria della Pomposa. This office he discharged with zeal and rectitude until 1733. In 1721, on the death of Bacchini, Muratori succeeded him as director of the Estense Library.

Like many scholars of his day, Muratori was a polymath gifted with the ability to write on a wide range of subjects. Not only was he an outstanding medievalist who compiled monumental works of scholarship, but a journalist and a writer on matters of religion, law, philosophy and critical subjects.

Soon after his return to Modena, Muratori produced a treatise entitled *Primi disegni della Repubblica Letteraria d'Italia* (1703). This was a programme for the correction of abuses and the reform of education, which advocated the intensification of the study of languages, both classical and modern, including Hebrew, the furtherance of the empirical and medical sciences, the study of mathematics, and the encouragement of the humanities through a plan for the restructuring of the academies of Italy, in the footsteps of the Arcadian reform, into a single sovereign and authoritative 'Republic of Letters'.

As a journalist, he contributed to the *Geiornale dei Letterati d' Italia* (see pp. 109–10) reviews and extracts from his works, and a spirited defence of Giovanni Orsi, the Bolognese philogist and critic of Padre Bouhours, under attack by the French rationalists in the *Mémoires de Trévoux* for his defence of Italian poetry. From 1740 on, Muratori also made several notable contributions to the Florentine *Novelle Letterarie*, directed by Giovanni Lami.

As a theologian, Muratori was the author of important treatises on religious matters, some of which he wrote in Latin, others in the vernacular. Among these the most influential were *De ingeniorum moderatione in religionis negotio* (1714), *Della carità cristiana in quanto è amore del prossimo* (1723), in which he provided a programme of work for his 'Compagnia della Carità', *De superstitione vitanda* (1740) and *Della regolata divozione dei cristiani* (1747). In these works, written in a spirit of religious toleration, Muratori combated prejudice and superstition. Though well received and highly esteemed, they rendered their Benedictine author suspect by the Jesuits. In the field of philosophy and education, Muratori produced *Filosofia morale esposta e proposta ai giovani* (1735), an expository work based on the principle of the capacity of human reason, aided by divine grace, to form the basis of moral philosophy. Later, as a lawyer anticipating the Age of Reforms, he wrote *Dei difetti della giurisprudenza* (1742), which was a plea for the codification of the chaotic mass of Italian law. In his last treatise, *Della pubblica felicità oggetto dei buoni principi* (1749), Muratori developed a variety of themes that were to become dear to the eighteenth century: questions of 'happiness' and the 'public good', and of government, especially in relation to the education of the ruling class, the use and abuse of wealth, the importance of agriculture, the military, and matters of public health.

Like Jean Mabillon, the Benedictine who inaugurated in France the scientific study of medieval documents, and by whose example he was doubtless greatly influenced, Muratori is especially renowned for his work on historical documentation, for his compilation of written records, and for his historical writings based thereon. His life-long labours in this field were intensive. After his appointment as court archivist at Modena in 1700 he devoted himself largely to the investigation of the fundamental history of the Dark and Middle Ages in Italy, periods at that time little understood and generally regarded with disdain.

As court archivist Muratori was first required to compile a genealogical account of the origins of the House of Este, on lines similar to those proposed by Leibniz for his history of the House of Brunswick. While preparing this work, however, which appeared under the title *Delle antichità estensi ed italiane* (2 vols., 1717, 1740), he availed himself of a band of erudite collaborators to put together the *Rerum italicarum scriptores*, a monumental collection of more than two thousand previously unpublished chronicles, statutes and letters from the various states of Italy between the years 500 and 1500. They were placed in chronological sequence and illustrated with commentaries and critical notices. This was a major corpus of medieval and Renaissance documentation unrivalled in its century and which remains, with its supplements, a fundamental and indispensable collection of source material. Begun in 1708, the first volume of *Rerum italicarum scriptores* appeared in 1723. Publication in Milan proceeded at regular intervals for nearly thirty years, and the last of the twenty-eight folio volumes issued bears the date 1751, a year after Muratori's death. The *Rerum italicarum scriptores* were subscribed to by the scholars, princes and higher nobility of Italy. Although threatened with censorship by the ecclesiastical authorities in Rome, the production was supported by the Emperor Charles VI, to whom it was dedicated.

Between 1738 and 1742, utilizing for the most part material drawn from the *Rerum italicarum scriptores*, Muratori brought out, in a further six volumes, a weighty collection of seventy-five original dissertations, with other minor chronicles and records, to which he gave the title *Antiquitates italicae medii aevi*. The dissertations illustrate the customs, political constitution, thought, commercial, legal and military relations of the Italian states in the Middle Ages. They refer to all topics of public and private interest, and, by reason of their scholarly use of source materials, constitute a landmark in the historical study of that period. In 1740 Muratori also began the *Annali d'Italia* (12 vols., 1744–9), a chronological history of Italy from the birth of Christ to the Treaty of Aix-la-Chapelle. The *Annali*, a vast repository of information, are characterized by lucid exposition and by a praiseworthy respect for facts, being based on first-hand examination of extant records. They were designed for a more general readership than Muratori's other historical publications and after his death they were continued, from year to year, by a number of subsequent Italian historians until well into the nineteenth century.

Muratori's other historical works include a sustained polemic (1708–20) with Giusto Fontanini, defender of the claims of the Church to the rights of dominion over Comacchio and Ferrara, in dispute between the House of Este and the court of Rome, and the *Novus thesaurus veterum inscriptionum* (6 vols., 1739–43), a large collection of Latin and medieval inscriptions supplementing the sources provided in the *Rerum italicarum scriptores.*

Throughout his life, Muratori also carried on a vast correspondence with his collaborators in Italy and in other parts of Europe, and with the principal literary and historical academies, of many of which he was a member. He also made a significant contribution to aesthetics and to literary criticism with three treatises entitled *Della perfetta poesia italiana* (4 vols., 1706), *Riflessioni sopra il buon gusto intorno le scienze e le arti* (1708) and *Della forza della fantasia umana* (1745).

Giambattista Vico (1668–1744)

While Muratori was working in Modena, in Naples and the south of Italy the two main representatives of Italian historical writing, whose work also entered the philosophical, political and religious spheres, were Giambattista Vico and his younger contemporary Pietro Giannone.

Vico, born in the heart of old Naples, the son of a bookseller, was a philosopher-historian interested essentially in legal and literary, rather than scientific, culture. His place in the history of thought is still uncertain: he was neglected in his day and the awakening of interest in his work was delayed, except in Italy, until well into the nineteenth century; nowadays, he is widely esteemed as one of the most ingenious thinkers of modern times. One of the great originators of the concept of growth in historical phenomena and the notion of the individuality of particular cultures, he was, as Sir Isaiah Berlin has pointed out, 'one of the earliest exponents of what might be called the class-war view of history'. He was also a philosopher whose 'ideas about the use of language, his very conception of language, form the foundations of comparative philology, comparative anthropology, comparative human sciences in general'. Vico's main title to fame is a work of synthesis and many-sided suggestion known as the *Scienza nuova*; it has been well-described as the *Novum organum* of politico-historical knowledge. First published in 1725, in extremely condensed form, it was later revised substantially for two subsequent editions known respectively as the *seconda* [second] *Scienza nuova* (1730) and the *terza* [third] *Scienza nuova* (1744). The full title of the *prima* [first] *Scienza nuova* was *Principj di una scienza nuova intorno alla natura delle nazioni, per la quale si ritruovano i principij di altro sistema del diritto universale delle genti* ['Principles of a New Science concerning the Nature of Nations, wherein the Principles of Another System of Jurisprudence are Discovered'].

Vico was an inveterate Platonist and traditionalist soaked in the eclectic thought of late Seicento Naples and he reacted against both rationalism and empiricism. He was a philosopher of history and culture whose writings, in both Latin and the vernacular, were suffused with a large dose of Christian humanism and the sense of a world ruled by divine ideas. At first a Gassendist, then a Cartesian interested in pedagogical matters, he later rejected the idea that mathematics is capable of expressing the ultimate truth of natural phenomena. Vico held that men can have no absolute knowledge of the physical world and he reacted against the rigid, mechanistic methodology of Descartes. Being profoundly versed in the legal science of ancient Rome, which he took to be exemplary, he became absorbed on the one hand in the origins and making of law, and on the other in the institutions and cultural manifestations of the remote and primitive past – ritual, divination and idolatry, the hieroglyphics of Egypt, the significance of Greek myth (which he regarded as a semi-fantastic form of knowing, an immature individualization of abstract concepts), the meaning of the Homeric heroes, theological patterns of society and patriarchal monarchy, the conflicts of patricians and plebeians, the beginnings of poetry and languages, the origins of names.

At the same time, he was also pondering a theory which he felt to be both new and grand. How was it that men emerged after the great Deluge (dated in accordance with current belief to the year of the world 1656) from their primal state of brutish savagery, which Vico postulated, with insight, as characteristic of that prehistoric epoch, into the condition of *humanitas*: the first civilized phase when, through salutary doses of terror, men became aware of conscience, developed a sense of shame, of religion and of family life; priests, wise men and law givers appeared; and people began to associate in a spirit of mutual co-operation? Vico believed that the history of the human race – which for Vico was essentially that of mental states – had been misunderstood through ignorance of its beginnings and that this knowledge could be supplied only by philosophy. The true nature of historical causation must also be found. Distinguishing between *verum* ('truth') and *certum* ('certitude') – that which is deducible from other propositions and certainty based on *de facto* observation – he sought patterns in history, the definition of cultures and axioms (*degnità*) of universal application, indicative of the factors common to all nations in their evolution. This he achieved through repeatedly amplifying, revising and recasting his writings until, in the later versions of the *Scienza nuova*, he finally brought together and fused into a system, however obscure and unreadable, his observations concerning the nature of nations and the foundations of their existence in the parabola of an 'eternal, ideal history of mankind', the idea of which he believed to have existed from eternity in the mind of God.

The best introduction to Vico is that provided by his own *Vita* (1728), first drafted in 1725 and subsequently continued to 1731. Writing in the third person, he traces with marked detachment and philosophic insight how, while preparing the *Scienza nuova*, he came to write as he did:

> meditating the causes, natural and moral, and the occasions of fortune; why even from childhood he had felt an inclination for certain studies and an aversion from others; what opportunities and obstacles had advanced or retarded his progress; and lastly the effect of his own exertions in right directions, which were destined later to bear fruit in those reflections on which he built his final work.[1]

Vico's early education was made irregular by a fall from a ladder at the age of seven, when he fractured his skull. At thirteen, in 1681, he left school almost completely to pursue his studies, under private tuition, in the seclusion of his father's bookshop. A clever and studious youth, with great powers of application, he began a philosophy course, studied canon and civil law, and gained experience in the law courts, to such effect that in 1686 he defended his father in a case brought against him by a fellow bookseller. For the next nine years (1686–95) he worked as a tutor for the Bishop of Ischia at Vatolla in the province of Salerno. Returning to Naples from time to time, he matriculated at the university law school (1689) and without attending the course of study appears in 1695 to have taken a doctorate in law at the University of Naples (Salerno). Three years previously he had

1. This and other translations from the *Vita* are cited from *The Autobiography of Giambattista Vico*, translated by M. H. Fisch and T. G. Bergin, Ithaca, NY, 1963.

been elected to membership of the Academy of the Uniti; and on his return to Naples in 1695 he soon began to form influential friendships, frequenting the salons, libraries and academies of the city, where he was strongly influenced by such eclectic, free-thinking intellectuals concerned with cultural renewal as the ageing Francesco d'Andrea, Leonardo di Capua and Tommaso Cornelio. In 1699 he was appointed to the chair of rhetoric an the university, a poorly paid teaching post concerned mainly with the provision of linguistic instruction for the higher courses. In the same year he married Teresa Caterina Destito, the daughter of a clerk in the criminal courts, who could neither read nor write. He was also received into the Academy of the Royal Palace, presided over by the Spanish Viceroy, the Duke of Medinaceli. In 1723 he competed for the chair of jurisprudence (civil law), a well-remunerated post on which he had long set his heart. His attempt was unsuccessful; but in 1734, when Spain restored the Bourbon rule to Naples, and Austria was ousted, Vico was selected to head the university delegation offering congratulations to Don Carlos III. In the following year, one of the first to benefit from the dynastic change, he was appointed to the newly created office of historiographer royal, with a modest honorarium and an increase in his basic salary. In 1737 he became *custode*, or keeper, of the Academy of the Oziosi. In 1741, having long been afflicted by an incurable illness, he relinquished his university chair in favour of his son Gennaro.

Prior to his first university appointment Vico wrote a quantity of commissioned pieces, including occasional verse. He also composed a powerful, self-probing *canzone* entitled *Affetti di un disperato* (1692) in which, in a moment of spiritual crisis, he gave voice to a hopeless pessimism. Vico's most important and influential writings, however, which culminated in the three versions of the *Scienza nuova*, all belong to the post-1699 period – the years of his slowly developing maturity. These include seven Latin 'Inaugural Orations', severe and reflective in tone, the *Liber metaphysicus*, which forms the first book of the unfinished *De antiquissima italorum sapientia ex linguae latinae originibus eruenda* ('On the Primitive Wisdom of the Italians to be Recovered from the Origins of the Latin Language'), *De rebus gestis Antonii Caraphaei* (1716), and a treatise on jurisprudence, in which he developed his historical theories, especially from the point of view of the history of law and the history of language; it was entitled *De universi iuris uno principio et fine uno* ('On the Single Principle and the Single Aim of Universal Law', 1720). To the latter Vico appended, in reply to his critics, a second part entitled *De constantiae iurisprudentiae* ('On the Consistency of Jurisprudence', 1721). These two parts, with a set of annotations, are often referred to under the collective title *Diritto* (or *Jus*) *universale* ('Universal Law').

Besides making a study of canon and civil law, of the medieval interpreters of the Roman civil law, of scholastic logic and classical rhetoric, as a young man, Vico read Homer, Dante and the Latin poets, especially Virgil and Horace. He also studied Greek ethics, beginning with Plato and Aristotle, the Stoics, Plutarch, the Florentine Neoplatonists, Ficino and Pico della Mirandola, geometry and the geometric method. But he soon became a partisan of two authors whom he studied equally and regarded as supreme: Plato, whom he read in Latin, and Tacitus. Plato, a mine of abstract and academic wisdom, Vico admired for considering man as he should be and because, in him, human wisdom seemed to come closest to Christianity. Tacitus, whose wisdom was that of a Roman historian and statesman, he regarded as equally supreme for contemplating man not as he ought to be but as he is, with an incomparably metaphysical mind. When, about 1707, Vico discovered the *Advancement of Learning* (1605), *De sapientia veterum* ('On the Wisdom of the Ancients', 1609) and the *Novum organum* (1620), he was able to add the name of Francis Bacon to his select list of model authors.

Much of Vico's thought in the early years of the eighteenth century can be found in his seven 'Inaugural Orations' (1699–1708), which were composed and delivered almost annually for the opening of studies at the university. In the first six of these, which deal with the ends of various studies, or with methods of study, Vico was accustomed, as he tells us in his autobiography, 'to propose universal arguments brought down from metaphysics and given social application'. In the first three orations he treated principally of the ends suitable to human nature; in the next two principally of the political ends; in the sixth of the Christian end. In 'Oration II' (1700) he turned over in his mind a theme which he was later to develop in the *Diritto universale*. 'Oration III' (1702) contained a plea for honesty in the Republic of Letters. 'Oration IV' (1703) was directed against false scholars. The theme of 'Oration VI' (1706) was that 'The knowledge of the corrupt nature of man invites us to study the complete cycle of the liberal arts and sciences, and propounds and expounds the true, easy and unvarying order in which they are to be acquired.' It contained a programme of systematic education, starting with languages and history to be taught to children, who memorize easily, and leading through subsequent study of the quantitative sciences and physics to Christian jurisprudence.

In 'Oration VI' (1708), *De nostri temporis studiorum ratione*, Vico entered somewhat belatedly into the quarrel of the Ancients and Moderns. The occasion was one of special import for the opening of studies at the university in the year following the change from Spanish to Austrian rule in the city. Vico had been reading *De sapientia veterum*, in which Bacon had purported to show that doctrines of natural philosophy were concealed in the Greek myths. Stimulated by this concept, Vico recast his previous six orations to deal with 'The Study Methods of our Time' as compared with the practice and methodology of the ancients. The lecture was revised, amplified and published in 1709. With it Vico closed one phase of his speculative activity and opened up another. Aiming to investigate a new field of knowledge, he remained a rationalist but drew increasing attention to the inadequacies of the methodology and basic doctrine of Descartes; and in his next work, the *Liber metaphysicus* of *De antiquissima italorum sapientia*, he assumed that the Latin language was a repository of profound philosophy awaiting elucidation through the meaning of words, and introduced his doctrine of 'metaphysical points', elaborated a theory of knowledge foreshadowing that of Kant, and raised questions concerning the relations of philosophy and history, which received their answers only years later in the *Scienza nuova*.

In 1710, shortly before the publication of the *Liber metaphysicus*, Vico was received into the Naples 'colony' of Arcadia. Another member of the same group, who had been introduced by Vico and whom he numbered among the inner circle of his friends, was Ippolita Cantelmo-Stuart, of the royal house of Scotland, whose marriage to Vincenzo Caraffa, Duke of Bruzzano, Vico had celebrated with a *canzone* as early as 1696. Adriano Caraffa, Duke of Traetta, one of Vico's pupils, had in his possession a quantity of papers relating to his uncle Marshal Antonio Caraffa, statesman and pillar of the Austrian monarchy, and the bloody suppressor of the Hungarian insurrection. In 1714 Adriano invited Vico to write his uncle's biography: a task which took him two years to complete and formed a parenthesis in his activity. But the labour was not in vain. As an aid to preparing *De rebus gestis Antonii Caraphaei* (1716), Vico was obliged to consult in depth *De jure belli ac pacis* by the Dutch jurist Hugo Grotius. Reading Grotius clarified Vico's own ideas and enabled him to add yet a further name to his list of supreme authors. The study revealed, moreover, what he had long been seeking, at least since the time of his early 'Inaugural Orations', and of which he now gained a fresh conception by perceiving that

there was not yet in the world of letters a system so devised as to bring the best philosophy, that of Plato made subordinate to the Christian faith, into harmony with a philology exhibiting scientific necessity in both its branches, that is in the two histories, that of languages and that of things; to give certainty to the history of languages by reference to the history of things; and to bring into accord the maxims of the academic sages and the practices of the political sages.

Vico's creative labours from 1719 on may perhaps best be construed, as Dario Faucci has suggested, as 'a progressive attempt to differentiate his thought from that of Grotius in point of natural or "universal" law, in order to replace Grotius's solution with his own'. Between 1720 and 1722, amplifying his 'Inaugural Oration' of 1719, he published in Latin the two parts, with Notes, of his *Diritto universale*. After this he began to write as with prophetic zeal. His prose, formerly calm and reflective, became more solemn, poetic and full of apophthegms, robust images and lapidary phrases. About the same time he completed a treatise, now lost, in which he appears to have explored the origins of civilization through a polemical refutation of Grotius, Puffendorf and the other jurists, and of the ancient and modern utilitarians. Vico considered this first draft of the *Scienza nuova* too 'negative', however; and having christened it 'Scienza nuova in forma negativa', he promptly rewrote it in severely condensed and more 'positive' form. He dedicated the revised treatise to Cardinal Lorenzo Corsini, later Pope Clement XII, and published it in Naples in 1725. Unfortunately, Vico received no subsidy from his patron and he was obliged to pay for the printing and binding of the *prima Scienza nuova* himself out of the sale of a ring, we are told, 'set with a five-grain diamond of the purest water'.

The *Scienza nuova*, in its various versions, constitutes an original philosophy of the stages and cycles of human society. In the first version this was presented as a method aimed at the construction of a new system of Natural Law, different from, but not contrary to, the already existing ones formulated by Grotius and his followers. For the *seconda Scienza nuova*, published in 1730, the *prima Scienza nuova* was amplified and completely recast, with the effect of making it more imposing as a system, but at the expense of great loss of clarity. The phrase 'natural law' was dropped and the title modified to read 'Five Books of the Principles of a New Science concerning the Common Nature of Nations, greatly enlarged and evolved in more pertinent Fashion'. The definitive *terza Scienza nuova*, published posthumously in 1744, was a somewhat retouched version of the *seconda Scienza nuova*, with additions.

In a curious allegorical engraving published with and illustrative of the *Scienza nuova*, a female figure with wings at her temples, representing Metaphysics, is seen standing on a globe of the world bound with the signs of the zodiac and resting on an altar. Rapt in contemplation, she gazes towards the Heavens. The rays of Divine Providence, issuing from an eye in the centre of a triangle, illumine a jewel on her breast, whence they are reflected towards the figure of Homer, represented as a statue mounted on a ruined base. Elsewhere are signs of auguries and divination, a torch, an urn, a rudder, a plough, a tablet with letters of an ancient alphabet, and other signs and symbols indicative of such civilizing practices and institutions as language, religion, matrimony, jurisprudence, agriculture and commerce, characteristic of the three worlds experienced by man as dealt with by Vico: the World of Nations, the World of Nature and the World of God.

The five books of the *Scienza nuova* are preceded by an 'Idea dell'Opera' in which the symbols of the allegory and the significance of its composition are explained, to enable the reader to gain an idea of the nature and scope of the treatise before reading it, and to understand it better. Book I, *Dello stabilimento dei principj*, contains a universal chronological table of pagan and sacred antiquity, with annotations, and a statement of philological and philosophical principles and methodology. The other four books, which are supplemented with a conclusion and four appendices, dealing especially with the Roman Law of the Twelve Tables, are entitled *Della sapienza poetica*, *Della discoverta del vero Omero*, *Del corso che fanno le nazioni* and *Del ricorso delle cose umane nel risurgere che fanno le nazioni*. Each of these, of which Book II is the bulkiest in the 1744 edition, is divided into a multiplicity of subsections.

In the annotations to his chronological table Vico describes, in accord with a tripartite scheme, three ages, or phases of cultural development, through which he believed archaic mankind to have evolved. With special reference to the history of language and the history of ideas, these are treated as the 'Age of the Gods', the 'Age of the Heroes' and the 'Age of Men'. The dividing lines between the periods are not always clear-cut: Vico had a subtle sense of the way in which one cycle of civilization might shade off into another. In his first age, however, which is that of the remotest pre-Homeric past, lost in the mists of antiquity and the cloud shapes of legend, men are regarded as having been neither rational nor sociable. After the great Deluge they lost their speech, communicated only by gesture, and were reduced to a state of brutish savagery, isolation and primitive fears. At first they were without moral conscience or religious feelings, and motivated primarily by the instincts. 'Poetry' was the first expression of humanity, not willed but spontaneous; and at its most exalted the eruption of fantasy. A 'divine' picture language is said to have been invented; men began to name the gods anthropomorphically; and the poets themselves were 'theological'. This age Vico regarded as 'divine' in the sense that its characteristic science was that of divination; and primitive mankind as a whole is considered to have received its eventual knowledge, language and authority from the gods. The 'Age of the Gods' is partly filled with events recorded in the Old Testament and by very ancient tradition. It runs from Noah's Flood in the year of the world 1656 to the 3,223rd year, when Hercules is reputed to have instituted the festival of the Olympic Games. It is the period of the Golden Age, interpreted by Vico as that of the discovery of agriculture, of the first legislator Minos, king of Crete, of the Spartan lawgiver Lycurgus, of Orpheus, Jason, Theseus and the Trojan War.

Vico's 'Heroic Age', the true interpretation of which it was his purpose to recover, starts before the end of obscure time, occupies the whole of fabulous time and continues after the foundation of states. Some six centuries in duration, it runs from the foundation of the Olympic Games to the second Punic War, when reliable recorded history and the more equilibrated, rational society of the 'Age of Men' begins. A period of the passions rather than of the instincts, it was characterized for Vico by a barbarous or semi-civilized existence; but it was free from the vices of later civilizations. An age of wars, it corresponds to the period of the Greek colonizations, the foundation of Rome, the flowering of Athens and of Greek art, science and philosophy, and the institution of the Roman Law of the Twelve Tables, which Vico found to represent a weighty testimonial of the natural law of the nation of Latium. The 'Age of the Heroes' was also rich in fables. The original 'divine' language was forgotten and the myths were given fictitious or lascivious meanings, to meet the demands of credulity, or for patriotic motives. This was the age of Homer, Aesop and Pythagoras, and later Herodotus, Socrates, Thucydides, Plato and Aristotle; it was the period of the Peloponnesian War and the battles of Alexander.

Book II of the *Scienza nuova* is divided into eleven sections and deals with the science of the 'poeti teologi', or the Poetic Wisdom of primordial cultures. In it the themes dealt with include 'Poetic Metaphysics', 'Poetic Morality', 'Poetic Politics' and 'Poetic Chronology'. Book III, 'The Discovery of the True Homer', is intended partly as an illustration of Book II. Vico puts forward the idea that 'Homer', whom he regarded as the 'primo autore della gentilità che ci sia pervenuto', was not so much an historical personage, as a mythological, or composite 'poetic' figure, a heroic symbol of the Greek people, who were the true authors of the *Iliad* and the *Odyssey*, works which were composed more than a lifetime apart. In the Homeric poems Vico found two treasure-troves of the customs, beliefs and institutions existent in primitive Hellenic civilization; and in Book II, besides querying the 'historical' Homer, he also dealt with substantial questions concerning the historical-poetic nature of the Homeric poems themselves, anticipating the theories of Wolff and Herder in viewing them as the culmination in the compilation of a tradition of oral 'folk' or ballad poetry handed down in debased form from the remotest antiquity to men who consciously sought historical-poetic material in the fables which had formerly been a folk language.

In Book IV of the *Scienza nuova* Vico offered the results of his discoveries concerning 'The Historical Course of Nations' in the light of the principles and axioms established in Books I–III. He distinguished between three kinds of human nature, three kinds of languages and three kinds of authority, each typical of one of the three ages into which he divided the chronology of pagan and sacred antiquity. Other aspects dealt with in tripartite division are 'Three kinds of Natural Law', 'Three kinds of government', 'Three kinds of jurisprudence' and 'Three kinds of judges'. In Book V, by comparing what he regarded as the semi-barbarity of medieval institutions with those of pre-classical Greece, Vico elaborated his theory of *ricorsi*, or cycles, to account for retrogressions and rebirth in the evolution of society. In periods when an apparent 'return to barbarism' takes place, Vico does not assume a complete loss of previous achievements, but at least a partial preservation of civilized values. In his 'Conclusion' he places this concept in a wider, philosophical context. Starting with a reference to Plato, he notes the rise and fall of civilizations, and considers the recurrence of an 'Eternal, natural commonwealth', perfect in all its aspects, conforming to an ideal prototype, or pattern, ordained by Divine Providence.

Vico's cyclical interpretation of history was a commonplace of classical and Renaissance thought; and his idea of the 'Three Ages' was likewise far from original, having been anticipated by Diodorus Siculus. As a 'philosopher of history', moreover, Vico has often been criticized not only for his excessive drive towards systematization and for his bias in taking Rome as the archetype of all nations and cultures, but also for his endless allusiveness and for his general obscurity. His terminology, which he does little to explain, has been regarded as uncouth; his Latinisms as too rugged; and his method of exposition as antiquated. Yet despite these evident shortcomings, initially through the labours of Benedetto Croce and Fausto Nicolini, and, more recently, many other scholars, Vico has at last been accorded his due. Nowadays he is often regarded not only as a philosopher who left a corpus of writings in which the germs of anthropology, the history of ideas, and the other sciences of social and cultural change can be found, but as a 'man born out of his time' whose ideas can everywhere be traced in modern disciplines as diverse as linguistic philosophy, comparative philology, biology, economics, psychology, sociology, phenomenology, philosophical pragmatism, existentialism and even structuralism. Such grandiose claims have naturally led to a certain distortion and exaggeration of Vico's achievement, which was essentially that of a late-seventeenth-century Neapolitan intellectual deeply versed in the legal and literary culture of his time and place. Vico was, however, a pioneer of what has been called 'conjectural history'. The ages of language and poetry, the foundation of privileges, the definition of the intuitive and the imaginative, or the non-rational faculties, were among the areas of his speculation; as were the importance of the economic factor in history, the origins and development of religious, political and civil institutions and of jurisprudence.

In the *Scienza nuova*, while conceiving history as the temporal expression of ideas that are eternal, and moved by a profound sense of the character of change in human affairs, Vico proposed to himself the task of distinguishing amid the infinite variety of thoughts and actions, languages and manners, which history presents, the regular from the accidental; the laws that govern the formation, growth and decay of societies. In doing this he regarded art as the prime operation of the human spirit; and he attempted by means of historical criticism to illustrate the interdependence of the sciences and the progress of each of them in relation to the others; he showed how their progress depends upon the general condition of society, and at the same time influences it. While holding that the actual state of society is the result of the free development of the human faculties, he further attempted to give a historical demonstration of the existence of Divine Providence directing the careers of nations.

Pietro Giannone (1676–1748)

Unlike Vico, whose works proved acceptable to authority, Pietro Giannone was a free-thinker, not unversed in north European modes of thought, who soon fell foul of the Holy Office as a result of his obstinate and passionate advocacy of his anti-clerical position. He was born at Ischitella, a town in Capitanata, and at the age of sixteen went to live in Naples, where, in 1698, a year before Vico's appointment at the university, he graduated in jurisprudence, having studied law – Roman, canon and feudal – history, ecclesiastical history and philosophy. Subsequently, while in practice as a lawyer, he laboured for some twenty years to produce *Istoria civile del regno di Napoli* (4 vols., 1723), a controversial historical survey tracing the evolution of the political, religious and legal institutions of Naples from Roman times to the end of the seventeenth century.

In the years of Giannone's youth Neapolitan society, especially in the confines of the academies and literary salons, was amongst the most free-thinking and eclectic in Italy. For two centuries, however, the kingdom had been governed as a province by Spanish viceroys (1509–1707). It was, furthermore, one of the Italian states most subject to the power of the Catholic priesthood, both Spanish and Roman, and the inquisitorial procedures of the Holy Office. The Church, indeed, had long regarded Naples as a vassal state. During the early eighteenth century, moreover, the kingdom was involved in the War of Spanish Succession, as a result of which dynastic changes took place. In 1707 Naples rose in support of Austria and the rule of Spain passed, until 1734, to the emperor in Vienna.

In his *Istoria* Giannone took his stand firmly for the independence of the lay state, menaced throughout the ages, as he repeatedly averred, through the extension and abuse of sacerdotal power. He presented Neapolitan history as one long struggle between the civil authorities and a corrupt, reactionary papacy. He supported the monocratic authority of the prince, and attacked the encroachments of the priesthood, clerical privilege, the Inquisition, the ecclesiastical courts, and the worldliness and self-seeking of monastic institutions.

To make his points Giannone was not always accurate or overscrupulous in the selection of his sources. His bitter polemic was so powerful, however, that when it was published the *Istoria* was promptly put on the *Index* and Giannone himself excommunicated. Obliged to flee from Naples, he sought refuge in Vienna where the Emperor Charles VI, to whom the *Istoria* was dedicated, took him under his protection.

While in Vienna Giannone was granted means of subsistence with a small pension. He was encouraged in his labours by the climate of sympathetic opinion among the scholars of his acquaintance; and with access to the imperial library, he defended his *Istoria* against the critics. He wrote an ironic *Professione di fede*, which further antagonized his adversaries, and in 1731 he began *Il Triregno* ('The Three Kingdoms';

first published 1895), a complex programme of anti-clerical reform, divided into three books corresponding to what Giannone identified as the three successive kingdoms or principal phases in the history of the Christian religion. These were: the Old Testament, the Gospel and the Papal periods. In the first, 'The Earthly Kingdom', he dealt, in the footsteps of Spinoza and John Toland, the Irish radical, with the civilization of the Hebrews, when good laws obtained and men, living in a 'state of nature', entertained no hopes of immortality. In 'The Kingdom of Heaven', which began with a consideration of John the Baptist, Giannone next examined the revelation of the Gospels, the 'state of grace', and such dogmas as that of the immortality of the soul. In the third book, reverting to his favourite theme, that of the papal abuses, he contemplated 'the Papal Kingdom' from the time of Constantine – when men built on to the primitive Church an institution which was, according to Giannone, utterly alien to its spirit. To recover the Kingdom of Heaven, and to ensure the emancipation and sovereignty of the state, Giannone asserted that it was necessary to suppress the papacy and the ecclesiastical hierarchy, deprive the clergy of temporal benefits and subordinate the Church to the state.

In 1734 when the Neapolitan crown passed back from Austria to Don Carlos, the Spanish Bourbon, the emperor lost interest in Giannone and his pension was terminated. Unable to return to Naples, he lived for a time first in Venice, then in Milan. Suspect, and a victim of clerical intrigue, he next sought refuge in Calvinist Geneva. During a visit in 1736 to Savoy, however, he was arrested and imprisoned first at Chambéry and later in Liguria at the castle of Miolans. His papers were sent to Rome; and subsequently, at Turin, he was constrained to sign an act of abjuration. But the promise that he would be given his liberty was not upheld. He was incarcerated at Ceva; and later, from 1744 until his death, in the citadel at Turin.

During his years of imprisonment Giannone was not denied the use of pen and ink, or access to books. Between 1736 and 1737, mainly at Miolans, he wrote his *Autobiography* 'per alleggerire in parte le noie e il tedio' of his incarceration. At Ceva he composed *Discorsi sopra gli Annali di Tito Livio* (1736–9) and the *Apologia de' teologi scolastici*, first drafted in 1739 and 1740. These were followed by *Istoria del pontificato di Gregorio Magno* (1742) and the curious *L'ape ingegnosa* (1743–4), a work of Giannone's old age, showing a new interest in Newton's *Mathematical Principles of Natural Philosophy*, in which, through a series of observations on the works of nature, he defended the themes previously developed in *Il Triregno*.

Apostolo Zeno (1668–1750) and Francesco Scipione Maffei (1675–1755)

In the Age of Arcadia the Italian Republic of Letters was composed of men of eclectic taste who were often gifted with the ability to write with erudition and understanding on a wide range of subjects. Such were Apostolo Zeno and Francesco Scipione Maffei, who lived and worked in Venice and Verona respectively, and confined themselves to no particular genre. Both were co-founders in 1710 of the *Giornale dei Letterati d'Italia*, the most distinguished journal of cultural popularization and divulgation of the period. Zeno was also a poet, scholar-historian and librettist, who spent many years at the imperial court in Vienna. Maffei was a palaeographer, archaeologist and playwright, whose verse-drama *Merope* (1713) is often regarded as the cornerstone of eighteenth-century Italian tragedy.[2]

As early as 1699 Zeno cherished the ambition of becoming a scholar-historian. Before Muratori, he collected the written records of the Middle Ages. He wrote biographies of Enrico Davila and Marcantonio Sabellico, and also one of the great Venetian printer Aldus Manutius. In later life he cultivated epigraphy and numismatics and corrected and enriched with erudite annotations Giusto Fontanini's *Biblioteca dell'eloquenza*, which had first been published in 1726. He also amplified and emended, in his *Dissertazioni vossiane* (2 vols., 1752–3), the third book of the *De historicis latinis*, a bibliography of Latin writers by the seventeenth-century Dutch theologian and classical scholar Gerardus Vossius. Between 1719 and 1731, Zeno lived in Vienna, as Poet Laureate to the imperial court. There he composed some fifty verse libretti on heroic themes, with which he aspired to restore dignity, nobility and regularity of structure to the *opera seria*, for which he is remembered as a distinguished precursor of Pietro Metastasio.

2. See pp. 287–8.

Scipione Maffei as a scholar-historian was especially interested in his native Verona, among the cities of Venetia second only to Venice for the importance and interest of its antiquities. In 1712 he had the idea of illustrating this attractive city. He immersed himself in the study of its sacred and secular erudition, its politics, literature and artistic life, its monuments and galleries, its customs and institutions throughout the centuries. In 1728 he published *Degli anfiteatri*, a treatise dealing in two parts with the history and architecture of amphitheatres, especially with that of Verona, the third largest and one of the best preserved examples of Roman architecture in existence. Four years later he reprinted this as Part IV of his masterpiece *Verona illustrata* (1732). The other three parts of this treatise deal respectively with the history of Verona and, in part, its province, from its origins until it was taken by Charlemagne in 774 (Part I); with the writers of Verona, more than eight hundred, dealt with mainly from the biographical point of view (Part II); and with memorable events in the life of the city (Part III). The third part also provides a wealth of information on the Roman, Christian and medieval antiquities of Verona, and on its modern structure.

Maffei's second contribution to historical scholarship was the *Museum Veronense* (1749), an imposing folio, set in antiquarian and oriental type, and decorated with illustrations by Giovanni Bettino Cignaroli, which were engraved by Francesco Zucchi. From modest beginnings in 1714, the Museo Lapidario, a collection of thirty tablets housed in the Academia Filarmonica, was fostered and developed by Maffei to become the first and most outstanding collection of Etruscan, Greek and Roman antiquities. In the *Museum Veronense*, which was written in Latin, Maffei reproduced and illustrated this collection, consisting of twenty-four Etruscan tablets and reliefs, and 104 Greek; 387 Latin inscriptions, eighteen Christian and medieval tablets and reliefs, and eleven Near Eastern antiquities. In the same volume he also dealt with the palaeographical and historical aspects of collections of antiquities in Turin and Vienna.

Maffei's other works of erudition, some of which dealt with theological matters, include the *Galliae antiquitates* (1733), twenty-five letters reporting the results of an archaeological tour of Provence; the *Istoria teologica delle dottrine e delle opinioni corse nei primi secoli della Chiesa in proposito della divina grazia, del libero arbitrio e della predestina-*

zione (1742), in which he entered on the side of orthodoxy in the controversy between the Roman Catholics and the Jansenists; and his polemical opposition to a pseudo science, *Dell'arte magica dileguata e dell'arte magica distrutta* (1749–50).

The pattern of scholarship set by the *eruditi* of the Age of Arcadia persisted throughout the eighteenth century into the Age of Reforms. In Florence, Etruscan studies were promoted by Anton Francesco Gori (1691–1757), author of the *Inscriptiones antiquae in Etruriae urbibus extantes* (3 vols., 1727–43) and the *Museum Etruscum* (1737–43); and at Pesaro by Giambattista Passeri (1694–1768), a pupil of Gravina. In Rome ecclesiastical studies flourished with the Jesuit Francesco Antonio Zaccaria (1714–95), a scholar who rendered great service to liturgical science with such works as the *Bibliotheca ritualis* (2 vols., 1776–81). In Venice Girolamo Zanetti (1713–82), author of numerous works of antiquarian and art scholarship, furthered regional historical studies with painstaking zeal. At the end of the century Ennio Quirino Visconti (1751–1808) produced in Rome his monumental *Museo Pio-Clementino descritto* (7 vols., 1782–1807), a major work of archaeological and classical erudition.

FROM THE AGE OF ARCADIA TO THE PERIOD OF REFORMS

Journalism

Between the Age of Arcadia and the Period of Reforms, journalism and allied activities, at times of a satirical nature, flourished, especially in the republic of Venice and at Florence, though notable gazettes and literary periodicals were also produced at Modena, Pisa, and in most other cultural centres of the peninsula. In character, this journalism naturally developed, as the years went by, from the phase of scholarship, typified by the *Giornale dei Letterati d'Italia*, to that of direct observation and critical attitudes consonant with the new spirit of the Enlightenment.

In the Age of Arcadia many Italian periodicals were largely composed of articles, reviews and news translated *verbatim* from the French, especially from the *Journal des sçavans*, the *Mercure historique et politique* and the *Mémoires de Trévoux*. One such was the *Mercurio storico e politico* (1718–73); others, also published in Venice, were the *Giornale de' Letterati Oltramontani* (1722–59) and *Il Gran Giornale d'Europa, o sia la biblioteca universale* (1725–6). The two latter were directed by Angelo Calogerà (1699–1768), the Benedictine of San Michele in Isola who is also remembered for his vast miscellany *Raccolta di opuscoli scientifici e filologici*. After 1740, also in Venice, a bibliographical bulletin, with reviews, was provided by the long-established *Novelle della Repubblica Letteraria* (1729–62). Other important Venetian journals were the *Memorie per servire all'Istoria Letteraria* (1753–8) and the *Nuove Memorie per servire all'Istoria Letteraria* (1759–61). Both were founded and edited by Calogerà and by Zaccaria Seriman (1709–83), an enlightened man-of-letters, who belonged to a wealthy Armenian merchant family settled in Venice since the seventeenth century. Both journals were compiled on the basis of letters on cultural topics addressed to the editors from correspondents all over Italy.

Another Venetian with journalistic talents at this time was the pseudo-epistolary writer and satirist Giuseppe Antonio Costantini, author of the *Lettere critiche, giocose, morali, scientifiche ed erudite alla moda ed al gusto del secolo presente*, written under the pseudonym of 'Conte Agostino Santi Pupieni'. Costantini, a failed lawyer, felt that the luxury and permissiveness of his day was the 'perniciosa sorgente di mille disordini'; and in his letters, which are presented as translations, he castigated almost every aspect of contemporary Venetian life: not only doctors, lawyers and adventurers; gaming; the carnival and fashion; but the educational system, the patrician contract of *mariage à la mode*, the simoniacal practices of the clergy, and all the innumerable abuses rife in 'the playground of Europe'. The *Lettere critiche* (1743–5) proved extremely successful and were frequently reprinted, an edition in eight volumes appearing between 1751 and 1756; by 1794, the letters had run into twelve editions in Venice alone.

In the early 1760s the best-known name in Venetian journalism was that of Gasparo Gozzi (1713–86), a professional man of letters who introduced a new style in Venetian periodic publications. The *Gazzetta Veneta*, the *Mondo Morale* and the *Osservatore Veneto* do not rely on learned contributions or on political happenings; but, in a manner suggested by such English papers of the Augustan period as the *Spectator* of Steele and Addison, they were largely composed of items dealing with practical moral issues, reflecting the manners and customs of the times by means of essays and anecdotes. The subjects and their treatment varied greatly in the three journals, from local gossip to philosophical fictions and matters of educational reform. The relationship between art and nature was discussed, as were medical matters, peasant customs, and the problems of conversation; all alternating with a wealth of fables, short stories, reveries and reportage of the *fait divers* of contemporary Venetian life.

Temperamentally Gozzi was a fair-minded man of humanistic outlook and inexhaustible invention who aspired to provide pleasant reading matter with a dose of moral instruction. He had a marked gift for sharp observation of life and manners and for reportage, coupled with a curious liking for allegorical modes of expression and for mythological allusions: qualities that were equally evident in his verse *Sermoni*, many of which were composed in the 1750s, and the vigorous *Difesa di Dante* (1758), which he wrote in reply to Saverio Bettinelli's savage attack on Dante in the *Lettere virgiliane* (1757).

Gozzi first gained experience as a journalist in 1756, when he replaced Girolamo Zanetti as assistant editor of Seriman's *Memorie per servire all'Istoria Letteraria*. But the great years of his journalistic activity were confined to the brief period 1760–62, when he brought out his own periodicals, as a commercial venture, in collaboration with the publishers Pietro Marcuzzi and Paolo Colombani. The *Gazzetta Veneta* (1760–61) and the *Osservatore Veneto* (1761–2) were issued twice weekly, on Wednesdays and Saturdays, and each ran to 104 numbers. The *Mondo Morale*, first issued on 5 May 1760, was hardly a periodical, but rather a curious hybrid made up on the one hand of an interminable, unfinished allegorical novel, and on the other of a wealth of discourses interspersed with the translation of eight dialogues by the Greek essayist Lucian and of Klopstock's poetic tragedy *Der Tod Adams* (1757). The characters and locations of this novel were the embodiment of such concepts as 'Innocence' ('Acacìa'), 'Heart' ('Cardìa'), 'Man' ('Adropo'), the 'Passions' ('Patossie'), 'Fraud' ('Dolossìa'), 'Head' ('Cèfalos') and 'Pleasure' ('Idonio'). It was read by a mysterious figure called 'La Pellegrina', and discussed by a group of twelve men and women described as the 'Congrega dei Pellegrini'.

The allegorical emphasis of the *Mondo Morale* was also present in the *Osservatore Veneto*. The *Gazzetta Veneta*, on the other hand, was primarily concerned with the curious happenings, either real or imagined, of Venetian daily life – the veracity of which it is nowadays extremely hard to verify or to disprove. The journal was made up of a mixture of letters addressed to the 'Gazzettiere', interspersed with musical, art and theatrical news, with reports of new inventions, scientific, industrial and commercial, with medical advice on wrinkles, gum diseases, bad breath, and even a horrific account of the extraction of a nasal polypus. It was also rich in instructive observations on family problems, advice to parents and to their erring children, and to friends, both real and fictitious. In the *Osservatore Veneto*, on the other hand, the Venetian framework was far less in evidence; and moral questions were treated on a less provincial level. This journal consisted, in the main, of literary and philosophical dialogues, character sketches (*ritratti*), allegories, fables and *novelle* urbanely satirizing depraved habits and bad taste. The dialogues were composed in the style of Lucian, with an amused, ironic view of life. The portraits, though based on contemporary figures, were influenced by the 'characters' of Theophrastus and La Bruyère.

The aim of Gozzi's journalism was didactic. Instructive matters were generally presented, however, in a well-written and entertaining manner. The *Mondo Morale* was tedious and a failure. But in the other two periodicals Gozzi wrote without prolixity or exaggeration, with the suggestion of a half-ironic smile at human fallibility, and with a charming lightness of touch.

In Florence during the first phase of Austrian rule the principal periodical was the *Novelle Letterarie* (29 vols., 1740–68), directed by Giovanni Lami (1697–1770) a scholar-theologian who also produced distinguished works of sacred erudition and illustrated the treasures of the Biblioteca Ricciardiana with his monumental *Deliciae eruditorum, seu veterum anecdotorum collectanea* (18 vols., 1736–69). As a young man, before his appointment as director of the Biblioteca Ricciardiana and to the chair of ecclesiastical history in Florence, Lami had travelled widely. He had lived in Vienna; served as a soldier and studied for two years in Paris. As a theologian he was of somewhat liberal persuasion and opposed to the Jesuits. He seems also to have been one of the first Florentines to join the clandestine Order of Free Masons. The *Novelle Letterarie*, as might be expected, was a scholarly but spirited journal which was open to new ideas. Its programme advocated study of the sciences and the liberal arts, while maintaining a high regard for the virtues of scholarship. It printed news from all over Europe and provided information especially on current works of science and erudition. The *Novelle Letterarie* welcomed the foundation in 1751 of the *Encyclopédie* of d'Alembert and Diderot, but it was also somewhat critical of the activity of the *philosophes*. Voltaire was reproved for his 'pensieri scellerati', though the clarity and brilliance of his prose was admired. Rousseau was criticized as ignorant and proud.

Francesco Algarotti (1712–64)

While still a student at the University of Bologna, Algarotti, a young Venetian of great personal charm and androgynous tastes, who has been described as the Italian polymath *par excellence*, became a staunch advocate of English experimentalism. He was attracted especially to the natural philosophy of Sir Isaac Newton, and in 1733, at the age of twenty-one, he began to draft the work which was to establish his reputation: *Newtonianismo per le dame*. Two years later he left Italy for Paris, where he met the noted mathematician Maupertuis, an able advocate of Newton's physical theory. Algarotti was invited by Maupertuis to join his expedition to Lapland to measure the degree of longitude, but he preferred to remain in Paris where he finished his treatise and showed it to Voltaire.

Newtonianismo per le dame was first published in 1737, at Padua and Milan simultaneously, under the false imprint of Naples. It ran into several editions and was published in its definitive, recast form in Berlin in 1752, with a letter of dedication to Frederick II of Prussia, under the more sober and suitable title *Dialoghi sopra l'ottica Neutoniana*. The treatise is in the form of six imaginary dialogues between the author and a philosophically minded young woman called the Marchesa di F —. They are conducted, tersely and without artifice, in a brilliant conversational style of striking modernity. The general principles of optics, the structure of the eye, and the manner of seeing are elucidated. The hypotheses of Descartes and his disciple Malebranche concerning the nature of light and colours are expounded and refuted. Dialogues III and IV are devoted to the Newtonian system of optics. The universal principle of attraction and the application of this to optics is explained in Dialogue V. The treatise concludes with further substantiation of the Newtonian system and the confutation of all other hypotheses concerning the nature of light and colours.

In 1736, before *Newtonianismo per le dame* was published, and again for two months in 1739, Algarotti visited London. He was promptly elected a Fellow of the Royal Society; and at the same time he won the hearts of both Lady Mary Wortley Montagu and Lord Hervey, who competed for his affections. In May of the same year Algarotti sailed from Gravesend to Petersburg in the entourage of Lord Baltimore, who had been invited to the Russian court to attend the marriage of the Princess of Mecklenberg. The journey lasted for three months, including four weeks at sea and visits to Helsingor, Revel, Kronstadt, Petersburg, Danzig and Hamburg. The outcome of this unusual adventure was *Lettere sulla Russia*, or *Viaggi di Russia*, as Algarotti preferred to call his book: an attractively written travel journal in the form of eight 'letters' addressed from various ports of call to Lord Hervey. The letters are of interest for the wealth of curious information they contain; for their observations on the Russian marine, and on the military, political and economic conditions of the Russian empire in the aftermath of the improvements previously wrought by the indomitable Peter the Great. Two letters (VII, VIII) dealt, at the request of Lord Hervey, with the war between Russia and Turkey (1736–9). Ten years later, in 1750 and 1751, Algarotti supplemented the *Viaggi* with four further communications on Russian and Persian affairs addressed from Berlin and Potsdam to Scipione Maffei.

On his return from Russia, Algarotti visited Frederick, the Crown Prince of Prussia, who was then surrounded by men of learning. On his accession to the throne in 1740, as King of Prussia, Frederick invited Algarotti to Potsdam, where he lived for two years. Between 1742–6 he was in Dresden; but he later returned to Potsdam, where Frederick elevated him to the rank of count, and subsequently made him his Lord Chamberlain. While in Dresden Algarotti negotiated on behalf of Augustus III, Elector of Saxony, the selection and purchase of Italian paintings for the Dresden Gallery. In 1753, being in ill-health, he returned to Italy where he lived first in Venice (1753–6), then at Bologna (1756–62). The last two years of his life were spent at Pisa.

Between 1740 and 1764 Algarotti wrote extensively and in many fields. He adopted especially, as his favourite genre, the *saggio*, one of the most characteristic literary forms of the Enlightenment. A number of his essays dealt with literary and linguistic matters; as, for example, the *Saggio sopra la lingua francese* (Berlin, 1750) and the *Saggio sopra la necessità di scrivere nella propria lingua* (Potsdam, 1750). In the *Saggio sopra la rima* (1752), he entered the lists in a long-standing debate and declared himself in favour of the *verso sciolto*, or blank verse hendecasyllable, rather than the rhymed couplet. Two years later in the *Saggio sopra il Cartesio* he recognized the merits of Cartesian geometry and its importance within the development of European thought.

Algarotti is best remembered as an essayist for three substantial pieces on the arts, all of which he wrote after his return to Italy. In the first of these, entitled *Saggio sopra l'architettura* (Bologna, 24 December 1756) he revealed himself as a moderate classicist, not averse to architectural ornamentation, citing the authority and practices of the greatest architects of the past – Vitruvius, Vignola and Palladio – to counter the ideas of the Venetian architectural theorist Carlo Lodoli (1690–1761), who is nowadays greatly esteemed as a pioneer of the 'functionalist' school. In the *Saggio sopra la pittura* (Bologna, 17 March 1762), which is addressed to the newly founded London Society for the Encouragement of the Arts, Manufactures and Commerce, Algarotti extolled Raphael, and advised a youthful aspirant to the practice of painting, the importance of whose artistic individuality he recognized, in the various aspects of the art from the study of anatomy and perspective to the concept of 'imitation' and the recreations necessary for a painter. The third essay, the *Saggio sopra l'opera in musica* (Pisa, 18 December 1762), was dedicated to the English statesman William Pitt, first Earl of Chatham. It constituted a rational plea for decorum in the musical theatre.

Algarotti was buried in the Camposanto at Pisa. His funerary monument, which was supplied by Frederick the Great, bears the solemn epitaph *Algarotto Ovidii aemulo, Newtonii discipulo, Fridericus rex.*

THE REFORMATORY ENLIGHTENMENT

Southern Italy – Genovesi, Galiani, Filangieri, Pagano

The first period of Bourbon rule in the kingdom of Naples, that of Don Carlos (1734–59) and the early years of the reign of Ferdinand IV (1759–1825), was characterized by a widespread movement for civil, economic and political reform. In 1776, however, after the elder statesman the Marquis Bernardo Tanucci (1698–1783) had been forced to resign his ministry, southern Italy fell under the Austrian influence of the resolute and ambitious queen Maria Carolina (daughter of the empress Maria Theresa), and her prime minister, Sir John Acton (1736–1811), an Irish adventurer born at Besançon, whose measures, prompted by his extreme hatred of the French, were cruel and intolerant.

In the Napoleonic period, dismayed by the Revolution, the Bourbons became increasingly reactionary. In January 1799 French land forces, under the command of General Championnet, overran the kingdom of Naples, Ferdinand was obliged to flee and Naples was proclaimed a republic. At this time, however, the protection of the city had been entrusted by the king to the British admiral Horatio Nelson, who was also commander-in-chief of the Neapolitan navy. Nelson accompanied the court to Palermo and organized the blockade of Naples. In June 1799 a loyalist uprising led to the fall of the so-called 'Parthenopean Republic'. After this, with the return of the king, thousands of citizens were arrested and some 120 leading republicans were executed.

The reformatory Enlightenment in Naples took root after the deaths of Vico and Giannone, when the two great currents of thought which had dominated Neapolitan culture in the early years of the century, Cartesianism and a renewed interest in Platonism, were becoming exhausted. It was a period of residual feudalism, Church interference, antiquated economic structures rooted in city or regional traditions, internal customs and the *annonario* system and inherited privileges of the nobility. On the other hand, in the 1740s and 1750s, the field was open to newcomers: men who had grown up in the new atmosphere of the southern Kingdom since Don Carlos had ousted the Austrians and had begun, through the efforts of Tanucci, to introduce uniformity of legislation and to diversify the organs of state administration.

The reformatory Enlightenment in southern Italy was largely the achievement of a small number of political economists, lawyers and savants who wished Naples to profit from the example of Holland, France and England, countries which, operating in a spirit of free enterprise and speculation during the seventeenth and early eighteenth centuries, had achieved remarkable prosperity through the pursuit of mercantile policies. All the civil reformers were interested, to a greater or less extent, in the two great problems of political economy: wealth and population. They concerned themselves with commerce, free trade and protectionism, value and currency reform, the development of unproductive zones, and recent advances in agricultural techniques, such as the system of drills introduced by the English farmer Jethro Tull. Towards the end of the century, new principles of judicial reform were also advocated.

The senior and most influential of the group of Neapolitan reformers, many of whom were his pupils, was the political economist and metaphysician Antonio Genovesi (1713–69), who is especially remembered for his *Discorso sopra il vero fine delle lettere e delle scienże* (1753) and for the *Lezioni di commercio, o sia d'economia civile* (2 vols., 1765, 1767). Born at Castiglione near Salerno, Genovesi studied jurisprudence at the university of Naples, where he was a pupil of the ageing Vico. In 1741 he was elected to a personal chair of metaphysics. Four years later he became professor of moral philosophy; and in 1754 he was appointed to the professorship 'di commercio e di meccanica' (the first of its kind in Europe), which was created for him on condition that the lectures were given in the vernacular, not in Latin, and that no friar should succeed him. The man responsible for the foundation of this chair, which met with considerable opposition, and for Genovesi's appointment to it, was Bartolomeo Intieri (1693–1757). Intieri was a Florentine agricultural administrator living in Naples; he was behind every effort to modernize the culture and institutions of the city and to inspire them with scientific principles and methods.

Younger than Genovesi, but equally active in the same period and rather more original as a thinker, was Ferdinando Galiani (1728–87), born at Chieti, whose diverse writings touched on basic topics of finance, literature, philosophy and social questions. Galiani's works include: an important treatise on the coinage and its circulation, *Della moneta* (1750); *Dialogues sur le commerce des blés* (1770, written in 1768); *Socrate immaginario* (1775), a masterpiece of Neapolitan *opera buffa*, written in collaboration with G. B. Lorenzi (music by Paisiello); and an important correspondence with Tanucci and with the French authoress Mme d'Épinay.

At an early stage in their development, both Genovesi and Galiani either made, or became interested in, translations into Italian from classic treatises by the English advocates of the mercantile system of political economy, by which their own writings were greatly influenced. Galiani, as a very young man, translated John Locke's pamphlet on *Some Considerations of the Consequences of Lowering Interest and Raising the Value of Money* (1692). Genovesi, on the other hand, was especially attracted to such works as *England's Treasure by Forraign Trade* (1664, written *c.* 1630) by the London merchant Thomas Mun (1571–1641), and *An Essay on the State of England, in Relation to its Trade, its Poor, and its Taxes* (1695; 3rd ed., 1745) by the Bristol merchant, William Cary.

In 1757, three years after his appointment to his chair of commerce, Genovesi brought out, in three volumes, the *Storia del commercio della Gran Bretagna*, which consisted of translations by Pietro Genovesi, a Neapolitan lawyer, from Cary and Mun, together with a substantial discourse and notes by himself on the trade and economy of the kingdom of Naples. The *Tesoro del commercio di Tommaso Mun* appeared in Volume II. The translation from Cary was based on a French version of the third English edition published in Paris, with the false imprint of London, in 1755, under the title *Essai sur l'état du commerce d'Angleterre*, by the French economist Georges Marie Butel Dumont.

Genovesi began his first course of lectures as professor 'di commercio e di meccanica' on 5 November 1754. The novelty and importance of these, and the eloquence of their presentation, attracted a large audience; and Neapolitan society soon began to speak only of agriculture, industry and commerce. In subsequent years he amplified and enriched his material, taking into account not only his knowledge of English and French mercantilism, but also the writings of such Spanish political economists as Geronimo Uztáriz and Bernardo Ulloa who, after the Treaty of Utrecht, had attempted to solve the economic problems of an ailing Spain.

The earliest extant version of the *Lezioni di commercio* – a manuscript preserved in the Biblioteca Nazionale, Naples – varies considerably from the definitive text published years later, from 1765 to 1767. The manuscript is divided into two parts which correspond with the lectures delivered during the academic sessions ending on 6 June 1757 and 10 June 1758 respectively. Part I is divided into thirteen sections, the first three of which deal with the 'natura', the 'necessità ed utilità' and with the 'spirito' of trade. A 'storia del commercio' follows, with an examination of the natural resources of the kingdom of Naples, its commerce and its arts. The essential features of a mercantile programme are next outlined. In the final section of Part I, which is headed 'Tre questioni importanti sulla semina dei grani', Jethro Tull's new system of agriculture is expounded. Part II of the same set of lectures was especially concerned with the problems of value and money.

In the published version of the *Lezioni di commercio* matters of mercantile and agricultural renewal, as dealt with over the years, were expanded to include substantial treatment of demographic questions, the development of trade and the advancement of industry and agriculture from the technical point of view. Many of the earlier lectures were revised; and the whole work was prefaced by a series of chapters on political institutions, the arts and sciences and the characteristics of the various social classes.

In his maturity Genovesi's studies were especially directed towards the identification of phenomena which lead to the wealth and the prosperity of nations. His investigations were influenced by a concept of life and the world seen as incessant activity directed towards the achievement of material and moral well-being, necessary for individual and collective happiness. He believed that the prime aspiration of a state should be to increase its population, not only by creating conditions favouring such an increase, but also by eliminating the causes of depopulation. On the practical level he wanted to see absolute freedom of trade; and he placed supreme importance on the improvement of agriculture. He advocated the abolition of feuds and the freeing of the peasants from their serfdom. He advised landowners to study agricultural economics. They should live on their land, consider its potential, and follow the examples of husbandry provided by the Florentine and the English landed gentry.

In his treatise *Della moneta* (1750), for which he had prepared himself with his translations from Locke, Ferdinando Galiani sought to establish, as a leading principle, that coin is a merchandise, and that its value and interest ought to be left free like other goods. His arguments were pursued with rigorous method, and they anticipated modern theories of value based on concepts of utility and rarity. Although Galiani was only twenty-two his doctrines were put into practice and, it is said, the financial ruin of Naples averted. Though now out-of-date, his ideas seemed novel at the time and the treatise was widely translated, subsequently being taken into consideration by Karl Marx in his analysis of capitalism.

After the publication of *Della moneta* Galiani visited the chief cities of Italy, and was everywhere acclaimed. From Pope Benedict XIV he received repeated proofs of favour; and he was eventually rewarded with the rich prebend of Amalfi. In 1759, however, he accepted an appointment as secretary to the Neapolitan Embassy in Paris, where his wit and vivacity made him a universal favourite. In 1767 he paid a visit to England, where he made a study of the social and political institutions. On his return to Paris, he wrote, in French, another treatise on political economy, entitled *Dialogues sur le commerce des blés* (1770, written in 1768). This work comprised eight dialogues on the corn trade, in which Galiani argued against both extreme protectionism and the absolute free-traders. Less interested than formerly in pure mercantile economics, and critical also of the rationalist abstractions of the Physiocrats, Galiani, in his *Dialogues*, made an important contribution to the theory of international trade, arguing the need for practical political economy to adapt to local circumstances.

On his return to Naples Galiani enjoyed the friendship of Tanucci, with whom he had long been in correspondence. He was appointed to posts of trust and authority, mainly of an economic nature. In his later years, besides *Socrate immaginario* (1775), he composed a number of substantial treatises, including *Doveri dei principi neutrali verso i principi guerreggianti e di questi verso i neutrali* (1782), with which he made an original contribution to international law.

Besides Genovesi and Galiani, other civil reformers of the same school, were Francesco Longano (1729–96), author of *Viaggi per la Capitanata* (1790), Francesco Antonio Grimaldi (1741–84), who wrote *Riflessioni sopra l'ineguaglianza tra gli uomini* (1779–80), and Giuseppe Maria Galanti (1743–1806), whose masterpiece was the *Nuova descrizione storica e geografica delle Sicilie* (1786–94). The most influential thinkers and publicists of the second generation, however, were Francesco Maria Pagano (1748–99), professor of criminal law at Naples University (1785), and Gaetano Filangieri (1752–88), who was regarded by Goethe, who met him in Naples, as a person who belonged 'to a group of young men worthy of all esteem, who do not fail to keep in view the happiness of mankind and a sound sense of liberty'. The chief works of Pagano were a collection of *Studi politici* (1783–5) and *Considerazioni sul processo criminale* (1787); that of Filangieri *La scienza della legislazione* (8 vols., 1780–91), a monumental treatise that applied liberal theories to the principles of government. Characterized by great fearlessness in the advocacy of reform, this work gained its author an international reputation; but it was promptly placed on the *Index* by the Roman Curia.

A soldier and man of the world, Filangieri was born at Naples of noble parentage, the son of Cesare Filangieri, Prince of Arianello, and the third of eleven children. As a young man he entered the army; but he soon resigned his commission in order to study morals, politics and legislation. In 1771, three years before he took his degree in law, he published a treatise entitled *Della pubblica e privata educazione*. In 1774 the promulgation by royal decree of certain judicial reforms, limiting the arbitrary jurisdiction of the courts, occasioned *Riflessioni politiche*. The reforms promulgated had met with fierce opposition from the legal officers; and Filangieri, who had written in support of the laws, at once attracted the favourable notice of the young king Ferdinand IV. Subsequently, between 1777 and 1783, he served at court and as an officer of the marine. In 1783, wishing to free himself from his obligations, he retired to Cava dei Tirreni, some twenty-five miles from Naples, where he devoted himself to the completion of his life's work. In 1788, however, at the time of his premature death, at the age of thirty-six, only four of the seven books planned for *La scienza della legislazione* had been published, though Book V was also in the press. Books VI and VII, still in manuscript, were destroyed in the Neapolitan upheavals of 1799.

The outcome of long and assiduous meditation on legal matters, *La scienza della legislazione* was a splendid monument to the enlightened sense of justice and to the exalted humanity of its author. It was not a treatise on actual legal practice so much as a work of pacific propaganda, pursued with rigorous method, in which law lost its historical and factual character and became an ideology. The work condemned despotism and advocated reform of the penal code, the abolition of privilege, the revitalization of agriculture, freedom of the individual before the law, and an obligatory system of free state education, all ordered within a new system of government. Book I is devoted to an analysis of the fixed ethics of legislation and of those principles which are modifiable. Book II, *Delle leggi politiche ed economiche*, deals with questions of wealth and population. The themes of Books III-V are respectively the criminal law in its widest extent, public instruction, and the laws that concern religious matters.

Mario Pagano, born at Brienza in Capitanata, was a liberal political philosopher and disciple of Genovesi, whose staunch Republican sentiments in the difficult years of Napoleon's Italian campaign (1796–7) soon rendered him suspect. In 1796 he was deprived of his teaching post for his defence of the Jacobins. He was imprisoned for two years and in 1798 expelled from the kingdom. With the entry of the French into Naples and the flight of the Bourbons, however, he was invited by General Championnet to return to Naples to take part in the formulation of the constitution of the Parthenopean Republic, the short-lived state on the Graeco-Roman model which was established on 23 January 1799. But in June of the same year, after the restoration of the monarchy, a violent reaction set in. The surrender terms of the revolutionaries were violated and the lives of the Neapolitan leaders were not spared. Admiral Francesco Caracciolo was hanged from the yardarm of Nelson's flagship; Pagano was arrested and was eventually executed (29 October) with other Republican sympathizers on the Piazza del Mercato. His friend Flaminio Massa wrote:

affrontò la morte impavidamente. Il suo coraggio fu sempre maggiore della sua sventura. Imperturbabile all'aspetto del patibolo, terminò con una serenità una carriera illustrata da tante virtù. Visse come Aristide e morì come Socrate.

Lombardy – Carli, Pietro Verri, Beccaria, Alessandro Verri

In the second half of the eighteenth century the Habsburgs were eager to increase the yield of their Lombard possessions; and under the 'benevolent despotism' first of Maria Theresa and subsequently of the emperor Joseph II, Milan shared in the work of reform achieved by the Austrian monarchy. The notable changes that took place, before the whole region was transformed by Napoleon, who set up the Cispadane and Transpadane Republics in 1796, have been succinctly recorded in the following passage by Luigi Salvatorelli:

> By the efforts of Count Beltrane Cristiani, followed by Count Firmian, the administration was reorganized, a census was taken, the taxes were equitably distributed, judicial procedure was improved, agriculture and industry were encouraged, and the economic development of the country was promoted; the Inquisition was abolished, the ecclesiastical censorship and the right of asylum were suppressed; beneficent institutions were founded, schools, theatres and libraries were opened; and the University of Pavia was an object of special solicitude. Joseph II, after the death of his mother, granted ample religious tolerance, suppressed numbers of convents, removed restrictions to commerce, and abolished the trade corporations.[3]

Most of the Lombard reformers in the time of Maria Theresa and Joseph II belonged by birth to the higher ranks of the Milanese privileged classes: a fact which enabled them to hold posts of influence and authority under the Austrian administration. Two of the most distinguished of these, who made an outstanding contribution to the reformatory movement, were the political economist Pietro Verri, editor and guiding light of *Il Caffè*, the polemical organ of the Società dei Pugni, and the jurist-criminologist the Marquis Cesare Beccaria. A third, and one of the most senior advocates of reform in northern

3. L. Salvatorelli, *A Concise History of Italy*, translated by B. Miall, London, 1940, pp. 485–6.

Italy, was the versatile and eclectic Gian Rinaldo Carli, author of the celebrated essay 'Della patria degli Italiani' (*Il Caffè*, III semestre), lamenting the lack of patriotism, but affirming the essential unity of the Italian people. Other figures of note were the cosmopolitan Paolo Frisi, mathematician and friend of d'Alembert, and the Marquis Alfonso Longo, author of the *Instituzioni economico politiche* (1773), both of whom, from 1766 and 1772 respectively, were employed as chief censors in Milan.

Gian Rinaldo Carli (1720–95), born at Capodistria, was educated first in Friuli and then at Padua University. He belonged to the Italian provincial nobility; and as a young man he came under the influence of Muratori and Maffei. At the age of twenty-four, he secured a post at Padua University teaching the history of navigation and astronomy (mainly from a mythological point of view). As a very young man he wrote the *Antichità di Capodistria* (1738). Five years later, echoing the polemics aroused earlier in the century by Maffei's tragedy *Merope*, he produced a critical work on the drama entitled *Indole del teatro tragico antico e moderno* (1743).

After teaching in Padua for seven years Carli returned to Istria, where he embarked on the compilation of *Delle monete e delle zecche d'Italia* (4 vols., 1754–69), dealing with the monetary history of Italy and the institution of the mints. A classic study, this treatise is profusely illustrated with the types of coins which had circulated in Italy between the fall of the Western Empire and the seventeenth century; and in it their value is compared with the price of provisions at various times. Between 1753 and 1756, while living in Milan, Carli became friendly with Pietro Verri though their relationship was later far from cordial. In 1757, at Pisa, he wrote *Saggio politico ed economico sopra la Toscana*. Subsequently, during the 1760s, he secured the patronage of Prince Kaunitz, the Austrian chancellor and diplomatist. As a result, he was appointed President of the Council of Commerce and Public Economy in Milan, and eventually President of the new Council of Finance and Public Instruction (1771). He also became the trusted adviser of Joseph II, whose decision to abolish the Inquisitorial Tribunal in Lombardy Carli influenced. In 1770 Carli published *Nuove osservazioni su la riforma delle monete* and in 1776 *Osservazioni preventive al piano intorno alle monete*. Four years later, by which time he was out of favour, he retired from political and administrative life. Not, however, before he had severely criticized the social theories of Rousseau in a treatise entitled *L'uomo libero, ossia ragionamento sulla libertà naturale e civile dell'uomo* (1778, written in 1776). Always a notable archaeologist, Carli brought out in five volumes the monumental *Antichità italiche* (1788–91), illustrating the antiquities of Italy from Etruscan times to the fourteenth century. His other works include *Lettere americane*, a utopian production dedicated to Benjamin Franklin, dealing especially with the empire of the Incas, and *Della disuguaglianza fisica, morale, civile fra gli uomini* (1794), in which he restated his views on social matters, previously expressed in *L'uomo libero*.

By temperament and upbringing Carli was a moderate; and in his old age he even became a reactionary. In contrast, Pietro Verri and Cesare Beccaria were far more radical in their outlook; as is perhaps to be expected, since both, especially Beccaria, belonged to a younger and more progressive generation.

Pietro Verri (1728–97), son of Gabriele Verri, a staid Milanese senator and magistrate of the old school, was educated in a variety of ecclesiastical establishments. As well as pursuing a *galant* social life in Milan during the 1750s, he took part in the 'enlightened' activities of the reformed Accademia dei Transformati, an ancient Milanese society which had been restored in 1743 by the wealthy and cultivated banker Count Giuseppe Maria Imbonati (1698–1768). The aim of this academy, which met informally, was to 'unire al diletto l'utile morale e civile'; and at its gatherings Verri came into contact with such diverse members of reformatory inclinations as the dialect poets Domenico Balestrieri and Carlo Tanzi; Gian Carlo Passeroni, author of *Il cicerone*; the very young Cesare Beccaria; and Giuseppe Parini, who was soon to become the outstanding 'civil' poet and satirist of his generation.[4]

In 1759, being of a restless and action-loving disposition, Verri left Milan for Vienna, where he enrolled as a volunteer in the Austrian army, at that time involved in the Seven Years' War. Soon disillusioned by the indiscipline and intrigues of military life, he resigned his captain's commission and set out for home: not, however, before he had come under the transforming influence of Henry Evans Lloyd, a Welsh military adventurer in the Austrian service, who became a distinguished military historian and died, with the rank of general,

4. See pp. 228–33.

while on pension from the British War Office. Lloyd was the author of commentaries on Montesquieu and Helvétius, and of a book on the theory of money. He struck Verri as a genius; and he was for long to be his mentor. He directed his attention to the English style of journalism of Addison and the *Spectator*; to Voltaire and to the writings of the other French *philosophes* and publicists of the period.

Back in Milan, at the age of thirty-three, and under the influence of Lloyd, Pietro Verri began his life's work for the regeneration of his country. With his younger brother, Alessandro, and with Cesare Beccaria, after a period of intense study, he founded in 1761 the Società dei Pugni ('The Punch-Hards'), which met in his house. He also started to write on literary, commercial, monetary and philosophical matters. At the same time he sought to interest Count Carlo di Firmian (1718–82), the Austrian Minister in Lombardy, in his proposals for legislative and administrative reform. At first the minister turned a deaf ear, finding Verri's writings ill-grounded. Later, being of an enlightened turn of mind, he brought Verri's activities to the notice of his government in Vienna. As a result, though Verri never obtained the more senior posts to which he aspired, or won the battles he fought for radical reform, he was soon appointed to high office in the Austrian administration. In 1765 he was nominated a representative of the government in the 'Ferma Mista' at Milan, and a counsellor in the Supreme Council of Political Economy. In 1778 he was appointed president of the Società Patriottica; and in 1780 president of the Chamber of Trade. In 1791 he was a member of the reformed municipality; and in 1796, after the French invasion, he served in the provisional government.

As an economist Verri was a free-trader and an advocate of industrial development; he was also concerned with the basic principle of the Enlightenment, which was that man, by taking thought, could organize rational happiness in this world. He attempted to define the concept of money and defended his government against protectionism. He recommended reforms based on the utilitarian and humanitarian criteria of the French Encyclopedists; and he also wrote, like Beccaria, on penal reform.

Verri's first work, published in 1763, was *Meditazioni sulla felicità*, which was followed in 1764 by two substantial pieces entitled *Saggio sulla grandezza e decadenza del commercio di Milano sino al 1750* and

Dialogo tra Frominio e Simplicio sul disordine delle monete dello Stato di Milano. Between June 1764 and May 1766 he subsequently contributed some thirty-seven articles to his polemical journal, *Il Caffè*. In the first issue, as editor, he clarified the title, which was intended to suggest an imaginary Milanese coffee-house, where the customers, under the guidance of an old Greek sailor, named Demetrio, discussed freely and freshly, in a spirit of free inquiry, unfettered by academic considerations, matters likely to appeal to an enlightened readership.

The object of *Il Caffè*, in Verri's words, was

> di far quel bene, che possiamo alla nostra patria . . . di spargere delle utili cognizioni fra i nostri concittadini, divertendoli, come già altrove fecero e Steele, e Swift, e Addison, e Pope, ed altri.

The articles in the journal, whether by Verri or his collaborators, were written 'con ogni stile che non annoi'. They opposed pedantry in all its forms and dealt on the one hand with literary and linguistic matters, and on the other with such topics as rural economy and the problems of agriculture, industrial production, legislation, jurisprudence, taxation, financial reform and the balance of trade. *Il Caffè* ran to seventy-four numbers; and to avoid the Austrian censorship, which was still vigilant at that time, it was printed at Brescia, in Venetian territory. It was discontinued, in May 1766, through the inability of Alessandro Verri and Cesare Beccaria to agree.

After the cessation of *Il Caffè*, Pietro Verri produced the works of his maturity. Besides *Osservazioni sulla tortura* (1769), in which he refuted the legitimacy of the infliction of severe bodily pain as punishment or as a means of persuasion, he is chiefly remembered for his *Memorie storiche sulla economia pubblica dello Stato di Milano* (1768), for *Delle leggi vincolanti principalmente il commercio dei grani* (1769) and for *Meditazioni sulla economia politica* (1771). In the sphere of philosophy his most influential work was *Discorso sull'indole del piacere e del dolore* (1773, written in 1772). In his later life, Verri devoted himself to historical writing, the outcome of which was the *Storia di Milano* (2 vols., 1783–98).

Born at Milan, where he spent the greater part of his life, Cesare Beccaria (1738–94) was the first child of a well-off and illustrious family. Like Pietro Verri he was educated by the Jesuits in the Collegio dei Nobili, Parma; and in 1758 he graduated in *utroque jure* at Pavia.

Three years later, in a state of poverty and frustration, he was befriended by the Verri brothers, with whom he soon became intimate. He helped to found the Società dei Pugni, began to study avidly the English and French rationalists, and from 1761, when he first read the *Lettres persanes* of Montesquieu, he became a 'convert' to the new culture of the Enlightenment. In the summer of 1762, with Pietro Verri, he read Rousseau's newly-published treatise *Du contrat social*. In the same period Helvétius, Buffon, Diderot, Hume, d'Alembert and Condillac became his favourite authors. The thought of Sir Francis Bacon, whose works he annotated, also played a vital role in his development.

In temperament Beccaria was morose and apprehensive; and throughout his life he demonstrated characteristic traits of neurotic instability. He experienced difficulty in working by himself; and his writings arose in great part from his friendship and collaboration with the *philosophes* of the Società dei Pugni. His early education he dismissed as 'fanatical'; and in 1761, against his father's wishes, he made an impetuous runaway marriage with Donna Teresa Blasco, the sprightly young daughter of a lieutenant-colonel in the engineers. Their relations cooled, and his wife soon became indifferent to him; but on her account he broke with his family for a time. In the Società dei Pugni Beccaria entered into economic discussions, debating especially the monetary problem which had vexed men's minds since 1748. In this area Pietro Verri encouraged him to produce his first little work: an essay on monetary reform entitled *Del disordine e de' rimedi delle monete nello Stato di Milano nel 1762* (Lucca, 1762). Verri also provided Beccaria with the subject of *Dei delitti e delle pene* ('On Crimes and Punishments'), the celebrated treatise on which his fame still rests. Verri himself, being committed to economic studies, was unwilling to tackle the law; but he gave advice to Beccaria and acted as midwife in the production of the treatise, correcting, encouraging and making suggestions as it was written. *Dei delitti e delle pene* was begun in March 1763. It was finished early in 1764 and began to circulate in the summer of that year after publication at Leghorn.

In *Dei delitti e delle pene* Beccaria protested against the severity and abuses of current penal procedure and undertook a systematic examination of criminal jurisprudence in the light of the humanitarian and philanthropic doctrines of Rousseau. He rejected what he regarded as the traditional 'barbaric' practices and arbitrary interpretations of the law going back to the time of Constantine; and in pursuit of 'the greatest happiness of the greatest number', he opposed the interests and privileges of the few and affirmed the 'rights of man' on behalf of the delinquent. The treatise opens with an appeal to the reader ('A chi legge') and with a brief introduction: two passages which, when read in conjunction, constitute, as Franco Venturi has pointed out, one of the fundamental texts of the Enlightenment. The rest of the book is divided into forty-seven numbered sections, some of which are little more than a paragraph in length. In general Beccaria advocated a reasoned and humane treatment of offenders; and required that the laws should be fixed, and that the functions of judge and prosecutor should be kept separate. He also sought the abolition of clandestine accusation, of arbitrary imprisonment and of secret trials. His basic principle was that punishment for crime should not be regarded as punishment for sin or as vengeance, but as a matter of social defence. Torture and the death penalty, especially, were neither useful nor necessary and both ought to be abolished. The book was one of the first to stress the beneficial influence of education in lessening crime. In his conclusion (XLVII) Beccaria enunciated a clear new rule for action which marked a notable departure from the usual penal practice and procedure at the time:

> . . . perché ogni pena non sia una violenza di uno o di molti contro un privato cittadino, dev'essere essenzialmente pubblica, pronta, necessaria, la minima delle possibili nelle date circostanze, proporzionata ai delitti, dettata dalle leggi.

Between 1764 and 1766 Beccaria contributed a few select pieces to *Il Caffè*. In one of these, 'Tentativo analitico su i contrabbandi', he applied algebra to economics to formulate a general theorem. In another essay, 'Frammento sullo stile', he provided a foretaste of his aesthetic theory. This was more fully developed in *Ricerche intorno alla natura dello stile*, the first part of which, written between 1767 and 1769, was published in Milan in 1770, to the surprise of his friends who were awaiting at that time a second treatise on jurisprudence or a book on political economy. Beccaria's other contributions to *Il*

Caffè included 'I piaceri dell'immaginazione' and the Addisonian essay 'De' fogli periodici'.

In these same years the rapid circulation of *Dei delitti e delle pene* brought Beccaria great notoriety and gave rise to much polemic. At first the treatise was regarded as a work of French propaganda, or as a plagiarism. It was fiercely attacked, especially by the clergy who regarded it as impious to deal with the concept of punishment separately from that of sin; and also by those who detected the germs of social and moral subversion in the attitudes expressed. In Rome, with a decree dated 3 February 1766, it was condemned by the Catholic Church and placed on the *Index*. In the previous year, however, it had been staunchly defended from the censure of the Vallombrosan Ferdinando Facchinei by Pietro Verri, who wrote a lively *Riposta ad uno scritto che s'intitola Note ed osservazioni sul libro Dei delitti e delle pene* (1765). In Milan Count Carlo di Firmian also supported Beccaria with his patronage. In Florence the influence of the treatise was extensive. Peter Leopold's reform of the penal code was on lines advocated by Beccaria; and in 1787 he even abolished capital punishment, the first monarch in Europe to take this radical step. Outside Italy *Dei delitti e delle pene* was promulgated both direct and through the medium of translation. A recast version in French, with textual modifications, by A. Morellet was published in Paris in 1765, under the false imprint 'Philadelphie, 1766'. Voltaire and various other *philosophes* wrote commentaries on it.[5] In England the anonymous translator of the first English version of 1767 applauded Beccaria's attempt to reduce the law 'to the standard of reason'. Its influence on the jurist Sir William Blackstone and the legal theorist Jeremy Bentham was notable, and through them, in the early nineteenth century, on the 'Philosophic Radicals' and the social philosophy of the Utilitarians. In Russia the reform of the penal code proposed by Catherine the Great in 1767 was entirely based on Beccaria's work, which the empress greatly admired. By the turn of the century the cavillings of Beccaria's enemies were effectively silenced; and despite the fundamental criticisms of Kant, subsequent reforms of the penal code in Europe have generally taken the direction first proposed in *Dei delitti e delle pene*.

5. See p. 54.

In June 1766 the last number of *Il Caffè* came out; and in October, at the invitation of the *philosophes*, Beccaria and Alessandro Verri left Milan for Paris, where they expected to remain for some four or five months. They met Morellet, Diderot, d'Alembert, d'Holbach and others; and everwhere they were accorded much adulation. Dissension, however, was in the air. Beccaria was a prey to morbid fears and he was worried by family matters. He disliked his new role as a celebrity; and in November, to the disgust of his friends, both old and new, he cut short his stay in France and returned to Milan after being away for only two months. A rift developed between Beccaria and Pietro Verri which never properly healed. But in 1767 Beccaria was invited to go to Petersburg to assist in the reform of the penal code. He hesitated; and to keep him in Milan, a state thought to be short of thinkers and philosophers, he was appointed by Kaunitz, on the advice of Count Firmian, to the newly created chair of political economy ('Scienze Camerali') in the Palatine Schools. He held this post for two years, after which he was succeeded by a friend and collaborator from the epoch of *Il Caffè*, the Marquis Alfonso Longo (1738–1804).

Beccaria's lectures for the years 1769 and 1770 dealt, like those of Genovesi, to whom he paid tribute, with questions of population, agriculture, trade and manufactures. They were well attended and he was invited to publish them. But in the event, through his apathy (always a predominant trait), they remained in manuscript until 1804, when they were published posthumously by P. Custodi in four parts under the title *Elementi di economia politica*.

In later life, like Pietro Verri and Gian Rinaldo Carli, Beccaria attained high office in the Austrian administration in Milan, where he devoted himself to the minutiae of reform. In 1771, at his own request, he was appointed to a vacancy on the Supreme Council of Political Economy. Seven years later he became a magistrate for the mint and a member of the committee on monetary reform. In 1786 he was chairman of the Third Department of the Government Council, concerned especially with agriculture, industry and commerce. Three years later he passed to the Second Department, where he dealt with jurisdictional matters. Finally, in 1791, he was appointed to the committee charged with reform of the criminal law.

*

Other figures of note – besides Carli, Beccaria and Longo – who gathered about Pietro Verri in the Società dei Pugni and contributed to *Il Caffè* were his younger brother Alessandro, Paolo Frisi (1728-84), one of the most typical representatives of the Enlightenment in the scientific field, the *abate* Sebastiano Franci, Count Luigi Stefano Lambertenghi, Pietro Francesco Secchi and Count Giuseppe Visconti. To *Il Caffè* Sebastiano Franci contributed 'Del lusso delle manifatture d'oro, e d'argento' and 'Osservazioni sulle questioni, se il commercio corrompa e costume, e la morale'. Alfonso Longo wrote 'Osservazioni su i fedecommessi'. Various articles on climatology and public health were the work of Giuseppe Visconti. The entries of Alessandro Verri (1741–1810) were almost as numerous as those of his brother; but he was far less concerned with civil and economic reform than with literary and linguistic topics and questions of pedantry and moral philosophy. After 1767, following his trip to Paris with Beccaria, and a subsequent visit to England and Germany, Alessandro Verri settled in Rome, where he became a man of letters of pre-Romantic sensibility, writing novels such as the *Avventure di Saffo* (1780), the *Vita di Eristrato* (1815, written in 1793), and the *Notti romane al sepolcro dei Scipioni* (1792–1804), a sequence of 'imaginary conversations' between the shades of the ancient Romans, influenced by the *Night Thoughts* of Edward Young.

Tuscany, the Papal States, Venice, Savoy-Piedmont

The movement for reform, so strong in Naples and in Lombardy, also took root in the second half of the eighteenth century, to a greater or less extent, in all the other states of the Italian peninsula. It was especially pronounced in Florence and Tuscany where, after the extinction of the House of Medici in 1737, beneficent reforms were eventually introduced under the House of Lorraine. But the reformatory movement was also felt even in those regions, such as the Papal States and the Republic of Venice, which seemed least susceptible, on the political level, to the innovatory ferment of the Enlightenment.

In Florence, in 1753, the Società del Georgofili, the first agrarian academy of its kind in Europe, was founded by Ubaldo Montelatici. A Tuscan precursor in matters of agricultural reform, however, was

Sallustio Antonio Bandini (1677–1760), archdeacon of Siena, president of the Accademia dei Fisiocratici, and author of the *Discorso sopra la Maremma di Siena*. This work was presented to Leopold of Lorraine, Grand Duke of Tuscany, as early as 1737; but it was not published until 1775, at the height of the Tuscan Enlightenment. In it Bandini opposed the exploitation and misgovernment of the desolate and malarious, but potentially fertile, wastes of the Tuscan Maremma by profiteers and monopolists; and he advocated the introduction of free trade and the freeing of agriculture from all economic and administrative fetters, to enable the inhabitants to make a living. Later in the century the Grand Duke Peter Leopold (1765–90), the younger brother of Joseph II, embarked upon a vast programme of agricultural, administrative and juridical reform. He abolished the old trade guilds, with their restrictive traditional practices, and introduced free trade, without restrictions of exports or imports. He began the costly reclamation of the Maremma, instituted public works, and reorganized the system of land tenure. Equality of taxation was introduced in 1770. He also founded schools, academies and museums; reformed the universities of Pisa and Siena; and was the first ruler in Europe to abolish torture, secret procedure and the death penalty. In his later years, with the support of Scipione de' Ricci, the Jansenist bishop of Pistoia, he entered the struggle for ecclesiastical reform.

Peter Leopold was aided in his programme of reform by a number of excellent ministers. Chief of these was the Florentine Francesco Maria Gianni (1728–1821), who held high office and drew up a plan for the constitution. Among his writings on economic and other matters Gianni is especially remembered for his *Pensieri sulla ricchezza nazionale* (1787) and *Memoria sulla costituzione di governo immaginata dal granduca Pietro Leopoldo* (1805, published 1825). Peter Leopold's other counsellors included Giulio Rucellai (1702–78), professor of civil institutions at Pisa; Pompeo Neri (1706–76) and Giovanni Fabbroni (1752–1822). Neri, a Florentine lawyer who had distinguished himself in Milan as chairman of the committee convoked for the compilation of the census there, was recalled to Tuscany in 1758, where he was appointed counsellor. His chief writings were *Osservazioni sopra il prezzo legale delle monete* (1751) and *Memoria sopra la materia frumentaria* (1766). Giovanni Fabbroni left, among other works, *Réflections sur l'état actuel de l'agricolture* (1780).

In Rome and the Papal States – a connected territory to the south and east of Tuscany, including the legations of Bologna and Ferrara, and bounded to the south by the kingdom of Naples – there was little trade and agriculture was neglected; commerce was in the hands of foreigners, and manufactures merely supplied the home market. There were two good harbours at Civitavecchia and Ancona; but apart from the Tiber and the Po, there were few navigable rivers, and other means of communication were undeveloped. Though physically diversified, much of the region was arid, mountainous, and in some areas extremely unhealthy; the marshy districts along the Tyrrhenian seaboard to the south of Rome were barely populated, and pestilential fevers were prevalent. The government, of which the head was a monarch elected by the college of cardinals, was in the hands of the clergy, who filled all the higher offices. And although the papal dominions were one of the most backward regions in Europe, they were also the territory where the Roman Catholic Church was established in its greatest splendour. The different religious orders were immensely rich; and convents were innumerable. The greater part of the landed property was in the hands of the clergy, who were divided into regular and secular. The former, like the nobility, were generally very wealthy and enjoyed great privileges; but the latter, except for the higher ranks, were poor and without influence. The peasantry of the region were oppressed and miserable.

Throughout the eighteenth century the Popes, generally worthy men of distinction, attempted to ameliorate conditions in Rome and the Papal States; but the strength of the church had been much sapped. The Jesuits and the Jansenists, who emphasized inner regeneration rather than external reorganization, had long been in conflict. In the other great European struggle affecting the Church, between the Bourbons and the Habsburgs, the Popes attempted to remain neutral, and they lost the support of both; and by the time of the French Revolution, a period of radical anti-clericalism, the Papacy had become an outworn and ineffectual institution.

Benedict XIV (Lambertini, 1740–58), a tolerant and scholarly man, much influenced by the Enlightenment, began his pontificate with useful and conciliatory measures. He encouraged agriculture and commerce, founded chairs of chemistry, physics and mathematics, revived academies, caused English and French books to be translated, dug out the obelisk in the Campus Martius, constructed fountains, and in many ways proved himself a munificent patron. His successor, Clement XIII (Rezzonico, 1758–69), was elected through the efforts of the Jesuits. But by this time the Society of Jesus had become extremely unpopular; and with Pope Clement XIV (Ganganelli, 1769–74), who yielded to pressure from the Bourbons, the Jesuits, already expelled from Portugal (1759) and from France (1762), were suppressed. At the end of the century, the relations of Pope Pius VI (Braschi, 1775–99) with the reformatory Emperor Joseph II and with the Grand Duke Leopold of Tuscany were far from cordial. His internal administration, however, was enlightened and judicious. He succeeded in draining and putting part of the Pontine marshes into cultivation at great expense. He improved the port of Ancona, completed the church of St Peter's, enlarged the museums of the Vatican (Museo Pio Clementino), and generally embellished Rome. But in 1793 a popular tumult gave the French Directoire an opportunity for hostile demonstrations. Three years later the French armies, under Napoleon, took possession of papal territory. In 1798 Rome itself was invaded and a revolutionary Republic set up. The Pope was called upon to renounce the temporal sovereignty; and on his refusal, he was seized and carried off first to Siena, then to Florence. In the following year he was transferred from the Certosa to Grenoble, and finally to Valence on the Rhône where, worn out with the privations of his confinement, he died at the age of eighty-two in the twenty-fourth year of his pontificate.

In Venice, throughout the eighteenth century, the old oligarchic structures were maintained with distrustful vigilance. It was an ageing republic, cut off from its hinterland through the policies of an outworn 'citizen economy' and in a state of military, political and economic exhaustion. In the Veneto, where for centuries manufactures had been discouraged to prevent competition with the industries of the Serenissima, the people were burdened with taxes and enjoyed no political rights. The republic was forced to maintain a prudent, though disastrous, neutrality, under which it aspired to live in political isolation from the crises that periodically convulsed the European scene. But even in Venice new ideas and attitudes were not wanting. From the 1730s on, men of the citizen class, and a sprinkling of the nobility, actively sought to animate the old maritime traffic. Public works were undertaken; rivers were diverted; and new industries were sited where power was plentiful and labour cheap. A movement also developed to open up the guilds to larger membership. Agricultural academies were founded. But the government itself, stubborn and hidebound, was hopelessly constricted by outworn social, political and economic concepts. It failed to revitalize itself through the assimilation of new blood; and the greater part of the reform movement in Venice failed.

Notable among the Venetian reformers was the theoretical economist Giovanni Maria Ortes (1713–90) who, though opposed to mercantilism, is remembered for his *Lettere sull'economia nazionale* (in part unpublished) and for his posthumous *Riflessioni sulla popolazione delle nazioni per rapporto all'economia nazionale* (1790). Antonio Zanon (1696–1770), author of *Dell'agricoltura, dell'arti e del commercio* (6 vols., 1763–66), devoted himself to the improvement of agriculture, the arts and industry; while the patrician Andrea Memmo (1729–93) applied himself to the unrewarding task of economic and administrative reform.

In the sphere of journalism and allied activities, from the time of the *Gazzetta Veneta* and the *Osservatore Veneto* of Gasparo Gozzi, the stream of Venetian periodicals flowed unceasingly. When the long-lived *Novelle della Repubblica Letteraria* and the *Nuove Memorie* died, to fill the gap *La Minerva, o sia nuovo Giornale de' Letterati d'Italia* (1762–7) was founded by the veteran Angelo Calogerà in collaboration with Jacopo Rebellini (1714–67). Though a journal of erudition, founded on the model provided by Apostolo Zeno's *Giornale dei Letterati d'Italia*, it took the enlightened view that the '*tre sorgenti principali, da cui deriva la Felicità dei Stati, sono l'Agricoltura, l'Arti ed il Commercio*'. The *Giornale d'Italia spettante alla Scienza Naturale* (12 vols., 1764–76) and its successor the *Nuovo Giornale* (8 vols., 1776–84) were conceived on similar lines by Francesco Griselini (1717–87). Each published articles on physics and mathematics, mechanics and medicine, agriculture, commerce and literary matters. *La Minerva* opposed the study of Latin in schools and praised the work of such Venetian reformers as Antonio Zanon. Other figures admired were the natural scientists Lazzaro Spallanzani, Alberto Fortis and the Frenchman Buffon; the Milanese satirist Giuseppe Parini; and the English Augustan poet Alexander Pope. Two further Venetian magazines of great influence, both of which cultivated a markedly 'philosophic' tone, were *L'Europa Letteraria Giornale* (1768–73) and its successor the *Giornale Enciclopedico* (1774–97). Both were issued monthly and were compiled by Domenico Antonio Caminer (1732–96) and his daughter Elizabetta Caminer (1751–96). Each contained articles and news on literary and scientific topics, both original and in translation from French. The *Giornale Enciclopedico*, which between 1777 and 1790 was published at Vicenza, was especially notable for the richness and variety of its material, for its theatrical notices and for its enlightened European outlook.

In Savoy-Piedmont, which took relatively little part in the intellectual and artistic life of eighteenth-century Italy, being essentially a military state, the free-thinking Ignazio Adalberto Radicati di Passerano (1691–1737), the 'Piedmontese Giannone', served Vittorio Amadeo II in his struggle against papal usurpation. He wrote twelve *Discorsi al Re* (1728), condemning theocracy; but before this, he suffered persecution and went into voluntary exile first to England (1726), then to Holland. Later in the century, under Carlo Emanuele III (1730–73) and Vittorio Amadeo III (1773–96), exile was normal for those Piedmontese, including Giuseppe Baretti and Vittorio Alfieri, who wished to think and write; alternatively, they cultivated clandestine activities in the masonic lodges and in Jansenist circles, out of which, at the time of Napoleon, emerged the Liberals and the Democrats, the Republicans and the Jacobins.

Three pre-eminent figures of the Piedmontese Enlightenment were the brothers Vasco and Carlo Denina. In 1769 Count Giambattista Vasco (1733–96), a distinguished economist, advocated granting the peasantry ownership of the land they worked, in a treatise entitled *La felicità pubblica considerata nei coltivatori di terre proprie*. His other writings include *Saggio politico delle monete* (1772), on the decimal system, and the French *Mémoire sur les causes de la mendicité et sur les moyens de la supprimer* (1790). His younger brother, Count Francesco Dalmazzo Vasco (1732–94), supported the Corsican independence movement of Pasquale Paoli, aspiring to give political body to his views, and suffered years of imprisonment. In 1790 he published *Saggio filosofico intorno ad alcuni articoli importanti di legislazione civile*. In the following year he was accused of professing seditious maxims in an essay, no longer extant, in which he attempted to formulate a democratic system of government. He was arrested and died in the fortress at Ivrea. Many of his works still exist only in manuscript.

Carlo Denina (1731–1813), born at Revello, near Saluzzo, was a graduate in theology at Milan (1756); but he devoted himself to historical writing and to literary history. In 1763, having already produced *Discorso sopra le vicende d'ogni letteratura* (1760) and *Saggio sulla letteratura italiana* (1762), he created *Il parlamento Ottaviano, ovvero Le Adunanze degli osservatori Italiani*, a minuscule periodical mirroring the intellectual world of Turin, which was soon suppressed for its interest, however moderate and circumspect, in the new types of political and social thought stemming from English and French encyclopedism. Denina's most influential publication, which had immense success, was *Delle rivoluzioni d'Italia* (twenty-five books in three volumes, 1769–70), to which, in the second edition, Denina added a further book, *L'Italia moderna*, covering the period from the Treaty of Utrecht to 1729. This was notable not only as the first complete history of Italy in a European context, making great use of material derived from Muratori, but for its linkage of political and economic issues, and for the frankness of some of its judgements on social, religious and educational matters. In the conclusion Denina made a series of proposals for reform, which attracted the wrath of both Church and state. In 1777 his attempt to publish *Dell'impiego delle persone*, developing his ideas, finally cost him his chair at Turin. In 1782 he went into exile; but he was invited to the Prussian court at Potsdam, where he was accorded high honours by Frederick II. Denina's later works, which were published at Berlin, include the apologetic *Essai sur la vie et le règne de Frédéric II* (1788), *La Prusse littéraire sous Frédéric II* (1790–91) and *Considérations d'un italien sur l'Italie* (1794–5). In 1804 Denina met Napoleon at Mainz. The emperor approved of his zeal for the Revolution and appointed him to the post of librarian in Paris, where he remained until his death.

PART TWO

POETRY

ONE

England

HAS there ever been a truly classical English poetry? If so, it must surely have been in the first half of the eighteenth century, with its foundations earlier in the Restoration period. The poetry of this time was undoubtedly ambitious of classical status. It was Roman in conception. It sought to create a new Augustan age in England. Dr Johnson succinctly defines the character of this poetry as it was established by John Dryden in the last thirty years of the seventeenth century: 'What was said of Rome, adorned by Augustus, may be applied by an easy metaphor to English poetry embellished by Dryden, *lateritiam invenit, marmoream reliquit*, 'he found it brick, and he left it marble' (*Lives of the English Poets*, 'Dryden'). Dryden was, in Johnson's opinion, the first English poet to appreciate the full expressive potential of the language and to use it with discrimination. Previously the language had been, according to Johnson, 'a heap of confusion'; Dryden got it into order, established a 'system of words' and 'rules' of taste, founded a 'poetic diction'. This was a far-reaching act, it was like reforming a nation: the neo-Augustan poetry which it inaugurated was all set to annexe a civilization. Johnson intimates as much in his life of Dryden: 'The new versification, as it was called, may be considered as owing its establishment to Dryden; from whose time it is apparent that English poetry has had no tendency to relapse to its former savageness.'

As Johnson indicates, Dryden's example was civilizing in that it brought order into a chaotic situation, and thereby made 'the proper choice of style' a matter not of happy accident or instinct but of systematic principle. 'All polished languages', he writes, 'have different styles, the concise, the diffuse, the lofty, and the humble', and the poet was henceforth going to be required to give full weight to those differences. Dryden brought into poetry (though he did not himself always live up to it) a sense of 'decorum', or 'system of propriety'. The different styles 'properly' belonged to the different 'genres' of poetry.

Dryden wanted his writing to be 'an imitation of human life, which is the very definition of a poem': he held it up to the light of real experience, and the different genres could be said to further this end by helping (as one critic puts it when describing a closely related aspect of Dryden's work) to 'discriminate between orders of experience that have been confused'.[1]

The theory of genres serves, then, to clarify and order experience. It also helps to clarify and regulate the work of the artist. It presupposes that he will be looking for unity and coherence, that he will put limits to his invention and ensure that every part of his work is consistent with his central intention. 'The design, the disposition, the manners, and the thoughts', these are in Dryden's view of primary importance: 'if the draught be false or lame, the figures ill disposed, the manners obscure or inconsistent, or the thoughts unnatural, then the finest colours are but daubing, and the piece is a beautiful monster at best' (Preface to the *Fables*). Thus the different genres, which exist only by virtue of their inner coherence and singleness of purpose, become prescriptive, become in effect a system of rules: there is only one way to represent life in, say, heroic or tragic or satiric terms and that is to obey the 'rules' for writing an epic, or a tragedy, or a comedy. At the same time, since these and other genres must be thought to have arisen spontaneously out of natural human responses, the rules they prescribe are not arbitrary. To obey them is really to obey a law of nature.

> Those RULES of old *discover'd*, not *devis'd*,
> Are *Nature* still, but *Nature Methodiz'd*;
> *Nature*, like *Liberty*, is but restrain'd
> By the same Laws which first *herself* ordain'd.
>
> (Pope, *An Essay on Criticism*, I, 87–91)

The genres are a way of formulating or systematizing our sense of reality. These, at any rate, are the lines on which Dryden argues in the Preface to his play *Troilus and Cressida* (an adaptation made in 1679 from Shakespeare's play). He has been outlining some of the rules governing the writing of tragedy and concludes ('because many

1. Martin Price, *To the Palace of Wisdom*, Illinois, 1970, p. 32.

men are shocked at the name of rules') by citing Rapin's *Reflections* on Aristotle:

> If the rules be well considered, we shall find them to be made only to reduce Nature into method, to trace her step by step, and not to suffer the least mark of her to escape us: 'tis only by these that probability in fiction is maintained, which is the soul of poetry. They are founded upon good sense, and sound reason, rather than on authority; . . . but 'tis evident, by the ridiculous and gross absurdities which have been made by those poets who have taken their fancy only for their guide, that if this fancy be not regulated, it is a mere caprice, and utterly incapable to produce a reasonable and judicious poem.

The Augustan poets, then, were hoping to achieve an ideal harmony between art and nature. From Dryden they got an indication of the strength and centrality offered by a revived classicism. They saw it as a way of channelling the creative energies, identifying and isolating the essential forms of feeling, and enhancing the powers of expression. It offered clarity and control, and an appreciation of the things that really mattered to all men. Order, clarity, definition, these were the desired qualities, and the word that covered them all, one of the key-words of the age, was *judgement*. 'No man', Dryden maintained, 'should pretend to write who cannot temper his fancy with his judgement: nothing is more dangerous to a raw horseman than a hot-mouthed jade without a curb' (Preface to *Troilus and Cressida*). There might be a specious charm in works extravagant in feeling, or undisciplined in expression, but 'whereas poems which are produced by the vigour of imagination only have a gloss upon them at the first which time wears off, the works of judgement are like the diamond; the more they are polished, the more lustre they receive' (The Dedication of Dryden's translation of the *Aeneid*, 1697). Naturally such writing is appreciated only by the judicious reader, and judgement is of course essential in a critic. But first it is essential to the poet, for it is not an entirely negative or restrictive influence, but a way of addressing all the faculties to the realization of important truths.

At the same time, as Dryden makes clear, the creative faculties do not actually arise out of the exercise of judgement. They even look like a contradiction of it. They represent something lawless and unpredictable in the mind, the activity of fancy, or the imagination: 'Judgement, indeed, is necessary', writes Dryden, in the preface to one of his plays, 'but 'tis fancy that gives the life-touches, and the secret graces to it.' And the word most often used to denote this other factor, another key-word of the period, is 'wit'. 'The composition of all poems is, or ought to be, of wit'; this is Dryden's view as expressed in a celebrated passage from the dedication of his early poem *Annus Mirabilis* (1666):

and wit in the poet, or *Wit writing* (if you will give me leave to use a school-distinction), is no other than the faculty of imagination in the writer, which, like a nimble spaniel, beats over and ranges through the field of memory, till it springs the quarry it hunted after; or, without metaphor, which searches over all the memory for the species or ideas of those things which it designs to represent. *Wit written* is that which is well defined, the happy result of thought or product of imagination.

Wit was certainly one of those words that became more difficult to pin down as it became more generally serviceable. Partly its meaning depended on its relation to what it was not: it belonged with its opposite, *judgement*. The two were contradictory, yet not hostile to each other. Each needed its opposite. Neither would be creative without the other. Pope writes of this balance of opposites in *An Essay on Criticism* (I, 80–84):

> Some, to whom Heav'n in Wit has been profuse,
> Want as much more, to turn it to its use;
> For *Wit* and *Judgement* often are at strife,
> Tho' meant each other's Aid, like *Man* and *Wife*.

Thus the 'classicism' of this neo-Augustan age had a complex character. It was generated by contradiction rather than harmony; it was held together by tension; it was always on the verge of becoming unlike itself. For, after all, the 'wit' that animated it was not historically very far removed from the wit of the seventeenth-century metaphysical poets. The writers of the generation before Dryden were all (even Milton) involved more or less closely in a tradition of 'wit-writing' which stemmed in the first place from John Donne (?1571–1631). The 'line of wit' from Donne, through Cowley and Marvell, and on to Dryden can still be traced (as modern critics have shown) in Pope.

But what is now admired was at that time viewed with some disquiet. What the Augustans noticed in seventeenth-century wit was its exaggeration, its forced logic and farfetched analogies. It seemed to them wilfully unnatural, and what they were looking for was quite different from that:

> *True Wit* is *Nature* to Advantage drest,
> What oft was *Thought*, but ne'er so well *Exprest*,
> *Something*, whose Truth convinc'd at Sight we find,
> That gives us back the Image of our Mind.

As Johnson pointed out, if that passage from Pope (*An Essay on Criticism*, I, 297–300) were thought to be a good description of wit then the metaphysicals would have to be rejected, 'for they endeavoured to be singular in their thoughts, and were careless of their diction'. Actually, in Johnson's opinion, this was *not* a good description of wit, and the shortcomings of metaphysical wit were in fact even more radical than had appeared:

> If by a more noble and more adequate conception that be considered as Wit, which is at once natural and new, that which, though not obvious, is, upon its first production, acknowledged to be just; if it be that, which he that never found it, wonders how he missed; to wit of this kind the metaphysical poets have seldom risen. Their thoughts are often new, but seldom natural; they are not obvious, but neither are they just; and the reader, far from wondering that he missed them, wonders more frequently by what perverseness of industry they were ever found.
>
> (*Lives of the English Poets*, 'Cowley')

With this line of argument neo-classical theory very rapidly reaches its limits. It cannot contain the idea that unity and truth to nature might be felt most strongly in the presence of what contradicts our expectations. For Johnson there was a perversity in the wit that functioned as a 'kind of *discordia concors*; a combination of dissimilar images, or discovery of occult resemblances in things apparently unlike'. What Coleridge was later able to see as a vital concern of the creative imagination, 'the balance or reconcilement of opposite or discordant qualities' (*Biographia Literaria*, xiv), was to Johnson the unnatural process by which 'the most heterogeneous ideas are yoked by violence together' (*Lives of the English Poets*, 'Cowley').

In this way the 'classicism' of the early eighteenth century was a force operating against its own inner nature. There was something unstable and ambivalent in it. Johnson recognized this in the work of Dryden, whose delight, he wrote, 'was in wild and daring sallies of sentiment, in the irregular and excentrick violence of wit'. Yet Johnson also considered that Pope, possessed of a firmer 'judgement', came short of Dryden in qualities vital to great poetry:

> Of genius, that power which constitutes a poet; that quality without which judgement is cold and knowledge is inert; that energy which collects, combines, amplifies, and animates; the superiority must, with some hesitation, be allowed to Dryden.
>
> (*Lives of the English Poets*, 'Pope')

The terms he is using define the inner contradictions of Augustan poetry.

Yet it does not follow that the precarious 'classicism' of this age must be said to lack artistic validity. It is not untroubled, but it is not therefore untruthful. On the contrary, it works towards an ideal the hard way, through a full experience of the forces that have to be reckoned with. It sustains the concept of order with an energy that encompasses disorder.

This, as one would expect, was not made explicit. What the Augustans intended can be seen by turning, once again, to Dryden's statement of the case: the ideal was to be found not just in the values of classical literature but in its highest values, in the ethos, the comprehensive vision and the artistic integrity of the epic. 'A Heroic Poem,' Dryden declares, in the opening sentence of his dedication of the translation of Virgil, 'A Heroic Poem, truly such, is undoubtedly the greatest work which the soul of man is capable to perform.' There is, Dryden says, handing on the architectural metaphor from Horace to Johnson, 'nothing to be left void in a firm building; even the cavities ought not to be filled with rubbish which is of a perishable kind, destructive to the strength, but with brick or stone, though of less pieces, yet of the same nature, and fitted to the crannies'. This is the kind of integrity that is especially characteristic of the epic: 'Even the least portions of them must be of the epic kind: all things must be grave, majestical, and sublime, nothing of a foreign nature . . .' (*ibid.*). And integrity of this order is really the only adequate way to give a true account of human nature. The 'novels' interpolated into Ariosto's romances are a relaxing and vicious distraction; stage plays are on too small a scale and their effects 'too violent to be lasting': 'tragedy is the miniature of human life; an epic poem is the draught at length'.

It was their ambition, then, to restore the possibility of epic poetry, bringing the artistic powers into harmony again. For the epic example would be found not only in Virgil but in Homer also, and whereas Virgil was the model of judgement and refinement, in Homer there was the inspiration of creative ardour, of 'invention'. This was the quality that Pope seized on as the essence of Homer's greatness: Homer has an 'unequall'd fire and rapture', a 'wild paradise', 'amazing invention'. Yet the important thing was that though Homer excelled in invention and Virgil in judgement, they both possessed both qualities in a high degree: 'each of these great authors had more of both than perhaps any man besides, and are only said to have less in comparison with one another' (Pope, Preface to his translation of the *Iliad*). Together they contain all the possibilities of the epic, and the epic in this way makes possible the full development of the creative powers in ideal harmony.

Yet the Augustans were hardly in a position to recreate the epic. As we have seen, they were caught in a historical situation that made it difficult to achieve a classical balance of the creative faculties. And they did not in fact achieve a new epic poetry. They translated, of course, and they provided, as Pope says of his translation of the *Iliad*, 'a more tolerable copy . . . than any entire translation in verse has yet done'. But their primary and unparalleled contribution to the history of the epic was to parody it, to submit it to ironic inversion and the demands of satire, to create the new genre of the 'mock-heroic'. At least the genre was new to England, and, though it had its origins in France in Boileau's *Le Lutrin* (1672–83), its extensive development in England, giving a distinctive character to the whole Augustan period, was unparalleled elsewhere. The mock-heroic is pre-eminently the Augustan contribution to English culture. It gets into all areas of Augustan literature: it is in John Gay's *The Beggar's Opera* (1728) and in the heroic couplets that he chooses as the medium for his *Trivia* (1716), his poem about the streets of London. It is in Dryden's satire of the poet and dramatist Shadwell, *MacFlecknoe* (1682), and it is in the 'comic epic poem in prose' that is Fielding's novel *Tom Jones* (1749). It is in the vigorous burlesque of Fielding's play, *The Covent-*

Garden Tragedy (1732) and in the refined subtleties of Thomas Gray's 'Ode on the Death of a Favourite Cat Drowned in a Tub of Gold Fishes' (1748). It is in Pope's *The Rape of the Lock* (1712 and 1714), an 'Heroi-Comical Poem', and his *The Dunciad* (1728 and 1743). It is at one level a habitual attitude widely shared, at another it is a formal principle in works of art. Since it is based on a sustained awareness of likeness in things which are thought to be unlike, sublimity and bathos, the elevated and the ordinary, it is, as Maynard Mack observes, a kind of metaphor, 'the metaphor of tone'.[2] And the significance of this 'great pervasive metaphor of Augustan literature' Mack takes to be its power, 'without the use of overt imagery at all', to hold together opposite or discordant qualities: 'the mock-heroic', he concludes, 'seems made on purpose to fit this definition of Coleridge's of the power of imagination'. It is in this oblique way, this sidelong equivocal celebration of the heroic idea, that Augustan poetry finds a way to make its inner contradictions work creatively.

It does this work of the imagination by simultaneously creating and destroying, or, more accurately, by creating images that at the same time are and are not what they seem to be – are true and yet not true, great and yet insignificant, important yet trivial. The process emerges with particular clarity and beauty in what is possibly the greatest of all mock-heroic creations, not a poem but an opera, Mozart's *Cosi Fan Tutte* (1790). The two heroines of this opera plead with their acquaintance, the 'philosopher' Don Alfonso, to tell them his bad news about their lovers: 'Are they dead?' 'Morti – non son': the reply exactly indicates the opera's theme: they are dead and not dead, they are and are not true to themselves when they reappear in disguise; love is and is not real, the opera itself is and is not 'serious'. Contradictions of this kind are basic to the ironic structure of a very similar work, Pope's *The Rape of the Lock*.

Alexander Pope (1688–1741) published the first version of this poem in 1712, and the second longer and more elaborate one two years later. It is a young man's poem, among the first of Pope's major works (*An Essay on Criticism* was published just before it, in 1711, and 'Windsor Forest' just after, in 1713). It is, indeed, a poem about youth, about flirtations taken lightly and trifles taken as tragedies,

2. 'Wit and Poetry and Pope', in T. L. Clifford, ed., *Eighteenth Century English Literature*, New York/Oxford, 1959.

about 'the moving toyshop of the heart', about a world which is all sparkling foreground and shallow perspectives. And it is, one might say, a family poem, prompted by a quarrel in the relatively circumscribed Roman Catholic circle to which Pope's own family belonged. It was meant to make light of the affair and restore goodwill and good relations between the families involved. It is a happy work. Even the darker tones are touched in lightly, and as if with pleasure: 'The hungry Judges soon the Sentence sign,/And Wretches hang that Jury-men may Dine' (III, 21–2). The poem does lead into issues that are deeply serious but it does so with a buoyancy that makes them appear easy to dispose of.

> What dire Offence from am'rous Causes springs,
> What mighty Contests rise from trivial Things,
> I sing – (I, 1–3)

The mock-epic 'proposition' at the beginning of the poem *really* indicates its scope: it is about dire effects, about the far-reaching consequences of trivializing the feelings. It opens up a frightening area of emotional nullity behind the giddy excitement of playing at love. At the same time it seems to be captivated by the surface brilliance of these lives, to invest them with amusement. It rejects the values of 'face', or reputation; but it is pleased with the world of the guardian Sylphs (mock-heroic representatives of the gods), a world of shifting and gleaming surfaces without substance.

In this way the poem simultaneously creates and supports two systems of value. The mock-heroic genre both enlarges and reduces the world it deals with: these battles, these weapons, are serious, but the things the characters take seriously, their 'heroics' are not. The intersecting ironies that are thus produced can be seen very clearly in the description of the heroine, Belinda, at the beginning of Canto II. We have just seen her in front of her mirror at her *toilette*, creating a 'face' for her triumphant progress up the Thames from London to Hampton Court:

> Not with more Glories, in th' Etherial Plain,
> The Sun first rises o'er the purpled Main,
> Than issuing forth, the Rival of his Beams,
> Launch'd on the Bosom of the Silver *Thames*,
> Fair Nymphs, and well-drest Youths around her shone,

But every Eye was fix'd on her alone.
On her white Breast a sparkling *Cross* she wore,
Which *Jews* might kiss, and Infidels adore.
Her lively Looks a sprightly Mind disclose,
Quick as her Eyes, and as unfix'd as those:
Favours to none, to all she Smiles extends,
Oft she rejects, but never once offends.
Bright as the Sun, her Eyes the Gazers strike,
And, like the Sun, they shine on all alike.
Yet graceful Ease, and Sweetness void of Pride,
Might hide her Faults, if *Belles* had Faults to hide:
If to her share some Female Errors fall,
Look on her Face, and you'll forget 'em all. (II, 1–18)

The extravagance of 'Not with more Glories' is demanded by the mock-heroic convention, but it does not sound simply mock-heroic. Belinda *is* all brightness and radiance. But then we see that her very brilliance is a kind of flaw; she is 'lively', 'sprightly', 'quick', all smiles, but she smiles indiscriminately on all; her 'quick' 'unfix'd' eyes see nothing but rather demand to be seen. 'Her Eyes the Gazers strike': they seem striking when gazed upon, or they strike the eyes blind that gaze on them; either way they are not themselves 'gazing' but 'striking'. Belinda exists to be looked at, and thus, with another ironic twist, we realize that to 'look on her Face' is exactly what she wants and will hardly dispose of the criticism associated with it. Yet in a way it does disarm criticism: this is her gift to us all, to make us her admirers: Belinda is and is not what she seems. The poem builds its whole significance on that kind of contradiction.

The Dunciad is a work of much more violence and an exacerbated imagination, but like *The Rape of the Lock* it employs the resources of mock-heroic to give heightened significance to the very things it rejects, to build up and demolish at the same time. Pope published in 1728 a poem in three books attacking what he believed to be the influences leading to a destruction of literary and cultural values. The poem was peopled with his enemies – poets, playwrights, scholars, critics, all lumped together as enemies of reason, nature and art – all 'dunces' and their epic story a 'dunciad'. Fourteen years later he produced a great satiric vision of a whole civilization falling under the paralysing power of the Goddess of Dulness, and this was *The New Dunciad.* The following year, 1743, he brought out a revised version of *The Dunciad*, in four books, with a new hero and with *The New Dunciad* as Book IV. This great and grotesque work, a labour of anger and enmity, went on through all the years of his maturity, from the age of forty to the year before his death at the age of fifty-six. It might seem a work of extreme paranoia, were it not for the imaginative energy and truth which the mock-heroic form made available.

Like Dryden's mock-heroic satire *MacFlecknoe* (1682) which must have been his model, Pope's *Dunciad* works by inflating its victims and making them into comic monsters. Particular individuals are elevated into a symbolic species; or, rather, their *names* – John Dennis, Oldmixon, Welsted, etc. – are enlarged into generic terms: ''Twas chatt'ring, grinning, mouthing, jabb'ring all,/And Noise and Norton, Brangling and Breval,/Dennis and Dissonance . . .' (II, 237–9). The poem is peopled by enormities created, as it were, to give identity and meaning to the names. Its most devastating satire is in the implication that its victims cannot really be said to exist unless the poem gives them existence. And yet the only existence it can give them is one that must be despised and ridiculed. It is their nullity, their inanity, that must be exposed. Thus the poem creates what it is demolishing, and it demolishes by the very act of creating. The mock-heroic ambiguousness of these 'dunces' is that they are powerful *because* of their impotence, enormously important because of their insignificance. They are the heroes of some kind of anti-life. The poem culminates in a final apotheosis of Dulness which abundantly demonstrates the resources of this Augustan 'metaphor', the mock-heroic.

> Lo! thy dread Empire, CHAOS! is restor'd;
> Light dies before thy uncreating word:
> Thy hand, great Anarch! lets the curtain fall;
> And Universal Darkness buries All.
>
> (IV, 653–6)

This closing vision is, taken in one way, the outcome of all the ironies created by mock-heroic celebration of the dunces and their instinct to spoil. But it is difficult to read it as irony. It is after all a fearful vision of night and the irresistible forces of darkness:

> Thus at her felt approach, and secret might,
> *Art* after *Art* goes out, and all is Night.
>
> (IV, 639–40)

This now seems the only way to assert the classical values of order, coherence, light: they can be sustained, if at all, in an irony precariously balanced on the edge of an appalling vision.

What is more, it seems possible that these classical values were felt to be menaced not only by external forces but by something within the personality, some inner irrationality. There is here something similar to the conflict between wit and judgement, but more radical and universal. It is presumably what Pope has in mind when he defines the 'two Principles in human nature' as 'Self-love, to urge, and Reason, to restrain' (*An Essay on Man*, II, 53–4). It is as modes of self-love, he believes, that the passions operate, and the passions are the source of energy and action. But to say this is, Pope admits, to say that these sources are virtually indefinable. 'Oft in the Passions' wild rotation tost, Our spring of action to ourselves is lost' (*Moral Essays*, I, 41–2). To locate it in the passions is to locate it in that area of our nature which is obscure, impenetrable, troubling. Significantly his argument draws on the analogy of sleep and dreams: when we try to identify this elusive factor we are in a territory where reason cannot operate:

> As the last image of that troubled heap,
> When Sense subsides, and Fancy sports in sleep,
> (Tho' past the recollection of the thought)
> Becomes the stuff of which our dream is wrought:
> Something as dim to our internal view,
> Is thus, perhaps, the cause of most we do.
>
> (*Moral Essays*, I, 45–50)

There is something governing all our actions which is itself ungovernable. And we cannot evade the uneasiness that this causes by having recourse to a theory of a ruling passion; we can see that if one passion dominates all the rest (ominously, 'like Aaron's serpent, swallows up the rest', *An Essay on Man*, II, 132) it will at least give direction and definition to the personality. But it does so in a fearful, cancerous way:

> As Man, perhaps, the moment of his breath,
> Receives the lurking principle of death;
> The young disease, that must subdue at length,

Grows with his growth, and strengthens with his strength:
So, cast and mingled with his very frame,
The Mind's disease, its ruling Passion, came;
(*An Essay on Man*, II, 133–8)

Thus Augustan thinking is dominated not only by external forces hostile to reason, but also by a deep sense of inner turmoil and unrest. Swift, for instance, writes of the way the balance of the personality can be overturned when 'a Man's Fancy gets *astride* on his Reason, when Imagination is at Cuffs with the Senses, and Common Understanding, as well as common Sense, is Kickt out of Doors' (*A Tale of a Tub*, ix). Claude Rawson, who quotes the passage in an illuminating essay on 'The Character of Swift's Satire'[3] notes how it resembles what Johnson has to say about 'that hunger of imagination which preys incessantly upon life'. 'No man', writes Johnson in *Rasselas*, 'will be found in whose mind airy notions do not sometimes tyrannize, and force him to hope or fear beyond the limits of sober probability. All power of fancy over reason is a degree of insanity . . .' (*Rasselas*, liii). As Rawson points out, the specifically satiric intentions of such statements do not preclude the possibility that in some degree they are universally true. They both carry the 'notion of a radical restlessness' and, what is more, they both reveal a 'personalized sense of it'. Both Swift and Johnson, Rawson maintains, were quick to feel that their idea of a universal 'madness' implicated themselves also: 'both men felt that even states of ordinary sanity are in a sense precarious and momentary victories of 'reason' over 'fancy', victories of a vigilance needing constant renewal, perhaps at times a matter not even of 'control' or 'repression' . . . but of show' (ibid.).

The Augustans, it seems, feel some deep inner disturbance which must be acknowledged though it can hardly be understood and hardly reconciled with the ideal of order and harmony they aspire to. It corresponds to something uncontrolled in their writing, the imagination racing, the feelings unable to engage with an adequate object. Thus the grotesque dreamlike images of *The Dunciad* may be an indication of some kind of disintegration that Pope feels as a personal threat: 'Nonsense precipitate, like running Lead,/That slip'd thro' Cracks and Zig-zags of the Head' (I, 123–4). The same may perhaps be said of the obscene 'epic' games in Book II of *The Dunciad*, and

3. C. J. Rawson, ed., *Swift: Critical Essays*, London, 1971, p. 18.

there is of course a correspondingly extreme and unbalanced imagination at work in Swift's satires, particularly in *A Tale of A Tub* (1704) and *Gulliver's Travels* (1726). His satire has an effect of physical revulsion, of nausea, going beyond the occasion. Take, for instance, the passage in which the diminutive Gulliver in Brobdingnag, the land of the giants, is carried off by a monkey, who stuffs its pap into his mouth:

> the Monkey was holding me like a Baby in one of his Fore-Paws, and feeding me with the other, by cramming into my Mouth some Victuals he had squeezed out of the Bag on one Side of his Chaps, and patting me when I would not eat . . .
>
> (II, v)

Here, and also in many of Swift's poems, there is a kind of violent reaction *against* the imagination, or a lacerating of the mind, what Ricardo Quintana has called 'a styptic to the imagination'. 'I pity wretched Strephon, blind/To all the charms of woman kind'; thus Swift concludes his poem on 'The Lady's Dressing-Room' (1730): 'His foul imagination links/Each dame he sees with all her stinks.' But Swift has nothing to propose in the place of this 'foul imagination', except romantic delusion and a stupid belief in beauty:

> He soon will learn to think like me,
> And bless his ravish'd eyes to see
> Such order from confusion sprung,
> Such gaudy tulips raised from dung.

In short the 'foul imagination' is a violent over-reaction to a kind of dread at the way in which imagination can only too easily subvert reason: disgust is at least a recognition of reality, and an indication that the mind has not gone spinning off into uncontrollable fancies. If reason cannot govern the mind then revulsion must:

> Corinna, in the morning dizen'd,
> Who sees, will spew; who smells, be poison'd.
>
> ('A Beautiful Young Nymph Going to Bed')

In the poetry of Johnson, finally, there is an element of inner unrest which rises above the dread and anger of Pope and Swift to achieve an almost tragic intensity. The whole tenor of *The Vanity of Human Wishes* (1749), an 'imitation' of Juvenal's Tenth Satire, is in fact determined by a kind of despair of ever being able to satisfy the 'hunger of imagination'. He approaches his theme, it is true, in grandly impersonal generalizations: 'Then say how Hope and Fear, Desire and Hate,/O'erspread with Snares the clouded Maze of Fate' (5–6). But the theme has a special emphasis for him and is brought home with concentrated force. There is a pattern many times repeated of power almost literally stifling itself, of febrile activity, uncontrollable ambition and the inevitable final cancellation: 'Delusive Fortune hears th'incessant Call,/They mount, they shine, evaporate, and fall' (75–6). In the poem this comes to seem an inescapable condition of life, a universal and self-destroying restlessness. Wolsey's 'restless wishes tow'r'; in the scholar 'the Fever of Renown/Burns from the strong Contagion of the Gown'; 'Madness fires [the] Mind' of Xerxes; in all cases Johnson allows no alternative ('Nor think the Doom of Man revers'd for thee'). All his creative energy goes into enforcing the realization of this universal madness. At the outset he appeals to Democritus, the laughing philosopher, to reappear 'With chearful Wisdom and instructive Mirth' and renew the satirist's laughter at folly. Yet Johnson's own response is far removed from laughter and scorn. He finds in this madness a reason for compassion, fellow-feeling, even a kind of awe. It is a tragic dilemma that men face, either impelled to go beyond their own powers or compelled to lapse into senseless torpor, either futile self-assertion or futile self-submission. Johnson's conclusion is that there *is* a way, and only one way, to escape from the tragic dilemma of being human, and that is by centring our lives on Heaven and turning our 'wishes' into prayers. The sincerity of this final resolution is undoubted. But it hardly conveys the same sense of tragic involvement as the rest of the poem does.

> Must helpless Man, in Ignorance sedate,
> Roll darkling down the Torrent of his Fate?...
> Enquirer, cease, Petitions yet remain,
> Which Heav'n may hear, nor deem Religion vain.
> Still raise for Good the supplicating Voice,
> But leave to Heav'n the Measure and the Choice.
> (345–52)

It is the answer Johnson needs, but not an answer he can make real. Like the other Augustans he has a haunted and perilous imagination.

With this in mind we should perhaps return to the question from which we started: 'Has there ever been a truly classical English poetry?' The more one discovers about the inner contradictions of Augustan poetry the more unlikely it begins to seem that *this* can be it. As we have seen, it can hardly sustain the epic qualities which were regarded as the highest expression of a classical ideal. And so also in satire, which was certainly one of the dominant features of the age, it is evidently not easy to appeal to shared classical values. Johnson's great poem turns away from its satiric model. Its dark tones are not those of *saeva indignatio* but of a personal insight into the 'doom of man'. What is shared is the irrationality; the belief in a higher spiritual order is one that calls for a new *inwardness*, in which 'celestial Wisdom calms the Mind,/And makes the Happiness she does not find'. The poem throws the individual back upon himself.

Even more in the satire of Pope and Swift we are conscious of a personal isolation. Of course the satirist's role is traditionally a lonely one: he is the single defender of virtue in a corrupt world. Thus Swift indicates the way in which he would hope to be recognized, after his death, as a man who

> In exile, with a steady heart,
> ... spent his life's declining part;
> Where folly, pride, and faction sway,
> Remote from St John, Pope, and Gay.

Yet the work in which he makes this claim, the poem 'On the Death of Dr Swift' (1731), gets its effect from envisaging the satirist as dead, hardly missed, soon forgotten, with only one, 'quite indifferent in the cause', to draw his character impartially. The poem finds in the satirist's lonely stance a deeper isolation. The satirist's importance derives almost entirely from his being in the eyes of the world a nonentity; he contradicts everything the world values and therefore can hardly be valued or even noticed by the world. He is therefore in a position of moral isolation, but he is far from feeling that this undermines his personal authority. It is in fact a preferred, a chosen isolation. It encourages him to cherish a sense of his own superiority, especially since it is disregarded and slighted by others. Here at the basis of the poetry of 'classical' detachment and poise is a 'romantic' stance, in which the individual finds his value by being set apart.

A similarly 'romantic' attitude colours Pope's great vindication of his role as a satirist, in '*An Epistle from Mr Pope to Dr Arbuthnot*' (1735). He makes basically the same claim as Swift does:

> That not for Fame, but Virtue's better end,
> He stood the furious Foe, the timid Friend,
> The damning Critic, half-approving Wit,
> The Coxcomb hit, or fearing to be hit.
>
> (342–5)

But he makes this claim with overt pride and without the protective irony of Swift's oblique statement:

> Not Fortune's Worshipper, nor Fashion's Fool,
> Not Lucre's Madman, nor Ambition's Tool,
> Not proud, nor servile, be one Poet's praise
> That, if he pleas'd, he pleas'd by manly ways.
>
> (334–7)

At the same time there is something in the poem that works against this sense of personal security and integrity. It can be felt, for instance, in the notoriously violent abuse of Lord Harvey in the character of Sporus, 'This painted Child of Dirt that stinks and stings' (310). This portrait so stridently represents all the things that Pope is not that it makes Pope's self-portrait also appear rather stridently defiant. And, in any case, the poem, wishing to establish a pattern of private virtue rather than public rhetoric, actually gives an impression of deep weariness and a desire to get away from the world rather than correct it.

> Oh let me live my own! and die so too!
> ('To live and die is all I have to do:')
> Maintain a Poet's Dignity and Ease,
> And see what friends, and read what books I please...
> Why am I ask'd, what next shall see the light?
> Heav'ns! was I born for nothing but to write?
> Has Life no Joys for me? or (to be grave)
> Have I no Friend to serve, no Soul to save?
>
> (261–73)

There is in the work of the Augustans an impression that to be isolated, set apart, is deeply desirable, a profound relief and a high privilege. What is more, this attitude finds itself reflected in a new relationship to the natural world. Admittedly much that is overtly and consciously 'romantic' at this time draws heavily on earlier examples. Pope's *Eloisa to Abelard* (1717), for instance, exploits the medievalism of the original letters of Abelard and Heloise, recently translated into English, the erotic religious imagery of the seventeenth-century metaphysical poet Crashaw, and especially the subjective landscapes of Milton's 'Lycidas' and 'Il Penseroso'. It is in fact the only occasion on which Pope shows any interest in wild nature as a setting for human feelings, and it is like a personal message carried from Milton to Gray.

There are many other instances in early eighteenth-century poetry of this kind of emotional landscaping. Even as late as the mid-1750s, those poets, including Mark Akenside (1721–70), Joseph Warton (1722–1800) and his brother Thomas (1728–90), and William Collins (1721–59), poets (as Johnson puts it) 'eminently delighted with those flights of imagination which pass the bounds of nature', were still working in a Miltonic atmosphere.

Even the 'Elegy Written in a Country Churchyard' (1751) by Thomas Gray (1716–71) hardly cuts loose from the images sanctioned by Milton:

> Haply some hoary-headed swain may say,
>   'Oft have we seen him at the peep of dawn
> Brushing with hasty steps the dews away
>   To meet the sun upon the upland lawn.'

The first stanza does indeed intimate something of the radical sense of loneliness felt by the Romantic poets in the presence of the natural world, especially in the final line, 'And leaves the world to darkness and to me'. There is something here that anticipates Keats's 'darkling I listen', a sense that the self is almost obliterated yet at the same time sharpened by its encounter with a different order of existence. But in Gray's poem this sense is soon dissipated, as the borrowed terminology gradually consolidates a persona for the poet and a pattern for the meditation.

Something the same is true of the most extended poem of natural description so far attempted in English poetry, James Thomson's *The Seasons* (1726–46). Thomson's subject is remarkable. It is the story not of human actions, character, destiny, but of natural events and processes, alteration and underlying continuity, the revolution of days and seasons, the pattern of climate and the changes of weather, the expressive features of landscape (its hills, fields, trees, rivers), the life of plants and animals. Yet even this poem, celebrated and influential throughout Europe (though less so in England), does not effect a radical displacement of the prevailing assumptions about man and nature. In some respects it is quite as much a poem about 'Man', about his place in the universal system and his moral life, as is Pope's *An Essay on Man*. Although Thomson is closely observant and faithful in his descriptions of nature, it is usually in terms that also invoke human values and a human scale of reference:

The cormorant on high
Wheels from the deep, and screams along the land.
Loud shrieks the soaring hern; and with wild wing
The circling sea-fowl cleave the flaky clouds.
Ocean, unequal pressed, with broken tide
And blind commotion heaves; while from the shore,
Eat into caverns by the restless wave,
And forest-rustling mountain comes a voice
That, solemn-sounding, bids the world prepare.
Then issues forth the storm with sudden burst,
And hurls the whole precipitated air
Down in a torrent.

('Winter', 144–55)

This is certainly evocative writing, but not without an anthropomorphic cast. The 'screams' and 'shrieks' of birds are noticeably a distortion of *human* sounds; the ocean's movement is 'blind', the storm approaches with a 'voice' (and a sublime one at that), and it 'hurls' the air as Jove might hurl a thunderbolt. All are ways of stressing that nature, seen in human terms, is wild and hard to comprehend. But all *are* ways of seeing nature in human terms. And, what is more, the anthropomorphic epithets often spread into similes and analogies with human life. And at the basis of it all is a still recognizable, Miltonic picture, redrawing the lines along which nature can be presented as an 'emblem' of the life of man:

Thrice happy he, who on the sunless side
Of a romantic mountain, forest-crowned,
Beneath the whole collected shade reclines;
Or in the gelid caverns, woodbine-wrought
And fresh bedewed with ever-spouting streams,
Sits coolly calm; while all the world without,
Unsatisfied and sick, tosses in noon.
('Summer', 458–64)

Yet, though some of the more consciously 'Romantic' poetry of this period hardly reveals a radical shift in attitude, there are in Augustan 'classical' poetry undercurrents of feeling which carry intimations of significant new developments. The preference for solitude, the privilege of being set apart, the cultivation of subjective experience, these much more than the deliberate choice of picturesque settings and the sympathetic accompaniment of the natural scene are the signs of a new kind of feeling. The less explicit, and much less poised loneliness felt in some of the poems of Swift, Pope and Johnson indicates a kind of watershed. From this point the going will be different. And the difference is going to be found not so much in a heightened sense of the picturesque (as for instance in *Eloisa*) but in the beginnings of a new kind of relationship between man and man, and therefore between man and nature. Indeed it begins to look as if the entry into Romantic poetry has to be described as a movement *away* from the natural world. *The Seasons* describes nature in terms of man, not because of some imperfection in the sensibility of the poet, but because man and nature are part of one system, vitally and organically interrelated. But the movement which begins to be apparent in Augustan poetry is one that tends to separate man from society and from the world around him. That is to say, the essence of Romantic poetry is in its sense of otherness, of an existence unique to the self. But that sense brings also a heightened awareness of sources of life outside the self, particularly in nature. There is something from which the individual, profoundly conscious of his individuality, is excluded. We may say that a fully realized poetry of nature is not possible unless man and nature have first become separated from each other.

The Romantic poets of the late eighteenth and early nineteenth centuries in England all speak of this separation. For Blake the starting-point of all human experience is an act of self-assertion which separates the individual from the eternal, either in ominous images of psychic disunity as in the conflict between Urizen and Los, or in the innocent joy with which the human soul discovers its identity in response to a question from some other being:

> I have no name;
> I am but two days old.
> What shall I call thee?
> I happy am,
> Joy is my name.
> Sweet joy befall thee.
> ('Infant Joy')

The outcome of this separation is Blake's 'mental strife' to achieve 'divine vision', and this becomes in fact a strife *against* nature, against the natural man and against the world of natural objects. But for Wordsworth and Coleridge a similar sense of separate identity is accompanied by the vital recognition of a living principle independent of and other than the human. Man is not now a part of nature, as when (even as late as Pope's *An Essay on Man*) he belonged to the 'great chain of being'. He is rather in a vital reciprocal relationship with nature, attached by many bonds of responsibility and love, not an adjunct of nature but for that very reason deeply responsive to it.

None of the eighteenth-century poets approaches nature quite in this way, but there are some striking anticipations of the Romantic vision. The attitude of mind which is adumbrated even in the most centrally Augustan poems becomes more explicit in some lesser known poems from the same period. Wordsworth himself draws attention to some of these by including them in a personal anthology made in 1819 for Lady Mary Lowther. This was a volume of *Poems and Extracts from the Works of Anne, Countess of Winchelsea and Others*; it draws together poems or passages from poems, by Thomson, Beattie, Armstrong, Akenside, Cowper, Smart and several seventeenth-century writers, nearly all of them centred on the theme of solitude and secluded meditation. But nearly a third of the volume is given up to poems by Lady Winchelsea (?1666–1720), and of these 'A Nocturnall Reverie', first published in her *Miscellany Poems* of 1713, is remarkable. True, it contains some traces of the kind of moral equation the Augustans made between man and nature: 'Their short-lived jubilee the creatures keep,/Which but endures while tyrant man does sleep.' But on the whole it is remarkable in that it is *not* intended to prove a point. It is really a discovery of something near and familiar yet unknown. It is an entry into a world which has a life of its own:

> In such a night when passing clouds give place,
> Or thinly veil the heaven's mysterious face;
> When in some river, overhung with green,
> The waving moon and trembling leaves are seen;
> When freshened grass now bears itself upright,
> And makes cool banks to pleasing rest invite,
> When springs the woodbine and the bramble-rose,
> And where the sleepy cowslip sheltered grows;
> Whilst now a paler hue the foxglove takes
> And chequers still with red the dusky brakes...

Everything now is seen and known with especial clarity, the 'sleepy' cowslip, the foxglove taking a 'paler hue', the odours which 'thro' temperate air uninterrupted stray', the 'loos'd horse' which approaches grazing and 'whose stealing pace, and lengthened shade we fear/ 'Till torn-up forage in his teeth we hear'. Hearing, in particular, becomes more acute: 'falling waters we distinctly hear', 'curlews cry beneath the village walls,/And to her straggling brood the partridge calls'. Everything is offered for what it is, and its separateness, its difference from human life is what makes it precious: 'In such a night let me abroad remain,/Till morning breaks and all's confused again.' The poet does not attempt to rationalize the experience, or to moralize it. Like many of Wordsworth's own experiences it eludes analysis or definition:

> But silent musings urge the mind to seek
> Something too high for syllables to speak;
> 'Till the free soul to a composedness charmed,
> Finding the elements of rage disarm'd,
> O'er all below a solemn quiet grown,
> Joys in the inferior world, and thinks it like her own.

The fact that one of the poems which most clearly anticipates the work of the great Romantic poets is itself a relatively minor work should warn us not to place too much weight on such anticipations. But the corresponding fact that even the greatest and most central poems from the Augustan period also carry the mind forward should prompt us to question their classical status.

TWO

France

EIGHTEENTH-CENTURY French poetry is, for the most part, vast in output but mediocre in quality. In many ways it resembles the history of tragedy on which the classical tradition had also exercised a sterilizing influence. The fact that poetic competence was accepted as a social accomplishment which facilitated entry into the *salons* is a further indication of its superficial nature; when it sought to be serious and profound, poetry lacked genuine inspiration and failed to free itself from the constricting influence of traditional social and literary attitudes.

At the beginning of the century the very survival of poetry was threatened by fierce attacks from philosophical critics. The question of the nature of poetry was raised by the famous Quarrel of the Ancients and Moderns. Beginning in the seventeenth century as a controversy concerning the role of *le merveilleux* in epic poetry (was Christianity to be allowed to compete with pagan mythology?), it flared up again in 1714 when Houdart de la Motte and Madame Dacier, who had translated Homer into prose and verse respectively, became involved in an argument about the essence of poetry. Laying great stress upon the progress made by reason in other spheres, the moderns (of whom Fontenelle was a particularly influential spokesman) maintained that the value of poetic imagery had to be tested by its intellectual content; Houdart de la Motte, for example, insisted on poetry's need to pay attention to 'the accuracy of its thoughts'. Since poetry thus seemed to have no distinctive subject-matter of its own, it was characterized mainly by its ability to overcome technical difficulties. To many critics this meant that, since it consisted of little more than mere 'rhyming', its eventual disappearance would be no great loss. With the advance of 'philosophy' there seemed no place for poetic frivolity. The philosopher Vauvenargues was probably not alone in his opinion that 'great poets could use their minds for something more useful than poetry'. A certain abbé de Pons expressed the same thought: 'I believe that the art of verse is a frivolous art; that if men agreed to banish it, not only should we lose nothing, but we should gain much.'

This controversy about the nature and existence of poetry did not ultimately check the activity of industrious versifiers and at least one major writer – Voltaire – protested against Fontenelle's strictures. The poet's task, he declared, was not simply to resolve technical difficulties, but also to produce 'beauties which please everybody'; in order to achieve this the poet had to be sensitive to the harmony and music of poetic language; even imagination and feeling did not by themselves constitute poetry, but became poetic only when they were embodied in a form that appealed to the ear as well as to the heart. In any case, Voltaire believed that technical difficulty ought to be an incentive, not a deterrent, to the production of fine verse. At the same time he conceded that poetry must be 'reasonable' in form and spirit and have a useful content.

His own attempts to set an example of serious poetry consisted of such works as *Le Mondain* (1736), a eulogy of luxury and civilized living and a condemnation of barbarism and grossness; *Discours sur l'homme*, a work perhaps suggested by the reading of Pope's *Essay on Man* and in which Voltaire's fluent alexandrines deal with the problems of equality, freedom, envy, pleasure and the nature of man; in his *Poème sur la loi naturelle* (1753) he appeals to the universal character of moral ideas as the true source of natural – as opposed to revealed – religion, whilst the *Poème sur le désastre de Lisbonne* (1755), written under the impact of the Lisbon earthquake, casts doubts on the beneficence or even existence of Providence.

As well as writing poetry with a philosophical content, Voltaire saw himself as a true heir to the classical tradition and tried to produce a great epic poem. He hoped that with *La Henriade* (which first appeared in 1723 as *La Ligue* and then in a revised form, with its present title, in 1728) he would rival Homer and Virgil; the hero, Henry IV of France, might seem a promising subject for a poem of this kind, but Voltaire failed to measure up to the demands of the genre, and posterity has condemned *La Henriade* as a failure, even though it contains some good passages and a number of the author's favourite ideas, including the condemnation of religious fanaticism. More successful than this largely conventional poem, but still falling short of true greatness, is *La Pucelle*, a mock-epic inspired by Ariosto's *Orlando Furioso* and intended as a disrespectful and at times licentious attack upon Joan of Arc; treated for a long time as a merely obscene satire, this poem has found some admirers among modern critics who consider it to be one of Voltaire's best poetic productions.

Voltaire's prestige as a poet inspired lesser writers to a diligent but essentially uninspired imitation of traditional forms. Such was the case with Écouchard Lebrun (1729–1870), known in his day as 'Lebrun-Pindare', the author of pretentious odes which brought him fame with his contemporaries but which, in spite of some technical skill, are now seen to lack genuine poetic inspiration. One of his odes, composed for the benefit of Corneille's poverty-stricken niece, was addressed to Voltaire, who interested himself in the case. Better than his odes (the first collected edition appeared posthumously in 1811) were his epigrams, which are sometimes pungent and witty. He even ventured into scientific poetry and wrote an ode on the causes of earthquakes!

Apart from Voltaire, perhaps the most admired author of serious poetry was Jean-Baptiste Rousseau (1671–1741) who was hailed by his contemporaries as 'the great Rousseau'. Accused of writing libellous verse, he was banished from France in 1707 and spent most of his remaining years in exile; his unhappy personal life was in striking contrast to his brilliant reputation as a poet. He was admired mainly for his odes on various topics, both general and personal, and for cantatas inspired by the Bible and ancient mythology; one of these, *Circé*, drawn from an adventure of Ulysses in the *Odyssey*, occasionally appears in anthologies. A much more genuine indication of his poetic talent is to be found in his epigrams, which were often prompted by personal feelings and circumstances and express resentment and bitterness at his own miserable situation. His light verse, usually of a satirical kind, is much more readable than his often tedious pseudo-classical poems.

Apart from being inspired by his own experience, such verse was much closer to the critical spirit of the age than the bombastic solemnity of works which sought to express philosophical ideas in classical form. Yet, like Voltaire, his reputation as a serious poet produced many imitators, including Lefranc de Pompignan (1709–84), who is now remembered for his quarrels with the *philosophes* (he was mercilessly satirized by Voltaire) rather than for his poetic achievement and whose work consisted mainly of religious poetry based on the Bible. He published two collections of *Poésies sacrées* (1734 and 1763).

At first, poetry seemed impervious to the new English influence which was beginning to affect so many other aspects of French cultural life. Admittedly, Pope's poetry became very popular; his *Essay on Man* (1733) was translated into French in 1736, 1737 and 1739 and, as we have seen, soon found an echo in Voltaire's *Discours sur l'homme*; Pope's influence eventually merged with that of the philosophical optimism associated with Leibniz. English 'pre-Romantic' poetry made a later impact and, even then, this tended to influence prose writers such as Jean-Jacques Rousseau and Prévost rather than poets. However, Thomson's *Seasons* were translated in 1759 and quickly found an imitator in *Les Saisons* (1769) of Saint-Lambert (1716–1803), a poet highly esteemed in his day but now remembered chiefly for his liaisons with Mme du Châtelet and Rousseau's great love, Mme d'Houdetot; posterity has not confirmed Voltaire's enthusiastic eulogy of *Les Saisons* as a 'masterpiece'. Roucher's *Le Mois* (1779) was another poem in the same vein – lengthy and uninspired, with a detailed account of rural activities. Poets such as these apparently wanted to create a new type of descriptive poetry based on the thoughts and feelings inspired by the world of physical nature, but they were too dependent on the old classical forms to be able to produce anything of lasting value. One of the best-known examples of this attempt to renew poetic inspiration was *Les Jardins* (1780) of Jacques Delille (1738–1813); influenced by Virgil and James Thomson, Delille published a verse translation of the *Georgics* (1770) before writing his own poems; during the French Revolution he left France for England and Germany, but on his return, he continued to produce descriptive poetry with such works as *l'Homme des champs* (1800) and *Les Trois Règnes de la Nature* (1809). Perhaps more clearly than any other poet of his time Delille expressed the melancholy feelings aroused by the contemplation of nature; his work is a curious combination of pre-Romantic feelings and a tenacious loyalty to the pseudo-classical tradition.

Translations of other English poets included Young's *Night*

Thoughts, which appeared in French as *Les Nuits*, Le Tourneur's version of Hervey's *Meditations* and Gray's famous 'Elegy Written in a Country Churchyard'. Subsequently, these works were to be completely overshadowed by the productions of the Celtic bard Ossian (really a Scotsman, Macpherson, who managed to pass himself off as the translator of an ancient poet); although many critics did not hesitate to compare Ossian to Homer, his influence became widespread only at the beginning of the nineteenth century. Yet these new tendencies encouraged indulgence in the melancholy emotions associated with the mountain mists of the north and with the effects of night, tombs and ruins; in a still more general way they helped to stimulate the development of a new sensibility. To this English influence should be added that of the Swiss poet Gessner (1730–88), the translation of whose *Idylls* (1762) earned him a European reputation: he extolled the virtues of rural simplicity and to his discreet descriptions of country scenery he added a belief in the natural goodness of man. All these translations thus helped to encourage the growing need to satisfy the heart rather than the mind.

Yet the influence of these foreign writers upon French poetry was very limited. It is discernible especially in elegiac poets whose inspiration already owed something to personal feelings. Such was the case with Nicolas-Germain Léonard (1744–93) whose unhappy life, combined with the influence of Gessner, Tibullus, Propertius and the English poets, led to the composition of *Idylles* (1766), which were marked by a nostalgic yearning for the lost possibilities of happiness; although his work anticipates in some ways that of Lamartine, Léonard rarely achieves more than a certain superficial charm. Evariste-Désiré de Parny (1753–1814) who, like several other poets of his time, came from the Ile Bourbon (now Réunion), published his main work just before the Revolution – the *Poésies érotiques*, inspired by unrequited love, and the *Chansons madécasses* (1787); like Léonard, he is more noteworthy for having foreshadowed a greater poet, Lamartine, than for the intrinsic value of his own work. The satirical poet Gilbert (1751–80), whose *Dix-huitième siècle* revealed him as a fierce opponent of the Encyclopedists, left one outstanding poem – an ode, *Adieux à la vie*, inspired by personal experience and a reading of the Psalms. Gilbert was to be presented (along with Thomas Chatterton and André Chénier) in Vigny's *Stello* (1832) as a remarkable example of genius destroyed by society, but such an interpretation of his career was without historical justification.

These persistent but ultimately barren efforts to produce serious poetry were accompanied by an extraordinary proliferation of light verse which is, in many ways, more typical of the period, even though it mostly lacks merit. Its practitioners are now largely forgotten and some – for example, the influential Président de Hénault (1685–1770) – devoted their lives to more serious pursuits; others such as Vadé (1719–57) and Voisenon (1708–75) are now known only to literary historians. Florian (1755–94), who tried his hand at various genres, including *Fables* (1792) (usually considered his best work, though greatly inferior to those of La Fontaine), comedies and historical and pastoral novels – produced some light-hearted poems. Louis Gresset (1709–77) attempted a more sustained piece of light poetry with his *Vert-Vert* (1734) which relates the story of a convent-trained parrot which is sent into the world for the edification of the pious but which, in its travels, acquires such terrible language that it has to be sent back to its original home; this witty poem was held in very high esteem by eighteenth-century readers and even secured Voltaire's approval. Charles Collé (1709–83) produced an abundance of songs and poetic pastiches. Both Gresset and Collé, however, were to achieve more durable fame with their plays, the former with *Partie de chasse de Henri IV* (1774) and the latter with *Le Méchant* (1747). Voltaire was probably the poet who produced the best light verse of the period, for he found it a suitable vehicle for his wit and biting irony. Typical of his manner was the famous poem directed against the journalist Fréron:

> L'autre jour au fond du vallon,
> Un serpent piqua Jean Fréron.
> Que pensez-vous qu'il arriva?
> Ce fut le serpent qui creva.

If for the most part the light poetry of the time remains superficial, it is more worthwhile than the uninspired versification based on the outworn techniques of the classical age.

Fortunately the century produced one major poetic figure – André Chénier (1762–94). Born at Constantinople, he was soon taken to Paris by his mother when his father became French consul in Morocco. He was educated at the Collège de Navarre and acquired an early enthusiasm for Greek literature, stimulated by his belief – now known to be mistaken – that his mother was of Greek origin. At the age of eighteen he entered the army, but because of poor health and an unstable temperament, he soon abandoned all idea of a military career. After a brief stay in Switzerland, he led an active life in his mother's *salon* where he met many of the leading cultural figures of the day, including the painter David, the philosopher Condorcet and the poet Lebrun. The feelings associated with his amorous exploits of this period are reflected in his *Élégies*. After a journey to Italy he went to London as secretary to the French Ambassador, but was unhappy there. In 1790 he returned to France to take part in the events of the Revolution. At first enthusiastic about the new political developments, he was eventually repelled by the excesses of the revolutionaries. After being arrested and imprisoned for a few months, he was guillotined two days before the fall of Robespierre. During his lifetime he published only two poems, both prompted by political events: *Le Serment du Jeu de Paume* and the *Hymne sur l'entrée triomphale des Suisses révoltés du régiment de Châteauvieux*. Since a collected edition of his works did not appear until 1819, early estimates of his achievement were distorted by the influence of the Romantic Movement. His ideas were, in fact, firmly rooted in the eighteenth century, although he was also strongly drawn to classical antiquity. It is probably the combination of these two influences, together with his own independent attitude, which helps to explain many characteristic features of his poetry.

As much of Chénier's work is fragmentary, for he was in the habit of beginning ambitious projects which he did not have time to complete, any attempt to judge the value of his embryonic large-scale works has to be based on an examination of surviving passages and sketches. He also worked assiduously at a variety of literary forms – odes, satires, comedies and tragedies. The early *Élégies*, mentioned above, do not seem to rise above the level of Lebrun's poetry, but their many classical elements reveal his deep affection for antiquity. Much more important were the Greek-inspired *Bucoliques*. Typical poems of this genre are *L'Aveugle*, in which the blind Homer relates to young shepherds episodes from the history of the world; *Le Mendiant*, which is taken from an incident in the *Odyssey*; *La Jeune Tarentine* describing the plight of a young girl doomed to a premature death; and various idylls inspired by Callimachus, Theocritus and Virgil. Apart from the Greek element already mentioned, Chénier was probably influenced by the neo-classical revival at the end of the eighteenth century – a revival which, in its turn, owed a great deal to the archaeological discoveries of Pompeii and Herculaneum. At the same time the presence of a sentimental strain in these poems may have been partly due to the Swiss poet Gessner, whose reputation has already been mentioned. It is, however, the classical influence which predominates in both form and content, for Chénier shows a marked preference for the alexandrine, which he occasionally treats with a certain freedom – for example, in his use of *enjambement* – and which produces an overall effect of musical harmony. Compared with the work of his contemporaries and immediate predecessors, such poems show a refreshing vigour and originality.

Although Chénier's modern poems, which are not restricted to any specific form, contain many classical elements, their subject-matter is inspired by the ideas and events of the day. In addition to the two poems published by Chénier himself, there are some *Hymnes* and a well-known *Ode à Charlotte Corday*. Particularly effective is *La Jeune Captive* which not only records a deep personal reaction to the unhappy lot of a fellow-prisoner but also considers the more general human problems of life and death.

Perhaps the most intensely felt of all the modern poems are the satirical *Iambes* in which Chénier castigates the Jacobin régime for the way it imposes tyranny in the name of freedom. As well as vibrating with a fierce indignation against the terrorists, Chénier makes a powerful plea for the basic human rights of justice and freedom. The *Iambes* are certainly a remarkable contribution to political satire, with their burning personal conviction, their powerful rhythms and the broad sweep and movement of the verse.

The projected philosophical poems included two vast epics, *Hermès* and *Amérique* – the former intended as an 'epopy of nature, man and societies' which proposed to trace the progress of humanity from primitive to modern times and to serve as an impressive act of confidence in the values of the Enlightenment, and especially in the beneficial effects of science; the latter poem was to deal with the exploration and colonization of the New World, and to stress also the familiar contrast between the simple life of nature and the complexity of civilized life; its other aim was to praise the virtues of natural religion and to condemn the intolerance and bigotry of traditional religious attitudes.

More important than either of these was *L'Invention* which expounded the aesthetic ideal of writing ancient poetry on modern ideas:

Sur des pensers nouveaux faisons des vers antiques.

The poet, insists Chénier, has to realize that he is living in a world very different from that of the ancients: 'everything has changed for us'. Why, he asks, should our writing be thoughtlessly determined by others and why should we paint a picture 'which our ideas have not seen'. The 'human sciences' cannot extend their domain without affecting 'the career of poetry'. As Chénier goes on to extol the achievement of scientists like Newton, Galileo and Buffon, he sees no reason why the achievements of modern culture should not form the subject-matter of genuine poetry. Nevertheless, invention does not mean arbitrary licence and individual caprice, but genuine respect for 'truth, good sense and reason'; feverish incoherence is not the mark of genius. Art must aim at beauty, but at a beauty purged of contradictions and incongruities. When they refused to mingle the genres, the ancients set us a good aesthetic precedent. In order to deal effectively with modern ideas, the poet needs to use the 'colours' of the ancients: 'Let us light our torches at their poetic fires.' Whether poetry be ancient or modern, 'nature is the source and model in us', we cannot escape from 'vast nature, nature herself'. Chénier, therefore, exhorts the 'young poet' to look to the future and to take advantage of the 'new treasures' at his disposal. In spite of the merits of ancient languages, the modern poet must use his native tongue; when handled with 'courage and genius', French can become a genuinely poetic language.

Il faut savoir tout craindre et savoir tout tenter.

Indeed it was the epigraph *Audendum est* ('we have to dare') which summed up the spirit of Chénier's view of poetic invention.

Although the precise manner in which he hoped to combine ancient and modern elements remained somewhat uncertain, Chénier, by both precept and example, brought new life to French poetry, not only by his extraordinary poetic range – and in this respect he recalls Ronsard – but also by the fervour of an often personal inspiration, which was to endear him to the Romantics. Still later in the nineteenth century the Parnassian poets, impressed by the plastic quality of his verse, treated him as a precursor; Chénier was certainly able to capture a striking pose or gesture and endow it with a kind of sculptural quality. At the same time his verse has an elusively melodious charm which, though owing much to his love of Greek poetry, reflects the individuality of his own poetic genius. Posterity can only regret that he did not live to fulfil his true potential as a great poet.

THREE

Germany

THE SHORTER FORMS

THE classification into shorter and longer poems is more appropriate to the special nature of German poetry in the eighteenth century than a division into epic and lyric verse. It is not until half-way through it that these conventional categories make their appearance, and yet poetry could hardly have been written more abundantly than it was in those fifty years. For verse was the accepted form of literature, and it was only gradually that prose, in the form of the novel, made headway in the field of creative writing. The use of prose was in fact virtually limited to philosophical exposition, literary criticism and polemic of all kinds.

Yet to all generalizations there are exceptions, and it so happens that the one lyric poet of the first half of the century belongs to its earliest years, a detached phenomenon exercising no influence on his contemporaries or immediate successors.

Johann Christian Günther (1695–1723)

Some musicians, like Schubert and Mozart, have managed to cram into a short life an *oeuvre* which would not, either in quantity or quality, be inadequate for three score years and ten. But the poets who have died young have almost all left a pathetic sense of unfulfilment. And of none is this truer than of Günther. In *Dichtung und Wahrheit*, Goethe concluded his paragraph on Günther with a reference to his lack of character (*Charakterlosigkeit*), followed by the magisterial pronouncement, 'Er wusste sich nicht zu zähmen, und so zerrann ihm sein Leben wie sein Dichten.'[1] This lapidary summation

1. 'He was unable to control himself, and so his life and his poetic talent melted away.'

appeared abruptly to cancel the praise which Goethe bestowed upon this unfortunate young man, who had been dead for nearly eighty years when these words were written.

Günther was not a weakling, but a victim of circumstances. The son of an austere father, he was never forgiven for an early love affair with a Leonore Jachmann, to whom he became secretly betrothed, and whom, in the face of his father's intransigent enmity, he eventually released from the engagement. He was, in fact, a sensitive, susceptible, passionate young man, whose devotion to poetry equalled that which he felt for the young woman who was the principal object of his affections. The view so widely held in the nineteenth century that a poet's *oeuvre* was in part a factual autobiography could well have drawn nourishment from Günther's poetry, as it undoubtedly did from Goethe's. Indeed, the two names can very properly be juxtaposed, for no other German poets of the eighteenth century have so directly and spontaneously and intimately expressed a relationship to a specific person in a given identifiable milieu. Günther's love poems use the poetic conventions of his time, but they are invigorated with deep feeling and linked to reality by many intimate threads, as well as by such obvious touches as the mention of Striegau and Schweidnitz (in Silesia), his own and Leonore's home towns. The vehicle for fluent, personal expression did not exist in Günther's day, but he went some way towards creating a direct and personal style of communication, though he remained without influence on others.

For all his innovations and explorations, the range and significance of which he probably did not fully grasp himself, Günther was fully in command of the formal style of his day, and wrote, sometimes to order and sometimes to attract notice, florid Baroque odes and occasional pieces, such as the ode written on the conclusion of peace between Austria and Turkey in 1718. In the pomp, flattery and fulsomeness of such poetry Günther was competing with others possessing an equal mastery in court poetry, such as the poets of the Saxon court Johann von Besser (1654–1729) and Johann Ulrich König (1688–1744). Günther's poetry, except for his formal show and parade pieces, was only known during his life to his intimates. His collected poems did not appear until after his death (*Deutsche und lateinische Gedichte*, 4 vols., 1724–35).

Friedrich von Hagedorn (1708–54)

When Günther died in a northern Austrian province in 1723, Friedrich von Hagedorn was a boy of fifteen growing up in the great north-western port of Hamburg. Hagedorn's father, a man of good Westphalian family and an official in the service of the Danish Crown, had lived in Hamburg for years and had died in 1722. With his death his emoluments were lost to the family, and the year of Günther's death is also the time at which young Hagedorn found himself relatively poor, no longer taught by a private tutor, but entered at the Hamburg grammar school. Like Günther, Hagedorn found himself in trouble with authority, being sent down from Jena University when he was nineteen. There any resemblance ends. Hagedorn had nothing of Günther's capacity for passionate love; he liked comfort, ease and the pleasures of good food, good wine and intelligent conversation. His peccadilloes in Jena had largely been a matter of debts contracted in order to satisfy these tastes. Fate was kinder to him than to Günther. After a visit to England to widen his experience Hagedorn received an appointment which, though not a sinecure, imposed only modest demands upon his time and industry, and provided him with a reasonable competence. He remained extravagant, married for money, and still ran into debt, but throughout his life pursued an even course of dining and wining, of pleasant rural excursions and hours of witty and instructive talk. He employed some of the time that he could spare from this agreeable way of life in writing poetry. One would not expect the verse of such a man, written in such circumstances, to be of a dynamic character. It is the work of a gifted dilettante. Yet, if Hagedorn's poems are neither weighty nor powerful, they are neat, mellifluous and elegant. His subjects are love, nature, wine and joy, not of rapture, but of contented ease. Conventions of form and substance are observed, but the resulting verse betrays no sign of constraint. If in the poems love is an agreeable pretence, the element of nature, which so frequently figures as a background, is free from artificiality. An excellent example of this is his poem *Die Vögel*:

In diesem Wald, in diesen Gründen
Herrscht nichts als Freiheit, Lust und Ruh.
Hier sagen wir der Liebe zu,

Im dicksten Schatten uns zu finden,
Da find ich dich, mich findest du.

Hier paaren sich Natur und Liebe,
Die Jugend und die Fröhlichkeit,
Die Lust und die Gelegenheit,
Und macht Gelegenheit ja Diebe,
So wird der Raub der Lust geweiht.

Die Vögel lieben hier und singen.
Es liebt, der in den Lüften schwebt,
Es liebt, was kaum der Fittich hebt,
Und suchet aus dem Nest zu dringen,
Weil alles nach der Freiheit strebt.

In the ensuing stanzas Hagedorn exemplifies his theme of love with the specific examples of nightingale, lark, quail, turtle dove and sparrow. *Der Mai* ranges even more widely among the birds, but also takes in details of landscape, and ends in a eulogy of the independence and vigour of the rural population. Hagedorn's most erotic poem, *Die Nacht*, contrives with elegance and wit to imply that which the night conceals. The links with reality, which enable the reader to take pleasure in this deftly written poetry, are made more obvious in Hagedorn's local topographical references, for instance to the Alster and Harvestehude. His fluency and command also enable him to write well-proportioned short narrative poems, and to handle with expertise the form which, in its didactic explicitness, was so dear to the early eighteenth century in Germany, the fable. In fact, those who know Hagedorn only through anthologies can rarely have read more than the fable *Johann der Seifensieder*. He deserves a revival, or at least the concession of several pages in collections, for he is a truly accomplished poet, possessed of humour and wit, and gifted with the ability to imply, whether he is serious or playful, more than he actually says. Whereas much poetry of the day might be called pharmaceutical, giving a thin coating to wholesome, but not particularly palatable medicaments, Hagedorn combines at his best the high-class *Delikatessengeschäft* and select *pâtisserie*. The factor of pleasure is considerable, and the quality is nourishing. It is sad, but perhaps appropriate, that Hagedorn should have died prematurely at forty-six as a consequence, apparently, of his indolent and epicurean mode of life.

Berthold Heinrich Brockes (1680–1747)

The third German poet of consequence in these early decades of the century was a somewhat older man, a Hanseatic like Hagedorn, but with a rather longer pedigree behind him. Brockes was by descent a Lübecker and by birth and adoption a Hamburger. He inherited a substantial fortune at fourteen, and in due course studied at Halle University and made the rich young man's grand tour, visiting the principal Italian cities from Rome northwards. He returned to Hamburg in 1704 and lived the life of an intelligent and educated man of means; in 1714 he married a well-to-do patrician's daughter, and appears to have led an equable and contented married life, which was blessed by numerous children. It would not be fair to call Brockes a specimen of the average man, but he was certainly a characteristic example of the patrician of means whose outlook was both rationalistic and pious, and whose behaviour was unostentatious and devoid of any hankering for self-aggrandizement or power. He had a gift for painting, which he had begun to cultivate while abroad, and this visual interest is clearly of great importance in the poetry which he was to write. Music, too, appealed to him strongly, and though he was not himself a composer, his first substantial published poetic work was his libretto for a Passion according to St John, *Der für die Sünden der Welt gemarterte und sterbende Jesus* (1712), which was first set by a local composer, Brockes's friend Reinhard Kaiser, and then in 1717 achieved fame when it was composed by G. F. Handel while on a visit to Germany. Its impact was further extended by a later musical version by G. P. Telemann and by the adoption by J. S. Bach of nine numbers from it for his St John Passion. This popularity with composers of a religious cast of mind speaks both for the musical planning of the work and for the evident devotion and sincerity of Brockes's writing.

Brockes was intellectually active, founding two literary societies, Die teutschübende Gesellschaft and Die patriotische Gesellschaft, the second of which published *Der Patriot*, a weekly along the lines of Addison's and Steele's *Spectator*. He wrote poetry for special occasions in the Free City of Hamburg and for his family and circle of friends, and he translated a seventeenth-century Italian religious poem, Marino's *La Strage degl' Innocenti* ('The Massacre of the Innocents').

In 1720 Brockes was elected to the Hamburg Senate, the governing body of the republic, and was several times employed on diplomatic missions. For fifteen years he led an active life in public affairs, yet this period is also that in which falls his most considerable and consistent poetic activity.

Between 1721 and 1748 Brockes published nine collections of verse, all with the same title, *Irdisches Vergnügen an Gott* ('Earthly Pleasure in God'). They appeared at irregular intervals, the last after Brockes's death. Their title represents a programme, the illustration of the pleasure Man can derive from contemplating the works of God, with which he is surrounded. It is an approach characteristic of the combination of rationalism and piety which is found in so many figures of the first half of the century. Brockes's output in the *Irdisches Vergnügen* is uneven in quality. He wrote too much and the result is often trite and sometimes ludicrous. But he brought something new to his more successful poems (e.g. *Der Schnee*, *Die auf ein starkes Gewitter erfolgte Stille*, and *Kirschblüte bei Nacht*')[2] in these collections – an eye for detail and a capacity for precise description.

Brockes took the responsibility of the man of enlightenment seriously, and many of his poems are overtly didactic. The result is sometimes bathos, but at his best he successfully integrates his poetic mission and his message of Christian edification.

These three poets, Günther, Hagedorn and Brockes, each in his own way extended the capacity of the German language for poetic expression and widened the range of sensibility, though Günther's achievements were not fully recognized for many years.

ANACREONTIC POETRY

The enlightened men of the eighteenth century were no gloomy Puritans. As men of reason they were wedded to a conception of a golden mean in human relationships as in other things. The enemy of the mean was passion, normally associated with sex or anger. But anger is fleeting and sex persistent, and so numerous writers of poems (for they were mostly scholars, doctors, lawyers, or gentlemen of

2. 'Snow', 'Quiet after a severe thunderstorm', 'Cherryblossom by night'.

means who liked to write poems) felt the need to admit love into their poetry, whilst making sure that it remained within bounds.

One solution is designated *Anakreontik*, or Anacreontic Poetry. Anacreon, a Greek poet of the sixth century BC, survives only in a few fragments, including some bitter satire, but also praise of wine, women and song. He was, however, much imitated in ancient times, and a collection of hedonistic poems, the general burden of which is *carpe diem* (or, in Herrick's words, 'Gather ye rosebuds while ye may'), was published as *Anakreonteia* in 1554. It is believed to be mainly the work of Latin poets. So-called Anacreontic poetry, more or less elegant verse, praising wine, or friendship, or beauties with Greek or Latin names, became fashionable in German middle-class and professional circles in the thirties and forties of the eighteenth century.

Examples of this playful, superficial poetry can already be found in the writings of Hagedorn, who, in fact, gave the title *Anakreon* to one of his odes. There were, however, numerous other exponents, few of them capable of so sure a touch as Hagedorn. In 1744 J. I. Pyra (1715–44) collaborated with his friend S. G. Lange (1711–81) in *Thyrsis und Damons freundschaftliche Lieder*, and in the same year J. W. L. Gleim (1719–1803), an amiable and generous character, but a mediocre poet, published the two volumes of his *Versuch scherzhafter Lieder*. J. P. Uz (1720–96) and H. N. Götz (1721–81), both friends of Gleim, produced *Die Oden Anakreons in reimlosen Versen* in 1746, and so took the first step towards a rejection of the rule, hitherto observed in eighteenth-century German verse, that all poetry must rhyme. Even so hard-headed a writer as Lessing wrote his share of this deliberately artificial form of literature. Gleim, a man of blameless life, anxiously forestalled puritanical criticism by emphasizing that Galatea, Doris and the other loved ones were figments of the imagination, and that such poetry was merely a mild and innocent entertainment. However vapid these poems now seem, they served in their day a useful purpose, flexing and lightening the German language, which at the beginning of the century had been a heavy and recalcitrant instrument for delicate expression. Gleim, it may be added, also invented patriotic poetry in his *Kriegs- und Siegeslieder der Preussen von einem preussischen Grenadier* (1758), so broadening the scope of poetry and bringing it into direct contact with the political events of the day, for its background is the Seven Years' War, then in progress.

Friedrich Gottlieb Klopstock (1724–1803)

From 1748 to 1771 Klopstock's considerable fame as a poet rested on his biblical epic *Der Messias*.[3] His numerous odes and short poems made little impression because they were scattered through various magazines and annuals, or remained unpublished. They were not a trivial feature of his writing, for by 1770 he had written approximately eighty shorter verse works, many of them substantial odes or descriptive poems which extended over several pages. He was of the generation of Uz and Götz and he shared their views on the triviality of rhyme and the nobility attainable by the use of classical prosody. Klopstock's high estimation of the poet's vocation rejected 'Anacreontic' themes as unworthy, though from time to time, in an unguarded moment, he could write a rococo poem such as *Das Rosenband*, and could do it so ingeniously as to leave open the question whether it rhymes or not.

Klopstock had a profound conviction that the poet must concern himself with matters of spiritual, moral or emotional weight, and many of his titles indicate their fundamental seriousness (*Dem Allgegenwärtigen*, *Das Anschaun Gottes*, *Die Gestirne*, *Der Tod*, *Mein Vaterland*, for example). Yet even where the subject was light, he loved to impart to it a sense of boding profundity, as may be seen in *Der Zürcher See*, which deals with a boating picnic, and *Der Eislauf*, a brief sermon on skating. Though it is easy to mock at touches of pomposity in these poems, they are generally successful (and were even more so at the time), because they treat the imposing background of mountain, lake or forest with a sense of awe which contrasted favourably with the artificial pastoral tone of most of his contemporaries.

Klopstock's shorter poems, collected and published in 1771 as *Oden*, were an eye-opener for the young men born in the mid or late 1740s, who, in their dissatisfaction with existing literary conventions, were more than ready to receive a new gospel. In Klopstock they learned to see a writer, who, though certainly middle-aged and widely respected as the author of a massive religious epic, could interpret nature, projecting himself into it with reverence and expressing his emotions in sublime and noble verse. Some impression of the influence exerted by

3. See p. 214.

the publication of the *Oden* can be seen in the rapt reference to *Die Frühlingsfeier* in Goethe's *Werther*. Klopstock cultivated emotion to a degree which later ages have considered excessive, but to the generation brought up on Hagedorn, Gleim, Uz and Götz, it showed a welcome responsiveness to neglected sentiments. *Empfindsamkeit* (sentimentality) was not then regarded as a sign of weakness, but as proof of a sensitive and warm personality.

Klopstock also wrote poems celebrating the remote Germanic past (*Hermann und Thusnelda*, *Kaiser Heinrich*, *Heinrich der Vogler*), and late in life he turned to topical and political subjects, especially in connection with the French Revolution (*Die États généraux*, *Ludwig der Sechzehnte*, *Die Jakobiner*). In addition to influencing Goethe, he was the inspiration, godfather and hero in one person of the Göttinger Hainbund. Though his reputation has declined since the eighteenth century, some of his strophes still exert their original hieratic or oracular spell, and a few of his shorter poems, of which *Die frühen Gräber* is the best, approach perfection.

Johann Wolfgang Goethe (*1749–1832*)

In the course of some four years (1766–70) Goethe covered the gamut of German lyric poetry of the three preceding decades and arrived at a kind of poetic writing which has virtually no adequate antecedents. He possessed an extraordinary basic facility for verse, which is discernible even in juvenile poems written in defective English. As a student at Leipzig (1765–8) he at first adopted the accepted formalistic standards, and wrote elegant verse of greater wit and subtlety than that of his models. And a poem such as *Die Nacht* (beginning 'Gern verlass' ich diese Hütte'), whilst adhering to some of the pastoral conventions, already contains a suggestion of the originality and depth which were to be fully disclosed a few years later. The transformation took place with great rapidity. In the spring of 1770 Goethe was sent to Strassburg University to finish his studies, interrupted at Leipzig by illness. A rural ride through Alsace aroused his interest in landscape and first showed his remarkable powers of empathy. The new extension of sense and feeling was powerfully reinforced by a love affair begun in October with Friederike Brion, daughter of the Protestant pastor of the village of Sesenheim. Her rural simplicity and naïve charm seemed to him at one with the scenes of nature which surrounded the remote manse, and it was precisely her essential rightness in her particular setting that released in Goethe in the summer of 1771 a succession of poems of unprecedented spontaneity, freshness and integrity, among them *Willkommen und Abschied*, and *Mailied*. These impulsive and ecstatic poems also possess a simplicity of form which derives in part from folk song.

In the winter 1770–71 Goethe assisted Herder, at that time in Strassburg undergoing treatment for a painful eye complaint, in the search for authentic Alsatian folk songs and grasped their homely and singable quality so well that his own poem *Heidenröslein* has often been taken for an actual *Volkslied*.

Goethe's lyric talent, once kindled in this way, developed rapidly and with remarkable versatility. In the next few years he wrote a handful of rhapsodic odes (often called 'Pindaric' odes or *Hymnen*), continuing a tradition established by Klopstock, but achieving a far greater sublimity and power and at times displaying a humour which to the older poet was intrusive and repellent. Particularly notable are the complementary poems of blasphemous defiance (*Prometheus*) and aspiration to divine union (*Ganymed*). The dynamic gestures and the rich emotions of these poems, paralleled also in *An Schwager Kronos* and *Wanderers Sturmlied*, are characteristic of the *Sturm und Drang*, which was largely Goethe's creation. They exhibit an extreme mobility of temperament, tumultuous feeling, a sense of violent physical exertion, and a mocking humour which the poet can direct at himself. This mobility was not, however, a sign of instability. A remarkable feature of Goethe's complex and probably unique personality was the capacity to change swiftly and unpredictably and yet to retain, so to speak, a fixed point of reference. This last is conspicuously lacking in the dramatist and minor poet J. M. R. Lenz, who exhibits a similar fluctuation, but lacks the fundamental stability of Goethe. Lenz's wayward originality is seen in his plays; his lyric poetry sometimes imitates Goethe in the latter's more gentle mood, but has not freed itself from the prevailing conventions.

Goethe, the poetic innovator of the 1770s, acquired within a few years a mastery in many poetic forms. There are noble strophic odes such as *Meine Göttin* (1780) and *Das Göttliche* (1783), meditations on human life, its mutability and continuity, such as *Gesang der Geister über den Wassern* (1779), and a continual outpouring of poems reflecting almost every aspect of his personal and official life, ranging from the love poetry of *Neue Liebe, Neues Leben* (1775) and *An den Mond* (1776–78), through impressions of fleeting moments of absorption in landscape in *Im Herbst* (1775, better known as *Herbstgefühl*) and '*Über allen Gipfeln*' (1780), to poems associated with actual incidents (*Harzreise im Winter*, 1777) or with the Weimar circle (*Ilmenau*, 1783).

It is not easy to assess the influence of Goethe's strikingly original poetry on his own generation. His first collected volume of poems did not appear until 1787, but in the 1770s many of his poems were published in magazines (especially *Iris*, edited by his friend, the minor prose writer, F. H. Jacobi), and others were circulated in manuscript. It is reasonable to assume that some of his contemporaries were sufficiently impressed by his work to adjust their styles, though allowance must also be made for a general change in the climate of literature which cannot be ascribed to any single individual.

Göttinger Hainbund

The group of lyric poets active in Göttingen was, at least in its early days, entirely independent. It consisted of young men of Goethe's generation, studying or teaching at Göttingen, who published poems in the Göttingen *Musenalmanach*, an annual of verse, and in 1772 established a formal association, drawing the designation 'the Grove' from Klopstock's poem *Der Hügel und der Hain*. Klopstock was, in fact, the hero of these young men, as Wieland was their *bête noire*. The original members were H. C. Boie (1744–1806), J. H. Voss (1751–1826),[4] J. M. Miller (1750–1814), G. D. Miller (1748–1821), L. H. C. Hölty (1748–76), L. P. Hahn (1746–1814) and J. T. L. Wehrs (1752–1806). Two brothers, the Counts Christian (1747–94) and Friedrich Leopold Stolberg (1750–1819), and J. A. Leisewitz (1752–1806) joined later, and G. A. Bürger (1747–94), though not a member, was associated with the group. Of these only Voss, Hölty and Bürger were poets of note, though J. M. Miller was a successful novelist and

4. See pp. 215f.

Leisewitz a promising dramatist. Voss's main achievements lay in longer forms, but Hölty and Bürger were genuine lyric poets, neither of whom, unfortunately, was to realize his full potential.

Hölty's life was brief and uneventful. The son of a Hanoverian pastor, he studied theology at Göttingen. Symptoms of tuberculosis appeared and grew worse after a visit to Leipzig. A visit with Voss to Hamburg to see Klopstock was a time of unalloyed happiness, but within a year he had died at Hanover. For several years he had known that his life would be short, and the awareness of imminent death is always present in his poetry, though it is often subdued or concealed. He hardly ever indulged in the solemn funereal broodings which Klopstock, at his best, could intone with so much dignity and weight. It may well be that Hölty, who was of Goethe's generation (he was nine months older), had learned something from Goethe's ecstatic outpourings and from his reverent sense of union with Nature; he can hardly have failed to read such poems as *Mailied* and *Ganymed.* If he did so, however, he used them, not as models to copy, but as an inspiration to follow his natural bent, which tended to move along similar lines; for Hölty possessed a natural gift for happiness, in spite of the misfortunes which beset him, and simultaneously a spontaneous and sympathetic appreciation of nature. Whilst he touches on a variety of themes connected with life, death and nature, the dominant motifs in his poetry are the month of May, the song of the nightingale and the light of the moon, occurring singly or, more often, in conjunction. Though joy may be muted by premonitions, it is not extinguished by them. Hölty was not only successful with simple verse of folk-song character, he also displayed a mastery in the handling of classical verse forms which surpasses that of Klopstock and foreshadows the work of the mature classical Goethe. To this more intricate category belong two of his best poems, *Die Mainacht* and the first of three odes entitled *An den Mond.*

G. A. Bürger (1747–94)

Bürger died in early middle age after a life in which intense brief joys alternated with periods of profound depression. In his private life he was his own worst enemy, taking decisions inimical to his own interests and drifting into impossible situations. His strong sexual impulses involved him in conflict with a respectable environment, and he possessed neither the discrimination to make the right choice nor the discretion to avoid giving public offence. Intended for the Church, he secretly studied law and also acquired at Halle and Göttingen an addiction to drink. Gleim and Boie helped him to pay his debts and he was appointed a magistrate. After neglecting the duties of his office, he had to resign, but was fortunate in being appointed in 1786 to a chair in Göttingen University. He was married three times, first to the wrong one of two sisters, then to the right one, who died within a year, and thirdly to an unbalanced woman who, after making him a laughing-stock, deserted him. Bürger's agitated and colourful life was reflected in a large number of spontaneous, quasi-autobiographical poems, resembling to some extent those of Günther and of the young Goethe. This poetic commentary on his own emotions was, for the most part, cast in the mould of folk song. He also created the modern 'folk ballad', writing ballads (of which *Lenore* is the most famous example) which had all the characteristics attributed by Herder to the ballad as a form of folk art. *Lenore*, published in the Göttingen *Musenalmanach* for 1774, had, with its galloping rhythm and uninhibited onomatopeia, an instant and lasting success.

Matthias Claudius (1740–1815)

Though he had some affinities with the poets of the Hainbund, and some personal sympathy for them, Claudius went his own idiosyncratic way in life as in poetry, defying categorization. He was primarily a journalist of a type rare in his own age and now extinct. His paper, *Der Wandsbecker Bothe*, intended primarily for the edification and education of the humble and simple, was composed entirely of his own contributions, including unpretentious anecdotes, plain reviews, letters, short news items and a number of poems of remarkable simplicity, both of feeling and of form. Like others of his generation Claudius caught the tone and movement of folk song, but no other poet came so close to the ordinary man and woman of farm, village or country town. His simple piety expresses a reverence for Nature as God's handiwork, an attitude plainly visible in the poem

Abendlied ('Der Mond ist aufgegangen') or in the less familiar *Die Sternseherin Lise.*

Friedrich Schiller (1759–1805)

In his youth Schiller was a poet quite unlike any of his contemporaries. Though he wrote a few light poems, these are not generally successful, and most of his effusions recall the style and attitudes of seventeenth-century baroque. Many powerful poems, including the strange love poems addressed to 'Laura', are obsessed with death and decay; and the poetic style in which he expresses his gloomy and anguished feelings is angular and elliptical, though it possesses undeniable strength. The uncharacteristic ode *An die Freude*, which perhaps marks the end of Schiller's youth, is a convivial song, which owes its fame to Beethoven's choice of it as the text for the last movement of his Ninth Symphony. Schiller later developed a capacity for ballad-writing, and his best examples (*Der Ring des Polykrates* and *Die Kraniche des Ibykus*) display a remarkable economy of means and intense dramatic power. The last, and perhaps most important, phase of his poetry occurs in alliance with Goethe and is classical.

The classical poetry of Goethe and Schiller

It was Klopstock who made the discovery that classical metres, which operated in Greek and Latin by quantity (long and short vowels), could be successfully adapted to German use, substituting stressed and unstressed syllables for the classical quantities. He wrote much good poetry in these forms, but his outlook had nothing to do with the classical ideal.

Goethe and Schiller, once hardly on speaking terms, were from 1794 close allies and met frequently in Weimar and Jena. They came to the conclusion that what they considered to be the confusion, triviality and mediocrity of the literary and fine arts in Germany could only be remedied by the deliberate adoption of an austere classicism, representing an ideal of order, balance and harmony. Their new policy first became apparent in their shorter poems, in which they abandoned rhyme and used the distichs (hexameter followed by pentameter) of classical elegiacs. Among the poems written by Schiller in this form are the moving threnody *Nänie*, *Der Tanz*, *Das Glück* and *Der Spaziergang*, which is a conspectus of human life viewed *sub specie aeternitatis*. Goethe composed a cycle of twenty well-wrought poems, originally published as *Elegien* in 1795 and, since 1810, usually known as *Römische Elegien* because of their association with his Italian journey (1786–8). They combine his pleasure in classical form with his delight in pagan freedom from sexual inhibition. In *Euphrosyne* he used the elegiac form to write a highly stylized lament.

Schiller's and Goethe's classical poems are only one aspect of the outlook which both of them developed and furthered in vigorous cooperative propaganda. The best-known phase of this campaign is represented by the *Xenien*, a collection of satirical distichs published in the Weimar *Musenalmanach auf das Jahr 1797*. The barbed epigrams of the *Xenien* provoked reprisals, and its publication did little to advance the aims of the authors. This classical movement, which Goethe and Schiller believed to be of the highest aesthetic and ethical value, represented a determined effort by a high-minded minority to convert authors and public, if necessary by browbeating, to a more elevated standard of taste. Such an authoritarian and esoteric attitude could hardly succeed even in eighteenth-century conditions. But at least the poetic writings of the two classical advocates reached a notable level of excellence, combining ideas, images and rhythm in a harmony which is controlled by unobtrusive discipline.

Friedrich Hölderlin (1770–1843)

If the classicism of Goethe and Schiller was a conviction rationally argued and intellectually defended (and so in a proper sense a product of the Enlightenment), that of Hölderlin was a profound emotional commitment and a mystic act of faith. Hölderlin's exalted, hypersensitive and vulnerable personality exposed him to stresses under which he broke down in his thirties, never fully to recover his sanity. Goethe's Greece was seen through the refractions of Roman antiquity, and Schiller's was an entirely intellectual construction. Hölderlin's classicism was a passionately cherished vision of a paradisal Antiquity to be revived in a new Heaven and a new Earth, and he expressed it with a command of classical measures so fluent and idiomatic that from his time these metres ceased to be exotic, becoming an accepted mode of German poetry. Some of his classical odes appeared in his novel *Hyperion* (1797–9) and some in magazines, but no volume of his poetry was published before 1826, by which time his mind had been clouded for twenty years. Hence his influence, immense in the late nineteenth and twentieth centuries, hardly affected his contemporaries. In addition to writing such accomplished yet moving classical poems as *Diotima*, *An die Parzen*, *Dichtermut*, *Menons Klagen um Diotima*, *Der Archipelagus* and *Brod und Wein*, Hölderlin raised to its highest pitch the form known as free verse (*freie Rhythmen*). It is a taxing, even intractable, form, since any flagging of tension causes it to lapse into the flattest prose; but the level of Hölderlin's inspiration is so uniformly high that his poems in this free verse, such as *Der Rhein*, *Am Quell der Donau*, *Patmos*, *Hälfte des Lebens*, are among his most sublime creations. In his later poems Christian elements are manifest, but the classical vision of a Germany transmuted into Hellas is a utopian sublimation of the highest aspirations of the Enlightenment.

THE LONGER FORMS

The earliest longer poem of note in the eighteenth century is *Die Alpen*, a descriptive poem by a Swiss patrician, Albrecht von Haller (1708–77), who later became professor of medicine at Göttingen University and a recognized authority in his field. The poem appeared in Haller's *Versuch Schweizerischer Gedichten* (1732), and was occasioned by an Alpine tour made in 1728. *Die Alpen*, comprising nearly 500 lines of alexandrine verse, opens up to poetry for the first time the landscape of forbidding peaks, sheer precipices and pathless valleys, hitherto shunned by poets and by tourists of the plains. It also initiated a fashion for descriptive poetry, of which, however, it remained the only notable example. More important is the way in which it foreshadows Rousseau. Haller is primarily interested in the tough, self-sufficient peasants of the Alpine valleys, and he contrasts their integrity and simplicity with the effete and corrupt civilization of the cities.

The authority of Aristotle (mostly seen in a French mirror) was valid for German writers through a large part of the eighteenth century, and it follows that epic poetry was conceived as the noblest genre. Yet serious epics were not numerous, and successful ones were few indeed. The 'discovery' of Milton's *Paradise Lost* provided the primary impulse. J. J. Bodmer of Zürich sang its praises and translated it into prose in 1732 as *Der Verlust des Paradieses.*[5] Among those inspired by Bodmer's eulogy and example was Klopstock, who, while still a schoolboy, made up his mind to compose the great biblical epic which German poetry lacked. *Der Messias*, written in classical hexameters, occupied Klopstock for more than a quarter of a century, but its tremendous impact came from the first three cantos, published in 1748. The acclamation with which they were received was accompanied by a sense of exultation that so great a poet should have arrived suddenly, in full majesty, on the scene of German literature. This famous poem, which is concerned with the Atonement and also depicts a conflict between the powers of Heaven and Hell, ending in the total rout of the latter, seems today to have appreciable *longueurs* and to be steeped in sentimentality. But the first three cantos revealed no tedium, and the public, weary with the desiccation of much rationalistic literature, was only too willing to share Klopstock's sentiment and to be moved by the figure of the repentant fallen angel Abbadona. Two cantos were added to make Volume One in 1751, but the full epic of twenty cantos was not completed until 1773, by which time it served rather for devotional than for poetic reading.

Klopstock did not lack imitators, and the most industrious of them was Bodmer, his one-time patron and friend, who published *Noah* in 1750 and several other biblical epics. C. M. Wieland (1733–1813), a later *protégé* of Bodmer, contributed *Der geprüfte Abraham* (1753) to the flood of so-called 'Patriarchaden'. The rival literary school of Gottsched countered with epics on subjects drawn from Germanic history, particularly *Hermann* (1751) and *Heinrich der Vogler* (1757), both by Baron C. O. von Schönaich (1725–1807), but none of the laboured productions of either side deserved or enjoyed the prestige of *Der Messias.*

Wieland, soon abandoning the religious vein, created a succession of light epic poems tinged with a rococo eroticism: *Idris und Zenide*

5. An earlier translation in 1681 went virtually unnoticed.

(1766), *Musarion* (1768), *Der neue Amadis* (1771), *Gandalin* (1776) and *Oberon* (1780). Of these the second and the last are outstanding examples. Wieland was not the first to exploit the comic epic, for as early as 1744 J. F. W. Zachariae (1726–77) had written an agreeable 'scherzhaftes Gedicht', *Der Renommist*, in which he deftly mocked both the preciosity of Leipzig manners and the boorishness affected by the students of Jena. Wieland, however, exactly blending humour and romance, wrote his light epics with an elegance and fluency which made them comparable with French works of similar character.

K. A. Kortum (1745–1824), in his 'Jobsiade' (*Leben, Meinungen und Taten des Hieronymus Jobs*, 1778), used the epic for broad and crude comedy, and the burlesque was attempted by A. Blumauer (1755–98) in *Virgils Äneis travestirt* (1783). Finally, Goethe made two attempts to write an epic, *Die Geheimnisse* in stanza form, (1783–4) and the strictly classical *Achilleis* (1799). Both remained fragments, and their abandonment betokens Goethe's recognition that the day of the epic was over.

Towards the end of the century, as the prospects of epic poetry faded, another classical form, the idyll, proved to be suitable to the habits of thought and feeling of the Enlightenment, as they had developed and modified with the growth of an extensive middle-class reading public. The leader in this field was J. H. Voss,[6] a schoolmaster in Eutin, who was a classical scholar well versed in the epic, having published a translation of the *Odyssey* in 1781 and of the *Iliad* in 1793. Voss made history in 1795 with his three-thousand line poem *Luise*, which he described as 'Ein ländliches Gedicht in drei Idyllen'. The three idylls were published separately in magazines and in the wrong order in 1783 and 1784, and the real impact of the poem dates from its publication in book form in 1795. It tells a simple tale of uneventful rural life, in which the birthday picnic of Luise, daughter of the pastor of Grünau, is the beginning of a courtship which ends with her marriage to young pastor Walter. It contains much realistic social detail and the setting, Grünau, is recognizably Malente in Holstein, but the picture is idealized, partly by Voss's careful selection of material and partly by the classical hexameters in which he tells the story. Voss wrote other idylls in hexameters, including *Der siebzigste Geburtstag* (1781), which some would rate above *Luise*, and *De*

6. See pp. 208f.

Winteravend (Low German for '*der Winterabend*'), which is notable for the combination of dialect with classical form. Also noteworthy is one of his earliest poems in this form, *Die Leibeigenen* (1776), in which he expresses his detestation of tyranny in a hexametrical dialogue between two serfs.

The outstanding idyll of the late eighteenth century is Goethe's *Hermann und Dorothea* (1797, in the *Taschenbuch für 1798*), though Voss thought *Luise* superior, an opinion not generally shared. *Hermann und Dorothea* has a topical background since it concerns the plight of a convoy of refugees fleeing from the French Revolution. Its concentrated action (limited to one day) consists essentially of the love at first sight of the innkeeper's son Hermann and the orphan refugee Dorothea, the opposition of his parents to the match, and their eventual ungrudging consent. Touching though this story is in itself, it is enhanced by deep compassion and by the effort to alleviate suffering to which both Hermann and Dorothea devote themselves. The poem, of slightly more than 2,000 hexameters, is divided into nine cantos, each dedicated to one of the Muses and bearing also a descriptive heading. It has been criticized for using Homeric means to tell a simple unheroic tale, but it may also be argued that the apparent disparity of means adds piquancy to the work and, further, that Goethe has, where necessary, imparted a winning quality to his hexameters. In its humanitarian outlook, its disciplined progress and its tenderness and grace it stands as a fitting monument to the measured compromise between reason and sentiment which the Enlightenment achieved.

FOUR

Italy

BETWEEN 1690 and 1800 – from the time of the foundation in Rome of the celebrated literary, social and cultural institution known as the Arcadian Academy to the end of the Period of Reforms a century later – lyric, didactic, satiric, mock-heroic, humorous and 'occasional' verse were all widely cultivated in Italy. The main verse forms and prosody employed were those of the sonnet, the ode (*canzone*), the *canzonetta*, the *septenarius*, the blank verse hendecasyllable (*verso sciolto*), *ottava rima*, *terza rima*, the *brindisi*, the dithyramb, the anacreontic, the epistle, the fable in verse and the epigram. At this time, verse, both rhymed and unrhymed, as distinct from prose, was also the favourite medium of the drama. The tragedies of Pier Jacopo Martello, the libretti of Pietro Metastasio for the *opera seria*, and the four Roman plays of Antonio Conti, for instance, are all in verse; as are Maffei's *Merope*, many popular comedies by Goldoni, and all the tragedies of Alfieri. Throughout the century there was also a significant production of dialect verse, especially in Milan, Venice and Sicily.

In the Age of Arcadia, when poetry in Italy was passing through a phase of late classicism, virtue in the creation of verse lay not in the cult of the 'marvellous' or in 'the spontaneous overflow of powerful feelings', but in the art of 'imitation' and of evocative quotation. The function of verse was to give pleasure and to be of use on the social level. Poets sought a return to the values of classical humanism, and to this end, for the expression of elevated thought and feeling in metre, the artistic traditions of the Renaissance were continually refined, rationalized and stylized. The Arcadian poets, therefore, in reaction against what was regarded as the 'bad taste', bombast and rhetoric of late Seicento trends, which were felt to have reduced poetry to confusion, looked less at the models provided by the conceits and verbal pyrotechnics of Giambattista Marino and turned for inspiration to a new range of authors in search of the 'simple' the 'musical' and the 'natural'. The result, for many years, was a spate of 'Arcadian' verses modelled on the poetry of Pindar, Anacreon and Theocritus amongst the Greeks; Virgil, Horace and Ovid amongst the Romans; and amongst the Italians, Petrarch, Sannazaro and the Neapolitan Petrarchists of the early Cinquecento. Some Arcadian verse was sweet and mannered in style; some of it was spirited; some more severely classical. Much of it was written to be set to music and sung. All of it was 'polite' and characterized by a notable limpidity of diction, metrical precision and musicality.

After 1740, and especially in the Period of Reforms, with the spread of the Enlightenment, and with the conflicting claims of neo-classic and pre-Romantic modes of thought, Italian poets turned their eyes increasingly towards foreign models. In this connection, the vogue for translations. at first from the English and French, and later from the German, was of seminal importance. Between 1742 and 1765 Pope's *Essay on Man* was rendered into Italian, both in prose and verse, on numerous occasions, and had a notable influence on the Italian Republic of Letters. The verse fables of John Gay, as well as those of La Fontaine, also achieved a wide circulation; as did the blank verse meditations of Edward Young, the polished 'sepulchral' and bardic poems of Thomas Gray, and the graceful idylls of the Swiss landscape painter-etcher Salomon Gessner. The most important document of Italian pre-Romanticism, however, which effected a revolution in taste, was the annotated translation in *versi sciolti* of James Macpherson's Ossianic fragments (1763–72) by the Paduan Melchiorre Cesarotti (1730–1808); the lugubrious sentiment and wild beauty of Ossian's poetry enjoyed an enormous vogue in Italy as elsewhere in Europe, influencing not only Vittorio Alfieri, Vincenzo Monti, Ippolito Pindemonte and Ugo Foscolo, but even such nineteenth-century poets as Leopardi, Tommaseo and Pascoli.

THE ARCADIANS

Arcadia took its name from the ancient and idealized rustic paradise in the mountainous regions of the Peloponnesus inhabited, in myth, by nymphs and shepherds. The Arcadian Academy, founded for the reform of Italian poetry from what were regarded as the excesses of the seventeenth-century style, was thus structured in the time and place of dream rather than of reality, and partook of the fantasies of the heroic and pastoral life played out in an ideal realm of values. Its emblem was the seven-piped syrinx of Pan surrounded by a garland of pine and laurel; its tutelary deity, the Infant Jesus. On aggregation, members were accorded the title to a symbolic three measures of land in Arcady and a pastoral designation, or academic name, to be used at all assemblies.

Arcadia was founded by a coterie of fourteen gentlemen, belonging mainly to the legal profession and to the ranks of the higher clergy, who had previously been members of the famous Roman salon of Queen Christina of Sweden. Two of the most influential of these were both doctors of law: Giovan Mario Crescimbeni (1663–1728) of Macerata, a priest who served the academy for thirty-eight years as its first keeper, or secretary-general (*custode*); and Gian Vincenzo Gravina (1664–1718), a Roman jurist, playwright and literary theorist, born at Roggiano in Calabria, who is especially remembered for his influential treatise *Della ragion poetica* (1708), concerning the origins and nature of poetry.

Crescimbeni ('Alfesibèo Cario' in Arcadia), was an indefatigable, but vainglorious pedant who became canon and eventually dean of the chapter in Santa Maria in Cosmedin. In 1695 he published his first book of *Rime*; and in 1697 the *Istoria della volgar poesia*, the first history of poetry in the language. He later brought out the *Vite degli Arcadi illustri* (1707–28), in five volumes, and the first nine volumes of the collected *Rime degli Arcadi* (1713–22). Four further official volumes of Arcadian verse were issued between 1747 and 1780.

Like Crescimbeni, Gravina ('Opico Erimantèo') spent more than twenty years furthering the aims of Arcadia. In 1696 he drafted ten laws, the *Leges Arcadum*, in archaic Latin, which were sculpted in marble and set up in the gardens on the Palatine belonging to the duke of Parma, where at that time the academy was accustomed to meet. The austere Gravina, however, far more than Crescimbeni, who was primarily interested in matters of literary taste, was a philosopher of severely classical stamp. He felt the need for a broad and far-reaching cultural renewal in all aspects of Italian life: not only in poetry, but in the moral, political and civil spheres as well. As a result, in 1711, a split developed in the ranks of Arcadia. Gravina seceded, taking with him more than twenty of his fellow academicians; and in 1714, with his young protégés Paolo Rolli and Pietro Metastasio, the principal lyric poets of the so-called second generation of Arcadia, he founded the rival, if short-lived Accademia Quirina.

Other founder-members of Arcadia were Silvio Stampiglia ('Palemone Licurio', 1664–1725) who later became Poet Laureate at the imperial court in Vienna, and Giambattista Felice Zappi ('Tirsi Leucasio', 1667–1719) of Imola, an assessor in the agricultural courts in Rome, who was one of the most representative poets in the early life of the academy.

Membership of Arcadia was open to any person of good family who was likely to bring it honour and renown. It was thought desirable that members should have reached the age of twenty-four, and be recognized as persons of learning. Lady members were also required to practise the art of poetry or some other aspect of humane letters. From the outset Arcadia enjoyed the favour of the Popes and the patronage of a notable succession of princely benefactors. Between 1690 and 1700 'colonies' of Arcadia, affiliated to the parent body in Rome, were established in Arezzo, Macerata, Camaldoli, Venice, Bologna and Ferrara; and such was Arcadia's phenomenal appeal in polite and cultured circles that between 1700 and 1740 further 'colonies' were instituted in most towns and cities throughout the length and breadth of the peninsula.

The first generation of Arcadia included among its members a number of scientists, lawyers, philosophers and mathematicians of literary inclination, who in age were either contemporaries of the founders of the academy or men of the older generation of established reputation. In the eighteenth century its membership embraced, besides the main Arcadian poets, many of the most distinguished men and women of science and letters, innumerable ecclesiastics and a high proportion of the Italian nobility.

Arcadia usually met in Rome seven times a year between 1 May and 7 October; small private gatherings might be arranged at any time. Each meeting was held in the open air and in a location which, wherever it might be, was designated the 'Parrhasian Grove' ('Bosco Parrasio'). Six of these assemblies were for the members in Rome; the seventh was reserved for those from other parts of Italy. Until 1725 the academy had no regular place of assembly. It first met at San

Pietro in Montorio on the Janiculum. The throng was so great, however, that subsequent meetings were held in the gardens of the duke of Paganico at San Pietro in Vincoli, where the poet-academicians, we are told, recited their compositions, some seated on the ground, others on rocks. Later assemblies met in the Palazzo dei Riari, now Corsini, and in the grounds of villas on the Palatine, Esquiline and Aventine. Finally, in 1725, a permanent seat was acquired, when a theatre and amphitheatre were constructed on the Janiculum, through the munificence of John V of Portugal.

At four-yearly intervals, at times calculated on the basis of the ancient Greek Olympiad, Arcadia organized elaborate ceremonies on the lines of the Olympic Games. These contests were not displays of athletic prowess, but of poetic skills, the winners of which were crowned with the laurel wreath at the first full moon next to the summer solstice after the end of each Olympiad. To preserve the semblance of social equality at these contests the Arcadians appeared masked and used only their academic names. During the contests they recited their compositions. At ordinary assemblies the chief of these was a discourse, on any theme, couched in pastoral guise. Each poet-academician then recited two eclogues of his own composition, one in Latin, the other in the vernacular; after which he might present an original lyric in one of the standard poetic forms. At the 'Olympic Games', however, the presentation of the compositions was strictly regulated in five main sections containing respectively a short discourse, eclogues, odes, sonnets, madrigals and epigrams.

Attempts to classify the Arcadian poets have at times been made on the basis of the subject-matter of their verses, their tendency to imitate a particular set of preferred models, or in relation to their use of specific metrical forms. Two of these, the sonnet and the madrigal, are often regarded as typical of the first or early phase of Arcadia; the *canzonetta* of the second phase; and the *verso sciolto* most characteristic of the third. Within the vast production of Arcadian verse, however, it is difficult, if not impossible, to generalize, since individual versifiers tended to compose in a variety of idioms and in any of the accepted poetic forms.

Poets characteristic of the first phase of Arcadia were Giovan Mario Crescimbeni, Giambattista Zappi and his wife Faustina Maratti Zappi ('Aglauro Cidonia'), all of whom lived in Rome, and

Eustachio Manfredi ('Aci Delpusiano'), mathematician and director of the astronomical observatory in the University of Bologna, the first edition of whose *Rime* came out in 1713. Each of these poets took the sonnets and *canzoni* of Petrarch as a model. Manfredi, especially, was regarded by his contemporaries as the most Petrarchizing of the Arcadians and the restorer of the Petrarchan tradition in its purest and most limpid form, as for example in the ode '*Donna, negli occhi vostri*', which is based on three *canzoni* in praise of Madonna Laura. Crescimbeni, however, was also influenced by Gabriello Chiabrera of Savona, the sixteenth-century author of innumerable light and sprightly verses, including the *canzonetta*. His first book of *Rime* (1695) is a miscellaneous selection of sonnets, madrigals, *capitoli*, *canzoni*, *canzonette*, *brindisi* and dithyrambs, in which love is a winged Cupid, his lady is compared to the sun, and her eyes dart rays. The taste of Giambattista Zappi was also eclectic. His verses are characterized by brilliance, rococo delicacy and sweetness, and they tend to oscillate between reminiscences of Seicento styles and the newer fashions. In contrast, the verses of Faustina Maratti Zappi, daughter of the painter-etcher Carlo Maratti, were more firmly set, like those of Manfredi, in the Petrarchan mould. They tell, in plangent and melancholy strains, of her love for her husband and of her grief after his death.

The most distinguished poets of the second generation of Arcadia were Paolo Antonio Rolli ('Eulibio Brentiatico'), Carlo Innocenzo Frugoni ('Comante Eginetico'), a Genoese by birth and a founder-member of the Brescian colony of Arcadia, and Pietro Metastasio ('Artino Corasio'). Rolli and Metastasio, both of whom were early befriended by Gravina in Rome, experienced the break with Crescimbeni and the foundation of the Accademia Quirina. Subsequently they spent much of their lives abroad: Rolli in England, from 1715 to 1744, and Metastasio in Vienna, from 1730 to 1782. Frugoni, who has been described as 'il più andante e disponibile, quanto esperto, artigiano rimatore della matura Arcadia' (C. Muscetta), made his name as court poet of the fashionable intelligentsia at Parma: the little duchy, first of the Farnese, then of the Bourbons, which was often regarded as the 'Athens of Italy'.

As a young man Rolli studied law in the studio of Giambattista Zappi. With his gift for improvising verses, and singing them to his own accompaniment, he soon became a favourite in fashionable circles. In 1715 he attracted the attention of Lord Pembroke, the English Maecenas and patron of the arts, who invited him to London, where he became Italian tutor at court and, in 1720, operatic librettist to the Royal Academy of Music. In London, where he worked for some thirty years, Rolli took a leading part in the Italianization of English taste. He composed the opera *Numitore* (1720) which was set to music by Giovanni Porta; and during the next quarter of a century he wrote more than a dozen verse libretti which were set by Handel, Bononcini, and other operatic composers working for the London stage. He also translated English works into Italian and edited the Italian classics for the English market. In 1716 he brought out the *Satire* and *Rime* of Ariosto; and these were followed by attractive and well-edited editions of works by Guarino, Berni, Firenzuola, Aretino and Lorenzo the Magnificent. His partial translation of *Paradise Lost* came out in 1735; and this was succeeded by Italian versions of the *Odes* of Anacreon (1739) and the *Bucolics* of Virgil. In 1744, while still active in his multifarious literary activities, Rolli left London for Italy and spent the rest of his life at Todi in Umbria.

As an original poet Rolli wrote with characteristic afflatus in a variety of styles. He modelled his verses, which were often intended to be sung, in part on the metres of Anacreon and Catullus, in part on Lucretius, and also on Horace and Martial. He had a taste for natural scenery, for female beauty and for mythological transformations; and he strove to capture a classical clarity and sensibility of expression. He is at his best in his drinking songs (*brindisi*), in some ninety-five epigrams referring with acute observation to his life in London, and in such pieces as the *canzonetta* '*La neve è alla montagna*' and the ode '*Solitario bosco ombroso*'. His first volume of *Rime*, which rendered him famous, came out in London in 1717, dedicated to Baron Bathurst, the distinguished statesman and generous patron of the poets and wits of the day. It was followed in 1727 by two equally celebrated volumes of *Canzonette* and *Cantate*. But it was not until 1753 that Rolli's collected *Poetici componimenti* were brought out in Venice in three volumes. These contained not only the early odes on amorous subjects, the elegies, *canzonette*, hendecasyllables, sonnets and cantatas, together with all the *melodrammi*, but also a notable new sequence of convivial rhymes known, after St Mary-le-bone, as the *Meriboniane*, and the *Tudertine*, a set of lyrics composed at Todi, in which the poet expressed his relief at returning to the Italian countryside after living for so long in London. The pungent *Marziale in Albion* was not published until 1776, more than a decade after Rolli's death.

Like Rolli, Pietro Metastasio also left Rome while still a young man. After the death of Gravina, in 1719, he went to Naples where he became the *protégé* of the operatic singer Marianna Bulgarelli, who introduced him to the leading exponents of the Neapolitan *opera seria*: the young male soprano Carlo Broschi, known as Farinelli, and the composers Niccola Porpora, Leonardo Vinci and Johann Adolph Hasse. Eleven years later, by which time he had himself become an accomplished poet, and the author of several lyric dramas, Metastasio left Italy for Vienna where he was invited to succeed Apostolo Zeno as Poet Laureate to the Austrian imperial court: a post which he held until the end of his life during the reigns first of the emperor Charles VI and later of the empress Maria Theresa.

The main poetic achievement of Metastasio lies in his sequence of operatic libretti, many of which were commissioned by the emperor to mark such recurrent state occasions as royal birthdays and weddings.[1] The lyricism and musicality of the arias and *ariette* in these heroic spectacles is likewise to be found in the considerable quantity of *canzonette*, *terzine*, *stanze* and epithalamia Metastasio also produced, and for which he has long been acclaimed as the foremost exponent of Arcadian lyricism.

A typical example of the Metastasian *canzonetta* is *La primavera*, written in Rome in 1719, addressed to a heartless young lady referred to, in pastoral guise, as 'Fille'. The poem consists of nine strophes of *settenari* arranged in coupled quatrains on a simple rhyme scheme (abbc–defc). In the poem, we are told, spring is returning 'Col suo fiorito aspetto': 'Già il grato zeffiretto/Scherza fra l'erbe e i fior.' Everywhere new life is bursting forth: on the mountains, in the fields, in the sea. But in the heart of the poet no new life is to be found, or any peace. The poet has sung the charms of Fille, but she has rejected him; he feels true love for her, but she is disdainful; he wants to be avenged for the wrongs she has done him, but he craves her pardon and he is content to be her slave. In *La primavera* the coldness of Fille is set in poignant contrast to the quickening of Nature. Yet the festive rebirth of spring and the frigidity and harshness of Fille are not set in

1. See pp. 289–95.

simple contrast. Underlying the poem is the poet's disquiet and sense of lurking danger. The presentation of spring itself is not without its ambiguities. It hovers between frost and the promise of new life: between bud and blight. The fields are bedecked with flowers, but they will be 'violated' by the cruel ploughshare. The swallow will fly to its nest; but it will be snared by the insidious bird-catcher.

Other typical Metastasian lyrics are *L'estate* (1724), *La libertà* (1733), *Palinodia a Nice* (1746) and *La partenza* (1746). All of these were written in lively strophes of *settenari* or *ottenari* arranged, like *La primavera*, in coupled quatrains according to a set rhyme scheme. In *L'estate* the poet dreams of accompanying Fille through the glories of Nature in summer-time until a ripe old age. The other three *canzonette* all refer to a certain 'Nice'.

The degree of involvement of Metastasio himself in the gallant sentiments expressed in his *canzonette* is, of course, a matter of doubt. They seem personal; but *La libertà* was in fact written at the request of Don Carlo Sanseverino in relation to Princess Strongoli. It should not be read in any sense as a personal statement. All the poems were designed to be set to music. *La libertà* was arranged as a cantata for soprano with string accompaniment; and the first two stanzas of *La partenza* were later used by Beethoven for his *Canzone per canto*.

In 1725 Carlo Innocenzo Frugoni gained the patronage of the cultured Farnese family, who were princes of Parma; but after the change in fortunes of the Farnese during the War of the Austrian Succession he lived for a time in Venice, where he was befriended by Algarotti. In 1748, when, by the peace of Aix-la-Chapelle, the duchy of Parma became a Bourbon possession in the hands of Philip, son of Philip V of Spain and Elizabetta Farnese, Frugoni returned to Parma, under the patronage of the duke and his minister Du Tillot. He spent the rest of his life there working in the multiple role of tutor to the young princes, director of the court theatre, Poet Laureate and secretary of the Academy of Fine Arts.

The name of Frugoni, unlike that of Rolli and Metastasio, is often associated with the *verso sciolto*, a type of unrhymed hendecasyllabic verse which became especially fashionable in Italy after the publication of *Versi sciolti di tre eccellenti autori* (Venice, 1757), a collection of occasional verses published anonymously by Frugoni, Algarotti and the Jesuit Saverio Bettinelli. Nowadays Frugoni's *versi sciolti* are little remembered; but he is still esteemed for some of his enormous output of rhymed verse in the form of *canzonette*, *carmi eroici*, odes and sonnets, in which he exploited to the full the rhythmical variety of the Arcadian style. Three typical poems are the *Navigazione di Amore* (1723) and the *Ritorno dalla Navigazione d'Amore* (1729) – on gallant themes recalling Watteau's 'Embarquement pour l'Isle de Cythère' – and the powerful, strident sonnet '*Ferocemente la visiera bruna*' (1767), in which the poet strikingly delineates Hannibal's first glimpse of Italy as he came over the Alps.

POETRY IN THE PERIOD OF REFORMS

Rolli, Frugoni and Metastasio all lived until well into the second half of the eighteenth century; and during their lifetime lyric verse of a predominantly Arcadian stamp continued to prosper. The Arcadian academy and its 'colonies' still attracted wide membership and a phenomenon of the period was the production of *Raccolte*, or 'Garlands of Verse', which, though often adversely criticized, became extremely fashionable. Throughout the century, all over Italy, no function or ceremony – the festival of a confraternity, a monk or nun taking the habit, a thesis or collegiate act – was complete without the production of a sonnet, or set of verses, to mark the occasion. With the gradual diffusion of the Enlightenment, however, with renewed interest in the classical world and especially with the discovery of English and German literature, Italian verse began to show unmistakable signs of new life. Didactic and philosophical poetry increased; satire, reflecting the most powerful impulses of the period, flourished with such poets as Giuseppe Parini, Gasparo and Carlo Gozzi, Giambattista Casti and the Sicilian dialect poet Giovanni Meli; while in the last decades of the century the lyric itself was transformed, through the assimilation of pre-Romantic modes, in the hands of Aurelio Bertola and Ippolito Pindemonte.

An early example of the eighteenth-century philosophical poem was *Aristippo*, a little-known work in *versi sciolti* published anonymously in Venice in 1744. Its author was Zaccaria Seriman (1709–84), the Venetian journalist and man of letters who later wrote *I viaggi di*

Enrico Wanton (4 vols., 1749–64), a witty and perceptive satire, couched in the manner of *Gulliver's Travels* in the popular form of an imaginary voyage to the 'Terra Australis Incognita'. In *Aristippo*, which was Seriman's first published work, the poet reveals how he has been transported in a dream to the Elysian Fields, where he has conversed with the ancient philosophers of the Cyrenaic school. He professes a cautious epicureanism, defines the correct use of intellect – too often misemployed by man – as a virile and powerful guide which 'ci conduca ad investigare il vero', and discusses the nature of happiness and of spiritual tranquillity.

In the 1740s didactic verse on agriculture and allied themes began to be produced, especially by a number of poets who lived in the Venetian provinces. Poetry of this type was often linked ideally to the Georgic tradition stemming from Virgil's work on husbandry and its sixteenth-century Italian derivatives, such as *Le api* (1539, written in 1524) by Giovanni Rucellai and Luigi Alemanni's *La coltivazione dei campi* (1546).

A good example of this type of didactic verse was *La coltivazione del riso* by Giambattista Spolverini (1695–1762) of Verona, whose interest in this subject arose from the fact that he was a gentleman farmer with estates at Campeggio, near Lake Garda, part of which consisted of rice fields. His poem, which is in *versi sciolti*, deals in four books with the husbandry of rice and provides an elegant portrayal of an industrious rural community from the point of view of a cultured nobleman whose main interest lies in the wise management and improvement of his estates, Spolverini wrote *La coltivazione del riso* at Malcesine (Garda) during the leisure of a period of public office. He had virtually completed it by 1746; but he continually revised the poem for more than a decade. It was first published in 1758.

Similar didactic poems were *Il canapaio* (1741) in eight books, on the cultivation of hemp, by Girolamo Baruffaldi (1675–1755) of Ferrara, a region noted for this product; *Il baco da seta* (1756) by Zaccaria Betti (1732–88); *La coltivazione dei monti* (1778) by Bartolomeo Lorenzi (1732–1822), professor of rhetoric in the seminary of Verona; and numerous works by the Jesuit Giovanni Battista Roberti (1719–86).

Zaccaria Betti, a friend of G. B. Spolverini, was a member of the Academy of Agriculture, Arts and Commerce in Verona, and also of the Georgofili in Florence. He devoted his time to the improvement of agriculture in his region and wrote numerous treatises on the subject. *Il baco da seta*, which is divided into four books, and accompanied by a wealth of erudite annotation, is designed to stress the value and usefulness of the silk-worm as the precious source of the rich agricultural economy of the Verona region.

Giovanni Battista Roberti wrote *Le fragole* (1752) and *Le perle* (1756). The former, which is in *ottava rima*, dealt with the cultivation of strawberries; the latter with the formation and fishery of pearls. Other didactic poems by Roberti include *La moda* (1746) and *La commedia* (1755), in defence of Goldoni's dramatic reforms.

In Milan the most distinguished poet who came to the fore in the years of the movement for civil, economic and cultural reform associated with the Lombard Enlightenment was Giuseppe Parini (1729–99), a countryman of sound good sense and a classical scholar who revered tradition, but who also felt the marked contrasts and injustices in the world about him. Parini, the son of an artisan silk-trader, was born at Bosisio, a village near Lake Pusiano (*il vago Eupili*) in the Brianza. While still a boy he was sent to Milan to live with his great-aunt, who on her death in 1741 left him a modest inheritance. Between 1740 and 1752 he studied with the Barnabites at the Arcimboldi schools, maintaining himself, at least in part, by copying manuscripts. In 1754 he took minor orders, adopted the title of *Abate*, and entered the household of Duke Gabrio Serbelloni where, until 1762, he was employed as a tutor.

During these years Parini engaged in a variety of literary activities. In 1752 he published pseudonymously *Prime poesie di Ripano Eupilino*, a set of eighty-six sonnets, some serious, some in the burlesque style, three *capitoli*, an epistle in *versi sciolti* and three piscatorial eclogues. As might be expected, this first volume of Parini's verses was markedly Arcadian in style, showing the influence on the one hand of Petrarch and on the other of the Tuscan Renaissance poet Francesco Berni. It gained him admittance, however, as a young poet of promise, to Count Giuseppe Maria Imbonati's reformed Accademia dei Trasformati, an elevated and enlightened group where he met such men as the young Pietro Verri, the Milanese dialect poets Domenico Balestrieri and Carlo Tanzi and the satirist Gian Carlo Passeroni.

In this environment Parini participated assiduously. Between 1756 and 1760 he engaged in two literary polemics: one concerning the *questione della lingua*, with Alessandro Bandiera (1756); the other defending the use of dialect in verse, with the purist Onofrio Branda (1760). In 1757 he also wrote, for the delectation of the Trasformati, the *Dialogo sopra la nobiltà*: an 'imaginary conversation' between a humble Poet and a Nobleman of ancient lineage and astounding pretensions, who by mischance find themselves buried together in the same tomb. The fantastic dialogue that ensues concerns the origins, rights and privileges of the aristocracy; and in it, with the wit and incisive vigour of a Jonathan Swift, the Poet gradually strips the Nobleman of his prejudices, showing him to have been blinded by false education and traditional assumptions, while revealing the positive virtues and obligations of an aristocracy of merit.

The moral and satirical attitudes embodied in the *Dialogo sopra la nobiltà*, which spring from Parini's humane awareness of a scale of values inherent, not in the rights of blood, but in the natural equality of men, the dignity of labour and of family life, are also to be found in his most extensive and important work, *Il giorno*, a satire in *versi sciolti* in four books in which, through the masterly use of irony, the poet castigates the vanity and profligacy of a social caste that has lost its function, under the pretext of instructing a languid young patrician (the 'Giovin Signore') how to beguile the tedium of his day and comport himself according to the rites of the *beau monde*.

The first two parts of *Il giorno*, entitled *Mattino* and *Mezzogiorno*, were published in 1763 and 1765 respectively.

In *Mattino*, after the dedication and proposition, and a reference to the artisans and the farm-labourers who have been hard at work in the fields since daybreak, the book begins with the 'Giovin Signore' waking up in the downy softness of his feather bed. Still exhausted from the round of pleasure of the previous evening – at the dinner party, the receptions, the gaming tables, and the theatre – he gives a little yawn and gently rubs the sleep from his eyes. His page brings him a cup of hot chocolate and he is then ready to receive his first visitors – the tailor, the dancing master, the French master and the violin master – to dismiss his creditors and to hold his levee. He then proceeds to the most elaborate ritual of the day, that of getting dressed. As the barber attends to his hair, he glances at the erotic illustrations and bindings of his favourite books, the rococo publications of eighteenth-century France. Then, like Achilles going into battle, he enters the powder room. After this, passing beneath the stern, reproving gaze of his forbears, he descends from the picture gallery, between the serried ranks of servants, to where his coach awaits. As he settles back on the cushions, with a taciturn, surly look, his coachman whips up the horses, and the *Mattino* ends with a searing vision of the contrast between the 'Giovin Signore' and the Pleb, and the savage spectacle of streaks of blood on the road where people were so foolish as not to get out of the way of the coach's flying wheels.

In *Mezzogiorno* the 'Giovin Signore' visits the lady of whom, in accordance with the sophisticated social codes of the period, he is the *cavalier servente*. Parini now introduces a charming satirical verse fable to explain the curious divorce between Love and Marriage in the patrician class. After which the 'Giovin Signore' leads his mistress to the dinner table, where the principal episodes of the *Mezzogiorno* are set. At table the 'Giovin Signore' occupies a place of honour among the other guests, whose appearance, phobias, obsessions and conversation provide the occasion for a wealth of critical ridicule of the current attitudes of fashionable cosmopolitanism, philosophism and mercantilistic economic theory. When the guests pass into the coffee-room, the beggars outside cluster round the doors and windows, waiting for the remnants of the meal.

In 1762, just before the publication of *Mattino*, Parini was dismissed from his post in the Serbelloni household; after which he passed through a period of hardship. Subsequently, he secured the patronage of Count Carlo di Firmian, the Austrian Imperial Minister in Lombardy, for whom he edited *La Gazzetta di Milano* (1768). In 1769 Parini, again sponsored by Count Firmian, was appointed professor of Greek and Latin in the Palatine Schools and subsequently at the Brera. When Mozart visited the city in 1771, he was commissioned to write *Ascanio in Alba*, a 'festa teatrale', set by the fifteen-year-old composer, to celebrate the wedding of the Archduke Ferdinand of Austria and Maria Beatrice d'Este. At the end of the century Parini, like Pietro Verri, took part for a time in the civic administration of the capital under the French.

Throughout these later decades Parini continued to compose *Il giorno*. It seems that he first intended to complete the satire with a third part only, *La sera*. But later this was split into two books, entitled *Vespro* and *Notte*, on which he continued to work until the time of his death; he also went on correcting and changing *Mattino* and *Mezzogiorno*, without ever deciding to publish the work as a whole. As a result *Vespro* and *Notte* were not published until 1801, when they first appeared, in fragmentary form, edited by Parini's friend, Francesco Reina.

In *Vespro*, which opens with an enchanting description of dusk and closes with an equally majestic account of nightfall, the main subjects dealt with are the ceremonial visits of the 'Giovin Signore' and the turn he takes with his mistress in their coach on the *Corso*. In *Notte*, the scene is the reception in a nobleman's palace and the subsequent gaming. The episode of the visit to the theatre, which was to have completed the satire was never written.

The protagonist of *Il giorno*, the 'Giovin Signore', is a languid and effete caricature creation reminiscent of some dissolute young aristocrat drawn from a print by Hogarth, rather than a character based on any specific Milanese nobleman of the period. *Il giorno* is not, however, merely an exercise in critical ridicule, but a true satire built on the moral and social contrast between the worlds of the 'Giovin Signore' and, on the one hand, that of the 'umil volgo' and, on the other, that of the protagonist's own aristocratic forebears. The imagery of the poem, especially that of the first two books, is precise and fully realized; the tone is flickering and ironic. To modern taste the style may seem excessively Latinized; but the whole poem has a moral intensity and vigour and sense of profound indignation and contained outrage that is barely kept in check. *Mattino* and *Mezzogiorno*, especially, are characterized by a Dantesque vigour of utterance; in *Vespro* and *Notte*, however, the animus which lies behind the verse is less intense, and the imagery is less powerfully charged.

Apart from *Il giorno*, Parini composed nineteen sage and measured odes, over the span of some forty years, which reflect in their variety and didactic aim the poet's civil, social and aesthetic adherence to aspects of the illuministic and neo-classic currents of his day. In them, two principal phases, consisting of eight and eleven poems respectively, may be distinguished: the first referring to the poems which were composed between *c.*1756 and 1777; the second to those belonging to the years 1783 to 1795.

In one of the earlier group of poems, *La salubrità dell'aria* (*c.* 1756–9), the poet contrasted the pollution, typical of the city, with the bracing air of the countryside, and defended recent measures introduced for the improvement of urban sanitation in Milan. In *L'educazione* (1764), which was written to mark the eleventh birthday of his pupil Carlo Imbonati, he offered advice on the education of the young. Not having any other gifts to bring, except the wisdom of the precepts in which he imagines Chiron the Centaur to have schooled Achilles, Parini propounds a programme of moral and physical education designed to promote the harmonious development of a healthy mind in a healthy body. In *L'innesto del vaiuolo* (1765) he praises, in the face of religious opposition, the enlightened and successful medical practice of variolation, at that time just gaining ground in Milan through the writings of Dr Gian Maria Bicetti (1708–78), a graduate of the University of Pavia, to whom the ode is dedicated. In *La musica* (1769) he deplores the long-standing practice of infant eviration as the means of producing male sopranos for the *opera seria*. In *La laurea* (1777), occasioned by the award of a degree in jurisprudence at Pavia to Maria Pellegrina Amoretti, he defends the rights of women in the sphere of higher education.

After *La laurea* several years were to pass before Parini again wrote in the form of the ode. Probably late in 1783, however, he composed *La recita dei versi*, on the use and abuse of declamation; and this was followed by the sequence of great odes of the second phase in which, while maintaining his habitual moral integrity, the poet seems to withdraw to some extent from his habitual involvement with the world about him. Some of these odes are still concerned with 'civil' and 'social' themes; others are more personal or deal with aesthetic questions.

On the 'personal' side, *La caduta* (1785) is of special interest: Parini, a cripple since childhood, has tripped over in the street. He is helped by a passer-by who, when he recognizes him, chides him because he ekes out a wretched, impoverished existence. Why does not Parini, the distinguished poet and noted classical scholar, take a leaf out of the book of many a poetaster who knows how to deploy his meagre talents to his best advantage? But Parini scorns such advice; and he indignantly traces the figure of his ideal citizen.

Turning to musical matters again, in *In morte del maestro Sacchini* (1786), Parini defended the good name of Antonio Sacchini, mediator in the polemics between the followers of Gluck and of Nicola Piccini, against charges of immorality. In *La gratitudine* (1790–91), he thanks Cardinal Angelo Maria Durini for placing a bust of Parini among the effigies of other famous men in his villa at Mirabellino, near Monza. In *Il messaggio* (1793), the ageing poet expresses his respect and admiration for the attractive young Countess Maria di Castelbarco, who had solicitously inquired if he had recovered from his illness during the winter of 1793. In *Sul vestire alla ghigliottina* (1795) – also known as *A Silvia* – he gently chides a perverse young lady of his acquaintance for adopting the grotesque garb, known as *à la victime*, which became fashionable in Paris during the Revolutionary period, in the aftermath of the Reign of Terror.

Parini's last Ode, *Alla Musa* (1795), was written for the Milanese patrician Febo d'Adda, a poet and former pupil of the master, who had recently married. In it Parini's aesthetic ideals, in their ultimate, neo-classic, evolution, are adumbrated. It is suggested that through his devotion to his wife, who is expecting her first child, the marquis has been neglecting his Muse. But the Muse herself intervenes. She admonishes Parini and reveals how the two loves of his old pupil are not incompatible and can easily be reconciled in symbolic association.

Apart from his poetry Parini in his later years also wrote a number of theoretical works defining, in the footsteps of Horace and the doctrines of eighteenth-century neo-classicism, the principles of art and letters, according to which he envisages poetry as 'l'arte d'imitare o di dipingere in versi le cose in modo chè sien mossi gli affetti di chi legge od ascolta, acciocché ne nasca diletto'.

Lyric, didactic, satirical and mock-heroic verse, in both Italian and in regional dialect, can be found in the work of a number of other interesting poets who flourished in the second half of the eighteenth century. Important regional centres were Milan and Venice: the former, the hub of the Lombard Enlightenment; the latter, an ageing state, constricted by outworn economic, political and social structures, but also the 'playground of Europe', to which visitors flocked.

In Milan, Gian Carlo Passeroni (1713–1803), a friend and benefactor of Parini, ridiculed the follies of contemporary Italian life in a curious burlesque composed in *ottava rima* entitled *Il cicerone* (6 vols., 1755–74). This vast poem, which was characterized by interminable satirical digressions, purported to be a translation in verse from an ancient manuscript life of the famous orator and commentator, Marcus Tullius, who was in the thick of the drama surrounding the death throes of the Roman Republic.

Throughout the eighteenth century several notable dialect poets flourished in Venice. Among these may be mentioned the patricians Angelo Maria Labia (1709–75), Giovanni Pozzobon (1713–85) and Angelo Maria Barbaro (1726–79). The most ill-famed was Giorgio Alvise Baffo (1694–1768), the last scion of an ancient patrician family and a patron of Casanova, whose sonnets, madrigals and *canzonette* constitute a corpus of the most impudently lubricious verse to have been produced by an eighteenth-century poet of distinction with the gift for spontaneity and a natural felicity of expression. Generally Baffo's verses circulated in private; and they enjoyed an enormous success. In some of his longer *canzoni* he lightly satirized the insidiously attractive venality of his native city.

Venetian poets of a more literary and respectable character than Baffo were Gasparo and Carlo Gozzi: two brothers of noble family, with markedly different personalities.

Gasparo Gozzi (1713–86), editor of the *Gazzetta Veneta* and the *Osservatore Veneto*,[2] was a professional man of letters, of humanistic tastes and moderately reformatory outlook who, besides his journalistic undertakings, composed nineteen blank verse *Sermoni*, or Horatian epistles (1750–82), Twelve of these, first published singly during the previous thirteen years, came out in a collected edition in 1763, with the false imprint of Bologna. The *Sermoni* are, in most instances, addressed to individual recipients. They are conversational in tone and elegant in diction; shrewd, contemplative and politely ironical. They have often been described as the foremost examples of *versi sciolti* to have been written in Italy prior to the verses of Parini. In some of the *Sermoni* (*Il gusto d'oggidì in poesia*, *La vera poesia*) Gozzi dealt with literary themes, especially with the nature of poetry, which he did not regard as a casual, or off-the-cuff activity, but as a serious intellectual pursuit, which demanded hard study. Other poems concern the misfortunes of their author, In one, first published in 1755 Gozzi courteously requested the publisher Zaccaria Seriman, author of *Aristippo* and the *Viaggi di Enrico Wanton*, to defend him from the

2. See pp. 133–5.

savage attacks of the literary critics. In another, published in 1760, he asked Marco Foscarini, procurator of St Mark's, to sponsor his appointment to the chair of Greek and Latin at the University of Pavia. The best of Gozzi's *Sermoni* are those in which he genially observed the effeminacy, the pretensions, and the general moral laxity of his fellow-citizens.

While Gasparo Gozzi was composing his *Sermoni*, his younger brother Carlo Gozzi (1720–1806)[3] was writing *Marfisa bizzarra*, a mock-heroic poem in twelve cantos, in *ottava rima*, which took its name from the fantastic warrior maiden whose singular exploits in the wars of Charlemagne were first narrated by Boiardo in *Orlando innamorato* and subsequently by Ariosto in *Orlando furioso*. In *Marfisa bizzarra*, however, the protagonist is no longer, as originally, simply a beautiful, good-natured, impetuous virago. An aged spinster, she has now become hysterical and eccentric in affairs of the heart – through living on values imbibed from her study of eighteenth-century books! Filonoro, her *cavaliere*, is a sort of Casanova, who is induced by Marfisa to embark on a thousand madcap adventures. The emperor is in his dotage; Rinaldo is a drunkard; and the other paladins of Charlemagne are old and corrupt. Religion and the heroic spirit have both been destroyed. The family is in decay; and adultery, which is everywhere prevalent, is a sign of sophistication. Eventually the state is sold to a foreign power; the Saracens pour in, and universal panic ensues. *Marfisa bizzarra* is full of allusions to contemporary figures and events. And apart from the general satire of contemporary society, which is threatened with extinction through the spread of 'enlightenment' and of subversive modes of thought, Gozzi's shafts of ridicule and wit are especially directed against the playwrights Pietro Chiari and Carlo Goldini, who figure in the poem as paladins of Charlemagne under the names of Marco and Matteo. The first ten cantos of *Marfisa bizzarra* were written in 1761; the last two in 1768, after Gozzi had been impressed and encouraged by the success of Parini's *Mattino* and *Mezzogiorno*, works of satire for which he professed a profound admiration. It was published in 1772 with a dedication to Caterina Dolfin Tron.

Satirists of a younger generation than the Gozzi brothers, the publication of whose works stretched into the Napoleonic period, were

3. See also pp. 318–24.

Giambattista Casti (1724–1803), a brilliant and bold-hearted man of great imaginative power, born at Acquapendente, near the Lake of Bolsena, in the Papal States, the Tuscan Lorenzo Pignotti (1739–1812), born at Figline in Val d'Arno; and Domenico Luigi Batacchi (1748–1802) of Pisa. Casti led a wayward and wandering life working as court poet at Florence, Vienna and St Petersburg. At times his peregrinations, whereby he gained a wealth of fruitful experience, took him as far afield as Berlin, Stockholm, the Iberian peninsula, Constantinople and Paris. Pignotti, who was a staunch admirer of English literature, became professor of physics and ultimately rector at the University of Pisa. Batacchi, an excise-man of impoverished but noble family, eked out a wretched exsitence writing his verses of lively fantasy, with broadly satirical intent, in racy Tuscan, while employed in the customs house at Leghorn.

Casti wrote libretti for the *opera buffa*, forty-eight scabrous *Novelle galanti* (1778–1802), drawn for the most part from Boccaccio, Firenzuola and Voltaire, and two works of social and political satire: the *Poema tartaro* (1783), in *ottava rima*, and his masterpiece, *Gli animali parlanti*, begun in 1793 and published in 1802. It consists of twenty-six cantos, in *sesta rima*, in which, through the conventions of a beast epic set in an antediluvian world peopled by animals endowed with reason and all the human passions, Casti satirized courtly intrigue – especially the struggle between absolutist and republican modes of thought in the revolutionary period. *Poema tartaro*, on the other hand, is set in 'Tartary' in the thirteenth century, at the time of the great conflict between the Emperor Frederick II and the Papacy; beneath the allegory of a fantastic plot in which Genghis Khan is Peter the Great and Caracora St Petersburg, the poet provides a satirical chronicle of the brutal autocracy and intrigues of imperial Russia, especially the government of the 'enlightened' Catherine II (the lascivious Turrachina).

Batacchi, whose poetry is noted for its scurrility, wrote in *sesta rima* and published under the pseudonyms of 'Padre Atanasio da Verrocchio' and 'Monaco Beda Tecchi'. His work is often regarded as even more licentious than that of Casti. His best, and most original, poem, published posthumously in Milan in 1812, under the false imprint of Siena 1779, was the mock-heroic comic parody *La rete di Vulcano*. His twenty-four *Novelle piacevoli* (1791 onwards), based on sources which include Masuccio Salernitano, Houdar de la Motte and the Bible, are almost all obscene; as are also the twelve cantos of the burlesque *Zibaldone* (Paris, 1805), celebrating, on a background of Tuscan social life, the exploits of Don Barlotta, the archpriest, in love with the maidservant Vespina.

Pignotti wrote *La tomba di Shakespeare* (1779), *L'ombra del Pope* (1782) and, in imitation of *The Rape of the Lock*, the mock-heroic *La treccia rubata* (1808). He is chiefly remembered for his set of verse fables (*Favole e novelle*, 1782), in which he ridiculed, with moral intent, the follies, hypocrisies and petty tyrannies of his time and place. Pignotti's fables were modelled partly on La Fontaine, and partly on such English masters of the genre as John Gay and Edward Moore.

One other characteristic satirist of the period, who wrote in Sicilian dialect, was Giovanni Meli (1740–1815), of Palermo: a versatile moralist of philosophical interests and enlightened aspirations. As a young man Meli became an enthusiastic advocate of the Italian epic. He wrote *La fata galanti* (1761–2), an Ariostesque fantasy in *ottava rima* with satirical digressions. In later life, besides a wealth of attractive anacreontics, bucolics and other lyric verse of unusual freshness and spontaneity, he composed *L'origini di lu munnu* (1768), *Lo specchio di lu disingannu* (1779), a set of incomparable *Favuli murali* (1810–14), and *Don Chisciotti e Sanciu Panza* (1785–7), in which Don Quixote figures as a social reformer defending the interests of the poor and the weak. In these works Meli reveals a restless spirit vacillating between anti-metaphysical attitudes, philosophic humanitarianism, a desire for social reconstruction and a bitter pessimism.

Exponents of purely didactic verse in the later eighteenth century tended to revitalize traditional forms with material provided by recent scientific and philosophic discoveries. Mercantilist theories of political economy also suggested the theme of a number of works. Among the writers influenced in this way were Giuseppe Colpani (1739–1822) of Brescia, a contributor to *Il Caffè*, the Jesuit Gaspare Cassola da Gravedona (1740–1809) and Carlo Castone della Torre di Rezzonico (1742–96), secretary to the Academy of Fine Arts in Parma and a friend of Condillac. In opposition to the physiocratic concepts advocated in *Il giorno*, Colpani and Cassola respectively wrote *Il commercio* (1766) and *L'oro* (1770), in praise of commerce. Colpani was also the author of poems entitled *Il gusto* (1767), *Le comete*, *Emilia, o l'educazione delle donne* and *La filosofia* (1776), reviewing the various schools of philosophy, both ancient and modern. Cassola later produced *L'astronomia* (1771) and *La pluralità dei mondi* (1774), based on Fontenelle. Rezzonico wrote *Il sistema dei cieli* (1775) and *L'origine delle idee* (1778), concerning the astronomical hypotheses of Copernicus and Newton and the sensationalism developed by Condillac in the footsteps of the English philosopher John Locke. *L'origine delle idee* was left incomplete.

The outstanding didactic poem at the end of the century was *Invito di Dafni Orobiano a Lesbia Cidonia* (1793), written in *versi sciolti* in the form of an epistle by Lorenzo Mascheroni (1750–1800), professor of algebra and geometry and rector of the University of Pavia. The recipient of this masterpiece, which was intended to exalt the faculty of science in the restored university, was the Bergamasque Countess Paolina Secco Suardi Grismondi – 'Lesbia Cidonia' in Arcadia – a celebrated poetess and a friend of the author. In the *Invito* Mascheroni reminded 'Lesbia Cidonia' of her promise to visit the university and he encouraged her to fulfil it. He provided an eloquent account of the distinguished scientists and doctors of the faculty, men such as the naturalist Lazzaro Spallanzani, Antonio Scarpa and the physicist Alessandro Volta. He then surveyed the wonders of the Athenaeum: the Museum of Natural History, the science laboratories, the library, the departments of comparative and human anatomy, and the botanical gardens. In reply Countess Grismondi accepted Mascheroni's invitation. She visited Pavia in 1793 and was accorded the homage of the university senate.

The lyric poets who flourished in the second half of the eighteenth century continued, as has been said, the general direction of Arcadia, developing in the main only through their imitation on the one hand of the Latin classics, especially of Horace, and on the other of selected foreign verse of the period. Prolific and versatile poets of this type were Giuliano Cassiani (1712–78), Ludovico Savioli Fontana (1729–1804), Onofrio Minzoni (1734–1817), Agostino Paradisi (1736–83), Luigi Cerretti (1738–1808), Angelo Mazza (1741–1817), Clemente Bondi (1742–1821), Jacopo Andrea Vittorelli (1749–1835) and Francesco Cassoli (1749–1812).

Two pre-Romantic poets of special note, who sought to widen their horizons through contact with English and German writers, such as Edward Young, Gray, Collins, and Salomon Gessner, were Aurelio de' Giorgi Bertola (1735–98) of Rimini, the author of critical essays disseminating his love of German verse, and Ippolito Pindemonte (1753–1828) of Verona.

Bertola wrote, in imitation of Young's *Night Thoughts*, the *Notti clementine* (1774) on the death of Pope Clement XIV. He is also remembered for his collection of erotic *Versi e prose* (1776), including idylls in the style of Gessner, and for a set of verse *Favole* (1783). As a young man Pindemonte composed the *Poesie campestri* (1788), two of the most typical of which were the sweetly reflective *La solitudine* and the frequently anthologized *La melanconia*. Subsequently he travelled throughout Europe and lived for a time in London. He translated the *Odyssey* (1805–18) and in 1806 he began, in *ottava rima*, the unfinished *I cimiteri*. This was continued in 1807 as the epistle *I sepolcri*, in response to Ugo Foscolo's ode of the same name occasioned by the Napoleonic decree that places of burial should be located only at some distance from communal habitation. Pindemonte later produced a series of melancholy verse *Sermoni* (1819) and the nostalgic *Il colpo di martello di San Marco* (1820).

In the years of political and social upheaval, between the outbreak of the French Revolution and the European settlements of 1815, the most influential Italian poets were Vincenzo Monti (1754–1828) and Ugo Foscolo (1778–1827). The older man was a somewhat paradoxical and contradictory, though highly esteemed figure, of fickle and vacillating disposition, who was already a long-established writer by the time Napoleon began the Italian campaign in 1796. Monti was a poet who clearly perceived the advantage of sailing with the wind in times of change; and he could speak with the voice of eulogy. But his verse as a whole, whether written in Rome before the Revolution, or in the Republican cause, or in honour of the Emperor Napoleon, is generally characterized by majestic imagery, by fiery sentiments, and by a superb technical virtuosity. His favourite metres were those of the Arcadian *canzonetta*, the Dantesque *terza rima*, and the blank verse hendecasyllable. Most of Foscolo's poetry, on the other hand, including the celebrated ode *De' Sepolcri* (1807, written in 1806), was composed after the turn of the century. Consideration of his work thus falls outside the scope of the present chapter.

Born at Fusignano, near Alfonsine in the Romagna, Monti went to school at Faenza, where he is said to have learned the *Aeneid* by heart. At the University of Ferrara he later studied both law and medicine. In 1775 he was admitted to Arcadia, for which he took the pastoral name 'Autonide Saturnino'. In the following year he composed the *Visione d'Ezechiello*, a Dantesque 'Vision', in *terza rima*, written under the influence of Alfonso Varano, which he sagaciously dedicated to Cardinal Scipione Borghese, the Papal Legate in Ferrara. The Cardinal was struck by Monti's promise as a poet and invited him to Rome, where he settled in 1778.

In Rome, where he lived for some twenty years, until 1797, Monti composed odes and a variety of lengthier works. He served as secretary to Duke Braschi, enjoyed favour at the court of the enlightened and judicious Pope Pius VI (Braschi), the uncle of his patron, and soon gained a leading position in Roman literary circles.

Soon after his arrival in Rome, two remarkable archaeological finds, the busts of Pericles and of Aspasia, unearthed at Tivoli and Civitavecchia respectively, provided the theme of the encomiastic *La Prosopopea di Pericle* (1779), Monti's first Roman ode. This was followed by *La bellezza dell'universo* (1781) and the *Ode al signor di Montgolfier* (1784). In the former, which is in *terza rima*, the beauties of Nature from the time of the Creation are depicted, in a sequence of magnificent images; the latter was written to mark the first ascent of the brothers Charles and Robert Montgolfier in their hydrogen balloon, which took off in the Tuilleries on 1 December 1783. The *Ode al signor di Montgolfier* is typically 'Montian' in its spirit of eulogy and in its exaltation of scientific enterprise within the context of Greek myth. As Orpheus sang long ago of the first naval expedition, that of Jason and the Argonauts, is it not now fitting, Monti inquires, that a modern poet should likewise sing of the first ascent of man in a hydrogen balloon and the conquest of the air? The invention is a triumph for science. The hydrogen gas which, enclosed in the bowels of the earth made the ground tremble, is now rendered harmless and is indeed useful to mankind. But what is now left for science to discover? The answer is provided in the final strophe: to prevent death and render man, like Jove, immortal. The *Ode al signor di Montgolfier*, which was composed in the form of a *canzonetta* with lines of seven syllables arranged in four-line stanzas, was recited in Arcadia in 1784, the year of its composition.

In the same year Monti began one of his most distinguished poems, *La Feroniade*, a mythological composition of Virgilian inspiration in which he extolled the plans of Pius VI for the drainage and reclamation of the Pontine marshes. The poem is in three cantos in *versi sciolti*. But although Monti worked on it occasionally throughout his life, it was left incomplete at the time of his death.

In the aftermath of the French Revolution Monti's verses became more political. At first he was a militant classicist and anti-revolutionary; but he later became an advocate of Romantic attitudes and an enthusiastic supporter of Napoleon. The subject of the *Bassvilliana* (1793), four cantos in *terza rima*, was provided by a political assassination: on 13 January 1793 Joseph Hugon, called Bassville, who had been sent to Naples as secretary to the French Legation to sustain the Republican cause, was stabbed to death by a mob stirred up against him by the reactionaries. At this time Monti deplored the excesses of the Revolution and the violence of the Jacobins, and in the poem, which has been characterized as 'il poema della reazione italiana', he turned the interest away from the protagonist to the unfortunate Louis XVI, who is presented as an innocent victim of the Revolutionaries.

The *Bassvilliana* was a great success and ran into many editions. With the Italian victories of Napoleon (1796–7), however, Monti gradually began to temper his political views and to write in a very different spirit. He broke with the Braschi; left Rome, where he had received so many favours; and eventually settled in Milan. Here he entered the French administration of the Cisalpine Republic and began to write verse in support of Napoleon, whom he then saw as the benefactor of humanity, as an ideal sovereign and the bringer of peace and civilization to the world. In 1802 Monti was appointed to the chair of eloquence and poetry in the University of Pavia; and in Milan itself he came to be regarded as the oracle of Italian letters. In these years Monti wrote *Prometeo* (1797), *In morte di Lorenzo Mascheroni* (1800), *Il beneficio* (1805), celebrating the coronation of the emperor,

Il bardo della selva nera (1806) – a classical-Romantic pastiche influenced especially by Ossian and the bardic verse of Thomas Gray – *La spada di Federigo* (1806), and various other works, in a variety of forms, in which Napoleon was either directly or indirectly honoured. His translation of the *Iliad* in *versi sciolti*, which appeared in 1810, is often regarded as the most beautiful of the Italian versions of this much-translated work and Monti's poetic masterpiece.

After the fall of Napoleon and the restoration of the Austrian power in Lombardy Monti continued to write and took an active part in the polemics between the Romantic and classic theorists. His later years were embittered by ill-health and by financial worries. He adopted a conservative standpoint and in his last poem, the *Sermone sulla mitologia* (1825), he roundly condemned Romantic aesthetics and defended the rights of the new literature to use mythological material, as he himself was doing in *Le nozze di Cadmo e d'Ermione* (1825).

One other poet expressive of the new ferment was Giovanni Fantoni (1755–1807), 'Labindo Arsinoetico' in Arcadia, a friend of Monti; like Monti, he has been both highly praised and severely condemned. Born of aristocratic lineage at Fivizzano in the territory of Lunigiana, belonging at that time to Tuscany, Fantoni early embarked on a military career by enrolling in the militia of the king of Sardinia. After imprisonment for debt, however, he dedicated himself to study; and he soon absorbed the most diverse classical and foreign cultural experiences. Between 1785 and 1788 he frequented the illustrious circles of the Neapolitan illuminists Gaetano Filangieri and Mario Pagano. Subsequently, during the Napoleonic period, he became an extreme democratic Republican and took an active part in political life.

Fantoni was known to his contemporaries as 'the Tuscan Horace', and he has often been regarded, on account especially of his metrical innovations, as a precursor of Giuseppe Carducci, the nineteenth-century poet and critic who aspired to revive the classical spirit of Italian literature, weakened, as he thought, through the influence of Romantic attitudes and of Christianity. He wrote erotic *canzonette* (*I baci di Lesbia*), Gessnerian idylls, and *Notti* in the melancholy and meditative vein of Young's *Night Thoughts*. But he is chiefly distinguished for his numerous odes in classical metres on themes suggested by contemporary historical events. Two of the most typical of these, which won him great acclaim, were *Al merito* (1782), concerning the English loss of Minorca to the French and Spanish forces during the American War of Independence, and *Sullo stato d'Europa nel 1787*. Both of these odes were composed in metres based on the four-line Sapphic stanza.

PART THREE

THEATRE

ONE

England

DRAMA

THE period in English literary history that saw the 'rise of the novel' also saw the decline and fall of the drama. It was the period, in other words, in which the English theatre lost its power to sustain a living poetic drama. It ceased to be able to reflect the inner, imaginative life of its society, or to create the myths which might define its ideals and its values. This is not simply to say that public taste had shifted (as indeed it had) from tragedy to comedy, but that the seriousness of both genres had been forfeited. Drama had become devalued; to what extent we can gauge by reference to the history of Shakespeare's plays in this period. It is true that they continued to be produced on the stage and, even more, to be *read* with admiration. But their position in the repertoire had moved somewhat from the centre: the comedies, for instance, were very seldom performed (at least before the mid-century) though in general at least three or four times as many comedies as tragedies were performed during the first half of the century. So, although Shakespeare's tragedies were in fact more popular than those of any other dramatist, and accounted for at least a third of all tragedies put on the stage, they amounted to no more than one part of a small minority of all plays performed. What is more, they were almost all presented in a more or less drastically revised form to suit the temper of the age: it was, that is, not exactly Shakespeare, but, say, *Macbeth* in the operatic version, or *Timon of Athens* in Shadwell's, or *Richard III* in Cibber's version, or the *Caius Marius* of Otway. Yet, in however impoverished a form, Shakespeare's plays, and those of some of his contemporaries, were virtually the only work of any lasting importance produced on the eighteenth-century stage. The theatre had not quite lost Shakespeare (and, indeed, under Garrick's influence set in motion the process of rediscovery which made it possible for the Romantics to appropriate him), but it missed the point of Shakespeare since it had begun to lose any conviction of the drama's centrality and necessity.

No doubt the change that overtook the drama in the eighteenth century was a change in the nature of society, the same change as gave rise to the novel, the transition from a predominantly aristocratic to a bourgeois society. The earlier Restoration period, in spite of the closure of the public theatres during the Commonwealth, had not quite lost touch with the Jacobean dramatic tradition; but it also, and more immediately, took its inspiration from the manners and the values of the newly restored court. It had access therefore to the dramatic tradition of France, and rapidly established on the basis of this a pattern of two antithetical types of drama, the Heroic Play and the Comedy of Manners, both equally coloured by aristocratic pretensions. The Heroic Drama, irresistibly popular for a generation or two, and then suddenly felt to be obsolete, is perhaps too easily undervalued now. Recent criticism has claimed that its exaggerated attitudes and its stiff confrontations of love, duty, honour and passion, do not preclude a serious presentation (both psychological and philosophical) of motives of power, dominance and possession. Be that as it may, the fact is that these plays make an overt appeal to the presumed ideals and values of the court: 'Heroes should only be judged by heroes; because they only are capable of measuring great and heroic actions by the rule and standard of their own' (Dryden's Dedication of *The Conquest of Granada*, 1672, to James, Duke of York). Similarly the comedy characteristic of the Restoration period, even when its range extended beyond the manners of 'high life', drew on courtly models. In this case it was a matter of style rather than action: the standard of value in this artificial world of raillery and cynical wit was less moral than linguistic, and the ideal aimed at was the courtly one of 'wit'. Thus Congreve, dedicating *The Way of the World* (1700) to the Earl of Montague, ascribed any success it might have to the 'Honour of Your Lordship's admitting me into Your Conversation, and that of a Society where everybody else was so well worthy of You'.

Yet even in this period, when the drama may be said still to have counted as a significant force in society, there are signs of an inherent instability. Since its two basic forms are so self-contradictory the drama seems bound to be divided against itself, its heroic ideals and its cynical realism inevitably working against each other. This is certainly the impression one gets from a revealing incident recorded by Pepys. He is describing a performance of the Earl of Orrery's play *The General*; Sir Charles Sedley in the audience keeps interrupting with witty ridicule, especially when it comes to a scene in which the general is ordered to rescue his rival in love: 'he after a great demurre', writes Pepys, 'broke out "Well I'll save my Rivall, and make her confess,/That I deserve her while he do but possess." "Why, what pox," says Sir Charles Sedley, "would he have him more, or what is there more to be had of a woman than the possessing her?"' (*Diary*, 4 October 1664). The scene has almost a symbolic force: aristocratic values working against each other, making the ideal seem hollow and the real cynically destructive, and all under the eye of another class, the emergent bourgeois, quick to adopt the tone of scepticism and ridicule.

The same pattern can, as it happens, be traced in a more specifically literary confrontation. A witty parody of heroic attitudes was acted on stage in 1671 in a play by George Villiers, second Duke of Buckingham (1628–87), called *The Rehearsal*. It obviously caught the right tone for the times, and indeed for the coming times, for it was not only immediately successful but also prompted imitations well into the eighteenth century. 'Rehearsal plays' thus turn out to be a genre in their own right: an 'author' rehearses his play and has to explain and justify it to his sceptical acquaintances on stage. Most of these plays, like most other plays of the period, are now quite unknown and likely to remain so. Sheridan's *The Critic, or A Tragedy Rehearsed*, produced as late as 1779 and printed in 1781, has not been utterly forgotten and still seems amusing, but it is not the best or the most important of these plays. For that we must go to Henry Fielding (1707–54), the novelist. He seems to have had a particular interest in the genre – its self-reflective structure, one play the subject of another play, has a significant effect (as we shall see on p. 342) on his development as a novelist – and in 1736 he produced one of the finest of such plays, a minor masterpiece, called *Pasquin, A Dramatic Satire on the Times*. Sheridan's buoyant humour, Fielding's brilliant and mordant talent, give the genre a kind of conviction that hardly allows us to feel that it is in fact self-defeating. But surely that is the case: as a genre it suggests that drama is becoming discredited. It is the *failure* of drama that has here become the subject for drama. In these farcical parodies and burlesques the theatre is enacting its own disintegration, for they denote the collapse of heroic drama and the shrinking of social comedy into an unfruitful self-mockery.

The process, we have seen, coincides with a shift in the balance of the social classes, and it is therefore tempting to conclude that the increasing influence of middle-class taste no longer allowed either for high tragedy or for high comedy. But it seems more likely that the middle class was not so much losing a sense of literary values as finding it in other media than the drama. The decline of the drama, perhaps, is not by mere coincidence associated with the rise of the novel. The drama could only develop with any credit in the direction of bourgeois realism, and that was after all the direction of the novel. The first major novelists do in fact seem to have sensed that they were inheriting from the dramatists the responsibility for reflecting, defining and enriching the life of their society. Fielding, for instance, builds the structure of his narratives on a theatrical metaphor: 'In this vast theatre of time are seated the friend and the critic; here are claps and shouts, hisses and groans, in short, everything which was ever seen or heard at the Theatre Royal' (*Tom Jones*, VII, i). And Richardson thinks of the letter-form of his novels as a dramatic rather than a narrative procedure.

Thus the drama was disinherited. With the notable exception of Oliver Goldsmith (?1730–74), himself a novelist, and Richard Brinsley Sheridan (1751–1816), the great creators of comedy in the eighteenth century are the novelists, Fielding, Smollett, Sterne, Jane Austen. They are at the centre; on the stage the undoubted success achieved by Goldsmith in *She Stoops to Conquer* (1773) and Sheridan in *The School for Scandal* (1780) lacks the support of a significant context. These authors stand on their own and have no successor until Wilde, a hundred years later. Thus comedy (as distinct from farce, or burlesque, or pantomime, all of which were abundant and popular) has almost ceased to be a dramatic tradition, and the tragic drama is eclipsed in an even more drastic way. Admittedly there *was* a tragic drama at the beginning of the century; indeed it may well be cited a the *only* tragic drama in England after the great era of Elizabethan and Jacobean tragedy, at least if we take it that the heroic plays of the Restoration period are a genre on their own, and that in the twentieth century we have a lyric rather than a tragic drama. And these tragedies of the early eighteenth century did in fact prove to be celebrated and influential outside England. They represent a new and necessary departure for the drama, a move towards a domestic or bourgeois tragedy, represented particularly by George Lillo's *The London Merchant: or, The History of George Barnwell* (1731) and the work of Nicholas Rowe (1674–1718). But here also, as with comedy, it appears that the drama could not contain and develop the new material. Bourgeois tragedy came to be represented (if at all in England) by the novel. Take for instance Rowe's best-known play, *The Fair Penitent* (1703). It is one of his so-called 'she-tragedies', especially celebrated for its portrayal in the character of Lothario of a libertine seducer: its importance now depends entirely on what Richardson was able to make of its theme and its characters in the story of Clarissa Harlowe and Lovelace.

In these ways the drama in England was almost bound to be replaced by 'theatre'. The fact is that the *theatre* flourished in the eighteenth century in an unparalleled way: it is, after the Elizabethan period the *great* age of English theatre. And this means not just that that theatrical spectacle, novelty, technical innovation, exuberant and fantastic invention became possible but that in particular it became a period of great *acting*. 'English drama' in this century might really be best represented as the story of the foundation and development of a great acting tradition, and of individual actors of genius, Garrick, Quin, Macklin, Mrs Oldfield, Kitty Clive.

There is, finally, one other important way in which the theatre in this period drew away from a purely literary development. Music had from the time of the Elizabethan masque been closely integrated with the drama. In the years when Dryden was the principal English dramatist one of the greatest of all English musicians, Henry Purcell (1658–95), was composing music of the highest distinction for the theatre. And later, in the age of Pope, the relation between music and drama was made even closer and more rewarding in the Italian operas of G. F. Handel (1685–1759). There was and is, of course, a good deal to be said against the absurd conventions and the artificiality of the form, the vanity of the singers, even the foreign-language libretto. John Gay's *The Beggar's Opera* (1728), itself the first and the liveliest of another form of music drama, the ballad opera, one of the most popular types of theatrical entertainment, has as its starting point the ridicule of the Italian opera. But what is now becoming abundantly clear as a consequence of sympathetic scholarship and persuasive new staging, is that Handel had a dramatic genius of a very high order.

Yet, after all, the Italian opera had a short-lived vogue. The ballad opera never again achieved anything like the ironic subtlety and satiric force of *The Beggar's Opera*. The eighteenth-century theatre seemed to have no room for a mature and responsible drama.

TWO

France

The eighteenth-century theatre in France is a very revealing expression of the old and new forces at work in the culture of the Enlightenment. While being in many ways reluctant to forsake the tradition which had been responsible for the glory of their classical predecessors, playwrights were becoming increasingly dissatisfied with the old formulae and many wanted to develop a view of the theatre that was closer to the requirements of the new age. Moreover, by the side of the serious theatre, were more popular dramatic entertainments which, though leaving little trace in histories of literature, were an important indication of contemporary taste: such was the *Théâtre de la Foire*, a popular out-of-door entertainment performed on improvised staging at the fairs of Saint-Germain and Saint-Laurent.

TRAGEDY

The most obvious feature of the eighteenth-century theatre was the continuing prestige of the classical tragedy and, at the same time, its growing mediocrity. It is perhaps no accident that for many years Voltaire's fame rested on his achievements in the theatre; in the eyes of his contemporaries he was a great writer of tragedies in the classical manner. Yet he lacked a true sense of the tragic; and he has left posterity with little more than museum-pieces. In spite of numerous attempts to recapture the glories of the past, the sense of tragic destiny was no longer strong enough to inspire works of genius and the age of the Enlightenment in general lacked a tragic vision. Man liked to think of himself as a being capable of measuring up to and controlling the forces of nature and so of determining his own destiny. Although tragedy was the genre still favoured by the aristocracy and most cultured people, it did not find any writers of genius and it no longer satisfied the demands of the new bourgeois *sensibilité*.

Tragedy in the classical manner was produced by the elder Crébillon, Prosper Jolyot de Crébillon (1674–1762), who found his inspiration in Greek mythology. He tried to give a new life to the old genre by introducing a strong element of horror into his plays; in *Atrée et Thyeste* (1707), for example, a father is given a cup containing the blood of his murdered son. Crébillon also liked complicated plots which relied on some violently romantic effects. His best play is generally considered to be *Rhadamiste et Zénobie* (1711), enthusiastically received by his contemporaries, but treated by later generations as an example of melodramatic violence without tragic grandeur.

Voltaire wrote many tragedies, the first of which, *Oedipe* appeared in 1718 and the last, *Irène* in 1778, the year of his death; in one of the best, *Zaïre* (1732), he tended to replace tragic feeling by sensibility, while in others he made use of an element of 'philosophical' propaganda; *Mahomet* (1742) is an attack (albeit a discreet one) upon religious fanaticism, and in 1745 Voltaire did not hesitate to dedicate the play to Pope Benedict XIV! He tried to inject fresh vigour into tragedy by using a much wider range of subjects than his predecessors; although he continued to draw upon classical themes, he also found inspiration in modern times and extended the scenes of his plays to Jerusalem (*Zaïre*), China (*L'Orphelin de la Chine*), America (*Alzire*); he also sought to widen and vary the subject-matter, often replacing love by political, religious or historical themes. While still remaining faithful to the classical tradition – his great model was Racine – he endeavoured to bring colour to the stage by increasing the amount of action and adding spectacular effects; (in *Eriphyle* and *Sémiramis*, for example, there is a ghost, while Caesar's corpse is brought on to the stage in *La Mort de César*). A number of less obvious reforms concerned the stage itself, as he experimented with a new style of declamation and the use of authentic period costumes. To some extent these innovations were due to the influence of Shakespeare, with whose work he had become familiar during his stay in England (1729–33). Yet Voltaire was more appreciative of Shakespeare's external effects than of his tragic vision and, while acknowledging the power of his genius, he condemned him for his barbarism and ignorance of classical rules – describing him as 'this genius full of strength and fertility, of naturalness and sublimity without the slightest spark of good taste or the least knowledge of the rules'. All Voltaire's efforts, however, were not enough to halt the decline of tragedy, for his innovations remained largely superficial and did not make up for the absence of tragic inspiration.

Meanwhile French interest in Shakespeare began to grow and in 1745–8 P. A. de Laplace included translations and analyses of eleven plays in his *Théâtre anglais*. Perhaps the most important contribution to the knowledge of Shakespeare in France was Letourneur's twenty-volume *Shakespeare traduit de l'anglais* (1776–82). Although not a very faithful translation, it enjoyed great popularity, whilst Letourneur himself hailed Shakespeare as the 'god of the theatre'. Jean-François Ducis (1733–1816), who did not know English, produced some curious adaptations which were intended to please French taste; he did not hesitate to change the colour of Othello's skin or replace the pillow by the allegedly more dignified weapon of the dagger! Interest in Shakespeare was given further stimulus by David Garrick's visits to Paris in 1751, 1763 and 1764, for they were accompanied by the performance of scenes or speeches from the plays. So great became the enthusiasm for Shakespeare that Voltaire grew alarmed; seeing in this English influence a grave threat to the purity of French taste (and perhaps a dangerous rival to his own plays!), he launched a vigorous campaign against Shakespeare, not only in his books (such as the *Dictionnaire philosophique*) but also in his correspondence; he even persuaded his friend d'Alembert to read a violent *Écrit sur les tragédies de Shakespeare* at one of the sessions of the French Academy.

COMEDY

Whereas tragedy was dominated by the memory of Racine and Corneille, comedy at first remained under the tutelage of Molière, although stress was laid on the social rather than on the human aspects. Regnard (1656–1710) is a good example of this socially orientated comedy, for *Le Joueur* (1696), as its title indicates, depicts the world of the gambler, whilst his best play, *Le Légataire universel* (1708) describes the ingenious efforts of a group of young people (including masters and servants) to persuade – and trick – an old man to make a will in their favour; thanks largely to the resourcefulness of the servant Crispin, who impersonates three of the characters, they achieve their aim. If Regnard's plays are marked by a superficial portrayal of character, they are full of gaiety, wit and dramatic movement. Dancourt (1661–1725) also describes social attitudes, especially in *Le Chevalier à la mode* (1696), for here and elsewhere he shows men striving for social advancement through the power of money and the exploitation of women. The element of direct social satire becomes much more apparent in Le Sage's *Turcaret* (1708), which makes a merciless attack upon the new social class constituted by the upstart financier – a theme already developed by La Bruyère in *Les Caractères*; Turcaret emerges as a character with practically no good quality – an ignorant, crude, corrupt and immoral figure who is mercilessly exploited by others; in a play such as this the comic element is to some extent tempered by the bitterness of the satire, although Turcaret ultimately shows himself to be as ridiculous as he is odious. *Turcaret* threatened to have such resounding repercussions that the financiers themselves tried to stop its performance. In spite of the play's popular appeal, their influence was great enough to prevent it receiving more than seven performances. Perhaps it was this frustration which finally caused Lesage to abandon the serious theatre and devote his dramatic energies to the composition of pieces for the *Théâtre de la Foire*.

In addition to this new social emphasis there was a growing tendency to concentrate on specific types of character. This is already apparent in Destouches (1680–1754): his best-known play, *Le Glorieux* (1732), portrays a count who creates great difficulties for himself by his obsession with his noble birth and his equally strong but contradictory desire to marry the daughter of a wealthy bourgeois for her money; the play thus represents a confrontation between the old aristocracy and the rising prosperous middle class. The description of a particular type is also to be found in Piron's *La Métromanie* (1738), an amusing play about an ageing poet's irresistible urge to write verse. In Gresset's *Le Méchant* (1747), the hero, Cléon, is a cynical egocentric who finds pleasure in creating dissension among those around him; such a character, devoid of any genuine feeling, has social significance as the embodiment of a typical contemporary attitude. If Cléon is finally condemned, however, it is not because of his rejection of traditional morality, but because his behaviour is opposed to the basic feelings of *les bonnes gens*.

The comedies of Marivaux, far more original than the work of the playwrights so far mentioned, do not fit easily into any specific category. In certain respects they are closer to Racine than to Molière, for their main theme is love and the principal roles are given to women. Avoiding, however, any temptation to indulge in tragic emotions, Marivaux is concerned above all with the subtle analysis of delicate feelings; his characters experience the burgeoning of love and yet struggle with the various obstacles – mostly psychological – which prevent or postpone acceptance of its reality; since such conflicts are never allowed to assume a tragic form, it is, in many cases, a question of overcoming a personal pride that is reluctant to acknowledge the existence of true love. *Le Jeu de l'amour et du hasard* (1730) is usually considered one of his best and most characteristic plays. Silvia's father, M. Orgon, wants her to marry his friend's son, Dorante, whom she has never met. In order to observe her suitor more closely, she takes the place of her servant Lisette. Unknown to Sylvia, Dorante has decided to assume the identity of his valet Arlequin. In spite of their disguise, Sylvia and Dorante fall in love with each other, while Arlequin and Lisette do likewise. Sylvia's ultimate triumph is to make Dorante confess his love and propose marriage to her while he still believes her to be a servant. The whole plot is developed with great skill and the emergence of Sylvia's love is portrayed with subtle delicacy as she gradually admits to herself the true nature of her feelings for Dorante. In *Les Fausses Confidences* (1737), another excellent example of Marivaux's skill, the heroine Araminte is eventually led, through the efforts of the valet Dubois, to recognize her love for Dorante.

Although these comedies of nascent love are among the finest, Marivaux did not restrict himself to this theme, for his other plays include social and political satire, *L'Île des esclaves* (1725) and *L'Île de la raison* (1727), and more sentimental moral topics such as *La Mère confidente* (1735) and *La Femme fidèle* (1755).

Although the appeal of Marivaux's plays is primarily psychological, it also rests on the effect of a very personal style which critics have called *le marivaudage* – a highly refined use of language which relies on a subtle combination of reflection and feeling; the characters seek to express the complexity of their feelings by playing on delicate nuances of verbal meaning. It is a style which, though very original, undoubtedly owes something to Marivaux's experience of the *salons* and is in a more general way connected with the tradition of 'preciosity'. In any case, it helps to create a highly individual mood and a kind of poetic comedy which critics have sometimes compared to the paintings of Watteau.

Although Marivaux always maintains a delicate balance between broad comedy and blatant emotion, eighteenth-century comedy reveals an increasing predilection for sentimentality. This is already obvious in Destouches, but it finds full expression in the works of Nivelle de la Chaussée (1692–1754), the creator of *la comédie larmoyante*. His best-known plays, *Le Préjugé à la mode* (1735) and *Mélanide* (1741), make an unashamed assault on the emotions of the spectators and seek to move them to virtue through the shedding of tears. The first play, for example, tries to show that it is not silly or degrading for a man to love his wife. It is not surprising that La Chaussée's preoccupation with moral sentiment caused one of his fellow-playwrights to call him 'le révérend père La Chaussée'. The eulogy of family relations and the indulgence in sentimentality are clear signs of the growing influence of bourgeois taste, so that La Chaussée's work must be seen against the wider cultural background of the time: instead of being an exceptional phenomenon, the popular sentimentality of his plays helped to reinforce the strong current of sensibility flowing from Prévost's novels and subsequent translations of Richardson.

Whereas La Chaussée was interested in the practice rather than in the theory of serious comedy, Diderot consciously strove to create a new genre which would be half-way between tragedy and comedy – *le drame bourgeois*. Like many other writers, Diderot was convinced that a modern audience could no longer remain content with a form that had been fashioned to suit a predominantly aristocratic taste. Although society was still determined by the old class system, the rise of the middle classes was beginning to have an important influence on the expression of literary taste. Diderot wanted to introduce a genre which would appeal directly to this emerging social class by combining the serious tone of the old tragedy with the more familiar atmosphere of a modern comedy that was related to the problems of everyday existence. He felt that, as soon as writers had found a literary form adequate for the purpose, the life of the new bourgeoisie would reveal just as many dramatic possibilities as the old aristocracy. Diderot developed his ideas on the subject in his *Essai sur la poésie dramatique* of 1758 and in his *Entretiens sur 'Le Fils naturel'* (1757). He wanted to create a 'domestic, bourgeois tragedy' which would replace the grandiose classical tragedy. He believed that domestic crises – for example, difficulties in family relations – could be much more interesting to a modern audience than the fate of kings and princes: tradesmen, merchants, shopkeepers were no less valuable to society than members of the aristocracy. Indeed, one important function of this new serious comedy would be to portray social conditions (including particular professions) and family relationships. In this respect the traditional classical emphasis upon character would give way to a new concern with social problems. In Diderot's words: 'Today the condition must become the main object and character only the accessory . . . It is the condition, its duties, advantages, embarrassments which must serve as the work's basis' (*Entretien*, III). An indication of his social intention is given in the titles of his own plays – *Le Père de famille* and *Le Fils naturel*. At the same time Diderot believed that this new social element ought to be accompanied by an equally serious concern with morality. The members of the bourgeosie had to show their involvement with moral problems: their very existence represented a more worthwhile contribution to morality than the frivolous life of the idle aristocracy: far from being shameful (as aristocrats like to believe), an honest devotion to one's profession could be ethically uplifting.

Diderot proposed to adapt the formal features of the new drama to these general requirements. Verse would give way to prose, whilst all plays would contain a strong visual element; the long speeches of the classical tragedy would give way to action supported by various kinds of physical aids, including stage-settings, and details of both background and dress; actors would make use of vivid gestures as well as of words; authors were, therefore, urged to give detailed instructions concerning facial expressions and gestures.

Diderot's own plays are not a very convincing proof of the validity of his precepts, for practice falls far short of theory, however interesting this may be in itself. On the whole the new genre failed to establish itself with any genuinely meritorious works. Diderot's obtrusive concern with moralizing prevented him from distinguishing between genuine dramatic emotion and sentimental bombast. Perhaps the only effective play in the genre was *Le Philosophe sans le savoir* (1765) written by Sedaine (1719–97). It is a pleasant little play with a merchant as one of its main characters and a plot revolving around family and professional relationships. It was, however, outside France that Diderot's theories aroused the greatest interest, especially in Germany, where Lessing became one of their most earnest advocates.

Eighteenth-century comedy does not end on a sentimental note, for Beaumarchais (1732–99) serves to remind us that the old comic spirit was not dead. The incredible energy of this clock-maker's son involved him in a life of intrigues and adventures, so that writing for the stage was only one of his many activities. Although he first became famous through four *Mémoires* (1773–4) written on the occasion of a legal dispute with the heirs of a financier who owed him money, he had already made his debut in the theatre with two sentimental comedies, *Eugénie* (1767) and *Les Deux Amis* (1771), in the style of *le drame bourgeois*; the first had been accompanied by an *Essai sur le genre dramatique sérieux* (1767) which took up and developed Diderot's views on *le drame*. Fortunately Beaumarchais's creative work did not continue in this vein, for he went on to write two plays of a genuinely comic inspiration: *Le Barbier de Séville* (1775) and *Le Mariage de Figaro* (1784). As he himself says of the first, he wanted to restore to French comedy 'the old frank gaiety', along with 'the light tone of our present jesting'.

In the first place, Beaumarchais revives the *comédie d'intrigue*: once again action and plot become important and the spectator is invited to interest himself in what is happening on the stage; the multiple plots of *Le Mariage de Figaro* form a complicated and not always coherent pattern; intrigues are apt to be started up or projected and then left without sequel; this is not very apparent in actual performance, for the spectator is carried along by the extraordinary rapidity of events and incidents. Moreover, Beaumarchais also pays great attention to the visual aspects of the play, giving precise stage-directions and details of decor and costume; there are also several songs and musical interludes and a vaudeville at the end. *Le Mariage de Figaro* thus constantly engages the spectator's attention by its variety, colour and incident.

Scholars have not been slow to point out that Beaumarchais borrowed a great deal from his predecessors – from Molière, from *le drame bourgeois* (for even *Le Mariage de Figaro* is not without its sentimental moments, especially when Marceline, who turns out to be Figaro's mother, is on the stage), and from opera. These borrowings, however, are much less important than Beaumarchais's own personal contribution. Figaro, to whom money and intrigue are of overriding concern, obviously embodies much of the author's own zest and energy; but Beaumarchais is also discernible in other characters such as the youthful Chérubin (a reminder of his own adolescence) and the Count, the promiscuous lover. The great law-scene clearly owes a great deal to his own frustrating experience of the legal profession.

If the plot of *Le Mariage de Figaro* sometimes lacks coherence, it is partly because of the many changes to which it was subjected while Beaumarchais struggled to get it performed, and partly because he wanted his play to be a vehicle for satire as well as a mere entertainment. Indeed, it was probably the topical allusions which greatly contributed to the success of the play with contemporary audiences. Figaro makes a direct attack upon specific abuses such as the corruption and inefficiency of the law and the immoral intrigues of political life, and this satirical element culminates in the long monologue in Act V, where he gives an embittered review of his career and the many injustices he has suffered; at this point the usually resilient valet gives way to a mood of bitter pessimism, for, as well as being temporarily demoralized by the uncertainty of his own position and future, he believes that he has been betrayed by his fiancée. No doubt the novelty of the satire should not be exaggerated, for many contemporary critics were much bolder than Beaumarchais in their denunciation of abuses, whilst Beaumarchais himself was not a revolutionary and certainly had no desire to overthrow the existing order; the play is more significant as an indication of the changes that were actually taking place in society than as a direct call for political action. Nevertheless, the impact of a controversial comic play was likely to be more sensational than that of the pamphlets in which such critical ideas were usually expressed.

Perhaps even more important than the direct satire are the social implications of the plot. It is a question of the conflict between the resourceful, intelligent and lively valet, Figaro, and the immoral aristocrat Almaviva, who wishes to use his power and position for his own unworthy ends and, more especially, for the seduction of Figaro's fiancée Suzanne. It is not simply a struggle between two individuals but between the representatives of two social classes, one of whom feels himself to be personally superior to the other, in spite of the enormous disadvantages of his lowly position. Figaro's success in eventually outwitting the Count seems to justify his confidence in himself.

The characterization of *Le Mariage de Figaro* has a certain originality, even though it is not primarily a comedy of character. Especially interesting is Beaumarchais's attempt to portray the amorous adolescent in the person of the young page-boy Chérubin who hovers around all women, including the deserted wife, the noble Countess, who, while remaining faithful to her husband, cannot resist the ambivalent feelings, half maternal, half-erotic, aroused by her attractive young godson. The vivacious Suzanne – Figaro's fiancée – also contributes to the gay spirit of the play.

Yet the liveliness and comic verve dominate not only the characters and their actions, but also their language. Far more important than any psychological innovation is the dazzling wit which pours out from the characters in a never-ending stream. It is a comedy of language as much as a comedy of intrigue and situation, and a worthy contribution to the theatre of the time. Indeed, it is the last important play to appear in France before the Revolution. Inevitably seen in retrospect as a forerunner of radical social changes, it is also a vigorous expression of the wit and gaiety still characteristic of the old society.

The changing nature of eighteenth-century dramatic taste is well brought out by the growing popularity of plays set to or accompanied by music. The out-of-doors *Théâtre de la Foire* added to its repertory the new genre of *opéra comique* (a comedy with musical interludes inserted between the scenes of spoken dialogue), to which such well-established authors as Le Sage, Piron and Sedaine willingly contributed. In 1762 the players of *la Foire* were joined by *les Italiens*, the Italian actors who, after being restricted to the performance of Italian works (*commedia dell'arte*) in Paris, had gradually included French scenes, often in the form of parody or satire; they then began to put on comedies with popular songs (*comédies en vaudevilles*) which were later transformed into *opéra comique*. In addition to these popular musico-dramatic entertainments there was a considerable development in the production of grand opera and ballet, with Jean-Philippe Rameau and

Gluck as two of the most outstanding composers. Although these innovations are only incidental to the formal literature of the period, they are an important indication of the way in which the rigid separation not only of literary genres but of different art-forms was breaking down. Audiences were henceforth to seek less pure aesthetic pleasures and to indulge in the enjoyment of hybrid emotions.

THREE

Germany

TRAGEDY

THE Aristotelean categories of tragedy and comedy, which provide a satisfactory basis for discussing German drama in the seventeenth century, no longer suffice in the Age of Enlightenment. This begins, as far as German drama is concerned, with a remarkably dark age. The tragedies of Gryphius and Lohenstein had been influenced by the French tradition, as embodied in the two Corneilles and Racine, but they had added to it a dimension of horror, which in Lohenstein amounted to distortion. He died in 1683. His successors were men of lesser calibre, such as C. F. Hunold (1680–1721), who was primarily a novelist but also provided libretti for tragic and horrific operas, and J. C. Hallmann (*c.* 1640–1704 or 1716), whose sadistic tragedies, of which *Mariamne* is an example, belong to his early manhood. Between these shadowy figures, whose plays still haunt the seventeenth century, and the 1730s there is a blank in which theatrical entertainment is provided at courts by foreign opera and in towns by the degenerate descendants of those troupes of English actors which had toured the Continent in the early years of the seventeenth century (*Englische Komödianten*). The actions of their plays were often debased versions of Elizabethan plays, which had long since lost their text, which was replaced by ranting or obscene extemporization.

It is not really surprising that the self-confident Professor J. C. Gottsched (1700–1766)[1] should not only have felt the need of a cleaning-up operation, but should have believed himself capable of supplying a replacement for what he proposed to sweep away. It may be supposed that two courses were open to him. Either he could cleanse the old drama, and build anew upon its foundations, or he could scrap the lot and introduce something entirely new. He chose the latter. Some twenty years later Lessing maintained that Gottsched

1. See p. 409.

had made the wrong decision, but Lessing spoke (as we do) with the benefit of hindsight. The intellectual climate of 1759 was very different from that of 1732. The first glimmerings of a historical outlook had begun to manifest themselves. Gottsched believed that drama, which had so greatly flourished in classical times, had been brought to perfection in France; this belief encouraged him in the idea that German drama might rapidly be brought to the same stage of advancement by the simple process of imitation. In order to prove his point he wrote a tragedy, *Der sterbende Cato* (1732), for which works by Deschamps and Addison provided the basis, and he persuaded Caroline Neuber, the talented directress of a troupe active in Leipzig, to back his efforts on the stage. His wife Luise Adelgunde cooperated by translating French plays and writing imitations, and before long he had a team of willing collaborators adapting and translating, so that between 1740 and 1745 he was able to publish the six volumes of *Die deutsche Schaubühne*, which he conceived as a basic repertoire of respectable and properly constructed plays for a reformed German theatre. He was patriotic rather than francophile, and believed that he was helping the ailing German drama to take a short cut to perfection. If he was not successful in this ambitious project, at least he made German drama and the German theatre respectable (if dull) and persuaded people to take it seriously.

The best example of tragedy as Gottsched understood it comes from a writer, Johann Elias Schlegel (1719–49), whose association with Gottsched was comparatively brief. Schlegel, who studied in Leipzig and in 1743 obtained an official appointment in Copenhagen, wrote a much-praised tragedy on early Germanic history (*Hermann*, 1741) during his student years in Germany and, not long after his removal to Copenhagen, a less well-known but better tragedy on early Danish history (*Canut*, 1746). Both plays are conventionally classical, observing the Aristotelean unities and employing alexandrine verse. *Canut* is a tragedy of ambition, the subject is the unsuccessful second revolt of Ulfo, King Canute's brother-in-law, after the king has already pardoned an earlier attempt. Though formally unenterprising, the portrayal of character has sufficient insight to leave room for diverging modern psychological interpretations.

In the 1740s Gottsched's personal reputation suffered a series of blows, largely of his own making, for his truculent and obdurate personality excluded any possibility of flexibility; it is, however, a mistake to consider that Gottsched's personal recession affected the prestige of the form of tragedy which he had advocated. Gottschedian tragedy persisted in Austria into the last quarter of the eighteenth century, and in other regions held its own at least to the late fifties. Johann Friedrich von Cronegk (1731–57) was at the time of his death writing a Gottschedian tragedy of martyrdom, *Olint und Sophronia*, which was finished by another hand, K. A. von Roschmann-Hörburg, (Cronegk was at the fourth act when he died) and published in 1760. Though savagely reviewed by Lessing some years later in the *Hamburgische Dramaturgie*, it was praised by reviewers at the time of its appearance.

The 1750s were, however, the years in which the climate of drama began to change. Wieland's rather feeble tragedy *Lady Johanna Gray* (1758) was perhaps a symptom of change, for it substituted blank verse for the alexandrine and used an English model by Nicholas Rowe (1674–1718).

Lessing's tragedy *Miss Sara Sampson* was first performed on 10 July 1755, and not in a capital city, but in a small university town, Frankfort-on-the-Oder. The impact on the audience is said to have been profound, and it may well be that the absence of a francophile aristocratic element in this provincial audience enabled the play to have a better send-off than it might have had in Leipzig or many larger cities. At any rate, once launched, it held its own. *Miss Sara Sampson* is a somewhat artificially constructed tragedy, as compact as any classical work, and is distinguished by three special features: it is in prose, its characters are relatively obscure country gentry instead of potentates, and it is set in England. Most of these features are not in themselves new. Prose dialogue and ordinary contemporary characters were familiar enough on the stage – but only in comedy. Lessing's innovation was to employ these elements in a tragedy, and in doing so he gave the model for a new type of play, the domestic tragedy or *bürgerliches Trauerspiel*, though Lessing himself used the simple description 'Trauerspiel'. As to the English setting, this is a pointer to a general broadening of the outlook of German literature and also to the growing familiarity of the German public with the English middle-class background represented in English novels, notably by those of Samuel Richardson. The depiction of the contemporary scene in a serious context on the stage was a symptom of a general social shift, a token of the increasing awareness of the middle-class citizen of his respectable standing and economic function. It coincides roughly with Diderot's similar preoccupations in *Le Fils naturel* and *Le Père de famille.*[2] The influence of *comédie larmoyante* (which Lessing called 'das weinerliche Lustspiel') is also recognizable in the sentimentality of situation and speech in *Miss Sara Sampson*, and is all the more remarkable coming from so unsentimental a person as Lessing. His play created a vogue, but evoked no masterpieces. Seventeen years were to pass before another outstanding (and much finer) play of this kind was to appear. This was Lessing's own *Emilia Galotti* of 1772. Of the many imitations which appeared in the intervening years the most notable is probably a sensational and implausible tragedy by J. W. von Brawe, *Der Freigeist*, published in 1758.

Emilia Galotti, though published and first performed in 1772, germinated in Lessing's mind as early as 1754, and so, in its origin, is closely associated with *Miss Sara Sampson*, but the lapse of years enabled Lessing, with his increasing maturity and experience, to produce an altogether more impressive play. Like the earlier tragedy, it is set abroad, but the background of a petty Italian state is much more easily translated into German terms than the English environment of *Miss Sara Sampson*. And so many of the readers and spectators understood it, for the political and social climate had undergone some change in the intervening seventeen years. The play itself had an intentional political aspect; for it has as one of its important characters a ruling prince, and it demonstrates unmistakably the havoc which can be wrought by absolute power. Lessing's prince is no conventional tyrant; he is merely self-indulgent, pleasure-loving, wilful, and heedless of the consequences of his actions. Such a man is a prey to flatterers and counsellors out to further their own interests. In the end he is shaken into at least some semblance of a sense of responsibility, but this is only achieved by the death of a man of integrity and rank and of a young woman of beauty and virtue as the unintended result of his misuse of his own powers. Any German reader or spectator would know of German princes who expected good-looking women to whom they took a fancy to be at their disposal, and would recognize the evil courtier Marinelli as an all-too-familiar and very dangerous

2. See p. 259.

type. Lessing's play is not, however, a political tract, nor even a powerful play directed solely against an unsatisfactory social structure. It is a well-made play full of tension, which rises to a first climax in the third act and to a second in the last, and it is peopled with characters, who, though each is representative of a type, nevertheless possess a convincing individuality. Indeed, the problem of motivation has continued to be a source of literary interpretation and controversy down to the present day, and the cause of this is not inadequacy on the part of the dramatist, but the real, and hence many-faceted, life with which he has endowed his characters. It is true (at least in the opinion of many) that the action creaks at one point in the fifth act, needing a slight, but noticeable, push from the author himself. The plot of *Miss Sara Sampson* is even more contrived for if Sara and her father had not been so artificially kept apart all would have ended happily – and rather too soon for an evening's entertainment. The fundamental fault of both the plays derives from Lessing's acceptance of the division of drama into tragedy and comedy. Both of these plays cry out to be turned into *Schauspiele*, that is serious plays which leave the future open and do not insist on a cathartically tragic effect in their final phase. But the *Schauspiel* was yet to be introduced, by the following generation of playwrights, some twenty years younger than Lessing.

Nevertheless it can be suggested that Lessing did, in fact, write a *Schauspiel. Nathan der Weise* (1779) discusses serious matters, above all religious intolerance, and does it in terms which bring it very close to racial intolerance. The play has an element of comedy, but this is certainly subordinated to high seriousness of purpose. And its ending is open. Lessing's sub-title, however, was 'dramatisches Gedicht'; it is one of the earliest German plays to use blank verse instead of the alexandrine. When *Nathan* was written Lessing was acquainted with a number of *Schauspiele* written by the generation of the *Sturm und Drang*. He did not approve of them, and his *Nathan* is quite different in tone and temper, but in this sermon in dramatic form he nevertheless demonstrates that at the end of his life he could still learn that an open ending, in serious drama, was a valid alternative to a tragic climax.

It was not until the 1770s that German drama showed true originality. No doubt the moment was ripe, but it was the meeting in

Strassburg in 1770 of Herder, who possessed a mind of great fertility, and Goethe, which precipitated the new movement. The '*Sturm und Drang*' ('*storm and stress*') movement was originally called the 'Age of Genius' (*Geniezeit*). It showed restless impatience with rules, controls, guidelines, precedents and tradition. Yet, for all its independence, it found its model in the past. Shakespeare, so long despised on the Continent, began, in the middle of the eighteenth century, to have an impact on German literature. *Julius Caesar* was translated in 1741 into alexandrines by C. W. von Borcke. Wieland's prose translation of twenty-two of Shakespeare's plays appeared in eight volumes between 1762 and 1766. It was, however, Herder's dynamic advocacy which first made Shakespeare a vital force in German literature. Herder's essay *Shakespear*, published in 1773 as part of his symposium *Von deutscher Art und Kunst*, depicts Shakespeare as a writer who created a new drama in accordance with the feelings, thought, and traditions of his own people; the essence of this new drama is, firstly, the penetrating presentation of a wide range of characters and, secondly, – instead of the artificially concentrated climactic structure of classical tragedy – a historical or chronicle form of drama, which is incidental and episodic rather than monolithic. Herder's thesis proves that he failed to grasp the principles of Shakespearean tragedy, but that was a matter of small moment. Each generation feels the need to find precedents to justify its own innovations, and it was necessary for the men of the Age of Genius to find an authority to whom, it seemed, rules had not mattered, one who had listened to his own inner voice and taken no notice of precept. In his view of Shakespeare and in his advocacy of 'folk' poetry (a category which for him, included Homer, the Bible and Ossian) Herder provided the *Sturm und Drang* with a warrant for the licence these writers desired.

Goethe, who for a time was hand in glove with Herder, put the lesson into practice on his return from Strassburg to Frankfort in the autumn of 1771. The first version of his play *Götz von Berlichingen* bore the title *Geschichte Gottfriedens von Berlichingen mit der eisernen Hand dramatisiert. Geschichte* is here the operative word. Goethe's aim was a chronicle of episodes in the supposedly Shakespearean manner. To his surprise it met with Herder's disapproval. Thrust on one side for a time, it was rewritten in 1773 in somewhat chastened form with the title *Götz von Berlichingen mit der eisernen Hand. Ein Schauspiel.*

Goethe had every justification for using the description *Schauspiel*. Though the play contains material which could be made into two tragedies, Goethe has abstained from making such use of his themes, and has presented the play both as a spectacle, and as a play which is serious but not tragic. Götz is conceived as a sixteenth-century Robin Hood who allows himself to be lured into a situation in which he is implicated in treason and atrocity. He is condemned to death, but Goethe does not allow him to die as a tragic sacrifice either to his ideals or to his betrayal. The death sentence is commuted, and Götz's death occurs from a sickness, aggravated, it is true, by his imprisonment, but caused by exhaustion in a life spent in all weathers, continually in the saddle or on the march under arms. And his last words '*Freiheit! Freiheit!*' are as much a promise for the future as a lament for past wrongs. Goethe had intended this play primarily to be read, imagining that its deliberately scrappy structure would debar it from the stage. He was mistaken. It was a great success in the theatre, as well as in the bookshop and the lending library. The public was ready and, albeit unconsciously, waiting for a new kind of drama which should break free from the old constrictions.

Goethe himself wrote a tragedy at this time, but *Clavigo* (1774) was a tame little affair, tossed off in a week; in later life he valued it mainly as a useful filler for gaps in a theatre's repertoire. His *Stella* of 1775 was hardly a better play, but it is a very striking example of the headway which the conception of the *Schauspiel* had made. Ferdinand is involved with two women at the same time, and chance brings him into a situation in which both are present. He can abandon neither, and the three accept the solution of a *ménage à trois*. There were possibilities for comedy or tragedy here, but Goethe would have neither. The whole play is serious and the ending entirely open. Many years later he was to think differently and prepared a stage version which ends with Ferdinand's suicide.

In the years between 1771 and 1775 another project preoccupied him and began to take shape. Stimulated partly by childhood recollections, partly by a study of the occult during an illness in 1769, partly by his experience of academic life in Leipzig and Strassburg and partly by his erotic adventures, he took up the story of Dr Faust, perhaps because of some vague or even unconscious sense that no subject could offer him greater or more varied potential. What he was to make it later lies outside the limits of this volume, for *Faust I* did not appear until 1808 and *Faust II* not until 1832. He did, however, in these early years write at least a draft of a play on Faust, some part of which he published, with additions (*Faust. Ein Fragment*, 1790). A copy of the draft, or of some of it, was first published in 1887 and is universally known as *Urfaust*. Goethe was obviously attracted to Faust by the latter's overpowering desire to extend the frontiers of his own knowledge, and in the opening scenes of *Urfaust* he appears as an explorer of dangerous magic and a rebel against conventional learning. But these scenes are at least as much satire as aspiration. Into them Goethe poured both his own sense of almost unlimited potentiality and his contemptuous impatience of contemporary university pedants. The play, however, quickly shifts its ground as Faust meets a beautiful and respectable girl, whom he is determined to possess. Instead of the *Schauspiel* of vast possibilities, which the legend of Faust at first seemed to offer him, we find ourselves involved in a powerful and enclosed domestic tragedy, the central figure of which is no longer Faust, but Gretchen, the girl whom he seduces and destroys. And so to the end of Goethe's *Sturm und Drang* years, say 1776, the pendulum swings between the open form of the *Schauspiel* and the traditional enclosed form of tragedy. Nevertheless Goethe breaks new ground in this play by abandoning verse in the final scene, *Kerker*, and writing a tragic climax of a power that no German verse play had yet been able to equal.

It would not be true to say that the *Sturm und Drang* was Goethe's handiwork. The intellectual, moral and social climate had changed, and in changing had influenced him; but he repaid the debt with interest. All but one of the writers of drama in that age were associates of Goethe, indeed they may be termed his satellites. Lenz, Klinger, H. L. Wagner, and Maler Müller were in close personal contact with him. Only Leisewitz, the author of a single play, belonged to the other circle, the Göttinger Hainbund,[3] which was primarily poetic and certainly very much tamer.

J. A. Leisewitz (1752–1806) was a careful and painstaking man, who in later life was a punctilious and considerate administrator, but in his twenties he had nursed literary ambitions and shown a talent which justified them. He wrote two brilliant short scenes in prose, *Die*

3. See pp. 208–10.

Pfandung (*Distraint*) and *Der Besuch um Mitternacht* (*The Midnight Visit*). In the former a married couple spend in lamentation their last night in the conjugal bed before their furniture is sold under a tyrannically issued distress warrant; in the second a tyrant is confronted by the spirit of the ancient Germanic hero Hermann (Arminius). Both scenes suggest a surprising trend of political criticism in view of Leisewitz's hesitant temperament and his impeccable official conduct. It is not known whether Leisewitz conceived them as scenes to be embodied in projected plays or whether they represent detached episodes complete in themselves. If the latter, Leisewitz created a new genre, and the fact that he had them both published in the Göttingen *Musenalmanach* (1775) lends some support to this view. On the other hand all his published literary papers were destroyed under the terms of his will, so the question of the possible incorporation of these scenes can never be settled. Leisewitz wrote, in addition to these sketches, one celebrated play. *Julius von Tarent* is the story of two brothers in love with the same girl. They are sons of the ruling prince of Taranto, they differ completely in temperament, each representing one aspect of the *Sturm und Drang* conception of man. Julius is the introspective melancholic brooder, Guido the man of sudden passion and dynamic action. Guido stabs Julius, as the latter attempts to carry Blanca off from a convent, repents too late, and submits to execution by his father, who thereupon abdicates, though he well knows that his Neapolitan successor will be an inhuman tyrant. This final touch is an echo of the anti-tyrannical feeling which is so strong in Leisewitz's two short scenes. *Julius von Tarent* is written in passionate prose, but its structure is largely conventional, that of a tragedy. No doubt Leisewitz was partly influenced in this acknowledgment of convention by the fact that his play was an entry for a theatrical competition, in which unconventional plays would probably be at a disadvantage. But he converted convention to his own use. If the men of the *Sturm und Drang* desired freedom and action, that desire corresponded to a condition of constriction and repression from which escape was sought. The enclosed nature of Leisewitz's tragedy sealed by the triple death and the further implication of the loss of freedom for all the prince's subjects very clearly emphasizes the tragic human situation as Leisewitz and his contemporaries saw it.

Leisewitz's successful rival in the competition was F. M. Klinger

(1752–1831), and Klinger's offering was *Die Zwillinge*, also a play dealing with two hostile brothers, sons of a nobleman and in love with the same woman. There seems some likelihood that Klinger had learned something of Leisewitz's intended entry, which would explain so striking a coincidence; but writers of the *Sturm und Drang*, aiming at extreme intensity of emotion, would, in any case, be conscious that the close-knit situation of a family offered special opportunities for such intensification. Klinger, in fact, screwed things to an even higher pitch by making the brothers twins and, since primogeniture is an important factor for their futures, casting a doubt on which of the two is really the elder. In this play, too, brother kills brother and the father puts an end to the life of his guilty son. The tragedy is, if anything, noticeably more claustrophobic even than in Leisewitz's play, though the extravagance of the dialogue, welcomed by contemporaries, comes close to caricature. Klinger, though he possessed more energy than Leisewitz, and a quicker eye and ear for what was fashionable, had neither Leisewitz's fine intelligence nor his sensitiveness.

In his first two plays he leaned heavily on more gifted writers. *Otto* (1775) was inspired by Goethe's *Götz von Berlichingen* and pushes formlessness to the point of chaos. Names and scenes are lifted from Goethe's play, characters and relationships from Shakespeare, especially from *King Lear* and *Othello*. Klinger's other play of 1775 (both were published anonymously) is *Das leidende Weib*, which in technique, and in the names of the characters, imitates *Der Hofmeister* of J. M. R. Lenz, but without Lenz's touches of comedy. His intention is to plumb the depths of desperation and suffering, but the exaggerated and repetitive tirades pall upon the ear.

This play was followed by Klinger's prize-winning *Die Zwillinge*, already mentioned, in which the hope of theatrical production has evidently exercised a measure of discipline. Klinger's high-pitched, obsessive and distorted world reappears in *Die neue Arria* (also 1776), oddly, though fashionably, called a *Schauspiel*, but, in fact, undoubtedly a tragedy. *Simsone Grisaldo* (1776) is, however, a *Schauspiel* in fact as well as name. The superhuman hero, of superhuman strength and courage, was intended by Klinger as a tribute to Goethe. The magnificent Grisaldo maintains his serenity through testing adventures and tribulations and finally triumphs over his enemies. There is a certain almost august quality about this play which raises it well above

Klinger's other works. His most frenetic *Schauspiel* is *Der Wirrwar*, which, when published (still in the fertile year 1776), was renamed *Sturm und Drang* and so, years later, provided the movement with its name. In it Klinger's attempts to express the extreme intensity of passion reach a new level of incoherence. At this point Klinger's explosiveness seems to have spent itself, however. The tragedy *Stilpo und seine Kinder* (1780) has reminiscences of the *Sturm und Drang*, but is comparatively tame, and his later plays, written to make a living, are for the most part conventional comedies. Though as a writer Klinger had many faults, he was a man of character; in 1780 he became an officer of Russian marines, rising eventually to the rank of general. His military duties did not prevent him from writing some novels towards the end of the eighteenth century.

J. M. R. Lenz (1751–92), a much more gifted man who moved in the same Goethean circle, never fulfilled his early promise, went out of his mind in his late twenties, and ended miserably in a Moscow street. It may well be that Lenz, a sensitive and subtle mind, wrote too much, as Klinger did, but was not tough enough to survive the pressure. He was closely associated with Goethe, whom he may almost said to have shadowed, even successively attaching himself to the various young and not so young women to whom Goethe was attracted. Lenz, who was one of the most articulate members of the *Sturm und Drang*, deliberately sought to free himself from the limitations imposed by classification, and his first full-length play (he had previously made adaptations of the comedies of Plautus), though described as a '*Komödie*', ranges widely between comic, tragic and grotesque elements, finally reaching a happy ending, though not for all its participants. Lenz had a strong didactic impulse and a lively social conscience. *Der Hofmeister, oder Vorteile der Privaterziehung* (1774) deals with a real social problem of the day, the situation of the poor ordinands employed by the rich and noble as tutors to their children and the dangers to all parties when the tutor's charges were attractive and nubile girls. Lenz's sub-title is ironical, for disaster overtakes his tutor, Läuffer, who in remorse castrates himself, though this is mitigated by his subsequent 'platonic' match with the country lass Lise. *Der Hofmeister* follows the technique of detached and episodic scenes which make their effect by accumulation, the method introduced by Goethe in *Götz von Berlichingen*, but he takes the bold step of applying it to a story which is contemporary both in its setting and its problems. Like almost all *Sturm und Drang* plays it appeared anonymously and was attributed by many to Goethe.

Lenz's most remarkable play, *Die Soldaten*, likewise styled '*Komodie*', may be variously interpreted as a *Schauspiel* or as a tragedy. If it is the former, it certainly lies close to the border territory of the more traditional form. Drawing on his own experiences as a companion of officers of the French garrison in Strassburg (by no means solely composed of Frenchmen) he has written a moving play of seduction in which the subsidiary figures are as real as the principal persons of the play. All the faults of Lenz's other works – changes of scene for their own sake, arbitrary shifts of level, irrelevant interpolations – consequences of his profound instability, are absent from this one work, which can rank in power and compassion with the early plays of Goethe. Yet *Die Soldaten*, like *Der Hofmeister*, is linked closely with Lenz's social conscience, and as in the earlier play, he is not content to let the events and emotions speak for themselves, but adds a didactic gloss. This is more blatant in *Die Soldaten*, which contains in the final scene the suggestion, apparently seriously intended, that such tragic seductions could be avoided if a company of heroic and self-sacrificing young women could be raised whose duty it would be to prevent the erotic impulses of young officers (and other ranks) from straying outside barracks. The proposal, which Lenz expanded in a short treatise, *Über die Soldatenehen* ('On Marriage for Soldiers', not published until 1914, is an indication of Lenz's ineptitude in dealing with the practical potentialities of life. This waywardness dominates the rest of his work, fragments and short plays and narratives, which help in the understanding of his mind, but in themselves give little satisfaction.

Heinrich Leopold Wagner (1747–79) was another one-time friend of Goethe, who had known him first in Strassburg and then in Frankfort. Wagner's gifts were not great; he exemplifies the lesser writer, who, inspired by contact with a group of authors of ability, can compose works which to the general public at least are as good, and perhaps better, than those of more gifted companions. Wagner's reputation, such as it is, rests on two plays, *Die Reue nach der Tat* (1775) and *Die Kindermörderin* (1776). The former is a garishly melodramatic work, in which a snobbish mother opposes her son's marriage, in consequence of which the girl takes poison and the son goes out of his mind. Remorse then drives the mother to insanity. *Die Kindermörderin* (the title is authentic, although there is only one victim of infanticide) is a much better and more powerful play. It owes something to Lenz's *Die Soldaten*, dealing with the dangerous relationship between a young officer and an attractive girl of lower rank. A child is born and the young mother, believing herself abandoned, puts an end to its life. But instead of the expected tragic conclusion the play ends with at least a ray of hope, for the young officer repents and sets out on a mercy mission to the king. Wagner has, in fact, written a social *Schauspiel*. A curious feature of both his plays is their organization in six acts, a gesture of defiance to the convention of five. Goethe resented Wagner's play, considering it to be a plagiarism of his draft of *Faust*,[4] the latter part of which is concerned with seduction and infanticide.

The remaining member of this group, Friedrich Müller (1749–1825), generally called Maler Müller, possessed a talent for drawing and painting which did not fulfil its early promise. His literary gifts were modest. He, too, contributed a play on Faust (*Fausts Leben dramatisiert*, 1778), but in it intention is more obvious than attainment. Müller did, however, discover a little niche for himself, which is neither tragedy, comedy nor *Schauspiel*; this was the prose idyll in dramatic form, and though *Die Schafschur* and *Das Nusskernen* do not fit into established categories, they are perhaps best considered under comedy (see below).

By 1778 the feverish dramatic activity of the *Sturm und Drang* had spent itself, and Goethe, the central star of the galaxy, had become a statesman (however small the state which he administered), and had developed to the point that he had come to despise much of his early work, which he now considered immature and undisciplined. In 1779 he wrote (but did not publish) the first version of his first unmistakably classical work, *Iphigenie auf Tauris*.

Before we consider this new and important trend, however, it is desirable to discuss Schiller's beginnings, since these constitute an altogether unforeseen and extremely powerful (though brief) resuscitation of *Sturm und Drang* drama. Of course long-forgotten playwrights continued for a time to produce exaggerated or devitalized imitations of the more important works of that period of six or seven

4. *Dichtung und Wahrheit*, Book 14.

years. In Schiller's early plays, however, although there may have been some exaggeration, there was certainly no lack of vitality. The reason for Schiller's delayed *Sturm und Drang* is to be found in two local factors: his cloistered education to the age of twenty-one in the Duke of Württemberg's private school-cum-university, and the absence of any centre of literary life or any tradition of taste in the duchy. His first play, *Die Räuber* (1781), has a slight link with historical fact. In Schiller's infancy a notorious gang of brigands had been active in Württemberg and their leader had surrendered; there is little doubt that Schiller often heard the story in his early childhood. His robbers are a mixed crowd ranging from scoundrels to men of misguided integrity. But their leader Karl Moor is a criminal of nobility, both in rank and motive, a man defrauded of his inheritance by a malevolent and scheming brother, aware of the wickedness of the course to which he has committed himself and seeking to retrieve something in the disaster by helping the honest poor and persecuting the unjust rich. But he cannot prevent his basest followers from committing atrocities, nor has he the omniscience which his moral stance demands. He stands condemned by the law and successfully resists, but when at last he is condemned by his own conscience he surrenders, performing one last act of virtue by ensuring that a poor man receives the reward for his capture. The violence of the language, its quivering rage and tormented despair, had a tremendous impact. Schiller achieved what Klinger had aimed at. But the play's success was brief, even in Schiller's own judgement. That kind of *Sturm und Drang* was five years too late.

Schiller next tried his hand with partial success at historical drama, but the problem he posed for himself in *Die Verschwörung des Fiesko zu Genua* (1783) proved almost insoluble, and he failed, in spite of repeated revisions, to bring the play to a satisfactory conclusion. His *Kabale und Liebe* (1784) showed that he had learned much from Lessing, especially in structure and discipline. And he far surpassed Lessing in his power to create character and to write dialogue of vitality. He chose a plausible story of love attempting to bridge the gap between classes and ending in tragedy; the effect of the tragedy is to destroy the head of the government and to discredit the social system. By using two families for his purpose Schiller made sure of obtaining the maximum emotional effect. Powerful satire goes hand in hand with heart-rending pathos. But Schiller himself was not satisfied and soon set out on a path which, in the end, was to bring him close to Goethe, to whom we must now return.

Goethe continued as the Duke of Saxe-Weimar's principal minister until 1787, years during which his already mature character acquired a new stature and authority. In literature he had turned his back firmly on the *Sturm und Drang* in 1776, and had felt his way with increasing conviction and assurance towards a classical standpoint. The essential qualities of this classical conception were harmony, balance and humanity. The views expressed by Winckelmann, both before and during his years in Italy, undoubtedly influenced Goethe, as they did many other intelligent and educated men of his generation. But the stress on humanity, and the accompanying serenity of outlook, were also affected by the circumstances of Goethe's life in Weimar, the ambience of courtesy and consideration, and above all the beneficent and soothing personality of Frau von Stein (1742–1827). The first embodiment of Goethe's new classical spirit was his *Iphigenie auf Tauris*, which was written in 1779 in prose and privately performed at court. Goethe was far from satisfied with this first version, but the essentials of the play are already present. The potentially tragic situation in which Iphigenia, for many years priestess of the Tauri, is faced with the obligation either of surrendering herself in a loveless and impious match with the king or of sacrificing to the gods her long-lost brother Orestes, is resolved entirely by her integrity and her serene spirit, which rejects alike the guile to which Orestes and his friend Pylades are willing to turn and the barbarous threats uttered by King Thoas. Aggression subsides and humanity prevails. Goethe rightly came to recognize that this work, in which the characters, rising above the dross of everyday, achieve a humane, harmonious equilibrium which is remote from human affairs, demanded something more exalted than the prose in which it was originally written. In 1786 he obtained leave of absence, turned his back on Weimar, and hastened to the Venetian frontier and from thence at an easier pace to Rome, which he conceived as the true fount of the classical. It was on this journey that he successfully turned the play into a poetic drama in smooth, even fluent, iambic verse. It was published in 1787 and received by the world at large with some surprise.

The successor to *Iphigenie*, conceived in the very next year 1780, was, at any rate at first sight, a much less obviously classical work. *Torquato Tasso*, inspired by the life of the Italian poet (1544–95) and therefore set in that happy hunting-ground of Romanticism, the Italian Renaissance, is clearly linked with the despairing misfits of the *Sturm und Drang*, of whom Werther[5] is the prime example. Indeed Goethe endorsed with satisfaction a pronouncement by J.-J.-A. Ampère establishing the relationship: 'Sehr treffend nennt er daher auch den *Tasso* einen gesteigerten *Werther*.'[6] Notwithstanding this, *Torquato Tasso* has an irrefutable claim to be considered an essential component of Goethe's classical phase. If *Iphigenie* represents the triumph of the still beauty of the Greek urn (a world to which Iphigenia herself belongs) over the harsh clashes and the turmoil of cross-currents in the Middle Ages, as embodied in *Götz von Berlichingen*, *Tasso* reveals to us the self-centred melancholic in the setting of a civilized court, in which classical harmony has been absorbed into a way of life. Tasso's attempts to adapt himself to the court life of Ferrara appear to succeed, but an ineradicable strain of artistic and personal egotism are revealed in the end under the delicate web of forbearance and self-restraint which alone make this refined existence possible. The iambic verse is as sensitive as that of *Iphigenie auf Tauris*; the conflict of the play ends, however, in a poignant dissonance.

Torquato Tasso was published in the sixth volume of Goethe's *Schriften* in 1790. The times were hardly propitious for his message of classical harmony, serenity and proportion. The French Revolution presented the educated public with events so unexpected and disturbing that the return to Greece or to Grecian Rome seemed remote from actuality. The Weimar court was unresponsive to his ideas, and it was even less willing to listen to him when he discovered the classical ideal of beauty in a young woman of humble birth and installed her in his house. In the decade which followed *Tasso* he wrote his splendid elegies,[7] his classical idyll *Hermann und Dorothea*,[8] and the novel *Wilhelm Meister Lehrjahre*,[9] setting forth a model of the development of a human personality, but in the field of the drama which involved contacts with people he wrote only trivialities, such as *Die Aufgeregten* and *Der Gross-Kophta*.

In 1794 Goethe made an ally. Schiller had lived in Weimar or at

5. See pp. 377–9. 6. Goethe, *Gespräche mit Eckermann*, 3 May 1827.
7. See p. 212. 8. See p. 216. 9. See pp. 381f.

near-by Jena since 1787 and in 1789 had married a lady connected with the court. But in spite of mediation by well-intentioned friends the two men long regarded each other with distrust. There was probably some jealousy on both sides. Schiller had the advantage of youth – he was twenty-seven when he came to Weimar, and Goethe chose to see in him a representative of what he now thought of as the baneful *Sturm und Drang*. Schiller, for his part, felt that life had been altogether too easy for Goethe, who had become lofty in manner as a result of constant adulation. He felt also that the verse drama, *Don Carlos*, which he had brought with him to Weimar, ought to have demonstrated that he was no longer the revolutionary of *Die Räuber*.

Don Carlos (which Schiller began in 1783 and published in 1787) grew out of (and outgrew) the *Sturm und Drang*. Schiller himself admitted the affinity of Carlos with the character of Leisewitz's Julius, and the family quarrel at its centre puts that of *Die Räuber* in the shade. But *Don Carlos* was historical, and its subject touched an important element of Protestant mythology, Philip II of Spain and the Spanish Inquisition. This in turn raised the question of freedom (clearly dear to Schiller on the evidence of his three previous plays), and especially freedom of thought. In the end *Don Carlos*, which is remarkable for its extraordinary flow of impassioned, yet controlled, blank verse, became a play of great complexity in which the playwright, though he does not waver in his convictions, frequently shifts the focal point of his enthusiasm. *Don Carlos*, as published in 1787, comprised 7,044 lines of blank verse - more than twice the length of the average five-act verse tragedy. It is not surprising that Goethe, faced with a work of such unaccustomed and unpractical magnitude, should have believed that Schiller was still a representative of the undisciplined *Sturm und Drang*. Schiller eventually reduced the play to 5,370 lines, exhibiting determination and a resourcefulness in cutting beyond that of most authors. Overgrown though *Don Carlos* was, it was nevertheless the turning-point. Schiller was not yet clear how to go ahead, but he resolutely turned his back on his early *Sturm und Drang* manner.

Several difficult years passed during which Schiller was silent as a creative writer, but successfully turned himself into a professional historian and then into a semi-professional philosopher. It was during a philosophical discussion in 1794 that Goethe and Schiller discovered each other to be conversable persons and, more than that, potential allies. Goethe's classicism and Schiller's Kantian idealism converged. As a consequence of this new-found unity Goethe was stimulated to take in hand once more his *Faust*, two sections of which, Act III (the union of Helen of Troy and Faust) and the 'klassische Walpurgisnacht' (classical witches' Sabbath) of Act II were to represent the ultimate consummation of his classical aspirations.

In contact with Goethe Schiller's abilities as a dramatist were re-awakened. He had now a solid foundation of historical knowledge on which to build, and clear aesthetic principles by which to set his course.[10] In the ten years of his life remaining to him, he wrote five plays, one of them a trilogy, and made substantial progress towards writing a sixth, and all of them can rank as masterpieces. Between 1796 and 1799 he wrote *Wallenstein*, consisting of the one-act prelude *Wallensteins Lager*, written in a deliberately archaic metre, and the two five-act dramas *Die Piccolomini* and *Wallensteins Tod*. The setting is the Thirty Years' War, on which Schiller was well informed, having written a history of it in 1793. This is verse tragedy on a scale hitherto undreamed of, for all the plays are closely interlocked. A rigid discipline of action and speech is maintained, and the whole work is an architectonic structure. Its classical quality lies in the cleanness of its lines, the tautness of its speech and the nature of the fall of its hero, who, through hubris, gets himself into a situation in which he is betrayed by an inner weakness of character. *Maria Stuart* (1800) is a brilliantly written tragedy of the opposition of legality and power. It has at its centre a bravura scene of confrontation between the two queens, Maria and Elisabeth. In the final act Maria, unjustly condemned to death, accepts her fate as a proper expiation of crimes by her in earlier years. *Die Jungfrau von Orleans*, Schiller's 'Saint Joan' (1801), was his own favourite play and still has its advocates today. On the other hand, the division between the historian's factual history and the idealizing dramatist's willingness to manipulate or disregard facts is nowhere so sharply discernible as in this play. One of its greatest merits lies in the use of pageantry and music, as well as metrical ingenuity, making a play which ends in a death harmonious rather than cathartic. With *Die Braut von Messina* (1803) Schiller undertook an apparently impossible task, the attempt to rival Greek tragedy on its own terms. Many consider that he failed.

10. See pp. 419–21.

He invented a story which has obvious points of contact with that of the *Oedipus* of Sophocles. He set it in Sicily at an unspecified medieval period. He introduced a Chorus which speaks in lyrical measures, and, though the greater part of the play is written in the blank verse which he used with such power and expertise, at two points he actually wrote in the trimeters which are the metre of Sophoclean tragedy. Somewhat surprisingly, since the play is in some sense a pastiche, the result is a classical tragedy of economy, authority and power. *Wilhelm Tell* (1804), made internationally famous by Rossini, is expressly a *Schauspiel*, and so is unique among Schiller's later works. It combines a study of a character under the strain of persecution with the portrayal of a popular movement attempting to restore usurped political liberties, an interesting version of the pursuit of liberty, this time under a conservative slogan. It is a thousand pities that Schiller's premature death robbed us of his *Demetrius*, the story of which is familiar through the opera *Boris Godounov*, for in the opinion of many, this play of guilt unwittingly incurred might well have proved the finest of his works. One of the drafts contains his boldest theatrical experiment, by which the audience would have been drawn into the play as members of the Polish Diet.,

COMEDY

The Comic Muse can rarely have felt happy in Germany in the eighteenth century. Antics were plentiful, wit was scarce. And the intelligent and gifted seem to have concentrated their attention mainly on serious drama. When the century began there existed some wooden imitations of French comedy (of Destouches rather than of Molière), but comedy on the whole was regarded merely as popular entertainment. A number of stereotyped actions could be combined or arranged so as to present a more or less plausible scenario, which depended for its success on the principal comic actor or *lustige Person*, who went by various names, of which Hanswurst and Pickelhering were the most frequent. The dialogue was rudimentary and supplemented by improvisation. The *lustige Person* made (or marred) the play by his powers of gesture and facial expression and his native wit. If these flagged, and it is likely that they often did, he could always fall back upon obscenity and so bring the house down. It is not surprising that comedy of this kind acquired a bad name.

One of Gottsched's self-imposed tasks in the 1730s and 1740s was to break this tradition and restore comedy to its proper place as a respectable branch of drama. He adopted the same policy for cleaning things up as he did in tragedy: imitation of the French. But being by nature a serious man he gave less attention to comedy, delegating it to his wife Luise Adelgunde (1713–62), who, though certainly not without gifts, was far from being a comic writer of genius. Her first comedy, *Die Pietisterei im Fischbeinrocke oder die Doktormässige Frau* (1736), was, as might have been expected, the translation of a French original (by an almost forgotten Jesuit named Bougeant). Her original comedies *Die Hausfranzösin* and *Das Testament* appeared in Gottsched's *Die deutsche Schaubükne* (1740–50). In his desire to make extemporized comedy obsolete Gottsched also took a more public step by organizing, in Frau Neuber's theatre in Leipzig, a ceremony in which Hanswurst was banished, an act which exposed him to subsequent ridicule by Lessing in the *Literaturbriefe*.

C. F. Gellert, a professorial colleague of Gottsched, but certainly not a sycophantic follower, also tried his hand at comedy in the 1740s. *Die Betschwester* (1745) has a plot in which lovers' affairs go awry only to come right in the end, but its real centre of interest is the hypocrite Frau Richardin (the Betschwester), whose exposure provides a measure of comedy and, even more, a clear didactic purpose. Gellert's *Das Los in der Lotterie* (1747), his most successful play in his day, is constructed on a similar pattern, makes its lovers happy and shows a free-thinker to be a man of low moral standards. *Die zärtlichen Schwestern* (1747), which, like Gellert's other comedies, conforms to Gottsched's view that comedy should be written in prose, inclines to *comédie larmoyante* (*weinerliches Lustspiel*) and is more tearful than comic. J. E. Schlegel, who departed from Gottsched's pattern by adhering to verse, wrote several comedies of note including *Der Geheimnisvolle*, *Der Triumph der guten Frauen*, and, perhaps his best work, the one-act play *Die stumme Schönheit* (1747); but though Schlegel was clearly emancipating himself from the precepts of Gottsched when he died in 1749 at the age of thirty, his creative works can only be reckoned as among the better works of a rather drab decade. His writings on aesthetic theory are a different matter.[11]

The most promising young writer of comedy in the late 1740s was Lessing. He began at least two comedies while still a schoolboy and finished them as a university student at Leipzig, where he matriculated in 1746. *Damon oder die wahre Freundschaft* (1747) is a triviality, but *Der junge Gelehrte* (1747) has some more or less witty satire of pedantry, which Lessing had no doubt experienced at first hand. This play was actually performed at the Leipzig theatre in 1748. Lessing wrote other comedies while he was at Leipzig, and two of them are noteworthy, not so much for wit or comic situations, but for the idea of tolerance which is the mainspring of both of them. *Der Freigeist* (1749) shows balance of character as the source of tolerance, rather than intellectual opinion. Lessing's mature and considerate Lutheran, Theophan, rises superior in moral stature to the irritable and arrogant free-thinker, Adrast. *Die Juden*, a one-act play written in 1749 and published in 1754, demonstrates the integrity and gentlemanliness of a Jew who rescues a country squire from the attentions of a pair of Christian thugs. None of these comedies of Lessing's early years succeeds in freeing itself from the conception that comedy is primarily concerned with improving morals or manners, and uses a measure of wit, humour and ridicule to achieve this end.

Lessing's *Minna von Barnhelm* (1767) belongs to a different world. It has a somewhat over-intricate plot, and follows tradition in doubling the principal lovers with a pair of servant counterparts. The truly remarkable feature of this play is the success with which an undoubtedly serious theme (an officer's honour and integrity) is combined with charm, wit and psychological subtlety. Lessing uses a well-worn theme, the pursuit of the reluctant man by the insistent woman, but does it with becoming discretion, so that Minna never departs sufficiently from true decorum to alienate the spectator. Both her performance and Tellheim's combine resolution with tact and delicacy in a psychologically convincing way, and *Minna von Barnhelm* has every title to rank as the first true comedy in German literature in the eighteenth century. It remained the only one.

Wieland (who ought to have been able to write elegant comedy) steered clear of the stage except for his one, unsuccessful, tragedy *Lady*

11. See pp. 410f.

Johanna Grey. Goethe wrote a number of amusing dramatic skits, parodies and burlesques, but his rare comedies are among his least inspired works. Schiller asserted in *Über naive und sentimentalische Dichtung* (1795–6) that comedy is a higher form of literary art than tragedy, but, except for the *Schauspiel Wilhelm Tell*, his own dramatic works are all tragedies. Not till two years before Schiller's death did a German comedy of some merit appear, though this play, *Die deutschen Kleinstädter* (1803) by A. von Kotzebue (1761–1819), is no serious rival to *Minna von Barnhelm*. Kotzebue's play is a very amusing farce with an element of social satire, but its motifs are well-worn commonplaces of comic tradition and its characters are conventional types.

In one German city and one alone, namely Vienna, did the old pre-Gottschedian tradition of extemporized folk drama maintain itself. Though for a time it was driven into the suburbs this tenacious form, usually described as the Wiener Volksstück, acquired in 1781 a theatre of its own, the Theater in der Leopoldstadt. These popular plays belonged to two principal genres, the magic play (*Zauberstück*) and the local comedy or farce (*Lokalposse*). The magic play gave an opportunity for spectacle, symbolism and contrast between a higher world and the antics of ordinary, and especially Viennese, mortals; its acme is Mozart's *Die Zauberflöte* (1791), the words of which are by E. Schikaneder (1751–1812). The *Lokalstücke*, strewn with dialect, humorous repartee and local allusion, held up to the Viennese a distorting mirror of their faults and quirks, a procedure in which they took immense delight. These popular plays are a vital part of theatrical history. Their literary merit up to the end of the eighteenth century was more dubious. Their real florescence was to come in the second quarter of the nineteenth century.

FOUR

Italy

TRAGEDY

Gravina, Martello, Maffei, Conti

THE creation of an Italian tragic theatre was a constant aspiration of the eighteenth century. This dream was to some extent realized in the Period of Reforms by Vittorio Alfieri, who is said to have found Italy Metastasian and left her Alfierian. But in the Age of Arcadia, in the heyday of the *opera seria*, half a century before the appearance of Italy's most outstanding tragedian, a number of writers and reformers of the Italian tragedy flourished. The most notable of these were four in number: Gian Vincenzo Gravina (1664–1718), who drafted the *Leges Arcadum* (1696) and subsequently founded in Rome the Accademia Quirina; the Bolognese Pier Jacopo Martello (1665–1727), a would-be emulator of the French, and the indefatigable author of thirty-four plays in all the dramatic genres then known, including one for the puppet theatre; Scipione Maffei (1675–1755), the Veronese antiquary, who achieved outstanding success with *Merope*, a tragedy of regicide, mistaken identity and revenge, first performed at Modena in 1713; and Antonio Conti (1677–1749), a Paduan mathematician of encyclopedic curiosity who spent the years 1713 to 1726 living mainly in Paris, Hanover and London. While abroad Conti acquired a considerable knowledge of both English and French literature. He had supreme regard for the works of Shakespeare, whom he esteemed as 'il Cornelio degl'Inglesi, ma molto più irregolare'. He made translations from Pope, and mediated in the famous controversy between Leibniz and Newton, both of whom were his friends.

Gravina and Martello were representative of the more conservative and innovatory trends respectively in the great debates of the day concerning the nature of the tragic genre, at a time when in France and Spain illustrious tragedians had emerged and England was still full of the echoes of the Shakespearian drama. Under the influence of the French neo-classic tragedians and the critical doctrines of Boileau, Martello sought to revitalize Italian tragedy with a series of works on biblical, oriental and classical themes in the French manner. These he enlivened with satirical touches and elements of Arcadian gallantry. Gravina, on the other hand, was opposed to the 'modern' manner. He criticized the French theatre, and its Italian imitators, in his treatise *Della tragedia* (1715); and he aspired with his own five tragedies (*Palamide*, *Andromeda*, *Servio Tullio*, *Appio Claudio*, *Papiniano*), all published in 1712, to restore to Italy the 'true' classicism of the Greek theatre.

Martello's tragedies include *Perselide*, *Perseo*, *Sisara*, *La morte di Nerone*, *Quinto Fabio*, *Marco Tullio Cicerone*, *Edipo tiranno*, *Alceste* and *Ifigenia in Tauri*. Several of these were written in a new and distinctive verse form, by which they are especially remembered, instead of the traditional blank verse hendecasyllable. This new metre was a rhyming couplet with lines of fourteen syllables, based on the French alexandrine. This type of verse is generally described as 'Martellian' after its creator. Martellian verse enjoyed a wide diffusion, but it did not gain complete acceptance; it was strongly criticized from the first by Gravina and Maffei. In the 1760s, Goldoni and Chiari, who used it for some of their verse comedies, were ferociously satirized on this account by Carlo Gozzi.

Gravina's *Tragedie cinque* were published together with a *Prologo*, spoken by Tragedy, in which a sort of history of the genre is traced from its peaks in Aeschylus, Sophocles and Euripides. The plays themselves deal with stern, civil themes, with moralistic intent. Legal arguments are employed and the author's love of justice is evident. The endings are enlivened by scenes of slaughter in the Senecan manner. To the modern reader, Gravina's tragedies may seem lacking in poetic merit. Their language, which sought to capture the classic rhythms, is Latinized and extremely difficult. The verses are unrhymed and the general effect is cold and remote; these austere dramas read like exercises in rhetoric and they have been little regarded.

Maffei's sole tragedy, the deeply felt and still affecting *Merope* (1713), was the product of a constructive programme of dramatic reform which took into account the achievement of both Gravina and

Martello. It was composed in blank verse hendecasyllables and based on a lost play by Euripides, of which Maffei believed he had recovered the plot. *Merope* is set in remote antiquity in the royal palace at Messene in the Peleponnesus. The events take place some fifteen years after the tyrant-usurper Polifonte has murdered Cresfonte, the husband of Queen Merope and two of her sons. When the play opens, Polifonte is seeking the hand of the outraged queen in marriage, in order to placate the factions of the turbulent populace, who remain faithful to their murdered king. A third son of Merope, long-lost and also named Cresfonte, is brought before the court in chains accused of theft and of slaying a brigand. He has been brought up in a distant land by a faithful servant. He is now is disguise, known only by the false name of Egisto. At first he is not recognized by Merope, who believes that the young man before her is in fact the murderer of her son Cresfonte. Polifonte, on the other hand, suspects that Cresfonte may be still alive; and eventually, at Merope's request, he willingly frees Egisto. Later, when Merope learns the true identity of Egisto, the two of them plot their revenge. Merope, in the meantime, has agreed to the hated nuptials. But at the height of the ceremony Egisto, armed with an axe, hurls himself upon his father's murderer and slays him, together with Adrasto, his perfidious counsellor. Merope then reveals that her son, the legitimate heir to the throne, has returned to Messene and the populace proclaim him king.

Noble in tone and psychologically convincing, *Merope* provides a harrowing and effective portrayal of turbulent passions in conflict. It was widely performed and ran into innumerable editions. It was translated into English by Pope and imitated by Voltaire. It is generally regarded as the best Italian tragedy of the Arcadian period.

The tragedies of Antonio Conti were four in number, though a fifth, *Cicerone*, was also projected. They were based on sources in Shakespeare, Plutarch, Livy and Tacitus; and they dramatize a sequence of political events in the history of ancient Rome, from the expulsion of the Tarquins to the poisoning of Drusus, son of Tiberius. All were composed in blank verse hendecasyllables. *Giunio Bruto* (1743) deals with the institution of Roman liberty and the Consulate; *Giulio Cesare* (1726), with the attempt to transform the republic into a monarchy; *Marco Bruto* (1743), with the assassination of Caesar; and *Druso* (1747), with the machinations of the base, self-seeking

Sejanus at the court of Tiberius. *Giulio Cesare* and *Marco Bruto*, which are the best of Conti's tragedies, were suggested by a reading of Shakespeare's *Julius Caesar*. But in them, as well as in his other two plays, being a strict observer of the dramatic unities, including that of 'interest', Conti 'corrected' what he regarded as the 'irregularities' of the Shakespearian text to conform with the conventions of the French classical theatre. Through his exaltation of tyrannicide and his interest in themes of liberty, Conti has often been regarded as a 'forerunner' of Alfieri; his place in the history of Italian tragedy has been much discussed.

Metastasio and the opera seria

While tragedy was being cultivated by a few dramatic theorists and reforming spirits such as Gravina, Martello, Maffei and Conti, the Italian theatre public was far more interested in two other characteristically Italian dramatic genres which had long enjoyed an immense success and which had largely ousted the classical written-out comedy and tragedy from the Italian stage. One of these was the *commedia dell' arte* (see pp. 305–6), performed since the sixteenth century by professional actor-companies of incredible virtuosity and skill, and much patronized by the lower classes. The other, favoured and supported by the higher levels of society, was the 'Italian opera': a costly and lavish spectacle, generally of a tragic-heroic or mythological kind, elevated in tone and formal in structure, in which music played an essential role. The dramatic foundation of the opera was a stage play, the libretto or '*dramma per musica*', which was furnished by a poet-librettist.

The eighteenth century *melodramma* or *opera seria* was thus the heir of a lengthy and developing operatic tradition. It had its roots at least as far back as the early 'music drama' of the Florentine Camerata dei Bardi, a group of poets and musicians of learning who, in the late Cinquecento, wanted to restore the musical accompaniment of the Greek tragedies, which, it was thought, had been sung. From the experiments of the Camerata one of the fundamental structures of the Italian opera had been born – recitative. This was a form of vocal composition in which melody and fixed rhythm were largely disregarded in favour of 'musical declamation' or 'sung speech' imitating the natural inflections of the human voice. Subsequently, the aria had developed, with its greater use of melody, repetition and contrast. In essence it consisted of a lengthy and developed piece in three sections of which the last repeated the first, and the middle offered a variety of key and a change of mood. Recitative of a more melodious kind, midway between recitative and aria, was known as *arioso*. An *arietta* was a shorter and simpler aria.

From the time of Claudio Monteverdi, the greatest of the early baroque opera composers, who employed both recitative and aria, opera developed rapidly. Opera schools were established, especially at Venice and Naples; and it has often been said that, between 1600 and 1800, the provision of opera was the principal activity of the Italian nation. As lavishness of spectacle and choreography came increasingly in vogue, the tendency of the practitioners of this hybrid and stylized form of entertainment was to gratify the tastes of the audience and the pretensions of the *virtuoso* singers. A race of public favourites arose; the adult male soprano whose voice was obtained by eviration came into being. In the late Seicento, the music and the singing of opera frequently touched the peaks of greatness. By the turn of the century the Italian opera was established as the fashionable, ceremonial and festive entertainment of the aristocracy in all the courts and capitals of Europe. But the libretto, formerly the source of dramatic strength and unity, had become largely subordinate; the opera itself had become over-spectacular, with comic interludes and with little artistic cohesion.

From time to time attempts were made to formalize the Italian opera. Poet-librettists sought to restore the genre to its early principles and especially to subordinate the music to the text. The most successful of these attempts was that of Ranieri Calzabigi (1714–95) who, in collaboration with Christian Willibald Gluck, director of the opera house at Vienna (1754–64), produced *Orfeo ed Euridice* (1762), *Alceste* (1767) and *Paride ed Elena* (1770): works which in their majesty and simplicity are comparable only to the first landmarks of the Italian opera, *Orfeo* (1607) and *L'Incoronazione di Poppea* (1642) by Monteverdi. Before the time of Gluck and Calzabigi, however, in the high summer of the Italian *opera seria*, other notable artificers of reform, especially of the libretto, were Apostolo Zeno (1668–1750) (see p. 130), who participated in most trends in the Arcadian culture of his day, and Pietro Metastasio (1698–1782) (see pp. 222–5), chief poet of the second generation of Arcadia and the author of some twenty *drammi per musica*, all composed between *c.* 1723 and 1740. In the footsteps of Zeno, whom he succeeded as 'Poeta Cesareo' at the imperial court, Vienna, where he lived from 1730 until his death, Metastasio sought to restore the Italian opera, in a suitably modified form, to the dignity, regularity and structure of the classical tragedy.

Zeno, the author of some fifty libretti on historical and heroic themes, first revealed his gifts as a poet as early as 1695, with *Gl'inganni infelici*. But his first popular success was *Lucio Vero*, on a Roman subject, performed in Venice in 1700, with music by Carlo Francesco Pollarolo, assistant chapel master at St Mark's. This was followed by *Temistocle* (Venice, 1701), performed to celebrate the birthday of the Emperor Leopold I, with music by Marc'Antonio Ziani, vice-director of music, Vienna. After this, Zeno became one of the most sought after Italian librettists of his day. His works were set by composers such as Francesco Gasparini, Domenico Scarlatti and others. But it was not until after the death of his wife that he finally accepted an invitation from the Emperor Charles VI to go to Vienna, where he collaborated at first with his friend Pietro Pariati (1665–1733), who had been Poet Laureate since 1714. In Vienna, where he lived from 1719 to 1731, Zeno wrote many libretti for the *opera seria*, which were mainly set to music by the Viennese composers of the period. Some of his most successful and influential works, besides the early *Lucio Vero* and *Temistocle*, were *Merope* (1711), which inspired Maffei's tragedy of the same name, *Eumene*, his first Viennese opera, *Semiramide in Ascalona* (1725) and *Griselda*, based on the *novella* of Boccaccio. In such works Zeno observed the dramatic unities and made a clear distinction between the recitative and the arias, which were well distributed; he also freed the opera from scurrility and put noble passions and noble protagonists on the stage. But in comparison with the works of Metastasio, Zeno's libretti are generally regarded as lacking in poetic merit and in musical harmony.

In the course of his long life, apart from his libretti for the *opera seria* – such as *Didone abbandonata* (first performed at Naples in 1724), and *Demetrio* (Vienna, 1731) – Metastasio composed a considerable number of less extensive 'azioni teatrali' (cantatas, oratorios and similar pieces), both sacred and secular. Many of his texts, which won universal acclaim, were set to music, sometimes by as many as fifty different composers, as diverse as Handel and Mozart. He is also remembered for a notable prose treatise, entitled *Estratto dell'Arte Poetica d'Aristotile*, in which, writing as a practising dramatist, he analysed 'La natura della Poesia, dell'Imitazione e del Verisimile', and incidentally demonstrated that his *drammi per musica* were the heirs of the classical tragedy and his arias of the Greek choric strophes.

It is evident from the *Estratto* that, on the authority of Plato and Aristotle, Metastasio took a lofty view of the dignity of his art and of his vocation. He viewed the act of poetic creation from what might nowadays be regarded as an excessively 'classical' point of view: as one of those 'imitations', or acts of *mimesis* – the basis of all the arts – to which men are drawn by Nature, and which universally give pleasure. For Metastasio there was no poetry without the discipline of verse. 'Free verse' was, for him, just prose. His view was that what makes poetry 'poetry' was the transformation by the poet of normal rational discourse into what he described as 'La misurata, numerosa, armoniosa favella, abile a dilettar per se stessa'. This musical speech idiom, to which he aspired in all his poetic compositions, was to be clear, harmonious, dignified, ordered and sublime: in a word, 'una lingua artificiosa imitatrice del discorso naturale'. This poetic medium was to be used on all occasions and for all subjects. Its style must never be altered. It was, for the poet, what a block of marble was for a sculptor; or for a painter, his range of colours. But to be what Metastasio regarded as a 'good poet', and not merely a 'poet', 'dottrina', 'buon giudizio', 'fantasia' and 'invenzione' were all essential.

Like Aristotle, and such tragedians of his own day as Gravina and Conti, Metastasio had a high regard for the dramatic unities; and he took great care that his *drammi per musica* should leave a simple and single impression. He divided his works into three acts, instead of the more usual five; and he believed that one illustrious action should provide the central interest of each. But he was not averse to the introduction of subordinate material, provided that this did not disturb the main development. The stage set was considered as an ample territory, sufficiently vast to contain within itself all the subsequent divisions and locations required by the individual scenes. In the first of these the dramatic situation was presented; usually with a subordinate action which contained the imminent catastrophe. The action as a whole, which observed the unity of time, took place within 'il termine d'un giro del sole'.

Textually Metastasio's libretti are composed of verse passages suitable for musical realization in terms of recitative and aria in their various forms: *arie cantabili*, *arie di portamento*, declamatory *arie parlanti*, and bold, virile *arie di bravura*, to name but a few. In tone the verses are lyrical, rather than dramatic; and, whether in the form of *settenari* or *endecasillabi*, or in lively bounding strophes, they are invariably characterized by a unique transparency of expression: a quality, especially cultivated by the author, and defined by him in the *Estratto*, as 'una specie di interno canto'.

The subjects of Metastasio's *drammi per musica*, with but one or two exceptions, were all drawn from the histories and fables of the Greco-Roman tradition: from sources on the one hand in such ancient authors as Virgil and Ovid, and on the other in the modern French playwrights, Racine and Crébillon. His favourite themes were Roman imperial, Greek in a few instances, and the remote world of the Trojan war and its aftermath. The operas are set in the Mediterranean, in pre-Christian times, in the exotic lands of Africa, the Levant, in Babylon, and in far-away, fabulous India.

In his treatment of his themes, Metastasio everywhere provided subjects concerning virtuous action in a hundred guises: triumphs of magnanimity, with personifications of Nobility and Clemency; themes of friendship, heroic gratitude, love of country, constancy in disaster, generosity with friends, and also with enemies. And out of the conflict, there usually emerged a moral. As a young man, under the stern eye of Gravina, by whom he had been educated, Metastasio had studied Aeschylus and Sophocles; but the violence, brutality and horror of the pure Greek tragedies had appalled him. Like the French tragedians of the *Grand Siècle*, he was interested primarily in the 'passions', or the *affetti* as they were called, especially when these were in conflict. He wanted an operatic drama which, though ideally linked to the ancient tragedy, would provide an experience less harrowing than that, and demonstrate some moral point.

Metastasio's *drammi per musica* are peopled with characters of a heroic, quasi-mythological stamp. Royalty of all types is the social norm; and a Roman hero is often found at the centre of the action. For the rest, the characters are either confidants, tutors, or military men of high rank. The plots are generally complicated; and they are resolved by such classical devices as 'recognition' and *peripeteia*. Disguises, the use of cover names, and mistaken identities abound; there are also false friends; a character may be cast in the role of a 'creduto figlio', an 'amante occulta', a 'nemico occulto', or as an 'amante ricusato'. Each character usually embodies some permanent element of human nature. Each is subtly motivated, possibly wilful, and endowed with emotions or passions, capable of the maximum expressive force. In number, in any one opera, the characters are normally extremely limited – usually six and, in a few later works, seven or eight. In general the characters, both male and female, are closely interlinked; and they tend to arrange themselves into symmetrical pairings of lovers. The vicissitudes of these cut across each other; and in this way the protagonists can express themselves through music, in the musical forms of the solo, or in the most varied combinations: in duets, trios and quartets. And it is in the infinite variety of contrasts and of conflicting passions, especially in the delicacy and subtlety of the shades of feelings within the passion of love, that part of the interest and appeal of the Metastasian *melodramma* resides.

Metastasio's first libretto for the *opera seria* was *Didone abbandonata*, based on the *Aeneid*, Book IV, in which Virgil had recounted the tragic love of Dido, queen of Carthage, for Aeneas. This drama of love versus duty describes the imminent departure of Aeneas and the abandonment of Dido and its sequel. Written at the behest of Marianna Bulgarelli, the Roman opera singer, known as 'La Romanina', the text was set to music by Domenico Sarro, *Maestro di cappella* of the Chapel Royal, Naples; and the opera was first performed at theTeatro San Bartolomeo, with Marianna Bulgarelli in the role of Dido, during Carnival in 1724. The appeal of *Didone abbandonata* was such that within a few years other versions were staged with music by such eminent composers as Domenico Scarlatti, Tomaso Albinoni and Leonardo Vinci. In 1736, Handel produced a score. The opera was soon performed all over Europe; and before the end of the Metastasian era a further fifty or sixty Italian and Italian-educated German composers had all written music to Metastasio's text.

Between 1724 and 1729 Metastasio wrote six more operatic libretti, five of which were first set to music by Leonardo Vinci: *Siroe* (1726), *Catone in Utica*, *Ezio* (with music by Pietro Auletta), *Semiramide*,

Alessandro nelle Indie and *Artaserse*. After this, finding himself famous, Metastasio was invited to Vienna, where he first joined and ultimately succeeded Apostolo Zeno in the role of 'Poeta Cesareo' at the imperial court.

In Vienna, between 1730 and 1740, Metastasio wrote libretti for the following operas: *Demetrio* (1731), *Issipile* (1732), *Adriano in Siria* (1732), *L'Olimpiade* (1733), *Demofoonte* (1733), *La Clemenza di Tito* (1734), *Achille in Sciro* (1736), *Ciro riconosciuto* (1736), *Temistocle* (1737), *Zenobia* (1740) and *Attilio Regolo* (1740). Each of these was commissioned either by the Emperor Charles VI or by the Empress Elizabeth to celebrate a royal birthday or some similar command performance, such as the wedding of the Archduchess Maria Theresa. In practically every instance the libretti were first set to music by the Venetian composer Antonio Caldara (1670–1736) who, after a lifetime of court service, had settled in Vienna with the appointment of vice-conductor and composer, under the ageing Austrian musical theorist Johann Joseph Fux. The Caldara–Metastasio operas were first performed with great splendour in the court theatre or, in the case of *L'Olimpiade*, in the gardens of *La Favorita*.

With the death of Charles VI, Metastasio's career suffered a setback. In 1740 the line of male succession was broken; and the almost automatic right of the Habsburgs to the crown of the Holy Roman Empire was ended. Worse still, the emperor's sprawling dominions were almost bankrupt. So when Maria Theresa came to the throne lean times set in for her Poet Laureate in some respects. She commissioned less of the costly heroic spectacles which Metastasio and his associates had been so capable of providing. In any case, times were changing; and after 1740 Metastasio became the purveyor of less frequent and more intimate entertainments than hitherto. These were mainly cantatas and oratorios. But he remained until his death, in 1782, the official poet of the Austrian nobility, writing verses designed to be set to music for royal birthdays, weddings and similar state occasions.

Vittorio Alfieri

In marked contrast to the somewhat timid Metastasio, who fitted in well at court, Vittorio Alfieri (1749–1803), born at Asti, in the dominions of the House of Savoy, was a 'literary lion' of pronounced individuality, who gradually came to personify his own ideal of a 'free writer' unshackled by social and political ties, especially by the impediments that dependence on a princely patron had traditionally implied. Anti-conformist, outspoken and impulsive in character, he was deaf to the exigencies of social and economic life, and highly critical of the aspirations of the Enlightenment and of the belief of the *philosophes* in prince-reformers. A proto-liberal at the beginning of the age of Romanticism, he helped to create the myth-image of the artist as the ideal 'free man', with the time to do anything he wished and a life-style beyond moral constraints. As a young man the Piedmontese dialect and French came more naturally to him than Italian until, at the age of twenty-seven, he took radical steps to remedy the defect. After this, having already had his first tragedy, *Cleopatra* (1774–5), performed with some success at the Teatro Carignano, Turin, he set out with characteristic zeal to write a further twenty-one, in which bitter and violent, if at times ingenuous, tragic effects were produced by the simplest and starkest means. With the exception of *Cleopatra* and the late *Alceste seconda* (1798) – an erudite re-handling of the *Alcestis* of Euripides – these greatly acclaimed and vibrant works were all published in a definitive edition by Didot, in Paris, between 1787 and 1789.

In their characters and themes, a few of Alfieri's tragedies had their origins in the writings of Machiavelli or in the lurid intrigues of sixteenth-century political history and legend. Among these may be mentioned *La congiura dei Pazzi*, *Filippo* and *Maria Stuarda*. The majority of his tragedies, however, were classical in subject and based on ancient sources: the Graeco-Roman theatre, Ovid and the Roman historians, Livy and Suetonius, and the *Lives* of Plutarch, in which the biographies of eminent Greek soldiers and statesmen were compared with their Roman counterparts. The Old Testament furnished the subject of his favourite masterpiece, *Saul*. In his treatment of his sources, Alfieri had no compunction in completely remodelling his material, or departing from historical reality. He was interested in extending and developing an elemental situation, either real or imagined, to extract its tragic potential in accordance with his own interests. These lay especially in themes of despotism and aspirations towards liberty; stark solitude and betrayal; egoism and hatred; dark passions and a bloody irreversible destiny. But in their form Alfieri's tragedies are scrupulously regular, according to the classical formula. They are in five acts; and the three unities are strictly observed: a matter which was easy to achieve in that all the plays deal with the culminating phase of the passionate conflicts with which they are concerned. Alfieri saw the past from which he drew his subjects as a sort of Plutarchan picture gallery of great figures waiting to be handled tragically. His characters, the range of which in any one play is often severely restricted (no more than four in the case of *Timoleone*), are lofty and superior beings. Their tone is earnest, gloomy and foreboding, and all are essential to the drama; the feelings expressed are heroic, exalted and at times ferocious. Power-seeking tyrants and their abused and suffering victims confront each other; and when it is no longer possible for liberty to be preserved, the victim commits suicide: an act that appears as a moral victory, a positive affirmation of essential freedom, and not as a sign of defeat.

Besides his tragedies, Alfieri produced in his maturity two politico-philosophical treatises, in which the influence of Machiavelli, Montesquieu and Rousseau is evident, six bizarre satirical comedies, one 'tramelogedia' (a form of drama mixing tragedy and opera invented by himself) and a notable quantity of miscellaneous pieces. The latter include seventeen satires (1777–97) in *terza rima,* deriding all that he saw in the life of the time that was keeping his countrymen from becoming capable of 'true freedom', five Pindaric odes celebrating the American War of Independence, and the splenetic *Il Misogallo* (1793–9), a violent expression of hatred and contempt for the excesses of the Gallic race, both before and after the Revolution, consisting of five prose passages, forty-six sonnets, sixty-three epigrams and an ode. In later life he also composed a masterly autobiography (*Vita scritta da esso*). This was first drafted in Paris in 1790; and subsequently completed in thoroughly revised form in Florence in 1803, with the addition of eleven new chapters bring the story of his life up to date. In these memoirs, which are self-revelatory and self-critical in style, Alfieri was concerned to idealize himself; and especially to stress the alleged contrast between what he presented as the ignorance and sterility of his youth spent in Piedmont, where he suffered 'otto anni d'ineducazione', and the maturity and sense of vocation of his later years when he came to recognize that his happiness and creative talents depended for their fulfilment on 'a worthy love' ('un degno amore'), as distinct from an 'unworthy' love, to occupy his heart, and 'a noble work' ('un qualche nobile lavoro') to occupy his mind.

Born into the provincial and conservatively minded aristocracy of Piedmont, Alfieri lost his father soon after his birth; and while still a boy, he inherited a fortune. At the age of nine, to his intense disgust, he was placed in the military academy at Turin; whence he emerged eight years later with the rank of ensign in the Asti regiment. In 1766, at the age of seventeen, he embarked on two journeys, with Francesco Elia, an attentive servant of dubious loyalty, which took him first to Florence, Rome and Naples, where he found little to admire; and then to France and England. Paris he viewed with disgust as a 'fetente cloaca'; England, in contrast, struck him as a 'fortunato e libero paese'. Back in Turin for a few months in 1768–9, he devoted himself to 'philosophical' studies, reading Plutarch avidly, and also Machiavelli and the French encyclopedists. Rousseau was not much to his taste; and he seems to have gained little from Voltaire. But Montesquieu, the theoretician of constitutional government, and Plutarch became his favourite authors. While in Turin Alfieri almost became engaged, but in May 1769, when the alliance was broken off, he again set out on his travels, undertaking a second, and longer, journey outside Italy.

He spent the summer at Vienna, where he took pains to avoid the ageing Metastasio; and he then proceeded to Berlin, where he was presented to Frederick the Great. But the ideal 'enlightened despot' of the Encyclopedists had no appeal for Alfieri; and the Prussian military state only confirmed his detestation of 'quell'infame mestier militare, infamissima e sola base dell'autorità arbitraria'. More at ease in Denmark and in Sweden, he was likewise appalled by the Petersburg of the Empress Catherine II. It was only in England, where in 1770 he became infatuated with the flighty Penelope Pitt, wife of Earl Ligonier, with whom he fought a duel in St James's Park, that he felt it possible to live comfortably and with humanity. Before returning to Turin in 1772, he also visited Spain and Portugal. He traversed the Andalusian plains partly on foot and partly on horseback, keeping his mind occupied by reading *Don Quixote*. At Lisbon, in the Piedmontese embassy, he met the astronomer and orientalist

Tommaso Valperga di Caluso, who awakened in him his latent love of poetry. This man, whom Alfieri esteemed as 'un Montaigne vivo', soon became one of his intimate friends and advisers. Ten years later Alfieri dedicated to him his tragedy *Saul*.

Alfieri first began his literary career on his return to Turin, where he settled in a luxurious apartment, frequented polite circles, set up an academy and took as his mistress the mature and obsessive Gabriella Falletti, wife of the marquis Turinetti di Prié. After a while, to amuse himself in a period of lethargy and sexual dissatisfaction, he drafted and three times versified his first tragedy, *Cleopatra*. In this theme of fatal passion he found much in common with his own situation; and through the characters of the Roman triumvir Mark Antony and the equivocal queen of Egypt, who is brutally disparaged, he depicted his own slavery to the 'odiasamata signora' he despised but was unable to renounce. *Cleopatra*, which was first performed in June 1775, was subsequently repudiated; and it remained unpublished until 1805. But it showed Alfieri his vocation and encouraged him in his determination to put aside his 'unworthy' love, to change his life and win fame as a tragedian.

Early in 1775, before the stage success of *Cleopatra*, Alfieri had already made a first draft of two other tragedies, *Filippo* and *Polinice*, both of which took six years to complete (1775–81). The former, which is set in the Escurial in the time of King Philip II, is a tragedy of unnatural hate. It deals with the fate of the Spanish Infante, Don Carlos, the king's son by Mary of Portugal, who was deprived of his right to the succession, and whose betrothal to Isabella of France was abruptly broken off when the king himself took the princess in marriage as his third consort. *Polinice* is a tragedy of regal ambition, which deals with the fratricidal strife of the sons of Oedipus for the throne of Thebes. In *Filippo*, which is one of Alfieri's best tragedies, the poet departed widely from historical testimony, like Schiller a few years later, who dealt with a similar theme in *Don Carlos* (1787). The tragedy is presented as one of 'lo snaturato inaudito odio paterno' of a cruel and hypocritical despot, who sees enemies everywhere, against a loyal and courageous son who is falsely accused of parricide. It was based on the popular *Histoire de Don Carlos* (1672) by Cesare Vichard, the Savoyard abbé de Saint-Réal. The play ends with the suicide of Don Carlos and of the ingenuous Isabella, both of whom stab themselves to death as the only noble course in the face of tyrannical oppression. Like most of Alfieri's early tragedies, *Filippo* was drafted first in French prose and then turned into Italian. It was subsequently versified on four distinct occasions. Even after 1781 Alfieri continued to correct and modify the text, as was his custom.

In the summer of 1775, with *Filippo* still in a French prose draft, Alfieri left Turin for Cézannes, at the foot of Montgenèvre, to take stock of himself as a budding tragedian. He was acutely aware of the inadequacies of his literary and linguistic preparation, his early knowledge of Italian being largely confined to books. He studied Latin and read the classic authors; and in the summer of 1776, to purge himself of his Piedmontese inheritance, and to learn to 'parlare, udire, pensare e sognare in toscano, e non altrimenti mai più', he went to live at Pisa. In the following year he settled first at Siena, then at Florence. In each town he enjoyed the friendship of the literary fraternity and worked diligently on his tragedies. In Florence he also contracted his most influential and long-lasting attachment. His 'worthy' love, from 1777 on, was the cultivated and attractive Louisa von Stolberg (1753–1824), the young wife of the ageing dipsomaniac Charles Edward Stuart, Count of Albany, the exiled 'Young Pretender', claimant to the Crown of England. In the same year, full of youthful impetuosity, he dashed off 'd'un solo fiato', *Della tirannide* (1777), a politico-philosophical treatise in two books defining the evils of arbitrary power in absolutist régimes – for Alfieri, any form of government which permitted the law to be broken with impunity. Subsequently, in *Del principe e delle lettere* ('The Prince and Letters', 1778–86), he attacked rationalism, exalted the natural impulse, delineated his ideal of the 'free writer', and was concerned to demonstrate that princely patronage could only lead to servility and to the detriment of a writer's art. In the meantime, with half a dozen new tragedies on the stocks, he strove to achieve poetic excellence; and in 1778, to free himself from subjectivity to Victor Amadeus III, he cut his ties with Piedmont definitively, by transferring his property, with the king's consent, to his sister, in exchange for an annuity.

Alfieri's tragedies, irrespective of their chronology, have often been grouped into five broad categories. These are: tragedies of passionate love and passionate hatred (*Cleopatra*, *Filippo*, *Rosamunda*, *Sofonisba*, *Ottavia*); tragedies of liberty versus tyranny (*Virginia*, *La congiura dei Pazzi*, *Timoleone*, *Agide*, *Bruto primo*, *Bruto secondo*); tragedies of regal ambition (*Polinice*, *Agamennone*, *Don Garzia*, *Maria Stuarda*); tragedies of fraternal, filial and maternal affection, locked in sombre conflict with tyrannical forces (*Antigone*, *Oreste*, *Merope*, *Alceste seconda*); and the dark interior tragedies of travailed souls (*Saul*, *Mirra*). The interest and originality of these works, in general, depends on three main factors: the nobility of the civil and moral aims by which they were inspired; their so-called 'subjectivity', the curious 'Alfierian' quality whereby the heroes and heroines, who are normally victims, partake of their author's state of mind; and the unusual harshness and vitality of the Italian blank verse which, in contrast to the musicality and sweetness of the Metastasian style, is often pithy and sententious, and makes few concessions to euphony.

Three of Alfieri's best tragedies, besides *Filippo* (already mentioned), are *Agamennone* (1776–81), which takes place in the royal palace at Argos, and the deeply affecting *Saul* (1782) and *Mirra* (1784): the latter, dedicated to the Countess of Albany, being his last masterpiece before his poetic powers began to wain. The protagonist of *Agamennone* is the wife of the king, the formidable Clytemnestra. Unable to forgive her husband for having sacrificed their daughter Iphigenia to avert the wrath of Artemis, she treacherously murders him in his sleep on his return from the Trojan War, egged on by her paramour, the perfidious Aegisthus, who has taken Agamemnon's place on the throne of Mycenae as well as in his bed. *Mirra*, a different type of play, is the original tragedy of a languid and stricken, but beautiful, Cypriot princess, Myrrha, the innocent victim of an atrocious vendetta brought against her by the goddess Venus, to whom Cyprus is sacred. She is betrothed to Peréo, prince of Epirus, who is driven to suicide when the nuptuals are bizarrely broken off on their wedding day; and Myrrha, the most touching and mutely desperate of Alfieri's heroines, is at last induced to betray the never-to-be-disclosed secret implanted in her heart. Torn between guilt and duty, she is torn by the mortal anguish of a tyrannical incestuous passion which makes her abhorrent to herself and a paradox of grief to her bewildered parents. In the catastrophe of Act V, frantic and hysterical, she transfixes herself on her father's sword; and she is dragged from the stage by him, like the carcass of an unclean beast, in loathing and disgust. The subject of *Mirra* was suggested by a mythological transformation, recounted in Ovid's *Metamorphoses* (X, 298–502), dealing with the daughter of Cinyras, king of Cyprus, who conceived a criminal passion for her father; and, with the assistance of her nurse, committed incest without being known.

Like *Mirra*, Alfieri's first tragedy of interior conflict, *Saul*, is also based on, though not contained by, an ancient source. It derives from the Old Testament narratives concerning the estrangement and subsequent contest between David, a man dearly beloved by God, and Saul, the Israelite king, who was defeated by the Philistines at the battle of Gilboa. David, later king of Judah, had first drawn attention to himself by slaying Goliath, the Philistine who had 'defied the armies of Israel'. Earlier still, he had acquired a reputation as a skilful harpist, and subdued by his music the paroxysms of insanity which afflicted Saul at certain seasons. Later, a fugitive from Saul's malice, he came to be regarded as a dangerous enemy and one to be persecuted – until the rivalry assumed the dignity of a civil war. Alfieri's *Saul* is set in the camp of the Israelites and takes place on the day of the battle of Gilboa. Besides Saul and David, the main characters are Jonathan and Micol, Saul's beloved son and daughter; and Abner, his treacherous cousin, and the captain of his army. Jonathan is David's 'bosom-friend'; Micol is compassionate towards her ailing father and to David a tender and loving wife. Saul himself is a monstrous, unpredictable tyrant, torn by the complexity of his vacillating love and jealousy, and dominated by a profound sense of his physical and moral decline and of his betrayal by all that he holds most dear. Acts I and II present the return of David, who wishes to redeem himself, from the Philistines to the Israelite camp. He is welcomed by Jonathan and Micol; and a reconciliation with Saul is attempted. But the deluded king, with the evil spirit still invading his heart and mind, suffers hallucinations and again wants to slay David. The latter is banished in Act IV; and the tragic isolation of Saul from his kinsfolk and from his God inexorably develops, until at last he stands alone with himself, like Lear, in his madness. In the battle in Act V Jonathan is slain; and the king falls on his sword, recognizing that everything is lost and that God is avenged, surrounded by a horde of yelling Philistines.

Saul is the most distinguished and complex of Alfieri's poetic dramas; and in it the author believed he had put the whole of himself. The protagonist is treated more as a subject of Greek than of Biblical tragedy. Ultimately Saul is the victim of his own character: a distraught and solitary despot, torn by conflicting passions, dominated by his sense of loss and by an inescapable destiny.

Besides *Saul* and *Mirra*, four other compelling tragedies by Alfieri are *Virginia* (1777–8), which was based on Livy, *Timoleone* (1779–81) and the Brutuses: *Bruto primo* and *Bruto secondo*, both first drafted in 1786, and referring respectively to the Republican hero, Lucius Junius Brutus, expeller of Tarquin the Proud, and the mysterious Marcus Junius Brutus, possibly the son of Julius Caesar, who joined the conspiracy for his assassination in 44 BC. Of the tragedies of regal ambition *Don Garzia* (1778–9) concerns the plot, now known to be legendary, of Piero, son of Cosimo I, Grand Duke of Tuscany, to murder his brother in order to inherit the succession. *Maria Stuarda* (1778–80), the theme of which was suggested by the Countess of Albany, deals with the murder of Darnley. *La congiura dei Pazzi* (1777–81), one of the tragedies of liberty versus tyranny, is taken from Machiavelli's *Istorie fiorentine*. In it the brothers Lorenzo and Giuliano dei Medici are cast in the role of tyrants. *Agide* (1784–6), which was written partly at Pisa and partly at Colmar, is set in Sparta in the fourth century BC and was dedicated to the memory of 'un re infelice e morto', Charles I of England.

The protagonist of *Virginia*, Alfieri's fifth tragedy and a favourite work, is a young plebeian betrothed to the Roman tribune Icilio. She is abducted by Appio Claudio, a patrician decemvir aiming at supreme authority and suppression of the Republic. Virginia's father and Icilio, a bitter adversary of despotism, incite the people to revolt. But Icilio is killed; the insurrection fails; and Virginia herself is menaced. To restore the concepts of honour and liberty, through an immensity of suffering, Virginia is stabbed to death by her own father. A similar defence of liberty is the concern of *Timoleone*, which was based on Plutarch's life of the great Greek general and statesman. In it Timoleone stands by while his brother, Timophanes, is assassinated because he has made himself tyrant of Corinth. The tragedy of *Bruto primo*, dedicated to George Washington, arose from an episode in the life of the first consul, who sacrificed his sons to save the emergent Republic, executing them when they were found guilty of conspiring to restore the Tarquins. Like two of Antonio Conti's tragedies, *Giulio Cesare* and *Marco Bruto*, and Shakespeare's *Julius Caesar*, *Bruto secondo* deals with the conspiracy and murder of Julius Caesar. The play was based on Plutarch and Suetonius, and dedicated 'al Popolo italiano futuro'. In it the tragic conflict, which is centred on the father–son relationship, is presented as a conflict between the death throes of the dying Republic, personified by Marcus Brutus, and the emergence of a dictatorship, with the rise of Caesar.

While writing his tragedies in the 1780s Alfieri was much encouraged by the Countess of Albany, without whom he could neither live happily nor compose. In 1781 he followed her to Rome, where she was living in a convent to avoid her husband; and after a trip to England in 1784 he joined her in Colmar. With the outbreak of the French Revolution, with the ideals of which he at first sympathized, he again spent a period in London. Later, from his experiences of rebellion in Paris at the time of the Terror, when his effects were sequestrated, he learned to fear and hate the violence of the revolutionary masses. His last years were spent in Florence, where he had apartments on the Lungarno Corsini, near Ponte di Santa Trinita, with the Countess of Albany. Here he tried to learn Greek, in order to read Homer, Hesiod and Euripides in the original, and he became increasingly absorbed in biblical and allegorical matters. He wrote his comedies and he also experimented further with a curious new form, mixing tragedy and opera, which he designated by the singular term of 'tramelogedia'. His sole success in this was *Abele* (1786–90), a curious composition, rich in allegory and symbolism, set at the time of Genesis, of which part was designed to be sung in the form of recitative and aria, and part to be declaimed as blank verse. The characters include, on the one hand, Lucifer, Beelzebub, Sin, Death and the Voice of God; and on the other, Adam and Eve, and the brothers Cain and Abel. *Abele* concludes with the triumph of the forces of Evil over the forces of Good.

Four of Alfieri's six comedies – *L'uno*, *I pochi*, *I troppi*, *L'antidoto* – have political themes. They are in hendecasyllables, and all were written in the last three years of his life. They develop allegorically with historical and fabulous characters drawn from antiquity, and deal satirically with the evils of despotic, oligarchic and democratic forms of government, and with their remedy, the 'antidote', constitutional monarchy. Of the other comedies, *La finestrina* is a moral allegory; and *Il divorzio* a satire on the marriage contract in high society and the curious phenomenon of *cicisbeismo*, 'fetor dei costumi italicheschi'.

COMEDY

The heritage of the 'commedia dell'arte'

For some two hundred years, from the mid sixteenth to the mid eighteenth century, the witty amalgam of mime, buffoonery, acrobatics, singing and bawdy known as the *commedia dell'arte*,[1] enjoyed a phenomenal success not only in Italy, where the genre was born, but also throughout Europe. In Italy itself the *commedia dell'arte* companies gained ascendancy in the comic theatre and their racy, improvised, knock-about farces entirely ousted the regular *commedia erudita*. The plots of the improvised comedy were intricate and existed only in the form of a *canovaccio* or *scenario*, a skeleton script comprising a series of stage instructions and the order of the scenes. The themes dealt with such popular matter as forced marriages, star-crossed lovers, and the intrigues of servants and their masters. Magic was much employed to resolve the plot. For generations the *commedia dell'arte* was performed by companies of professional actors, frequently of outstanding talent and technical virtuosity, who specialized in fixed character parts with clearly defined roles. Besides the Innamorato and the Innamorata, two languishing lovers at the centre of the comedy, some of the most typical character players were a greedy bombastic Neapolitan (Pulcinella), a boastful, singing vagabond from Calabria (Coviello), a crusty Venetian business man in his dotage (Pantalone), a pedant from Bologna (Dottor Balanzon), two comic servants, or *zanni* (the wily Arlecchino and the cunning Brighella), and the Canterina and the Ballerina, whose duty was to sing and dance. Most of the players, apart from the Innamorati, habitually wore a grotesque leather mask on the stage. Their dialogue, with strict observance of current speech idioms, was for the most part improvised, though much use was made of memorized poetic formulas, especially for exits

1. Alternative names for this type of comedy were *commedia all'improvviso*, *commedia di maschere*, *commedia a soggetto*, *commedia a braccio* and *commedia buffonesca*.

(*uscite*) and entrances (*entrate*). Pantalone spoke in Venetian; the doctor in Bolognese macaronics; and the *zanni* in two distinct versions of Bergamasque.

In the age of Arcadia, with the growing rejection of the past so typical of the period, there gradually emerged a few Italian playwrights who wished to adapt the Italian comedy to changed conditions. The excessive influence of the *commedia dell'arte* companies was criticized; it was felt that the same kind of jokes, told by Brighella and Arlecchino, had raised the same coarse laughs by the same buffoonery and the same gestures of obscenity for far too long. As a result of this, the history of the Italian comic theatre from the Age of Arcadia to the Period of Reforms, is one of two strictly interrelated phenomena, which were accompanied, especially at Venice where the changes were acutely felt, by an unparalleled spate of theatrical polemics and bitter recriminations. One of these phenomena was the slow eclipse of the *commedia dell'arte*, and its subsequent brief revival in the 1760s, through the initiative of Count Carlo Gozzi, the creator of a new dramatic form – the *fiaba teatrale* – and the self-appointed guardian of tradition and of the moral order. The other was the gradual creation of a vast corpus of regular, written-out comedies of a 'classical' stamp, which, largely on the pretext of imitating the seventeenth-century French theatre, especially Molière, held up the twin mirrors to 'character' and 'manners' with the aim of correcting defects and making vice detestable. This trend culminated, between 1738–62, despite fierce opposition in the 1750s, first of the ex-Jesuit *abate* Pietro Chiari and later of Carlo Gozzi, in the so-called 'reform' of Carlo Goldoni (1707–93), one of the most prolific and genial of playwrights, the greater part of whose multifarious works were informed by an estimable intent: the advancement and elevation of honourable sentiments and deeds, and the flagellation of vices.

In the course of his long life, the last thirty years of which were spent in France, at Paris and Versailles, Goldoni wrote some 120 comedies, both in prose and verse, in Italian, Venetian dialect and French, and an almost equal number of other theatrical compositions. The latter included *scenari* for the *commedia dell'arte*, musical *intermezzi*, tragi-comedies, lyric and heroic dramas, *melodrammi giocosi* and *comédies larmoyantes*. These works defy simple classification; and the comedies are perhaps best seen on the one hand in relation to the new taste beginning to affirm itself in Goldoni's day, and on the other in relation to the various strata of Italian social life with which the plays were concerned. Some of the comedies lightly satirized the nobility; others mirrored the customs and manners of the middle classes; others again were set in the vibrant, open-air world of the common people. The rest of the comedies have often been classified as 'sentimental', 'historical' and 'exotic'.

In his last years, while living in France, Goldoni also wrote a notable volume of *Mémoires*, in French, which provide an invaluable, if somewhat prosaic, account of his life, his theatre and the stages of his reform.

Carlo Goldoni

A striking aspect of Goldoni's reform – which involved not only renewal of the text of the comedy and its content, but also the re-education of the actors and of the audience – was the inordinate slowness and hesitancy with which it was achieved. Though he started to write at the age of eight, as a young man Goldoni was only incidentally connected with the theatre and with theatre folk; and it was not until 1748, at the age of forty-one, after being widely employed in theatrical undertakings for many years, that he finally decided to turn professional playwright, with a contract to provide eight new plays a season for the troupe of Gerolamo Medebach, actor-manager of the Teatro Sant'Angelo, Venice.

Born at Venice on 25 February 1707, the son of a medical practitioner, Goldoni went to school at Perugia and Rimini, where between 1720 and 1721 he followed courses with the Dominican fathers. Later, he was placed in the Collegio Ghislieri, Pavia (1723–5), whence he was expelled for a satire against the ladies of the town. Destined to become a lawyer, he worked for a time in the legal office of an uncle in Venice; and in 1731 he graduated in law at Padua University. He was then admitted to the Venetian bar and subsequently employed at various record offices. In 1733 and 1734 he held a post at the Venetian embassy at Milan. Between 1740 and 1743 he served as Genoese consul in Venice; and from 1744 to 1748 he practised as an advocate at Pisa, seemingly settled in his career as a lawyer.

Throughout these years Goldoni's interest always lay with the theatre. At the age of fourteen he ran away from the school at Rimini with a troupe of *commedia dell'arte* players who were visiting the town. At Pavia, he preferred reading the classical comedy, both ancient and modern, especially Machiavelli and Molière, to his more formal studies. And in the winter of 1729–30, while in the record office at Feltre, he wrote, as a diversion, the text of two entertaining musical interludes (*intermezzi*), the one 'comic', the other 'satiric', that were performed between the acts of the *opera seria*, but which also enjoyed a vitality of their own. In 1732, on his way to Milan, he carried in his pocket the manuscript of his first lyric tragedy, *Amalasunta*. And in 1734, having met the Genoese actor-manager Giuseppe Imer and his company at Verona, and interested them in his tragi-comedy *Belisario*, he was soon engaged as a playwright for the Teatro San Samuele, Venice, by its proprietor, the Venetian patrician Michele Grimani. From then on he produced numerous *libretti*, more *intermezzi*, and a number of *scenari* for the *commedia dell'arte*.

From his earliest years, however, Goldoni had felt a sense of discontent at the dearth of regular, scripted comedy in Italy. He had assimilated the lesson of the classics; as he was later to become interested in the sentimental and didactic literature of contemporary England and France. In Italy he disliked especially the habitual use of improvisation and the convention of wearing a mask on the stage. He also disapproved of the outworn use of the stock *commedia dell'arte* characters; their dialogue with its fixed poetic formulas; and the intricacy, fantasy and unnaturalness of the plots. In place of the *commedia dell'arte* Goldoni wanted a theatre that would delineate the realities of social life in as natural a manner as possible and permit him to put on the stage characters caught in the fulness of their humanity. While working for Imer the opportunity for which Goldoni had been looking first presented itself when two new actors joined the company – Antonio Sacchi, famous for his interpretation of the part of Truffaldino, and the expressive Francesco Golinetti, who habitually played the part of Pantalone. For these players, in 1738, Goldoni composed *Momolo cortesan*: a *scenario*-type play with which he began the Herculean task first of suppressing improvisation and then of removing the mask. In it he wrote out the dialogue, which he required Sacchi and Golinetti to memorize instead of improvising. The success of *Momolo cortesan*, the original text of which has not survived, was followed in 1740 by *Momolo sulla Brenta, ossia il prodigo*; and in 1743 by *La donna di garbo*, the first example of a play by Goldoni in which all the parts were entirely scripted. 1745 saw the ever-popular *Il servitore di due padroni*. But it was not until 1750, when Goldoni was contracted to Medebach at the Teatro Sant'Angelo, that with *Pamela nubile*, a sentimental drama, based on the novel *Pamela* by Samuel Richardson, Goldoni finally put a play on the stage in which none of the characters was required to wear a mask.

While working for Medebach, between 1748–53, Goldoni produced his first masterpiece of 'character' comedy, *La locandiera* (written in 1752 and performed in 1753), which is often regarded as the culmination of his apprentice years. His first brilliant success, however, was *La vedova scaltra* (1748), a somewhat artificial comedy in three acts, with both 'character' and *commedia dell'arte* parts, which ran for twenty-five evenings, with Teresa Raffi-Medebach in the title-role of the spirited and independently minded young widow, Rosaura. The latter is not averse to marrying again; and the claimants to her hand are a jealous but faithful Italian count, a boorish Spanish grandee, who is entirely obsessed with his sense of caste and the twenty-four generations of his family tree, a gallant and ridiculous Frenchman, and a dry and laconic English milord on the Grand Tour. Each of these four well-contrasted national types is subjected to a test of fidelity and in the end, only her fellow-countryman, the Conte di Bosco Nero, who courts her for herself alone, surmounts the test and wins her hand.

La vedova scaltra was a transitional play still steeped in elements typical of the *commedia dell'arte*, such as the use of the masks and frequent disguises, but its innovations gave rise to fierce polemics. In 1749 Pietro Chiari, resident playwright at the rival Teatro di San Luca, produced for the Imer company *La scuola delle vedove*, a savage parody of *La vedova scaltra*, accompanied by an offensive manifesto, which led to the suppression of both plays and the introduction of censorship into the Venetian theatre. Polemics, parodies and censorship, however, did not stop Goldoni in his course. Two other plays of the 1748 season stand out for their novelty, *La putta onorata* and its sequel *La buona moglie*. For the 1749–50 season he wrote, among other works, *Il cavaliere e la dama*, satirizing *cicisbeismo*, and *La famiglia dell'antiquario*, a domestic drama of which the protagonist, as a result of his mania for collecting antiquities, neglects his family and lets his household run to ruin. The season ended with the sensational failure of *L'erede fortunato*.

The heroine of *La putta onorata* is Bettina, a Venetian orphan of modesty and charm who is in love with Pasqualino, a poor young man thought to be the son of a gondolier, but whose real father turns out to be Bettina's protector, the wealthy merchant Pantalone. In the meantime, Lelio, a rake, and the supposed son of Pantalone turns up from Leghorn, while Bettina is abducted by the marquis Ottavio, with the aid of her sister Catte and her brother-in-law Arlecchino, both of whom are very dubious characters. Bettina resists every attempt at seduction. Her honour is saved and the plot is resolved happily when Lelio turns out to be the son of Menego, the gondolier, and Pasqualino of Pantalone, who is glad to reward the virtue of Bettina by welcoming her as his daughter-in-law. In *La buona moglie*, Bettina is a virtuous wife, while Pasqualino spends his time at the gaming table and dissipates his resources with the help of Catte and Arlecchino. He does not mend his ways, despite the affection and despair of Bettina, until Lelio is stabbed to death in a brawl in a tavern.

After the failure of *L'erede fortunato*, in order to win back his audience for the 1750–51 season, Goldoni undertook the formidable task of providing not eight, but sixteen 'New Comedies', of which one, *Il teatro comico*, was designed to provide a programme, dramatized, of his ideas on theatrical reform. The plot of this play is very simple. In it use is made of the device, previously employed by Molière in *L'Impromptu de Versailles* (1663), of a play within a play. The actors are rehearsing, with Medebach, the 'primo amoroso', a short comedy entitled *Il padre rivale del figlio*. The set is the stage of the theatre and the action takes place, without footlights, in the daytime. From behind the scenes we witness the arrival of the players: Placida, the 'prima donna', called Rosaura; Eugenio, the 'secondo amoroso', called Florindo; Vittoria, 'servetta di teatro', called Colombina; Tonino, a Venetian who plays Pantalone; Petronio, the doctor in the farce; and Anselmo and Gianni, who play respectively Brighella and Arlecchino. Some of these players feel that their profession and traditional roles are menaced; others welcome the suppression of improvisation. Medebach, who plays Orazio, and later Ottavio, is especially in favour of the new ideas, and he serves as a mouthpiece for Goldoni, proferring advice to all and sundry. In the meantime Lelio arrives, a hack poet who tries to interest the players in a new *scenario* he has written in the traditional style. But he, like Eleonora, a virtuoso singer who also offers her services, is bitterly ridiculed. In the course of *Il teatro comico*, which is in three acts, the titles of Goldoni's sixteen new plays are announced, and the old style of performance and the pretensions of the *commedia dell'arte* players are criticized. A wealth of advice is given on acting techniques; and the audience is instructed on the type of comedy to expect from the plays produced by Goldoni for the new season.

In 1753, when *La locandiera*, interpreted by the *servetta* Maddalena Marliani in the role of Mirandolina, achieved its clamorous success, Goldoni, dissatisfied with his remuneration, left Medebach and accepted an offer from Francesco Vendramin to write for the Teatro San Luca. In exchange Pietro Chiari took Goldoni's place with Medebach at the Teatro Sant'Angelo. After this the two theatres entered a period of fierce competition, unleashing upon the public a succession of bitter polemics. In 1757 Carlo Gozzi also entered the lists, launching his diatribes against both Goldoni and Chiari. There ensued for Goldoni a period of exhaustion and boredom. He left Venice for a time, and spent seven months in Rome and Bologna, where he wrote *Gl'innamorati*, a play which heralded the advent of his greatest creative period. Subsequently he returned to Venice where he remained until 1762.

While contracted to the Teatro San Luca, between 1753 and 1762, Goldoni developed in various directions. After the definitive affirmation of his reform while working for Medebach, he produced, in rivalry with Chiari and largely in response to popular taste, a number of 'exotic' tragi-comedies in 'Martellian' verse, set in distant lands, especially the Orient. One of the best of these was *La sposa persiana* (1753), which obtained a great success, with Caterina Bresciani in the title-role. Others were *Ircana in Julfa* (1755) and *Ircana in Ispahan* (1756), which offered occasion for adventure and spectacular dramatic effects. But this kind of comedy was not to Goldoni's true taste. And his most effective and successful works of the mid-1750s were a number of clean, swift dialect comedies of Venetian popular life, often written as pot-boilers for the end of Carnival, such as *Le massere* and *Le donne di casa soa*, both of 1755, and the inimitable *Il campiello*, of 1756. It was not until 1760, however, at the beginning of his greatest period, before he left Venice for Paris, that he produced the work that is often regarded as his masterpiece, *I rusteghi*: a comedy of conflicting atmospheres set in the gloomy household of Sior Lunardo, a merchant and domestic tyrant of the old school, who aspired to keep his womenfolk in claustrated subjection.

Il campiello and *I rusteghi* were both written in Venetian dialect and rooted in the customs and manners of the Republic at Carnival time in the mid eighteenth century. The time was one in which new ideas had made a little headway. The differences between the plays, however, apart from the fact that one is in verse, the other in prose, are very marked. The former is one of Goldoni's most brilliant 'collective' comedies of Venetian popular life; the latter, which is set at a more elevated social level in the merchant class, is informed with a sense of tragedy more poignant and intense than elsewhere.

The fixed set of *Il campiello* represents a piazza in one of the poorer quarters of the city; and the characters belong, for the most part, to the lively, plebeian world of street-sellers, waiters and small traders. Other characters are distinguished from the locals by reason of social class. There are four houses to left and right, and an inn backstage. All have balconies and a roof-terrace, permitting great mobility and a variety of action at different levels. To the left live Lucietta with her mother Donna Catte, and Gasparina with her uncle Fabrizio, an elderly gentleman of means, who is irritated by his environment and its rowdy and disrespectful inhabitants. Lucietta is a sprightly and outspoken girl of eighteen and Gasparina a rather bored and disconsolate orphan with a lisp. She is disliked by all the other women, who regard her as affected. Her uncle's main desire is to get Gasparina off his hands so that he can lead a quiet, retired life, immersed in his books. To the right of the square live Orsola, a pancake-seller, with her son Zorzetto, and Donna Pasqua with her daughter, the flighty Gnese. A newcomer to the neighbourhood is the *cavaliere* Astolfo, an impoverished Neapolitan gallant, who is staying at the inn and hoping to adjust his fortunes. The action of *Il campiello* takes place four days before the end of the Carnival. It deals with the flirtation of the young people, Lucietta and the haberdasher Anzoletto, Gnese and Zorzetto, and with the events which lead to the betrothal of Gasparina and Astolfo. All the women of the square, both young and old, with the exception of Gasparina, are sturdily independent. The dialogue, which is based on a fluid alternation of rhymed and unrhymed *settenari* and *endecasillabi*, is vigorous, colloquial and full of witty repartee. The atmosphere is festive; and the humour, especially that provided by Donna Catte and Donna Pasqua – both widowed and prematurely aged, but eager to remarry – grotesquely comic. The main appeal of *Il campiello* lies in its skilful artistry, and in Goldoni's seemingly effortless portrayal, without a trace of condescension, of a tight-knit, but mixed, local community, shot through with brawls and bickering, malicious gossip and screaming rows.

In contrast with the free and easy world of the common people in *Il campiello*, that of *I rusteghi* is one of claustral, middle-class stuffiness. The title of *I rusteghi* derives from a Venetian epithet (*rustego*) which was applied, as Goldoni explains, to a man who was 'aspro, zotico, nemico della civiltà, della cultura, e del conversare'. It might be rendered in English 'The Squares'. The four principal male parts, apart from the young Felippetto, are all men of this type, the incarnation, in their various ways, of an impotent, reactionary and authoritarian mentality in a time of change. Behind the laughter of *I rusteghi* there lies the pathos of a serious drama arising out of the conflict of the *rusteghi* with their women folk: a conflict of sentiment versus egoism, of domestic tyranny and the right to a freer life, and of the young versus the old.

The action takes place entirely indoors, within two rooms at the home of old Lunardo, a sharp-tongued merchant and the surly embodiment of Venetian domestic conservatism, who has betrothed his daughter, Lucietta, to Felippetto, the son of his fellow-*rustego*, Maurizio. According to custom, Lunardo insists that the young couple shall on no account meet, or even be informed of the proposed marriage, until the last possible moment. Margarita, Lucietta's young stepmother, utterly disapproves of this situation. And Felice, the wife of Canciano, and Marina, the wife of Simon, both of whom wish to break out of the pattern of domestic servitude which regulates their activities, arrange for Lucietta and Felippetto to meet clandestinely. It is Carnival time; and with the help of an accomplice, Count Riccardo, Felippetto, masked and dressed as a woman, is stealthily introduced into the home of Lunardo; at a time, however, when unknown to Margarita, whom he has not bothered to inform,

Lunardo has invited his fellow *rusteghi* in to celebrate. The presence of Felippetto is soon disclosed; the severe laws of honour and reputation (notwithstanding the innocence of the encounter) have been brutally shattered. Lunardo and Maurizio wish to break off the betrothal; but reason and common sense prevail. Through the arguments of Felice the situation is brought to a happy conclusion, and the *rusteghi* are eventually persuaded to permit the marriage that they themselves had first arranged.

Between 1760 and 1762 – the years not only of *I rusteghi*, but of *La casa nova* (1760), the *Villeggiatura* cycle, satirizing the pretensions of the middle classes apeing the rich, *Sior Todero brontolon* (1762) and *Le baruffe chiozzotte* ('The Brawls at Chioggia', 1762), a marvel of popular comedy regarded by Carlo Gozzi as one of the most scandalous examples of Goldoni's 'plebeian' manner – the artistic vigour of the playwright seemed inexhaustible. Goldoni was now so practised in his art that when he had visualized a good plot and worked it out, he could write out a play from start to finish at one sitting. These years, however, were still ones of rivalry and of bitter polemic. The success of Goldoni's works served only to increase the envy and jealousy of his enemies. More fanatical than ever, in 1761, Carlo Gozzi staged the first of his 'fiabe teatrali', *L'amore delle tre melarance*, in which both Goldoni and Chiari are pilloried. About the same time Goldoni received a letter, couched in very flattering terms, inviting him to Paris. The letter was written at the instigation of a high-placed personage in the service of King Louis XV and sent by Francesco Antonio Zanuzzi, the 'primo amoroso' of the Italian *commedia dell'arte* company playing in Paris at the Comédie Italienne. Goldoni, who was an adventurer at heart, welcomed the invitation with enthusiasm and would probably have left at once had he not been bound by contract to the Teatro San Luca. He therefore gradually freed himself from his obligations and in the meantime wrote a number of other comedies, all of which were performed with outstanding success. Then, on 15 April 1762, with his wife Nicoletta Conio and his nephew Antonio, Goldoni set out from Venice for Paris. The journey lasted four months and eleven days. He arrived in Paris on 26 August 1762, where he was welcomed by Zanuzzi and the players of the Comédie Italienne. From then on Goldoni never returned to Italy.

For two years, in Paris, Goldoni spent his time writing or reelaborating old-type *scenari* for the *commedia dell'arte*, as the public expected works of this type from the Italian players at the Comédie Italienne. His 'reform' was not understood or little appreciated; and it was not until several years later, when he had gained a complete mastery of French, that he produced a number of distinguished new 'character' comedies in that language, the best of which are almost as highly regarded as his most distinguished works in Italian or in Venetian dialect. One of these was *Le bourru bienfaisant*; another *L'avare fastneux*. The former was performed with outstanding success at the Comédie Française in 1771. In the meantime Goldoni had been welcomed at court and accepted an appointment as Italian master to Maria Adelaide, the eldest daughter of Louis XV. In 1769 he was granted a court pension and from then on he lived partly in Paris and partly at Versailles. In 1787 he put the finishing touches to his *Mémoires*, which were subscribed to by the court. His last years, howwere, were overshadowed by the Revolution. In 1792, his pension was abolished and he was deprived of all means of subsistence. Subsequently the pension was restored, through the spirited pleading of the dramatist Marie Joseph Chénier, but Goldoni had died on the previous day. Subsequently, again at the insistence of Chénier, La Convention Nationale voted Nicoletta Conio, Goldoni's destitute widow, a pension of 1,500 livres; and she also received a substantial sum from a benefit performance of *Le bourru bienfaisant*.

Precursors and Rivals of Goldoni

Goldoni's reform of the Italian comedy was not an isolated phenomenon. In the Age of Arcadia, when Goldoni was still in his infancy, a number of notable attempts were made by playwrights of the older generation to adapt the *commedia dell'arte* to changed conditions. These dramatists, most of whom lived and worked in Tuscany, have generally been considered less in their own right than as the so-called 'precursors' of the Venetian master. One of them was the Florentine Giambattista Fagiuoli (1660–1742), the author of nineteen regular comedies, four of which are in verse, beginning with *Gl'inganni infelici* (1706) and *Il cicisbeo sconsolato*, a comedy of manners that ran for thirteen evenings in Florence in 1708. Two other comedy writers of the period, both Sienese, were Girolamo Gigli (1660–1722) and Jacopo Angelo Nelli (1673–1767). Nelli wrote *La serva padrona* (1709), which was followed by many other comedies in a popular satirical style, freely imitating both the *commedia dell'arte* and Molière in their characters, dialogue and plots. Gigli was the author of *Don Pilone* (1711), a rehandling of Molière's *Tartuffe*, attacking religious hypocrisy; which he followed up with the farcical *La sorellina di Don Pilone* (1712). Other notable comedies of the pre-Goldonian period were *Il Femia sentenziato* (1724), a personal satire of the Veronese antiquary Scipione Maffei, by Pier Jacopo Martello; and two social satires, of a literary nature, by Maffei, entitled *La cerimonie* (1727) and *Raguet* (1747). The former pilloried ceremonious forms of address; the latter was an attack on the vogue in Italy for imitation of French manners and customs.

In the 1750s, when Goldoni was writing for Medebach at the Teatro Sant'Angelo and subsequently for Imer at the Teatro San Luca, his main rival was the *abate* Pietro Chiari (1711–85), who has often been dismissed as a literary hack, but was nevertheless a competent and prolific writer with a flare for filling the theatres. The subject of a play by Chiari, which usually mingled comic and tragic elements, was often determined by that of a popular success of Goldoni, whom Chiari persistently parodied, as for instance in *La scuola delle vedove* (1749), *Il buon padre di famiglia* (1750) and *La schiava cinese* (1753), suggested respectively by *La vedova scaltra, Il padre di famiglia* and *La sposa persiana.*

Born at Brescia, of impoverished military family, Chiari as a young man developed a taste for the philosophical, the pathetic and the picaresque. He was especially interested in foreign subject-matter, including the Oriental, of which he later made striking use. While teaching literature at Modena, in the 1730s, he was greatly influenced by such seminal works as the *Lettres persanes* (1721) of Montesquieu, and the *Lettres philosophiques* (1734) of Voltaire. In 1740, having travelled extensively, he settled in Venice, where he determined to make a living by his pen, with such works as the *Lettere scelte di varie materie piacevoli critiche ed erudite scritte ad una dama di qualità* (1749–52) in imitation of G. A. Costantini's pseudo-epistolary *Lettere critiche.* From 1749 on Chiari also wrote comedies, operas and farces for the companies of Imer and Casali playing at the Grimani theatres of San

Samuele and San Giovanni Grisostomo. Four years later, in succession to Goldoni, he entered the service of Girolamo Medebach, first at the Teatro Sant'Angelo (1753–60), then at the Teatro San Giovanni Grisostomo (1760–62). The dramatic and personal rivalry of Chiari and Goldoni which developed in these years led to the division of the Venetian theatre-going public into two bitterly opposed factions of *chiaristi* and *goldonisti*. The rivalry was probably fostered more for commercial than for artistic reasons. Though mocking in his attitude, Goldoni maintained throughout a tone of affability and indulgence towards Chiari; and in 1757, and again in 1761, when Carlo Gozzi virulently attacked them both, the two joined forces in mutual defence against the common enemy.

As a playwright Chiari is nowadays little studied, though he was extremely successful in his day. While contracted to Imer and Casali, he composed some thirty comedies in prose, with masks, sixteen of which were published. His plays for Medebach, on the other hand, were in verse, mainly Martellian, and designed for performance in the new style, without the masks. Many of Chiari's plays are now known only from their titles; and their exact chronology has not as yet been established.

Two typical plays of Chiari, both in five acts, were *L'orfana o sia la forza della virtù* and its sequel *L'orfana riconosciuta o sia la forza del naturale*. Both were composed in emulation of Goldoni's *Pamela* and performed at the Teatro San Samuele in 1750. The theme of *L'orfana* and its sequel was derived from Marivaux's *La Vie de Marianne* (1731–41).[2] To Chiari, however, the heroine of the novel did not seem sufficiently romantic and pathetic, so for his plays he invented various new characters and had the excellent idea of placing Marianna between two fires by giving the hypocritical Climal an equally dissolute and violent son. Both try to seduce Marianna, the one by means of gifts, the other by force. In the sequel, before her marriage to the young and brilliant Valville, a match which is strongly opposed, Marianna is seized and taken to the Bastille. In the outcome the heroine is vindicated and she is recognized as not of lowly birth, but as the niece of a Scottish nobleman and the daughter of the Marquis Flaoour.

Other notable plays by Chiari are a prose trilogy portraying the history of a foundling whose frank and impulsive nature leads him

2. See pp. 359–60.

into a long series of adventures, based on Fielding's *Tom Jones* (1749), and *Il filosofo veneziano* (1754) imitating *Il filosofo inglese* of Goldoni. *L'orfano perseguitato* and *L'orfano ramingo*, which constitute the first and second parts of the trilogy, deal respectively with Tom's love for the charming and heroic Sophia, and with the flight of Sophia and Tom's adventures prior to his arrival in London. *L'orfano riconosciuto*, which completes the work, dramatizes the happenings in the capital and the marriage of Tom and Sophia.

Besides his innumerable plays, Chiari also wrote some forty tales of love and adventure, many of which are narrated by a foreign lady of rank and presented as a translation in the pseudo-epistolary or in the memoir form. The first of these was *La filosofessa italiana* (1753). Three other striking romances were *La ballerina onorata* (1754), *La cantatrice per disgrazia* (1754) and *La commediante in fortuna* (1755), which constitute a fascinating trilogy of contemporary theatre life. Other novels by Chiari were written in imitation of Swift and Montesquieu (*L'uomo d'un altro mondo*, 1760) and of Rousseau's *Julie ou la Nouvelle Héloïse* (*La donna che non si trova*, 1762). As a successful journalist, between 1761 and 1762 Chiari edited the *Gazzetta Veneta* in succession to Gasparo Gozzi.

Carlo Gozzi

Goldoni's second great rival, Count Carlo Gozzi (1720–1806), who also attacked Pietro Chiari as 'uno scrittore il più goffo e ampolloso che adornasse il nostro secolo', was a bizarre genius, with a marked gift for parody and vituperation, and somewhat younger than his playwright-victims. Between *c.* 1756 and 1765, beginning with a series of satirical skirmishes in verse, at times extremely personal and offensive, Gozzi sought to counter Goldoni's theatrical reform, equalize the achievement of his adversaries and revitalize the *commedia dell'arte* on the Venetian stage. A master of zany humour and buffoonery, who detested Goldoni's naturalistic and low-life character comedies, Gozzi was the author at this time of ten highly successful and influential stage entertainments, part fairy-tale, part philosophy, full of hidden meanings, in a novel idiom which he variously designated 'fiaba teatrale tragicomica', 'tragedia fiabesca', 'fiaba filosofica' or 'fiaba serio-faceta'. In these works, through the medium of prose and verse, Italian and Venetian dialect, and a larger or smaller dose of improvisation, the princes and magicians of the folk imagination are grotesquely intermingled with the old Venetian masks. In the first of them, *L'amore delle tre melarance* ('The Love of the Three Oranges', 1761), which was based on a fairy-tale recorded by Giambattista Basile in *Lu cunto de li cunti* (1632–4; also known as *Il Pentamerone*), beneath the fantasy and slapstick of an improvised extravaganza, the underlying intent was to parody and satirize the plays, and especially the *versi martelliani*, of his rivals, and the theatrical battles of the period.

Belonging to a branch of an ancient and numerous family, with estates in Friuli, Gozzi was a *rustego* out of sympathy with the intellectual trends of his century. Rebelliously anxious to defend the traditional values of Venetian life and letters against the spirit of subversion implicit in the diffusion of foreign *moeurs*, he clamorously opposed the innovations of his rivals. He dreamed of a literature that would be free from foreign influences, linguistically 'pure' and a bastion of faith and morality. Witty, acrimonious and misanthropic by nature, he was superbly indifferent to the susceptibilities of his compatriots; and he passed much of his life involved in polemic with his enemies, both real and imagined. Gozzi's hostility towards Goldoni was thus not simply a personal matter, but social, philosophical, literary and even political in its ramifications, though doubtless an element of jealous animosity at Goldoni's phenomenal success was also present. In Gozzi's view, that of a fanatical reactionary, 'born to sail alone, against the current' (E. Rho), Goldoni was one of the most trivial and 'incorrect' writers in the Italian language: a miserable scribbler who had presumed to play the philosopher and moralist, without having studied either philosophy or morals. Through his suppression of the art of improvisation, and with his cultivation of sentiment and naturalism in the drama, Goldoni had proved, furthermore, to be a dangerous innovator. His activities had resulted, in Gozzi's estimation, not only in the extirpation of the Italian impromptu comedy, and in great hardship to the extempore players, but they were also a menace to the established order. He had satirized and given offence to the patriciate; and he had flattered the lower classes by putting the dregs of the population on the stage. His language was 'impure'; he even reproduced popular speech overheard in the streets.

When a young man Gozzi spent three years in Dalmatia as a cavalry cadet. On his return to Venice, at the age of twenty-four, he found his patrimony dissipated and his family in dire financial straits. In 1747, with his elder brother Gasparo, he became a leading figure in the Accademia dei Granelleschi. A bulwark of Venetian conservatism, this ultra-purist academy opposed literary and linguistic innovation, while seeking to preserve intact the 'lingua letteral italiana' as employed by the Tuscan authors of the Renaissance. Ten years later, incensed by the popularity of the plays of Goldoni and Chiari, especially by such radical achievements as *Pamela nubile*, *Le massere* and *Il campiello*, each of which he abhorred, Gozzi began his campaign against the two playwrights – a deadly and ultimately successful offensive, which reached its peaks of insolence and animosity on the one hand in *L'amore delle tre melarance* and on the other in the mock-heroic epic *Marfisa bizzarra* (1761–8; publ. 1772).[3]

Gozzi entitled his first diatribe against Goldoni and Chiari *La Tartana degli influssi per l'anno bisestile 1756* (1757; 'The Tartan, an Almanac of Influxes for the Leap Year 1756'); and this was followed by *Il teatro comico all'Osteria dei Pellegrini*, a satirical poem parodying the various types of plays Goldoni was then producing, and the burlesque in verse, *I sudori d'Imeneo* ('The Labours of Hymen'). The *Tartana degli influssi* was made up of a set of verses, many of which were composed in the humorous and satirical vein of the fifteenth-century barber-poet, Il Burchiello, and took the form of prophesies for the various months of the year. The collection was arranged in the antiquated form of an old Venetian almanac, *Lo Schieson*, and dedicated to Daniele Farsetti, the Maecenas of the Granelleschi. In the verses Gozzi expounded the uses and abuses of the times. In conclusion he declared himself an enemy of the modern comedy and especially of Chiari and Goldoni. The former he nicknamed 'Saccheggio', the latter 'Originale', characterizing both as mountebanks fighting each other with wooden swords and dividing the spoils.

For many years, from the time of *La Tartana degli influssi*, Gozzi was the friend and patron of Antonio Sacchi, a comic *improvvisatore* of genius, who had played at one time for Goldoni, in *Momolo cortesan*. During the 1750s Sacchi and his troupe had prospered in Lisbon, at the court of the king of Portugal. After the terrible earthquake, how-

3. See p. 325.

ever, they had returned to Venice and settled at the San Samuele theatre. And it was for Sacchi and the San Samuele players, then impoverished and in the doldrums of neglect, that Gozzi created *L'amore delle tre melarance*, which was a largely extempore *fiaba*, first performed during Carnival on 21 January 1761. Believing that any subject, however trivial, would attract an audience, Gozzi set his extravaganza in the imaginary kingdom of Silvio, king of Coppe, where the cast are gorgeously attired in the costumes of the court figures in a pack of playing-cards. Tartaglia, the hereditary prince, has for a decade been afflicted by hypochondria, which is diagnosed by Truffaldino as a severe case of indigestion brought on by a surfeit of Martellian verses. The only cure is to make him laugh and spew the verses forth. Truffaldino, a part created by Sacchi, is the equerry of Prince Tartaglia; Chiari and Goldoni figure in the fantastic roles of the wicked Fata Morgana and the wizard Celio, both of whom possess magic powers. The former is the king's enemy; the latter the protector of Tartaglia. The *fiaba* opens with a doleful Prologue announcing that the extempore actors are perplexed and full of shame, and that the long-suffering audience are bored with the current repertoire. It is proposed, therefore, to try out a new and more lively form of entertainment than Goldoni's character comedies. In Act I, in his efforts to make Tartaglia laugh, Truffaldino pushes Fata Morgana head over heels in a slapstick *lazzo* of marked obscenity. In revenge, in the hope that the prince will perish miserably while on the quest, the sorceress casts a spell, condemning Tartaglia to fall in love with three huge 'Oranges' kept in the power of Creonta, a giant witch living in a magic castle two thousand miles away. In Act II Tartaglia and Truffaldino set out to seize the mysterious fruits, which must not be cut open, they are informed, unless they are near a fount of water. In an atmosphere of transformations and diabolical forces, conjured up by Celio Mago, the prince and his equerry are blown on their way by Farfarello; they eventually reach Creonta's castle, which is guarded by a rusty gate, a ravenous dog, a well with a tangle of rotten rope and a grotesque bakeress sweeping her oven. When Tartaglia has secured the fruits, and is making his escape, the castle reverberates to the sound of Martellian verses. Creonta, lumbering in pursuit, is blasted by a thunderbolt. Subsequently, Truffaldino is assailed by a prodigious thirst. He cuts open one of the oranges, and out of it steps a beautiful maiden, who piteously asks for a drink, but immediately expires. The same happens in the case of the second fruit. But Tartaglia recalls the instructions of Celio Mago; and when out of the third orange there steps Ninetta, an orange-princess, Tartaglia immediately assuages her thirst by filling his iron shoe with water from a near-by lake and offering it to her to drink. The princess's life is saved and the couple fall in love. In Act III, at the instigation of Clarice, Tartaglia's envious sister, Smeraldina Mora plants a magic hat-pin in Ninetta's head, whereby she is changed into a white dove. In the meantime, back at the palace of the king of Coppe, Truffaldino has been put in charge of the kitchens. While he is turning his spit, the dove Ninetta appears to him in a dream. He catches the dove, extracts the hat-pin, and with the charm broken the princess reappears in human shape. The amazement is very great. The king comes down to the kitchen and he gravely threatens Truffaldino for being late with the roast. The rumbustious entertainment ends with the confounding of Tartaglia's enemies, a wedding and the restoration of happiness at court.

The text of *L'amore delle tre melarance* was not written out at first, but designed as a *scenario* to be improvised by Sacchi and his players; and in this Gozzi remained faithful to the traditional techniques of the *commedia dell'arte*. Years later, when the *fiaba* was published, together with his other works, Gozzi invented the curious and original form of what he termed the 'analisi riflessiva' of *L'amore delle tre melarance*. In this he published not merely the *scenario*, but a draft of the whole spectacle. The action is described by the author, with an interpolated commentary, an explanation of the hidden meanings and information concerning the reactions of the audience.

The success of *L'amore delle tre melarance* was so outstanding that it was in part responsible for Goldoni's decision to leave Venice in 1762 and seek his fortune in France. In the meantime Gozzi consolidated his triumph by producing in rapid succession a number of other *fiabe* on similar lines, although in them he abandoned the principle of improvised comedy by writing out their dialogue in full. The first of these, a tragi-comedy of sorcery and witchcraft, in five acts, mixing prose and verse, Italian and Venetian dialect, the rigid schemes of the classical theatre and the improvisation and buffoonery of the *commedia dell'arte*, was *Il corvo* ('The Raven'), first performed in Milan, and then in Venice on 24 October 1761. *Il re cervo* ('The King turned Stag', 1762), Gozzi's third *fiaba*, is a spectacle, based on an eastern folk-tale, of magical transformations of men into beasts and into other men.

Of Gozzi's other seven *fiabe*, two of the most admired for their flashes of profundity were *Turandot* (1762), well-known for the operatic versions based upon it, notably that of Puccini (Milan, 1926), and *L'augellino belverde* ('The Pretty Green Bird', 1765), a satire of 'enlightened' philosophy, which is often regarded as his masterpiece. His other *fiabe*, most of which were characterized by sorcery, witchcraft and grotesque transformations, were entitled *La donna serpente* ('The Woman Snake', 1762), *La Zobeide* (1763), *I pitocchi fortunati* 'The Lucky Beggars', 1764), *Il mostro turchino* ('The Blue Monster', 1764) and *Zeim re de' Geni* (1765).

In *Turandot*, of which the story is of very ancient origin and found in many languages, a beautiful and passionate, but misanthropic princess will give her hand only to the suitor who resolves three riddles. Those who fail are decapitated. In Gozzi's version, which is set in a fabulous and cruel Peking, the masks of the *commedia dell'arte* are cast in the roles of the emperor's secretary (Pantalone), the Grand Chancellor (Tartaglia), the Master of the Pages (Brighella) and the Chief of the Eunuchs (Truffaldino). In *L'augellino belverde*, which was presented by Gozzi as a *fiaba filosofica*, the characters and situations go back with those of *L'amore delle tre melarance*. In the absence of Prince Tartaglia, the queen-mother condemns Ninetta to be buried alive for giving birth to Renzo and Barbarina. The twins are brought up by their foster-mother, Smeraldina, the wife of Truffaldino, a sausage-seller. As they grow older, they dedicate themselves to the study of French encyclopedism, especially the materialists Helvétius and d'Holbach. As a result of their 'enlightenment', they become hard, egotistical and cruel, the walking embodiments of *amour-propre*. They reject their kindly foster-mother and devote themselves to a life of pleasure. Renzo sets out to catch the 'Pretty Green Bird', but he is turned into a statue. In the outcome, of course, through a complexity of fantasy and spectacle, Renzo and Barbarina learn the error of their thinking. The 'Pretty Green Bird' turns into a prince; Tartaglia recovers the entombed Ninetta; and the wicked queen-mother is transformed into a tortoise.

In his later years, in the Napoleonic period, Gozzi wrote an apologia for his life, an outstanding and original autobiography, in three parts, which he ironically entitled *Memorie inutili scritte per umiltà* (1797). Bitter and vituperative in tone, and at times facetious and self-denigratory, these memoirs are full of shrewd observations, and they provide a fascinating documentation of their author's early life in Dalmatia, the origins of his literary polemics, his poverty, his phobias and his theatrical innovations. They are also memorable for their portrayal of Gozzi's relations with the actors and actresses of the Sacchi troupe, by which the *fiabe* were performed, and for the account of the infamous Gozzi–Gratarol scandal, which convulsed Venice in 1777, subsequent to the production of the *Droghe d'amore* ('The Love-Potions'). In that comedy Gozzi had caricatured Pier Antonio Gratarol, secretary to the Venetian Senate and ambassador-elect to the court of Naples, his rival in a jealous squabble for the favours of Gozzi's flirtatious *protégée* and leading lady, the actress Teodora Ricci. As a result Gratarol became the laughing-stock of Venice. He was forced to flee to Stockholm, where he produced a pamphlet defaming Gozzi and other Venetian patricians. His estates were confiscated and he died in obscurity.

Italian comedy in the late eighteenth century followed more in the footsteps of Goldoni than of Gozzi. In the 1770s Gozzi, still working with the Sacchi company, put his *teatro fiabesco* to one side and adapted various seventeenth-century Spanish plays for the Venetian stage. At this time, too, the Bolognese Marquis Francesco Albergati Capacelli (1728–1804), one of the most distinguished playwrights of the period, published *Il nuovo teatro comico* (5 vols., Venice 1774–8), with which he aspired to enrich the Goldonian theatre. A further notable development, with which Albergati was associated, was the systematic elaboration of the 'tearful' or 'lachrymose' drama, plays of sentiment and pathos, often in an urban setting, in the style established by the French dramatist Nivelle de la Chaussée and advanced by the dramatic theories of Diderot.

Since the period of Romanticism, the fortune of Gozzi's *fiabe* in Europe has been very striking. They were soon translated into German and acclaimed by such influential men of letters as Lessing, Goethe and Schiller. In France they were imitated and admired on the authority of Madame de Staël. More recently they have proved a fertile soil for the operatic librettist and for transposition to the lyric stage. In 1917 Busoni set *Turandot* to music. (Weber had previously, in 1809, written incidental music to Schiller's translation.) In 1926, in Puccini's popular opera, the same work was treated as a romantic melodrama. Prokofiev's *Love for Three Oranges* (1921), with a Russian text, is a brilliant romp making propaganda out of the *commedia* ingredients. Casella's setting of *La donna serpente* (1931) was less successful. In this spectacular *fiaba*, which had previously fascinated Wagner, the symbolic parts were taken as a joke and the fantasy failed to appeal. Hans Werner Henze's second opera, *König Hirsch* ('King Stag'), is based on a libretto by Heinz von Cramer drawn from *Il re cervo*. This dark and sombre 'morality', which exists in several revised versions, was first performed in Berlin in 1956.

Of the character comedies of Goldoni's immediate followers, two of the best were *Il ciarlatore maldicente* and *Le convulsioni*, both by Albergati. The protagonist of the former, the Marquis Alfonso Rovinati, is reminiscent of Don Marzio, the infamous Neapolitan scandal-monger of indefatigable vitality, who dominates *La bottega del caffè*. The lively satire of the latter is directed against the follies of a pretentious and capricious gentlewoman who is given to tantrums. In Rome another imitator of Goldoni, Gian Gherardo de Rossi (1754–1827), wrote sixteen plays, the most successful of which were *Il calzolaio inglese a Roma* and *La commedia in villeggiatura*.

An early Italian example of the *dramma lacrimoso* was, of course, Goldoni's *Pamela nubile*: his first play with no masks and one of the sixteen 'New Comedies' performed by the Medebach troupe during the 1750–51 season, which was a milestone in the dramatist's career. The heroine, a modest but well-educated lady's maid in the household of Milord Bonfil, was derived from the protagonist of Samuel Richardson's *Pamela, or Virtue Rewarded* (1741). In Goldoni's adaptation Pamela remains a paragon of virtue and sensibility. She is beautiful, tender and excessively prone to tears. Frank and outspoken when necessary, she repels the imprudent advances of her master, even though she is secretly in love with him. And her delicacy forbids her to marry Bonfil until it is revealed that, unlike her prototype, she is not a person of humble country stock, but the daughter of a Scottish nobleman living incognito for his rebellion against the British Crown.

After Goldoni two of the most successful champions of the *dramma lacrimoso* were Giovanni de Gamerra (1743–1803) and Camillo Federici (pseudonym of G. B. Viassolo, 1749–1802). De Gamerra, who flourished first at Vienna and subsequently at the court of Naples, is best remembered for *I solitari*, *La madre colpevole* and *Il parricida*. Federici, who worked mostly at Padua and Venice, was the author of some seventy plays, including *I pregiudizi dei paesi piccoli* and *Il delatore*, the pathetic drama of a sick woman tended by her two sons, and their ruses to obtain money.

Two other playwrights, both of whom worked in Venice at the end of the eighteenth century, were Alessandro Pepoli (1757–96) and Simeone Antonio Sogràfi (1759–1818). Pepoli wrote *I pregiudizi dell'amor proprio* and *La scommessa*, but he is best-known for his tragedies (*Agamennone*, *Sofonisba*), with which he sought to obscure the fame of Alfieri. Sogràfi was the prolific author of more than one hundred stage works. Some of these were farces (*L'amor platonico*, *L'anglomania in Italia*); others were sentimental dramas (*Carlotta e Werther*); others were character comedies in the style of Goldoni (*La donzella di Oxford*). His most notable play, which brought the life of the actors on the stage, was *Le convenienze teatrali* (1794).

PART FOUR

THE NOVEL

ONE

England

IN England the novel was virtually an eighteenth-century discovery. It was evidently the form that suited the times, the scepticism and tolerance of that age. It was (and was felt to be) a discovery of the commonplace: Dr Johnson described it in such terms in a *Rambler* essay:

> The works of fiction, with which the present generation seems more particularly delighted, are such as exhibit life in its true state, diversified only by accidents that daily happen in the world, and influenced by passions and qualities which are really to be found in conversing with mankind.
>
> (*Rambler*, no. iv)

'*Really* to be found': the words confirm the common assumption that the eighteenth-century novel was a discovery of 'realism'. But this is an assumption that must be submitted to question. Did the novel in fact reveal a new attitude to reality? And was the 'representation of reality' the only, or even the dominant, characteristic of the genre. First we ought to bear in mind that this 'new' form was defined in terms that were not at all new. The word 'novel' was no novelty. It had a history. It represented a long-standing resistance to certain kinds of fiction, the improbable tales of idealized heroes and heroines, the exaggerated sentiments and unreal values of the 'romance'. Congreve, in the preface to his own novel *Incognita* (written in 1691, though not published until 1713), defines the novel by its marked unlikeness to the Romance:

> Romances . . . elevate and surprise the reader into a giddy delight, which leaves him flat upon the ground whenever he gives off . . .
>
> Novels are of a more familiar nature; come near us, and represent to us intrigues in practice, delight us with accidents and odd events, but

not such as are wholly unusual or unprecedented, such which not being so distant from our belief bring also the pleasure nearer us.

Romances give more of wonder, novels more delight.

There are distinct echoes of this language in the opening chapters of Fielding's *Tom Jones*, where Squire Allworthy is apparently in danger of becoming an idealized figure, 'a human being replete with benevolence'. Fielding undercuts this figure and in so doing establishes his genre, the novel: 'Reader, take care, I have unadvisedly led thee to the top of as high a hill as Mr Allworthy's and how to get thee down without breaking thy neck, I do not well know. However, let us e'en venture to slide down together . . .' (I, iv). But this calculated descent into the novel occurs some fifty years after Congreve had shown the way, and Congreve's formula in its turn harks back to something written forty years earlier still. Paul Scarron in *Le Roman comique* (1651) aligns his work with the 'Spanish' tradition of the 'Novel', as distinct form the 'French' form, the 'Romance', with its 'heroes of Antiquity who grow tedious and troublesome by being overcivil and virtuous'. (The English translation quoted here dates from 1665.) That view of the matter reminds us that to find the prototype of all these 'comic romances', and arguably the most influential novel ever published, we have to go back another fifty years to *Don Quixote*.

Thus, when the eighteenth-century English novelists ventured to define what they were doing, it was in terms that were almost trite. Fielding set out to create, in *Joseph Andrews*, a 'comic romance' which would be a *re*-creation of what Cervantes had done in that book 'which records the Atchievements of the renowned D. Quixotte', and he is clear that this will distinguish it from the products of 'those Persons of surprising Genius, the Authors of immense Romances, or the modern Novel and *Atalantis* Writers, who without any Assistance from Nature or History, record Persons who never were, or will be, and Facts which never did nor possibly can happen . . .' (III, i). In a similar manner Richardson has Pamela, the heroine of his first novel, dissociate herself from the heroines of 'romance' who would be expected to 'climb walls, leap precipices, and do twenty other extravagant things, in order to show the mad strength of a passion [they] ought to be ashamed of . . .' (*Pamela*, II, Letter CII).

Bearing in mind the antecedents of such statements it looks as if we can hardly describe the eighteenth-century novel as the emergence of a *new* sense of reality.

Realism is a product of its literary antithesis, romance. Indeed the novels of this period display a certain timidity in the face of reality, as if uncertain how to deal with it in its raw state. The 'anti-romances' are full of a sense of what they are *not*: their ambition to 'copy nature' is felt as a reply to some other, quite different possibility. The one determines and defines the other. And therefore these novels relate as much to the experience of other literature as to ordinary life: from *Shamela* to *Northanger Abbey* the prevailing mode is parody and burlesque.

In these ways the eighteenth-century novel may well frustrate the expectations of the modern reader. Its views appear cramped; it is based on assumptions that interfere with the sense of reality. At the same time these assumptions cannot be said to be invalid. If they do not to the modern reader seem productive, the reason is likely to be that they conflict with the assumptions that *he* makes about immediacy, psychological realism and intimacy in the novel. In fact, by virtue of their bias towards the literary, their concern with style and procedure, they have much value in calling these more recent assumptions into question. Though the eighteenth-century novel discovers itself by continuing an old and well-worn debate, it does discover things about the form of the novel that are important. If it works quite excessively through parody, finding itself in comically distorted reflections of other literary works, it also works by reflecting on itself. It is in fact not by virtue of any ambition for realism but rather by its very literariness, its literary self-consciousness, that it achieves its interest and its influence.

The mainspring of this achievement is, as we have seen, in the past, in the subtle and manifold self-reflections of *Don Quixote*. In this respect *Don Quixote* is anything but the relic of a dead past. It is one of the first manifestations of the modern mind, the mind that works through self-consciousness, detachment, scepticism, irony. E. C. Riley points to the significance of Cervantes's prologue to the novel, in which he dissociates himself from his own creation whilst recognizing that to do so is itself a way of continuing and completing that creation: 'like Velasquez in *Las Meninas* . . . he realized artistically an act of mental detachment which is a distinguishing mark of European thought around 1600. It was a similar act, "essayed" earlier by Montaigne, that produced the first axiom of the philosophy of Descartes'.[1]

This demonstration of self-awareness was the thing that made Cervantes important to Fielding, Smollett and Sterne. At the same time those writers, like Defoe and Richardson, who were not directly influenced by Cervantes, may also be seen to be developing an art which could accommodate self-consciousness, an art of analysis and reflection, if not exactly of detachment. If the art learned from Cervantes was Cartesian, Richardson's art can be said to be at the beginning of what Georges Poulet calls 'the strictly modern form of the *cogito*', existentialism.

Thus the 'discovery' of old forms is after all a discovery of new ways of feeling. But, though these new ways of feeling give a new significance to the ordinary, the world of the commonplace, and therefore endorse a new realism, it is not the realism as such that is important. The novel engages with the everyday world, the 'real' world, but its 'social realism' is not an end in itself but the means to achieve another, more elusive and critical end. The end that the eighteenth-century novelists have in view is to develop a literary form that will truly reflect moral experience. This calls for 'realism' – it will have to be a form capable of getting the whole range of experience in, particularly that which has always seemed comically 'low' – but more importantly it calls for a new philosophical sense, a sense of the kinds of knowledge the novel makes available. It was there waiting to be discovered; the novel as epistemology. The power that was in the literary form could not be released without the convergence of another power, the 'power of the moment', the impulse of the age towards self-analysis, the questioning of experience, the examining of motives and the complicating of moral issues. In other words the anti-romantic impulse now presented itself as the appropriate form for new modes of consciousness. The 'novel', that form at once familiar and unprecedented, lodged in the past but alive with future possibilities, offered a rich opportunity to explore the subjective and moral experience of life in society.

It is in this way that the eighteenth-century novelists *are* the founders of the modern novel and do not disappoint the modern reader. It is not the 'realistic' surface of their novels we value, but the organiza-

1. E. C. Riley, *Cervantes's Theory of Fiction*, Oxford, 1962, p. 223.

tion of different modes of experience, both introspective and social, reflective and practical, personal and general. The essence of their discovery was that the novel has these complications of experience inherent in its very nature. It is a mirror of social life yet, unlike the drama, a private activity. It speaks with the subjectivity of the author and appeals to the subjective response of the reader, and this 'inter-subjectivity' is valued for its intimacy and privacy; at the same time, being the telling of a story, it is, as D. W. Harding has said, a 'quasi-social experience', a 'convention for enlarging the scope of the discussions we have with each other about what may befall'.[2] Any attempt to render the subjective life in writing is going to enter on these complications, and, as several recent studies have shown, the Puritan 'spiritual autobiographies' of the seventeenth century anticipate many of the complexities of the novel. These deeply introspective accounts of spiritual experience, of intense conflicts and closely analysed doubts and beliefs were an important source for the inwardness of both Defoe and Richardson. But they are essentially committed to the idea of private, individual experience; they lack the public or social dimensions of the novel. The eighteenth-century novelists were the first writers (at least in England) to conceive the possibility of the novel as a kind of conversation, a means of externalizing and extending into the social sphere our subjective moral experience. In other words, the true 'rise of the novel' begins when writers begin to be aware of the complications inherent in the negotiations with 'reality'. There was an abundance of prose fiction, of course, before Fielding and Richardson, but hardly any sense that it could clarify and extend the sense of reality. We may take as an example the work of Mrs Manley (1663–1724). She was not without a sense of the novel's obligations to realism, and her transparent fictions about scandals at court and in society (her *New Atlantis* of 1709, for example) may be taken to exploit sexual fantasy for the purpose of political satire – to this extent she may be said to have some measure of social responsibility – but her work has hardly any pretensions to literary sophistication. It is characteristic in fact of the whole area of sub-literature which J. J. Richetti has brilliantly analysed; he makes the point that prose fiction at this popular level has merely (using Leslie Fiedler's term)

2. D. W. Harding, 'Psychological processes in the reading of fiction', in *British Journal of Aesthetics*, II, 1962, pp. 133–47.

'symbolic' or 'demonstration' literacy: '... the fiction of the period can best be described as fantasy machines, which must have appeared to the educated literate élite of the eighteenth century precisely what comic books and television seem to the contemporary guardians of cultural standards'.[3] And this essentially was the scope of the novel for almost the first half of the eighteenth century. The 'rise of the novel', the discovery of its potential significance, did not occur until the early 1740s with the publication of Richardson's *Pamela* (1740) and Fielding's *Joseph Andrews* (1742).

DEFOE

There is one novelist of almost a generation earlier whose work demands attention, even though it seems on the face of it as undeveloped and unliterary as most popular fiction. Daniel Defoe (?1660–1731), towards the end of a long and active career as political and religious journalist, polemicist, manufacturer, economist, found himself (almost by accident it seems) also a novelist. He was nearly sixty when he wrote his first work of fiction, *Robinson Crusoe* (1719); in the last decade of his life he wrote another half dozen or so novels, including *The Fortunes and Misfortunes of the Famous Moll Flanders* (1722). Of his more than 500 published works these few are the ones that are still read. They throw his career out of perspective; they cause the creator, the myth-maker, to loom large. They persuade us that Defoe was essentially an imaginative artist; they lead us to expect artistic unity and coherence in his work. We assume that he only became fully himself when he 'progressed' from journalist to novelist.

There is no reason to think that Defoe would have taken this view. The fictions of his later life hardly represent a new literary dimension for him. They are well-nigh indistinguishable from his narratives of real people (John Sheppard, for instance, or Jonathan Wild, both notorious criminals) or of real events, like the great plague of 1665. There is invention and imaginative insight in such works: Defoe, who was only five years old in 1665, produces a supposedly first-hand account of the events of that year and achieves an effect of overwhelming authenticity. But this is fiction turned to the service of

3. J. J. Richetti, *Popular Fiction before Richardson*, London, 1969, p. 9.

fact; and fact is valuable, Defoe evidently believes, to the extent that it can be turned to practical use. From the early *Essay upon Projects* (1697) to the novels of the 1720s Defoe sticks to one principle, to find what can and should be done to make the conditions of life better. His fictions have the same intention as his social or political or religious tracts: he recommends *Moll Flanders* to 'those who know how to read it', that is to those who know 'how to make the good uses of it which the story all along recommends to them' (Preface). No doubt this need not be taken as an adequate guide to the scope of his novel, but it does not suggest that Defoe's concept of the author's function in society has substantially altered. He is not interested in any of his books as 'aesthetic objects'; his writing extends into the life of society, it has the weight and force of action. Unlike all the other major eighteenth-century novelists Defoe has no theory of fiction; but he has a theory of social value, of probity, enterprise and cooperation in social conduct, and the novels conduce to this.

All the same it would be absurd to argue that Defoe's novels lack imaginative force. His fictions are stubbornly factual yet at the same time poetic, mythic even. So indeed are his non-fictional works. It is not so much that Defoe *created* myths as that he inherited a tradition, that of the Puritan dissenters of the seventeenth century, in which the conduct of life was charged with symbolic intensity. Critics in the last few years have been questioning the prevailing opinion that Defoe is interested only in *Homo economicus*, only in the values of commerce and cash; they point rather to the influence on him of Puritan 'spiritual autobiographies' with their intense introspection, their strenuous examination of motive and conduct, their pattern of guilt, doubt and conversion. Defoe is close to Bunyan, they maintain. Crusoe's narrative is a spiritual history of rebellion, isolation and renewal. Moll Flanders's life as a self-confessed criminal, like Bunyan's as 'the chief of sinners', can have exemplary value. Such readings hardly dispose of the many ambiguities and contradictions in the novels – Moll's history, for instance, gives a decidedly ambivalent interpretation of 'grace abounding' – but they do help to account for the intensity with which his characters project themselves.

Even more telling is Defoe's sense of the symbolic force that operates through inanimate objects. His world is full of things, intractable or malleable, potentially useful, but demanding effort, labour, resource. Their importance to Defoe is that they elicit work and thus become a source of value. Crusoe's story makes this plain. But this potential wealth in the material world suggests to Defoe a powerful image, the image of gold, which works to the destruction of a sense of value. It is through this image that he rises again and again to poetic intensity. He is fascinated by it; it is a compelling and malign influence in all the novels. Gold is irresistible, yet in itself worthless; it symbolizes wealth yet it undermines value. It is a parody of wealth, just as greed is a parody of work. In a famous passage Crusoe makes us aware of the confusing power it exercises; he has salvaged some from the wreck and at first is struck by its worthlessness in his present situation: '"O drug?" said I aloud, "what art thou good for? Thou art not worth to me, no, not the taking off of the ground; one of these knives is worth all this heap . . ." However upon second thoughts, I took it away.' Later, in a passage less often cited, Defoe shows that the effect of this episode was calculated and deliberate: the gold *is* useless and Crusoe knows that it is, yet he keeps it: 'I had not the least advantage by it, or benefit from it; but there it lay in a drawer, and grew mouldy with the damp of the cave in the wet season . . . no manner of value to me because of no use.' Defoe makes us intensely aware of the inner contradictions of the acquisitive nature.

His novels, then, make a sort of poetry out of their active contribution to social and spiritual improvement. But they are important above all for the way they contribute to the development of a 'modern' self-consciousness and detachment. The great interest of Defoe's novels derives from the way they connect the experience of literature and the experience of life, and especially from the way they confront the reader with an unflattering reflection of his own nature and experience.

They are in fact based on an irony; not an irony which is contained within the narrative – such an irony, which Defoe does not permit himself, would arise, for instance, from any implied criticism of Moll Flanders's protestations of repentance – but an irony arising out of the act of reading the book, an irony which has the effect of displacing the reader's criticism and directing it back upon himself. Such irony is not an entirely literary device. It could almost be described as a political manoeuvre, resembling the way in which Brecht compels his audience to recognize its own political character and its social morality. It is not an artistic but a social conscience that is at work. In this way Defoe's novels *are* of a piece with the rest of his writing, political and polemical. They turn social disapproval back upon itself. In *Moll Flanders*, for instance, the reader is meant to censure the heroine: she *is* a criminal, she makes no secret of the fact, she knows herself and she is always reproaching herself. Defoe does not encourage us to see this as ironic. On the contrary he wants the unquestioned fact of Moll's criminality to throw back an ironic light on our own lives. The irony in the novel is at the reader's expense: he is induced to recognize in Moll his own motives and his own attitudes to society. She wants to be accepted in society, to become a 'gentlewoman', and she is accepted. Yet she is a confessed liar, a thief, a whore. Dishonesty and fraud succeed: her story forces us to recognize this. At the same time the entire candour with which she brings about this recognition is inimical to the 'decencies' of society, its secrecy, concealment, silence. So her narrative (the very fact indeed, that there is such a narrative) separates her from the reader who belongs to that society. The result is that the reader cannot get out of the double trap of being both like and unlike Moll. In Moll there is a reflection of social values which the reader can hardly avoid subscribing to, yet can hardly afford to have brought into the open. It is in these shifting reactions of involvement, recognition, rejection, that Defoe's novels are at their most impressive, and convince us that they are the 'appropriate form' for displaying some of the complexities of moral experience in society.

RICHARDSON

Defoe was the first writer of fiction in English to attain this degree of fidelity to moral experience. He went beyond the schematization of allegory and the simplifications of romance or fantasy to create the first modern novels. But he is not really the founder of the modern novel. He gave nothing to the novel that later writers did not find elsewhere. When Fielding and Smollett, for instance, became attracted to the picaresque it was Le Sage rather than Defoe they had in mind. When, twenty years after the publication of *Robinson Crusoe*, Richardson embarked on his first novel, *Pamela* (1740), it was not Defoe's work that served as a model but perhaps Marivaux's *Marianne*. Samuel

Richardson (1689–1761) considered himself an innovator, the creator of a 'new species of writing' which he called 'writing to the moment'. What he meant was that his narrative was contained in letters supposed to have been written immediately after the event by the people who had been involved. In many ways this was *not* a new species: Richardson was drawing on a quite well established and copious body of fiction in letter-form. But his sense of the psychological and dramatic and, indeed, moral significance of this form *was* new. He seized on the real artistic purpose of this kind of narration. He had an artist's sense of responsibility to his form. He was the first English novelist to take the novel seriously as a work of art. One way and another the whole history of modern fiction is bound up with his having done so.

He is the founder of the modern novel, and he may also be described as the first modern novelist – not exactly the same thing. It is true there are many ways in which he seems quite un-modern, and most of all in his didacticism. His novels are meant to enforce a moral, and the moral is usually very hard to identify with any of the moral values that seem important to the modern reader. For instance, his intention in his second novel, his masterpiece *Clarissa* (1747–8), was twofold: first 'to admonish Parents against forcing their Children's Inclinations' in marriage, and secondly to 'explode . . . that pernicious Notion, that a Reformed Rake . . . makes the best Husband' (*Selected Letters*, p. 73). There is something repugnant to the modern reader (indeed there was even to his contemporaries) in the prudential virtue he endorsed in the novels, and in the moral casuistry that allowed him to square his professed purity of motive with his erotic fantasies. And this feeling is made more acute for the modern reader by his sense that the moralizing drastically interferes with Richardson's imaginative insight and psychological intuition. At the same time Richardson concerns himself again and again with questions of personality, identity, will, the impulse to dominate – all of which are specially characteristic of modern life, and in my view, this concern reveals itself in his narrative form, the 'new species of writing'.

The letter-form of the narration is the main thing in Richardson. It is, of course, supremely artificial, especially to the modern reader unfamiliar with the deliberate and articulate self-expression that letter-writing stimulates. The unnaturally complete and coherent self-expression of these practised letter-writers does make them seem abnormally literary. Clarissa dauntingly presents herself in this light:

> And indeed, my dear, I know not how to *forbear* writing. I have now no other employment or diversion. And I must write on, although I were not to send it to anybody. You have often heard me own the advantages I have found from writing down everything of moment that befalls me; and of all I *think*, and of all I *do*, that may be of future use to me; for besides that this helps to form one to a style, and opens and expands the ductile mind, every one will find that many a good thought evaporates in thinking ...
>
> (vol. II, Letter xxxvi)

This studied self-consciousness also makes it hard to accept the view of many critics that the letter-form of narration gives the novels a dramatic effect. The different personalities and points of view are not in fact brought into dramatic confrontation by this method. They do not interact but remain each absorbed in their own self-realization. In fact the most dramatic parts of the novels occur in the scenes remembered and recounted by the characters in their letters. But here the dramas are distanced from us, they are subject to the bias of the narrators, and, after all, in their verbatim completeness they only reinforce the impression of unusual literary flair in the writers.

In short, when it is proposed that the letter-form is the main thing, it must be assumed that the novels have a lot to do with the *act* of writing, with *l'écriture*, with the need to trust in the written word and at the same time to recognize its untrustworthiness. Richardson's characters, like Richardson himself, want to be able to believe that letter-writing is profoundly communicative, a way for heart to speak directly to heart. Yet the characters in the novels, after all, write because they are separated from each other. Lovelace has persuaded Clarissa to elope with him and they are living in the same house, yet there is no communication between them directly. Lovelace records his frustration in the letters to his friend John Belford; Clarissa confesses her fears to her confidante Anna Howe. But these letters only intensify the realization that the recipients are powerless to intervene: the writers are close only to people excluded from their world. At the same time the letters, which confirm their isolation, make them vulnerable to each other, for they are revealing and their revelations can be intercepted and tampered with. 'This perverse lady', Lovelace writes, 'keeps me at such a distance that I am sure something is going on between her and Miss Howe. . . . I *must* come at correspondence so disobediently carried on . . . I shall never rest till I have discovered, in the first place, where the dear creature puts her letters' (vol. II, Letter lxxv). Meanwhile Miss Howe is writing to Clarissa: 'You have exceedingly alarmed me by what you hint of his attempt to get one of my letters . . . I wish you could come at some of his letters' (vol. II, Letter lxxviii).

Letters, then, express both isolation and danger. They do not bring people close to each other, they isolate and expose them. They are expressive of the need to protect oneself and to assert oneself, to impose one's own will or succumb to the will of another. So Richardson's constant themes, the conflict between the sexes and the struggle for power, are directly reflected in his artistic method. But his method carries other implications as well. It indicates that his characters are divided not only from each other but from themselves. This is the real significance of their writing 'to the moment', since, as Richardson notes in the preface to his last novel *Sir Charles Grandison* (1753–4), this is a matter of writing not merely in the present tense, but 'whilst the heart is agitated by hopes and fears, on events undecided'. The events they are writing about have only just occurred, but they *have* occurred and nothing can be done to alter them. The characters look back on their actions with dismay, because their consequences are incalculable. Clarissa tells the story of her elopement and then breaks off: 'for now I am come to this said period of it my indiscretion stares me in the face; I hope his heart cannot be so deep and so vile a one: I hope it cannot!' (vol. I, Letter xciv). Her reflections are full of self-reproach for what has happened and anxiety for what may happen. They are written in the present tense, that is in a mode fraught with crisis, hemmed in between the errors of the past and the fears for the future. And in this way particularly they adumbrate the modern consciousness. They have a close resemblance to what Poulet describes as the Cartesian moment: 'separated from the external world, the past and the future, the Cartesian consciousness can exist only in the narrowest confines, those of the present moment'.[4]

The characters cannot extricate themselves from the words they write. Richardson's novels also cannot dissociate themselves from the

4. *Le Point de Départ*, Paris, 1964, p. 218.

words they are written in. Of course all novels are written in words, but these novels are written in *written* words: they cannot help reminding both writer and reader that they themselves are in much the same position as the writers and readers of the letters. The reader sees himself duplicated in the text of the novel, his reactions anticipated and repeated: 'I am all impatience for particulars,' writes Miss Howe, 'Lord have mercy upon me! – but can it be?' (vol. I, Letter xciii). It is true that in the end the reader of the novel, unlike the readers *in* the novel, is possessed of all the letters, and has therefore the privilege of omniscience, but at each stage, like the characters, he is caught up in suspense and uncertainty. He is made to feel what the characters feel, to share their anxieties and only to have the kind of advantage over them that comes from a sense of dramatic irony. Thus Richardson makes the reader highly conscious of the conditions imposed by the words on the page. His novel makes itself felt as a medium. And poignantly it does this by returning again and again to something that cannot actually be expressed in terms of that medium. It offers an image of another kind of communication, not through written or even spoken words, but by the eyes, with glances or searching looks, involuntary betrayals of feeling, that are possible only when the characters confront each other directly and without equivocation. Clarissa is a 'great observer of eyes', Lovelace knows that the eyes are 'the casement the heart looks out of', they are 'both great watchers of each other's eyes'. But what the eyes reveal cannot be continued into the written word, the opaque medium of the letters and the novel. Their language extends beyond the language of the novel, which is therefore almost bound to follow a pattern of alienation, of words placed at one remove from reality and of characters separated from themselves and each other. It is in this way that Richardson's novels are self-reflective. They reflect in their form as well as in content the need to unify experience and, at the same time, the difficulty of surmounting personal loneliness and anxiety. Richardson in effect has discovered what the novel will be called on to do in the modern world. He is the first English novelist to become conscious of the novel's awkward stance, balanced between the subjective individual and society, between reflection and action, between literature and life.

FIELDING

Richardson's novels were much imitated (though more in France and Germany than in England) but the first and most significant effect they had was to prompt Fielding into writing novels of a quite different kind. Henry Fielding (1707–1754) was a copious and resourceful writer, the author of a large number of stage plays (farces, burlesques, ballad-operas, comedies), essayist and journalist, lawyer, philosopher, moralist, satirist; but he seems not to have had any incentive to turn to novel-writing until Richardson began publishing novels. His immediate reaction to the publication of *Pamela* was the outrageous burlesque of *Shamela* (1741). But within the year he had produced a further and more formidable challenge to the ascendancy of *Pamela* in his first real novel, *Joseph Andrews* (1742). His second and finest novel, *Tom Jones*, published in 1749, was written between 1746 and 1748 when Richardson had already completed his second novel *Clarissa* and was arranging for its serial publication (in 1747–8). Fielding's last novel, *Amelia*, appeared in December 1751 (though dated 1752). The only prose fiction he wrote before Richardson, *Jonathan Wild* (published in 1743 but probably begun in 1740 or earlier) is an ironic satire in the manner of Swift rather than a novel.

Yet Fielding's novels are of a piece with his other work: their significance is not just that they aim to surpass Richardson but that in them Fielding surpasses himself. This can be seen very clearly in the transition from his stage plays (all written in the 1730s) to the novels of the 1740s. Richardson's work seems to have given him the clue for the form he really needed and had been striving for in his plays. In several of his works for the stage he had experimented with the possibilities of a self-reflexive art modelled on the 'rehearsal' plays initiated by Buckingham's satirical comedy, *The Rehearsal* (1672). In plays like the masterly *Pasquin, A Dramatick Satire on the Times* (1736) Fielding exhibits the failure of the drama, and then insists that such failure is the true witness to a general failure in society. That is to say, the important thing is the relation that exists between artistic form and social values. To grasp Fielding's meaning we have to be attentive to the various ways in which art connects with life.

This complicated art, reflecting itself in a distorting mirror and then reflecting the real world in those distortions, is the art that we find first and above all in Cervantes's great novel. But Fielding's only attempt to put Cervantes's hero on the stage, in the ballad-opera *Don Quixote in England* (1734), gives no idea of Cervantes's art or of the use that Fielding would eventually find for it. And in a play like *Pasquin* he is not in a position to draw directly on Cervantes as a model. Without realizing it Fielding was, we may say, on the verge of writing a novel like *Don Quixote*. It needed Richardson's first, quite un-Cervantean novel to show Fielding the sort of novel he wanted to write.

A significant part of his intention in *Joseph Andrews* must have been, as it was for Cervantes, to throw light on the relations between literature and life. At the very centre of the novel there is an encounter that reveals what is at issue throughout: an innkeeper's claim that travel gives the best knowledge of men is hotly disputed by Parson Adams, a man who resembles Quixote at least in deriving his knowledge of the world from books. Adams maintains that 'the only way of travelling by which any Knowledge is to be acquired' is in books; it is reading that provides the fullest experience of life. But Fielding's own view is not identical with Adams's. In fact he shows Adams to be often out of touch with reality. Like Quixote Adams is a reader, and he naïvely expects life to sustain the impressions derived from his reading. He is able, as it happens, to convince us that it would be better if reality could match up to literature. His reading is not, after all, in the 'Romances' but in Homer and Aeschylus; his expectations are an implicit criticism of the life which falls short of them. Yet, like Quixote, he is unfitted to survive in the real world. His being in the right constitutes an irony at his own expense: he is a comic martyr who manages to uphold the values derived from his reading by refusing to recognize that they do not obtain in reality. He is the instrument of a satire on the age, but he is also the victim of a situation that satire cannot alter; like Quixote he is so placed as to feel the full force of the dislocation between literature and life. There is behind the relaxed comedy of this novel, a sense of disappointment at such dislocation, a sense that cannot be dispelled by turning it into satire.

The character of Parson Adams tells us something about the troubled relationship of books to life. But Fielding makes it plain that the way in which Adams tries to square his reading with the life round about him must be comparable with the way we react as readers of his novel. There are, for instance, those occasions when we find we are reading a story which is also being told to Adams. We hardly know how to take these interpolated stories. Adams accepts them entirely, just as *we* accept Fielding's story about *him*; but, precisely because we are aware of Adams's naïve 'reading' of these stories we cannot ourselves take them in that way. We are made conscious of their artificiality. We cannot enter their world as Adams can; to us they are opaque. At the same time they appear to be part of *our* book; they continue the printed text of our novel. Thus they are a kind of literature which demands but cannot be given the same kind of attention as the rest of the book. They disturb our simple acceptance of the novel as 'true' or 'real'. They make us ask the same questions about our reading as Fielding asks about Adams's. But this is not something that destroys our belief in the values of fiction. On the contrary it alerts us to the element of unreality, the element of play and invention, only in order to clarify the nature and the function of fiction. Quixote's madness is that he cannot conceive of a fictional truth, but only of literal fact. His mind is so possessed with the creatures of fiction that he cannot understand that they *are* fictional. He is not, as is often said, more imaginative than other people, but less. He thinks there is an identity between the world of the imagination and the real world. Cervantes sees him as a victim, therefore, of delusions, just as Fielding sees Adams as a martyr. Both authors expect the reader to extricate himself from that kind of failure. They both work to make the reader conscious of his own role, conscious of the correspondences and contradictions set up between his reactions to fiction and his experience of real life.

Fielding does in fact make *Joseph Andrews* a 'way of travelling': reading it is a series of encounters with the unknown, with unnamed people, 'a gentleman', 'a young lady', 'a solemn Person riding into the Inn', 'two horsemen', strangers who represent a question and a challenge to one's judgement. The book reflects the way in which in reality we acquire knowledge and come to terms with our environment; but the essential difference is that it reflects it without menace or threat, through the play of imagination in fiction. Parson Adams and Joseph are often at risk as they travel into the West Country. We journey with them in the way that fiction allows, with a clear sense that their reality is not forced on us but is a possibility made available to us by the imagination. In his first novel Fielding has achieved the kind of book that can really improve the 'taste' of his reader, the ability, that is, to bring the imagination and the judgement into harmony.

Similarly, in *Tom Jones*, Fielding develops a plot structure which both reflects and clarifies the experience of the reader. Too much attention has been given to the elaborate mechanical perfection of the plot in this novel. One of the central motifs of the story is the idea of pursuit, and the fact is that, as the plot unfolds its riddles and false clues, the reader, like the characters in the story, is involved in a blind pursuit of mistaken ends. Looking back on the whole story he is, it is true, struck by its formal order and coherence, but in the process of reading he is teased by unanswerable questions, unforeseeable outcomes, open-ended possibilities. And again Fielding's intention is to imitate the confusions of real experience, for these are the conditions in which we have to be responsible to ourselves and to others, and to exercise 'prudence' and good judgement. The characters in the novel, and especially the magistrate Squire Allworthy, are constantly being asked to pass judgement, to decide on moral issues, to arbitrate. The reader is neither exempted from this responsibility, nor given the privilege of omniscience: he is as much in the dark as the characters themselves. Yet he has after all the assurance that this is a fiction, a rehearsal of his moral faculties in an imagined world. And the advantage of this is that it frees him from the pressure of circumstance and allows him to become aware of what is involved. In one of his essays Fielding writes: 'The understanding like the eye (says Mr Locke) whilst it makes us see and perceive all other things, takes no notice of itself; and it requires art and pains to set it at a distance, and make it its own object' (*The Champion*, no. 47). Fielding's art is addressed to this task of providing what, as he says, 'no Narcissus hath hitherto discovered, [a] Mirrour for the Understanding'.

SMOLLETT

Tobias Smollett (1721–71) is often bracketed with Fielding by virtue of his satire, his realism, his violent 'anti-romantic and picaresque novels. And it is true that he too had affinities with Cervantes. He not only translated *Don Quixote* (in 1755) but, in *Sir Launcelot Greaves* (1762), he recreated Quixote as a crusading satirist, an idealistic champion of reason and virtue, no madman but a relentless antagonist of 'the foes of virtue and decorum'. Yet this offers a more limited concept of Cervantes's art than Fielding had, and in general Smollett is simpler (not to say cruder) than Fielding. Where Fielding is subtle, elusive, provocative Smollett is impetuous, violent, single-minded. Smollett, it seems, cannot reconcile himself to Fielding's relaxed good humour: reality is too oppressive, it cannot be distanced, it has a suffocating closeness. If Smollett's is the more restricted art it is also the more urgent, more desperate even.

His novels are full of physical violence, fights, beatings, assaults, but all apparently a matter for manic excitement and wild laughter. They have the dimensions of farce or of animated cartoons rather than satire. But the farce and the laughter do not represent a release from the oppressive reality of his world. His heroes are perpetually at war with their world. Everything is against them. They suffer hostility, malicious accusation, physical attack. Yet, as Roderick Random says, they are 'far from being subdued by this infernal usage'. They have enormous resilience: it seems appropriate that Roderick's mother should have dreamed 'she was delivered of a tennis-ball': Roderick is a survivor, he keeps on bouncing back.

Since Smollett's theme is conflict his novels have to keep renewing the occasions of conflict. The heroes cannot afford to be subdued. The pattern of his novels can only be a continual succession of violent encounters. In Fielding's novels the picaresque form impels the reader to move forward into the unknown. They too present a series of encounters, but it is a series shaped by a moral intention; it is a journey that tests the reader's judgement and extends his moral experience. Fielding's plots are, in fact, a kind of alternative to the idea of a life dominated by chance, or 'Fortune'. 'Life may as properly be called an art as any other,' he writes in the first chapter of *Amelia*; 'As Histories of this kind, therefore, may properly be called models of Human life; so by observing minutely the several incidents which tend to the catastrophe or completion of the whole, and the minute causes whence these incidents are produced, we shall best be instructed in the most useful of all arts, which I call the art of life.' But Smollett's novels can hardly claim this kind of purpose. He seems to see no way of rationalizing experience; it is a recurring sequence, not a progressive one; it typically holds all the characters 'subject to those vicissitudes of disposition which a change of fortune usually creates'. Thus Roderick Random, for instance, knows no more of the meaning of his life at the end of the book than he did at the beginning. He is in the hands of Fortune from start to finish: at the outset he has 'an intoxicating piece of good fortune', and then almost at once is lamenting 'my reverse of fortune'; on the very last page he has reached no other conclusion than that 'fortune seems determined to make ample amends for her former cruelty'. That is to say, the novels deal with experience, but not with knowledge.

We have been examining the way in which the first major English novelists sought to develop a form which would truly reflect moral experience. Smollett's novels, with one exception, tend rather to reflect a desire to *have* intense experiences. The pattern of conflict has to be kept going, not because it has a moral importance – related for instance to 'that generous indignation' which, according to Smollett, 'ought to animate the reader against the sordid and vicious disposition of the world' (Preface to *Roderick Random*) – but because it keeps on generating intense reactions and renewing the capacity for feeling. Everything in Smollett is in extremes. The exception to all this is Smollett's last novel, *Humphry Clinker* (1771). Here, uniquely in his work, he achieves detachment and ironic balance. The letter-form of narrative here has a different effect from that produced by Richardson, for Smollett is not proposing to write 'to the moment' but to display the incongruities produced by differing views of the same scenes and events. The novel aims at a balance of the different temperaments and is therefore able to get outside the claustrophobic experience of the separate characters. Here, therefore, Smollett's comedy is for once without the violence and the bitterness that colours most of his work. It is a novel which reflects not only the real world but the world of his own novels and, in the figure of Matt Bramble, his own nature.

STERNE

Laurence Sterne (1713–1768) also uses the novel as a medium for reflecting his own nature, and he does so by reflecting on the various roles offered to him as a writer, and then catching the reflections of these roles in the roles played by his readers. His novels thus become an account in fiction of the operations of fiction. More than any other novelist he understands and develops the true meaning of Cervantes's art. His two novels, *The Life and Opinions of Tristram Shandy, Gentleman* (1760–1767) and *A Sentimental Journey* (1768), together typify and transcend the eighteenth-century novel: they renew the significance of its origins and they extend its possibilities into the twentieth century and, in particular, the work of James Joyce and Virginia Woolf.

Sterne's art is highly self-conscious, at the opposite extreme from the involuntary self-revelation of Smollett's black comedy. Yet it would be wrong to think of it as introspective, wrapped up in self-scrutiny. That would be to mistake Tristram Shandy, defeated in his efforts to get himself, his 'life and opinions', into the book he is writing, for Sterne, who is telling the story of the writing of that book. Tristram's narration starts from and returns to the self; Sterne's enlarges the possibilities open to the self. Sterne experiments with various versions of the self, and Tristram is in fact one of those versions: Tristram's dilemma as a writer and his predicament as a man are like, yet unlike, Sterne's own. For instance Tristram re-enacts the painful comedy of Sterne's tubercular disease and of his desperate race with death in his travels through Europe. Yet in the novel these travels become a symbol of something beyond Tristram's scope, a release of creative energy and a discovery of the creative power of joy. Thus Tristram's life, which he can hardly cope with, is a kind of analogue of things that would be overwhelming in Sterne's life, were it not that, projected in this way as comedy, they lose their menace and take the form of play. Tristram, that is, allows Sterne to envisage his own life as a fiction. Tristram is overwhelmed by reality, he can neither control nor escape from the circumstances of his life; but the contemplation of his self-imprisonment becomes for Sterne a form of freedom.

This freedom to experiment with his own nature allows Sterne to assume the identity not only of Tristram but simultaneously of the radically different Yorick. This is in some ways a much bolder thing to do: Sterne would have many precedents for identifying himself with his own narrator (and actually Yorick *is* the supposed author of *A Sentimental Journey*) but Yorick is hardly able even to get into the action of *Tristram Shandy*. Indeed almost the first thing that is told us in the novel is that Yorick is dead. Whereas there is nothing in the book that is not part of Tristram's story, there is nothing in it of the story of Yorick. At the same time Yorick is centrally important in the novel, his influence is felt at the start and remains potent throughout, and he speaks the final words of the novel: 'L—d! said my mother, what is all this story about? – A COCK and a BULL, said *Yorick* – And one of the best of its kind, I ever heard.' Yorick embodies all the things that are beyond Tristram's scope and yet are part of Sterne's nature: the mischievous and disreputable humour, the manic disregard of self-interest, the charity, the eccentricity. He represents that part of Sterne's nature that is a contradiction of Tristram. It is as if he represents the kind of person who *could* have written the sort of book that Sterne is writing, though that kind of person is virtually unable to get into the book that Tristram is writing. Sterne, wittily, is excluding the creative side of his nature from the book. Yet, having done so, he reverses the situation by printing the whole of one of his own sermons, supposing it to have been written by Yorick, and submitting it to the judgement of the characters in the novel. So Sterne invents a fictional world in which his own nature, even his own work, takes on a different aspect, a different emphasis. The sermon which was preached by Sterne becomes a sermon written by Yorick. (After the success of the first two volumes of *Tristram Shandy* in 1760 Sterne in fact published the first two volumes of *The Sermons of Mr Yorick*.) Out of an imaginary volume in the hands of a fictional character flutter the leaves of an actual sermon whose real author thus becomes a fiction in his own novel. These are the ways in which Sterne uses the novel form to play with the relations between fiction and reality.

He goes further. He experiments not only with his own role as writer but with the various ways in which the part played by the reader will affect his work. Here too there are reflections and resemblances between the actual reader and his various fictional counterparts. Corporal Trim reads Sterne's 'Yorick's sermon', and *we* read it also; we react in one way to it, Uncle Toby, Dr Slop and Walter Shandy in another. The sermon is being read on two levels simultaneously. The fictional reading, like Tristram's fictional writing, is inadequate: it reveals an inability in the characters to imagine any other situation but their own. By contrast our reading is of its very nature an exercise of the imagination, for we are to imagine, as we read, a different reading from our own; we are reading both the sermon and the reading of the sermon. Indeed, not only are we expected to envisage and enter this fictional world, we are also invited to consider various fictional versions of our own activities as readers. Thus Sterne directly addresses several supposed readers ('madam', 'ye critics'). He imagines, and therefore requires us to imagine, not only the events in the story but events in the reading of the story as when one reader who has missed the point is instructed to go back to the beginning of the chapter and read it again whilst the rest of us read on. Again Sterne takes an example of incompetence and offers it as a creative experiment: he teases the reader into rearranging his reading and becoming, like the book itself, both 'digressive and progressive at the same time'. In effect Sterne is asking us to discover as readers the same creative vitality as he has found as writer. He goes so far in fact as to ask us to 'write' two of the chapters which are offered first as blank pages and only later become part of the text of the book (obeying, in Tristram's words, 'the necessity I was under of writing the 25th chapter of my book, before the 18th', Chapter 25 of Volume IX contains the text of 'The Eighteenth Chapter' and 'Chapter the Nineteenth'). Similarly the reader has to be able and willing to supply the words indicated only by asterisks, and thus to 'write' the obscenities that Sterne can avoid writing. The reader is being invited to collaborate in the creating of Sterne's book. At the same time he recognizes that the roles made available to him are of Sterne's creation, suggesting that Sterne wishes to collaborate in the reading of his book. The reader is asked to imagine the fictional world of the novel and this involves imagining himself in various roles, recreating himself in the reading of the book as Sterne was in the writing.

Viktor Shklovsky describes *Tristram Shandy* as a 'parodying novel' which reveals the aesthetic laws lying behind its compositional processes: it is thus 'the most typical novel of world literature'.[5] It is an extraordinarily complete image or reflection of the many experiences which come together in the writing and reading of a novel. It mediates between literature and life, not primarily by its touching and humorous images of human behaviour, but by its sensitive exploration of the points at which reality and fiction meet and enrich each other. In this it is only doing with more dazzling ease and confidence what most of the major eighteenth-century novelists had set themselves to do. The ambition to enter and occupy the region in which fiction and reality overlap was what produced in England the 'rise of the novel'.

5. Laurence Sterne, *A Collection of Critical Essays*, ed. John Traugott, New Jersey, 1968, p. 89.

TWO

France

THE development of the novel is a particularly interesting aspect of eighteenth-century French literature, for it represents a change from a comparatively despised and neglected genre to a serious and well-established art form with a remarkable future. The novel ultimately benefited from what at first sight seemed a grave disadvantage – its lowly status – for it constituted a genre for which the classical theorists had not laid down firm rules: being unknown to the ancients, it was not judged worthy of serious critical attention. Admittedly, this position of inferiority meant that the novel had to struggle for acceptance and to justify itself in the face of stern opposition: there was considerable hostility towards a genre which was widely held to be not only of dubious aesthetic value but also morally reprehensible. Georges May has shown in his important study of the subject[1] that this consciousness of critical opposition was an important factor in the formation of the novelists' outlook and probably explains the prefaces by which they usually sought to justify the moral value of their work. At the same time the existence of these prefaces shows that novelists, though freed from rigid aesthetic rules, were aware of the growing need to give their work greater truth and authenticity. Consequently, they were faced with the technical problem of developing a literary form which would enable them to achieve this end.

In general the eighteenth-century novel shows a remarkable change from the artificiality of its seventeenth-century predecessors as exemplified by the aristocratically romantic and pseudo-historical novels of Mlle de Scudéry and La Calprenède or by the coarse and grotesque popular novels of Scarron and Sorel. As in England, there was a broad movement towards a more 'realistic' conception of the novel, not in the restricted nineteenth-century manner of Balzac or Zola, but in the sense of a literary form which tended increasingly to find its

1. *Le Dilemme du roman au XVIIIe siècle: étude sur les rapports du roman et de la critique*, *1715–61*, New Haven, 1963.

inspiration in its contact with everyday life and human experience, at both the psychological and the social level. Not only was there a greater interest in the portrayal of human feelings and passions (so that in certain respects the novel took over the role of classical tragedy), but there was also a serious attempt to replace the pseudo-historical or pastoral background of the previous century by an interest in recent history and contemporary life. In some ways the novel was deemed to be closer to everyday reality than traditional history, because it dealt with ordinary people and their problems rather than with exceptional characters of the remote past. It must be added, however, that the older type of novel, with its use of romantic and *merveilleux* elements, survived into the eighteenth-century; to some extent it was given a new impetus by Galland's extended translation of the *Arabian Nights* which appeared between 1704 and 1717. Nevertheless, serious writers tended to move away from this escapist mood towards a greater concern with recognizable human and social reality.

The desire to guarantee the apparent veracity of the novel probably accounts for the rapid development of the first person narrative and the 'memoir'. When using the memoir form, novelists may well have been thinking of the popularity of the genuine historical memoirs of the preceding age: a first-person narrative was perhaps deemed to be more credible than a story told in the third person. Although the modern reader will find this assumption naïve, the early-eighteenth-century novelist's preoccupation with the problem of defending the truth of his work led him to emphasize its historical aspects. It will be recalled that certain seventeenth-century writers (Scudéry, for example, in *Le Grand Cyrus* and *Clélie* with its significant subtitle of 'histoire romaine') had already used historical characters and events as a means of providing an acceptable framework for their narratives, even though the element of authenticity thereby introduced was very limited because of the absence of genuine human content. Other writers such as Courtilz de Sandras (1644–1712), the author of the *Mémoires de M. d'Artagnan* (1700) had presented fictional narratives as genuine historical accounts.

When the memoir form proved somewhat limited in scope, novelitst turned to the epistolary medium, which had the apparent advantage of retaining the illusion of direct personal testimony and yet of presenting more than one point of view. It is worth noting that two of the most famous novels of the later decades of the period, Rousseau's *La Nouvelle Héloïse* (1761) and Laclos's *Les Liaisons dangereuses* (1782), were written in this form, while Montesquieu had already used the epistolary medium in his *Lettres persanes* of 1721.

Another important influence upon the development of French fiction was that of the foreign novel. Apart from the continuing popularity of the Spanish tradition of Cervantes and the picaresque novels, a major new factor was the emergence of the fertile English novel. Even though its effect upon French writers was not always beneficial, its great popularity helped to increase the widespread English influence which was already affecting so many other aspects of French culture. Prévost's translations of Samuel Richardson appeared towards the middle of the century – *Pamela* (1742), *Clarissa* (1751) and *Sir Charles Grandison* (1755) – and in 1761 Diderot was prompted to compose his enthusiastic *Éloge de Richardson*. About the same time Fielding's work appeared in translation. Other widely read translations were those of Defoe's *Robinson Crusoe* (the only book which Rousseau would allow his young Émile to read) and Oliver Goldsmith's *The Vicar of Wakefield* (1767). Sterne's work became known between 1760–67 and may have encouraged Diderot's deliberate experimentation with the novel form in a work such as *Jacques le fataliste*. Towards the end of the period the work of Horace Walpole, Anne Radcliffe and 'Monk' Lewis encouraged the development of a new and more sombre 'pre-Romantic' novel. Translation, however, often meant adaptation, so that the work known to French readers differed considerably from the original, these differences being due as much to considerations of taste as to the change in language. The English novel as seen through the French eyes of the time would undoubtedly have appeared somewhat odd to English readers.

The new emphasis on real life is strikingly illustrated in one of the first important novels of the period: *Les Illustres Françaises* (1713) of Robert Chasles (or Challes), which enjoyed considerable success in the early part of the eighteenth century but then practically disappeared from view until it was 'rediscovered' in 1959. (It was translated into English by Mrs Penelope Aubin in 1727 under the title of *The Illustrious French Lovers.*) It has an unusual form, for it consists of seven different stories linked together by a narrative in which the main characters reappear, thus giving the work an effective unity and yet allowing for the different points of view of the various narrators. For the most part the characters are drawn from the upper bourgeoisie and are not intended to be exceptional; they are also depicted in real-life situations. The author makes a considerable effort to set the stories in authentic backgrounds, many of them taking place in an easily recognizable Paris. Even more important is the way in which the characters are involved in serious attempts to solve the genuine moral problems and conflicts forced upon them by their environment. In particular, Chasles is interested in the individual's attempts to reconcile a legitimate desire for happiness with the demands of social life; he has to face up to the injustice of many institutions (for example, legal and ecclesiastical) without denying the fundamental claims of society itself; if, therefore, the rights of the individual are stressed, society is also shown as an inescapable and ultimately justifiable aspect of every human existence. Running through the whole work is an earnestness and sincerity which is markedly absent from the artificial novels of Chasles's predecessors. Even though *Les Illustres Françaises* has been criticized for a certain lack of depth (the psychological motives of the characters are not given detailed analysis), it is a work of considerable originality in both form and content, and, in this respect, well ahead of its time.

The work of Le Sage (1668–1747) is an interesting example of a writer who still felt the need to follow foreign models and yet wanted to relate his work to contemporary life. With the possible exception of *Le Diable boiteux* (1707), directly inspired by a Spanish writer, Luis Velez de Guevera, Le Sage, as a novelist, is remembered solely for *l'Histoire de Gil Blas de Santillane* (1715–35). His indebtedness to the Spanish picaresque novel shows that he was not unmindful of the popular appeal of the *roman d'aventures*. When he is seventeen years old, Gil Blas is sent by an uncle-priest to study at the University of Salamanca, but he never reaches his destination, for he is captured by robbers; thereafter he experiences a bewildering variety of adventures as social pressures force him to seek survival by resourceful if dubiously moral means; he becomes a doctor, a servant to the Archbishop of Granada and, afterwards, to the prime minister of Spain, the Duke of Lerma. Corrupted by prosperity, he eventually falls from favour and is imprisoned. On his release, he withdraws into the country and marries. After his wife's death, he returns to political life in Madrid and serves the new prime minister, Olivares, this time avoiding his previous mistakes, so that he is finally able to retire again to the country, remarry and lead a peaceful life. In spite of the many vicissitudes of his existence, Gil Blas differs from the traditional hero in one very significant respect: in spite of the often remarkable nature of his experiences, he remains an unexceptional person, retaining many of the characteristics of the average man struggling to cope with adversity by his innate wit, intelligence and good humour. At the same time Gil Blas does not have the lowly status of the Spanish *picaro*, for he is a frequenter of polite society. The witty, ironical style of the book also shows that it was intended to appeal to a far more educated public than the readers of Scarron's *Roman comique*.

More important than this attempt to relate the hero's adventures to the world of everyday humanity is the author's interest in society. The thin Spanish veneer cannot conceal the French society which Le Sage has constantly before his eyes. The story is set in the period of the French Regency with its various social types: the court, the nobility, the ecclesiastical hierarchy, the doctors and many others with their good and bad qualities. Yet, as critics have frequently observed, Le Sage, though looking back in some ways to La Bruyère and the classical tradition of character portrayal, is also aware of the significance of telling details and his preoccupation with types does not exclude interest in his characters as individuals. It is, however, in its satirical portrayal of social – rather than psychological or moral – reality that the novel makes its impact.

The extraordinary change in moral climate which accompanied the advent of the Regency, with its abandonment of the old austerity for an often hectic pursuit of money and pleasure, greatly influenced the novel as a whole, and, apart from *Gil Blas*, at least two other famous works reflect the mood of the time. In Montesquieu's *Lettres persanes* (1721) two Persian visitors to France, Usbek and Rica, write to each other and their friends in Persia in order to report on their impressions of western life and obtain news of the disturbing events happening in Usbek's harem at home. The extraordinary success of the book owed almost as much to its appearance at the right moment as to its undoubted literary qualities. It made a strong appeal to the newly awakened interest in the Near East by setting the letters within the framework of a harem intrigue which coincided with the master's visit to France. The popular travel books of Tavernier and Chardin (especially the latter's *Voyages en Perse* of 1711) had already stimulated curiosity about Persia and though fairly superficial, Montesquieu's use of an oriental background helped to give the work an exotic flavour. Moreover, the oriental theme was accompanied by erotic details well calculated to titillate the feelings of readers already influenced by the immorality of the Regency period. More important, however, than these two factors was the satirical analysis of contemporary society which many Frenchmen were also beginning to consider with disillusioned eyes. The apparently unsophisticated attitude of the Persians, who still believed that they were living in accordance with the principles of 'nature', served to emphasize the corruption and perversity of a society which assumed its way of life to be that of normal people. In particular, critical attention was focused on the monarchy, with Louis XIV seen as a potential despot and a king led astray by the influence of women and with the Pope as a powerful 'magician' who can make people believe that 'three are only one'; there are also many detailed satirical pictures of French society, with all its whims and foibles. At the same time the *Lettres persanes* discuss a variety of topics, including the value of the arts and sciences, divorce and population. Especially interesting from the point of view of the history of ideas are the letters on the origin of society, which recount the story of the Troglodytes; in them Montesquieu apparently takes issue with Hobbes's theory of pre-social life as a state of war. Also present in the work are political ideas (for example, on republicanism and the English constitution) which he was to develop more fully in *De l'esprit des lois*, while behind these specific discussions are several fundamental notions (nature, virtue and freedom) which were to play an important part in the thought of the Enlightenment. Moreover, the pungent, ironic style of the work as well as its skilful use of different literary forms (portraits, conversation-pieces, dramatic scenes, short narratives, etc.) make it one of the most revealing expressions of the spirit of the early Enlightenment as well as of the Regency period.

Another novel set in the Regency period, the abbé Prévost's *Histoire du chevalier des Grieux et de Manon Lescaut* (1731), though clearly describing the immorality of the time, places its main emphasis on a human problem, for it traces the consequences of a human dilemma

– the overwhelming love of a young man for a girl who is unworthy of him. Prévost (1697–1763) was an extremely prolific writer: as well as being an enthusiastic journalist (he published, among other ventures, *Le Pour et le contre*, 1733–40, a journal devoted to the diffusion of knowledge of English culture) and an indefatigable translator who introduced Richardson's *Pamela*, *Clarissa Harlowe* and *Charles Grandison* into France (1742–55), he wrote a series of very long novels. Although *Cleveland* (which purported to describe the life of an illegitimate son of Cromwell) was Rousseau's favourite novel, *Manon Lescaut* is the only one which has retained its popularity. Compared with the other works, which tend to be long and rambling, this is remarkable for its concision. As critics have suggested, perhaps Prévost put into it some of his own personal tensions and inner conflicts as a one-time Benedictine monk who fled from his monastery in order to participate in the life of the world; even if it is scarcely autobiographical in the strict sense, for the author describes a career and situations which were different from his own, the work undoubtedly embodies a good deal of personal feeling and experience. The young Des Grieux, an apparently upright and promising young seminary student, becomes the victim of a helpless and degrading passion for a girl whose main interest is the pursuit of pleasure. Devoid of any genuine moral sense, and knowing that pleasure requires money, Manon does not heed her lover's passionate desire for fidelity. This does not prevent him from sacrificing everything for her, and he ultimately accompanies her to the American colonies to which she has been deported for immorality. Realizing at last the depth of her lover's devotion, she wishes to become his wife; but through misfortune and misunderstanding, they are compelled to flee to the desert where Manon dies of exhaustion, leaving the unhappy Des Grieux to return to European life, alone and yet to some extent fortified by his bitter experience.

In its portrayal of the social background of the time and even in its emphasis upon Manon as a typical girl of the Regency period, the novel shows the same interest in social reality as the other works already mentioned. A considerable part of the action takes place in Paris and although Prévost does not place undue emphasis on the physical background, he seeks to make it recognizably authentic, whilst the feverish concern with money and the unscrupulous ways of obtaining it clearly indicate the mood of the time. However, the social background is less important than the human content of the book, and, as critics have already observed, the portrayal of irresistible passion has at times a Racinian intensity; for the first time a French novel is imbued with a genuinely tragic element. Moreover, the restrained analysis of physical and psychological elements reveals the classical aspect of a work which, on the whole, shuns rhetoric and bombast. Yet the portrayal of Des Grieux as a young man who feels himself to be cut off from society by his exceptional passion, marks him out as a precursor of the Romantic hero with his *passion fatale*. At the same time the *sensibilité* of *Manon Lescaut* retains a certain ambiguity in so far as it reflects the attitude of many eighteenth-century writers towards passion: whilst recognizing its tragic and immoral character, Prévost cannot bring himself wholeheartedly to condemn it and ultimately gives it a redemptive power. The attempt of his 'Préface' to justify the work as a 'terrible example of the evil effects of the passions' is unconvincing, being little more than a means of forestalling the criticism of contemporary moralists. In so far as the book has a deeper moral purpose, it would seem to be contained in the idea that although Manon dies in the end, she is not unredeemed, having found salvation through the Chevalier's untiring devotion.

No doubt the form of the work, with its rapid series of often melodramatic adventures, still retains close links with the *roman d'aventures*, but the human content lifts it above the mediocrity of that genre. Moreover, the sordidness of the theme is offset by a certain poetic charm emanating from the youthfulness of the main characters.

The two unfinished novels of Marivaux, *La Vie de Marianne* (1731–41) and *Le Paysan parvenu* (1735–6) also reflect, though in a highly individual way, the new psychological and social dimensions of the genre. The unfinished character of these works already suggests that their author was not concerned primarily with a well-constructed plot; although they tend to move on different social planes, both novels reveal the same subtle and distinctive psychological approach; narrated in the first person, they betray the same kind of self-consciousness, as though the characters are both performers and commentators of the actions they record: in spite of their involvement with events, they analyse their situations and moods with considerable finesse. Unlike Prévost, Marivaux does not move in the domain of the tragic, for he seeks to explore the unexpected aspects of ordinary human feelings: *La Vie de Marianne* describes the life and adventures of a young orphan girl of unknown but seemingly very reputable parentage, but the events are much less important in themselves (the plot moves forward very slowly and is often interrupted by secondary episodes) than the psychological analyses to which they give rise; Marianne tries to disentangle the true impulses of her heart from evanescent and often artificial feelings. Some contemporary critics were irritated by her persistent habit of personal reflection, although others were fascinated by her attempt to understand the elusive complexity of her feelings. Jacob, the narrator of *Le Paysan parvenu*, describes with subtlety and good-humour his rise from humble peasant origins to a high place in society, acknowledging that the main cause of his success is his powerful sexual attraction which allows him to exploit women (usually older than himself) shamelessly for his own advantage. Like Marianne, he is given to constant reflection and he analyses his reactions and state of mind as he passes from one woman to the next.

Both novels also accord an important place to the observation of society and depict a considerable number of social classes and situations. *La Vie de Marianne*, for example, contains impressions of Parisian life, including some very lively street scenes, whilst *Le Paysan parvenu* draws a very vivid picture of ageing women addicted to *la fausse dévotion*. Once again it is contemporary France, and not the remote historical past, which occupies the novelist's attention. Moreover, this sharpened perception of social reality involves, as Dr Vivienne Mylne points out,[2] a much greater range of visual references than is found in other novelists of the time: physical objects, clothes and gestures are all noted with precision. However, the social background is rarely described for its own sake, but tends to be subordinated to the human reality in which the author is primarily interested.

Marivaux imparts a peculiar flavour to his work by a very original style which, in some ways, continues the tradition of *la préciosité*. Although it is given a more dramatic and forceful form in his plays, the novels also contain the *marivaudage* which so faithfully reflects the mental attitude of the main characters: it is a style in which psycho-

2. *The Eighteenth-Century French Novel: Techniques of Illusion*, New York, 1965.

logical reactions and linguistic usage become very closely connected. Marivaux certainly seems to aim – more deliberately than any other novelist so far analysed – at a very highly individual use of language.

By the middle of the century some of the characteristic preoccupations of the Enlightenment were already becoming evident in the novel. Voltaire in particular used *le roman philosophique* as a vehicle for the critical exposition of ideas. Like other writers of the time, he adapted a traditional form (the *roman d'aventures* and the picaresque novel) to his own purpose. In the most famous of these tales, *Candide ou l'Optimisme* (1759) which was written at a time when he was moving towards a very pessimistic and disillusioned view of human existence, he sought to demolish what he considered to be the complacent optimism of rationalist thinkers and writers, especially Leibniz and Pope, by confronting it with the grim realities of everyday life. The naïve hero Candide, who had uncritically imbibed the philosophical teaching of his master Pangloss that 'this is the best of all possible worlds', is subjected to an almost endless series of misfortunes which are intended to show that the cruelty of real life bears no resemblance to the shallow pretensions of abstract philosophizing. In the course of the novel Voltaire also delivers fierce attacks on various professions and institutions (doctors, lawyers, journalists) which he considered to be inimical to the spread of enlightenment. In the end, however, Candide is made to see that practical effort (not metaphysical speculation) is the best way to alleviate human misery and that it is more profitable to 'cultivate one's garden' than to construct philosophical systems. An earlier tale, *Zadig ou la Destinée* (1748) is also intended as a corrective to the passive acceptance of intellectual or religious ideas which are not tested by experience. Zadig, a likeable young man endowed with many fine qualities, is convinced that a virtuous life leads to happiness and well-being. His many misfortunes, however, show him that evil is an inescapable part of human existence, that evil-doers usually triumph over the good and that women turn out to be even more dishonest than men. As Voltaire admitted in his correspondence, 'Providence' rather than 'Destiny' would have been a more suitable subtitle for his work, had not fear of censorship made him cautious. Admittedly, from time to time, Zadig is led to see that 'the immutable order of the universe' is ultimately greater than the 'insects' who are so busy devouring each other, but the intractable problem of the unhappiness of the just still remains. When Zadig's situation is most desperate, he is visited by the angel Jesrad. Unfortunately the latter's attempts to allay Zadig's doubts by means of three moral stories are not free from serious difficulties, even though they are intended to show that the universe is greater than man. Zadig greets them with a 'But –', as he falls on his knees in humble submission. Other thought-provoking philosophical tales are *Micromégas, histoire philosophique* (1752), which has a predominantly social and political emphasis, *Le Monde comme il va* (1748) and *Le Taureau blanc* (1774).

Needless to say, these works contain little serious characterization, for we are presented with mere puppets embodying some essential idea; Voltaire is more interested in putting forward a point of view than in depicting real-life situations. His main weapon is his remarkable mastery of irony, which is revealed not only in the basic conception of these books as a contrast between the abstract and empty pretensions of intellectual concepts and the cruelty and ruthlessness of real existence, but also in his remarkable gift of lively and varied literary expression.

When he tried to justify the publication of his epistolary novel, *Julie ou la nouvelle Héloïse* (1761), Rousseau was embarrassed by his earlier condemnation of contemporary society and his severe criticism of its culture. As he said in the *Confessions*, he feared that he might be incurring 'the shame of contradicting himself so clearly and so openly'. However, he consoled himself with the thought that he was producing a useful work with a serious purpose – one which would help those of his fellow-men who had not yet been completely corrupted by the 'vices of society': he proposed to 'analyse the human heart in order to distinguish in it the true feelings of nature'. Probably still more important in the genesis of the novel was Rousseau's need to find a medium through which he could express some of his deepest aspirations and feelings: as he admitted, it originated in the frustrations of his dream of perfect love during his rural sojourn at Montmorency in 1756. The first part of *La Nouvelle Héloïse* is the story of a true and noble passion thwarted and then tainted by the prejudices of society: in spite of their genuine love and striking affinity of character, Julie and her young tutor Saint-Preux are refused permission to marry by a father who will not accept a commoner as a son-in-law. Julie then marries a much older man, her father's friend, M. de Wolmar, who eventually takes the surprising step of inviting Saint-Preux to share his family life at Clarens; he is convinced that he can 'cure' the young man of his 'unhappy passion' and bring him moral fulfilment by showing him that Julie de Wolmar, wife and mother, is no longer the same person as the young girl, Julie d'Etange. The last part of the book thus describes the redemption and rehabilitation of the two main characters. Throughout the whole work, however, the main emphasis is upon the characters' feelings rather than upon striking events: Rousseau prided himself upon having sustained his readers' interest throughout a long novel which had a very simple subject, few characters and no 'romantic adventures or wickedness of any kind'. Yet the absence of external incidents was counterbalanced by the fervent idealism and deep sincerity of the feelings portrayed.

Although the characters of *La Nouvelle Héloïse* are exceptional in so far as they are 'great' or 'beautiful souls', they are not intended to be superhuman; they are people struggling with the problems of life and love and hoping for eventual happiness and fulfilment. Moreover, their story unfolds against an authentic background. After considering the possibility of using a more exotic setting (such as the Borromean Islands), Rousseau finally decided to choose a Swiss valley with which he was familiar. Included in this background is a detailed account of the domestic life of Clarens which, as an ideal community, contains a curious amalgam of imaginative and realistic elements: it is a self-sufficient society relying on its own inherent strength and resources and offering to its members a happy, ordered and dignified existence; it is, however, paternalistic in spirit, for it is ultimately controlled by M. de Wolmar and his wife.

As well as being a story of love and passion, *La Nouvelle Héloïse* is also a didactic work with a strong moral purpose. M. de Wolmar is convinced that he can make Saint-Preux an acceptable member of the community of Clarens by putting him through a series of 'tests'. Moreover, Julie herself becomes a major figure in the later stages of the novel and is the source of truth and wisdom. It is not without reason that she is described as 'une âme prêcheuse', for she gives her views on all kinds of topics – education, morality, religion. At the same time *La Nouvelle Héloïse* is a novel about friendship, for Julie has a very close and intensely devoted friend Claire, while Saint-

Preux wins the affection and esteem of an English aristocrat Lord Edward Bomston, with whom he exchanges views on such topics as suicide and other moral problems. Towards the end of the book the religious theme becomes increasingly prominent and is very closely identified with Julie who finally dies after saving one of her children from drowning and, through her death, opens up the ultimate spiritual perspective from which everything has to be viewed.

In spite of its edifying conclusion *La Nouvelle Héloïse* is not without its ambiguity, for Julie's death is in some respects an admission of her failure to solve the conflict between duty and passion – between her life as a devoted wife and mother and her suppressed desire for Saint-Preux's love; in spite of her firm religious principles, she is tormented by a need for the absolute and, unable to find complete fulfilment in her everyday life, she is given to mystical contemplation. The danger still lurking in her heart is revealed in her farewell letter to Saint-Preux in which she confesses that she may not have completely overcome her love for him.

Although *La Nouvelle Héloïse* is complex and uneven, combining moments of great poetry and charm with pages of tedious didacticism, its new *sensibilité*, which involves the intense inner life of the characters and their relations to the physical world of nature, represents an important stage in the development of the novel; it is also an invaluable document for the deeper understanding of the genius of Rousseau himself, since he has expressed in it some of his most intimate and contradictory longings.

Of the major novelists of the Enlightenment, Diderot was certainly the boldest experimenter, although some of his best work was not published during his lifetime. Beginning with an immoral work, *Les Bijoux indiscrets* (1748), which also contained important philosophical ideas as well as satirical elements, he went on to write *La Religieuse* (1760, published 1796), a first-person narrative about an unfortunate girl who is forced to enter a convent against her will, and *Jacques le fataliste* (published posthumously in 1796), the most original of all his experiments. Reminiscent of Voltaire in so far as it has a satirical philosophical purpose (Diderot tries to do to Spinoza and philosophical fatalism what Voltaire had done to Leibniz and philosophical optimism in *Candide*), this last novel not only deals with the problem of the relationship of fiction and reality, but does not hesitate to involve the reader directly in a discussion of the problem. Within the loose framework which takes the form of a rambling conversation between Jacques and his master about the former's love-life and the various adventures to which it gives rise, are included some striking secondary episodes which add to the complexity and remarkable creative vitality of the work: the most remarkable of these is the story of the ruthless Mme de la Pommeraye who wreaks savage vengeance on an unfaithful lover, the Marquis d'Arcis. The unorthodox, experimental nature of the novel suggests that Diderot may not have been unmindful of Sterne's *Tristram Shandy*.

Le Neveu de Rameau (probably written between 1761 and 1774, but published from the original manuscript only in 1891, having been preceded by a German translation by Goethe in 1805 and a French re-translation in 1823) is one of the undoubted masterpieces of the century, but difficult to classify. It is certainly not a novel in the conventional sense, since it takes the form of a dialogue set against the background of a Parisian café and contains passages of description and personal action as well as stories; its main emphasis is upon the confrontation of two radically different points of view as represented by the bohemian Nephew, who is a self-confessed parasite, and his interlocutor 'Moi', the virtuous *philosophe*. The work is short but extremely complex as it ranges over a wide variety of attitudes and themes; it is dominated by the intellectual and linguistic vitality of the chief protagonist, Rameau, who develops the extreme consequences of a self-centred materialism that not only gives priority to man's animal appetites but also seeks to justify indulgence in them by an appeal to the degradation of contemporary social values. *Le Neveu de Rameau* is an interesting example of the dilemma confronting an author who wanted to reconcile the apparently conflicting demands of materialism and morality.

If the eighteenth-century novel was characterized by a new psychological dimension in its concern with the analysis of passion and feeling – a concern that sometimes (as with Prévost and Rousseau) involved an uneasy alliance with morality – certain authors betrayed a growing tendency to establish a more cynical and deliberate antithesis between sexuality and moral values, love being rejected in favour of a careful exploration of the reflective aspect of erotic experience. Already Crébillon *fils* (1717–77) had developed the theme of eroticism, often seeking to hide its sinister implications beneath a superficial elegance of thought and language. Nevertheless, he gave a detailed analysis of the psychological reactions of his characters, for whom 'love' was the mere occasion for the subtle expression of erotic reactions. In Crébillon's novels men simply use women for the satisfaction of their own vanity and desires, considering themselves as the masters and women as their servants. Crébillon uses various literary forms, including the letter novel, memoir and short narrative. His most successful work was *Les Égarements du coeur et de l'esprit* (1736–8) which was written in the first person. The main character Meilcour is initiated into the art of seduction by the experienced Versac, who teaches him that love owes as much to the mind as to the heart. Meilcour becomes involved with three different women, each of whom introduces him to hitherto unknown aspects of amorous experience. This novel seeks to stress the complexity of an attitude that involves different and often conflicting elements of the personality; in the main, sensual appetite tends to take precedence over genuine feeling. At the same time, erotic experience is treated as an essential aspect of 'la science du monde' and as a man's way of adapting himself to the demands of society, usually in defiance of 'reason and honour'.

The theme of *libertinage* is also examined by Duclos (1704–72) in his *Confessions du comte de* *** (1741) and his *Histoire de Madame de Luz* (1740). The former work has a certain interest as an attempt to describe a man–woman relationship not based primarily on sex. Mme de Selves encourages her friend in his amorous exploits and discusses their implications with him; the two finally give up the world in order to live together in quiet contentment. The *Histoire de Mme de Luz* is the story of a thrice-raped woman and her reactions to the experience. As might be expected from an author who also wrote *Considérations sur les moeurs de ce siècle* (1750), which is probably his most important work, Duclos tends to write *romans de moeurs* portraying the immoral aspects of contemporary society. Although not a major writer, he reveals the growing complexity of sexual attitudes and, in this respect, he can be treated as a forerunner of the Marquis de Sade.

Laclos (1741–1803) produced only one major work – *Les Liaisons dangereuses* (1782) – but it is now regarded as a masterpiece, both for its psychological content and for its brilliant use of the letter-form.

The main protagonists, Mme de Merteuil and the Vicomte de Valmont, are accomplices and rivals in their ruthless desire to dominate through sexual conquest. The dissolute aristocrat Valmont's chief aim is to satisfy his vanity by the seduction of a highly virtuous woman of the upper bourgeoisie, Mme de Tourvel, whilst Mme de Merteuil carries on her intrigues under the cloak of eminent respectability. Ultimately, however, their ruthless and cunning efforts to dominate other people involve Valmont and Mme de Merteuil in a fatal struggle for mastery over each other – a struggle which ends with Valmont's death in a duel and Mme de Merteuil's public disgrace and physical disfigurement by disease. In spite of its moral ending, the novel presents a vivid and yet lucid picture of vice in action, the innocent and virtuous becoming the victims of the calculating seducers who plan their campaigns with great efficiency, as Valmont's use of military terms constantly stresses. An interesting aspect of the work is the way in which Mme de Merteuil is made to appear as the more reflective and careful of the two characters, for if her immorality has become a way of life and a means of affirming her superiority, this has to be achieved through the skilful and systematic use of deceit and hypocrisy: until she is unmasked at the end she is revered as an eminently virtuous and respectable woman.

If Valmont is eventually destroyed, it is not only because of Mme de Merteuil's greater control of herself and the situation, but also because this would-be Don Juan becomes the unwitting victim of his own scheming as his reactions to Mme de Tourvel take the form of deep feelings which he is unwilling to acknowledge to himself. Psychologically, therefore, the novel is a masterly study of eroticism as a mental as well as a physical attitude. At the same time the vanity of Valmont's character and Mme de Merteuil's determination to conform outwardly to conventional attitudes bring out the social significance of the novel as a study of an aristocracy that had no other outlet for its energies than the cultivation of a perverse eroticism.

Laclos's extremely effective exploitation of the letter-form is one of the work's outstanding literary merits: it shows itself not only in the organization of the letters but also in his ability to write in the style appropriate to the different characters, ranging from the effusions of the naïve Cécile to the sophisticated elegance of Valmont, who takes as much delight in demonstrating his cleverness to Mme de

Merteuil as in deceiving his victims. Many of the letters – especially Valmont's, which have one meaning for the writer, another for the recipient and yet another for the reader – are fine examples of irony. The language of seduction thus becomes as important as the experience, for the victims' letters reveal them to be as ignorant of their true situation as those of the seducers prove them to be masters of their art.

The world of Restif de la Bretonne (1734–1806), a peasant's son and a painter, was not that of Laclos's aristocratic characters, for he drew most of his inspiration from his own life and experience; more especially he sought to convey through his writings the nature of his own complex erotic feelings. *Monsieur Nicolas ou le coeur humain dévoilé* (1794–97) is in many ways a disguised autobiography. This and other works such as *Ingénue Saxancour* (1789), *Le Paysan perverti* and *La Paysanne pervertie* (1775–6) reveal the same personal inspiration which often assumes the form of a curious obsession with the memory of the various women whom Restif has loved and who often turn out to be daughters born to him from former liaisons! Desire and reality are very strangely mingled and sometimes assume the form of a perverse eroticism. Apart from the exploration of unusual erotic feelings, Restif gives a remarkably varied picture of society, especially in *Les Nuits de Paris* (1788). The vigour and detail of his social descriptions – for example, in his portrayal of peasant life in *La Vie de mon père* (1779) – are very striking; it has been calculated that he gives details of no less than two hundred different trades and professions. This element of social realism has led several critics to compare his work to that of Balzac and Zola in its detailed and yet imaginative portrayal of everyday life.

As an aristocrat who witnessed the destruction of his class and suffered imprisonment, the notorious Marquis de Sade (1740–1814) takes libertinism much further than any other novelist of the time. By placing great emphasis on sexual perversion, he represents a deliberate attack upon traditional morality and the elevation of evil into the supreme human value: nothing matters except the pleasure of the individual who is allowed to seek it in any way he sees fit and, if necessary, through the infliction of pain upon other people. Sade's novels, however, make no concession to the superficial elegance of style and form which marks the work of most of his contemporaries and it is not surprising that many of his works have been condemned as pornographic, for their lurid subject-matter cannot conceal their mediocre literary quality. Of the large-scale novels *Justine ou les malheurs de la vertu* (1779) is perhaps the most characteristic. (The first part was preceded by two other versions entitled *Les Infortunes de la vertu*, which were not published in the author's lifetime). *Justine* is probably the grossest and most detailed expression of sexual sadism, whilst *La Nouvelle Justine ou les malheurs de la vertu* takes us, in the words of Coulet, to the 'very heart of sadistic truth'. Sade's nihilistic view of human existence stems not only from his own inner life and experience but from his philosophical conception of nature as a cosmic impersonal force which uses the principle of destruction as a means of creating new life. This means that no activity, however perverse, can be the object of moral censure, for pleasure, whatever its particular form, is the sole criterion of conduct.

It would be misleading to see the novel developing solely in the direction of greater immorality and perversity, for the success of Bernardin de Saint-Pierre's *Paul et Virginie* (1788) shows that primitivism and idealism still retained a wide appeal. Regarded today as little more than a faded museum-piece, *Paul et Virginie* is an interesting survival of one significant aspect of eighteenth-century sensibility. For Bernardin himself, however, authorship was only one aspect of a very active and varied life which included service as soldier and engineer and a great deal of travelling. His first significant work was a travel-book, the *Voyage à l'Île de France* (1772), which was eventually followed by a more ambitious production, the *Éléments de la Nature* (1784) in which he tried to combine the interpretation of the physical world as the creation of Providence and the expression of 'final causes' with a detailed description of nature. *Paul et Virginie* appeared in the fourth volume of this work and enjoyed enormous popularity. It is the story of two children who are brought up by their mothers on the island of Mauritius, far away from the corruption and evil of European life. Although they love each other and seem destined to marry, Virginie is summoned to France by a wealthy and imperious aunt who wishes to educate her for social life and a rich marriage. Growing increasingly unhappy, Virginie decides to return to her family, only to perish in a shipwreck as she is approaching the shores of the island.

The most striking feature of the work is to be found in its descriptions of nature: it is a vivid evocation of the vegetation and geography of an island known to Bernardin himself and recalled with colourful precision and poetic emotion. (In fact, some of the descriptive material is drawn from his earlier *Voyage*.) From this point of view the work marks a decisive stage in the development of the 'exotic' novel and anticipates the later achievements of Chateaubriand. Yet picturesque description is only one element in a book which continues in many ways the 'pastoral' tradition developed by a contemporary such as Florian (1755–94); it was customary for such escapist novels to portray the happy simplicity and innocence of rural life. To this conventional literary source Bernardin, as a disciple of Jean-Jacques Rousseau, added his own moral and social intention to portray the superiority of the life of nature over the corruption of European civilization. Admittedly, this moral aim is sometimes expressed in very sentimental terms: and in this respect it recalls not only the influence of Gessner, but also the emotional moralizing of many other writers of the time. Occasionally, however, Bernardin manages to introduce into this idyllic atmosphere a more serious psychological note, as, for example, when he subtly describes the confusion of Virginie's adolescent feelings. The catastrophic ending which includes the shipwreck and the eventual death of all the main characters also reveals Bernardin's determination to bring a tragic element into his story, while references to such authentic contemporary problems as the enslavement and exploitation of the negroes limit still further the mere sentimentality of the pastoral theme. Although it is more complex than appears at first sight and is imbued with a genuine poetic content derived from the author's own frustrated dreams and aspirations, *Paul et Virginie* may still deserve no more than a limited place in the history of the French novel; nevertheless, it is an interesting example of some of the themes that were dominating French culture on the eve of the Revolution.

THREE

Germany

IN the second half of the seventeenth century the novel had sprung unexpectedly to life in Germany. It immediately developed, however, a dual existence based on social distinctions. The conventionalized adventures, the unremittingly artificial tone and the hierarchical gradations of the long courtly novels of Lohenstein, Ziegler und Kliphausen, Duke Anton Ulrich of Brunswick and others clearly appealed to the aristocracy of the time, but now seem merely tedious to the majority of readers. The racy and often bawdy narratives of Grimmelshausen and Beer (both of whom wrote pseudonymously and were identified many years later, Beer in this century) must have appealed primarily to the literate members of the middle order, though they may have had a limited and perhaps clandestine public in the princely courts.

Both of these classes of novel died out about the turn of the century. The cumbersome and stilted courtly novels gave way, among those of the aristocracy who were not solely occupied with farming or hunting, to French literature of a much more up-to-date character. And the vulgarity of Beer's entertaining novels became repugnant to the gravity and self-conscious dignity of the rising middle class. The opinion of the age regarded prose as a suitable vehicle for philosophical and theological exposition, for literary criticism, for aesthetic theory and for pulpit oratory, but rated its aesthetic value as minimal. Verse alone was suitable as a means of creative literary expression, the only exception being comedy, for which verse was sometimes used but was not considered to be mandatory. The higher forms of literary art were the epic, tragedy, the didactic poem, odes and other shorter poetic forms. In such an intellectual climate the novel withered away, and the century was well advanced before tentative attempts were made to restore it.

It was characteristic of the low repute of the genre that novels, at any rate of the more vulgar sort, were invariably pseudonymous. And so it is not surprising that the first important novel of the eighteenth century was apparently written by one Gisander, an obvious *nom de plume*. The name concealed the identity of J. G. Schnabel, though this was not discovered until the nineteenth century. Schnabel could on occasion write with liveliness and he had a gift for sustaining a narrative, but above all he had a clear awareness of what the public was ready to receive. His second (also pseudonymous) novel was a picaresque story full of erotic incidents, but *Der im Irrgarten der Liebe herumtaumelnde Cavalier* (1738) substitutes elegance and piquancy for the forthrightness of its seventeenth-century predecessors. It is, however, Schnabel's earlier novel, known since the nineteenth century by the simplified title *Die Insel Felsenburg* (1732) which marks the starting-point of the modern German novel. The original title was descriptive and occupied the entire title-page, beginning: *Wunderliche Fata einiger Seefahrer, absonderlich Alberti Julii, eines gebohrnen Sachsens/ welcher in seinem 18ten Jahre zu Schiffe gegangen, durch Schiff -Bruch selbste an eine grausame Klippe geworffen worden/nach deren Übersteigung das schönste Land entdeckt* . . . continuing thus for another eighty-odd words. A title of this character and dimension brings home the novelty of the task which Schnabel had undertaken. From the middle of the eighteenth century onwards a reader had some idea what a novel was; he would at once form certain expectations and would be content with a brief title, perhaps a name, followed by a slightly longer, explanatory subtitle. But in 1732 Schnabel's potential readers had no idea what they might find between the covers of the book, and the author therefore found it necessary to omit what we would call a title and to issue a prospectus instead.

Die Insel Felsenburg, the more convenient title by which the work is now known, was not only a novelty by the mere fact of being a novel. It can be confidently asserted that, if Defoe had not published in 1719 *The Life and Strange Surprising Adventures of Robinson Crusoe*, Schnabel's story would never have been written. He cashed in on a great European success (*Crusoe* was translated into German as early as 1720), but *Die Insel Felsenburg*, in spite of owing its conception to Defoe's work, is not a plagiarism. It leans on Defoe in its early stages, although the adventures on board ship before the wreck are of a different character; after the disaster, however, it becomes not a record of moral courage in solitude, but the story of the creation of a Utopian state.

Die Insel Felsenburg shows patience and persistence visibly prospering under the immediate protection of God, as a reward for undeviating virtue. Albertus Julius, who tells his story to his admiring great-nephew, displays the virtue of chastity in respecting the wish of the widow Concordia not to marry but to mourn her husband in celibacy. When, however, his devotion causes her to relent, the pair become the progenitors of an ideal community which multiplies and prospers until it consists of three hundred virtuous souls, living in peace, concord and useful activity. All joyfully accept the rule of their patriarch Albertus Julius, 'der liebe Altvater'. Though much in this novel is tedious, it may be said to contain something for everyone. It is less imaginative than *Robinson Crusoe* but it moralizes, if anything, rather more, so providing the profoundly moral middle class with acceptable reading matter of a new and intriguing kind. Moreover, since the story is 'reported' by a descendant, this pioneering work also introduces the 'frame technique' (as it is called in German, using the word *Rahmen*) which was to play so important a part in German fiction over the two following centuries.

Die Insel Felsenburg, important landmark though it is, did not immediately set numbers of other writers on the way to writing novels and achieving fame. Within a few years, however, French, and still more, English examples of the novel excited emulation and whetted the appetite of the public. It may well be that the decisive date is 1742, the year in which Richardson's *Pamela or Virtue Rewarded* was published in German translation. *Das Leben der schwedischen Gräfin von G . . .*, published anonymously in two volumes (1747–8) is no imitation of *Pamela*. But in its moral stance it belongs to the middle-class tradition which Richardson represented and sought to encourage. It is the work of C. F. Gellert (1715–69), the Leipzig professor who enjoyed so wide a repute as a counsellor in matters of morality. Gellert is on the side of both sentiment and reason and is totally opposed to passion. *Das Leben der schwedischen Gräfin* purports to be autobiography. The countess tells her own story, dealing briefly with her childhood and at some length with her marital history. She loves and marries Count G—, with whom she lives happily. War brings news of his death on active service, and since the countess is subject to the unwelcome attentions of Prince S—, she flees with Herr R—, a friend of her deceased husband, to Holland, where, after the lapse of a number of years she becomes the wife of R—. The news of the count's death proves, however, to be false and the countess finds that she has unwittingly entered into a bigamous union. The matter is easily solved. Each gentleman loves the countess, but each is willing to retire in favour of the other. The countess, however, sees it as her clear duty to return to her true husband, and the union is resumed as if no interruption had occurred. In the course of time G— dies, and again, after a decent period of mourning, the countess marries R—. The three characters set an example of self-control, unselfishness and sensible behaviour. Enclosed within this autobiography is a story of the tragic end of another pair of lovers who will not listen to the voice of reason and surrender completely to their passion. Gellert asserts his message of moderation and makes sure that it shall not be misunderstood. His novel is very much of its time and could only attract readers so long as its passivity was generally accepted.

A less parochial and more urbane world is revealed in the work of C. M. Wieland (1733–1813). Arguably his best novel is *Geschichte des Agathon*, published in two volumes in 1766–7. Its breadth of vision, its cosmopolitanism and its remote classical setting debarred it from immediate success in the narrow world which had found satisfaction in reading Schnabel and Gellert. It never became a best-seller, but it succeeded in establishing itself as an essential item in the library of any German reader of intellectual pretensions.

Lessing, no advocate of Wieland's early sentimental and pietistic works, went out of his way, not merely to praise *Agathon*, but to place it in a category above all rivals. After quoting from the work at length in his *Hamburgische Dramaturgie*[1] Lessing goes on to acknowledge that the extract is drawn 'from a work . . . which is unquestionably one of the most notable of our century', and sums up his critical opinion a few lines later in the words: 'It is the first and only novel for the thoughtful reader with classical taste.' With this judgement Lessing not only gave Wieland's *Agathon* a certificate of merit which carried all the weight of the most feared critic in Germany in that age, he raised the novel into the category of serious literary art, which had hitherto been reserved for tragedy and the epic.

Wieland's *Agathon* is still a readable work, though the competition of other and later works of fiction is so intense that it probably finds

1. 69, Stück, 25 December 1767.

very few readers, which is a pity, for, in its urbanity, it is highly civilized. Its setting in classical antiquity, one of the factors which commended it to Lessing, is probably an obstacle to its enjoyment in an age when Latin and Greek are losing ground. The book is not without incident. Piracy, enslavement, conspiracy and an unsuccessful revolution mark stages in the plot. The real subject of the work, however, is the intellectual and spiritual growth of Agathon, the book's hero. It is a pilgrim's progress, albeit a secular one. Agathon, who possesses a personal beauty which is seductive to the most diverse persons who come into contact with him, threatens to succumb to the temptations of hedonism, succeeds in freeing himself from the danger, and develops into a man of humane virtue who devotes himself to the welfare of his fellow-men. It is the serious discussion of philosophical attitudes which makes *Agathon* a landmark among early German novels, and it is undoubtedly this aspect which evoked Lessing's powerful eulogy.

Agathon was not Wieland's only novel, nor his first. In 1764 he had published *Der Sieg der Natur über die Schwärmerei oder Die Abenteuer des Don Sylvio von Rosalva*, in which the hero is cured of romantic obsessions, but it is a lightweight work obviously intended only as an occupation for idle hours. *Der goldene Spiegel* (1772) is set in an imaginary Orient. It is in intention a serious work setting out the duties of the ruler, as the age of Enlightenment (and hence of enlightened despotism) saw them. It earned Wieland an appointment as tutor to the two young princes of Saxe-Weimar, the elder of whom was three years later to invite Goethe to Weimar. But Wieland was more proficient at theoretical than at practical education and was soon relieved of his post to his great advantage, since he received a permanent pension and remained an honoured member of the literary circle of the dowager Duchess. In spite of its beneficial effects on the life of its author and perhaps also on his patrons and others, *Der goldene Spiegel* is not a successful novel. It is only in *Agathon* that Wieland succeeded in integrating his story and his messsage. From *Der goldene Spiegel* on, the reader is aware that the ideas, though of interest and rationally justifiable to the author, are not held with any passionate conviction, and so are less powerfully expressed; neither does Wieland greatly trouble himself in his later fiction to tell his tale so as to achieve the 'willing suspension of disbelief'. His work is non-illusionary, and employs a number of more or less diverting, playful conventions. Of the later works *Die Geschichte der Abderiten* (1774), a satire on provincialism, is probably the best; it is certainly the most entertaining. As a satirist, Wieland indulges in mocking wit, leaving lofty indignation to more committed authors. His late philosophical novels, *Geheime Geschichte des Philosophen Peregrinus Proteus* (1791), *Agathodämon* (1799) and *Aristipp* (1800–1801) fail in the attempt to blend entertainment and instruction. By this time much of importance had happened to the novel, and Wieland had become a rather old-fashioned figure.

The swing of taste away from Wieland's philosophical and often flippant novels had already been suggested by Sophie von La Roche's *Geschichte des Fräuleins von Sternheim* (1771). Frau von La Roche (1731–1807) was a cousin of Wieland and had been, some twenty years before her novel appeared, the subject of his adoration. She had married in 1754 a nobleman in the service of the Electoral Archbishop of Mainz, but she had not quarrelled with her cousin, who, in 1765, himself made a happy marriage, and when she completed her novel, it was Wieland who took on the task of getting it published. The authoress concealed her identity, posing as a friend who makes the heroine's letters known. Fräulein von Sternheim is orphaned in adolescence and persecuted by her guardian, a worldly aunt, who brings her into touch with a scheming English lord, who induces the girl to go through a ceremony of marriage which turns out to be void. She is lured to Scotland and is for a time in mortal danger, but is rescued by humble crofters. In the end the wicked lord is providentially removed by death, and Sophie marries a more amiable and virtuous member of the British aristocracy. Frau von La Roche's modest, yet distinct, literary talents might never have been discovered, if she had not lapsed into melancholy when her daughters were sent away to boarding-school at Strassburg. Disconsolate for a time, she eventually cured herself by writing this once very successful novel. It is almost entirely composed of letters written by Sophie, and so follows a contemporary French fashion, but it seems quite likely that fictitious letter-writing afforded the lonely mother special solace. The result, with its mixture of the sensational and the sentimental, is very much of its time and deficient in lasting power, but a reader who is prepared to make concessions and cares for a period flavour may still read it with moderate pleasure. Frau von La Roche, however, was doing more than she realized. She foreshadowed one of the literary sensations of the century, Goethe's *Werther*.

In the spring of 1772 Goethe, sent to Wetzlar to study the procedures of the highest court of the Holy Roman Empire, the Reichskammergericht, found the task heavy going and chose rather to divert himself, both poetically and socially. In June he made the acquaintance of an attractive eighteen-year-old girl, Charlotte (or Lotte) Buff, with whom he at once fell deeply in love, only to discover that she was already betrothed to another. The fiancé was tolerant, Lotte kind and perhaps flattered, and Goethe spent three months of mingled ecstasy and torment, before wrenching himself away in September. He continued to correspond with the couple, who married in April 1773, and it seemed that a crisis had passed and declined without leaving any literary precipitate.

Experiences, however, can work by delayed action. This became clear to Goethe's friends. At the autumn book fair of 1774 appeared what was perhaps the greatest success of the century, *Die Leiden des jungen Werthers*, a novel by Goethe, which was praised to the skies by many and damned to the depths by some. This was not a work which Goethe had been painstakingly composing since he left Wetzlar. He began it in February 1774 and by May it was finished. It is a short novel, but an extraordinarily vital one, communicating a sensation of immediate experience, and it seems astonishing that eighteen months of quite other activity and diverse occupation should lie between the work and the original experience. For though *Werther* is not a self-portrait, throughout the first book (there are two) it follows with remarkable fidelity the phases of the strange triangular love affair which had played itself out at Wetzlar in the summer of 1772. This first book is given entirely in letters, all written by Werther to a friend; they recount Werther's passion, using the real names Lotte and Albert for the affianced couple and adhering to the actual dates in 1772. Any modern reader will know that Lotte and Albert in the book are not the Lotte and the Albert of real life, but contemporaries, inexperienced in the subtleties of the novelist, could not be expected to refrain from identifying the characters with the real persons. Indeed Lotte and Kestner themselves took umbrage, for they felt exposed and betrayed. Book Two, however, though it still gave offence, drew on a different set of facts, which had no connection with Lotte Kestner, née Buff. In October 1772 an acquaintance of Goethe, K. W. Jerusalem, took his life in Wetzlar. In November Goethe obtained from Lotte's husband, whose pistols Jerusalem had borrowed in order to end his life (though Kestner had no idea of the purpose behind the request), a full account of the suicide with some of the background, which included disappointed love and a snub which led to friction with his superiors.

This episode provided Goethe with the continuation which his own disappointment in love in Wetzlar could not give. But this was not immediately apparent to him. The process of creation proceeded subconsciously to the point that the work suddenly emerged virtually complete, demanding to be written down. The success of *Werther* extended beyond the boundaries of Germany, and it is one of the few novels which can be seen to have had a direct influence on the lives of a number of its readers. Young men of means set their tailors to work making 'Werther suits', the blue tail-coat and the yellow breeches described in the novel. More important was the influence the book exercised upon people's minds. More than one suicide was laid to its charge, and Goethe himself in 1777 made a journey in order to attempt to dispel the melancholia into which a young man had sunk after reading the book. It is not surprising that *Werther* came in for much moral reprobation, which naturally increased its circulation. Lessing's friend Nicolai, who was both fascinated and repelled by it, even re-wrote it with a happy ending. The most celebrated reader of *Werther* is Napoleon, who, when Goethe was received in audience at Erfurt in 1808, asserted that he had read the book seven times.

What Goethe did in this novel was to give a voice to a new generation, for which enlightenment was not enough. Its passionate intensity broke through the existing literary conventions and endowed contemporary life with unsuspected heights and depths. And the final tragedy was thrown into striking relief by the cool and sober detachment of the narration, which allowed facts to speak for themselves. Many of the readers, of course, accepted *Werther* as a moving tale of unhappy love, which it is. But many of the leading spirits of the age saw further into it, perceiving its deeper tragedy of immense potentiality destroyed by a world which will not allow it to unfold.

The imitations of *Werther* were love stories, and numerous though they were; they have all passed into oblivion save one, *Siegwart* (1776) by J. M. Miller (1750–1814), a Protestant ordinand from Ulm, who had learned while a student at Göttingen to express his sentimental enthusiasm through association with the poets of the Hainbund.[2] *Siegwart*, like *Werther*, was a novel of contemporary life. But, in order to achieve a high degree of pathos, Miller introduced an element which was distinctly old-fashioned – except perhaps in the imaginations of northern Protestants in the late eighteenth century. He called his book 'Eine Klostergeschichte', a tale of monastic and conventual life; it has little to do with the routine of the cloistered life, but seeks to exploit the possibilities of pathos inherent in the situation of a pair of lovers separated for ever by vows and enclosure. Xaver Siegwart becomes a monk of his own free will, only to regret it when he becomes acquainted with Mariane Fischer. She is consigned to a convent by her stern father, Xaver returns to his monastery and the two pine and die. It is a tale of ready-made sentimentality, and if that were all, it could be forgotten. Miller, however, has counterbalanced this sad, even maudlin, tale with the story of Siegwart's sister Therese and his friend Kronhelm. These two face difficulties almost as great as those of the other couple but they face them resolutely and prevail. Miller has contrasted two types of temperament and so presented in some measure a considered conspectus of the age. His literary skill is, of course, much inferior to that of Goethe and hence this worthy, yet not fully convincing, work has declined into an obscurity which it scarcely deserves.

To the same decade as *Werther* and *Siegwart* belongs the long, tedious and well-meaning novel of Nicolai, *Leben und Meinungen des Herrn Magisters Sebaldus Nothanker* (1773–6). Through three volumes it exemplifies true charity and humility and castigates the intolerance of the orthodox Lutherans of the day. The repellent figure of Pastor Stauzius is said to be modelled on Lessing's persecutor, Pastor Goeze. It embodies the ideals of Enlightenment, but, as it doggedly plods on its way, it fails to invest them with any semblance of life.

A much more original novel and perhaps the true inheritor of *Werther* is *Anton Reiser* (1785–90) by K. P. Moritz (1756–93). This work is almost as closely autobiographical as the first part of Goethe's novel, but covers a much longer span. Moritz passed a hard and

2. See pp. 208f.

unhappy childhood, and *Anton Reiser* recounts the hero's early miseries at home and as an apprentice to the hatter Lohenstein, his unexpected good fortune in being sent to a grammar school and his experiences there, the penury into which he falls, and the collapse of his hopes of becoming an actor. The importance of the action in this novel resides in the emotions which accompany it. *Anton Reiser* is described in the preface as 'Ein psychologischer Roman', and it thoroughly deserves this (for 1785) unheard of description. It is a work of profound introspection, developing into a thorough-going study of neuroses, which can hardly be paralleled in the Age of Enlightenment, though the religious crises through which Anton passes must have been experienced by many humble Protestants of the time. In its fundamental honesty Moritz's *Anton Reiser* is greatly superior to the wayward imitation of Sterne offered a few years earlier by S. G. Hippel (1741–96) in his unfinished autobiographical novel *Leben in aufsteigender Linie* (1778–81). Both works, in their authentic detail, are of sociological value, and *Anton Reiser* has a further interest in that it preserves the responses of a sensitive young man to the literature of his day.

Schiller is so prominent as a dramatist, an aesthetic theorist and a poet, that his fiction is easily overlooked, which is a pity, for it does not fall below the standards which he maintained in more familiar works. It consisted in the main of a story of thirty-odd pages and a substantial fragment of a novel. The story, *Der Verbrecher aus verlorener Ehre* (1786), is a well-wrought piece of narration which has a marked, and for its day advanced, ethical content showing, how society, in its treatment of a minor offender, turns him into a desperate criminal. It is characteristic of Schiller's conception of Enlightenment that Christian Wolf's acquired wickedness is eroded by his conscience, so that in the end he gives himself up. Schiller did not invent this ending, for the story is based closely on recorded fact, but that he should choose it and treat it with such liberality of mind is significant. Schiller's novel *Der Geisterseher* (1787–9) was, for a year or two, the most popular of his works. It has a story of dynastic and religious intrigue, in which the conversion to Roman Catholicism of the heir to a Protestant German state is the aim. It is set in Venice and reflects the current interest in occultism and mysticism, though Schiller gives a rational explanation of his mystery. He shows a power of sustaining suspense, which is perhaps not surprising in a great dramatist. What is astonishing is the fact that one who began a novel so successfully and powerfully could not be bothered to finish it in spite of pleas from frustrated readers and a pecuniary offer from an intending patron. *Der Geisterseher* remained unfinished and we are left merely with tantalizing glimpses of the novelist Schiller might have become.

J. J. W. Heinse (1746–1803) made his appearance as a novelist in the same year as Schiller, but instead of publishing in instalments which petered out, he published his two-volume work complete in 1787. *Ardinghello, und die glückseeligen Inseln* contrasts greatly with Schiller's fragment. Tension and detachment are replaced by effusiveness and passion. Schiller had had his phase of *Sturm und Drang*, had rejected it and was on the way to adopting the discipline of classicism. Heinse (who in age is of the original generation of *Sturm und Drang*) may be seen as an unexpectedly late fulfilment of the attitudes and ideas of the mid-1770s. Ardinghello, who tells his story mainly through letters, is both a painter and a man of action. He is, so to speak, a cousin of the powerful heroes of the *Sturm und Drang*, of Faust, Guido of Taranto, or Guelpho (in *Die Zwillinge*), but whereas they, encountering the established strength of the real world, fail tragically, Ardinghello, finds bliss in sensual fulfilment in an Aegean Utopia of love, in which he lives in a free sexual union with adoring and responsive women. Naïve though this consummation of the novel seems, it proves the lengths to which the descendants of the Enlightenment were prepared to carry the doctrine of Nature, at least in fantasy.

Hölderlin's only novel, *Hyperion oder Der Eremit in Griechenland* (1797–9) shares with *Ardinghello* the enthusiasm for Greece and an element of Utopianism (here unfulfilled). Classicism has undeniable affinities with the Enlightenment, but Hölderlin's passionate and hopeless addiction to his ideal Greece renounces the values of the *Aufklärung* and substitutes for it a poetic and tragic vision.

The final stage of the German Enlightenment in the novel is perhaps achieved by Goethe's *Wilhelm Meisters Lehrjahre* (1795), which has tended in recent years to sink into rather undeserved neglect. Its pace is slow and its style deliberate. Moreover, without being unduly sententious, it contains much wisdom, which is now somewhat at a discount. Its range and appreciation of character are impressive, the ability to depict incident convincing. What might also still endear it to the twentieth century is its preoccupation with education. For it traces gradually but relentlessly the process by which Wilhelm is changed from an impetuous youth into a man of judgement and character. The rationalistic beginnings of Enlightenment are here forgotten, but the enlightened man is fully realized as a character with impeccable credentials.

PART FIVE

AESTHETIC IDEAS

ONE

England

THE transitional character of much eighteenth-century thought is very clearly brought out in the development of aesthetic theory. Though still revered, the classical tradition gradually gave way to new pressures, while constantly re-affirming its claim to be the final arbiter in all disputes about literary judgement. Yet the new intellectual and social forces of the time, too powerful and insistent to be ignored, exerted a steadily increasing influence upon the theory as well as upon the practice of literature and are often discernible in writers who were firm defenders of the old ideal.

Respect for neo-classicism was often accompanied by a surprising independence. This independent attitude towards a widely accepted classical tradition was particularly evident in England. Pope's *Essay on Criticism* (1711) was rightly regarded as a powerful defence of classical principles, but in his later work – for example, in his observations on Homer and Shakespeare – Pope extolled the rights of genius and imagination with an almost 'Romantic' fervour. Another supporter of neo-classicism, Joseph Addison (1672–1719) was also an admirer of Locke's philosophy, so that the *Spectator* not only defended classical doctrines but also called attention to some of their limitations and to the need for a broader view of literature: particularly important were his articles on 'The Pleasures of the Imagination', which helped to provide a new psychological dimension in literary criticism – in spite of the rather narrow conception of imagination itself as a purely visual faculty. Addison also stressed the decisive role of 'taste' as 'the faculty of the soul which discerns the beauties of an author with pleasure and the imperfections with dislike.'

Other writers were to echo this interest in the nature of the imagination. Joseph Warton (1722–1800) in the Dedication to *An Essay on the Genius and Writings of Pope* (1756) pointed out that the true poet was endowed with 'a creative and glowing imagination, *acer spiritus ac vis*, and that alone can stamp a writer with this exalted and uncommon character, which so few possess, and of which so few can properly judge'. In his view, Pope did not have this supreme quality, while Shakespeare, Milton and Spenser did. Bishop Richard Hurd (1720–1808) also praised the imagination when he pointed out that 'the poet has a world of his own, where experience has less to do than consistent imagination', and 'where all is marvellous and extraordinary' without necessarily being 'unnatural' since it involves 'magical and wonder-working Natures'. He admitted that poetry was of different kinds, but insisted that it was 'the more sublime and creative poetry' which 'addressed itself solely or principally to the imagination (a young and credulous faculty, which loves to admire and to be deceived).' Akenside's poem *The Pleasures of the Imagination* scarcely lives up to the promise of its title, but it at least bears witness to Addison's influence. Although such developments as these fall far short of the later achievement of Coleridge in this field, they are interesting indications of a new attitude towards the problem of literary creation.

Apart from this new psychological and affective emphasis, the recognition of national differences helped to create a more liberal attitude towards literature. Dryden's *Essay on Dramatic Poetry* (1668) had already pointed out that Shakespeare's originality could not be accounted for in terms of classical norms and the eighteenth century was to witness a remarkable advance in the interpretation of Shakespeare. This was helped by the emergence of a more scholarly attitude towards the text. Lewis Theobald (1688–1744), with his *Shakespeare Restored* (1726) and his 1733 edition of the plays, made an outstanding contribution to textual criticism. Even a supporter of neo-classicism like Dr Johnson did not allow his principles to obstruct his common sense; from the outset he insisted that the appreciation of Shakespeare could not be effectively separated from an understanding of the Elizabethan age. Although his own knowledge of this historical background was inadequate, his preface to his edition of Shakespeare showed a surprising breadth of outlook for a critic who saw poetic perfection in Dryden and Pope. Johnson strongly objected to any slavish adherence to the rules and maintained that it was necessary to distinguish rules based on 'reason and necessity' from those 'enacted by despotic antiquity.' He thoroughly endorsed Shakespeare's disregard for the classical unities and he defended tragi-comedy as a valid genre. Characteristically he maintained that 'no man ever yet became great by imitation'.

In the second half of the century the historical study of literature gained momentum: there was a growing interest in Celtic and Scandinavian antiquity as well as in the literature of the Middle Ages and the Renaissance. Percy's *Reliques of Ancient English Poetry* (1765) called attention to the merits of the old ballads, while Thomas Warton's *Observations on the Faery Queen of Spenser* (1754) made a remarkable effort to relate that work to its social and historical background; his unfinished *History of English Poetry from the Close of the Eleventh to the Commencement of the Eighteenth Century* (1774–78) was a still more ambitious and far-ranging attempt to see English literature not only in its strictly chronological development but also in its European context and in relation to cultural factors such as mythology and folk-lore. Bishop Hurd, the author of *Letters on Chivalry and Romance* (1762), was another scholar with an interest in antiquity; he pointed out that Gothic literature – like Gothic architecture – could not be judged by the standards of the Greeks. To later readers works of the past may seem 'marvellous and extraordinary', but to the authors themselves they were not 'unnatural'.

A broader view of criticism is also very apparent in Robert Lowth's *De Sacra Poesi Hebraeorum* (1753) – subsequently translated and published in 1787 as *Lectures on the Sacred Poetry of the Hebrews*. As J. W. H. Atkins points out,[1] Lowth, in his examination of a poetic tradition which lay outside the Greco-Roman world, not only recognized its unique character but also called attention to the need for a broader outlook and for sound critical and historical principles in the scrutiny of unfamiliar literatures.

Apart from these developments in the psychological and historical aspects of literary criticism, the most striking reactions against the old classical emphasis upon rules and fixed principles was the increasing attention being devoted to the nature of genius. In addition to the comments of Pope, Addison and Johnson who, in spite of their innovations, remained defenders of the classical spirit, there was the interesting work of Edward Young (1683–1765), *Conjectures on Original Composition* (1759), which stressed the importance of genius as an

1. J. W. H. Atkins, *English Literary Criticism: 17th and 18th Centuries*, London, 1951, pp. 189–92.

original force and relegated imitation to a subordinate place in the artistic process. While in no way seeking to denigrate the classics, Young insists that they should 'nourish' not 'annihilate' our own creative efforts. Since Nature is common to them and to us, why should we not go directly to its source? 'Genius is a master-workman, learning is but an instrument and an instrument, though most valuable, yet not always indispensable.' 'Unexampled beauties', he says in the same work, 'and an unexampled eloquence, which are characteristics of genius, lie without the pale of learning's authorities and laws; which pale, genius must leap to come at them.' He also affirms: 'A genius differs from a good understanding as a magician from a good architect: that raises his structure by means indivisible; this by the skilful use of tools.' Genius can, therefore, dispense with rules, for 'rules, like crutches, are needful to the lame, though an impediment to the strong'. Finally, 'originals shine, like comets; have no peer in their path; are rivalled by none, and the gaze of all'.

This emphasis upon the role of genius undoubtedly owed something to the renewal of interest in 'Longinus' and his treatise *On the Sublime* – already known in Boileau's translation of 1674. Although consistent with certain aspects of neo-classicism, Longinus's ideas called attention to the view that genius went beyond the confines of regularity and precision. Addison had also observed with Longinus that 'the products of a great genius, with many lapses and inadvertencies, are infinitely preferable to the works of an inferior kind of author, which are scrupulously exact and conformable to all the rules of correct writing'.

Reflection upon the nature of genius sometimes merged with attempts to develop the broader philosophical implications of aesthetic experience, even though the term 'aesthetics' did not appear until Baumgarten used it in 1735. Philosophers such as Shaftesbury (1671–1713), in his *Characteristics* (1711) and Frances Hutcheson (1694–1746) in *An Inquiry into the Original of our Ideas of Beauty and Virtue* (1725) sought to analyse the notion of beauty in non-rationalist terms by relating it to a special kind of feeling, animated, in Shaftesbury's case, by a response to 'the perfection of nature' and its exquisite harmony: the artist fixes his gaze on 'that consummate grace, that beauty of Nature, and that perfection of numbers which the rest of mankind, feeling only by the effect whilst ignorant of the cause, term the *je ne scay quoi* . . . and suppose to be a kind of charm or enchantment of which the artist himself can give no account'. Hutcheson tried to make a careful distinction between the perception of beauty and other impulses such as desire or knowledge. Although both thinkers believe that aesthetic experience depends on some special inner disposition, they do not regard it as a purely subjective emotion but as a universal characteristic of human nature. It was especially with the publication of Edmund Burke's *A Philosophical Enquiry into the Origin of our Ideas of the Sublime and the Beautiful* (1756) that the nature of beauty received a deeper analysis: beauty is sharply distinguished from the 'sublime', which evokes the idea of power, pain and infinite greatness; whereas beauty is associated with objects which are 'comparatively small and smooth and polished', sublime objects are 'vast in their dimensions' and 'rugged and negligent', the intensity of their effect often depending upon 'obscure and indefinite presentation'.

As Burke's comments reveal, thinkers were coming to see that aesthetic experience could not be separated from man's reactions to different aspects of the physical world; the broadening of the critical approach to literature was obviously connected with the artist's ever-increasing interest in nature. It was no accident that Young should not only be the author of the *Conjectures* just mentioned, but also the long poem *Night Thoughts* which was to give him a European reputation. Other nature poets such as Thomson, Gray and Ossian also helped to encourage both artist and critic to look at the outside world in a different light. Even the changing attitudes towards landscapes and gardens, with the formal classical style giving way to a taste for 'natural' gardens, was a further indication of this new attitude.

Lord Kames's *Elements of Criticism* (1762) is a good example of the philosophical attempt to analyse and classify the different kinds of literary taste. Not only did he define literary terms with greater accuracy, but he also took his illustrations from a wide range of material, both ancient and modern, English and foreign; at the same time he tried to relate literary criticism to man's essential nature, stressing in particular the primary importance of emotions and passions.

The broadening of critical interest in the second half of the eighteenth century was accompanied by sporadic efforts to relate literature to the other arts. The *Discourses* (1769–90) of Joshua Reynolds (1723–

92) were not confined to painting, but elucidated general aspects of the aesthetic process through the comparison of different arts. Firmly classical in so far as he believed in an 'ideal beauty' based on nature, he recognized that a work of art had to please by appealing to the imagination as well as to the judgement and that merely mechanical or rigid imitation could never be enough to produce a great work which was often 'full of disproportion'.

Although it had not been uncommon for critics to compare literature and painting (and so follow the Horatian dictum *Ut pictura poesis*), literature was henceforth to be associated with music, as is evident from James Harris's *Dialogue on Music, Painting and Poetry*; it is also interesting to note that the word 'Music' was added to the English translation of the abbé Du Bos's *Réflexions critiques sur la poésie et la peinture* which will be discussed below.

These changes in critical emphasis were not of course confined to one country. In Italy, for example, critics such as Gravina, in his *Della ragion poetica* (1708) and Muratori, in *Della perfetta poesia italiana* (1706) combined adherence to neo-classicism with a rejection of rigid rules, while later in the century Parini, in *Dei principi delle belle lettere* (1773–75) reacted against the rationalist outlook by stressing the role of the senses and emotions in literary appreciation; Melchiorre Cesarotti (1730–1808) struck a new note by translating Ossian's Celtic poems; Guiseppe Baretti (1719–89), known in England for his relations with Dr Johnson, criticized outmoded contemporary ideas in the name of life and common sense, as René Wellek points out,[2] and helped to diffuse knowledge of English, French and Spanish literatures; appropriately enough, during his stay in England he published works on Italian language and literature. One of the most original Italian thinkers of the period was certainly Vico, but his ideas were largely ignored in his day and, in any case, his interest in literature was largely derived from wider historical preoccupations which belong more properly to the literature of ideas than to literary criticism in the strict sense, for he saw poetry as one of the early manifestations of the human spirit.[3]

2. R. Wellek, *A History of Modern Criticism*, vol. 1, *Late Eighteenth Century*, New York and London, 1955, chapter 7, 'Italian Criticism', upon which the paragraph is based.

3. See pp. 116–27.

TWO

France

AT first sight French literary criticism of the eighteenth century seems to carry a markedly philosophical emphasis. Even though it was left to the German thinker Baumgarten to coin the term 'aesthetics'[1] there was a considerable effort to situate literary problems in a wider intellectual context. An indication of this new trend in aesthetic criticism is already provided by the attempt of Jean-Pierre de Crousaz, a Swiss writing in French, to define the nature of beauty in his *Traité du beau* (1715). This treatise identifies beauty with 'unity in variety' and emphasizes the idea of the human mind as a very mutable principle which none the less yearns for uniformity and permanence: beauty results from the conjunction of these two different principles of change and permanence. Behind 'reason' and 'feeling', which so often seem to be in conflict, there is a natural harmony which has to be developed through education. Another example of this rationalist approach to aesthetic problems is père André's *Essai sur le beau* (1741). Determined to eschew the use of specific examples. André proposes to rely solely upon 'the general principles of reason and good taste'. He defines beauty in very vague terms, equating it with 'excellence, charm (*agrément*), perfection'; it is a quality which we 'esteem in others and should like in ourselves'. The beautiful is 'what is entitled to please reason and reflection by its own excellence, by its clarity and precision, and, if this expression is permitted, by its intrinsic charm' (p. 58). So wide is André's conception of beauty that it embraces all man's higher powers, including his capacity for morality, science and politics. A great part of the treatise is devoted to the classification of various forms of beauty; a distinction is made between 'le beau essentiel', 'independent of all – even divine – institution'; 'le beau naturel', 'independent of men's opinions'; and 'le beau d'institution humaine' which is 'arbitrary up to a certain point'. Then follow other subdivisions – 'le beau sensible' which is revealed through reason 'atten-

1. See p. 411.

tive to the senses' and 'le beau intelligible', revealed through reason 'attentive to the ideas of the mind'. 'Le beau sensible' can itself be divided into two categories – 'le beau visible' and 'le beau acoustique'. An essential feature of beauty is unity: to be called beautiful, works of poetry or eloquence must exhibit a unity between their various parts; this principle includes unity of proportion between the style and subject-matter as well as unity of propriety or 'la bienséance' between the person who speaks, the things he says and the tone in which he says them. Already an enthusiastic admirer of Descartes at a time when the philosopher was viewed with disfavour by the Jesuits, André shows a strong Cartesian influence when he maintains that the true instrument for the perception of beauty is reason; yet reason does not exclude the imagination or the heart, but controls them both. The strong rationalistic bias of André's work tends to make it abstract and superficial, for it fails to make any significant distinction between art and other forms of beauty. The *Essai sur le beau*, however, was widely read in the eighteenth century and was re-published three times during the author's lifetime and twice after his death.

One of the best-known philosophical treatments of art in the eighteenth century was the abbé Charles Batteux's *Les Beaux-Arts réduits à un seul principe* (1746). The author's search for a single principle capable of explaining the essence of all the arts led him to look upon himself as the Newton of the fine arts: just as Newton used the principle of gravitation to explain the behaviour of physical phenomena, so did Batteux hope to reduce all art-forms to a sole explanatory principle. Bringing, as he believed, Aristotle up-to-date, he invoked the notion of the imitation of nature or, more precisely, the imitation of 'la belle nature'; the artist does not imitate nature as she is, but as she can be, and as 'she can be conceived by the mind'. As Diderot was to point out, Batteux's attempt to explain what he meant by 'la belle nature' remained somewhat vague. However, he did stress both its subjective and objective aspects: 'beautiful nature is, according to taste, (1) what has the closest relation to our perfection, advantage and interest, and (2) what is at the same time the most perfect in itself'. He goes on to point out that the taste which enables us to judge works of art is rooted in feeling and, more specifically, in a feeling that is a source of pleasure. Nevertheless, the man of taste needs reason in order to understand the nature of the intimate relationship existing between himself and the objects which arouse his interest. Because the imitation of nature affects both heart and mind, it is 'good' and 'beautiful', moral and pleasurable. Moreover, the variety and elevation of great art does not exclude an essential unity expressed through qualities of symmetry and proportion. In spite of the various forms of art and the limitations of the human mind and heart, the 'voice of feeling' has always enabled men to recognize that objects 'perfect in themselves' have been 'the same in all times': the constant presence of 'perfection' in true art prevents it from being capricious and arbitrary. The very fact that feeling – which, in this matter, is much more reliable than 'subtle metaphysics' – shows us the relevance of these works of art to the 'preservation and perfection of our own being' and to 'the nature of our soul and its needs', proves, in Batteux's opinion, their universal and objective quality.

Much more important than these rather dry and abstract works were the *Réflexions critiques sur la poésie et la peinture* by the abbé Jean-Baptiste Du Bos (1670–1742) – one of the century's most important contributors to aesthetic criticism. Du Bos starts with the assumption that one of man's greatest enemies being boredom, his primary need is to 'keep his mind occupied'. Unlike the baleful habit of trying to escape from boredom through indulgence in violent passions, which merely destroys all possibility of happiness, art provides an opportunity for the experience of intense passions and yet purifies them of their harmful element. This explains why it is possible to contemplate with tranquillity scenes which would be unbearable in real life. The test of artistic value is, however, feeling, not reason, because feeling can seize directly what reason fails to grasp by more circuitous methods. The merit of a poem is decided by the 'impression' it makes upon the reader and not by any mere intellectual analysis of its qualities. Yet, far from being a merely subjective phenomenon, the feeling involved in artistic appreciation is a form of subtle perception, capable of great precision and delicacy; quite different from the wayward emotions of everyday life, it is a 'sixth sense' or a special 'taste' which is stimulated by contact with works of art. 'There is in us a sense meant to judge the merit of those works which consist of the imitation of objects drawn from nature.' This sixth sense is not some purely individual activity, but a characteristic which exists in all men, though with varying degrees of perfection. No doubt it has to be educated, so that reason may eventually be able to account for the 'decision of feeling', but this in no way affects the primacy of this 'sixth sense' as the source of artistic judgement.

As far as the famous Quarrel between the Ancients and Moderns was concerned, Du Bos separated himself from the moderns on one important point: he refused to allow that they were more talented than the ancients, for they simply enjoyed certain fortuitous historical advantages. It was very doubtful, according to Du Bos, whether modern man had any greater natural aptitude than his predecessors for judging the value of works of art. Not only did Du Bos reject the rational criterion by which the moderns set so much store, but he believed that the excellence of the works of antiquity had been guaranteed by the approbation of many generations of cultured people. Such a consensus of opinion was not likely to be mistaken. 'The poem which has pleased all past ages and peoples really deserves to please.' Ultimately it is the public, not 'les gens du métier', who are the best judges of literary excellence; the opinions of many successive generations of people of good taste are a far more reliable guide to artistic excellence than the theoretical discussions of professional critics who often lack genuine feeling for the works they analyse. By 'public' Du Bos means a kind of aristocracy of cultivated people – people who have acquired enlightenment, whether through reading or human intercourse. In spite of the proved excellence of the works of the past, they have to be valued for their own sake and not simply for their antiquity. There is no reason for supposing that the past is superior to the present; time and experience have simply allowed us to see the true extent of its achievements. In one sense all great works rise above the vicissitudes of time. Du Bos tends to see history as alternating periods of greatness and decadence, or urbanity and barbarism. He believes that there were at least four great periods – those of Alexander, Augustus, Leo X and Louis XIV – which saw the perfect expression of literary taste. Yet this does not mean that taste is subject to indefinite progress; it is a recurrent rather than a permanently developing phenomenon.

In spite of his respect for the ancients, Du Bos puts genius above technical knowledge and skill. The significance and value of the work of art rest ultimately upon the innate genius which has produced it. This genius is 'an idle frenzy' ('une fureur oisive') or enthusiasm which undoubtedly has physical causes; 'it is a quality of the blood joined to the fortunate disposition of the organs'. Du Bos thus seems to return to the Renaissance idea of genius as 'divine enthusiasm'. Moreover, genius may take many forms, revealing itself in war and medicine as well as in art. At the same time, the physiological basis of genius suggests that there is a connection between emotional response and the physical world. Art is not the result of abstract speculation, but the effect of specific physical causes acting upon the mind and body, so that literary judgements must be traced back to their physical origins. Of the external causes, climate, in Du Bos's opinion, is one of the most important. The earth gives out 'emanations' and 'exhalations' which may be either favourable or inimical to artistic endeavour; he believes, for example, that genius cannot flourish in cold, damp climates. Later on, Montesquieu was to apply the same principle – though in a more detailed way – to the analysis of law.

These physical factors do not exclude psychological and moral influences. Genius will flourish only in an environment that is favourable to its free expression. Although Du Bos is vague about the nature of these environmental causes, he insists that artists must have 'an opportunity of perfecting their genius, because these causes make their work easier and, by emulation and rewards, incite them to study and application'. No doubt the encouragement of an enlightened monarch would be, in Du Bos's eyes, a powerful stimulus to artistic production.

Du Bos is an interesting example of a critic's attempt to combine absolute and relative elements in the appreciation of art. On the one hand, he believes that taste is governed by a special sense having universal validity, but, on the other, he clearly attaches considerable importance to cultural variations and modifications. To understand the true meaning of a work of art, we have in some way to make ourselves contemporary with it, and consider it in the light of its origins. Historical understanding is thus added to direct and absolute emotional enjoyment.

The very title of Du Bos's work also shows that he is not interested in literature alone, but that he is trying to elaborate principles applicable to all the fine arts. Here again he anticipates the comparative outlook of later aesthetic criticism. The literary work should not be considered in isolation from other cultural phenomena. Du Bos compares, for example, the appreciation of poetry with that of painting;

he concludes that painting has a more immediate effect because it relies on the sense of sight which is simpler and more direct in its operation than the complex responses involved in literary appreciation. Since he also gains from his use of 'natural' instead of 'artificial' signs, a painter can reproduce the object without the use of linguistic or other mental intermediaries.

As French philosophers became increasingly influenced by the empiricist philosophy of Locke, their view of art was correspondingly modified. Condillac is an instructive example of the new philosophical tendencies, even though his *Essai sur l'origine des connaissances humaines* (1746) was not concerned primarily with aesthetic questions. It will be recalled that, as a disciple of Locke and Newton, Condillac wished to explain all mental and psychological phenomena in terms of a single principle – sensation.[2] He claimed that sensation was developed largely through the association of ideas – 'the connection of ideas, either with signs, or among themselves'. It was man's power to use particular 'signs' (language) that made him capable of such apparently complicated mental activities. What is particularly relevant for the explanation of art, however, is Condillac's use of the genetic method inherited from Locke. He believed that it was necessary to retrace the development of language from its primitive origins; this did not require the extensive use of historical or scientific research, but could be achieved through a hypothetical reconstruction of its development. Although Condillac was interested mainly in the origin of language, he linked it up with a wider view of culture. He insisted that the emergence of language did not involve a definite break in man's psychological development; it was associated, like other processes such as imagination and attention, with the activity of sensation. The earliest form of language, according to Condillac, was not the language of communication as it is now understood, but 'le langage d'action' inspired by instinct alone; although imitative, it involved man's whole being, including gestures and cries. Articulated language appeared at a much later stage of man's mental history. In other words, primitive human language was expressive rather than merely communicative, in so far as it sought to externalize inner feeling. That is why primitive language, according to Condillac, was associated with dancing – 'la danse des gestes', and, later on, 'la danse

2. See p. 79.

des pas'. Accordingly, early language was often linked with music. In the oldest cultures dancing, music and poetry were merely different aspects of the same essential process. Poetry and music, in particular, were used to teach people about religion, the laws and patriotism. At a later stage the visual element became important and a special use of language led to the appearance of writing: men's need to communicate ideas about absent objects or persons made them invent pictorial writing as a means of representing 'the images of things'. Condillac's main point is that language and the arts are rooted in the same desire for human expression; both spring from one fundamental need. The nature of language and literature cannot be understood by an analysis of its modern forms, but only through an examination of their origins in man's primordial psychological experience. With Condillac, therefore, questions of literary principle were removed from the domain of merely metaphysical speculation and related closely to a kind of philosophical psychology, which at the same time allowed an important place to the idea of development. Even so, Condillac did not advocate mere cultural relativism, for, ultimately, 'nature' guarantees the order of the universe and man's place in it.

These philosophical speculations were too far removed from the specific concerns of creative writers to have any decisive effect upon their work. Yet the pervasive influence of the rationalist spirit had already been revealed in the discussion of particular genres at the beginning of the century. The philosophical outlook was particularly striking in the controversy about the nature of poetry, to which a brief reference has already been made in an earlier section.[3] The advance of the philosophical and scientific outlook seemed at first sight to augur ill for the future of poetry, as the Quarrel of the Ancients and Moderns had already shown. Fontenelle tried to bring poetry closer to reason by suggesting that it should use 'intellectual ideas' or 'spiritual images' instead of the traditional 'adornments'. In his view, it should deal with such lofty conceptions as 'the general order of the universe, space, time and *les esprits*'; the determining principles of modern poetry would be Cartesian in spirit, stressing order, clarity and precision, which he hoped would be extended to 'the whole domain of letters'. The same ideas were to be developed later by the abbé Trublet who declared that poets would eventually become

3. See p. 188.

philosophers, since reason was henceforth to be the supreme guide. De la Motte also insisted that the decisive quality of a poem was its intellectual content and that reason, not enthusiasm, was the supreme poetic value. There was a growing belief that any poetry which did not have this philosophical purpose was a merely frivolous activity, capable perhaps of amusing empty-headed courtiers but unworthy of serious-minded people.

The ultimate effect of these views was to threaten the very existence of poetry as a distinct literary form, since the idea of a special poetic style (as developed from the time of the Pléiade onwards) was rejected in favour of a genre that was in many ways indistinguishable from prose. 'Our age', wrote d'Alembert, 'no longer recognizes anything as good verse except what it would find to be excellent in prose.'[4] The abbé Trublet went so far as to maintain that it would be a good idea to change the best verse into prose, while La Motte suggested that Racine's tragedies could be turned into prose without any great loss! The truly poetic qualities of imagination and feeling, it was alleged, were more suited to prose than to verse. A vigorous attack was made upon the whole idea of versification; because of its dependence on rhyme, verse – when it was not simply monotonous – created unnecessary difficulty and obscurity; rhyme was an artificial device that merely added to the difficulty of verse without bringing any corresponding benefits. Since art was based on the principle of imitation, the expression of true feeling would gain from the disappearance of a special poetic form. This attitude probably helps to explain the enormous popularity of Fénelon's *Télémaque* which many considered to be a perfect example of this poetic use of prose. Perhaps the ultimate objection to poetry at this period was inspired by the conviction that its 'enthusiasm' was incompatible with the truly rational spirit of modern culture. By the very nature of its inspiration, poetry seemed to threaten the supremacy of reason as man's greatest attribute. There was a widespread conviction that those art-forms which lent themselves to rational development ought to be encouraged in the modern age.

The strength of this attack on poetry was not due solely to philosophical influences. Although it is difficult to determine its precise

4. Quoted in P. van Tieghem, *Petite histoire des grandes doctrines littéraires en France*, Paris, 1954, p. 93.

effects, the social atmosphere of the time probably helped to weaken attachment to traditional principles. The death of Louis XIV had been followed by a period of reaction in which austerity and seriousness gave way, at least for a time, to immorality and frivolity as well as to a new critical spirit which was to become increasingly hostile to old values. The weakening of authority in the face of reason caused writers to abandon the earlier aesthetic viewpoint for a rational attitude inspired largely by the development of the sciences, and, in a more general way, by the spread of Cartesianism: confidence in the intrinsic power of reason meant that works of art had to be justified in their own right and not simply by comparison with the allegedly perfect models of antiquity. At the same time the traditional social and aristocratic values which had sustained classicism in its most creative and fertile period were now beginning to lose their hold. The rising bourgeoisie, as it became more conscious of its needs, was imbued with a more practical and mundane spirit than the carefree and leisurely attitude of the aristocracy; an intellectual curiosity directed upon the acquisition of useful knowledge was quite willing to sacrifice the apparent irrelevance of traditional poetry to the needs of modern life.

Needless to say, this revolutionary and iconoclastic view of poetry was not allowed to go unchallenged. Some of the leading writers of the age – Voltaire, Diderot and d'Alembert amongst others – came to the defence of tradition. Moreover, this 'philosophical' attack upon poetry did not seriously affect the abundance of poetic production, even though most of it is now judged to be of mediocre quality. As poets regained their confidence, new views began to emerge concerning specific types of poetry. The eclogue is a good example of the new elements which were coming to the fore and which were eventually to be reinforced by foreign influences, especially English 'pre-Romantic' poetry.

The theatre, as we have already seen, is another subject which was stimulating fresh thinking. Although the influence of Racine and Corneille was still too great to permit any serious re-appraisal of classical tragedy, which continued to enjoy considerable prestige and attract the creative efforts of a writer like Voltaire, it did not prevent the eventual emergence of a new type of play – *la comédie larmoyante* and (somewhat later) *le drame bourgeois* – along with elaborate theorizing by such practitioners as Diderot and Beaumarchais.[5] The novel, of course, showed a yet more spectacular rise in status; from being a lowly and despised genre, it rose to a position of eminence by the end of the century.

This increasing interest in literary thought, along with the general broadening of cultural outlook, was encouraged not only by the establishment of new *académies* and *salons*, but also by the rapid development of the press. New journals such as *Le Mercure galant* of Donneau de Visé (which became in 1724 the better-known *Mercure de France*), the Jesuit *Journal de Trévoux*, Fréron's *Lettres sur quelques écrits de ce temps*, which in 1754 were to be transformed into the *Année littéraire*, often devoted considerable space to book reviews and questions of literary criticism. Yet a further extension of literary interest was provided by the creation of journals concerned mainly with foreign culture – the abbé Prévost's *Le Pour et contre*, which dealt with English literature; the *Journal littéraire* (1713–36), the *Bibliothèque anglaise* and the *Journal étranger*, gave information about the latest cultural developments outside France. To these should be added the *Correspondances littéraires* of Pierre Clément (1748–52), of Grimm and Meister (1753–90) and La Harpe (1774) which were sent out to special subscribers. Not all these journals were in favour of the newest ideas, for some were staunch supporters of conservative values: Fréron, for example, was a zealous enemy of the *philosophes* and a steadfast defender of classical ideals; deploring the decadence of the modern age, he extolled the artistic perfection of the seventeenth century and of antiquity. In his *Observations*, Desfontaines made vigorous attacks against various kinds of innovations, including linguistic neologisms. Even an apparently progressive publication like the *Encyclopédie* often showed surprising conservatism in literary matters; although they discussed new genres such as *le drame bourgeois* or *la comédie larmoyante*, Marmontel's articles were often very timid in their approach. In any case, a good deal of this journalism was ephemeral and one-sided; but, whatever its particular emphasis or bias, it provided a powerful stimulus to the growing curiosity about different cultures and eventually led to fresh thought about the implications of literary activity. As readers became aware of cultures

5. See pp. 258ff.

other than their own, their allegiance to the idea of absolute literary values was gradually weakened.

It is instructive to examine the literary criticism of two major writers – Voltaire and Diderot – in the light of these general developments. At first sight Voltaire seems to adopt an independent attitude towards authority, for he does not hesitate to subordinate observance of the rules to artistic pleasure; a feeble line of poetry, he maintained, does not sin against the rules but against genius. In other words, taste is the ultimate criterion in judging the value of a literary work. Moreover, Voltaire's wide-ranging curiosity enabled him to recognize the importance of foreign literatures: he admitted that each country had its own genius and that there was no reason to suppose that an Englishman's taste should be the same as a Frenchman's: he reacted against a narrowly pedantic and one-sided approach to literature. Nevertheless, all this did not prevent him from being an essentially conservative figure. He insisted that, though taste had to be based on feelings, it could never be arbitrary; a person of taste followed universal principles which in turn reflected the true nature of man. Moreover, Voltaire's man of taste turns out to bear a very close resemblance to the Frenchman of the classical age. In spite of its liberal aspects, Voltaire's own taste was firmly rooted in the age of Louis XIV which he considered to be one of the perfect moments of civilization: it was a time when society and culture achieved a completely satisfactory synthesis. It is not surprising, therefore, to find that the eight writers whom Voltaire would allow into this literary 'paradise' were all Frenchmen of the classical age – Fénelon, Bossuet, Corneille, Racine, La Fontaine, Boileau, Molière and Quinault; of these Racine was, in his opinion, the greatest. The qualities which Voltaire admired in literature were elegance, decorum, propriety – qualities which appealed to the aristocratic taste of *l'honnête homme*; no work of art could be acceptable if it offended the canons of correct style and form. Voltaire might indeed make a brave effort to understand the culture of other countries and to relate the notion of genius to something more fundamental than mere rules, but he ultimately tended to base his judgements on the standards of the seventeenth century.

Voltaire's attitude towards Shakespeare is very revealing. He rightly claimed to have been one of the first French writers to introduce

Shakespeare to the general public. (Earlier accounts of Shakespeare in France had been limited to learned journals.) The *Lettres philosophiques* of 1734 praise the genius of Shakespeare for its remarkable fecundity and power; but the dramatist is severely criticized for his lack of taste and his ignorance of the rules, his tragedies being no more than 'monstrous farces'. Voltaire admits that after two centuries this author's 'bizarre and gigantic ideas' have earned the right to be treated as 'sublime', but, as he was to say later, Shakespeare had produced a 'chaotic tragedy' in which there were 'a hundred flashes of light'. Gradually, however, Voltaire's hostility to Shakespeare increased and, during the last years of his life, he delivered frenzied attacks upon him, denouncing him as 'a monster', 'barbarian' and 'a village buffoon'. It has been said that Voltaire saw in Shakespeare's rising reputation a threat to the popularity of his own tragedies, but more than this was involved: although Voltaire himself had incorporated a number of Shakespeare's elements into his own plays, these were for the most part fairly superficial visual effects or attempts to bring more life and action into the traditional genre; they did not affect the basis of Voltaire's classical loyalties.[6] There is no doubt that his ultimate condemnation of Shakespeare – and, for that matter, of Milton also – was due to his belief that a few isolated beauties did not compensate for what he considered to be a lack of artistic simplicity and unity. In spite of his moments of genius, Shakespeare offered a serious threat to the classical taste which Voltaire admired so passionately and which he believed was being threatened by the cultural changes he saw around him. Open though he was to so many of these new influences in philosophy and other intellectual domains, Voltaire never abandoned his devotion to the old aesthetic ideals; to the very end he saw himself as the defender of that classical taste which had achieved perfect expression in seventeenth-century France.

If Voltaire tends to look towards the past for his standards of taste, Diderot in many ways anticipates the future, though often in a sporadic and inconsistent way. As in the case of his philosophy as a whole, he never worked out a complete aesthetic system, but he approached the problem of art in a far more independent and original way than most of his contemporaries. Not only was he led to ponder aesthetic problems by his involvement with the *Encyclopédie* and his

6. See pp. 254–5.

activity as a creative writer (both novelist and dramatist), but he became very interested in painting when his friend Grimm asked him to supply art reviews for the privately circulated *Correspondance littéraire*; Diderot was asked to report on the various art exhibitions which were being held in Paris, the result being the voluminous *Salons* he produced between 1761 and 1781.

Diderot's aesthetic thought is difficult to summarize because of its scattered and frequently tentative nature; in the course of his life he sometimes changed its emphasis, if not its guiding principles, tending to move from an insistence upon the importance of sensibility towards a greater sympathy for the traditional notion of imitation. One of his first important essays on the subject was the long article 'Beau' which he contributed to the *Encyclopédie* in 1752. Like his rationalist predecessors, Crousaz, André and Batteux, Diderot sought an all-embracing principle which would explain the various artistic expressions of beauty. He located it in the general principle of 'relations' expressed as order, proportion and harmony, although he insisted that such relations take on meaning only when they involve the perceiving subject. Later on he came to realize the excessively abstract nature of this definition, but he never abandoned the notion of orderly relationships as an integral aspect of all aesthetic activity.

After this initial excursion into general aesthetics, Diderot began to place greater stress upon the importance of sensibility and feeling. 'Touch me, astonish me, tear me apart', he demanded of the artist. His predilection for sensibility was undoubtedly encouraged by his reading of Richardson, as his brief but eloquent *Éloge de Richardson* makes clear. Likewise, his interest in domestic drama led him to accord priority to the emotional impact of stage-performances. His reflections on language, and especially poetic language, also convinced him that barbarian nations were more essentially poetic than civilized nations, because they made a more spontaneous use of language; this meant too that they obeyed the impulse of the imagination and strove for visual metaphorical effects. In this connection Diderot worked out an interesting theory of poetic language as 'emblem' or 'hieroglyph'; the impact of sense and feeling causes poetic language to follow the inner movement of the soul which expresses itself in emblematic or symbolic sign-language through its fundamental response to the physical world.

Diderot is eventually led to interpret genius as a spontaneous primordial urge which ignores all rules and takes a man from the 'town and its inhabitants' in order to plunge him into the midst of nature – that 'fertile source of all truths'. The sight of a true 'object of nature' will inspire enthusiasm (it is the 'moment of enthusiasm' which sets in motion the poet's genius), and stir both imagination and passion. Such is the power of genius that it may manifest itself in the most violent physical symptoms – the shuddering of the whole body and onset of a heat which, as Diderot puts it in the *Entretien* on *Dorval et Moi*, 'sets him alight, makes him pant, consumes him, kills him, gives soul and life to all he touches'. At its most intense it would make the artist 'see ghosts' and raise his passion 'almost to the point of fury'. Finally, in the essay *De la poésie dramatique*, he points out that genius is rare in modern times, since it usually appears in moments of great national calamities or 'extraordinary events'.

However 'Romantic' and forward-looking this conception of genius may have been, it never led Diderot to abandon his faith in the principle of order; he affirmed that poetic order must always be based on 'the universal order of things'. Even the genius, who at times seems so bizarre and unpredictable, perceives a higher order to which ordinary people are blind. Indeed the true genius, though following his sensibility, always remains in control of it. In the *Paradoxe sur le comédien*, Diderot went so far as to condemn sensibility and suggest that the actor was an observer with an orderly and disciplined mind which allowed him to perceive the higher truth contained in the play he was performing. The presentation of apparent chaos and disorder – for example, the portrayal of a distraught character – must always involve a certain detachment and a power to rise above natural emotions.

If his reactions against excessive sensibility led Diderot to stress the traditional notion of 'imitation', he did so in an original way. The artist does not imitate nature as it is, but an 'inner model' which exists in himself and is derived from his perception of hidden relationships. This notion, however, raises difficulties because the relationships observed by the artist and recreated through the 'inner model' are not static but dynamic; the model does not remain fixed, but involves affinities and structures which are to be understood as forces rather than geometrical relations. Yet the artist is creative because it is his mind which produces the inner model which does not simply 'exist' in nature. Like genius itself, it may come to the fore in times of internal disruption and conflict – for example, when barbarism has destroyed the traditional forms of society, so that new aesthetic possibilities and associations are able to emerge. In this respect Diderot's views on art link up with his philosophical concept of perpetual creation and destruction and his cosmic vision undoubtedly influenced his ideas about art.[7] The different elements of the universe are involved in a permanent process of interpenetration and participation. 'All beings participate in the existence of all other beings' and it is the genius who has a valid insight into this process.

In spite of the originality of his aesthetic ideas, Diderot remained a life-long admirer of the ancients, particularly of Homer and Greek tragedy. He saw art as a continuous process of creation with its roots in the past. Unless he makes a sustained effort to appreciate the great achievements of the past, the modern artist will never produce anything truly great. At the same time, he has to remember that the sublime models of the past are not revered simply for their own sake, but as the successful efforts of former artists to express their 'inner model'. The modern artist's intuitive perception of hidden relations and his subsequent attempts to recreate them in his own work can be given shape and coherence only through a clear-sighted understanding of the sublimity of former times.

The role of painting in the later stages of Diderot's views of art ought not to be forgotten, for his art criticism led him to see the importance of structure, composition and arrangement. Yet the greatest painter does not merely copy nature – even the 'beautiful nature' extolled by Batteux. Every artist has to start with his inner vision, even though he knows that this is related to the world outside him – but to a world that is in the constant process of growth and development. This is why the great artist so often appears, in Diderot's view, to be ahead of his time.

If Diderot's original, forward-looking views made him an exceptional figure, he also paid respect to the well-established principle of imitation, while interpreting it in his own way. In general, the influence of this principle was too powerful to permit the acceptance of a creatively 'Romantic' attitude towards art. Far more characteristic

7. See pp. 67ff.

of the period were the persistent attempts to bring the 'imitation' of art closer to the reality of life by relating it to the non-rational aspects of the self or its historical, social and physical origins. It was not until the end of the century, however, that there appeared a more comprehensive and far-reaching attempt to establish closer contact between art and society: this was with the publication in 1800 of Mme de Staël's *De la littérature considérée dans les rapports avec les institutions sociales*. A consideration of this work, however, belongs more properly to the early Romantic period than to the last decades of the Enlightenment.

THREE

Germany

It is often maintained that in German literature theory precedes practice, with the implication that, since it conforms with precepts, it is deficient in originality and therefore somehow inferior. The source of this legend is to be found in an extended bout of polemics concerned with literary theory in the 1730s, which, though certainly not without importance, has undoubtedly been inflated in many of the traditional accounts of eighteenth-century German literature.

The name which looms largest in this prolonged squabble is that of J. C. Gottsched (1700–1766). Gottsched had a warm admiration for French literature, which he repeatedly praised, but his francophilia was in no way a new phenomenon. The seventeenth-century theorist and poet Martin Opitz (1597–1639) established the French alexandrine as the principal measure for German poetry for more than a century, and the literary societies (of which the Fruchtbringende Gesellschaft, 1617, is the best known), founded to benefit German literature, accepted French principles as a necessary basis. After all, the primacy of Greece and Rome in poetic writing (including the drama) had been recognized since the beginning of the Renaissance, and the French had succeeded in establishing themselves as the true inheritors and correct interpreters of the Classical Age and especially of Aristotle, its most prominent theorist. The European prestige of Paris and Versailles under Louis XIV led also in the numerous courts of Germany to the currency of French literature and even to the adoption for most purposes of the French language. Even a work such as A. von Haller's *Die Alpen* (written 1728–9), which looks forward to Rousseau, adhered to the accepted French verse form.

It was in Switzerland, however, that the first stirrings against French domination in German literature became apparent. Two men, of very different character but working in concert, began almost imperceptibly and all but unintentionally a reorientation of German literature. They were the mercurial J. J. Bodmer (1698–1783) and the stolid theologian J. J. Breitinger (1701–76), both professors at the Zürich classical grammar school, who as early as 1721 collaborated in a weekly periodical, the *Diskourse der Mahlern*, based on an English model, *The Spectator*. The *Diskourse* was a tame production and petered out in 1723; but at least it indicated that English literature had come within the field of view and established the cooperation of Bodmer and Breitinger, who came to be known as 'the Swiss' ('die Schweizer'). They turned away from French literature, though they had not the temerity to attack the principles on which it was based, and they found a completely new object of enthusiasm in Milton. Zürich, of course, was a stronghold of the Reformed Church, and it is not surprising that the biblical epic of *Paradise Lost* should seem to them a more worthy enterprise than the succession of pagan subjects to which French classical tragedy, with few exceptions, confined itself. Bodmer set about translating Milton's poem. He used prose, completing his version in 1724, though it was not printed until 1732.

Meanwhile Gottsched was busy establishing himself in Leipzig as an arbiter of taste. Though it may seem to us now that he did not always use it to best effect, there is no doubt about his intellectual capacity, and he had in addition organizational and administrative gifts of a high order. He had also considerable pride and belonged to the group of people in whom success brings out latent rigidity and dogmatism. The academic climate of the age also fostered pedantry in all but the most liberal minds, and Gottsched could never be reckoned among these. He was thorough, systematic and formal, and all these qualities were manifested in the treatise published in 1730 which is his best-known work, *Critische Dichtkunst vor die Deutschen*. The first virtue of this work is its clarity. It may not be elegant, but it is unambiguous. Gottsched accepts French models and principles but justifies them by his own homely and even naïve arguments. His order of merit for genres puts epic poetry first, tragedy second and comedy third. The lyric does not come within his purview. Prose is expository and has nothing to do with 'Dichtung'.

Gottsched, like almost all his contemporaries, held that the function of poetic writing was to demonstrate important truths in a way which gave pleasure to the reader or spectator. Poetry imitates Nature, but Nature in this context means essential truth, and has not the remotest connection with landscape. Remoteness from the irrelevances of present-day life is indispensable in the epic and in tragedy. The stories of antiquity, made familiar by the Renaissance and especially by French classical tragedy, provide the only satisfactory subject-matter. Gottsched provides instructions on the writing of such works, occasionally expressing himself so naïvely as to give the impression of being a literary Mrs Beeton. His tone is imperative, and he provides directions rather than advice. The criterion by which he justifies classical literature is that of common sense. Nowhere is this clearer than in his exposition of the unities of time and place. The spectator sits in the same seat in the same building for a period of two to three hours. It is ridiculous to ask him to believe that the place on the stage changes while he remains motionless, and equally absurd to ask him to assume that years have passed, when he knows perfectly well that only half an hour has gone by. Though he did not realize what he was doing and therefore did not draw the full consequences, Gottsched was applying the criterion of an extreme realism, more stringent even than that of the late-nineteenth-century Naturalists.

For a decade Gottsched's writ was almost unchallenged. Imitations of French classical tragedy were written wholesale, and practically all of them have passed into a well-deserved oblivion. Yet Gottsched's aim was a laudable one, however mistaken his method. He wished to see German literature raised to European rank. French literature had achieved this status. It followed that German literature could reach an equivalent standing by making itself as much like French literature as possible. The errors in Gottsched's assumptions were exposed before a generation had passed, and his treatise survives mainly because his forceful and truculent personality imposed his views for a few years on almost the whole of Germany and for a much longer period on Austria. His critical naïveties should not, however, blind us to the services which he undoubtedly rendered to German literature. He did much to purify and standardize German literary language (*Grundlegung zu einer deutschen Sprachkunst*, 1748) and, as we have already seen,[1] in *Erste Gründe der gesamten Weltweisheit* (1733–4) he provided the general reader with a concise summary of the popular philosophy of his day.

If Gottsched had been able to maintain his hegemony for long, German literature would have declined into a state of petrification.

1. See p. 98.

But in the 1740s the virtual dictatorship slipped from his grasp. The *Versuch einer critischen Dichtkunst* had contained a chapter 'Von dem Wunderbaren in der Poesie', but it had confined this concept to classical gods and their works, and to hyperbole, rejecting the supernatural and miraculous in modern contexts, and conceding them only reluctantly with the ancients. In 1740 Bodmer went into action with a treatise which expressly contradicted the Gottschedian view: *Kritische Abhandlung von dem Wunderbaren in der Poesie und dessen Verbindung mit dem Wahrscheinlichen in einer Vertheidigung des Gedichtes Joh. Miltons von dem verlorenen Paradiese.* The Swiss Calvinist in Bodmer could not deny the suitability of biblically authenticated miracles as subjects for poetry. This was the basis of a dispute with Gottsched which lasted for approximately a decade at the end of which the Leipzig professor had completely lost the dictatorial position, which he had used (unintentionally, of course) to reduce German literature to a uniform level of mediocrity. The Swiss critics were, however, no effective replacement for the discredited authority of Gottsched. Except on the biblical question, their views scarcely differed from his, and their vision and attitudes were decidedly more provincial. They had not even won the battle by themselves. What gave Gottsched's standing the final blow was the warm public reception accorded to the first three cantos of Klopstock's biblical epic *Der Messias* on their publication in 1748.

The only aesthetic theorist to rise above the platitudes and irrelevancies which characterize the contentious writings of Gottsched, Bodmer and Breitinger was Johann Elias Schlegel, whose residence in Denmark from 1743 until his early death in 1749 partly explains why his views did not evoke any appreciable contemporary resonance in Germany. His importance has only been realized (and sometimes exaggerated) in the twentieth century. In 1745 Schlegel published in the *Bremer Beiträge* (a series of publications put out by defectors from the Gottsched party) an essay entitled *Abhandlung, dass die Nachahmung der Sache, der man nachahmet, zuweilen unähnlich werden müsse.* Schlegel here struck a blow against the widely accepted view (held by Gottsched and the Swiss alike) that art is an imitation of reality, and that its merit increases according to the degree of exactness of the imitation. His conception of literary art was set out more fully in the substantial essay *Gedanken zur Aufnahme des dänischen Theaters* written in Copenhagen in 1747, but delayed by his marriage and appointment to a new post in 1748. It was not in fact published until 1764, when its originality was no longer obvious. Schlegel made two significant points. He insisted on the importance of the pleasure given by art, rejecting the view, held by most early representatives of Enlightenment, that pleasure was merely the sugar-coating which made the bitter moral pill palatable. He firmly maintained that pleasure in itself was a proper aim of poetry, though not its only aim. His second point is that a country should evolve its own literature and not slavishly imitate that of another, which reflects different national conditions. In this environmental approach Schlegel anticipates in some degree later views powerfully expressed by Lessing and Herder.

It was, however, a disciple of Wolff, Alexander Gottlieb Baumgarten (1714–62) who initiated the specialized study of aesthetics in Germany as a distinct branch of philosophy, not by the introduction of original ideas, since he drew largely on Wolff and the abbé Batteux, but by adopting the term as the title of a treatise (*Aesthetica acroamatica*, uncompleted, 2 vols., 1750–58) and creating a terminology. He had also used the term in the text of his earlier *Meditationes philosophicae de nonnullis ad poema pertinentibus* (1735).

Though the persuasive voice of Herder was heard by 1767, it may reasonably be said that criticism and aesthetics in the two decades 1750–70 were dominated by Lessing. His first critical writing appeared in 1750, and by 1752, at the age of twenty-three, he was a regular and effective reviewer. Simultaneously he embarked on various enterprises in critical journalism which, though financially unsuccessful, contained the germ of some of his later views on critical theory. Most notable was the assertion in *Das Neueste aus dem Reiche des Witzes* that the so-called rules of art are not static but movable, being subject to continual alteration as writers of genius take new directions: 'The rules in fine arts have been derived from observations of works of art. These observations have been augmented from time to time, and continue to be augmented each time a genius strikes out a new path or continues an old one beyond the limits it has hitherto reached.' The importance of this statement, put out in an obscure periodical, is evident. The critics of the eighteenth century, though paying lip-service to inspiration and original talent, had written on the assumption that literature was a craft with easily handled materials and that an intelligent person, possessed of a thorough knowledge of its rules, could not fail to produce work of merit. In striking his first tentative blow for originality Lessing was not only following his own mother wit, but was responding to the drabness and inadequacy of most of the numerous works of literature which streamed from the presses of the booksellers who were the publishers of the age. Throughout his life he never diverged from the view that the genius is the pioneer of literature, and both by precept and example sought to establish the activity of the writer as a combination of originality and professionalism, though others were later to exalt genius in a more flamboyant tone.

For many years Lessing's not inconsiderable influence continued to be exercised through periodical journalism and through occasional short essays. In the *Theatralische Bibliothek* (founded 1754) he began to draw attention to British drama in a short life of the Scottish poet and dramatist James Thomson (1700–1748) and in a lengthy essay on the plays of Dryden. In a preface written for a German translation of Thomson's tragedies (1756) he rejected the view, shared alike by Gottsched and the Swiss, that the aim of tragedy was to impart moral instruction. Instead he boldly affirmed that it can have no other purpose but to move the heart – to call forth 'tears of pity and of sympathetic humanity'. It was, however, in the widely read *Briefe die neueste Literatur betreffend* (1759), generally abbreviated to the *Literaturbriefe*, that Lessing went beyond informing the public on English poetry and drama and energetically asserted its congeniality with the German mind. In the Seventeenth Letter he mounts a withering attack upon Gottsched (hardly worth the trouble, for Gottsched's reputation had faded and Gottschedism was in retreat in all quarters except Austria), denouncing imitation of French eighteenth-century tragedy, proclaiming the greatness of Shakespeare, and emphasizing that, if models are necessary, the affinities of English and German culture would render English literature much more suitable for the purpose than French. He scathingly rejects the widely held current idea, propagated by the French, that Shakespeare was a worthy person, possessed of poetic gifts, who had the misfortune to be sadly lacking in education and to be born into an age which had no notion of the principles of drama as formulated by the ancients and interpreted by the French of the seventeenth century. As he vigorously put it:

Even if we decide the matter in accordance with the models provided by the Ancients, Shakespeare is a much greater tragic dramatist than Corneille, although the latter was well acquainted with the Ancients and the former hardly at all. Corneille is closer to them in the mechanics of tragedy, Shakespeare in its essence . . . After Sophocles's *Oedipus* no play has been written which has such power over our passions as have *Othello*, *King Lear*, *Hamlet*, etc.

Correctness and refinement have gone by the board, and Lessing, setting the pace for the *Sturm und Drang*, which still lay in the future, comes down unambiguously for the direct expression of human passion, however disturbing or indecorous it may be.

Lessing's final statement on the drama is contained in the periodical which he founded in Hamburg in 1767 and subsequently re-published in collected form in the two volumes of the *Hamburgische Dramaturgie* (1767–9). In addition to comparing Voltaire with Shakespeare (to the former's disadvantage), it contains, in a continuous argument running through Nos. 74–84, Lessing's definitive interpretation of a celebrated passage on tragedy in Aristotle's *Poetics*. The sentence (in Bywaters's translation) runs: 'A tragedy, then, is the imitation of an action that is serious and also, as having magnitude, complete in itself; in language with pleasurable accessories, each kind brought in separately in the parts of the work; in a dramatic, not in a narrative form; with incidents arousing pity and fear, wherewith to accomplish its catharsis of such emotions.' This statement is only controversial in its last section, the phrase concerning pity, fear and catharsis (which some authors translate as 'purgation' and the *Greek–English Lexicon* of Liddell and Scott defines as 'a cleansing, purification'). Lessing sets himself the following problems: what is meant by fear, who experiences it, how is it connected with pity, and what is the nature of the catharsis?

Lessing's views on fear and pity are succinctly expressed in No. 75 of the *Hamburgische Dramaturgie*:

He [Aristotle] speaks of pity and fear, not of pity and terror; and his fear is by no means the fear which impending evil threatening another arouses in us for this other person, it is the fear which, because of our affinity with the suffering person, we experience for ourselves; it is the fear that the misfortunes which we see happening to others could befall ourselves; it is the fear that we ourselves could become the object of pity; in a word, this fear is pity applied to ourselves.

Rejecting the almost Lucretian idea of contemplating the sufferings of others from a safe distance, Lessing involves the spectator himself personally and deeply in the action.

Catharsis Lessing interprets as purification ('Reinigung'), giving to the word a rather unusual signification.

Now, as this purification, to put it briefly, consists simply and solely in the transformation of passions into virtuous qualities, and as every virtue, according to our philosopher Aristotle, consists in a mean between two extremes, so tragedy, if it is to transform our pity into virtue, must be capable of purifying us from the extremes of pity; and in like manner it operates with regard to fear.

It will be seen that the two main points of Lessing's interpretation of Aristotle, though not openly contradictory, have differing implications. The theory of personal involvement looks beyond the strict sphere of Enlightenment to the depths of emotion probed by Rousseau in France and shortly to be thoroughly explored by the *Sturm und Drang* in Germany. The interpretation of catharsis, however, remains firmly rooted in the age of reason, which abhorred extremes of emotion and opted for a regulated moderation of feeling. In fairness to Lessing, it should also be pointed out that his theory of catharsis may also be seen as foreshadowing the conception of psychological balance, which was to be one of Schiller's great contributions to aesthetics and was to be echoed in the twentieth century by the pioneering work of I. A. Richards and C. K. Ogden.

Though the *Hamburgische Dramaturgie* was a journalistic enterprise, the influence of Lessing's views on the aesthetics of drama is largely due to its subsequent publication in book form. Lessing's other great contribution to aesthetic theory was conceived from the outset as a book. *Laokoon*, which is perhaps the work by which Lessing is best known outside Germany, was a book written with a personal aim. Lessing wished to justify himself as a man of learning by publishing a work of solid erudition, the consequence of which, he hoped, might be appointment by Frederick the Great of Prussia to the vacant post of royal librarian. To his chagrin the job went to an obscure Frenchman without noticeable qualifications. Perhaps as a consequence, the work remained unfinished, but torso though it is, it remains a treatise of considerable importance. It was Lessing's habit of mind to write his critical works in contradiction. He had to seek out some real or imagined adversary, and among others Gottsched, Voltaire, Pierre Corneille, Madame Dacier and the abbé Batteux had already served in this capacity. They were not necessarily enemies; some of them might be regarded as opponents in a fencing match, and from time to time Lessing was prepared to honour their skill and integrity. So it was with *Laokoon oder Über die Grenzen der Mahlerei und Poesie* (1766), for which he chose Winckelmann as his antagonist.

J. J. Winckelmann (1717–68) was one of the prodigies of the eighteenth century. A cobbler's son growing up in the poorest circumstances, he possessed or acquired, no one knows how, a passionate admiration for classical Greece. After years spent as an indigent schoolmaster teaching by day and studying Homer at night, he secured the patronage of a wealthy nobleman, attracted the attention of others and in 1755 obtained a grant for a visit to Rome. He spent the rest of his life in Italy, except for brief stays in Germany, and devoted himself to the study of classical art, becoming best known for his work in the excavation of the archaeological sites in southern Italy, but above all significant as the founder of the modern study of classical sculpture and architecture. His great work was the *Geschichte der Kunst des Altertums* (1764), but Lessing's *Laokoon* takes as a springboard an extended essay, *Gedancken über die Nachahmung der griechischen Werke in der Malerei und Bildhauerkunst*, published in 1755 at a time when Winckelmann only knew Greek art through his bookish studies in Germany.

In this essay Winckelmann had been at pains to demonstrate the moral superiority of the Greeks in comparison with the Romans; and he chose to illustrate his point by setting side by side the silently suffering Laocoön in the (supposedly) Greek statue (now in the Vatican) and the shrieking Laocoön in Virgil's account in the *Aeneid* (Book II). Winckelmann's evidence and argumentation are not confined to this example, but it is referred to in a particularly important passage, to which Lessing took exception. As Lessing saw it, Winckelmann's argumentation was fallacious. The solution was not moral but aesthetic. Statues and paintings are static; the bodily posture and the facial expression remain fixed. The sculptor of the Laocoön would, by eighteenth-century standards of taste, have committed a grave error if he had shown his central figure with mouth wide open to utter a shriek, so rendering the features ugly. Laocöon, said Lessing, is silent or almost so, not because he is a stoic, but because he is a statue. Virgil on the other hand, is a poet, concerned with the process of time. The shrieks are uttered, but they do not persist, and the beholder is not repelled by a frozen yell. The Virgilian Laocoön is not a hysterical exhibitionist, he is as he is because he conforms with the principles of poetry.

Lessing pronounced his conclusions with characteristic clarity: 'Objects which exist adjacent to one another are termed bodies. And so bodies with their visible properties are the subject of painting.[2] Objects which occur successively, or whose acts so occur, are termed actions. Hence actions are the proper subject of poetry' (Chapter 4). This dictum was in large part directed against descriptive poetry, which, through a misunderstanding of Horace's phrase *ut pictura poesis*, was widely practised in the eighteenth century. In Lessing's view descriptive verse was a contradiction in terms, since it attempted to render in time that which ought to be represented spatially. It was obvious (even to Lessing himself) that, in practice, many qualifications to his pronouncement were inevitable. Yet the basic principle underlined in *Laokoon* was true and had been lost sight of. What was even more important is that Lessing discerned that the various arts could simply not be put into one bundle and cultivated in accordance with one single set of principles. He reminded poets, painters and the public that the practitioners of an art must take into account the properties of the materials in which they work.

Johann Gottfried Herder (1744–1803), fifteen years younger than Lessing, had not the same capacity for precise distinction and crystalline clarity, nor did he share Lessing's preference for the *reductio ad absurdum* as a weapon for controversy. But, if his thought was less sharply focused, and its edges blurred, its scope was broader and its fertility greater. Lessing's thought was an almost entirely intellectual activity, Herder's was heavily charged with emotion. Herder grew up at a time when the electrical effect of Rousseau's writings was making itself felt in France. He read them in his East Prussian solitude and

2. Although Lessing speaks of painting, he intends to comprehend all plastic arts.

was so deeply affected that he resigned his pastoral office in Riga in May 1769 and set out by sea for France, landing at Nantes where he stayed for some months before spending the winter of 1769–70 in Paris. During this journey Herder set down a record of his thoughts, and feelings, which reflects the emotional turmoil and the intellectual fertility of these months. Had it been published at the time it would have been a most influential document, but it remained among his papers until 1846. No other work of his is so obviously the immediate product of his wayward and dynamic personality.

Herder's influence upon Goethe, exerted in their frequent discussions in Strassburg in 1770 and 1771, has already been mentioned,[3] and an important result of it appeared in 1773, the collection of essays bearing the title *Von deutscher Art und Kunst*, intended as the manifesto of a new literary creed. Of the five essays, three are particularly important: Herder's 'Auszug aus einem Briefwechsel über Ossian und die Lieder alter Völker' and 'Shakespeare', and Goethe's panegyric of gothic architecture 'Von deutscher Baukunst'. For Herder Ossian, folk song and Shakespeare all typify the natural unspoiled poetry of periods on which intellectual factors have not yet imposed their restraint.

Herder's opinions on art and civilization are contained in a series of substantial works: *Abhandlung über den Ursprung der Sprache* (1772), *Auch eine Philosophie der Geschichte zur Bildung der Menschheit* (1774), *Älteste Urkunde des Menschengeschlechts* (1774–6), *Ursachen des gesunkenen Geschmacks bei den verschiedenen Völkern* (1775), *Vom Geist der ebräischen Poesie* (1782–3) and *Ideen zur Philosophie der Geschichte der Menschheit* (1784–91). A turgid style and a rather heavy-weight presentation restricted their public, but they penetrated, directly or indirectly, to many of the most active minds, and some of their ideas are the basis of attitudes still widely held.

Herder was largely responsible for the enthusiasm for Shakespeare manifested by the *Sturm und Drang* and, ultimately, for his establishment as a virtual German classic; for an appreciation of the literary aspect of the Bible; for the warm acceptance of Ossian as a poet of primitive Celtic romanticism, and for enabling people to see folk songs as poems of simple beauty instead of naïve relics of barbarism. More than anyone else he preached the cult of genius, though he owed

3. See pp. 207 and 269.

his views on this subject in part to the eccentric thinker J. G. Hamann (1730–88).[4] In emphasizing the autonomy of genius he was one of the founders of the modern conception of the artist. Furthermore Herder thought in environmental terms, seeing literature as a part of the life of the age, and asserting that the contemporary conditions are a factor in the growth of literature. To an age satisfied with itself and contemptuous of tradition, he brought a habit of historical thought, a sense of continuity, which made a whole of past, present and future. And for rationalistic assumptions of progress he substituted the so-called *Organismus-Gedanke*, the conception that each phase of history has its semblance of a life-cycle, birth, childhood, youth, maturity, decline and fall. Though so many of these ideas, in which aesthetics and history are inextricably mingled, have become common-places, their popularity stems ultimately from Herder's work, in which they were passionately and persuasively advocated.

As far as the *Sturm und Drang* is concerned, Herder's praise of genius, of natural simplicity, and of unrestrained emotion were the principal factors underlying its aesthetic attitude. Minor contributions came also from H. W. von Gerstenberg and from J. M. R. Lenz. Gerstenberg (1737–1823) published, in the years 1766–70, *Briefe über Merkwürdigkeiten der Literatur*, a periodical similar to Lessing's *Briefe, die neueste Litteratur betreffend.* They are noteworthy for their unqualified approval of Shakespeare, expressed some years before the appearance of Herder's better-known essay. Lenz, in his *Anmerkungen übers Theater* (1774), rejects unity and proportion in favour of multiplicity of detail, opts for the portrayal of real characters (or even caricatures) in preference to idealized figures, and stresses the subjectivity of drama. A play, he claims, is not 'a picture of nature, but of his [that is to say the dramatist's] own soul'.

The revolutionary explorations of the *Sturm und Drang* gave way from about 1780 to an idealized form of literary art which develops classical leanings and reaches its extreme point about the turn of the century in explicit imitation of Hellenic models; examples of such work are Goethe's tragedy *Die natürliche Tochter* (1804), his epic *Achilleis* (1799), both works unfinished, and Schiller's tragedy *Die Braut von Messina* (1803). Both men subsequently seceded from this extreme position to an idealized form of modern drama and poetry.

4. See pp. 102f.

Schiller, who by temperament inclined more readily to theory than did Goethe, plunged in 1795 into the study of Kantian philosophy and remained immersed in it until 1797, when he transferred all his energies to *Wallenstein*. Schiller's position was one of general agreement with the idealistic metaphysics of Kant, but in ethics and aesthetics (which for him were closely associated) he had important reserves to make. Schiller's contributions to aesthetics are contained in a number of essays and treatises, of which the most significant are *Über Anmuth und Würde* (1793), *Über die ästhetische Erziehung des Menschen in einer Reihe von Briefen* (1795) and *Über naive und sentimentalische Dichtung* (1795–6), though *Über das Pathetische*, *Vom Erhabenen* (both 1793), *Über das Erhabene* (1801) and *Über den Gebrauch des Chors in der Tragödie*, a preface to the first edition of *Die Braut von Messina*, are also of considerable importance.

Schiller's theoretical approach was based on the Kantian theory of cognition.[5] Schiller was not only convinced by Kant's argumentation, he was also temperamentally receptive to this view. Since for him art, in the widest sense, was a moral activity, it was a gateway to reality, a means of presenting truth freed from the distortions and accretions produced by sensual perception and personal bias. All his theoretical writings were devoted, directly or indirectly, to this elevated view of the role of art and its responsibility.

The basic principle of Schiller's aesthetics is best illustrated by a quotation from his last work on the subject, *Über den Gebrauch des Chors in der Tragödie*:

> True art does not aim merely at transitory entertainment, it is its serious purpose, not to translate man into a momentary dream of freedom, but to make him really and truly free. It does this by arousing, exercising and developing a capacity to remove the sensual world, which otherwise oppresses us as crude raw material and weighs upon us as a blind force, into an objective remoteness, transforming it into the free work of our own spirit and enabling us to attain mastery over matter through ideas.

This insistence on the moral and metaphysical role of art is further amplified in the following passage taken from the same source:

5. See pp. 105f.

> Nature itself [by which Schiller means true reality] is only an idea of the mind, and is inaccessible to the senses. It is covered over by perceptual appearances, but never itself appears. Only to idealistic art is given the capacity, and indeed the task, of grasping this spirit of the universal and of fixing it in a corporeal form. Even art cannot present reality to the senses, but by its creative power it can reveal it to the imagination, and thereby become truer as an everyday reality and more real than any experience.

And so art in Schiller's view (and it is particularly literary art that he has in mind) becomes a form of revelation and achieves in a perceptual sphere what in Kant's philosophy was only apprehensible by the abstract moral sense.

The form of literature with which Schiller was primarily concerned was tragedy. He conceived a psychological ideal, which he termed the 'beautiful soul' ('schöne Seele') and which was characterized by a complete harmony of moral duty and inclination. The 'schöne Seele' willed that which was right and so was exempt from all internal conflict. Only approximations to such a character can exist in the sensual world (examples of such personalities in his works are Thekla Wallenstein and Max Piccolomini in *Wallenstein*). In the world of experience the conflict is always there in greater or lesser degree. The function of tragedy was to present the conflict between duty and inclination in an extreme situation in which the character is faced with inescapable death. The true tragic hero is the man who, while suffering the mortal ills of the world of the senses, maintains his spiritual integrity intact. Schiller puts it aphoristically in *Vom Erhabenen*: 'The man who overcomes what is terrible is great. The man who, though succumbing to it, does not fear it is sublime.' And this sublimity is the climax of tragedy. The distinction between the 'false' or distorted reality of experience and the ideal reality made accessible by art is made exceptionally clear in *Die Braut von Messina* by the use of a chorus, which Schiller describes in the preface as a living wall separating the two worlds.

Finally Schiller devised a typology of artists, using the terms naïve and sentimental, though not quite with their usual signification (it should be noted that instead of *sentimental* which has the same meaning in German and in English, Schiller coined the term *sentimentalisch*). The poets of ancient Greece were naïve, by which Schiller signified that they were at one with the world around them. The sentimental is the characteristic of the modern poet, who is conscious of the rift which separates him from nature and yearns for a reunion which he cannot achieve. In expounding this view in *Über naive and sentimentalische Dichtung*, Schiller had himself in mind as a sentimental and Goethe as a partially naïve poet. Approaching the critical problem of poetry, as it were, from opposite sides, they attained a unified classical idealism. This is the final position of aesthetic theory reached by the Age of Enlightenment in Germany, and it came at a time when the drift in a contrary Romantic direction was just beginning to be perceptible.

Chronological Table

	History	Science	England
1702	War of Spanish Succession (–1713)		
1703			
1704	Battle of Blenheim	Newton, *Optics*	Swift, *Battle of the Books*
1706	Battle of Ramillies		
1707			
1708			
1709			
1710			Berkeley, *Principles of Human Knowledge*
1711	Reign of Charles VI, Emperor of Austria (–1740)		Pope, *Essay on Criticism* Shaftesbury, *Philosophical Writings*, incl. *Characteristicks* Steele-Addison, *Spectator* (–1712)
1712			Pope, *Rape of the Lock*

France	*Germany*	*Italy*
		Muratori, *Primi disegni della Repubblica Letteratia d'Italia*
		Muratori, *Della perfetta poesia italiana*
		Filicaia, *Poesie toscane* Crescimbeni, *Vite degli Arcadi illustri*, I (–1728, V)
		Gravina, *Della ragion poetica* Vico, *De nostri temporis studiorum ratione* (Oration VI) Muratori, *Riflessioni sopra il buon gusto*
Le Sage, *Turcaret*		Martello, *Del verso tragico* Muratori, *Anecdota greca* Nelli, *La serva padrona*
		Martello, *Canzoniere* Vico, *De antiquissima italorum sapientia* *Giornale dei Letterati d'Italia*, Venice, co-founded by Zeno and Maffei (–1740) Gigli, *Don Pilone* Gigli, *La Sorellina di Don Pilone*
Birth of Jean-Jacques Rousseau		Gravina, *Tragedie cinque*

	History	Science	England
1713	Kingdom of Naples assigned to Austria by Peace of Utrecht. Bull Unigenitus Peace of Utrecht (–1715)		Berkeley, *Dialogues between Hylas and Philonous* Addison, *Cato* Collins, *Discourse on Free Thinking*
1714	Reign of George I (–1727)		
1715	Death of Louis XIV Regency of Duc d'Orléans (–1723)		Pope's translation of the *Iliad* (–1720)
1716	Bank of France founded		
1717	West India Company founded	'sGravesande teaches Newtonian physics at Leyden	
1718		Halley demonstrates movement of fixed stars	
1719		'sGravesande, *Physices elementa*	Defoe, *Robinson Crusoe*
1720			Swift, *Miscellaneous Works* (including *Tale of a Tub*)
1721	Innocent XIII (Conti) Pope		
1722			Defoe, *Moll Flanders*
1723	Reign of Louis XV (–1774)		

France	*Germany*	*Italy*
Abbé de Saint-Pierre, *Projet de paix perpétuelle*		Crescimbeni, *Rime degli Arcadi*, I (–1722, IX)
		Manfredi, *Rime*
		Maffei, *Merope*
Fénelon, *Lettre à l'Académie*		*Accademia Quirina*, Rome, founded by Gravina
		Martello, *L'impostore*
Le Sage, *Gil Blas* (–1735)		Gravina, *Della tragedia*
		Martello, *Della tragedia antica e moderna*
		Vico, *De rebus gestis Antonii Caraphaei*
		Muratori, *Delle antichità estensi ed italiane*, I (–1740, II)
		Rolli, *Rime*, pub. London
		Metastasio, *La primavera*
Du Bos, *Réflexions critiques sur la poésie et la peinture*	Wolff, *Vernünftige Gedanken von Gott, der Welt und der Seele* (followed by two volumes with similar titles, 1720–21, and other works, 1723–40)	
Club de l'Entresol founded		Vico, *De universi iuris principio et fine uno*
Montesquieu, *Lettres persanes*	J. J. Bodmer, *Diskurse der Mahlern* (–1723)	Vico, *De constantiae iurisprudentiae*
Marivaux, *Le Spectateur français*		
		Martello, *Opere*, I (–1735, VII)
		Giannone, *Istoria civile del Regno di Napoli*

	History	Science	England
1723 (*cont.*)			
1724	Benedict XIII (Orsini) Pope		
1725	Death of Peter the Great, Emperor of Russia		Hutcheson, *An Inquiry into the Original of our Ideas of Beauty and Virtue* Pope's translation of the *Odyssey*
1726	Ministry of Cardinal de Fleury		Swift, *Gulliver's Travels*
1727	Reign of George II (–1760)		Chambers, *Cyclopedia* Hutcheson, *Essay on Passions*
1728		Pemberton, *A View of Sir Isaac Newton's Philosophy*	Pope, *Dunciad* Gay, *Beggar's Opera*
1729			
1730	Clement XII (Corsini) Pope	Réaumur invents the thermometer	Thomson, *The Seasons*
1731	Treaty of Vienna (–1733)		Lillo, *The London Merchant*

France	*Germany*	*Italy*
		Muratori, *Rerum italicarum scriptores*, I (–1751, XXVIII) Metastasio, *Didone abbandonata* (music Sarro; perf. Naples 1724)
	J. C. Günther, *Gedichte* (posthumous 1724–35)	Martello, *Il Femia sentenziato* Metastasio, *L'estate*
		Vico, *Scienza nuova I*
		Conti, *Giulio Cesare* Metastasio, *Siroe* (music Vinci)
		Maffei, *Le cerimonie* Metastasio, *Catone in Utica* (music Vinci)
Prévost, *Mémoires et aventures d'un homme de qualité* (–1731)		Vico, *Vita* Maffei, *Degli anfiteatri* *Raccolta di opuscoli scientifici e filologici*, Venice, directed by Calogerà (–1757) Metastasio, *Semiramide* (music Vinci) Metastasio, *Alessandro nelle Indie* (music Vinci) *Novelle della Repubblica Letteraria*, Venice (–1762)
Marivaux, *Jeu de l'amour et du hasard*	Gottsched, *Versuch einer critischen Dichtkunst vor die Deutschen*	Vico, *Scienza nuova II* Metastasio, *Artaserse* (music Vinci)
Prévost, *Manon Lescaut* Marivaux, *Vie de Marianne* (–1741)		Nelli, *Commedie*, I (–1758, V) Giannone, begins *Il Triregno*, pub. 1895

	History	Science	England
1732		Maupertuis, *Discours sur les différentes figures des astres*	
1733	War of Polish Succession		Pope, *Essay on Man*
1734	Don Carlos, King of Naples (–1759)	Réaumur, *Histoire des insectes*	
1735		Boerhaave, *Treatise on Venereal Disease*	
1736		Linnaeus, *Systema naturae*	Butler, *Analogy of Religion*
1737	Francis, Duke of Lorraine, assigned the Grand Duchy of Tuscany		
1738		Bernouilli, *Hydrodynamics*	

France	Germany	Italy
Voltaire, *Zaïre* Prévost, *Le Philosophe anglais ou l'histoire de Cleveland* (–1739)	Gottsched, *Der sterbende Cato* Haller, *Die Alpen* (*Ein Versuch schweizerischer Gedichte*)	Maffei, *Verona illustrata* Metastasio, *Adriano in Siria* (music Caldara) Goldoni, *Amalasunta*
Voltaire, *Le temple du goût* Prévost, *Le Pour et contre* (–1740)		Maffei, *Galliae antiquitates* Metastasio, *La libertà*; *L'Olimpiade*; *Demofoonte* (music Caldara)
Voltaire, *Lettres philosophiques* Montesquieu, *Considérations sur la grandeur des Romains* Marivaux, *Le Paysan parvenu* (–1735) Saint-Simon, *Mémoires*		Metastasio, *La clemenza di Tito* (music Caldara) Goldoni, *Belisario*
Desfontaines, *Observations sur les écrits modernes* (–1743)		Muratori, *Filosofia morale* Rolli, partial Italian translation of *Paradise Lost*
Voltaire, *Le Mondain* Crébillon fils, *Les Égarements du coeur et de l'esprit* (–1738)		Giannone's autobiography written in prison (–1737) Metastasio, *Achille in Sciro* (music Caldara)
Marivaux, *Les Fausses Confidences*		Zeno, *Ezechia* Bandini, *Discorso sopra la Maremma di Siena* (–1743; pub. 1775) Algarotti, *Newtonianismo per la dame*
Voltaire, *Éléments de la philosophie de Newton* Voltaire, *Discours en vers sur l'homme*		Goldoni, *Momolo cortesan* (–1739) Algarotti, *Viaggi di Russia* (–1739) Carli, *Antichità di Capodistria*

	History	Science	England
1739	War between Great Britain and Spain Wesley founds Methodism		Hume, *Treatise of Human Nature*
1740	Benedict XIV (Lambertini) Pope Three Silesian Wars (–1743) Reign of Maria-Theresa, Empress of Austria (–1780) Reign of Frederick II, King of Prussia (–1786)		Richardson, *Pamela*
1741	War of Austrian Succession (–1748) Dupleix, Governor of Pondicherry (–1754)		Hume, *Moral and Political Essays*
1742		Heilbronner, *History of Mathematics*	Young, *Night Thoughts* Fielding, *Joseph Andrews*
1743		d'Alembert, *Traité de Dynamique*	
1744	France declares war on England	Euler, *Treatise of Differential Calculus*	Collins, *Eclogues* Akenside, *Pleasures of the Imagination*
1745	Battle of Fontenoy Charles Stuart's rebellion		

France	*Germany*	*Italy*
	Breitinger, *Critische Dichtkunst*	Muratori, *Novus Thesaurus veterum inscriptiones*, I (–1743, VI)
	Frederick II, *L'Anti-Machiavel* J. J. Bodmer, *Critische Abhandlung von dem Wunderbaren*	*Novelle Letterarie*, Florence, directed by Lami (–1768) Metastasio, *Attilio Regolo*, perf. Dresden 1750 (music Hasse) Goldoni, *Momolo sulla Brenta*
Duclos, *Confession du Comte de*** La Chaussée, *Mélanide*		Baruffaldi, *Il canapaio*
Prévost, translation of *Pamela* Voltaire, *Mahomet* Crébillon fils, *Le Sopha*		Muratori, *Dei difetti della giurisprudenza* Maffei, *Istoria teologica* First Italian translation of Pope's *Essay on Man*
		Conti, *Giunio Bruto*; *Marco Bruto* Goldoni, *La donna di garbo* Carli, *Indole del teatro tragico antico e moderno* Costantini, *Lettere critiche*, I–VIII (1743–56)
		Vico, *Scienza nuova III*, pub. posthumously Muratori, *Annali d'Italia*, I–XII (1744–9) Seriman, *Aristippo*
Maupertuis, *Vénus physique* La Mettrie, *Histoire naturelle de l'âme*		Muratori, *Della forza della fantasia umana* Goldoni, *Il servitore di due padroni*

	History	*Science*	*England*
1746	French conquest of Madras Battle of Culloden		T. Warton, *Odes on Various Subjects*
1747			Collins, *Odes* Richardson, *Clarissa Harlowe* (–1748) Samuel Johnson, *Dictionary* (–1755)
1748	Peace of Aix-la-Chapelle	Euler, *Introduction to Infinitesimal Calculus*	Smollett, *Roderick Random*
1749			Fielding, *Tom Jones*

France	Germany	Italy
Vauvenargues, *Maximes: Introduction à la connaissance de l'esprit humain* Batteux, *Les Beaux Arts réduits à un seul principe* Diderot, *Pensées philosophiques* Condillac, *Essai sur l'origine des connaissances humaines* Prévost, *Histoire générale de voyages*	Gellert, *Fabeln und Erzählungen*	Metastasio, *Palinodia a Nice* Metastasio, *La partenza* Roberti, *La moda*
Voltaire, *Zadig* La Mettrie, *L'Homme machine*	Klopstock, *Oden* (published in periodicals; –1773)	Muratori, *Della regolata divozione dei cristiani* Maffei, *Raguet* Conti, *Druso*
Rousseau, *Lettre à d'Alembert* Diderot, *Les Bijoux indiscrets* Montesquieu, *De l'esprit des lois*	Gottsched, *Grundlegung einer deutschen Sprachkunst* Klopstock, *Der Messias* (I–III)	Goldoni, *La vedova scaltra*
Diderot, *Lettre sur les aveugles* Buffon, *Histoire naturelle* (*Théorie de la Terre*) Condillac, *Traité des systèmes* Duclos, *Considérations sur les moeurs* Buffon, *Histoire naturelle* (–1790)	E. von Kleist, *Der Frühling*	Muratori, *Della pubblica felicità* Maffeì, *Museum Veronense* Maffei, *Dell'arte magica* (–1750) Goldoni, *Il cavaliere e la dama* Goldoni, *La famiglia dell'antiquario* Chiari, *La scuola delle vedove* Chiari, *Lettere scelte . . . ad una dama di qualità* (–1752) Seriman, *Viaggi di Enrico Wanton*, I–II (–1764, IV) Goldoni, *Il treatro comico*

	History	Science	England
1750			Johnson, *The Rambler* (–1752)
1751		Linnaeus, *Philosophia botanica*	Smollett, *Peregrine Pickle* Fielding, *Amelia* Gray, *Elegy Written in a Country Churchyard*
1752			
1753		Linnaeus, *Species plantarum*	Hogarth, *Analysis of Beauty* Richardson, *Charles Grandison*
1754		Maupertuis, *Essai sur la formation des corps organisés*	J. Warton, *Observations on the 'Fairie Queen' of Spenser* Hume, *History of Great Britain* (–1761)

France	*Germany*	*Italy*
		G. Gozzi, *I sermoni* (–1782) Galiani, *Della moneta*
Rousseau, *Discours sur les sciences et les arts*	A. G. Baumgarten, *Aesthetica acroamatica* (–1758)	
Encyclopédie, Vol. I (including d'Alembert's *Discours préliminaire*) Prévost, translation of *Clarissa Harlowe* Voltaire, *Siècle de Louis XIV*		Metastasio, *Il re pastore* (music Bonna)
Voltaire, *Micromégas*		Zeno, *Dissertazioni vossiane*, I (–1753, II) Goldoni, *La locandiera*, perf. 1753 Algarotti, *Dialoghi sopra l'ottica Neutoniana* (recast ed. of *Newtonianismo per le dame*) Roberti, *Le fragole* Parini, *Prime poesie di Ripano Eupilino*
Buffon, *Discours sur le style*	Wieland, *Der geprüfte Abraham*	Rolli, *Poetici componimenti* Goldoni, *La sposa persiana* Chiari, *La schiava cinese* Chiari, *La filosofessa italiana* *Memorie per servire all'Istoria Letteraria*, Venice (–1758) Genovesi, *Discorso sopra il vero fine delle lettere e delle scienze*
Condillac, *Traité des sensations* Diderot, *Pensées sur l'interprétation de la Nature* Grimm, *Correspondance littéraire*		Chiari, *Il filosofo veneziano* Carli, *Delle monete e delle zecche d'Italia*, I (–1769, IV)

	History	*Science*	*England*
1755	Lisbon earthquake	Euler, *Institutiones calculi differentialis*	Johnson, *Dictionary of the English Language*
1756	Seven Years' War (–1763)		Edmund Burke, *Philosophical Inquiry into the Origin of Our Ideas of the Sublime and Beautiful* J. Warton, *Essay on the Genius and Writings of Pope*
1757	Battle of Plassey	Haller, *Elementa Physiologiae* (–1765)	
1758	Clement XIII (Rezzonico) Pope Choiseul French foreign minister (–1770)		Blackstone, *Commentaries*
1759	English capture Quebec		Sterne, *Tristram Shandy* Johnson, *Rasselas* Edward Young, *Conjectures on Original Composition* Alexander Gerard, *An Essay on Taste*

France	Germany	Italy
Prévost, translation of *Charles Grandison* Morelly, *Code de la Nature* Rousseau, *Discours sur l'inégalité*	Lessing, *Miss Sara Sampson* Winckelmann, *Gedanken über die Nachahmung der griechischen Werke* Nicolai, *Briefe über den itzigen Zustand der schönen Wissenschaften in Deutschland*	Goldoni, *Ircana in Julfa*; *Le massere*; *Le donne di casa soa* Chiari, *La commediante in fortuna* Passeroni, *Il cicerone*, I (–1774, VII) Roberti, *La commedia*
Voltaire, *Poème sur le désastre de Lisbonne* Rousseau, *Letter to Voltaire on 'Providence'* Voltaire, *Essai sur les moeurs*	S. Gessner, *Idyllen*	Goldoni, *Ircana in Ispahan* Goldoni, *Il campiello* Chiari, *Commedie in versi*, I (–1762, X) Algarotti, *Saggio sopra l'architettura* Roberti, *Le perle* Parini, (?) *La vita rustica* Parini, *La salubrità dell'aria* (–1759?) Betti, *Il baco da seta*
Diderot, *Le Fils naturel* Diderot, *Entretiens sur le fils naturel*	M. Mendelssohn, *Über die Haupgrundsätze der schönen Künste und Wissenschaften*	Genovesi, *Storia del commercio della Gran Bretagna* Bettinelli, *Versi sciolti di tre eccellenti autori* (Algarotti, Frugoni, Bettinelli) Bettinelli, *Lettere Virgiliane* C. Gozzi, *La Tartana degli influssi* Parini, *Dialogo sopra la nobiltà*
Helvétius, *De l'esprit* Diderot, *Le père de famille* Diderot, *Discours sur la poésie dramatique*	Gleim, *Kriegs und Siegeslieder der Preussen* S. Gessner, *Der Tod Abels*	G. Gozzi, *Difesa di Dante*
Voltaire, *Candide* Diderot, *Salons* Diderot, *Lettre sur les sourds et muets* Diderot, *La Religieuse* (pub. 1796)	Lessing, *Briefe die neueste Literatur betreffend*	Goldoni, *Gli innamorati* *Nuove Memorie per servire all'Istoria Letteraria*, Venice (–1761)

	History	Science	England
1760	English capture Montreal Reign of George III (–1820)		Ossian, *Poems and Fragments of Ancient Poetry translated from the Gaelic* Goldsmith, *Citizen of the World* (–1762)
1761			
1762	Execution of Calas Catherine II, Empress of Russia (–1796)		R. Hurd, *Letters on Chivalry and Romance* Kames, *Elements of Criticism*
1763	Peace of Paris		

France	Germany	Italy
		Goldoni, *I rusteghi*; *La casa nova* G. Gozzi, *Gazzetta Veneta* (–1761); *Mondo Morale* Parini, *Contro il padre Branda*
Diderot, *Éloge de Richardson* Rousseau, *La Nouvelle Héloïse* Marmontel, *Contes Moraux* Diderot, *Le Neveu de Rameau* (–1776; pub. 1823)		Goldoni, *Le smanie per la villeggiatura* G. Gozzi, *Osservatore Veneto* (–1761) C. Gozzi, *L'amore delle tre melarance*
Rousseau, *Contrat social* Rousseau, *Émile*	Hamann, *Dei Kreuzzüge eines Philologen*	Goldoni, *Le baruffe chiozzotte* Goldoni, *Sior Todero brontolon* Goldoni moved to Paris as director of the *Comédie Italienne* Chiari, *La donna che non si trova* Algarotti, *Saggio sopra la pittura*; *Saggio sopra l'opera in musica* C. Gozzi, *Il re cervo*; *Turandot*; *La donna serpente* Denina, *Saggio sulla letteratura italiana* Beccaria, *Del disordine e de' rimedi delle monete nello Stato di Milano* *La Minerva, osia Nuovo Giornale de' Letterati d'Italia*, Venice (–1767)
Voltaire, *Traité sur la tolérance* Rousseau, *Lettre à M. de Beaumont*		Zanon, *Dell'Agricoltura, dell'Arti e del Commercio*, I (–1766, VI) Baretti, *La frusta letteraria* (–1765) C. Gozzi, *La Zobeide*

	History	Science	England
1763 (*cont.*)			
1764	Dissolution of Jesuits in France		Reid, *Inquiry into the Human Mind* Walpole, *Castle of Otranto*
1765	Peter Leopold, Grand Duke of Tuscany (–1790) Reign of Joseph II, Emperor of Austria (–1790)	Spallanzani, *Saggio di osservazioni microscopiche concernenti il sistema della generazione*	Johnson, Preface to *Plays of William Shakespeare* Goldsmith, *Vicar of Wakefield* Percy, *Reliques of Ancient English Poetry*
1766	Lorraine becomes French		Swift, *Journal to Stella* Colman and Garrick, *The Clandestine Marriage*
1767	Jesuits expelled from France, Spain and Uruguay Bougainville's journey round the world (–1769)	Priestley, *History of Electricity*	

France	*Germany*	*Italy*
		P. Verri, *Meditazioni sulla felicità* Parini, *Il giorno: Mattino* (1763), *Mezzogiorno* (1765), *Vespro* and *Notte* (pub. post. 1801) Cesarotti, Italian translation of Macpherson's *Ossian* (–1772)
Rousseau, *Lettres de la montagne* Voltaire, *Dictionnaire philosophique* Diderot, *Essais sur la peinture* (pub. 1796)	Winckelmann, *Geschichte der Kunst des Altertums*	*Giornale d'Italia spettante alla Scienza Naturale*, Venice, directed by Griselini (–1776) C. Gozzi, *I pitocchi fortunati*; *Il mostro turchino* P. Verri, *Saggio sulla grandezza e decadenza del commercio di Milano* Parini, *L'educazione* Beccaria, *Dei delitti e delle pene* *Il Caffè*, Milan, directed by P. Verri (–1766)
Sedaine, *Le Philosophe sans le savoir*		Goldoni, *Il ventaglio* C. Gozzi, *Zeim re de' Geni*; *L'augellino belverde* Genovesi, *Lezioni di Commercio*, I (–1767, II) Parini, *L'innesto del vaiuolo*
Voltaire, *Commentaire sur les délits et peines de Beccaria*	Lessing, *Laokoon* Wieland, *Geschichte des Agathon* (–1767)	Bettinelli, *Lettere inglesi* Colpani, *Il commercio*
Voltaire, *Le Philosophe ignorant* D'Holbach, *Le Christianisme dévoilé* Beaumarchais, *Eugénie*; *Essai sur le genre dramatique sérieux*	Lessing, *Minna von Barnhelm* Goethe, *Annette* Herder, *Über die neuere deutsche Literatur*	Colpani, *Il gusto*

	History	*Science*	*England*
1768	Corsica becomes French	Euler, *Institutiones calculi integralis* *Lettres à une Princesse d'Allemagne*	Sterne, *Sentimental Journey* Goldsmith, *The Good-Natured Man* Robertson, *History of Charles V* Reynolds, *Discourses* (–1790)
1769	Clement XIV (Ganganelli) Pope		
1770			
1771			R. Cumberland, *The West Indian* *Encyclopaedia Britannica*, First Edition Smollett, *Humphry Clinker*
1772	First partition of Poland	Priestley, *Observations on Air*	
1773	Suppression of Jesuits		

France	Germany	Italy
		Galiani, *Dialogues sur le commerce des blés*, pub. 1770 P. Verri, *Memorie storiche sulla economia pubblica dello Stato di Milano* *L'Europa Letteraria Giornale*, Venice, directed by Caminer (–1773)
Diderot, *Le Rêve de d'Alembert* (first pub. 1830)	Herder, *Critische Wälder*	Bettinelli, *Dell'entusiasmo delle belle arti* P. Verri, *Osservazioni sulla tortura* Parini, *La musica* Denina, *Delle rivoluzioni d'Italia*, I (–1770, III)
d'Holbach, *Système de la Nature*	Goethe, 'Sesenheimer Lieder'	Beccaria, *Ricerche intorno alla natura dello stile*, I Cassola, *L'oro*
		Goldoni, *Le bourru bienfaisant* P. Verri, *Meditazioni sulla economia politica* Parini, *Ascanio in Alba* (music Mozart) Filangieri, *Della pubblica e privata educazione*
Diderot, *Supplément au voyage de Bougainville* (pub. 1796) Helvétius, *De l'homme* Raynal, *Histoire philosophique des deux Indes*	Lessing, *Emilia Galotti* Herder, *Über den Ursprung der Sprache*	Goldoni, *L'avare fastueux* (–1773) C. Gozzi, *La Marfisa bizzarra* (wr. 1761–8) Tiraboschi, *Storia della letteratura italiana*, I (–1782, XIII)
B. de Saint-Pierre, *Voyage à l'Île de France* Diderot, *Jacques le fataliste* (pub. 1796) Diderot, *Paradoxe sur le comédien* (–1778; pub. 1830)	Herder/Goethe, *Von Deutscher Art und Kunst* Goethe, *Götz von Berlichingen*	P. Verri, *Discorso sull'indole del piacere e del dolore*

	History	Science	England
1774	Ministry of Turgot (–1776) Reign of Louis XVI (–1793)	Mesmer, *Animal Magnetism*	Thomas Warton, *History of English Poetry* (–1781)
1775	Pio VI (Braschi) Pope War of American Independence (–1783)		Sheridan, *The Rivals*
1776	Declaration of Independence by United States Necker's first ministry		Gibbon, *Decline and Fall of the Roman Empire* Adam Smith, *Wealth of Nations*
1777			Cook, *Voyage Round the World* Sheridan, *School for Scandal* Hume, *Dialogues concerning Natural Religion* Chatterton, *Poems*
1778	France enters American War		

France	*Germany*	*Italy*
	Wieland, *Die Abderiten* G. A. Bürger, *Lenore* Goethe, *Clavigo* Goethe, *Die Leiden des jungen Werthers* Möser, *Patriotische Phantasien* (–1778)	Albergati Capacelli, *Il nuovo teatro comico*, I (–1778, V) *Giornale Enciclopedico*, Venice, Vicenza, directed by Caminer (–1797) Alfieri, *Cleopatra*, perf. Turin 1775, pub. 1805 Filangieri, *Riflessioni politiche*
Restif de la Bretonne, *Le Paysan perverti* Beaumarchais, *Le Barbier de Séville*	F. H. Jacobi, *Eduard Allwills Papiere* Lavater, *Physiognomische Fragmente* (–1778)	Bertola, *Notti clementine* Bettinelli, *Risorgimento d'Italia* Galiani, *Socrate immaginario* Alfieri begins *Filippo* and *Polinice* (–1781) Monti, *Visione d'Ezechiello*
	Leisewitz, *Julius von Tarent*	Rolli, *Marziale in Albion*, pub. post. *Nuovo Giornale*, Venice, directed by Griselini (–1784) Alfieri, *Agamennone* begun (–1781) Bertola, *Versi e prose*
		Parini, *La laurea* Alfieri, *Della tirannide*; *Virginia* (–1778); *La congiura dei Pazzi* (–1781) Alfieri, *Satire* (–1797)
Death of Rousseau and Voltaire		Carli, *L'uomo libero* Casti, *Novelle galanti* (–1802) Rezzonico, *L'origine delle idee*

	History	*Science*	*England*
1779			Beattie, *Essay on Poetry and Music* Johnson, *Lives of the Poets* (–1781)
1780		Spallanzani, *Dissertationi de fisica animale e vegetale*	Goldsmith, *The Deserted Village*
1781		Herschel discovers planet Uranus Watt invents steam-engine	
1782			
1783	Treaty of Versailles	Herschel, *Discourse on the Movement of the Solar System*	
1784			

France	Germany	Italy
		Alfieri begins *Don Garzia* (–1779), *Maria Stuarda* (–1780) and *Del principe e delle lettere* (–1786)
Restif de la Bretonne, *La Vie de mon père*	Lessing, *Nathan der Weise*	Pignotti, *La tomba di Shakespeare* Grimaldi, *Riflessioni sopra l'ineguaglianza tra gli uomini* (–1780) Alfieri, *Timoleone* begun (–1781) Bertola, *Idea della poesia alemanna* Monti, *La Prosopopea di Pericle*
	Lessing, *Die Erziehung des Menschengeschlechts* Wieland, *Oberon*	A. Verri, *Le avventure di Saffo* Filangieri, *La scienza della legislazione* begun
	Schiller, *Die Räuber* Kant, *Kritik der reinen Vernunft*	Tiraboschi, *Biblioteca Modenese*, I (–1786, VI) Monti, *La bellezza dell'universo*
Rousseau, *Confessions; Dialogues; Rêveries* Laclos, *Les Liaisons dangereuses*	Schiller, *Die Verschwörung des Fiesco zu Genua*	Pignotti, *L'ombra del Pope*; *Favole e novelle* Alfieri, *Saul*
		Casti, *Poema tartaro* Bertola, *Favole*
		Goldoni, *Mémoires* (–1787) Alfieri, *Mirra: Agide* begun (–1786)
Death of Diderot Bernardin de Saint-Pierre, *Études de la Nature* (3 vols.) Rivarol, *Discours sur l'universalité de la langue française*	Kant, *Beantwortung des Frage: Was ist Aufklärung?* Schiller, *Kabale und Liebe* Herder, *Ideen zur Philosophie der Geschichte der Menschheit* (–1791)	Monti, *Ode al signor di Montgolfier* Fantoni, *Odi*, I (–1786, III)

	History	Science	England
1784 (*cont.*)			
1785			Paley, *Principles of Moral and Political Philosophy* Reid, *Essay on the Intellectual Powers of Man*
1786			Burns, *Poems*
1787	Russo-Turkish War		
1788		Lagrange, *Mécanique analytique*	
1789	Beginning of French Revolution Fall of Bastille		Bentham, *Introduction to the Principles of Morality and Legislation* Blake, *Songs of Innocence*
1790			Blake, *Marriage of Heaven and Hell* Burke, *Reflections on the French Revolution*
1791			Boswell, *Life of Johnson*

France	*Germany*	*Italy*
Beaumarchais, *Le Mariage de Figaro* Restif de la Bretonne, *La Paysanne pervertie*		
	R. E. Raspe, *Wunderbare Reisen . . . und lustige Abenteuer des Freiherrn von Münchhausen* Kant, *Grundlegung zu einer Metaphysik der Sitten* K. P. Moritz, *Anton Reiser* (–1790)	Parini, *La caduta* Cesarotti, *Saggio sulla filosofia delle lingue* Cesarotti, *Saggio sulla filosofia del gusto* M. Borsa, *Del gusto presente in letteratura italiana* Pindemonte, *Poesie campestri*, pub. 1788
		Parini, *La tempesta*; *In morte del maestro Sacchini* Alfieri begins *Bruto primo* (–1789), *Bruto secondo* (–1789) and *Abele* (–1790)
Bernardin de Saint-Pierre, *Paul et Virginie* (in *Études de la Nature*, IV)	Goethe, *Iphigenie auf Tauris* Schiller, *Don Carlos*	Parini, *Il pericolo* Alfieri, definitive ed. of 19 tragedies, Paris, Didot (–1789) Pepoli, *Teatro*, I (–1788, VI)
Death of Buffon	Kant, *Kritik der praktischen Vernunft* Herder, *Volkslieder* (–1789)	Carli, *Antichità Italiche*, I (–1791, V)
Chénier, *Le Serment du Jeu de Paume* Rivarol, *Petit Dictionnaire des grands hommes de la Révolution*	Kant, *Kritik der Urteilskraft* Jean Paul, *Leben des vergnügten Schulmeisterleins Maria Wuz*	Parini, *Il dono* Parini, *La gratitudine* (–1791) Longano, *Viaggi per la Capitanata* Alfieri begins the *Vita* (–1803) G. G. de Rossi, *Commedie*, I (–1798, IV)
Sade, *Justine ou les malheurs de la vertu*		Pepoli, *Tragedie*, I (–1796, VI)

	History	*Science*	*England*
1792			
1793	Second partition of Poland		
1794			Ann Radcliffe, *Mysteries of Udolpho* Paley, *Evidences of Christianity*
1795			
1796	The invasion of Italy by Napoleon Bonaparte	Laplace, *Système du Monde*	
1797			
1798			Austen, *Northanger Abbey* Wordsworth, *Lyrical Ballads*
1799		Laplace, *Mécanique céleste*	
1800			

France	*Germany*	*Italy*
Beaumarchais, *La mère coupable*		A. Verri, *Le notti romane al sepolcro dei Scipioni* (–1804)
	Herder, *Briefe zur Beförderung der Humanität* (–1797)	Casti, *Gli animali parlanti* (–1802) Alfieri, *Il misogallo* (–1799) Mascheroni, *Invito a Lesbia Cidonia*
Chénier, *Iambes* (pub. 1819)		Monti, *La Bassvilliana*
		Carli, *Della disuguaglianza fisica, morale, civile fra gli uomini* Denina, *Considérations d'un italien sur l'Italie* (–1795) Sogràfi, *Le convenienze teatrali*
Condorcet, *Esquisse d'un tableau historique des progrès de l'esprit humain* Sade, *Aline et Valcour*	Schiller, *Über naïve und sentimentalische Dichtung* Goethe, *Wilhelm Meisters Lehrjahre* (–1796)	Parini, *Sul vestire alla ghigliottina* Parini, *Alla Musa* Pindemonte, *Prose campestri*
Restif de la Bretonne, *Monsieur Nicolas* (–1797)		
Sade, *La Nouvelle Justine* Rivarol, *De l'homme intellectuel et moral*		C. Gozzi, *Memorie inutili* Monti, *Prometeo*
Restif de la Bretonne, *L'Anti-Justine*		Alfieri, *Alceste seconda*
Mme de Staël, *De la littérature*		Alfieri, *Commedie* (–1803) Monti, *In morte di Lorenzo Mascheroni*

Bibliography

GENERAL

Cassell's Encyclopaedia of World Literature, 3 vols., London, 1973.

Penguin Companion to Literature, Vol. 2, *Europe*, Harmondsworth, 1969.

The Year's Work in Modern Language Studies (published yearly for the Modern Humanities Research Association), 1931 onwards.

New Cambridge Modern History, Vols. VI–VIII, 1969.

Histoire générale des civilisations, ed. M. Crouset, Vol. V.

Le XVIIIe siècle, révolution intellectuelle, technique et politique. By R. Mousnier, E. Labrousse and M. Bouloiseau, Paris, 1933.

Anderson, M. S., *Europe in the 18th Century 1713–89*, London, 2nd ed., 1976.

Beloff, M., *The Age of Absolutism, 1660–1815*, London, 1954.

Berlin, Isaiah, *The Age of Enlightenment; the 18th Century Philosophers*, New York, 1956.

Vico and Herder: Two studies in the history of ideas, London, 1976.

Bury, J. B., *The Idea of Progress*, London, 1928.

Gay, Peter, *The Enlightenment: An Interpretation*, 2 vols., London, 1967–70.

Ginsberg, M., *The Idea of Progress*, London, 1953.

Hampson, N., *The Enlightenment* (Pelican History of European Thought, Vol. IV), Harmondsworth, 1968.

Hazard, P., *The European Mind (1680–1715)*, tr. J. L. May, London, 1953.

European Thought in the 18th Century, tr. J. L. May, London, 1954.

Ogg, D., *Europe of the Ancien Régime: 1715–1783* (Fontana History of Europe), London, 1965.

Pollard, S., *The Idea of Progress: History and Society*, London, 1968.

Préclin, E., *Le XVIIIe Siècle* (Clio Series), Paris, 1952.

Sampson, R. V., *Progress in the Age of Reason*, London, 1956.

Smith, Preserved, *The Enlightenment, 1687–1776* (A History of Modern Culture, Vol. II), New York, 1934.

Talmon, J. L., *The Rise of Totalitarian Democracy*, Boston, 1952.

Tieghem, P. van, *Le Préromantisme: Études d'histoire littéraire européenne*, 2 vols., Paris, 1924–30.

Venturi, F., *Utopia and Reform in the Enlightenment*, Cambridge, 1971.
White, R. J., *Europe in the 18th Century*, London, 1965.
Willey, B., *The Eighteenth-Century Background*, London, 1940.
Wolf, A., *A History of Science, Technology and Philosophy in the Eighteenth Century*, 2 vols., London, 1938.

I. ENGLAND

(i) *General*

Clifford, J. L., ed., *Eighteenth-Century English Literature: Modern Essays in Criticism*, New York/London, 1959.
Dobrée, B., *English Literature in the Early Eighteenth Century* (Oxford History of English Literature, Vol. VII), London, 1959.
Bredvold, L. I., *The Literature of the Restoration and the Eighteenth Century*, New York, 1950.
Ford, B., ed., *From Dryden to Johnson* (Pelican Guide to English Literature, Vol. IV), Harmondsworth, 1957.
Fussell, P., *The Rhetorical World of Augustan Humanism*, New York, 1965.
Hilles, F. W., and Bloom, H., eds., *From Sensibility to Romanticism*, New York, 1965.
Hilles, F. W., ed., *The Age of Johnson*, New Haven and London, 1949.
Humphreys, A. R., *The Augustan World*, London, 1954.
Lonsdale, R., ed., *Dryden to Johnson* (Sphere History of Literature in the English Language, Vol. IV), London, 1971.
Price, M., *To the Palace of Wisdom*, New York, 1964.
Price, M., ed., *The Restoration and the Eighteenth Century*, (Oxford Anthology of English Literature), New York, 1973.
Rogers, P., *Grub Street: Studies in a Sub-Culture*, London, 1972.
Stephen, L., *English Literature and Society in the Eighteenth Century*, London, 1904.
Tucker, Susie I., *Enthusiasm: A Study in Semantic Change*, Cambridge, 1972.
Willey, B., *The Eighteenth-Century Background*, London, 1940.

(ii) *Poetry*

Chalker, J., *The English Georgic: A Study in the Development of a Form*, London, 1971.

Davie, D., *Purity of Diction in English Verse*, London, 1952.
Davie, D., ed., *The Late Augustans: Longer Poems of the Later Eighteenth Century* (an anthology), London, 1958.
Jack, I., *Augustan Satire*, London, 1952.
Johnson, S., *Lives of the Poets*, London, 1779–81.
Rogers, P., *The Augustan Vision*, London, 1974.
Røstvig, Maren-Sofie, *The Happy Man: Studies in the Metamorphosis of a Classical Ideal, Vol. ii, 1700–1760*, Oslo, 1958; 1971.
Sutherland, J., *A Preface to Eighteenth-Century Poetry*, London, 1948.
Trickett, Rachel, *The Honest Muse: A Study in Augustan Verse*, London, 1967.

(iii) Novel

Alter, R., *Rogue's Progress: Studies in the Picaresque Novel*, Cambridge, Mass., and London, 1964.
Braudy, L., *Narrative Form in History and Fiction*, Princeton, 1970.
Brissenden, R. F., *Virtue in Distress: Studies in the Novel of Sentiment from Richardson to Sade*, London, 1974.
Iser, W., *The Implied Reader*, Baltimore and London, 1974.
Kettle, A., *An Introduction to the English Novel*, Vol. I, London, 1951.
McKillop, A. D., *Early Masters of English Fiction*, Lawrence, 1956.
Paulson, R., *Satire and the Novel in Eighteenth-century England*, New Haven and London, 1967.
Preston, J., *The Created Self, The Reader's Role in Eighteenth-Century Fiction*, London, 1970.
Pritchett, V. S., *The Living Novel*, London, 1946.
Richetti, J. J., *Popular Fiction before Richardson*, London, 1969.
Scott, W., *Lives of the English Novelists*, 1821–4.
Spearman, Diana, *The Novel and Society*, London, 1966.
Spector, R., ed., *Essays on the Eighteenth-Century Novel*, Indiana, 1965.
Van Ghent, Dorothy, *The English Novel, Form and Function*, New York, 1953.
Watt, I., *The Rise of the Novel*, London, 1957.
Wurzbach, Natascha, *The Novel in Letters*, London, 1969 (a selection of texts).

(iv) Drama

Bateson, F. W., *English Comic Drama, 1700–1750*, London, 1929.

Donaldson, I., *The World Upside-Down: Comedy from Johnson to Fielding*, London, 1970.
Loftis, J., *Comedy and Society from Congreve to Fielding*, Stanford, 1959.
The Politics of Drama in Augustan England, New York/London, 1963.
Nicoll, A., *A History of English Drama*, 6 vols., Cambridge, 1952–9.
Taylor, W. D., ed., *Eighteenth-Century Comedy*, 1929 (a selection of texts, rev. S. Trussler, London, 1969).
Trussler, S., *Burlesque Plays of the Eighteenth-Century*, London, 1969.
Waith, E. M., *The Herculean Hero*, London, 1962.
Ideas of Greatness: Heroic Drama in England, London, 1971.

(*v*) *Aesthetic Ideas*

Allen, G. W., and Clark, H. H., *Literary Criticism from Pope to Croce* (selections), Detroit, 1962.
Atkins, J. W. H., *English Literary Criticism: 17th and 18th Centuries*, London, 1951.
Bate, W. J., *From Classic to Romantic. Premises of Taste in 18th century England*, Cambridge, Mass., 1946.
Folkierski, W., *Entre le classicisme et le romantisme*, Paris, 1925.
Kames, Lord, *Elements of Criticism*, 3 vols., London, 1962.
Ker, W. P., *Taste and Criticism in the 18th Century*, Oxford, 1900.
Monk, S. M., *The Sublime*, London, 1935.
Needham, H. A., *Taste and Criticism in the 18th Century*, London, 1952 (selection of texts).
Robertson, J. C., *Studies in the Genesis of Romantic Theory in the 18th Century*, Cambridge, 1923.
Winsatt, W. K., and Brooks, C., *Literary Criticism: A Short History*, London, 1957.

(*vi*) *Authors*

CONGREVE

Complete plays, ed. H. Davis, Chicago, 1967.

DEFOE

Novels and Selected Writings, Oxford, 1927–8.
Robinson Crusoe (Oxford English Novels), ed. J. D. Crowley, London, 1977.
Moll Flanders (Oxford English Novels), ed. G. A. Starr, London, 1972.
Earle, P., *The World of Defoe*, London, 1976.

Hunter, J. P., *The Reluctant Pilgrim. Defoe's Emblematic Method and Quest for Form in Robinson Crusoe*, Baltimore, 1966.

Moore, J. R., *Defoe: Citizen of the Modern World*, Chicago, 1958.

Novak, M., *Defoe and the Nature of Man*, London, 1963.

Richetti, J. J., *Defoe's Narratives*, London, 1975.

Starr, G. A. L., *Defoe and Casuistry*, Princeton, 1971.

Defoe and Spiritual Autobiography, Princeton, 1965.

DRYDEN

Poetical Works, ed, J. Kinsley, London, 1958.

Harth, P., *Contexts of Dryden's Thought*, Chicago, 1968.

King, B., ed., *Dryden's Mind and Art*, Edinburgh, 1969.

Kinsley, J. and H., eds., *Dryden: The Critical Heritage*, London, 1971.

Miner, E., *Dryden's Poetry*, Bloomington, Indiana, 1967.

Van Doren, M., *Dryden: A Study of his Poetry*, Bloomington, Indiana, 1946.

FIELDING

Complete Works, ed. W. E. Henley *et al.*, 1903, reprinted London, 1967.

Complete Works, ed. W. B. Coley *et al.* (The Wesleyan Edition, not yet completed), London, 1967.

Alter, R., *Fielding and the Nature of the Novel*, Cambridge, Mass., 1968.

Battestin, M. C., *The Moral Basis of Fielding's Art: A Study of Joseph Andrews*, Middletown, Conn., 1959.

Digeon, A., *Les Romans de Fielding*, Paris, 1923.

Ehrenpreis, I., *Fielding's 'Tom Jones'*, London, 1964.

Harrison, B., *Henry Fielding's 'Tom Jones': The Novelist as Moral Philosopher*, Brighton, 1975.

Hatfield, G. W., *Henry Fielding and the Language of Irony*, Chicago, 1968.

Hunter, J. P., *Occasional Form: Henry Fielding and the Chains of Circumstance*, Baltimore and London, 1975.

Paulson, R., ed., *Fielding: A Collection of Critical Essays*, Englewood Cliffs, NJ, 1962.

Paulson, R., and Lockwood, T., *Henry Fielding: The Critical Heritage*, London, 1969.

Rawson, C. J., *Henry Fielding and the Augustan Ideal under Stress*, London, 1972.

Wright, A., *Henry Fielding, Mask and Feast*, London, 1965.

GAY

Poetry and Prose, ed. V. A. Dearing and C. E. Beckwith, London, 1974.

Empson, W., *Some Versions of Pastoral*, London, 1935.

Gagey, E. M., *Ballad Opera*, New York, 1937.
Schulz, W. E., *Gay's 'Beggar's Opera'*, New Haven, 1923.
Spacks, Patricia M., *John Gay*, New York, 1965.

GOLDSMITH

Collected Works, ed. A. Friedman, London, 1966.
Poems, ed. R. Lonsdale, Harlow, 1969 (with Gray and Collins).
Ginger, J., *A Notable Man*, London, 1977.
Halsband, R. H., *The True Genius of Oliver Goldsmith*, Baltimore, 1969.

GRAY

Poems, ed. R. Lonsdale, Harlow, 1969 (with Collins and Goldsmith).
Spacks, Patricia M., *The Poetry of Vision*, Cambridge, Mass., 1967.
Starr, H. W., ed., *Elegy Written in a Country Churchyard* (Merrill Literary Casebook Series), 1968.
Twentieth-century Interpretations of Gray's Elegy, Englewood Cliffs, NJ, 1968.

JOHNSON

Works (Yale Edition), ed. A. T. Hazen *et al.*, New Haven, 1958– .
Complete English Poems (Penguin English Poets), ed. J. D. Fleeman, Harmondsworth, 1971.
Bate, W. J., *The Achievement of Samuel Johnson*, New York, 1955.
Boswell, J., *The Life of Johnson*, ed. G. B. Hill, rev. L. F. Powell, London, 1934–65.
Boulton, J. T., ed., *Johnson: The Critical Heritage*, London, 1971.
Bronson, B. H., *Johnson and Boswell*, Berkeley, 1944.
Clifford, J. L., *Young Samuel Johnson*, New York, 1955.
Greene, D., *Samuel Johnson*, New York, 1970.
Hilles, F. W., ed., *New Light on Dr Johnson*, New Haven, 1960.
Wimsatt, W. K., *The Prose Style of Samuel Johnson*, New Haven, 1941.

POPE

Poems (Twickenham Edition), ed. J. Butt and others, London, 1939–67.
Prose Works, ed. N. Ault, Oxford, 1935.
Brower, R. A., *Alexander Pope: The Poetry of Allusion*, London, 1959.
Hunt, J. D., ed., *Pope, The Rape of the Lock: A Casebook*, London, 1968.
Knight, G. W., *Poetry of Alexander Pope, Laureate of Peace*, London, 1954.
Mack, M., *The Garden and the City*, London, 1970.
Mack, M., ed. *Essential Articles for the Study of Alexander Pope*, Hamden, Conn., 1964.
Rogers, P., *An Introduction to Pope*, London, 1976.

Rousseau, G. S., ed., *Twentieth-Century Interpretations of The Rape of the Lock: A Collection of Critical Essays*, Englewood Cliffs, N.J., 1969.
Sitter, J. E., *The Poetry of Pope's Dunciad*, Minnesota/London, 1971.
Spacks, Patricia M., *An Argument of Images: The Poetry of Alexander Pope*, Cambridge, Mass., 1971.
Spence, J., *Observations, Anecdotes and Characters of Books and Men*, 2 vols., ed. J. M. Osborn, London, 1966.
Tillotson, G., *On the Poetry of Pope*, 1938; 2nd ed., London, 1950.
Williams, A. L., *Pope's Dunciad*, London, 1955.

RICHARDSON

Novels, Oxford, 1929–31.
Pamela, ed. T. C. Duncan Eaves and B. Kimpel, 1971 (based on the first edition).
Selected Letters, ed. J. Carroll, London, 1964.
Brissenden, R. F., *Samuel Richardson* (Writers and their Work), London, 1958.
Brophy, Elizabeth B., *Samuel Richardson: The Triumph of Craft*, Knoxville, Tennessee, 1974.
Carroll, J., ed., *Samuel Richardson: A Collection of Critical Essays*, Englewood Cliffs, NJ, 1969.
Doody, Margaret A., *A Natural Passion: A Study of the Novels of Samuel Richardson*, London, 1974.
Duncan Eaves, T. C., and Kimpel, B., *Samuel Richardson*, London, 1971.
Fiedler, L. A., *Love and Death in the American Novel*, New York, 1960.
Golden, M., *Richardson's Characters*, Ann Arbor, 1963.
Gopnik, I., *A Theory of Style and Richardson's Clarissa*, The Hague, 1970.
Kinkead-Weekes, M., *Samuel Richardson: Dramatic Novelist*, London, 1973.
Konigsberg, I., *Samuel Richardson and the Dramatic Novel*, Lexington, 1968.
McKillop, A. D., *Samuel Richardson, Printer and Novelist*, N. Carolina, 1936.

SMOLLETT

Novels, Oxford, 1925–6.
Boucé, P.-G., *The Novels of Tobias Smollett*, London, 1976.
Knapp, L. M., *Smollett: Doctor of Men and Manners*, Princeton, 1949.
Martz, L. L., *The Later Career of Smollett*, 1942.
Rousseau, G. S., and Boucé, P.-G., *Tobias Smollett: Bicentennial Essays Presented to Lewis M. Knapp*, New York, 1971.
Spector, R. D., *Tobias Smollett*, New York, 1968.

STERNE

Tristram Shandy, ed. J. A. Work, 1940.

Cash, A. H., *Sterne's Comedy of Moral Sentiments*, Pittsburgh, 1966.

Cash, A. H., and Stedmond, J. M., eds., *The Winged Skull: Papers for the Laurence Sterne Bicentenary Conference at the University of York*, London, 1971.

Fluchère, H., *Laurence Sterne from Tristram to Yorick*, London, 1965.

Traugott, J., *Tristram Shandy's World: Sterne's Philosophical Rhetoric*, Berkeley, 1954.

Traugott, J., ed., *Laurence Sterne: A Collection of Critical Essays*, Englewood Cliffs, N.J., 1968.

SWIFT

Prose Works, ed. H. Davis, London, 1939–64.

Poems, ed. H. Williams, 2nd ed., London, 1958.

Ehrenpreis, I., *The Personality of Jonathan Swift*, London, 1958.

Swift: The Man, His Work and the Age, London, 1962– .

Harth, P., *Swift and Anglican Rationalism*, Chicago, 1961.

Price, M., *Swift's Rhetorical Art*, New Haven, 1953.

Quintana, R., *The Mind and Art of Jonathan Swift*, New York, 1936.

Rawson, C. J., ed., *Focus: Swift*, London, 1971.

Williams, Kathleen, *Swift and the Age of Compromise*, Lawrence/London, 1959.

THOMSON

The Seasons, ed. J. Sambrook, London, 1972.

Cohen, R., *The Unfolding of the Seasons*, Baltimore, 1970.

2. FRANCE

(*i*) *Bibliography*

Cabeen, D. C., *A Critical Bibliography of French Literature*, Vol. IV, *The Eighteenth Century*, ed. G. R. Havens and D. F. Bond, 1951; *Supplement*, ed. R. A. Brooks, Syracuse, New York, 1968.

Giraud, Jeanne, *Manuel de bibliographie littéraire pour les XVIe, XVIIe et XVIIIe siècles français*, Paris, 1939.

Klapp, O., *Bibliographie der französichen Literaturwissenschaft*, Frankfurt am Main, 1960.

Lanson, G., *Manuel bibliographique de la littérature française moderne, XVIIIe siècle*, 1923 (with *Supplément*).

(*ii*) *General*

The Oxford Companion to French Literature, ed. Paul Harvey and H. J. H. Heseltine, London, 1959.

Dictionnaire des lettres françaises, ed. G. Grente, 2 vols., Paris, 1960.

Histoire des littératures, ed. R. P. Queneau, Vol. 5 (*Littératures françaises*), Paris, 1958.

Le Dix-huitième Siècle, Paris, 1969– (annual publication).

Studies on Voltaire and the 18th Century, ed. T. Besterman, Geneva and Banbury.

The Age of the Enlightenment: An Anthology of 18th Century French Literature, ed. O. E. Fellows and N. L. Torrey, New York, 1942.

Abraham, P., and Desné, R., *Histoire littéraire de la France*, Vol. III (1715–89), Paris, 1969.

Adam, A., and Lerminier, G., *La Littérature francaise*, 2 vols., Paris, 1968.

Atkinson, G., *The Extraordinary Voyage in French Literature from 1700 to 1720*, New York, 1922.

Le Sentiment de la nature et le retour à la vie simple, 1690–1740, Geneva, 1960.

Atkinson, G., and Keller, A. C., *Prelude to the Enlightenment: French Literature, 1690–1740*, London, 1971.

The Sentimental Revolution: French Writers from 1690–1740, Seattle, London. 1965.

Barber, E. G., *The Bourgeoisie in 18th Century France*, Princeton, NJ, 1955.

Barber, W. H., and others, *The Age of the Enlightenment: Studies Presented to Theodore Besterman*, Edinburgh, London, 1967.

Berlin, I., *The Age of the Enlightenment: The 18th Century Philosophers*, New York, 1956.

Brulé, A., *Les Gens de lettres*, Paris, 1929.

Chinard, G., *L'Amérique et le rêve exotique au XVII etc au XVIIIe siècles*, 1913.

Cobban, A., *A History of Modern France*, Vol. I, 1715–99, Harmondsworth, 1957.

Cruickshank, J., ed., *French Literature and its Background*, Vol. III, *The Eighteenth Century*, London, 1968.

Etiemble, R., *L'Orient philosophique au XVIIIe siècle*, Paris, 1958.

Fabre, J., *Lumières et romantisme*, Paris, 1963.

Ford, F. L., *Robe and Sword: The Regrouping of French Aristocracy after Louis XIV*, Cambridge, Mass., 1953.

Gay, P., ed., *Eighteenth Century Studies presented to Arthur M. Wilson*, Hanover, New Hampshire, 1972.

Glotz, M., and Maire, M., *Les Salons au XVIIIe siècle*, Paris, 1949.

Gooch, G. P., *Four French Salons*, London, 1951.

Goyard-Fabre, S., *La Philosophie des lumières en France*, Paris, 1972.

Green, F. C., *Minuet: A Critical Survey of French–English Literary Ideas in the Eighteenth Century*, Cambridge, 1935.

Eighteenth Century France: Six Essays, New York, 1964.

Grimsley, R., *From Montesquieu to Laclos: Studies in the French Enlightenment*, Geneva, 1974.

Laufer, R., *Style rococo, style des lumières*, Paris, 1963.

Launay, M., and Mailhos, G., *Introduction à la vie littéraire au XVIIIe siècle*, Paris, 1968.

Leroy, M., *Histoire des idées sociales en France*, Paris, 1946.

Lough, J., *An Introduction to Eighteenth Century France*, London, 1960.

Manuel, F., *The Eighteenth Century Confronts the Gods*, Cambridge, Mass., 1959.

Prophets of Paris, New York, 1965.

Martino, P., *L'Orient dans la littérature française du XVIIe au XVIIIe siècle*, Paris, 1906.

Monglond, A., *Histoire intérieure du préromantisme français*, 2 vols., Paris, 1929.

Moore, W. G., and others, *The French Mind: Studies in Honour of G. Rudler*, Oxford, 1952.

Niklaus, R., *A Literary History of France: The Eighteenth Century*, London, 1970.

Pellisson, M., *Les Hommes de Lettres au XVIIIe siècle*, Paris, 1911.

Perkins, J., *The Concept of the Self in the French Enlightenment*, Geneva, 1969.

Pomeau, R., *L'Europe des lumières*, Paris, 1965.

Poulet, G., *Études sur le temps humain*, Paris, 1949.

La Distance intérieure, Paris, 1952.

La Mesure de l'instant, Paris, 1968.

Le Point de départ, Paris, 1964.

Sagnac, P., *La Formation de la société francaise moderne*, 2 vols., Paris, 1945–6.

Sée, H., *La France économique et sociale au XVIIIe siècle*, Paris, 1925.

Trahard, P., *Les Maîtres de la sensibilité française au XVIIIe siècle*, 4 vols., Paris, 1931–3.

Vier, J., *Histoire de la littérature française, XVIIIe siècle*, 2 vols., Paris, 1965, 1970.

(iii) Literature of Ideas

Adam, P., *Le Mouvement philosophique dans la première moitié du XVIIIe siècle*, Paris, 1967.

Barber, W. H., *Leibniz in France, from Arnauld to Voltaire*, Oxford, 1955.

Becker, C., *The Heavenly City of the Eighteenth Century Philosophers*, New Haven, Connecticut, 1960.

Belin, J. P., *Le Mouvement philosophique de 1748 à 1789*, Paris, 1913.

Bonno, G., *La Culture et la civilisation britannique devant l'opinion française au XVIIIe siècle*, Philadelphia, 1948.

Brumfitt, J. H., *The French Enlightenment*, London, 1972.

Brunel, L., *Les Philosophes et l'Académie française au XVIIIe siècle*, Paris, 1884.

Brunet, P., *L'Introduction des théories de Newton en France au XVIIIe siècle*, Paris, 1931.

Buchdahl, G., *The Image of Locke and Newton in the Age of Reason*, London, 1961.

Callot, E., *La Philosophie de la vie au XVIIIe siècle*, Paris, 1965.

Carré, J. R., *La Philosophie de Fontenelle ou le sourire de la raison*, Paris, 1932.

Cassirer, E., *The Philosophy of the Enlightenment*, trans. F. C. A. Koelln and J. P. Pettegrove, Princeton, NJ, 1951.

Cobban, A., *In Search of Humanity*, New York, 1960.

Crocker, L. G., *The Age of Crisis: Man and World in Eighteenth Century French Thought*, Baltimore, 1959.

Nature and Culture: Ethical Thought in the French Enlightenment, Baltimore, 1963.

Delvolvé, J., *Religion, critique et philosophie positive chez P. Bayle*, Paris, 1906.

Desné, R., *Les Matérialistes français de 1750 à 1800*, Paris, 1965.

Dieckmann, H., *Le Philosophe: texte and interpretation*, Saint-Louis, 1948.

Dupront, A., *Les Lettres, les sciences et les arts dans la société française de la deuxième moitié du XVIIIe siècle*, Paris, 1963.

Dupront, A., Ehrard, J., and others, *Livre et société*, Paris, 1965.

Ehrard, J., *L'Idée de la nature en France dans la première moitié du XVIIIe siècle*, 2 vols., Paris, 1963

Fontenelle, B. le B. de, *Entretiens sur la pluralité des mondes*, ed. R. Shackleton, London, 1955.

Fox, J., ed., and others, *Studies in French Literature Presented to R. Niklaus*, Exeter, 1975.

Frankel, C., *The Faith of Reason: Its Idea and Progress in the French Enlightenment*, New York, 1940.
Gay, P., *The Party of Humanity. Studies in the French Enlightenment*, New York, 1964.
Grégoire, F., *Fontenelle, une philosophie désabusée*, Nancy, 1947.
Grosclaude, P., *Malesherbes: témoin et interprète de son temps*, 1961.
Guy, B., 'The French image of China before and after Voltaire', in *Studies on Voltaire, XXI*, 1963.
Hampson, N., *The Enlightenment*, Harmondsworth, 1968.
Hastings, H., *Man and Beast in French Thought of the Eighteenth Century*, Baltimore, 1936.
Havens, G. R., *The Age of Ideas*, New York, 1955.
Hazard, P., *La Crise de la conscience européenne*, 3 vols., Paris, 1935.
La Pensée européenne au XVIIIe siècle de Montesquieu à Lessing, 3 vols., Paris, 1936.
Hearnshaw, F. J. C., *Social and Political Ideas of French Thinkers of the Age of Reason*, London, 1930.
Kiernan, C., 'Science and the Enlightenment in 18th century France', in *Studies on Voltaire*, LIX, 1968.
Labrousse, E., *Pierre Bayle*, 2 vols., The Hague, 1963–4.
Lichtenberger, A., *Le Socialisme au XVIIIe siècle*, Paris, 1895.
Lively, J. F., *The Enlightenment* (selected texts), London, 1966.
Lovejoy, A. O., *The Great Chain of Being*, Cambridge, Mass., London, 1936.
Essays in the History of Ideas, Baltimore, 1948.
McCloy, S. T., *The Humanitarian Movement in 18th Century France*, 1957.
Martin, K., *French Liberal Thought in the 18th Century*, London, 1929.
Mason, H. T., *P. Bayle and Voltaire*, London, 1963.
Mauzi, R., *L'Idée du bonheur au XVIIIe siècle*, Paris, 1960.
Mercier, R., *La Réhabilitation de la nature humaine (1700–50)*, Villemomble, 1960.
Meslier, J., *Oeuvres complètes*, ed. J. Deprun, etc., 3 vols., 1969–70.
Mornet, D., *Les Origines intellectuelles de la Revolution française*, Paris, 1934.
La Pensée française au XVIIIe siècle, Paris, 1932.
Les Sciences de la Nature au XVIIIe siècle, Paris, 1911.
Mousnier, R., *Progrès scientifique et technique au XVIIIe siècle*, Paris, 1958.
Palmer, R. R., *Catholics and Unbelievers in 18th Century France*, Princeton, NJ, 1939.
Pappas, J., ed., *Essays on Diderot and the Enlightenment in Honour of Otis Fellows*, Geneva, 1974.
Réau, L., *L'Europe française au siècle des lumières*, Paris, 1938.

Rex, W., *Essays on P. Bayle and Religious Controversy*, The Hague, 1965.

Roger, J., *Les Sciences de la vie dans la pensée française du XVIIIe siècle*, Paris, 1963.

Roustan, M., *Les Philosophes et la société française au XVIIIe siècle*, Paris, 1906.

Saulnier, V. L., *La Littérature française du siècle philosophique* (Que sais-je? series), Paris, revised ed., 1958.

Spink, J. S., *French Free-Thought from Gassendi to Voltaire*, London, 1960.

Starobinski, J., *L'Invention de la liberté*, Geneva, 1965.

Vartanian, A., *Diderot and Descartes, A Study of Scientific Naturalism in the Enlightenment*, Princeton, NJ, 1953.

Vernière, P., *Spinoza et la pensée française avant la Révolution*, 2 vols., Paris, 1954.

Vyverberg, H., *Historical pessimism in the French Enlightenment*, Cambridge, Mass., 1958.

Wade, I. O., *The Clandestine Organization and Diffusion of Philosophic Ideas in France from 1700 to 1750*, Princeton, NJ, 1938.

White, R. J., *The Anti-Philosophers, A Study of the Philosophes in 18th Century France*, London, 1970.

D'ALEMBERT

Oeuvres philosophiques, historiques et littéraires de d'Alembert, 5 vols., Paris, 1821.

Discours préliminaire de l'Encyclopédie, ed. F. Picavet, 1894.

Grimsley, R., *Jean d'Alembert, 1717–83*, London, 1963.

Hankins, T. L., *Jean d'Alembert: Science and the Enlightenment*, London, 1970.

BUFFON

Oeuvres complètes de Buffon, ed. Lanessan and N. de Buffon, 14 vols., Paris, 1884–5.

Oeuvres philosophiques, ed. J. Piveteau, M. Fréchet and C. Bruneau, Paris, 1954.

Histoire naturelle, générale et particulière, 44 vols., Paris, 1749–1804.

Histoire naturelle des minéraux, 5 vols., Paris, 1783–8.

Les Époques de la Nature, crit. ed. J. Roger, Paris, 1962.

De l'homme, ed. M. Duchet, Paris, 1971.

Correspondance générale, ed. H. de Buffon, 2 vols., Paris, 1885.

Bertin, L., *et al.*, *Buffon*, Paris, 1952.

Fellows, O. E., and Milliken, S. F., *Buffon*, New York, 1972.

CONDILLAC

Oeuvres philosophiques, ed. G. Le Roy, 3 vols., Paris, 1947–51.

Essai sur l'origine des connaissances humaines [ed. C. Porset], *précédé de L'Archéologie du frivole par J. Derrida*, Paris, 1973.
Knight, I. F., *The Geometric Spirit. The Abbé de Condillac and the French Enlightenment*, New Haven, Connecticut, 1968.
Lefèvre, R., *Condillac ou la joie de vivre* (avec choix de textes), Paris, 1966.
Le Roy, G., *La Psychologie de Condillac*, Paris, 1937.

CONDORCET
Oeuvres de Condorcet, ed. A. Condorcet-O'Connor and F. Arage, 12 vols., Paris, 1847–9.
Sketch for a Historical Picture of the Progress of the Human Mind, ed. J. Barraclough and S. Hampshire, New York, 1955.
Baker, K. M., *Condorcet: from Natural Philosophy to Social Mathematics*, Chicago, 1975.
Bouissounouse, J., *Condorcet: le philosophe dans la Révolution*, Paris, 1962.
Cahen, L., *Condorcet et la Révolution française*, Paris, 1904.
Cento, A., *Condorcet e l'idea di progresso*, Florence, 1956.
Granger, G. G., *La mathématique sociale du marquis de Condorcet*, Paris, 1956.
Manuel, F. E., *The Prophets of Paris*, Cambridge, Mass., 1962.
Schapiro, J. S., *Condorcet and the rise of Liberalism*, New York, 1934.

DIDEROT
Oeuvres complètes, ed. J. Assézat and M. Tourneux, 20 vols., Paris, 1875–7.
Oeuvres complètes, édition chronologique, ed. R. Lewinter, 15 vols., Paris, 1969.
Oeuvres complètes, ed. H. Dieckmann, Hermann, Paris, 1975– . (To be completed in 33 volumes.)
Oeuvres esthétiques, ed. P. Vernière, Paris, 1959.
Oeuvres philosophiques, ed. P. Vernière, Paris, 1956.
Oeuvres politiques, ed. P. Vernière, Paris, 1963.
Oeuvres romanesques, ed. P. Vernière, Paris, 1959.
Diderot: interpreter of nature: selected writings, trans. J. Stewart and J. Kemp, New York, 1963.
Rameau's Nephew and d'Alembert's Dream, trans. L. Tancock, Harmondsworth, 1966.
Correspondance, ed. G. Roth, 16 vols., Paris, 1955–70.
Salons, ed. J. Seznec and J. Adhémar., 4 vols., Paris, 1957–67.

Diderot Studies, ed. O. E. Fellows, N. L. Torrey, 1949–.

Belaval, Y., *L'Esthétique sans paradoxe de Diderot*, Paris, 1950.

Benot, Y., *Diderot, de l'athéisme à l'anticolonialisme*, Paris, 1970.

Cartwright, M. T., 'Diderot critique d'art et le problème de l'expression', in *Diderot Studies*, XIII, 1969.

Crocker, L. G., *Diderot the Embattled Philosopher*, Michigan, 1954.

Diderot's Chaotic Order: Approach to Synthesis, Princeton, NJ, 1974.

Two Diderot Studies: Ethics and Aesthetics, Baltimore, 1952.

Chouillet, J., *La Formation des idées esthétiques de Diderot, 1745–63*, Paris, 1973.

Cru, R. L., *Diderot as a Disciple of English Thought*, New York, 1913.

Dieckmann, H., *Cinq Leçons sur Diderot*, Geneva, 1959.

Doolittle, J., *Rameau's Nephew. A Study of Diderot's 'Second Satire'*, Geneva, 1960.

Duchet, M., and Launay, M., *Entretiens sur 'Le Neveu de Rameau'*, Paris, 1967.

Freedman, A. G., *Diderot and Sterne*, New York, 1955.

Funt, D., 'Diderot and the Aesthetics of the Enlightenment', in *Diderot Studies*, XI, .

Gorny, L. A., *Diderot un grand européen*, Paris, 1971.

Guyot, C., *Diderot par lui-même*, Paris, 1953.

Hermand, P., *Les idées morales de Diderot*, Paris, 1923.

Josephs, H., *Diderot's Dialogue of Gesture and Language*, Ohio, 1969.

Kempf, R., *Diderot et le roman ou le Démon de la Présence*, Paris, 1964.

Le Gras, J., *Diderot et l'Encyclopédie* (Grands Événements Littéraires), Paris, 1942.

Luxembourg, L. K., *Francis Bacon and Denis Diderot: Philosophers of Science*, Copenhagen, 1967.

May, G., *Quatre Visages de Denis Diderot*, Paris, 1951.

Diderot et 'La Religieuse', New Haven and Paris, 1951.

Mayer, J., *Diderot, l'homme de science*, Rennes, 1959.

Mesnard, P., *Le Cas Diderot*, Paris, 1952.

Mornet, D., *Diderot, l'homme et l'oeuvre*, Paris, 1966.

Mølbjerg, H., *Aspects de l'esthétique de Diderot*, Copenhagen, 1964.

Mortier, R., *Diderot en Allemagne*, Paris, 1954.

O'Gorman, D., *Diderot the Satirist: 'Le Neveu de Rameau' and related works*, New York, 1971.

Proust, J., *Diderot et l'Encyclopédie*, Paris, 1962.

Lectures de Diderot, Paris, 1974.

Schwartz, J., *Diderot and Montaigne*, Geneva, 1966.

Sherman, C., *Diderot and the Art of Dialogue*, Geneva, 1976.

Strugnell, A., *Diderot's Politics*, New York, 1973.

Thomas, J., *L'Humanisme de Diderot*, Paris, 1933.

Vartanian, A., *Diderot and Descartes, a Study of Scientific Naturalism in the Enlightenment*, Princeton, 1953.
Venturi, F., *Jeunesse de Diderot*, Paris, 1930.
Wilson, A. M., *Diderot*, New York, 1974.

THE ENCYCLOPÉDIE

The Encyclopédie of Diderot and d'Alembert: Selected articles, ed. J. Lough, Cambridge, 1954.

Auroux, S., *L'Encyclopédie: 'grammaire' et 'langue' au XVIIIe siècle*, Mame, 1973.
Barber, G. G., *Book-making in Diderot's Encyclopédie*, Farnborough, 1973.
Le Bicentenaire de l'Encyclopédie (*Education nationale*, special number, Vol. 16, May 8, 1952).
Delorne, S., and Taton, R., eds., *L'Encyclopédie et le progrès des sciences et des techniques*, Paris, 1952.
Deuxième centenaire de l'Encyclopédie française (*Annales de l'Université de Paris*, special number, Vol. 22, October 1952).
L'Encyclopédie et son rayonnement à l'étranger (*Cahiers de l'Association internationale des études françaises*, Vol. 2, 1952.)
Gordon, D. H., and Torrey, A. L., *The Censoring of Diderot's Encyclopédie and the Re-established Text*, New York, 1974.
Grosclaude, P., *Un Audacieux message: L'Encyclopédie*, Paris, 1951.
Guyot, C., *Le rayonnement de l'Encyclopédie en Suisse française*, Neuchâtel, 1955.
Hubert, R., *Les sciences sociales dans l'Encyclopédie*, Paris, 1923.
Legras, J., *Diderot et l'Encyclopédie*, Paris, 1928.
Lough, J., *The Contributors to the Encyclopédie*, London, 1973.
The Encyclopédie, London, 1973.
The Encyclopédie in Eighteenth Century England and other studies, Newcastle-upon-Tyne, 1970.
Proust, J., *L'Encyclopédie*, Paris, 1965.
Schargo, N., *History in the Encyclopédie*, New York, 1947.
Venturi, F., *Le origini dell'Enciclopedia*, Florence, 1946.

HELVÉTIUS

De l'esprit, ed. Guy Besse, Paris, 1959.
De l'homme, de ses facultés intellectuelles et de son éducation, 1772.
Le Bonheur (poem), 1772.
Oeuvres complètes, ed. La Roche, 14 vols., 1795 and 1818.

d'Andlau, B., *Helvétius seigneur de Vore* (*avec des documents inédits*), Paris, 1939.

Cumming, I., *Helvétius: His Life and Place in the History of Educational Thought*, London, 1955.

Horowitz, C., *Helvétius, philosopher of democracy and enlightenment*, New York, 1954.

Keim, A., *Helvétius, sa vie et son oeuvre*, Paris, 1907.

Momdzhian, K. N., *La philosophie d'Helvétius*, trans. from Russian by M. Katsovitch, Moscow, 1959.

Smith, D. W., *Helvétius: a study in persecution*, London, 1965.

D'HOLBACH

Most of his works were published anonymously or under other names.

[Boulanger] *Le Christianisme dévoilé*, 1767.

[Mirabeau] *Le Système de la nature*, 1770.

Système social, 1773.

Politique naturelle, 1774.

Éléments de morale universelle, 1790.

Hubert, R., *D'Holbach et ses amis*, Paris, 1928.

Naville, P. P., *Thiry d'Holbach et la philosophie scientifique du XVIIIe siècle*, Paris, 1943.

Topazio, V. W., *D'Holbach's moral philosophy; its background and development*, Geneva, 1956.

Wickwar, W. H., *Baron d'Holbach, a prelude to the French Revolution*, London, 1935.

LA METTRIE

La Mettrie, Oeuvres philosophiques, London (Berlin), 1751.

L'homme machine: a study in the origins of an idea, critical edition with introduction and notes by A. Vartanian, Princeton, NJ, 1960.

Man a Machine, tr. G. Bussey (bilingual ed.), London, 1912, reprinted 1977.

Histoire naturelle de l'âme, The Hague, 1745.

Discours sur le Bonheur, critical ed. by J. Falvey, in *Studies on Voltaire*, CXXXIV, 1975.

Boissier, R., *La Mettrie, médicin, pamphlétaire et philosophe*, Paris, 1931.

Falvey, J., 'The individualism of La Mettrie', in *Nottingham French Studies*, Vol. 4, 1965.

Lemée, P., *Une figure peu connue: Offray de la Mettrie, 1709–51*, Saint-Servan, Haize, 1925–7.

Rosenfield, L. C., *From beast-machine to man-machine* (preface by P. Hazard), New York, 1941.

MAUPERTUIS

Oeuvres, ed. G. Tonelli, 4 vols., Hildesheim, 1965 (reprint edition).

Maupertuis, le savant et le philosophe (selected texts), edited by E. Callot, Paris, 1964.

Maupertuis, Turgot, Maine de Biran: Sur l'origine du langage, Étude suivie de trois textes, edited by R. Grimsley, Geneva, 1971.

Bachelard, S., *Les polémiques concernant le principe de moindre action au XVIIIe siècle*, 1961.

Brown, H., 'Maupertuis philosophe: Enlightenment and the Berlin Academy', in *Studies on Voltaire*, XXIV, 1963.

Brunet, P., *Maupertuis*, 2 vols., Paris, 1939.

Callot, E., *La philosophie de la vie au XVIIIe siècle*, Paris, 1965.

Dufrenoy, M. C., 'Maupertuis et le progrès scientifique', in *Studies on Voltaire*, XXV, 1963.

MONTESQUIEU

Oeuvres complètes, ed. R. Callois (Bibliothèque de la Pléiade), 2 vols., Paris, 1949–51.

Oeuvres complètes, ed. D. Oster (Éditions du Seuil), Paris, 1964.

Considerations on the Causes of the Greatness of the Romans and their Decline, trans. D. Lowenthal, New York, 1965.

Lettres persanes, ed. P. Vernière, Paris, 1960.

The Persian Letters, edited and translated by J. Robert Loy, New York, 1961.

De l'esprit des lois, ed. R. Derathé, 2 vols., Paris, 1973.

The Spirit of Laws, trans. T. Nugent, introduced by F. Neumann, New York, 1949.

Cabeen, D. C., *A Montesquieu Bibliography*, New York, 1947.

'A Supplementary Montesquieu Bibliography', in *Review internationale de Philosophie*, IX, 1955.

Académie Montesquieu, *Études sur Montesquieu: philosophie sociale et politique* (Archives de lettres modernes), Paris, 1970.

Académie Montesquieu, *Études sur Montesquieu* (Archives des lettres modernes, 158), Paris, 1975.

Actes du Congrès Montesquieu réuni à Bordeaux, 1955, Paris, 1956.

Althusser, L., *Montesquieu: la politique et l'histoire*, Paris, 1959.

Barrière, P., *Un Grand Provincial: Charles de Secondat, baron de la Brède*, Bordeaux, 1946.

Courtney, C. P., *Montesquieu and Burke*, Oxford, 1963.

Dargan, E. P., *The Aesthetic Doctrine of Montesquieu*, Paris, 1907.

Dedieu, J., *Montesquieu, l'homme et l'oeuvre*, Paris, 1943.

Durkheim, D., *Montesquieu and Rousseau, Forerunners of Sociology*, Michigan, 1965.

Ehrard, J., *Politique de Montesquieu, textes choisis*, Paris, 1965.

Montesquieu, critique d'art, Paris, 1965.

Fletcher, F. T. H., *Montesquieu and English Politics*, London, 1939.

Goyard-Fabre, S., *La Politique de Droit de Montesquieu*, Paris, 1973.

Granpro-Molière, J. J., *La Théorie de la Constitution anglaise chez Montesquieu*, Leyden, 1972.

Kassem, B., *Décadence et absolutisme dans l'oeuvre de Montesquieu*, Paris, 1964.

Levin, L. M., *The Political Doctrine of Montesquieu's 'Esprit des Lois': Its Classical Background*, London, 1936.

Loy, J. R., *Montesquieu*, New York, 1968.

Mason, S. M., *Montesquieu's Idea of Justice*, The Hague, 1976.

Merry, H. J., *Montesquieu's System of Natural Government*, Lafayette, Indiana, 1970.

Pangle, T., *Montesquieu's Philosophy of Liberalism: A Commentary on the 'Spirit of the Laws'*, Chicago, 1973.

Shackleton, R., *Montesquieu: a Critical Biography*, London, 1961.

Starobinski, J., *Montesquieu par lui-même*, Paris, 1953.

Vlachos, G., *La Politique de Montesquieu: notion et méthode*, Montchrestien, 1974.

Waddicor, H., *Montesquieu and the Philosophy of Natural Law*, The Hague, 1970.

ROUSSEAU

Oeuvres complètes, ed. B. Gagnebin and M. Raymond (Bibliothèque de la Pléiade), Vols. I–IV, Paris, 1959–70. (Vol. V has yet to be published).

La Nouvelle Héloïse, ed. D. Mornet, 4 vols., Paris, 1925.

The two following works are not yet included in the Pléiade edition:

Lettre à d'Alembert sur les spectacles, ed. M. Fuchs, Geneva, 1948.

Essai sur l'origine des langues, ed. C. Porset, Bordeaux, 1968.

Political Writings, ed. C. E. Vaughan, 2 vols., Cambridge, 1915.

Religious Writings, ed. R. Grimsley, London, 1970.

Correspondance complète de Jean-Jacques Rousseau, ed. R. A. Leigh, Geneva and Banbury, 1965– .

Correspondance générale, ed. T. Dufour and P. P. Plan, 20 vols., Paris, 1924–34.

Émile, trans. B. Foxley, new ed. with introduction by P. D. Jimack (Everyman's Library), London, 1974.

The Social Contract and Discourses, trans. G. D. H. Cole, revised by J. H. Brumfitt and J. C. Hall (Everyman's Library), London, 1973.
The Social Contract, trans. M. Cranston, Harmondsworth, 1968.
Du contrat social, ed. R. Grimsley (French text, with introduction and notes in English), London, 1973.
The Confessions, trans. J. M. Cohen, Harmondsworth, 1953.

Annales de la Société Jean-Jacques Rousseau, Geneva, 1905 onwards.

De Beer, G., *J. J. Rousseau and his World*, London, 1972.
Broome, J. H., *Rousseau: A Study of his Thought*, London, 1963.
Blanchard, W. H., *Rousseau and the Spirit of Revolt: a Psychological Study*, Michigan, 1967.
Burgelin, P., *La Philosophie de l'Existence de Jean-Jacques Rousseau*, Paris, 1950.
Cassirer, E., *The Question of J. J. Rousseau*, trans. P. Gay, Bloomington, Indiana, 1963.
Charvet, J., *The Social Problem in the Philosophy of Rousseau*, Cambridge, 1974.
Cobban, A., *Rousseau and the Modern State*, new ed., London, 1964.
Crocker, L. G., *Jean-Jacques Rousseau*, 2 vols., New York, 1968, 1973.
Rousseau's Social Contract: An Interpretive Essay, Cleveland, 1968.
Derathé, R., *J. J. Rousseau et la science politique de son temps*, Paris, 1950.
Le Rationalisme de Rousseau, Paris, 1948.
Eigeldinger, M., *J. J. Rousseau et la réalité de l'imaginaire*, Paris, 1962.
Einaudi, M., *The Early Rousseau*, Ithaca, NY, 1967.
Ellenburg, S., *Rousseau's Political Philosophy: An Interpretation from Within*, Ithaca, NY, 1976.
Ellrich, R. J., *Rousseau and his Reader: the Rhetorical Situation of the Major Works*, Chapel Hill, 1969.
Gouhier, H. *Les Méditations métaphysiques de J. J. Rousseau* Paris, 1970.
Grimsley, R., *Jean-Jacques Rousseau: a Study in Self-Awareness*, new ed., Cardiff, 1969.
The Philosophy of Rousseau, London, 1973.
Rousseau and the Religious Quest, London, 1968.
Guehenno, J., *Jean-Jacques Rousseau*, trans. J. and D. Weightman, 2 vols., London, 1966.
Hall, J. C., *Rousseau: An Introduction to his Political Philosophy*, London, 1973.
Hendel, C. W., *Jean-Jacques Rousseau, moralist*, 2 vols., London, 1934.
Hubert, R., *Rousseau et l'Encyclopédie*, Paris, 1928.
Huizinga, J. H., *The Making of a Saint: The Tragi-Comedy of J. J. Rousseau*, London, 1975.

Launay, M., *J. J. Rousseau: Écrivain politique, 1712–62*, Geneva, 1971.
Lecercle, J. L., *Rousseau et l'art du roman*, Paris, 1969.
McDonald, J., *Rousseau and the French Revolution*, London, 1965.
Masson, P. M., *La Religion de J. J. Rousseau*, 3 vols., Paris, 1916.
Masters, R. D., *The Political Philosophy of J. J. Rousseau*, Princeton, NJ, 1968.
May, G., *Rousseau par lui-même*, Paris, 1961.
Munteano, B., *Solitude et contradictions de J. J. Rousseau*, Paris, 1975.
Osborn, M. A., *Rousseau and Burke*, London, 1940.
Polin, R., *La Politique de la solitude: Essai sur J. J. Rousseau*, Paris, 1971.
Raymond, M., *Jean-Jacques Rousseau, la quête de soi et la rêverie*, Paris, 1962.
Roddier, H., *J. J. Rousseau en Angleterre au XVIIIe siècle*, Paris, 1950.
Roussel, J., *J. J. Rousseau en France après la Revolution*, 1795–1830, Paris, 1972.
Shklar, J. N., *Men and Citizens: A Study of Rousseau's Social Theory*, Cambridge, 1969.
Spink, J. S., *Rousseau et Genève*, Paris, 1935.
Starobinski, J., *Jean-Jacques Rousseau: La transparence et l'obstacle*, new ed., Paris, 1970.
Trousson, J., *Rousseau et sa fortune littéraire*, Paris, 1971.
Vallette, G., *J. J. Rousseau, Genevois*, Paris, 1908.
Voisine, J., *J. J. Rousseau en Angleterre à l'époque romantique*, Paris, 1956.
Wright, E. H., *The Meaning of Rousseau*, London, 1929.

TURGOT

Oeuvres de Turgot et documents le concernant, ed. G. Schelle, 5 vols., Paris, 1913–23.

Dakin, D., *Turgot and the Ancien Régime in France*, London, 1939.
Neymarck, L., *Turgot et ses doctrines*, 2 vols., Paris, 1885.

VOLTAIRE

Oeuvres complètes, ed. Moland, 52 vols. Paris, 1877–85.
The Complete Works of Voltaire, ed. T. Besterman, W. H. Barber and others (in course of publication, Geneva and Banbury, 1968– . This includes a new edition of the *Correspondence*.)
Mélanges, ed. J. van den Heuvel (Bibliothèque de la Pléiade), Paris, 1965.
Candide, ed. R. Pomeau, Paris, 1959.
Candide, critical edition by C. Thacker, Geneva, 1968.
Candide and other tales, trans. Smollett, ed. J. C. Thornton (Everyman's Library), London, 1937.

Candide or Optimism, trans. J. Butt, Harmondsworth, 1941.
Dictionnaire philosophique, ed. J. Benda and R. Naves, Paris, 1954.
Lettres philosophiques, ed. F. A. Taylor, Oxford, 1943.
Traité de metaphysique, ed. H. T. Patterson, 1937.
Correspondence, ed. T. Besterman, 107 vols., Geneva, 1953–65.
Correspondance, ed. T. Besterman (Bibliothèque de la Pléiade), Paris, 1964– .

Barr, M. M. H., *Bibliography of Writings on Voltaire 1825–1925*, reprinted New York, 1972.
Quarante années d'études voltairiennes 1926–1965, Paris, 1968.
Bengesco, G., *Voltaire: Bibliographie de ses oeuvres*, 4 vols., Paris, 1882–90.
Besterman, T., *Some 18th Century editions unknown to Bengesco*, new ed., Banbury, 1974.

Studies on Voltaire and the 18th century, ed. T. Besterman, Geneva and Banbury, 1959– .

Aldridge, A. O., *Voltaire and the Century of Light*, Princeton, NJ, 1975.
Barber, W. H., *Voltaire's 'Candide'*, London, 1960.
Bellessort, A., *Essai sur Voltaire*, Paris, 1926.
Besterman, T., *Voltaire*, London, 1969.
Brailsford, H. N., *Voltaire*, London, 1933.
Brumfitt, J. H., *Voltaire historian*, London, 1958.
Carré, J. R., *La Consistance de Voltaire le philosophe*, Paris, 1939.
Choptrayanou, G., *Essai sur Candide*, reprinted Paris, 1969.
Collins, J. C., *Voltaire, Montesquieu and Rousseau in England*, London, 1908.
Conlon, P. M., 'Voltaire's Literary Career from 1728 to 1750', in *Studies on Voltaire*, XIV, Geneva, 1961.
Dédéyan, C., *Voltaire et la pensée anglaise*, Paris, 1956.
Deschanel, E., *Le Théâtre de Voltaire*, Paris, 1886.
Desnoiresterres, G., *Voltaire et la Société française au XVIIIe Siècle*, 8 vols., Paris, 1871–6.
Faguet, É., *La Politique comparée de Montesquieu, Rousseau et Voltaire*, Paris, 1902.
Gaillard, P., *Candide: analyse critique* (Profil d'une oeuvre, 34), Paris, 1972.
Gay, P., *Voltaire's Politics: The Poet as Realist*, Princeton, NJ, 1959.
Guiragossian, D. S., *Voltaire's 'Facéties'*, Geneva, 1963.
Havens, G. R., *Voltaire's Marginalia on the Pages of Rousseau*, reprinted New York, 1966.
Hearsey, J. E. N., *Voltaire*, London, 1976.

Lanson, G., *Voltaire*, Paris, 1919; new ed. revised by R. Pomeau, Paris, 1960.

Lantoine, A., *Les 'Lettres philosophiques' de Voltaire* (Grands Evénements littéraires), Paris, 1931.

Lounsbury, T., *Shakespeare and Voltaire*, New York, 1902.

Maestro, M., *Voltaire and Beccaria as Reformers in Criminal Law*, New York, 1942.

Mason, H. T., *Pierre Bayle and Voltaire*, London, 1963.

Voltaire, London, 1973.

Mitford, Nancy, *Voltaire in Love*, New York, London, 1957.

Morize, A., *L'Apologie du luxe au XVIIIe siècle et 'le Mondain' de Voltaire*, Paris, 1909, reprinted Geneva, 1970.

Naves, R., *Le Goût de Voltaire*, Paris, 1938.

Voltaire et l'Encyclopédie, Paris, 1938.

Voltaire l'homme et l'oeuvre, Paris, 1942.

Nixon, Edna, *Voltaire and the Calas Case*, New York, 1961.

Pappas, J. N., *Voltaire and d'Alembert*, Bloomington, Indiana, 1962.

Pomeau, R., *Politique de Voltaire*, Paris, 1963.

La Religion de Voltaire, Paris, 1956.

Voltaire par lui-même, Paris, 1955.

Ridgway, R. S., 'La Propagande philosophique dans les tragédies de Voltaire', in *Studies on Voltaire*, XV, Geneva, 1961.

Rihs, C., *Voltaire: recherches sur les origines du matérialisme historique*, Droz, 1962.

Rowe, C., *Voltaire and the State*, New York, 1955.

Sareil, J., *Voltaire et la critique*, New Jersey, 1966.

Topazio, V. W., *Voltaire: a critical study of his major works*, New York, 1967.

Torrey, N. L., *The Spirit of Voltaire*, New York, 1938.

Voltaire and the English Deists, New Haven, Connecticut, 1930.

Van den Heuvel, *Voltaire dans ses Contes de 'Micromégas' à 'l'Ingénu'*, Paris, 1967.

Wade, I. O., *The Intellectual Development of Voltaire*, Princeton, 1969.

The Search for a New Voltaire, Philadelphia, 1958.

Studies on Voltaire, Princeton, NJ, 1947, reprinted New York, 1963.

Voltaire and Candide: A Study in the Fusion of History, Art and Philosophy, Princeton, NJ, 1959.

Voltaire and Madame du Châtelet, Princeton, NJ, 1941.

Voltaire's 'Micromégas': A Study in the Fusion of Science, Myth and Art, Princeton, NJ, 1950.

Waldinger, R., *Voltaire and Reform in the Light of the French Revolution*, Geneva, 1959.

Williams, D., 'Voltaire Literary Critic', in *Studies on Voltaire, XLVIII*, Geneva, 1966.

(*iv*) *Poetry*

Allem, M., ed., *Anthologie poétique française, XVIIIe siècle*, Paris, 1966.
Barquissau, R., *Les poètes créoles du XVIIIe siècle*, Paris, 1949.
Cameron, M. M., *L'Influence des 'Saisons' de Thomson sur la poésie descriptive en France*, Paris, 1927.
Delille, J., *Oeuvres complètes*, Paris, 1818.
Dimoff, P., *La Vie et l'oeuvre d'André Chénier jusqu'à la Revolution*, Paris, 1936.
Dupont, P., *Houdar de la Motte*, Paris, 1898.
Duviard, F., *Anthologie des poètes du XVIIIe siècle*, Paris, 1948.
Fabre, J., *André Chénier, l'homme et l'oeuvre*, Paris, 1955.
Faguet, E., *Histoire de la poésie française*, Vols. VI–IX, 1932–6.
Finch, R., *The Sixth Sense: Individualism in French Poetry 1686–1760*, Toronto, 1966.
Florian, J.-P. C. de, *Oeuvres*, Paris, 1797.
Fusil, C. A., *La Poésie scientifique de 1750 à nos jours*, Paris, 1917.
Gilbert, N. J. L., *Oeuvres complètes*, 2 vols., Paris, 1802.
Gilman, M., *The Idea of poetry in France from Houdar de la Motte to Baudelaire*, Cambridge, Mass., 1958.
Gresset, J. B. L., *Oeuvres choises*, ed. L. Derome, Paris, 1883.
Grubbs, H. A., *J. B. Rousseau: His Life and Works*, Princeton, NJ, 1941.
La Motte, Houdar de, *Oeuvres complètes*, Paris, 1754.
Lefranc de Pompignan, *Oeuvres complètes*, 4 vols., Paris, 1784.
Leonard, N. C., *Oeuvres*, ed. V. Campenon, 3 vols., Paris, 1798.
Le Tourneur, P. P. F., Translations of Young (*Oeuvres diverses*, 1770, and *Oeuvres complètes*, 1796), Hervey (*Méditations sur les tombeaux*, 1770) and Ossian (1777).
Parny, E. D. de F., *Oeuvres complètes*, 2 vols., Paris, 1797.
Le Chevalier de Parny et ses poésies érotiques, ed. L. de F. Parny, 1949.
Piron, A., *Poésies diverses et poésies fugitives*, London, 1779–83.
Potéz, H., *L'Élégie en France avant le romantisme*, Paris, 1897.
Roucher, J. A., *Les Mois*, 2 vols., Paris, 1779.
Rousseau, J. B., *Oeuvres complètes*, 5 vols., Paris, 1820.
Saillard, G., *Florian, sa vie, son oeuvre*, Toulouse, 1912.
Saint-Lambert, Marquis de, *Les Saisons*, Paris, 1769.
Scarfe, F., *André Chénier, His Life and Work 1762–94*, London, 1965.

Van Tieghem, P., *La Poésie de la nuit et des tombeaux en Europe au XVIIIe siècle*, Paris, 1921.

(*v*) *Theatre*

Albert, M., *Les théâtres de la Foire (1660–1789)*, Paris, 1900.

Arnould, E. J., *La Genèse du 'Barbier de Séville'*, Dublin, 1965.

Attinger, G., *L'Esprit de la commedia dell'arte dans le théâtre français*, Paris, 1950.

Beaumarchais, *Théâtre: Lettres relatives à son théâtre* (Bibliothèque de la Pléiade), Paris, 1957.

Breitholz, L., *Le théâtre historique en France jusqu'à la Révolution*, Upsala, 1952.

Crébillon, P. J., *Théâtre*, 2 vols., Paris, 1750.

Dancourt, F. C., *Oeuvres*, 12 vols., Paris, 1760.

Deloffre, F., *Une préciosité nouvelle: Marivaux et le marivaudage*, Paris, 1955.

Destouches, P. N., *Oeuvres dramatiques*, Paris, 1957.

Drack, *Le Théâtre de la Foire, la Comédie Italienne et l'Opéra-Comique*, Paris, 1889 (selection of plays performed between 1658 and 1720).

Foire, Théâtre de la, *Le Théâtre de la Foire ou l'Opéra-Comique*, 10 vols., Paris, 1721–37.

Fontaine, L., *Le Théâtre et la Philosophie au XVIIIe siècle*, Versailles, 1878.

Gaiffe, F., *Le Drame en France au XVIIIe siècle*, Paris, 1921.

Le Mariage de Figaro, Paris, 1928.

Greene, E. H. J., *Marivaux*, Toronto, 1965.

Gresset, J. B. L., *Oeuvres choisies*, Paris, 1866.

Gunther, *L'Oeuvre dramatique de Sedaine*, Paris, 1908.

Hankiss, J. P. N., *Destouches, l'homme et l'oeuvre*, Debreczen, 1918.

Lancaster, H. C., *French Tragedy in the Time of Louis XV and Voltaire 1715–74*, 2 vols., 1950.

French Tragedy in the reign of Louis XVI and the early years of the French Revolution, 1774–92, Baltimore, 1953.

Lanson, G., *Esquisse d'une histoire de la tragédie française*, 1920.

Nivelle de la Chaussée et la comédie larmoyante, 1887.

Larroumet, G. *Marivaux, sa vie et ses oeuvres*, Paris, 1882.

Lemaître, J., *La Comédie après Molière et le théâtre de Dancourt*, Paris, 1882.

Letourneur, P., *Oeuvres de Shakespeare*, Paris, 1776–82.

Lenient, C., *La Comédie en France au XVIIIe siècle*, 2 vols., Paris, 1888.

Lintilhac, E., *Histoire générale du théâtre en France*, Paris, 1909 (especially Vol. IV).

Lioure, M., *Le Drame*, Paris, 1963.
Lough, J., *Paris Theatre Audiences in the 17th and 18th Centuries*, Cambridge, 1957.
Marivaux, *Théâtre complet* (Bibliothèque de la Pléiade), ed. M. Arland, Paris, 1949.
McKee, K. N., *The Theatre of Marivaux*, New York, 1958.
Moffat, M. M., *La Controverse sur la moralité du théâtre*, Paris, 1930.
Morel, J. *La Tragédie*, Paris, 1964.
Myers, R. L., *The dramatic theories of E. C. Fréron*, Geneva, 1962.
Niklaus, R., *Beaumarchais: Le Barbier de Séville*, London, 1968.
Pomeau, R., *Beaumarchais, l'homme et l'oeuvre*, Paris, 1956.
Proschwitz, G. von, *Introduction à l'étude du vocabulaire de Beaumarchais*, Paris, 1956.
Pugh, A. R., *Beaumarchais: Le Mariage de Figaro* 1968.
Ratermanis, J. B., and Irwin, W. R., *The Comic Style of Beaumarchais*, Seattle, 1961.
Ratermanis, J. B., *Étude sur le comique dans le théâtre de Marivaux*, Geneva, 1961.
Richard, P., *La Vie privée de Beaumarchais*, Paris, 1951.
Schérer, J., *La Dramaturgie de Beaumarchais*, Paris, 1954.
Sedaine, M. J., *Oeuvres dramatiques*, 4 vols., Paris, 1776.
Trahard, P., *Les Maîtres de la sensibilité française (1715–89)*, Vol. I, Paris, 1931.
Van Tieghem, P., *Beaumarchais par lui-même*, Paris, 1960.
Voltz, P., *La Comédie*, Paris, 1964.

(*vi*) *Novel*

Etiemble, R., ed., *Romanciers du XVIIIe siècle* (Bibliothèque de la Pléiade), 2 vols., Paris, 1960–65.
Roy, C., ed. *Quatre romans dans le goût français*, Paris, 1959. Novels by Mme de Genlis, Mme de Tencin, Duclos (*Madame de Selves*) and Vivant Denon (*Point de Lendemain*).
Actes du Colloque d'Aix-en-Provence, 1963, Orphrys, 1965 (Prévost).
d'Almeras, H., *Paul et Virginie, histoire d'un roman*, Paris, 1937.
Arland, M., *Marivaux*, Paris, 1963.
Billy, A., *Un Singulier bénédictin: l'abbé Prévost*, Paris, 1969.
Brooks, P., *The Novel of Worldliness: Crébillon, Marivaux, Laclos, Stendhal*, Princeton, NJ, 1969.
Bégué, A., *État présent des études sur R. de la Bretonne*, Paris, 1948.
Chadbourne, M., *R. de la Bretonne ou le siècle prophétique*, Paris, 1958.

Chasles (Challes), Robert, *Les Illustres françaises*, ed. critique par F. Deloffre, 2 vols., Paris, 1959.
Cherpack, C., *An Essay on Crébillon Fils*, Durham, North Carolina, 1962.
Clarétie, L., *Essai sur Lesage romancier*, Paris, 1890.
Coulet, H., *Marivaux romancier*, Paris, 1975.
Le Roman jusqu'à la Révolution, 2 vols., Paris, 1967.
Crébillon fils, *Les Égarements du coeur et de l'esprit*, ed. Etiemble, Paris, 1961.
Dawes, C. R., *The Marquis de Sade, his life and works*, 1927.
R. de la Bretonne, 1734–1806, London, 1946.
Drummond, W., *Philosopher of Evil* [Marquis de Sade], Evanston, 1962.
Dedeyan, C. A. R., *Lesage: Gil Blas*, Paris, 1956.
Deloffre, F., *Une Préciosité nouvelle, Marivaux et le marivaudage*, Paris, 1955, new edition, 1967.
Deloffre, F., and Picard, R., *Manon Lescaut* (with introduction and notes), Paris, 1965.
Dupé, G., *Le Marquis de Sade*, in *Oeuvres libres*, Paris, 1957.
Engel, C. E., *Le véritable abbé Prévost*, Monaco, 1958.
Funke, H. G., *Crébillon fils als Moralist und Gesellschaftskritiker*, Heidelberg, 1972.
Gorer, G., *The Marquis de Sade*, new ed., New York, 1963.
Green, F. C., *French Novelists: Manners and Ideas from the Renaissance to the Revolution*, London, 1929.
Havens, G. R., *The Abbé Prévost and English Literature*, New York, 1965 (reprint).
Hazard, P., *Études critiques sur Manon Lescaut*, Chicago, 1935.
Jaccard, J., *Manon Lescaut: le personnage-romancier*, Paris, 1975.
Jones, S. P., *A List of French Prose fiction (1700–50)*, New York, 1939.
Klossowski, P., *Sade mon prochain*, Paris, 1947.
Koppen, E., *Laclos's Liaisons dangereuses in der Kritik (1782–1850)*, Wiesbaden, 1961.
Laclos, *Oeuvres complètes* (Bibliothèque de la Pléiade), ed. M. Allem, Paris, 1943.
Lasserre, E., *'Manon Lescaut' de l'abbé Prévost*, Paris, 1930.
Laufer, R., *Lesage ou le métier de romancier*, Paris, 1971.
Le Breton, A., *Le Roman français au XVIIIe siècle*, Paris, 1898.
Lesage, A.-R., *Histoire de Gil Blas*, ed. M. Barden, 2 vols., Paris, 1942.
Mathé, R., *Manon Lescaut: analyse critique* (Profil d'une oeuvre 9), Paris, 1970.
May, G., *Le Dilemme du roman au XVIIIe siècle*, New Haven, 1963.
Meister, P., *Charles Duclos (1704–72)*, Paris, 1956.

Milner, M., *Le diable dans la littérature française de Cazotte à Baudelaire, 1772–1861*, 2 vols., Paris, 1960.

Montesquieu, *Les Lettres persanes*, ed. P. Vernière, Paris, 1960.

Morillot, P., *Le roman français*, 1892, revised edition, Paris, 1921.

Monty, J. R., 'Les romans de l'abbé Prévost' in *Studies on Voltaire*, LXXVIII, 1970.

Mornet, D., ed., *Rousseau: La Nouvelle Héloïse*, 4 vols., Paris, 1924. (The first volume deals with the history of the eighteenth-century novel before Rousseau.)

Mylne, V., *The 18th Century French Novel, Techniques of Illusion*, Manchester, 1965.

Prévost, *Prévost's Manon Lescaut*, London, 1972.

Prévost, *Oeuvres*, 39 vols., Geneva, 1969 (reprint of 1810–16 ed.).

Porter, C. A., *Restif's novels: or an autobiography in search of an author*, New Haven, Connecticut, 1967.

Restif de la Bretonne, *Oeuvres*, ed. H. Bachelin, 9 vols., Paris, 1930–32.

Monsieur Nicolas ou le coeur humain dévoilé, new ed., 6 vols., Paris, 1960.

Les Nuits de Paris (facsimile reprint), ed. H. Bachelin, Paris, 1960.

Les Nuits de Paris, or the nocturnal spectator: a selection, translated by L. Asher and E. Fertig, New York, 1964.

La Paysanne pervertie, ou les dangers de la ville, preface by A. Maurois, Paris, 1959.

La Vie de mon père, ed. J. Desmeuzes, Paris, 1960.

Roddier, H., *L'Abbé Prévost, l'homme et l'oeuvre*, Paris, 1955.

Rosbottom, R. C., *Marivaux's novels*, New Jersey, 1974.

Rousset, J., *Forme et signification: essais sur les structures littéraires*, Paris, 1962.

Sade, Marquis de, *Oeuvres complètes*, ed. G. Lely, Paris, 1966–7.

Centre d'Aixois d'études sur le XVIIIe siècle: Le Marquis de Sade, Paris, 1968.

Saint-Pierre, B. de, *Paul et Virginie*, ed. P. Trahard, Paris.

Saintsbury, G., *History of the French Novel*, 2 vols., 1917–19.

Seylaz, J. J., *Les Liaisons dangereuses et la création romanesque chez Laclos*, Geneva, 1958.

Sgard, J., *Prévost, romancier*, Paris, 1968.

Showalter, E. *The Evolution of the French Novel*, 1641–1782, Princeton, NJ, 1972.

Souriau, M., *B. de Saint-Pierre d'après ses manuscrits*, Paris, 1905.

Stewart, P. R., *Imitation and Illusion in the French Memoir Novel, 1700–50*, New Haven, Connecticut, 1969.

Thelander, D. R., *Laclos and the Epistolary Novel*, Geneva, 1963.

Thody, P., *Laclos's Les Liaisons dangereuses*, London, 1970.

Trahard, P., *Les Maîtres de la sensibilité française*, 3 vols., 1933.
Vaillard, R., *Laclos par lui-même*, Paris, 1968.
Versini, L., *Laclos et la tradition*, Paris, 1968.
Voltaire, *Romans et contes* (Classiques Garnier), ed. H. Bénac, Paris, 1964.
Ware, J. N., *The Vocabulary of B. de Saint-Pierre*, Baltimore and Paris, 1927.

(*vii*) *Aesthetic Ideas*

André, Yves, *Essai sur le beau*, Paris, 1741.
Batteux, C., *Les Beaux-Arts réduits à un seul principe*, Paris, 1946.
Bayer, R., *Histoire de l'esthétique*, Paris, 1961.
Chouillet, J., *L'Esthétique des lumières*, Paris, 1974.
Coleman, F. X. J., *The Aesthetic Thought of the French Enlightenment*, Pittsburgh, 1971.
Crousaz, J. P. de, *Traité du Beau*, Amsterdam, 1715.
Dacier, Anne F., *Des causes de la corruption du goût*, Paris, 1714.
Dubos, J. B., *Réflexions critiques sur la poésie et la peinture*, Paris, 1719.
Fayolle, R., *La Critique littéraire*, Paris, 1964.
Folkierski, W., *Entre le classicisme et le romantisme*, Cracow, 1925.
Fontaine, A., *Les Doctrines d'art en France de Poussin à Diderot*, Paris, 1909.
Fontenelle, J. G., *Oeuvres complètes*, Paris, 1790.
Gerrard, A., *Essai sur le goût*, Paris, 1766.
Lombard, A., *L'Abbé du Bos un initiateur de la pensée moderne*, Paris, 1913.
Marmontel, *Éléments de littérature*, Paris, 1781 (collection of articles written for the *Encyclopédie*).
Moreau, P., *La Critique littéraire en France*, Paris, 1960.
Mustoxidi, T. M., *Histoire de l'esthétique française, 1700–10*, Paris, 1920.
Rocafort, J., *Les Doctrines littéraires de l'Encyclopédie*, Paris, 1890.
Saintsbury, G., *A History of Criticism and Literary Taste in Europe*, 3 vols., Edinburgh and London, 1900–1904.
Saisselin, R. G., *Taste in 18th century France: critical reflections on the origins of aesthetics*, Syracuse, 1965.
Schneider, R., *L'Art français: XVIIIe siècle*, Paris, 1926.
Smith, L. P., 'Four Romantic Words', ['Romantic', 'Originality', 'Creative' and 'Genius'] in *Words and Idioms*, London, 1925.
Van Tieghem, P., *Petite Histoire des grandes doctrines littéraires en France*, Paris, 1954.
Wellek, R., *A History of Modern Criticism*, 4 vols., London, 1955–66.

3. GERMANY

(*i*) *General*

The Oxford Companion to German Literature, London, 1976.

Stammler, W., ed., *Deutsche Philologie im Aufriss*, 3 vols., Berlin, 1952; 2nd ed., 1966–7; *Register* (Index), 1969.

Merker, P., and Stammler, W., *Reallexicon der deutschen Literaturgeschichte*, 3 vols., Berlin, 1925– ; revised W. Kohlschmidt, 1958–77. (A fourth volume is to be published by instalments.)

Bruford, W. H., *Culture and Society in Classical Weimar, 1775–1806*, Cambridge, 1962.

Germany in the Eighteenth Century, Cambridge, 1935.

Burger, H. O., ed., *Annalen der deutschen Literatur*, 2nd. ed, Stuttgart, 1970.

Closs, A., *The Genius of the German Lyric*, revised ed., London, 1962.

Goedeke, K., *Grundriss zur Geschichte der deutschen Dichtung*, 2nd ed., Berlin, 1884–1953, with continuation 1955– .

Hansel, J., *Bücherkunde für Germanisten*, Berlin, 1961.

Personalbibliographie zur deutschen Literaturgeschichte, Berlin, 1967.

Kohlschmidt, W., *Geschichte der deutschen Literatur von Barock bis zur Klassik*, Stuttgart, 1965.

Körner, J., *Bibliographisches Handbuch des deutschen Schrifttums*, 1949; 2nd ed., Berne and Munich, 1966.

Köster, A., *Die deutsche Literatur der Aufklärungszeit*, Heidelberg, 1925.

Martini, F., *Deutsche Literaturgeschichte*, Stuttgart, 1949.

Raabe, P., *Einführung in die Bucherkunde zur deutschen Literaturwissenschaft*, 1961.

Robertson, J. G., *A History of German Literature*, Edinburgh and London, 1902; 6th ed., 1970.

Schneider, F. J., *Die deutsche Dichtung zwschen Barock und Klassizismus*, Stuttgart, 1924.

Stahl, E. I., and Yuill, W. E., *German Literature in the 18th and 19th Centuries*, London, 1970.

(*ii*) *Authors*

BROCKES

Irdisches Vergnügen in Gott (selection), ed. A. Eschenbroich, Stuttgart, 1966.

BÜRGER

Werke, ed. L. Klain-Klook and S. Streller, 1962.

CLAUDIUS

Sämtliche Werke, ed. J. Perfahl and H. Platschek, Munich, 1968.

GESSNER, S.

Sämtliche Schriften, ed. M. Birchner, 3 vols., reprinted 1972, 1974.

Idyllen, Kritische Ausgabe, ed. E. T. Voss, Stuttgart, 1973.

Hibberd, J., *Saloman Gessner: His Creative Achievement and Influence*, Cambridge, 1976.

GOETHE

Gedenkausgabe, ed. E. Beutler, 24 vols., Zürich, 1948–60.

Werke (Hamburger Ausgabe), ed. E. Trunz, 14 vols., 1948–60.

Der junge Goethe, ed. O. Morris, rev. H. Fischer-Lamberg, 6 vols., Berlin and New York, 1963–74.

Geeth, H. J., *J. W. Goethe*, Stuttgart, 1972.

Graham, I., *Goethe and Lessing*, London, 1973.

Müller, G., *Kleine Goethe-Biographie*, Bonn, 1947.

Robertson, J. G., *Goethe*, London, 1932.

Staiger, E., *Goethe*, 3 vols., Zürich and Freiburg, 1952–9.

Wilkinson, E. M., and Willoughby, E. A., *Goethe: Poet and Thinker*, London, 1970.

GOTTSCHED

Schriften zur Literatur, ed. H. Steinmetz, Stuttgart, 1972.

GÜNTHER

Gesamtausgabe, ed. W. Krämer, 6 vols., 1930–37.

Dahlke, H., *J. C. Günther*, 1960.

HAGEDORN

Gedichte, ed. A. Anger, Stuttgart, 1968.

Stix, G., *P. Hagedorns Menschenbild und Dichtungsauffassen*, Rome, 1961.

HAMANN

Sämtliche Werke, ed. J. Nadler, 6 vols., Vienna, 1949–57.

Schriften, selected and ed. K. Widmaier, Leipzig, 1921.

HERDER

Sämtliche Werke, ed. K. Suphau, 33 vols., Berlin, 1877–1913.

Gillies, A., *Herder*, Oxford, 1945.

Lohmeier, D., *Herder und die Aufklärung*, 1968.

HÖLDERLIN

Sämtliche Werke, ed. F. Beissner, 7 vols., Stuttgart, 1943–72.

Böckmann, P., *Hölderlin und seine Götter*, 2nd ed., 1970.

Ryan, L., *Hölderin*, Stuttgart, 1962.

KANT

Gesammelte Schriften, ed. Proussische Akademie der Wissenschaften, 23 vols., Berlin, 1900–1955.

Körner, S., *Kant*, London, 1955.

KLEIST, E. VON

Sämtliche Werke, ed. J. Stenzel, Stuttgart, 1971.

KLOPSTOCK

Werke und Briefe, ed. H. Grone, Berlin and New York, 1974– .

Oden, ed. F. Muncker and J. Pawel, 2 vols., Stuttgart, 1899.

Muncker, F., *Klopstock*, Stuttgart, 1888.

LEIBNIZ

Brüggemann, F., ed., *Das Weltbild der deutschen Aufklärung*, Leipzig, 1930.

Reihe Aufklärung, Vol. 2, Leipzig, 1930 (also for texts by Wolff, Gottsched, Brockes and Haller).

Saw, R. L., *Leibniz*, Harmondsworth, 1954.

LENZ

Gesammelte Schriften, ed. F. Blei, 5 vols., Munich, 1900–1915.

Rosanow, N., *J. M. R. Lenz, Leben und Werke*, Leipzig, 1909.

LESSING

Kritische Gesamtansgabe, ed. K. Lachmann and F. Muncker, 23 vols., Stuttgart, 1886–1924.

Werke, ed. J. Petersen and M. von Olshausen, 30 vols., Berlin and Leipzig, 1925–35.

Werke, ed. H. G. Göpfert and others, 8 vols., Munich, 1970–79.

Garland, H. B., *Lessing, the Founder of Modern German Literature*, London, 2nd ed., 1968.

Graham, I., *Goethe and Lessing*, London, 1973.

SCHILLER

National-Ausgabe, various editors, Weimar, 1943– , 43 vols. (26 vols. published to 1979).

Sämtliche Werke, ed. G. Fricke and H. G. Göpfert, 5 vols., Munich, 1958–60.

Garland, H. B., *Schiller*, London, 1949.

Schiller, the Dramatic Writer, London, 1969.

Graham, I., *A Master of the Tragic Form*, 1972.

Stahl, E. L., *F. Schiller's Drama, Theory and Practice*, London, 1954.

Storz, G., *Der Dichter Friedrich Schiller*, Stuttgart, 1959.

Wiese, B. von, *Schiller*, Stuttgart, 1959.

SCHLEGEL

Canut, ed. H. Steinmetz, Stuttgart, 1967.

WIELAND

Werke, selected and ed. F. Martini and H. W. Seiffert, 5 vols., Stuttgart, 1973.

Sengle, F., *Wieland*, Stuttgart, 1949.

STURM UND DRANG

Sturm und Drang, ed. K. Freye, 4 vols., Berlin and Leipzig, 1911 (selection of texts).

Sturm und Drang, Kritische Schriften, ed. E. Loewenthal, Heidelberg, 1949.

Sturm und Drang, Dramatische Schriften, ed. E. Loewenthal and H. Schneider, 2 vols., Heidelberg, 1959.

Garland, H. B., *Storm and Stress*, London, 1952.

Pascal, R., *The German Sturm und Drang*, Manchester, 1952.

4. ITALY

(i) *Bibliography and General*

Petronio, G., ed., *Dizionario enciclopedico della letteratura italiana*, 6 vols., Bari and Rome, 1966–70.

Compagnino, G., Nicastro, G., and Savoca, G., *Il Settecento. L'Arcadia e l'età delle riforme*, 7 vols., 1973–4, in *Letteratura Italiana Laterza*, directed by C. Muscetta, Bari, 1971– (extensive history of Italian literature, with anthologies and bibliographies, by numerous specialists).

Natali, G., *Il Settecento*, 2 vols., 6th rev. ed., Milan, 1964.

Problemi ed orientamenti critici di lingua e letteratura italiana, ed. A. Momigliano, Milan, 1948–9: (i) *Notizie introduttive e sussidi bibliografici*, 2nd ed. 1958–60; (ii) *Tecnica e teoria letteraria*, 2nd ed., 1951; (iii) *Questioni e correnti di storia letteraria*, 2nd ed., 1963; (iv) *Letterature comparate*, 1949.

Letteratura italiana (*Orientamenti culturali*), ed. A. Momigliano, Milan, 1956–61: (i) *Le Correnti*; (ii) *I Maggiori*; (iii) *I Minori*.

Storia della letteratura italiana, ed. E. Cecchi and N. Sapegno, Vol. VI, *Il Settecento*, Milan, 1968.

Binni, W., and Scrivano, R., *Introduzione ai problemi critici della letteratura italiana*, Messina and Florence, 1967.

Puppo, M., *Manuale critico-bibliografico per lo studio della letteratura italiana*, 12th ed., Turin, 1972.

Dizionario biografico degli italiani, Rome, 1960– .

Stych, F. S., *How to find out about Italy*, Pergamon Press, 1970.

A substantial anthology of eighteenth-century Italian authors, with an important introduction, is G. Petronio, ed., *Il Settecento e l'Ottocento (1°)*, Milan, 1968 (Vol. IV of *Antologia della letteratura italiana*, directed by M. Vitale). The selections are annotated and the sections prefaced with critical-biographical-bibliographical information.

Art and Ideas in Eighteenth-Century Italy, Rome, 1960 (Pubblicazioni dell'Instituto Italiano di Londra, IV).

Binni, W., *L'Arcadia e il Metastasio*, Florence, 1963.

Classicismo e neoclassicismo nella letteratura del Settecento, Florence, 1963.

Preromanticismo italiano, Naples, 1959.

Settecento maggiore, Milan, 1979.

Bosco, U., 'Preromanticismo e romanticismo', in *Questioni e correnti di storia letteraria*, Milan, 1963 (cf. *Problemi ed orientamenti critici* above).

Candeloro, G., *Storia dell'Italia moderna*, Vol. I, *Le origini dell Risorgimento, 1700–1815*, Milan, 1956.

Compagnini, G., *Gli Illuministi Italiani* ('Letteratura Italiana Laterza', 35), Bari, 1974.

Compagnini, G., and Savoca, G., *Dalla vecchia Italia alla cultura europea del Settecento* ('Letteratura Italiana Laterza', 32), Bari, 1973.

Consoli, D., *Dall'Arcadia all'Illuminismo*, Bologna, 1972.

Croce, B., *La Letteratura italiana dell Settecento*, Bari, 1949.

Dorris, G. F. *Paolo Rolli and the Italian circle in London, 1715–1744*, The Hague, 1967.

Duchartre, P. L., *The Italian Comedy*, tr. R. Weaver, New York, 1968.

Fubini, M., *Dal Muratori al Baretti*, 2nd ed., Bari, 1954.

Fubini, M., 'Arcadia e Illuminismo', in *Questioni e correnti di storia letteraria*, Milan, 1963 (cf. *Problemi ed orientamenti critici* above).

Fubini, M., ed., *La cultura illuministica in Italia*, 2nd ed., Turin, 1964.

Giannessi, F., 'Illuminismo e romanticismo', in *Le Correnti*, Vol. II, Milan, 1956 (cf. *Letteratura italiana* (*Orientamenti culturali*) above).

Giazotto, R., *Poesia melodrammatica e pensiero critico nel Settecento*, Milan, 1952.

Graf, A., *L'Anglomania e l'influsso inglese in Italia nel secolo XVIII*, Turin, 1911.
Kennard, J. S., *The Italian Theatre*, Vol. II: *From the Close of the Seventeenth Century*, New York, 1932; reprinted 1964.
Goldoni and the Venice of his Time, New York, 1920; reprinted 1968.
Muscetta, C., ed., *Poetiche e poeti del Settecento*, 2nd ed., Catania, 1969.
Nicastro, G., *Goldoni e il teatro del secondo Settecento* ('Letteratura Italiana Laterza', 37), Bari, 1974.
Metastasio e il teatro del primo Settecento ('Letteratura Italiana Laterza', 33), Bari, 1973.
Vittorio Alfieri ('Letteratura Italiana Laterza', 38), Bari, 1974.
Noether, E. P., *Seeds of Italian Nationalism, 1700–1815*, New York, 1951.
Oreglia, G., *The Commedia dell'Arte*, London, 1968.
Petronio, G., *Parini e l'illuminismo lombardo*, Milan, 1961.
Piromalli, A., ed., *L'Arcadia*, Palermo, 1963.
Rota, E., *Le origini del Risorgimento: 1700–1800*, Milan, 1948.
Salvatorelli, L., *Il pensiero politico italiano dal 1700 al 1870*, Turin, 1949.
'Italy under Spanish Domination', 'The Eighteenth Century' and 'From the Revolution to the Restoration', in *A Concise History of Italy*, tr. B. Miall, London, 1940.
Savoca, G., *Parini e la poesia arcadica* ('Letteratura Italiana Laterza', 34), Bari, 1974.
Scalia, G., *L'Illuminismo*, Palermo, 1966.
Schippisi, R., 'L'Arcadia' in *Le Correnti*, Vol. I, Milan, 1956 (cf. *Letteratura italiana* (*Orientamenti culturali*) above).
Valsecchi, F., *L'Italia nel Settecento: dal 1714 al 1788*, Milan, 1959 (Vol. VII of the Mondadori *Storia d'Italia*; also rev. ed. in Mondadori 'Edizione Economica', 1971).
Vaussard, M., *Daily Life in Eighteenth Century Italy*, trans. M. Heron, London, 1962.
Venturi, F., *Italy and the Enlightenment: Studies in a Cosmopolitan Century*, ed. S. Woolf, trans. S. Corsi, London, 1972.
Vianello, C. A., *Il Settecento Milanese*, Milan, 1934.
Ziccardi, G., *Forme di vita e d'arte nel Settecento*, Florence, 1947.

(ii) *Literature of Ideas*

SCHOLARS AND HISTORIANS

Giannone, P., *Illuministi Italiani*, I, *Opere*, ed. S. Bertelli and G. Ricuperati, Milan and Naples, 1971.
The Civil History of the Kingdom of Naples, trans. J. Ogilvie, 2 vols., London, 1729–31.

A.E.(G) – 22

Maffei, S., *Verona illustrata*, ed. G. Donadelli, 2 vols., Milan, 1825–6.
Opere, 21 vols., Venice, 1790.
Muratori, L. A., *Opere*, ed. G. Falco and F. Forti, Milan and Naples, 2 vols., 1964 (an ample anthology).
Vico, G. B., *Tutte le opere*, ed. F. Nicolini, B. Croce and G. Gentile, 8 vols., Bari, 1914–41.
Opere, ed. F. Nicolini, Milan and Naples, 1953. (A useful collection of Vico's main works. The Latin texts are translated into Italian.)
The New Science of Giambattista Vico, revised translation of the 3rd ed. (1744) by T. G. Bergin and M. H. Fisch, Ithaca, NY, 1968.
The Autobiography of Giambattista Vico, trans. M. H. Fisch and T. G. Bergin, Ithaca, NY, 1963.
On the Study Methods of our Time, trans. E. Gianturco, Indianapolis, 1965.
Zeno, A., *Dissertazioni vossiane . . . libro De historicis latinis*, reprinted in 2 vols., Farnborough, Hants., 1970.

FROM THE AGE OF ARCADIA TO THE PERIOD OF REFORMS

A representative selection of articles from Venetian periodicals will be found in: *Giornali veneziani del Settecento*, ed. M. Berengo, Milan, 1962. See also L. Piccioni, ed., *Giornalismo letterario del Settecento*, Turin, 1949, which includes extracts from the *Giornale dei Letterati d'Italia*, *L'Osservatore Veneto* and Lami's *Novelle Letterarie*.
Algarotti, F., *Sir Isaac Newton's theory of light and colours and his principle of attraction, made familiar to ladies*, trans. E. Carter, 2 vols., London, 1742.
Bonora, E., ed., *Illuministi Italiani*, II, *Opere di Francesco Algarotti e di Saverio Bettinelli*, Milan and Naples, 1969, contains Algarotti's *Dialoghi sopra l'ottica Neutoniana*, the *Viaggi di Russia*, and the most important *Saggi*.
Gozzi, G., *La Gazzetta Veneta*, ed. A. Zardo, 1915; rev. ed. F. Forti, Florence, 1957.
L'Osservatore Veneto, ed. N. Raffaelli, 3 vols., Milan, 1965.
Scritti scelti, rev. ed. N. Mangini, Turin, 1967.

THE REFORMATORY ENLIGHTENMENT

Selections of texts by Genovesi, Galiani, Filangieri, Pagano and other reformers in southern Italy, together with fundamental introductory material, are contained in the 'Storia e Testi' *Illuministi Italiani* series: Vol. V, *Riformatori napoletani*, ed. F. Venturi, Milan and Naples, 1962; Vol. VI, *Opere di Ferdinando Galiani*, ed. F. Diaz and L. Guerci, Milan and Naples, 1975.

Beccaria, *Dei delitti e delle pene*, ed. F. Venturi, Turin, 1965; *Of Crimes and Punishments* (Oxford Library of Italian Classics), trans. J. Grigson, 1964.

Opere, ed. S. Romagnoli, 2 vols., Florence, 1958.

Carli, G. R., *Opere*, 19 vols., Milan, 1784–95.

Filangieri, G., *La scienza della legislazione*, 6 vols., Milan, 1822; tr. R. Clayton, 2 vols., London, 1806.

Romagnoli, S., ed., *Il Caffè*, Milan, 1960.

Venturi, F., ed., *Illuministi Italiani*, III, *Riformatori lombardi piemontesi e toscani*, Milan and Naples, 1958, contains *Dei delitti e delle pene* and extracts from works by many Lombard reformers, including Carli, Longo and Frisi, but excludes the Verri brothers.

Verri, A., *Opere scelte*, Milan, 1822.

Verri, P., *Del piacere e del dolore e altri scritti*, ed. R. De Felice, Milan, 1964, includes *Della economia politica* and *Riflessioni sulle leggi vincolanti principalmente nel commercio dei grani.*

Osservazioni sulla tortura, ed. G. L. Barni, Milan, 1961.

Meditazioni sulla economia politica, ed. G. R. Carli and others, Rome, 1967 (reprint).

Texts by reformers in Tuscany, the Papal States, Venice and Savoy-Piedmont are contained in two fundamental anthologies: F. Venturi, ed., *Illuministi Italiani*, III, cited above, and *Illuministi Italiani*, VII, *Riformatori delle antiche Repubbliche, dei Ducati, dello Stato Pontificio e delle Isole*, ed. G. Giarrizzo, G. F. Torcellan and F. Venturi, Milan and Naples, 1965.

SCIENCE

Adelmann, H. B., *Marcello Malpighi and the Evolution of Embryology*, 5 vols., Ithaca, NY, 1967.

Cristofolini, P., ed., *Redi Vallisnieri Spallanzani. La scuola galileiana e l'origine della vita*, Turin, 1968.

Magalotti, L., *Saggi di naturali esperienze*, ed. T. P. Salani, Milan, 1976.

Malpighi, M., *Opere scelte*, ed. L. Belloni, Turin, 1967.

Manfredi, E., *Delle opere matematiche*, 2 vols., Bologna, 1749–55.

Mascheroni, L., *La geometria del compasso*, ed. G. Fazzari, Palermo, 1901.

Morgagni, G. B., *Opera omnia*, 5 vols., Venice, 1765.

The Seats and Causes of Diseases investigated by Anatomy, trans. W. Cooke, 2 vols., London, 1822.

Redi, F., *Scritti di botanica, zoologia e medicina*, ed. P. Polito, Milan, 1975.

Spallanzani, A., *An Essay on Animal Reproduction*, trans. M. Maty, London, 1769.

Le Opere, 6 vols., Milan, 1932–6.

Spallanzani, L., *Tracts on the Natural History of Animals and Vegetables*, trans. J. G. Dalyell, 2nd ed., 2 vols., Edinburgh, 1803.

Vallisnieri, A., *Opere fisico-mediche . . . raccolte da Antonio suo figliuolo*, 3 vols., Venice, 1733.

Volta, A., *Opere*, 7 vols., Milan, 1918–27.

(*iii*) *Poetry*

ANTHOLOGIES

Poesie del Settecento, ed. C. Muscetta and M. R. Massei, 2 vols., Turin, 1968, provides an excellent selection of eighteenth-century Italian verse from Arcadia to the Period of Reforms, including *Il Giorno* and *Le Odi* of Parini, extracts from popular and dialect writers, and representative dramatic texts. *Lirici del Settecento*, ed. B. Maier, in collaboration with M. Fubini, D. Isella and G. Piccitto, Milan and Naples, 1959, is another fundamental, well-annotated anthology. See also C. Calcaterra, ed., *I lirici del Seicento e dell'Arcadia*, Milan, 1936. The *Appendice* in G. Parini, *Poesie e prose*, ed. L. Caretti, Milan and Naples, 1951, offers a convenient selection of satiric and didactic verse by Passeroni, Baruffaldi, Roberti, Betti, Spolverini, Lorenzi, Rezzonico, Mascheroni and others. For the fable writers, see *Favolisti del Settecento*, ed. M. Sansone, Florence, 1943. A good sample of Venetian dialect verse is given in *Il fiore della lirica veneziana*, II, *Seicento e Settecento*, ed. M. Dazzi, Venice, 1956.

POETS

Baffo, G., *Opere*, ed. E. Bartolini, 2 vols., Milan, 1971.

Batacchi, F., *Le Novelle*, ed. F. Giannessi, Milan, 1971.

Bertola, A., *Poesie e prose*, 3 vols., Florence, 1818.

Casti, G. B., *Gli animali parlanti*, 3 vols., Milan, 1966; *The Court and Parliament of Beasts*, tr. W. S. Rose, London, 1819.

See Maier anthology and appendix to P. Metastasio, *Opere*, ed. M. Fubini, cited below.

Cesarotti, M., *Poesie di Ossian*, ed. G. Balsamo Crivelli, Turin, 1924; extracts in E. Bigi, ed., *Dal Muratori al Cesarotti*, IV, *Critici e storici della poesia e delle arti nel secondo Settecento*, Milan and Naples, 1960.

Colpani, G., *Opere*, 5 vols., Vicenza, 1784–90.

Crescimbeni, G. M., *Opere*, ed. A. and P. C. Zeno and A. F. Seghezzi, Venice, 1730–31.

Fantoni, G., *Poesie*, ed. G. Lazzari, Bari, 1913.

Frugoni, C. I., *Opere poetiche*, ed. C. G. della Torre di Rezzonico, Parma, 1779.

Gozzi, C., *La Marfisa bizzara*, ed. M. Ortiz, Bari, 1911.

Gozzi, G., *Poesie e prose*, ed. A. Pippi, 1901; revised ed. E. Falqui, Florence, 1967.

Gravina, G. V., *Della ragione poetica*, ed. G. Natali, Lanciano, 1933.

Opere italiane, 3 vols., Naples, 1756–8.

Mascheroni, L. *L' "Invito a Lesbia Cidonia" ed altre poesie*, ed. G. Natali, Turin, 1918.

Meli, G,, *Opere*, ed. G. Santangelo, 2 vols., Milan, 1965–8.

Metastasio, P., *Opere*, ed. M. Fubini, Milan and Naples, 1968, selections, with an important introduction.

Tutte le opere, ed. B. Brunelli, 5 vols., Milan, 1943–54.

Monti, V., *Opere*, ed. M. Valgimigli and C. Muscetta, Milan and Naples, 1953.

Parini, G., *The Day. Morning, Midday, Evening, Night*, trans. H. M. Bower, London, 1927.

Opere, ed. G. M. Zuradelli, 2 vols., Turin, 1965 (I, *Il Giorno e le Odi*; II, *Poesie minori e prose*). New critical editions are *Il Giorno*, 2 vols., and *Le Odi*, ed. D. Isella, Milan and Naples, 1969–76.

Passeroni, G. C., *Il Cicerone*, Venice, 1845; also Caretti and Maier anthologies. above.

Pignotti, L., see Maier and Sansone anthologies above.

Pindemonte, L., *Opere*, 4 vols., Milan, 1832–3.

Rezzonico, C. G., della Torre di *Opere poetiche*, ed. E. Guagnini, Ravenna, 1977.

Rime degli Arcadi, 13 vols, Rome, 1915–80.

Rolli, P., *Liriche*, ed. C. Calcaterra, Turin, 1926.

Spolverini, G. B., *La coltivazione del riso*, ed. V. Mistruzzi, Milan, 1929.

(*iv*) *Theatre*

TRAGEDY

Anthologies: Representative dramatic texts by Zeno (*Griselda*), Maffei (*Merope*), Metastasio (*Olimpiade, Attilio Regolo*), and Alfieri (*Saul, Mirra*), will be found in *Poesie del Settecento*, ed. C. Muscetta and M. R. Massei, 2 vols., Turin, 1968. *Drammi per musica*, ed. A. della Corte, 2 vols., Turin, 1958, provides a good selection of libretti from Rinuccini to Zeno. *Teatro Italiano*, Vols. II and III, ed. S. D'Amico, Milan, 1955–6, contain *Merope, Didone abbandonata, Olim-*

piade, *Saul* and *Mirra*. *L'Opera per musica dopo Metastasio* in Appendix to P. Metastasio, *Opere*, ed. M. Fubini, Milan and Naples, 1968, includes Calzabigi's *Alceste*.

Alfieri, V., *Memoirs*, revised trans. E. R. Vincent, London, 1961.
Opere, 11 vols., Turin, 1903.
Opere, ed. V. Branca, Milan, 1965, is a useful anthology.
The Prince and Letters, trans. B. Corrigan and J. A. Molinaro, Toronto, 1972.
Tragedie, ed. P. Cazzani, Milan, 1958.
The Tragedies, trans. C. Lloyd, 3 vols., London, 1815; trans. E. A. Bowring, 2 vols., London, 1876.
Tutte le opere, 20 vols., Asti, 1951– (in progress).
Calzabigi, R. de, *Poesie*, 2 vols., Leghorn, 1774.
Conti, A., *Le quattro tragedie*, Florence, 1751.
Gravina, G. V., *Opere italiane*, 3 vols., Naples, 1756–8.
Maffei, S., *Merope*, ed. C. Garibotto, Turin, 1963; trans. Mr Ayre, London, 1740.
Martello, P. J., *Opere*, 7 vols., Bologna, 1723–35.
Metastasio, P., *Dramas and other Poems*, trans. J. Hoole, 3 vols., London, 1800.
Tutte le opere, ed. B. Brunelli, 5 vols., 1943–54.
Zeno, A., *Drammi scelti*, ed. M. Fehr, Bari, 1929.
Poesie drammatiche, ed. G. Gozzi, 10 vols., Venice, 1744.

COMEDY

The Italian improvised comedy is fully documented in V. Pandolfi, ed., *La commedia dell'arte. Storia e testi*, 6 vols., Florence, 1957–61. Extracts from the comedies of Gigli, Fagiuoli, Nelli, Maffei, Albergati Capacelli and Sografi are given in Appendix to C. Goldoni, *Opere*, ed, F. Zampieri, Milan and Naples, 1954. *Teatro Italiano*, Vol. III, ed. S. D'Amico, Milan, 1956, includes Goldoni's *La Locandiera* and *Il campiello*, and Gozzi's *L'augellino belverde*.

Capacelli, F. Albergati, *Opere*, 12 vols., Venice, 1783–5.
Chiari, P., *Commedie in versi*, 10 vols., Venice, 1756–62.
Nuova raccolta di commedie in versi, 2 vols., Venice, 1763–4.
Fagiuoli, G. B., *Commedie*, 7 vols., Florence, 1734–6.
Federici, C., *Opere*, 13 vols., Florence, 1826–7.
Gamerra, G. de, *Nuovo teatro*, 8 vols., Pisa, 1789–90; 18 vols., Venice, 1790.

Gigli, G., *Don Pilone, La sorellina di Don Pilone, Il Gorgoleo*, ed. M. Manciotti, Milan, 1963.
Opere, 3 vols., L'Aja [Lucca], 1797–8.
The Coffee House, trans. H. B. Fuller, New York, London, 1925.
Commedie, 3 vols., Turin, 1971.
A Curious Mishap, The Beneficent Bear, The Fan, The Spendthrift Miser, trans. in *The Comedies of Goldoni*, ed. H. Zimmern, London, 1892.
The Liar, trans. G. Lovat Fraser, London, 1922.
Memoirs, trans. J. Black, 2 vols., London, 1814; reprinted, ed. W. A. Drake, London, 1926.
Mine Hostess, The Impresario from Smyrna, The Good Girl, The Fan, trans. in *Four Comedies*, ed. C. Bax, London, 1922.
The Servant of Two Masters, trans. E. J. Dent, 2nd ed., Cambridge, 1952.
Tutte le opere, ed. G. Ortolani, 14 vols., Milan, 1935–56.
Venetian Twins, Artful Widow, Mirandolina, Superior Residence, in *Four Comedies*, trans. F. Davies, London, 1968.
Gozzi, C., *The Blue Monster*, trans. E. J. Dent, Cambridge, 1951.
Memorie inutili, ed. D. Bulferetti, 2 vols., Turin, 1928 (abridged); trans. J. A. Symonds, 2 vols., London, 1890, rev. and abridged ed. P. Horne, London, 1962.
Opere, Teatro e polemiche teatrali, ed. G. Petronio, Milan, 1962.
Scritti, ed. E. Bonora, Turin, 1977.
Maffei, S., *Opere drammatiche e poesie varie*, ed. A. Avena, Bari, 1928.
Martello, P. J., *Il Femia sentenziato*, ed. P. Viani, Bologna, 1869; reprinted 1968.
Nelli, J. A., *Commedie*, ed. A. Moretti, 3 vols., Bologna, 1883–9.
Pepoli, A., *Teatro*, 6 vols., Venice, 1787–8; *Tragedie*, 6 vols., Parma, 1791–6.
Rossi, G. G. de, *Commedie*, 4 vols., Bassano, 1790–98.
Sografi, S. A., *Commedie*, Milan, 1831.

Index

MORE ABOUT PENGUINS AND PELICANS

Penguinews, which appears every month, contains details of all the new books issued by Penguins as they are published. It is supplemented by our stocklist, which includes almost 5,000 titles.

A specimen copy of *Penguinews* will be sent to you free on request. Please write to Dept EP, Penguin Books Ltd, Harmondsworth, Middlesex, for your copy.

In the U.S.A.: For a complete list of books available from Penguins in the United States write to Dept CS, Penguin Books, 625 Madison Avenue, New York, New York 10022, U.S.A.

In Canada: For a complete list of books available from Penguins in Canada write to Penguin Books Canada Ltd, 2801 John Street, Markham, Ontario L3R 1B4.

In Australia: For a complete list of books available from Penguins in Australia write to the Marketing Department, Penguin Books Australia Ltd, P.O. Box 257, Ringwood, Victoria 3134.

Pelicans provide an enormous range of expert books for the amateur reader. On the following pages you will find a selection of the titles to be published in the next few months.

THE DUTCH REVOLT

Geoffrey Parker

'The first comprehensive history of the Revolt by an English historian, unquestionably supersedes Geyl' – H. G. Koenigsberger in *The Times Literary Supplement*

'Performs the near miracle of giving a portrait and an explanation of a large and long event of immense complexity and enormous importance in only 330 pages' – H. H. Rowen in *Sixteenth-Century Journal*

'Brings clarity and thorough scholarship to these complex events. It is a fine blend of descriptive and analytical history' – *Economist*

VIABLE DEMOCRACY

Michael Margolis

Professor Margolis describes his project in these words: 'We must build up a theory of viable democracy, one that preserves traditional concerns for individual self development through political participation, but one that also takes into account the realities of the bureaucracy, the military and corporate establishment, and the environment'. If democracy is to resist onslaughts from both right and left, major reforms are essential. *Viable Democracy* both recognizes this and offers a challenging possibility for the future.

PHILOSOPHY AS IT IS

Edited by Ted Honderich and Myles Burnyeat

The editors set out to fulfil four aims: to represent philosophy as it is; to represent it through clear, non-technical, reasonable essays on central problems; to represent recent developments in philosophy; to give the reader in an introduction to each essay an admirably lucid résumé of its arguments. Where the essays become difficult the editors say so, but in most cases the general reader will find that – among others – Bernard Williams on Utilitarianism and moral integrity, Richard Wollheim on art as a form of life or Alvin Plantinga on God, freedom and evil offer a stimulating, but not insuperable, challenge.

LOOK OUT FOR THESE FROM PELICANS

VANISHING BIRDS

Their Natural History and Conservation

Tim Halliday

Since the Dodo died three centuries ago, about 130 species of bird have joined it in extinction, and many others have become dangerously rare – mostly through the fault of man.

Dr Halliday looks at the way birds have evolved in order to identify what it is that makes some species particularly vulnerable to changes in their environment and thus tragically susceptible to human influences. The histories of several extinct species, such as the Great Auk and the Passenger Pigeon, are discussed in detail, and the book is beautifully illustrated by Dr Halliday's paintings and drawings.

WILL THE SOVIET UNION SURVIVE UNTIL 1984?

Andrei Amalrik

First published in 1970, Amalrik's essay was hailed by the *Guardian* as 'a brave unique voice from the Soviet Union coolly and pessimistically explaining the reality of that society and (a little less coolly) outlining his vision of the apocalypse to come, with the rise of China and the revival of nationalism among the non-Russian Soviet peoples': while the *Sunday Times* called it 'literally the first piece of serious political analysis, based on experience, observation and undogmatic deduction, to have emerged from Russia for fifty years'.

POVERTY IN THE UNITED KINGDOM

Peter Townsend

Peter Townsend first gives the history of poverty and its study, and then, using the findings from a nationwide survey and from four area surveys in Belfast, Glasgow, Salford and Neath, goes on to analyse the relationship between deprivation and poverty, showing that poverty is more extensive than is generally believed. He spells out the elaborate hierarchy from rich to poor, and traces the interconnections between wealth, income and non-cash benefits. He also shows how poverty and deprivation are systematically *imposed* upon social minorities such as the elderly, the unemployed, the low-paid, one-parent families and disabled people.

PELICAN HISTORY OF EUROPEAN THOUGHT

Volume 3
FROM HUMANISM TO SCIENCE
Robert Mandrou

The cultural heritage at men's disposal at the end of the fifteenth century was rich in traditions that were contrasting, even contradictory. The upheavals of the time profoundly transformed intellectual life. Robert Mandrou has reconstructed the role played by the new intellectuals, from Erasmus, Copernicus and Budé to Newton, Leibnitz, Bayle and Locke, within the institutions consecrated to them and in society at large. He has succeeded in combining imaginative flair with a meticulous and comprehensive synthesis of this crucial period in European Intellectual development.

Volume 4
THE ENLIGHTENMENT
Norman Hampson

Norman Hampson follows through certain dominant themes of the Enlightenment of the eighteenth century, and describes the contemporary social and political climate, in which ideas could travel from the salons of Paris to the court of Catherine the Great – but less easily from a master to his servant. On such vexed issues as the role of ideas in the 'rise of the middle class' he provides a new and realistic approach linking intellectual and social history.

Volume 6
THE AGE OF THE MASSES
Michael D. Biddiss

This comprehensive review of the last hundred years ranges widely over the fields of natural science, philosophical and religious thought, social and political ideas, literature and the arts. A major unifying theme is the emergence of mass society, together with the advance of mass politics and mass culture, which raised a complex of problems that no sphere of intellectual or artistic endeavour could altogether ignore.

THE PELICAN GUIDES TO EUROPEAN LITERATURE

The Pelican Guides to European Literature offer an approach to the literature of the western world from a European rather than a purely national viewpoint. Each volume is devoted to the major figures and movements of a specific period and to the historical, intellectual and imaginative contexts in which they appeared. No strict framework has been imposed and the editors will bring to their respective volumes the approaches that seem most appropriate and most fruitful.

THE CONTINENTAL RENAISSANCE

Edited by A. J. Krailsheimer

The Continental Renaissance 1500–1600 is concerned with the century of Ronsard and Ariosto, Rabelais and Machiavelli, Erasmus, Luther and Calvin. It was a period in which new ideas and new forms in art burgeoned to an unprecedented extent, and in which the modern world began to take recognizable shape. This volume is divided into six main sections: The Cultural and Historical Background, Poetry, Drama, Prose Fiction, The Literature of Ideas and Manners, and Popular Literature.

THE AGE OF REALISM

Edited by F. W. J. Hemmings

The Age of Realism examines, country by country, the literature generated by new social forces in nineteenth-century Europe – from the beginnings of the realist novel in Balzac and Stendhal, the burgeoning of the form in Tolstoy, Flaubert, Dostoyevsky, Galdos, Fontane and Zola, to its demise at the end of the century.

MODERNISM

1890–1930

Edited by Malcolm Bradbury and James McFarlane

Few historical phases contain such an extraordinary wealth of major writers as the Modernist period – Apollinaire, Brecht, Joyce, Kafka, Strindberg, Yeats – and few have to such an extent broken down traditional national frontiers in matters of literary and cultural concern. This book examines the ideas, the groupings, the social tensions, out of which Modernism emerged.